WEBSTER'S NEW WORLD POCKET DICTIONARY

David B. Guralnik
EDITOR IN CHIEF

WEBSTER'S NEW WORLD
New York

WEBSTER'S NEW WORLD

Simon & Schuster, Inc.
15 Columbus Circle
New York, NY 10023

SIMON AND SCHUSTER, TREE OF
KNOWLEDGE, WEBSTER'S NEW
WORLD and colophon are
trademarks of Simon & Schuster.

DISTRIBUTED BY PRENTICE HALL TRADE SALES

Manufactured in the United States of America

12 13 14 15 16 17 18 19 20

ISBN 0-671-41826-2

This book is based upon and in-
cludes material from WEBSTER'S
NEW WORLD DICTIONARY,
SECOND COLLEGE EDITION
copyright © 1970, 1972, 1974,
1976 by Simon & Schuster and
WEBSTER'S NEW WORLD DIC-
TIONARY, COLLEGE EDITION
copyright 1953, 1954 © 1955,
1956, 1957, 1958, 1959, 1960,
1962, 1964, 1966, 1968 by Simon
& Schuster.

KEY TO PRONUNCIATION

Symbol	Key Word		Symbol	Key Word
a	fat		u	up
ā	ape		ū	use
ã	bare		ûr	fur
ä	car		ə	a *in* ago
e	ten			e *in* agent
ē	even			i *in* sanity
ê	here			o *in* comply
ẽr	over			u *in* focus
i	is		ch	chin
ī	bite		ŋ	ring
o	lot		sh	she
ō	go		th	thin
ô	horn		*th*	then
ōō	tool		zh	azure
oo	book		'	*as in*
oi	oil			apple (ap''l)
ou	out			season (sē'z'n)

ABBREVIATIONS USED IN THIS DICTIONARY

a.	adjective		**Obs.**	obsolete
adv.	adverb		**orig.**	originally
alt.	alternate		**pl.**	plural
Am.	American		**Poet.**	poetic
Ar.	archaic		**pp.**	past participle
Biol.	biology		**ppr.**	present
Br.	British			participle
c.	circa, century		**pref.**	prefix
cf.	compare		**prep.**	preposition
Col.	colloquial		**pron.**	pronoun
con.	conjunction		**pt.**	past tense
cu.	cubic		**R.C.**	Roman
Dial.	dialectal		**Ch.**	Catholic Church
esp.	especially		**sing.**	singular
etc.	et cetera		**Sl.**	slang
fem.	feminine		**sp.**	spelling
Gr.	Greek		**spec.**	specifically
int.	interjection		**suf.**	suffix
masc.	masculine		**Theol.**	theology
Mus.	music		**TV**	television
n.	noun		**v.**	verb

Other abbreviations will be found on pages 303–305.

EDITORIAL STAFF

Supervising Editor: Samuel Solomon

Editors: Clark C. Livensparger, Thomas Layman,
Andrew N. Sparks, Eleanor Rickey,
Paul B. Murry

Assistants: Irene T. Kauffman, Shirley M. Miller

RULES FOR SPELLING

Words that end in a silent "-e" usually drop the -e when a suffix beginning with a vowel is added [Ex.: *file—filing*]. However, before the suffixes -able and -ous, the -e is usually kept if it follows a soft c or g [Ex.: *outrage—outrageous*]. The -e is usually kept when a suffix beginning with a consonant is added [Ex.: *time—timely*].

Words that end in a single consonant preceded by a single vowel usually double that consonant when a suffix beginning with a vowel is added, if: a) the word is a monosyllable [Ex.: *sin—sinning*], or b) the word has more than one syllable but is accented on the last syllable [Ex.: *refer—referring*]. If the final consonant is preceded by something other than a single vowel or, in American usage, if the last syllable is not accented, the final consonant is usually not doubled [Ex.: *hurl—hurling*; *travel—traveling*].

Words that end in a double letter usually drop one letter when a suffix beginning with the same letter is added [Ex.: *free—freest*].

Words that end in "-y" preceded by a consonant usually change the -y to an i when a suffix that does not begin with i is added [Ex.: *marry—married*]. If preceded by a vowel, the -y is usually kept [Ex.: *play—played*].

Words that end in "-ie" change the -ie to a y when the suffix -ing is added [Ex.: *lie—lying*].

Words that end in "-c" usually take on a k when a suffix beginning with i or e is added [Ex.: *picnic—picnicker*].

Words containing "ie" or "ei." The combination ei is usually used following the letter c and is always used to represent the sound (ā). In most other native English words the combination ie is used.

The word "full" when used as a suffix drops one l [Ex.: *cupful*].

Verbs ending in "-cede" and "-ceed." Three common verbs (exceed, proceed, and succeed) end in -ceed. Most other verbs end in -cede.

RULES FOR FORMING PLURALS

Most nouns in English form the plural by adding -s or -es. When the singular noun ends in a sound that allows a -s to be added and pronounced without the formation of a new syllable, -s is used [Ex.: *book—books*]. When the singular noun ends in such a sound that -s cannot be joined to it and pronounced without the formation of an additional syllable, -es is used [Ex.: *kiss—kisses*; *torch—torches*].

The chief exceptions to this basic rule are listed below.

Words that end in "-o" usually form the plural by adding -es [Ex.: *hero—heroes*]; however, some of them do so by adding -s [Ex.: *solo—solos*]. There is no rule that deals with the distinction; only experience can serve as a guide.

Some words that end in "-f" form the plural by dropping the -f and adding -ves [Ex.: *wolf—wolves*].

Words that end in "-y" preceded by a consonant usually form the plural by dropping the -y and adding -ies [Ex.: *lady—ladies*]. If the -y is preceded by a vowel, they form the plural regularly, by adding -s [Ex.: *day—days*].

Some words form the plural by a vowel change. Among the commonest examples are: *foot, feet; man, men; tooth, teeth; woman, women.*

Some words have special plurals to which none of the above general statements apply. Among them are words such as: *alumna, alumnae; child, children; phenomenon, phenomena; radius, radii.*

A

a, *a., indefinite article* 1. one. 2. each; any one.

a-, *pref.* not.

aard'vark (ärd'-) *n.* African mammal that eats ants.

ab-, *pref.* away; from; down.

a·back', *adv. & a.* [Ar.] back. **—taken aback**, surprised.

ab'a·cus, *n.* frame with beads for doing arithmetic.

ab·a·lo'ne, *n.* sea mollusk.

a·ban'don, *v.* 1. give up entirely. 2. to desert. **—n.** lack of restraint.

a·base', *v.* to humble.

a·bash', *v.* embarrass.

a·bate', *v.* lessen. **—a·bate'ment**, *n.*

ab·at·toir' (-a-twär') *n.* slaughterhouse.

ab·bé (ā-bā') *n.* priest's title in France.

ab'bess, *n.* woman who is head of a nunnery.

ab'bey (-i) *n.* [*pl.* -BEYS] monastery or nunnery.

ab'bot, *n.* man who is head of a monastery.

ab·bre'vi·ate, *v.* shorten, as a word. **—ab·bre'vi·a'tion**, *n.*

ab'di·cate, *v.* give up, as a throne. **—ab·di·ca'tion**, *n.*

ab'do·men (*or* ab-dō'-) *n.* part of the body between chest and pelvis. **—ab·dom'i·nal** (-dom'-) *a.*

ab·duct', *v.* kidnap. **—ab·duc'tion**, *n.* **—ab·duc'tor**, *n.*

a·bed', *adv.* in bed.

ab·er·ra'tion, *n.* deviation from normal, right, etc.

a·bet', *v.* [ABETTED, ABETTING] to help, esp. in crime. **—a·bet'tor**, *a·bet'ter*, *n.*

a·bey'ance (-bā'-) *n.* temporary suspension.

ab·hor', *v.* [-HORRED, -HORRING] shun in disgust, hatred, etc. **—ab·hor'rence**, *n.*

ab·hor'rent, *a.* detestable.

a·bide', *v.* [ABODE *or* ABIDED, ABIDING] 1. remain. 2. [Ar.] reside. 3. await. 4. endure. **—abide by**, keep (a promise) or obey (rules).

a·bil'i·ty, *n.* [*pl.* -TIES] 1. a being able. 2. talent.

ab'ject, *a.* miserable.

ab·jure', *v.* renounce on oath. **—ab'ju·ra'tion**, *n.*

a·blaze', *adv. & a.* on fire.

a'ble, *a.* 1. having power (*to* do). 2. talented; skilled. **—a'bly**, *adv.*

-able, *suf.* 1. that can or

should be. 2. tending to.

a'ble-bod'ied, *a.* healthy.

ab·lu'tion, *n.* a washing of the body, esp. as a rite.

ab'ne·gate, *v.* renounce; give up. **—ab'ne·ga'tion**, *n.*

ab·nor'mal, *a.* not normal. **—ab·nor·mal'i·ty** [*pl.* -TIES] *n.* **—ab·nor'mal·ly**, *adv.*

a·board', *adv. & prep.* on or in (a train, ship, etc.).

a·bode', *n.* home.

a·bol'ish, *v.* do away with.

ab·o·li'tion, *n.* an abolishing, spec. [A-] of slavery in U.S. **—ab·o·li'tion·ist**, *n.*

A'-bomb', *n.* atomic bomb.

a·bom'i·na·ble, *a.* 1. disgusting. 2. very bad. **—a·bom'i·na·bly**, *adv.*

a·bom'i·nate, *v.* loathe. **—a·bom'i·na'tion**, *n.*

ab·o·rig'i·ne (-rij'ə-nē) *n.* native of original stock. **—ab·o·rig'i·nal**, *a. & n.*

a·bor'tion, *n.* miscarriage. **—a·bor'tive**, *a.*

a·bound', *v.* be plentiful.

a·bout', *adv.* 1. around. 2. near. 3. in an opposite direction. 4. nearly. **—a.** astir. **—prep.** 1. around. 2. near to. 3. just starting. 4. concerning.

a·bout'-face', *n.* a reversal.

a·bove', *adv.* 1. higher. 2. earlier on a page. **—prep.** 1. over. 2. higher than. **—a.** mentioned above.

a·bove'board', *a. & adv.* in plain view; honest(ly).

a·brade' (ə-brād') *v.* scrape away. **—a·bra'sive**, *a. & n.*

a·bra'sion, *n.* 1. an abrading. 2. abraded spot.

a·breast', *adv. & a.* side by side.

a·bridge', *v.* shorten, as in wording; lessen. **—a·bridg'ment**, **a·bridge'ment**, *n.*

a·broad', *adv.* 1. far and wide. 2. outdoors. 3. to or in foreign lands.

ab'ro·gate, *v.* abolish; repeal. **—ab'ro·ga'tion**, *n.*

a·brupt', *a.* 1. sudden. 2. brusque. 3. steep.

ab'scess (-ses) *n.* inflamed, pus-filled area in body.

ab·scond' (-skond') *v.* flee and hide to escape the law.

ab'sent, *a.* 1. not present; away. 2. lacking. **—v.** (ab-sent') keep (oneself) away. **—ab'sence**, *n.*

ab·sen·tee', *n.* absent person.

ab'sent-mind'ed, *a.* 1. not attentive. 2. forgetful.

ab'so·lute, *a.* 1. perfect. 2. complete. 3. not mixed; pure.

4. certain; positive. 5. real.
—**ab·so·lute'ly**, *adv.*

ab·so·lu'tion, *n.* 1. forgiveness. 2. remission (*of* sin).

ab·solve', *v.* to free from guilt, a duty, etc.

ab·sorb', *v.* 1. suck up. 2. engulf wholly. 3. interest greatly. —**ab·sorp'tion**, *n.* —**ab·sorp'tive**, *a.*

ab·sorb'ent, *a.* able to absorb moisture, etc.

ab·stain', *v.* to do without; refrain. —**ab·sten'tion**, *n.*

ab·ste'mi·ous (-stē'-) *a.* not eating or drinking too much.

ab·sti'nence, *n.* an abstaining from food, liquor, etc.

ab·stract', *a.* 1. apart from material objects; not concrete. 2. theoretical. —*v.* summarize. —*n.* (ab'strakt) summary. —**ab·strac'tion**, *n.*

ab·stract'ed, *a.* preoccupied with or lost in thought.

ab·struse', *a.* hard to understand.

ab·surd', *a.* ridiculous. —**ab·surd'i·ty** [*pl.* -TIES] *n.*

a·bun'dance, *n.* more than is needed. —**a·bun'dant**, *a.*

a·buse' (-būz') *v.* 1. use wrongly. 2. mistreat. 3. berate. —*n.* (-būs') 1. wrong use. 2. mistreatment. 3. vile language. —**a·bu'sive**, *a.*

a·but', *v.* [ABUTTED, ABUTTING] to border (*on* or *upon*).

a·but'ment, *n.* part supporting an arch, strut, etc.

a·bys'mal (-biz'-) *a.* too deep to be measured.

a·byss' (-bis') *n.* deep or bottomless gulf.

a·ca'cia (-kā'sha) *n.* tree with yellow or white flowers.

ac·a·dem'ic, *a.* 1. of schools or colleges. 2. of liberal arts. 3. theoretical. —**ac·a·dem'i·cal·ly**, *adv.*

a·cad'e·my, *n.* [*pl.* -MIES] 1. private high school. 2. school for special study. 3. society of scholars, etc.

a·can'thus, *n.* plant with large, graceful leaves.

ac·cede' (-sēd') *v.* 1. agree (*to*). 2. enter upon the duties (of an office).

ac·cel'er·ate (-sel'-) *v.* 1. increase in speed. 2. make happen sooner. —**ac·cel·er·a'tion**, *n.* —**ac·cel'er·a'tor**, *n.*

ac'cent, *n.* 1. stress on a syllable in speaking. 2. mark showing this. 3. distinctive way of pronouncing. 4. rhythmic stress. —*v.* emphasize.

ac·cen'tu·ate (-choo-) *v.* to

accent; emphasize; stress.

ac·cept', *v.* 1. receive willingly. 2. approve. 3. agree to. 4. believe in. —**ac·cept'ance**, *n.*

ac·cept'a·ble, *a.* satisfactory. —**ac·cept'a·bly**, *adv.*

ac·cess', *n.* 1. right to enter, use, etc. 2. means of approach.

ac·ces'si·ble, *a.* 1. easy to enter, etc. 2. obtainable.

ac·ces'sion, *n.* 1. an attaining (the throne, etc.). 2. an addition or increase.

ac·ces'so·ry, *n.* [*pl.* -RIES] 1. thing added for decoration, etc. 2. helper in a crime.

ac'ci·dent, *n.* 1. unexpected happening. 2. mishap. 3. chance. —**ac'ci·den'tal**, *a.*

ac·claim', *v.* greet with applause. —*n.* great approval.

ac'cla·ma'tion, *n.* 1. great applause. 2. spoken vote of "yes" by many.

ac·cli'mate (ə-klī'mit *or* ak'-li·māt') *v.* get used to a new climate or situation: also **ac·cli'ma·tize**.

ac·co·lade', *n.* high praise.

ac·com'mo·date, *v.* 1. adjust. 2. do a favor for. 3. have room for; lodge. —**ac·com'mo·da'tion**, *n.*

ac·com'pa·ny, *v.* 1. go with. 3. play music supporting a soloist. —**ac·com'pa·ni·ment**, *n.* —**ac·com'pa·nist**, *n.*

ac·com'plice (-plis') *n.* partner in crime.

ac·com'plish, *v.* do; complete. —**ac·com'plish·ment**, *n.*

ac·cord', *v.* 1. agree. 2. grant. —*n.* agreement. —**according to**, 1. consistent with. 2. as stated by. —**of one's own accord**, voluntarily. —**ac·cord'ance**, *n.*

ac·cord'ing·ly, *adv.* 1. in a fitting way. 2. therefore.

ac·cor'di·on, *n.* musical instrument with a bellows.

ac·cost', *v.* approach and speak to.

ac·count', *v.* 1. give reasons (*for*). 2. judge to be. —*n.* 1. *pl.* business records. 2. worth. 3. explanation. 4. report. —**on account of**, because of. —**take into account**, consider.

ac·count'a·ble, *a.* 1. responsible. 2. explainable.

ac·count'ing, *n.* the keeping of business records. —**ac·count'ant**, *n.*

ac·cou′ter (-kōō′-) v. equip.

ac·cred′it, v. 1. authorize; certify. 2. believe in.

ac·crue′ (-krōō′) v. be added, as interest on money.

ac·cu′mu·late, v. pile up; collect. —**ac·cu′mu·la′tion**, n.

ac′cu·rate (-rit) a. exactly correct. —**ac′cu·ra·cy**, n. —**ac′cu·rate·ly**, adv.

ac·curs′ed, a. damnable.

ac·cuse′ (-kūz′) v. 1. to blame. 2. charge with doing wrong. —**ac′cu·sa′tion**, n.

ac·cus′tom, v. make familiar by habit or use.

ac·cus′tomed, a. 1. usual; customary. 2. used (to).

ace, n. 1. playing card with one spot. 2. expert. —a. [Col.] first-class.

a·cer′bi·ty (-sûr′-) n. sourness; sharpness.

ac′e·tate (as′-) n. salt or ester of an acid (**a·ce′tic acid**) found in vinegar.

ac′e·tone, n. liquid solvent for certain oils, etc.

a·cet′y·lene (-set′l-) n. gas used in a blowtorch.

ache (āk) n. dull, steady pain. —v. have such pain.

a·chieve′, v. 1. do; accomplish. 2. get by effort. —**a·chieve′ment**, n.

ac′id (as′-) n. 1. sour substance. 2. chemical that reacts with a base to form a salt. —a. 1. sour; sharp. 2. of an acid. —**a·cid′i·ty**, n.

a·cid′u·lous (-sij′oo-) a. somewhat acid or sour.

ac·knowl′edge, v. 1. admit or recognize. 2. respond to (a greeting, etc.). 3. express thanks for. —**ac·knowl′edg·ment**, n.

ac′me (-mē) n. highest point.

ac′ne (-nē) n. pimply skin.

ac′o·lyte, n. altar boy.

a′corn, n. nut of the oak.

a·cous′tics (-kōōs′-) n. 1. science of sound. 2. qualities of a room that affect sound: with pl. n. —**a·cous′tic**, a.

ac·quaint′, v. 1. make familiar (with). 2. inform.

ac·quaint′ance, n. 1. personal knowledge. 2. person one knows slightly.

ac·qui·esce′ (-kwi-es′) v. consent without protest. —**ac·qui·es′cence**, n. —**ac·qui·es′cent**, a.

ac·quire′ (-kwīr′) v. get as one's own. —**ac·quire′ment**, n.

ac·qui·si′tion (-kwə-zish′-) n. 1. an acquiring. 2. something acquired. —**ac·quis′i·tive** (-kwiz′-) a.

ac·quit′, v. [-QUITTED, -QUITTING] 1. declare not guilty. 2. conduct (oneself). —**ac·quit′tal**, n.

a·cre (ā′kēr) n. measure of land, 43,560 sq. ft. —**a′cre·age** (-ij) n.

ac′rid, a. sharp or bitter.

ac′ri·mo′ny, n. bitterness, as of manner or speech. —**ac′ri·mo′ni·ous**, a.

ac′ro·bat, n. performer on the trapeze, tightrope, etc. —**ac′ro·bat′ic**, a.

ac′ro·bat′ics, n.pl. acrobat's tricks.

a·cross′, adv. from one side to the other. —prep. 1. from one side to the other of. 2. on the other side of. 3. into contact with.

act, n. 1. thing done. 2. doing. 3. a law. 4. division of a play or opera. —v. 1. perform in a play, etc. 2. behave. 3. function. 4. have an effect (on).

act′ing, a. substitute.

ac·tin′ic, a. designating rays causing chemical change.

ac′tion, n. 1. a doing of something. 2. thing done. 3. pl. behavior. 4. way of working. 5. lawsuit. 6. combat.

ac′ti·vate, v. make active. —**ac′ti·va′tion**, n.

ac′tive, a. 1. acting; working. 2. busy; lively; agile. —**ac·tiv′i·ty** [pl. -TIES] n.

ac′tor, n. one who acts in plays. —**ac′tress**, n.fem.

ac′tu·al (-chōō-) a. existing; real. —**ac′tu·al′i·ty**, n.

ac′tu·al·ly, adv. really.

ac′tu·ar·y, n. [pl. -IES] insurance statistician. —**ac′tu·ar′i·al**, a.

ac′tu·ate, v. 1. put into action. 2. impel to action.

a·cu′men (-kū′-) n. keenness of mind.

a·cute′, a. 1. sharp-pointed. 2. shrewd. 3. keen. 4. severe. 5. critical. 6. less than 90°: said of angles.

ad, n. [Col.] advertisement.

A.D., of the Christian era.

ad′age (-ij) n. proverb.

a·da′gio (-dä′jō) adv. & a. Music slow(ly).

ad′a·mant, a. unyielding.

Ad′am's apple, bulge in the front of a man's throat.

a·dapt′, v. fit or adjust as needed. —**a·dapt′a·ble**, a. —**ad′ap·ta′tion**, n.

add, v. 1. join (to) so as to

increase. 2. increase. 3. find the sum of. 4. say further.

ad·den'dum, *n.* [*pl.* -DA] thing added, as an appendix.

ad'der, *n.* small snake, sometimes poisonous.

ad·dict', *v.* give (oneself) up (*to* a habit). —*n.* (ad'ikt) one addicted, as to a drug.

ad·di'tion, *n.* 1. an adding. 2. part added. —**ad·di'tion·al**, *a.*

ad'dle, *v.* make or become confused. —**ad'dled**, *a.*

ad·dress', *v.* 1. speak or write to. 2. write the destination on (mail, etc.). 3. apply (oneself *to*). —*n.* 1. a speech. 2. (*or* ad'res) place where one lives. —**ad·dress·ee'**, *n.*

ad·duce', *v.* give as proof.

ad'e·noids, *n.pl.* growths in the throat behind the nose.

a·dept', *a.* highly skilled. —*n.* (ad'ept) an expert.

ad'e·quate (-kwit) *a.* enough or good enough. —**ad'e·qua·cy**, *n.*

ad·here', *v.* 1. stick fast. 2. give support (*to*). —**ad·her'ence**, *n.* —**ad·her'ent**, *n.*

ad·he'sive, *a.* sticking. —*n.* sticky substance, as glue. —**ad·he'sion**, *n.*

a·dieu (ə-dū') *int. & n.* [Fr.] good-by.

ad in·fi·ni·tum (-nī'-) [L.] endlessly.

a·dios (ä-dyōs') *int. & n.* [Sp.] good-by.

ad'i·pose (-pōs) *a.* fatty.

ad·ja'cent, *a.* near or next.

ad'jec·tive (-tiv) *n.* word that qualifies a noun. —**ad'jec·ti'val** (-tī'-) *a.*

ad·join', *v.* be next to.

ad·journ' (-jûrn') *v.* suspend (a meeting, etc.) for a time. —**ad·journ'ment**, *n.*

ad·judge', *v.* judge, declare, or award.

ad·ju'di·cate (-jōō'-) *v.* act as judge (*in or on*).

ad'junct, *n.* a nonessential addition.

ad·jure', *v.* 1. order solemnly. 2. ask earnestly.

ad·just', *v.* 1. alter to make fit. 2. regulate. 3. settle rightly. —**ad·just'a·ble**, *a.* —**ad·just'ment**, *n.*

ad'ju·tant, *n.* assistant, esp. to a commanding officer.

ad-lib', *v.* [-LIBBED, -LIBBING] [Col.] improvise (words, etc.).

ad·min'is·ter, *v.* 1. manage; direct. 2. give; attend (*to*). —**ad·min'is·tra'tor**, *n.*

ad·min·is·tra'tion, *n.* 1. an administering. 2. executive officials; management. —**ad·min'is·tra'tive**, *a.*

ad'mi·ra·ble, *a.* worth admiring. —**ad'mi·ra·bly**, *adv.*

ad'mi·ral, *n.* high-ranking naval officer.

ad'mi·ral·ty, *n.* department of naval affairs.

ad·mire', *v.* have high regard for. —**ad'mi·ra'tion**, *n.*

ad·mis'si·ble, *a.* acceptable.

ad·mis'sion, *n.* 1. an admitting. 2. entrance fee. 3. confession or concession.

ad·mit', *v.* [-MITTED, -MITTING] 1. let enter. 2. concede or confess. —**ad·mit'tance**, *n.* —**ad·mit'ted·ly**, *adv.*

ad·mix'ture, *n.* mixture.

ad·mon'ish, *v.* 1. warn or advise. 2. reprove mildly. —**ad·mo·ni'tion**, *n.* —**ad·mon'i·to·ry**, *a.*

a·do' (-dōō') *n.* fuss; trouble.

a·do'be (-dō'bi) *n.* unburnt, sun-dried brick.

ad·o·les'cence, *n.* time between childhood and adulthood; youth. —**ad·o·les'cent**, *a. & n.*

a·dopt', *v.* 1. take legally as one's child. 2. take as one's own. —**a·dop'tion**, *n.*

a·dore', *v.* 1. worship. 2. love greatly. —**a·dor'a·ble**, *a.* —**ad·o·ra'tion**, *n.*

a·dorn', *v.* decorate; ornament. —**a·dorn'ment**, *n.*

ad·re'nal glands, two ductless glands on the kidneys.

ad·ren'a·lin, *n.* hormone that is a heart stimulant, etc.

a·drift', *adv. & a.* floating aimlessly.

a·droit', *a.* skillful and clever. —**a·droit'ly**, *adv.*

ad·u·la'tion (aj'ə-) *n.* too high praise.

a·dult', *a.* grown-up; mature. —*n.* mature person.

a·dul'ter·ate, *v.* make impure by adding things. —**a·dul·ter·a'tion**, *n.*

a·dul'ter·y, *n.* sexual unfaithfulness in marriage. —**a·dul'ter·ous**, *a.*

ad·vance', *v.* 1. bring or go forward. 2. pay before due. 3. rise or raise in rank. —*n.* 1. a move forward. 2. *pl.* approaches to get favor. —**in advance**, ahead of time. —**ad·vance'ment**, *n.*

ad·van'tage, *n.* 1. superiority. 2. gain; benefit. —**take advantage of**, use for one's own benefit. —**ad'van·ta'geous**, *a.*

ad·ven·ti·tious (-tĭ´-) *a.* not inherent; accidental.

ad·ven·ture, *n.* 1. dangerous undertaking. 2. exciting experience. —ad·ven´tur·er, *n.* —ad·ven´tur·ous, *a.*

ad·verb, *n.* word that modifies a verb, adjective, or other adverb. —ad·ver´bi·al, *a.*

ad·ver·sar·y, *n.* [*pl.* -IES] foe; opponent.

ad·verse (*or* ad´vĕrs) *a.* 1. opposed. 2. harmful.

ad·ver·si·ty, *n.* [*pl.* -TIES] misfortune.

ad·vert´, *v.* refer (to).

ad·ver·tise (-tīz) *v.* tell about publicly to promote sales, etc. —ad·ver´tis·ing, *n.*

ad·ver·tise·ment (*or* ad·vûr´tiz-) *n.* public notice, usually paid for.

ad·vice´, *n.* opinion on what to do.

ad·vis·a·ble (-vĭz´-) *a.* being good advice; wise. —ad·vis´a·bil´i·ty, *n.*

ad·vise´, *v.* 1. give advice (*to*). 2. offer as advice. 3. inform. —ad·vis´er, ad·vi´sor, *n.* —ad·vi´so·ry, *a.*

ad·vis·ed·ly, *adv.* with due consideration.

ad·vise·ment, *n.* careful consideration.

ad·vo·cate, *v.* support or urge. —*n.* (-kit) one who supports another or a cause. —ad´vo·ca·cy (-ka-si) *n.*

adz, adze, *n.* axlike tool.

ae·gis (ē´jĭs) *n.* sponsorship.

ae·on (ē´ən) *n.* very long time.

aer·ate (âr´-) *v.* expose to air. —aer·a´tion, *n.*

aer·i·al (âr´-) *a.* 1. of or like air. 2. of flying. —*n.* radio or TV antenna.

aero–, aero–, *pref.* 1. air; of air. 2. of aircraft.

aer·o·nau·tics (-nô´-) *n.* aviation. —aer´o·nau´ti·cal, *a.*

aer·o·space, *n.* earth's atmosphere and outer space.

aes·thet·ic (es-thet´-) *a.* 1. of beauty or aesthetics. 2. sensitive to art and beauty. —aes´thete (-thēt), *n.*

aes·thet·ics, *n.* study or philosophy of beauty.

a·far´, *adv.* far away.

af·fa·ble, *a.* pleasant; sociable. —af·fa·bil´i·ty, *n.*

af·fair´, *n.* 1. matter; event. 2. *pl.* business matters. 3. amorous episode.

af·fect´, *v.* 1. act on; influence. 2. stir emotionally. 3. like to wear, use, etc. 4. pretend to feel.

af·fec·ta·tion, *n.* pretense.

af·fect·ed, *a.* 1. artificial. 2. diseased. 3. influenced. 4. emotionally moved.

af·fec·tion, *n.* 1. fond feeling. 2. disease.

af·fec·tion·ate (-it) *a.* tender and loving.

af·fi·da·vit (-dā´-) *n.* sworn statement in writing.

af·fil·i·ate, *v.* join as a member; associate. —*n.* (-it) affiliated member. —af·fil´i·a´tion, *n.*

af·fin·i·ty, *n.* [*pl.* -TIES] 1. close relationship or kinship. 2. attraction.

af·firm´, *v.* assert or confirm. —af´fir·ma´tion, *n.*

af·firm·a·tive, *a.* affirming; positive. —*n.* assent.

af·fix´, *v.* attach. —*n.* (af´-) thing affixed, as a prefix.

af·flict´, *v.* cause pain to; distress. —af·flic´tion, *n.*

af·flu·ence, *n.* 1. plenty. 2. riches. —af·flu·ent, *a.*

af·ford´, *v.* 1. have money enough for. 2. provide.

af·front´, *n.* & *v.* insult.

af·ghan (-gan) *n.* crocheted or knitted wool blanket.

a·field´, *adv.* away; astray.

a·fire´, *adv.* & *a.* on fire.

a·flame´, *adv.* & *a.* in flames.

a·float´, *a.* 1. floating. 2. at sea. 3. current.

a·foot´, *adv.* & *a.* 1. on foot. 2. in motion; astir.

a·fore·said´, *a.* said before.

a·foul´, *adv.* & *a.* in a tangle.

a·fraid´, *a.* 1. frightened. 2. regretful.

a·fresh´, *adv.* anew; again.

Af´ri·can, *a.* of Africa. —*n.* native of Africa.

Af·ro, *n.* buoffant hair style.

aft, *a.* & *adv.* near the stern.

af·ter, *adv.* 1. behind. 2. later. —*prep.* 1. behind. 2. in search of. 3. later than. 4. because of. 5. in spite of. 6. in imitation of. 7. for. —*con.* later than. —*a.* later.

af·ter·birth, *n.* placenta, etc. expelled after childbirth.

af·ter·math, *n.* (bad) result.

af·ter·noon´, *n.* time from noon to evening.

af·ter·thought, *n.* thought coming later or too late.

af·ter·ward(s), *adv.* later.

a·gain´, *adv.* 1. once more. 2. besides.

a·gainst´, *prep.* 1. opposed to. 2. so as to hit. 3. next to. 4. in preparation for.

a·gape´, *adv.* & *a.* with mouth wide open.

ag´ate (-it) *n.* hard semi-

age, *n.* 1. length of time of existence. 2. time of getting full legal rights. 3. stage of life. 4. old age. 5. historical period. —*v.* grow old or make old.

-age, *suf.* act or state of; amount of; place of or for.

a'ged, *a.* 1. old. 2. (ā'jd) of the age of.

a'gen·cy (-jən-si) *n.* [*pl.* -CIES] 1. action or means. 2. firm acting for another.

a·gen'da (-jen'-) *n.* list of things to be dealt with.

a'gent, *n.* 1. force, or cause of an effect. 2. one that acts for another.

ag·gran'dize (*or* ə-gran'-) *v.* increase in power, riches, etc. —**ag·gran'dize·ment**, *n.*

ag'gra·vate, *v.* 1. make worse. 2. [Col.] vex; annoy. —**ag'gra·va'tion**, *n.*

ag'gre·gate (-git; *for* -gāt) *a., n.* total; mass. —**ag'gre·ga'tion**, *n.*

ag·gres'sion, *n.* unprovoked attack. —**ag·gres'sor**, *n.*

ag·gres'sive (-siv') *a.* 1. quarrelsome. 2. bold and active. —**ag·gres'sive·ly**, *adv.*

ag·grieve' (-grēv') *v.* offend.

a·ghast' (-gast') *a.* horrified.

ag'ile (aj'əl) *a.* quick; nimble. —**a·gil'i·ty** (-jil'-) *n.*

ag'i·tate (aj'-) *v.* 1. stir up. 2. disturb. 3. talk to arouse support (*for*). —**ag'i·ta'tion**, *n.* —**ag'i·ta'tor**, *n.*

a·glow', *adv. & a.* in a glow.

ag·nos'tic, *n.* one who doubts the existence of God.

a·go', *adv. & a.* (in the) past.

a·gog', *a.* eager; excited.

ag'o·ny, *n.* great suffering.

a·grar'i·an, *a.* of land and farming.

a·gree', *v.* 1. to consent. 2. be in harmony or accord. —**a·gree'ment**, *n.*

a·gree'a·ble, *a.* 1. pleasing. 2. willing to consent.

ag'ri·cul'ture, *n.* farming. —**ag'ri·cul'tur·al**, *a.*

a·ground', *adv. & a.* on or onto the shore, a reef, etc.

a·gue (ā'gū) *n.* fever with chills.

ah, *int.* cry of pain, delight, etc.

a·head', *adv. & a.* in front; forward; in advance.

a·hoy', *int.* Naut. hailing call.

aid, *v. & n.* help.

aide (ād) *n.* military officer assisting a superior: also

aide-de-camp [*pl.* AIDES-]

ail, *v.* 1. to pain. 2. be ill.

ai'le·ron (ā'-) *n.* hinged flap of an airplane wing.

ail'ment, *n.* chronic illness.

aim, *v.* 1. direct (a gun, blow, etc.). 2. intend. —*n.* 1. an aiming. 2. direction of aiming. 3. intention; goal. —**aim'less**, *a.*

ain't, [Col. or Substandard] am not; is not; are not.

air, *n.* 1. mixture of gases around the earth. 2. appearance. 3. *pl.* haughty manners. 4. tune. —*v.* 1. let air into. 2. publicize. —*a.* of aviation. —**on the air**, broadcasting on radio.

air conditioning, controlling of humidity and temperature of air in a room, etc.

air'craft, *n.sing. & pl.* machine or machines for flying.

air'field, *n.* field where aircraft can take off and land.

air line, air transport system or company.

air'man, *n.* [*pl.* -MEN] 1. aviator. 2. enlisted person in U.S. Air Force.

air'plane, *n.* motor-driven or jet-propelled aircraft.

air'port, *n.* airfield with facilities for repair, etc.

air raid, attack by aircraft.

air'ship, *n.* dirigible.

air'sick, *a.* nauseated because of air travel.

air'tight, *a.* too tight for air to enter or escape.

air'y, *a.* [-IER, -IEST] 1. open to the air. 2. flimsy as air. 3. light; graceful. 4. gay. —**air'i·ly**, *adv.*

aisle (īl) *n.* passageway between rows of seats.

a·jar', *adv. & a.* slightly open.

a·kim'bo, *adv. & a.* with hands on hips.

a·kin', *a.* similar; alike.

-al, *suf.* 1. of; like; fit for. 2. act or process of.

al'a·bas'ter, *n.* whitish, translucent gypsum.

a la carte, with a separate price for each dish.

a·lac'ri·ty, *n.* quick willingness; readiness.

a la mode, 1. in fashion. 2. served with ice cream.

a·larm', *n.* 1. signal or device to warn or waken. 2. fear. —*v.* frighten.

alarm clock, clock with device to sound at set time.

a·larm'ist, *n.* one who expresses needless alarm.

a·las', *int.* cry of sorrow, pity.

alb, *n.* priest's white robe.

al'ba·core, n. kind of tuna.

al'ba·tross, n. large, web-footed sea bird.

al·be'it (ôl-) con. although.

al·bi'no (-bī'-) n. [pl. -NOS] individual lacking normal coloration.

al'bum, n. blank book for photographs, stamps, etc.

al·bu'men (-bū'mən) n. white of an egg.

al·bu'min, n. protein in egg, milk, muscle, etc.

al'che·my (-kə-) n. chemistry of the Middle Ages. —**al'che·mist,** n.

al'co·hol, n. colorless, intoxicating liquid got from fermented grain, fruit, etc.

al'co·hol'ic, a. of alcohol. —n. one addicted to alcohol.

al'cove, n. recess; nook.

al'der (ôl'-) n. small tree of the birch family.

al'der·man, n. [pl. -MEN] member of a city council.

ale, n. kind of beer.

a·lert', a. watchful; ready. —n. an alarm. —v. warn to be ready. —**a·lert'ness,** n.

al·fal'fa, n. plant used for fodder, pasture, etc.

al'gae (-jē) n.pl. primitive water plants.

al'ge·bra, n. mathematics using letters and numbers in equations. —**al'ge·bra'ic,** a.

a'li·as (ā'-) n. assumed name. —adv. otherwise named.

al'i·bi (-bī) n. [pl. -BIS] 1. plea that the accused was not at the scene of the crime. 2. [Col.] any excuse. —v. [Col.] give an excuse.

al·ien (āl'yən) a. foreign. —n. foreigner.

al'ien·ate, v. make unfriendly. —**al'ien·a'tion,** n.

a·light', v. 1. dismount. 2. land after flight. —a. lighted up.

a·lign' (-līn') v. 1. line up. 2. make agree. —**a·lign'ment,** n.

a·like', a. similar. —adv. similarly. 2. equally.

al'i·men'ta·ry canal, the passage in the body that food goes through.

al'i·mo'ny, n. money paid to support one's former wife.

a·live', a. 1. living; in existence. 2. lively. —**alive with,** teeming with.

al'ka·li (-lī) n. [pl. -LIS, -LIES] substance that neutralizes acids. —**al'ka·line,** a. —**al'ka·lize,** v.

al'ka·loid, n. alkaline drug from plants, as cocaine.

all, a. 1. the whole of. 2. every one of. 3. complete. —pron. 1. [with pl. v.] every one. 2. everything. 3. every bit. —n. a whole. —adv. entirely. —**after all,** nevertheless. —**at all,** in any way.

Al'lah, n. God: Moslem name.

all'-a·round', a. having many abilities, uses, etc.

al·lay', v. to calm; quiet.

al·lege' (-lej') v. declare, esp. without proof. —**al'le·ga'tion** (-gā'-) n. —**al·leg'ed·ly,** adv.

al·le'giance (-lē'jəns) n. loyalty, as to one's country.

al'le·go'ry, n. [pl. -RIES] story in which things, actions, etc. are symbolic. —**al'le·gor'ic,** a.

al·le'gro, a. & adv. Music. fast.

al·ler'gy, n. [pl. -GIES] sensitive reaction to certain food, pollen, etc. —**al·ler'gic,** a.

al·le'vi·ate (-lē'-) v. relieve; ease. —**al·le'vi·a'tion,** n.

al'ley, n. [pl. -LEYS] 1. narrow street. 2. bowling lane.

al·li'ance (-lī'-) n. 1. an allying. 2. association; league.

al·lied', a. 1. united by treaty, etc. 2. related.

al'li·ga'tor, n. large lizard like a crocodile.

al·lit'er·a'tion, n. use of the same initial sound in words.

al'lo·cate, v. allot.

al·lot', v. [-LOTTED, -LOTTING] 1. distribute in shares. 2. assign. —**al·lot'ment,** n.

all'-out', a. thorough.

al·low', v. 1. to permit. 2. let have. 3. grant. —**allow for,** leave room, time, etc. for. —**al·low'a·ble,** a.

al·low'ance, n. 1. thing allowed. 2. amount given regularly.

al'loy, n. metal mixture. —v. (ə-loi') mix (metals).

all right, 1. satisfactory. 2. unhurt. 3. correct. 4. yes.

all'spice, n. pungent spice from a berry.

al·lude', v. refer; mention.

al·lure', v. tempt; attract. —**al·lur'ing,** a.

al·lu'sion, n. indirect or casual mention.

al·ly' (-lī') v. [-LIED, -LYING] unite; join. —n. (al'ī) [pl. -LIES] country or person joined with another.

al'ma ma'ter, college or school that one attended.

al'ma·nac, n. calendar with miscellaneous data.

al·might'y, a. all-powerful. —**the Almighty,** God.

al·mond (ä'mənd) n. edible,

nutlike, oval seed of a tree of the peach family.

al'most, *adv.* very nearly.

alms (ämz) *n.* money, food, etc. given to the poor.

al'oe (-ō) *n.* African plant whose juice is a laxative.

a·loft', *adv.* high up.

a·lo'ha, *n. & int.* love: Hawaiian "hello" or "goodby."

a·lone', *a. & adv.* with no other. —**let alone**, not to mention.

a·long', *prep.* on or beside the length of. —*adv.* 1. onward. 2. together (*with*). 3. with one. —**all along**, from the beginning.

a·long'side', *adv.* at the side. —*prep.* beside.

a·loof', *adv.* apart. —*a.* cool and reserved.

a·loud', *adv.* loudly.

al·pac'a (-pak'ə) *n.* 1. kind of llama. 2. cloth from its long, silky wool.

al'pha, *n.* first letter of the Greek alphabet.

al'pha·bet, *n.* letters of a language, in the regular order. —**al'pha·bet'i·cal**, *a.*

al'pha·bet·ize', *v.* arrange in alphabetical order.

al·read'y, *adv.* by or before the given time; previously.

al'so, *adv.* in addition; too.

al'tar (ôl'-) *n.* table, etc. for sacred rites, as in a church.

al'ter, *v.* change; modify. —**al'ter·a'tion**, *n.*

al'ter·ca'tion, *n.* a quarrel.

al'ter·nate (-nit) *a.* 1. succeeding each other. 2. every other. —*n.* a substitute. —*v.* (-nāt) do, use, act, etc. by turns. —**al'ter·na'tion**, *n.*

al·ter'na·tive (-tiv) *n.* choice between two or more. —*a.* giving such a choice.

al·though' (-thō') *con.* in spite of the fact that.

al·tim'e·ter, *n.* instrument for measuring altitude.

al'ti·tude, *n.* height, esp. above sea level.

al'to, *n.* [*pl.* -TOS] lowest female voice.

al'to·geth'er, *adv.* wholly.

al'tru·ism, *n.* unselfish concern for others. —**al'tru·ist**, *n.* —**al'tru·is'tic**, *a.*

al'um, *n.* astringent salt.

a·lu'mi·num, *n.* silvery, lightweight metal, a chemical element: also [Br.] **al'u·min'i·um**, *n.*

a·lum'nus, *n.* [*pl.* -NI (-nī)] former student of a certain school or college. —**a·lum'**-

na [*pl.* -NAE (-nē)] *n.fem.*

al'ways, *adv.* 1. at all times. 2. continually.

am, *pres. t.* of **be**, with *I.*

A.M., **a.m.**, before noon.

a·mal'gam, *n.* alloy of mercury and another metal.

a·mal'ga·mate, *v.* unite. —**a·mal'ga·ma'tion**, *n.*

am'a·ranth, *n.* plant with showy flowers.

am'a·ryl'lis (-ril'-) *n.* bulb plant with lilylike flowers.

a·mass', *v.* pile up; collect.

am'a·teur (-choor) *n.* 1. one who does something for pleasure. 2. unskillful person. —**am'a·teur'ish**, *a.*

am'a·to'ry, *a.* of love.

a·maze', *v.* astonish; surprise. —**a·maze'ment**, *n.*

am'a·zon, *n.* strong woman.

am·bas'sa·dor, *n.* top-ranking diplomatic official.

am'ber, *n.* 1. yellowish fossil resin. 2. its color.

am'ber·gris (-grēs) *n.* waxy secretion of certain whales, used in perfumes.

am·bi·dex'trous, *a.* using both hands with equal ease.

am·big'u·ous, *a.* having two or more meanings; vague. —**am'bi·gu'i·ty** [*pl.* -TIES] *n.*

am·bi'tion, *n.* 1. desire to succeed. 2. success desired. —**am·bi'tious**, *a.*

am·biv'a·lence, *n.* simultaneous conflicting feelings. —**am·biv'a·lent**, *a.*

am'ble, *v.* move in an easy gait. —*n.* easy gait.

am·bro'sia (-zha) *n. Gr. & Rom. myth.* food of the gods.

am'bu·lance (-byoo-) *n.* car to carry sick or wounded.

am'bu·late, *v.* walk.

am'bu·la·to'ry, *a.* 1. of walking. 2. able to walk.

am·bus·cade', *n. & v.* ambush.

am'bush, *n.* 1. a hiding for a surprise attack. 2. the hiding place or troops. —*v.* to attack from hiding.

a·me'ba (-mē'-) *n.* amoeba.

a·mel'io·rate (-mēl'ya-) *v.* improve. —**a·mel'io·ra'tion**, *n.*

a·men', *int.* may it be so!

a·me'na·ble (-mē'nə-, -men'ə-) *a.* willing to obey or heed advice; responsive. —**a·me'na·bly**, *adv.*

a·mend', *v.* 1. to correct. 2. improve. 3. revise, as a law. —**a·mend'ment**, *n.*

a·mends', *n.* a making up for injury, loss, etc.

a·men'i·ty, *n.* [*pl.* -TIES] 1.

pleasantness. 2. *pl.* cour-
tesies.

A·mer'i·can, *a.* 1. of America. 2. of the U.S. —*n.* 1.
native of America. 2. U.S.
citizen.

A·mer'i·can·ize', *v.* make or
become American.

am'e·thyst (-thist) *n.* purple quartz for jewelry.

a·mi·a·ble (ā'-) *a.* good-
natured; friendly.

am'i·ca·ble, *a.* friendly;
peaceable. —**am'i·ca·bly,**
adv.

a·mid', **a·midst',** *prep.*
among.

a·mid'ship(s), *adv.* in or toward the middle of a ship.

a·mi'no acids (-mē'-) basic
matter of proteins.

a·miss', *adv. & a.* wrong.

am'i·ty, *n.* friendship.

am'me'ter, *n.* instrument
for measuring amperes.

am·mo'ni·a, *n.* 1. acrid gas.
2. water solution of it.

am·mu·ni'tion, *n.* bullets,
gunpowder, bombs, etc.

am·ne'sia (-zha) *n.* loss of
memory.

am'nes·ty, *n.* general pardon for political offenses.

a·moe'ba (-mē'-) *n.* [*pl.* -BAS,
-BAE (-bē)] one-celled ani-
mal. —**a·moe'bic,** *a.*

a·mong', **a·mongst',** *prep.*
1. surrounded by 2. in the
group of. 3. to or for each of.

a·mor'al (ā-) *a.* with no
moral sense or standards.

am'o·rous, *a.* 1. fond of making love. 2. full of love.

a·mor'phous, *a.* 1. shape-
less. 2. of no definite type.

am'or·tize, *v.* provide for
gradual payment of.

a·mount', *v.* 1. add up (*to*).
2. be equal (*to*). —*n.* 1.
sum. 2. quantity.

a·mour' (-moor') *n.* love
affair.

am'pere (-pêr) *n.* unit of
electric current.

am·phib'i·an, *n.* 1. land-
and-water animal, as the
frog. 2. land-and-water vehicle. —*a.* amphibious.

am·phib'i·ous, *a.* adapted
to both land and water.

am'phi·the·a·ter, *n.* open
theater with central space
circled by tiers of seats.

am'ple, *a.* 1. large. 2. adequate; plenty. —**am'ply,** *adv.*

am'pli·fy, *v.* make stronger,
louder, or fuller. —**am'pli-
fi·ca'tion,** *n.* —**am'pli·fi-
er,** *n.*

am'pli·tude, *n.* 1. extent or

breadth. 2. abundance.

am'pu·tate (-pyoo-) *v.* to
cut off, esp. by surgery.
—**am'pu·ta'tion,** *n.*

am·pu·tee', *n.* one who has
had a limb amputated.

a·muck', *a. & adv.* in a mad
rage to kill.

am'u·let (-yoo-) *n.* charm
worn against evil.

a·muse', *v.* 1. entertain. 2.
make laugh. —**a·mus'ing,**
a. —**a·muse'ment,** *n.*

an, *a., indefinite article* 1.
one. 2. each; any one.

-an, *suf.* 1. of. 2. born in;
living in. 3. believing in.

a·nach'ro·nism (-nak'-) *n.*
thing out of proper historical
time. —**a·nach'ro·nis'tic,**
a.

an·a·con'da, *n.* large S.
American boa snake.

a·nae'mi·a (-nē'-) *n.* anemia.

an'a·gram, *n.* word made by
rearranging the letters of
another word.

a'nal, *a.* of the anus.

an'al·ge'sic (-jē'-) *n. & a.*
(drug) that eases pain.

a·nal'o·gy (-ji) *n.* [*pl.* -GIES]
similarity in some ways.
—**a·nal'o·gous** (-gos) *a.*

a·nal'y·sis (-ǝ-sis) *n.* [*pl.* -SES
(-sēz)] 1. separation of a
whole into its parts to find
out their nature, etc. 2.
psychoanalysis. —**an'a·lyst**
(-list) *n.* —**an·a·lyt'i·cal,** *a.*
—**an'a·lyze** (-līz) *v.*

an'arch·ism (-ēr·kiz'm) *n.*
opposition to all government.
—**an'arch·ist,** *n.*

an'arch·y, *n.* 1. absence of
government and law. 2. great
disorder. —**an·ar'chic,** *a.*

a·nath'e·ma, *n.* 1. person or
thing accursed or detested.
2. ritual curse. —**a·nath'e-
ma·tize',** *v.*

a·nat'o·my, *n.* 1. science of
plant or animal structure.
2. structure of an organism.
—**an·a·tom'i·cal,** *a.*

-ance, *suf.* 1. action or state
of. 2. a thing that (is).

an'ces·tor (-ses-) *n.* person
from whom one is descended.

an'ces·try, *n.* 1. family descent. 2. all one's ancestors.
—**an·ces'tral,** *a.*

an'chor (-kēr) *n.* metal
weight lowered from a ship
to prevent drifting. —*v.*
hold secure. **at anchor,**
anchored. —**an'chor·age,** *n.*

an'cho·rite (-kǝ-) *n.* hermit.

an'cho·vy (-chō-) *n.* [*pl.*
-VIES] tiny herring.

an'cient (-shǝnt) *a.* 1. of

times long past. **2.** very old.
—**n.** [in *pl.*] people of ancient times.

an·cil·lar·y, *a.* auxiliary.

and, *con.* **1.** also. **2.** plus. **3.** as a result.

an·dan·te, *a. & adv. Mus.* moderately slow.

and·i·rons, *n.pl.* metal stands for logs in a fireplace.

an·dro·gen (-jan) *n.* male sex hormone.

an·ec·dote, *n.* brief story.

a·ne·mi·a (-nē′-) *n.* deficiency of red blood cells.
—**a·ne′mic,** *a.*

an·e·mom′e·ter, *n.* gauge measuring wind velocity.

a·nem′o·ne (-nē) *n.* plant with cup-shaped flowers.

a·nent′, *prep.* concerning.

an·es·the′sia (-zha) *n.* loss of the sense of pain, touch, etc.

an·es·thet′ic, *n. & a.* (drug, gas, etc.) that produces anesthesia. —**an·es′the·tize,** *n.* —**an·es′the·tist,** *n.*

an·gel (ān′jal) *n.* messenger of God, pictured with wings and halo. —**an·gel′ic** (an-) *a.*

angel (food) cake, light, spongy, white cake.

an′ger, *n.* hostile feeling; wrath. —*v.* make angry.

an·gi′na pec′to·ris (-jī′-) heart disease with chest pains.

an′gle, *n.* **1.** space formed by two lines or surfaces that meet. **2.** point of view. —*v.* **1.** bend at an angle. **2.** fish with hook and line. **3.** use tricks to get something. —**an′gler,** *n.*

an′gle·worm, *n.* earthworm.

An′gli·cize (-sīz) *v.* make English in form, sound, etc.

An·glo-, *pref.* English (and).

An′glo-Sax′on, *n.* **1.** native of England before 12th c. **2.** person of English descent. **3.** Old English.

An·go′ra, *n.* wool from long-haired goat or rabbit.

an′gry, *a.* [-GRIER, -GRIEST] **1.** feeling anger; enraged. **2.** stormy. —**an′gri·ly,** *adv.*

an′guish (-gwish) *n.* great pain, worry, or grief.

an′gu·lar (-gyoo-) *a.* having angles. —**an′gu·lar′i·ty,** *n.*

an′i·line (-′l-in) *n.* oily liquid made from benzene, used in dyes, etc.

an′i·mad·vert′, *v.* criticize. —**an′i·mad·ver′sion,** *n.*

an′i·mal, *n.* **1.** living organism able to move about. **2.** any four-footed creature. —*a.* **1.** of an animal. **2.** bestial.

an′i·mate, *v.* **1.** give life to. **2.** make gay. —*a.* (-mit) **1.** living. **2.** lively. —**an′i·mat′ed,** *a.* —**an′i·ma′tion,** *n.*

an·i·mos′i·ty, *n.* strong hatred; ill will.

an′i·mus, *n.* ill will.

an′ise (-is) *n.* plant whose seed is used as flavoring.

an′kle, *n.* joint connecting foot and leg.

an′nals, *n.pl.* historical records, year by year.

an·neal′ (-nēl′) *v.* toughen (glass or metal) by heating and then cooling slowly.

an·nex′, *v.* attach or join to a larger unit. —*n.* (an′eks) something annexed. —**an′nex·a′tion,** *n.*

an·ni′hi·late (-nī′ə-) *v.* destroy. —**an·ni′hi·la′tion,** *n.*

an·ni·ver′sa·ry, *n.* [*pl.* -RIES] yearly return of the date of some event.

an′no·tate, *v.* provide explanatory notes for. —**an′no·ta′tion,** *n.*

an·nounce′, *v.* make known; tell about. —**an·nounc′er,** *n.* —**an·nounce′ment,** *n.*

an·noy′, *v.* to bother or anger. —**an·noy′ance,** *n.*

an′nu·al, *a.* yearly. —*n.* **1.** plant living one year. **2.** yearbook. —**an′nu·al·ly,** *adv.*

an·nu′i·ty, *n.* [*pl.* -TIES] investment yielding fixed annual payments.

an·nul′, *v.* [-NULLED, -NULLING] make null and void. —**an·nul′ment,** *n.*

an·ode (-ōd) *n.* positive electrode.

an′o·dyne (-dīn) *n.* anything that relieves pain.

a·noint′, *v.* put oil on, as in consecrating.

a·nom′a·ly, *n.* [*pl.* -LIES] unusual or irregular thing. —**a·nom′a·lous,** *a.*

a·non′, *adv.* **1.** soon. **2.** at another time.

a·non′y·mous (-i-mas) *a.* with name unknown or withheld; unidentified. —**an′o·nym′i·ty** (-nim′-) *n.*

an·oth′er, *a. & pron.* **1.** one more. **2.** a different (one).

an′swer (-sēr) *n.* **1.** thing said or done in return; reply. **2.** solution to a problem. —*v.* **1.** reply (to). **2.** serve or suit. **3.** be responsible. —**an′swer·a·ble,** *a.*

ant, *n.* small insect living in colonies.

-ant, *suf.* 1. that has, shows, or does. 2. one that.

ant·ac'id, *n. & a.* (substance) counteracting acids.

an·tag'o·nism, *n.* hostility. —**an·tag'o·nis'tic,** *a.*

an·tag'o·nist, *n.* opponent.

an·tag'o·nize, *v.* incur the dislike of.

ant·arc'tic, *a.* of or near the South Pole. —*n.* antarctic region.

an'te (-ti) *n.* player's stake in poker. —*v.* [-TEED or -TED, -TEING] put in one's stake.

ante-, *pref.* before.

ant'eat'er, *n.* long-snouted mammal that feeds on ants.

an'te·ced'ent (-sēd'-) *a.* prior. —*n.* 1. thing prior to another. 2. word or phrase to which a pronoun refers.

an'te·date', *v.* occur before.

an'te·di·lu'vi·an, *a.* 1. before the Flood. 2. outmoded.

an'te·lope, *n.* horned animal like the deer.

an·ten'na, *n.* [*pl.* -NAE (ē), -NAS] 1. feeler on the head of an insect, etc. 2. [-NAS] wire(s) for sending and receiving radio waves.

an·te'ri·or, *a.* 1. toward the front. 2. earlier.

an'te·room', *n.* room leading to another room.

an'them, *n.* religious or patriotic choral song.

an'ther, *n.* pollen-bearing part of a stamen.

an·thol'o·gy, *n.* [*pl.* -GIES] collection of poems, stories, etc. —**an·thol'o·gist,** *n.*

an'thra·cite, *n.* hard coal.

an'thrax, *n.* disease of cattle.

an'thro·poid, *a.* manlike. —*n.* an anthropoid ape.

an'thro·pol'o·gy, *n.* study of the races, customs, etc. of mankind. —**an'thro·pol'o·gist,** *n.*

anti-, *pref.* 1. against. 2. that acts against.

an'ti·bi·ot'ic, *n.* substance produced by some microorganisms, able to kill or weaken bacteria.

an'ti·bod'y, *n.* [*pl.* -IES] substance produced in body to act against toxins, etc.

an'tic, *n.* silly act; prank.

an·tic'i·pate (-tis'-) *v.* 1. expect. 2. act on before. —**an·tic'i·pa'tion,** *n.*

an·ti·cli'max (-klī'-) *n.* sudden drop from the important to the trivial.

an'ti·dote, *n.* remedy to counteract a poison or evil.

an'ti·freeze', *n.* substance used to prevent freezing.

an'ti·his'ta·mine' (-mēn') *n.* drug used to treat allergies.

an'ti·mo'ny, *n.* silvery metal in alloys, a chemical element.

an'ti·pas'to (-päs'-) *n.* [It.] appetizer of spicy meat, fish, etc.

an·tip'a·thy (-thi) *n.* [*pl.* -THIES] strong dislike.

an·tip'o·des (-dēz) *n.pl.* opposite places on the globe.

an'ti·quar'i·an (-kwär'-) *a.* of antiques or antiquaries. —*n.* antiquary.

an'ti·quar'y, *n.* [*pl.* -IES] collector or student of antiquities.

an'ti·quate, *v.* make obsolete. —**an'ti·quat'ed,** *a.*

an·tique' (-tēk') *a.* 1. of a former period. 2. out-of-date. —*n.* piece of furniture, etc. of earlier times.

an·tiq'ui·ty (-tik'wə-) *n.* [*pl.* -TIES] 1. ancient times. 2. great age. 3. ancient relic, etc.

an'ti·Sem'i·tism, *n.* prejudice against Jews. —**an'ti·Se·mit'ic** (-mit'-) *a.*

an'ti·sep'tic, *a.* preventing infection by killing germs. —*n.* antiseptic substance.

an'ti·so'cial, *a.* 1. not sociable. 2. harmful to society.

an·tith'e·sis, *n.* [*pl.* -SES] exact opposite.

an'ti·tox'in, *n.* serum that counteracts a disease.

an'ti·trust', *a.* regulating business trusts.

ant'ler, *n.* branched horn of a deer, elk, etc.

an'to·nym (-nim) *n.* word opposite in meaning.

a'nus, *n.* opening at rear end of the alimentary canal.

an'vil, *n.* block on which to hammer metal objects.

anx·i'e·ty (aŋ·zī'-) *n.* [*pl.* -TIES] 1. worry about what may happen. 2. eager desire.

anx'ious (aŋk'shəs) *a.* 1. worried. 2. eagerly wishing. —**anx'ious·ly,** *adv.*

an'y, *a.* 1. one of more than two. 2. some. 3. every. —*pron. sing. & pl.* any person(s) or amount. —*adv.* at all.

an'y·bod'y, *pron.* anyone.

an'y·how, *adv.* 1. in any way. 2. in any case.

an'y·one, *pron.* any person.

an'y·thing, *pron.* any thing. —**anything but,** not at all.

an'y·way, *adv.* anyhow.

an'y·where, *adv.* in, at, or to any place.

a·or'ta (ā-) *n.* main artery leading from the heart.

a·pace', *adv.* swiftly.

a·part', *adv.* 1. aside. 2. away from (one) another. 3. into pieces. —*a.* separated.

a·part'ment, *n.* room or set of rooms to live in.

a·pa'thy, *n.* lack of feeling or interest. —**ap·a·thet'ic**, *a.*

ape, *n.* large, tailless monkey. —*v.* imitate.

ap·er'ture (-chēr) *n.* opening.

a'pex, *n.* highest point.

a'phid, *n.* insect that sucks the juices of plants.

aph'o·rism, *n.* wise saying.

aph'ro·dis'i·ac, *n.* & *a.* (drug, etc.) arousing sexual desire.

a·pi'a·ry, *n.* [*pl.* -IES] collection of beehives.

a·piece', *adv.* to or for each.

a·plomb' (ə-plom') *n.* poise.

a·poc'ry·phal, *a.* of doubtful authenticity.

a·pol'o·gist, *n.* defender of a doctrine, action, etc.

a·pol'o·gy (-ji) *n.* [*pl.* -GIES] 1. expression of regret for a fault, etc. 2. defense of an idea, etc. —**a·pol'o·get'ic**, *a.* —**a·pol'o·gize**, *v.*

ap'o·plex'y, *n.* paralysis caused by a broken blood vessel in the brain. —**ap·o·plec'tic**, *a.*

a·pos'tate, *n.* one who abandons his faith, principles, etc. —**a·pos'ta·sy**, *n.*

A·pos'tle (-pos'l) *n.* 1. any of the disciples of Jesus. 2. [a-] leader of a new movement. —**ap'os·tol'ic**, *a.*

a·pos'tro·phe (-fi) *n.* sign (') indicating: 1. omission of letter(s) from a word. 2. possessive case.

a·poth'e·car'y, *n.* [*pl.* -IES] druggist.

ap·pall', **ap·pal'** (-pôl') *v.* to dismay. —**ap·pal'ling**, *a.*

ap'pa·ra'tus (-râ'- *or* -ra'-) *n.* 1. tools, etc. for a specific use. 2. complex device.

ap·par'el, *n.* clothes. —*v.* clothe; dress.

ap·par'ent, *a.* 1. obvious; plain. 2. seeming. —**ap·par'ent·ly**, *adv.*

ap·pa·ri'tion, *n.* ghost.

ap·peal', *n.* 1. request for help. 2. attraction. 3. request for rehearing by a higher court. —*v.* 1. make an appeal. 2. be attractive.

ap·pear' (-pēr') *v.* 1. come into sight. 2. seem. 3. come before the public. —**ap·pear'ance**, *n.*

ap·pease', *v.* quiet by satis-

fying. —**ap·pease'ment**, *n.*

ap·pel'lant, *n.* one who appeals to a higher court.

ap·pel'late court (-it) court handling appeals.

ap·pel·la'tion, *n.* a name.

ap·pend', *v.* add or attach.

ap·pend'age (-ij) *n.* attached part, as a tail.

ap'pen·dec'to·my [*pl.* -MIES] *n.* surgical removal of the appendix.

ap·pen·di·ci'tis, *n.* inflammation of the appendix.

ap·pen'dix, *n.* [*pl.* -DIXES, -DICES (-də-sēz)] 1. extra material at the end of a book. 2. small, closed tube attached to large intestine.

ap·per·tain', *v.* pertain.

ap'pe·tite, *n.* desire (esp. for food).

ap'pe·tiz'ing, *a.* stimulating the appetite; savory. —**ap'pe·tiz'er**, *n.*

ap·plaud', *v.* show approval, esp. by clapping the hands; praise. —**ap·plause'**, *n.*

ap'ple, *n.* round, fleshy fruit. —**ap'ple·sauce**, *n.*

ap·pli'ance, *n.* device or machine, esp. for home use.

ap'pli·cant, *n.* one who applies, as for a job.

ap·pli·ca'tion, *n.* 1. an applying. 2. thing applied. 3. formal request.

ap·pli·qué' (-kā') *n.* decoration of one fabric on another.

ap·ply', *v.* [-PLIED, -PLYING] 1. to put on. 2. put into use. 3. devote (oneself) diligently. 4. ask formally. 5. be relevant. —**ap'pli·ca·ble**, *a.*

ap·point', *v.* 1. set (a time, etc.). 2. name to an office. 3. furnish. —**ap·point'ee'**, *n.* —**ap·poin'tive**, *a.* —**ap·point'ment**, *n.*

ap·por'tion, *v.* portion out. —**ap·por'tion·ment**, *n.*

ap'po·site (-zit) *a.* fitting.

ap'po·si'tion, *n.* placing of a word or phrase beside another in explanation. —**ap·pos'i·tive**, *a.* & *n.*

ap·praise', *v.* estimate the value of. —**ap·prais'al**, *n.* —**ap·prais'er**, *n.*

ap·pre'ci·a·ble (-shi-) *a.* enough to be noticed. —**ap·pre'ci·a·bly**, *adv.*

ap·pre'ci·ate (-shi-) *v.* 1. value; enjoy. 2. recognize rightly or gratefully. —**ap·pre'ci·a'tion**, *n.* —**ap·pre'ci·a·tive**, *a.*

ap·pre·hend', *v.* 1. arrest. 2. understand. 3. fear. —**ap·pre·hen'sion**, *n.*

ap·pre·hen′sive, *a.* anxious.

ap·pren′tice (-tis) *n.* helper who is being taught a trade. —*v.* place as apprentice. —**ap·pren′tice·ship**, *n.*

ap·prise′, ap·prize′ (-prīz′) *v.* 1. inform; notify.

ap·proach′, *v.* 1. come nearer (to). 2. speak to. —*n.* 1. a coming near. 2. way of beginning. 3. access.

ap′pro·ba′tion, *n.* approval.

ap·pro′pri·ate, *v.* 1. take for one's own use. 2. set (money) aside for some use. —*a.* (-it) suitable. —**ap·pro′pri·ate·ly**, *adv.* —**ap·pro′pri·a′tion**, *n.*

ap·prove′, *v.* 1. consent to. 2. have a favorable opinion (of). —**ap·prov′al**, *n.*

ap·prox′i·mate, *v.* be about the same as. —*a.* (-mit) nearly exact or correct. —**ap·prox′i·ma′tion**, *n.*

ap·pur′te·nance, *n.* 1. adjunct. 2. additional right.

ap·pur′te·nant, *a.* pertaining.

a′pri·cot (ā′- *or* a′-) *n.* small peachlike fruit.

A′pril, *n.* fourth month.

a′pron, *n.* garment to protect the front of clothes.

ap·ro·pos′ (-pō′) *a.* fitting. —**apropos of**, regarding.

apt, *a.* 1. fitting; suitable. 2. likely (*to*). 3. quick to learn.

ap′ti·tude, *n.* 1. ability. 2. quickness to learn.

aq′ua·ma·rine′ (ak′wə-) *n. & a.* bluish green.

aq′ua·plane′, *n.* towed board ridden in water sports.

a·quar′i·um (-kwâr′-) *n.* tank, etc. for keeping fish or other water animals.

A·quar′i·us, *n.* 11th sign of the zodiac; Water Bearer.

a·quat′ic (-kwät′-) *a.* 1. living in water. 2. taking place in water.

aq′ue·duct (ak′wi-) *n.* large pipe or channel bringing water from a distance.

a′que·ous (ā′kwi-) *a.* of or like water.

aq′ui·line (ak′wə-līn) *a.* curved like an eagle's beak.

Ar′ab, A·ra′bi·an, *n.* one of many nomadic people native to Arabia, etc. —**Ar·a′bic**, *a. & n.*

Arabic numerals, figures 1, 2, 3, 4, 5, 6, 7, 8, 9, and 0.

ar′a·ble, *a.* fit for plowing.

a·rach′nid (-rak′-) *n.* small, eight-legged animal, as the spider or mite.

ar′bi·ter, *n.* judge; umpire.

ar′bi·trar′y, *a.* using only one's own wishes or whim. —**ar′bi·trar′i·ly**, *adv.*

ar′bi·trate, *v.* settle (a dispute) by using or being an arbiter. —**ar·bi·tra′tion**, *n.* —**ar′bi·tra′tor**, *n.*

ar′bor, *n.* place shaded by trees, shrubs, or vines.

ar·bo′re·al, *a.* of, like, or living in trees.

ar′bor·vi′tae (-vī′tē) *n.* small kind of pine tree.

ar·bu′tus, *n.* evergreen trailing plant.

arc, *n.* 1. curved line, as part of a circle. 2. band of light made by electricity leaping a gap.

ar·cade′, *n.* 1. covered passage, esp. one lined with shops. 2. row of arches or columns.

arch, *n.* curved structure over an opening. —*v.* form (as) an arch. —*a.* 1. chief. 2. mischievous; coy.

arch-, *pref.* chief; main.

ar′chae·ol′o·gy (är′ki-) *n.* study of ancient peoples, as by excavation of ruins. Also sp. **archeology**. —**ar′chae·o·log′i·cal**, *a.*

ar·cha′ic (-kā′-) *a.* 1. out-of-date. 2. now seldom used.

arch′an·gel (ärk′-) *n.* angel of the highest rank.

arch′bish′op (ärch′-) *n.* bishop of the highest rank.

arch′en·e·my, *n.* chief enemy.

arch′er·y, *n.* a shooting with bow & arrow. —**arch′er**, *n.*

ar′che·type (-kə-) *n.* original model.

ar′chi·pel′a·go′ (-kə-) *n.* chain of islands in a sea.

ar′chi·tect (-ki-) *n.* one who designs buildings.

ar′chi·tec′ture (-chēr) *n.* science of designing and constructing buildings. —**ar′chi·tec′tur·al**, *a.*

ar′chives (-kīvz) *n.pl.* public records or place to store them.

arch′way, *n.* passage under an arch.

arc′tic, *a.* of or near the North Pole. —*n.* arctic region.

ar′dent, *a.* passionate; eager. —**ar′dent·ly**, *adv.*

ar′dor, *n.* passion; zeal.

ar′du·ous (-jōō-) *a.* laborious or strenuous.

are, pres. t. of **be**, used with *you, we,* and *they.*

ar′e·a, *n.* 1. region. 2. total

surface, measured in square units. 3. scope.

a·re'na (-rē'-) n. 1. center of amphitheater, for contests, etc. 2. area of struggle.

aren't, are not.

ar'gon, n. chemical element, gas used in radio tubes, etc.

ar'go·sy, n. [Poet.] large merchant ship or fleet.

ar'got (-gō, -gət) n. special vocabulary, as of thieves.

ar·gue, v. 1. give reasons (for or against). 2. dispute; debate. —**ar'gu·ment,** n. —**ar'gu·men·ta'tion,** n. —**ar'gu·men·ta'tive,** a.

a'ri·a (är'i-, âr'i-) n. solo in an opera, etc.

-arian, suf. one of specified age, belief, work, etc.

ar'id, a. 1. dry. 2. dull. —**a·rid'i·ty,** n.

Ar'i·es (-ēz) n. 1st sign of the zodiac; Ram.

a·right', adv. correctly.

a·rise', v. [AROSE, ARISEN, ARISING] 1. get up; rise. 2. come into being.

ar'is·toc'ra·cy, n. 1. government by an upper class minority. 2. upper class. —**a·ris'to·crat,** n. —**a·ris'to·crat'ic,** a.

a·rith'me·tic, n. science of computing by numbers. —**ar'ith·met'i·cal,** a.

ark, n. Bible boat in which Noah, etc. survived the Flood.

arm, n. 1. upper limb of the human body. 2. anything like this. 3. weapon. 4. military branch. 5. pl. heraldic symbols. —v. provide with weapons. —**up in arms,** indignant. —**with open arms,** cordially.

ar·ma'da (-mä'-) n. fleet of warships.

ar'ma·dil'lo, n. [pl. -LOS] tropical mammal covered with bony plates.

ar'ma·ment, n. often in pl. military forces & equipment.

ar'ma·ture (-chēr) n. revolving coil in an electric motor or dynamo.

arm'chair, n. chair with supports for one's arms.

arm'ful, n. [pl. -FULS] as much as the arms can hold.

ar'mis·tice (-tis) n. truce.

ar'mor, n. protective covering. —**ar'mored,** a.

ar·mor'i·al, a. heraldic.

ar'mo·ry, n. [pl. -IES] 1. arsenal. 2. military drill hall.

arm'pit, n. the hollow under the arm at the shoulder.

ar'my, n. [pl. -MIES] 1. large body of soldiers. 2. any very large group.

a·ro'ma, n. pleasant odor. —**ar'o·mat'ic,** a.

a·rose', pt. of **arise.**

a·round', adv. & prep. 1. in a circle (about). 2. on all sides (of). 3. to the opposite direction. 4. [Col.] near by.

a·rouse', v. wake; stir up.

ar·raign' (-rān') v. 1. bring to court for trial. 2. accuse. —**ar·raign'ment,** n.

ar·range', v. 1. put in a certain order. 2. plan. 3. adjust; adapt. —**ar·range'ment,** n.

ar'rant, a. out-and-out.

ar·ray', v. 1. place in order. 2. dress finely. —n. 1. orderly grouping. 2. impressive display. 3. finery.

ar·rears', n.pl. overdue debts. —**in arrears,** behind in payment.

ar·rest', v. 1. stop or check. 2. seize. 3. seize and hold by law. —n. an arresting.

ar·rest'ing, a. interesting.

ar·rive', v. 1. reach one's destination. 2. come. —**ar·riv'al,** n.

ar'ro·gant, a. haughty; overbearing. —**ar'ro·gance,** n.

ar'ro·gate, v. seize arrogantly. —**ar'ro·ga'tion,** n.

ar'row, n. 1. pointed shaft shot from a bow. 2. sign (→) to show direction.

ar'row·head, n. pointed tip of an arrow.

ar'row·root, n. starch from a tropical plant root.

ar·roy'o, n. [pl. -OS] n. 1. dry gully. 2. stream.

ar'se·nal, n. place for making or storing weapons.

ar'se·nic, n. silvery-white, poisonous chemical element.

ar'son, n. crime of purposely setting fire to property.

art, n. 1. skill; craft. 2. aesthetic work, as painting, sculpture, music, etc. 3. pl. academic studies. 4. cunning; wile. —v. [Ar.] form of **are,** used with **thou.**

ar·te'ri·o·scle·ro'sis, n. hardening of the arteries.

ar'ter·y, n. [pl. -IES] 1. tube carrying blood from the heart. 2. a main road. —**ar·te'ri·al** (-têr'i-) a.

art'ful, a. 1. skillful; clever. 2. crafty; cunning.

ar·thri'tis, n. inflammation of joints. —**ar·thrit'ic,** a.

ar'ti·choke, n. 1. thistle-like plant. 2. its flower head, cooked as a vegetable.

ar'ti·cle, n. 1. single item. 2. separate piece of writing, as in a magazine. 3. section of a document. 4. any of the words a, an, or the.

ar·tic'u·late, v. 1. speak clearly. 2. join. —a. (-lit) 1. clear in speech. 2. jointed. —**ar·tic'u·la'tion,** n.

ar'ti·fice (-fis) n. 1. trick or trickery. 2. clever skill.

ar·ti·fi'cial, a. 1. made by man; not natural. 2. not genuine; affected. —**ar·ti·fi'ci·al'i·ty,** n.

ar·til'ler·y, n. 1. mounted guns, as cannon. 2. military branch using these.

ar'ti·san (-z'n) n. skilled craftsman.

art'ist, n. person with skill, esp. in any of the fine arts.

ar·tis'tic, a. 1. of art or artists. 2. skillful. —**ar'tist·ry,** n.

art'less, a. 1. unskillful. 2. simple; natural.

art'y, a. [-IER, -IEST] [Col.] affectedly artistic.

as, adv. 1. equally. 2. for instance. —con. 1. in the way that. 2. while. 3. because. 4. though. —pron. that. —prep. in the role of. —**as for** (or **to**), concerning.

as·bes'tos, n. fibrous mineral used in fireproofing.

as·cend' (-send') v. go up; climb. —**as·cen'sion,** n.

as·cend'an·cy, as·cend'en·cy, n. domination. —**as·cend'ant, as·cend'ent,** a.

as·cent', n. 1. an ascending. 2. upward slope.

as·cer·tain' (-sĕr-tān') v. find out with certainty.

as·cet'ic (-set'-) a. self-denying. —n. one who denies himself pleasures. —**as·cet'i·cism,** n.

as·cor'bic acid, vitamin C.

as'cot, n. scarflike necktie.

as·cribe', v. assign or attribute. —**as·crip'tion,** n.

a·sep'tic, a. free from disease germs.

a·sex'u·al, a. sexless.

ash, n. 1. often pl. grayish powder left from something burned. 2. shade tree. —**ash'en,** a. —**ash'y,** a.

a·shamed', a. feeling shame.

a·shore', adv. & a. to or on shore.

A'sian (-zhən), **A'si·at'ic,** a. & a. (native) of the continent of Asia.

a·side', adv. 1. on or to one side. 2. away. 3. apart. —n.

actor's words spoken aside. —**aside from,** except for.

as'i·nine (-nīn) a. stupid; silly. —**as'i·nin'i·ty** (-nin'-) [pl. -TIES] n.

ask, v. 1. call for an answer to. 2. inquire of or about. 3. request. 4. invite.

a·skance', adv. 1. sideways. 2. with suspicion.

a·skew' (-skū') adv. & a. awry.

a·slant', adv. & a. on a slant. —prep. slantingly across.

a·sleep', a. 1. sleeping. 2. numb. —adv. into sleep.

a·so'cial (ā-) a. not social; avoiding others.

asp, n. poisonous snake.

as·par'a·gus, n. plant with edible green shoots.

as'pect, n. 1. look or appearance. 2. side or facet.

as'pen, n. poplar tree with fluttering leaves.

as·per'i·ty, n. [pl. -TIES] harshness; sharpness.

as·per'sion (-pūr'-) n. a slur; slander.

as'phalt, n. tarlike substance used for paving, etc.

as·phyx'i·ate (fik'si-) v. ov-ercome by cutting down oxygen in the blood. —**as·phyx'i·a'tion,** n.

as'pic, n. jelly of meat juice, tomato juice, etc.

as·pi·ra'tion, n. ambition.

as·pire', v. be ambitious (to). —**as·pir'ant,** n.

as'pi·rin, n. drug that relieves pain or fever.

ass, n. 1. donkey. 2. fool.

as·sail', v. attack.

as·sail'ant, n. attacker.

as·sas'sin, n. murderer.

as·sas'si·nate, v. murder, esp. for political reasons. —**as·sas'si·na'tion,** n.

as·sault' (-sôlt') n. & v. attack.

as·say', n. & v. test; analyze.

as·sem'ble, v. 1. gather in a group. 2. put together. —**as·sem'blage** (-blij) n.

as·sem'bly, n. [pl. -BLIES] 1. an assembling. 2. group. 3. [A-] legislative body.

as·sent', v. & n. consent.

as·sert', v. 1. declare. 2. defend, as rights. —**as·ser'tion,** n. —**as·ser'tive,** a.

as·sess', v. 1. set a value on for taxes. 2. impose a fine, tax, etc. —**as·sess'ment,** n. —**as·ses'sor,** n.

as'set, n. 1. valuable thing. 2. pl. property, cash, etc.

as·sev'er·ate, v. declare.

as·sid'u·ous, a. diligent. 2.

as·sign', v. 1. designate. 2.

appoint. 3. allot; give. —**as·sign'ment**, n.

as·sim·i·late, v. merge; absorb. —**as·sim·i·la'tion**, n.

as·sist', v. & n. help; aid. —**as·sist'ance**, n. —**as·sist'ant**, a. & n.

as·so'ci·ate, v. 1. join. 2. connect in the mind. 3. join (with) as a partner, etc. —n. (-it) partner, colleague, etc. —a. (-it) associated. —**as·so'ci·a'tion**, n.

as'so·nance, n. likeness of sound.

as·sort'ed, a. 1. miscellaneous. 2. sorted.

as·sort'ment, n. variety.

as·suage (a-swāj') v. ease (pain, hunger, etc.).

as·sume', v. 1. take on (a role, look, etc.). 2. undertake. 3. take for granted. 4. pretend to have. —**as·sump'tion**, n.

as·sure' (-shoor') v. 1. make sure; convince. 2. give confidence to. 3. promise. 4. guarantee. —**as·sur'ance**, n. —**as·sured'**, a.

as'ter, n. daisylike flower.

as'ter·isk, n. sign (*) used to mark footnotes, etc.

a·stern', a. & adv. at or toward the rear of a ship.

asth'ma (az'-) n. chronic disorder characterized by coughing, hard breathing, etc. —**asth·mat'ic**, a.

a·stig'ma·tism, n. eye defect that keeps light rays from focusing to one point.

a·stir', adv. & a. in motion.

as·ton'ish (a-ston'-) v. fill with sudden surprise. —**as·ton'ish·ing**, a. —**as·ton'ish·ment**, n.

as·tound', v. astonish greatly. —**as·tound'ing**, a.

a·stray', adv. & a. off the right path.

a·stride', adv., a. & prep. with a leg on either side (of).

as·trin'gent, n. & a. (substance) contracting body tissue and blood vessels.

as·trol'o·gy, n. pseudo science of effect of stars, etc. on human affairs. —**as·trol'o·ger**, n. —**as'tro·log'i·cal**, a.

as'tro·naut, n. traveler in outer space. —**as'tro·nau'tics**, n.

as·tron'o·my, n. science of the stars and other heavenly bodies. —**as·tron'o·mer**, n. —**as'tro·nom'i·cal**, a.

as·tute', a. shrewd; keen.

a·sun'der, adv. & a. apart.

a·sy'lum, n. 1. place of safety. 2. institution for the mentally ill, aged, etc.

at, prep. 1. on; in; near. 2. to or toward. 3. busy with. 4. in the state of. 5. because of.

a'va·tism, n. a throwback.

ate, pt. of eat.

-ate, suf. 1. make, become, or form. 2. to treat with. 3. of or like.

at'el·ier (-yā) n. studio.

a'the·ism (-thē-) n. belief that there is no God. —**a'the·ist**, n. —**a·the·is'tic**, a.

a·thirst', a. eager.

ath'lete, n. one skilled at sports requiring strength, speed, etc. —**ath·let'ic**, a. —**ath·let'ics**, n.pl.

athlete's foot, ringworm of the feet.

a·thwart', prep. & adv. 1. across. 2. against.

a·tilt', a. & adv. tilted.

a·tin'gle, a. tingling.

at'las, n. book of maps.

at'mos·phere, n. 1. the air surrounding the earth. 2. general feeling or spirit. —**at·mos·pher'ic**, a.

at·oll' (-ōl) n. coral island surrounding a lagoon.

at'om, n. smallest particle of a chemical element, made up of electrons, protons, etc. —**a·tom'ic**, a.

atomic (or **atom**) **bomb**, bomb whose immense power derives from nuclear fission.

atomic energy, energy released from an atom in nuclear reactions.

at'om·iz·er, n. device for spraying liquid in a mist.

a·tone', v. make amends (for). —**a·tone'ment**, n.

a·top', a., adv. & prep. on the top (of).

a·tro'cious (-shas) a. 1. cruel or evil. 2. [Col.] very bad. —**a·troc'i·ty** (-tros'-) —[pl. -TIES] n.

at'ro·phy, v. [-PHIED, -PHYING] waste away or shrink up. —n. a trophying.

at·tach', v. 1. fasten; join. 2. tie by devotion. 3. seize by legal order. —**at·tach'ment**, n.

at'ta·ché (-shā'), n. member of a diplomatic staff.

at·tack', v. 1. fight or work against. 2. undertake vigorously. —n. 1. an attacking. 2. fit of illness.

at·tain', v. 1. gain; achieve. 2. arrive at. —**at·tain'a·ble**, a. —**at·tain'ment**, n.

at'tar (-ēr) *n.* perfume made from flower petals.

at·tempt', *v. & n.* try.

at·tend', *v.* 1. be present at. 2. pay attention. 3. go with. —**attend to**, take care of. —**at·tend'ant**, *n.*

at·tend'ance, *n.* 1. an attending. 2. number present.

at·ten'tion, *n.* 1. a giving heed. 2. heed; notice. 3. *pl.* kind acts. —**at·ten'tive**, *a.*

at·ten'u·ate, *v.* thin out; weaken. —**at·ten'u·a'tion**, *n.*

at·test', *v.* 1. declare to be true. 2. be proof of.

at'tic, *n.* space just below the roof; garret.

at·tire', *v.* clothe; dress up. —*n.* clothes.

at'ti·tude, *n.* 1. bodily posture. 2. way of looking at things, or manner.

at·tor'ney (-tūr'-) *n.* [*pl.* -NEYS] lawyer: also **attorney at law**.

attorney general, chief law officer of a government.

at·tract', *v.* 1. draw to itself. 2. make notice or like one. —**at·trac'tion**, *n.* —**at·trac'tive**, *a.*

at·trib'ute, *v.* think of as belonging or owing (to). —*n.* (at'rə-būt) characteristic. —**at·trib'ut·a·ble**, *a.* —**at'tri·bu'tion**, *n.*

at·tri'tion (-trī'-) *n.* a wearing down bit by bit.

at·tune', *v.* bring in tune.

a·typ'i·cal, *a.* not typical.

au'burn, *a. & n.* red-brown.

auc'tion, *n.* public sale in which items go to the highest bidder. —*v.* sell at auction. —**auc·tion·eer'**, *n. & v.*

au·da'cious (-shəs) *a.* 1. bold; reckless. 2. insolent. —**au·dac'i·ty**, *n.*

au'di·ble, *a.* loud enough to be heard. —**au'di·bly**, *adv.*

au'di·ence, *n.* 1. group seeing or hearing a play, concert, radio or TV show, etc. 2. formal interview.

au'di·o, *a.* of the sound portion of a TV broadcast.

au'dit, *v.* examine and check (accounts). —*n.* an auditing. —**au'di·tor**, *n.*

au·di'tion, *n.* a hearing to try out a singer, actor, etc. —*v.* try out in an audition.

au'di·to'ri·um, *n.* hall for speeches, concerts, etc.

au'di·to'ry, *a.* of hearing.

au'ger (-gēr) *n.* tool for boring holes in wood.

aught (ôt) *n.* 1. anything.

2. naught. —*adv.* in any way.

aug·ment', *v.* increase. —**aug'men·ta'tion**, *n.*

au gra·tin (ō grä') [Fr.] with browned cheese crust.

au'gur (-gēr) *v.* foretell. —**au'gu·ry** (-gyēr-i) *n.*

Au'gust, *n.* eighth month.

au·gust', *a.* imposing.

au jus (ō zhōō) [Fr.] in its natural gravy.

auk, *n.* diving sea bird.

aunt, *n.* 1. sister of one's parent. 2. uncle's wife.

au'ra, *n.* radiance or air about a person or thing.

au'ral, *a.* of hearing.

au're·ole, *n.* halo.

‡**au re·voir** (ō'rə-vwär') [Fr.] good-by.

au'ri·cle, *n.* 1. outer part of the ear. 2. an upper chamber of the heart.

au·ro'ra, *n.* dawn.

aurora bo·re·a'lis (-al'is) luminous bands in the northern night sky.

aus'pic·es (-pis-iz) *n.pl.* patronage.

aus·pi'cious (-pish'əs) *a.* favorable; of good omen. —**aus·pi'cious·ly**, *adv.*

aus·tere', *a.* 1. strict. 2. very plain; severe. —**aus·ter'i·ty** [*pl.* -TIES] *n.*

Aus·tral'ian (-trāl'-) *n. & a.* (native) of the continent or country of Australia.

au·then'tic, *a.* true, real, genuine, etc. —**au·then'tic'i·ty** (-tis'-) *n.*

au·then'ti·cate, *v.* 1. make valid. 2. verify. —**au·then'ti·ca'tion**, *n.*

au'thor, *n.* writer or originator. —**au'thor·ship**, *n.*

au·thor'i·tar'i·an, *a.* enforcing or favoring strict obedience to authority.

au·thor'i·ta·tive, *a.* having or showing authority.

au·thor'i·ty, *n.* [*pl.* -TIES] 1. power to command. 2. *pl.* persons with such power. 3. expert; reliable source.

au'thor·ize, *v.* 1. give official approval to. 2. empower. —**au'thor·i·za'tion**, *n.*

au'to, *n.* [*pl.* -TOS] [Col.] automobile.

auto-, *pref.* self.

au'to·bi·og'ra·phy, *n.* [*pl.* -PHIES] one's own life story written by oneself. —**au'to·bi·o·graph'i·cal**, *a.*

au'to·crat, *n.* ruler with unlimited power. —**au·toc'ra·cy**, *n.* —**au'to·crat'ic**, *a.*

au'to·graph, *n.* signature.

—v. write one's signature on.

au·to·mat, n. restaurant dispensing food from coin-operated compartments.

au·to·mat·ic, a. 1. done without conscious effort. 2. operating by itself. —**au·to·mat·i·cal·ly**, adv.

au·to·ma·tion, n. automatic system of manufacture, as by electronic devices.

au·tom·a·ton, n. robot.

au·to·mo·bile, n. car propelled by its own engine, for use on streets and roads. —**au·to·mo·tive**, a.

au·ton·o·my, n. self-government. —**au·ton·o·mous**, a.

au·top·sy, n. [pl. -SIES] examination of a corpse to find cause of death, etc.

au·tumn (-tam) n. season after summer, when leaves fall. —**au·tum′nal** (-n'l) a.

aux·il·ia·ry (ôg-zĭl′yə-ri) a. 1. helping. 2. subsidiary. —n. [pl. -IES] auxiliary group, etc.

auxiliary verb, helping verb, as has in "he has gone."

a·vail′, v. be of use or help (to). —n. use or help. **avail oneself of**, make use of.

a·vail·a·ble, a. that can be got or had. —**a·vail·a·bil′i·ty**, n.

av′a·lanche (-ris) n. great fall of rock, snow, etc. down a hill.

a·vant-garde (ä′vän-gärd′) n. [Fr.] vanguard.

av′a·rice (-ris) n. greed for money. —**av·a·ri′cious**, a.

a·vast′, int. Naut. stop!

a·venge′, v. get revenge for. —**a·veng′er**, n.

av′e·nue, n. 1. street. 2. way to something; approach.

a·ver′ (-vûr′) v. [AVERRED, AVERRING] declare to be true.

av′er·age, n. 1. sum divided by the number of quantities added. 2. usual kind, amount, etc. —a. being the average. —v. 1. figure the average of. 2. do on the average. —**on the average**, as an average amount, rate, etc.

a·verse′, a. unwilling.

a·ver′sion, n. dislike.

a·vert′, v. 1. turn away. 2. prevent.

a′vi·a·ry (ā′-) n. [pl. -IES] large cage for many birds.

a′vi·a′tion, n. science or work of flying airplanes. —**a′vi·a′tor**, n.

av′id, a. eager or greedy.

av′o·ca′do (-kä′-) n. [pl. -DOS] thick-skinned tropical fruit with buttery flesh.

av′o·ca′tion (-kā′-) n. hobby.

a·void′, v. keep away from; shun. —**a·void′a·ble**, a. —**a·void′ance**, n.

av·oir·du·pois (av′ĕr-də-poiz′) n. weight system in which 16 oz.=1 lb.

a·vouch′, v. assert; affirm.

a·vow′, v. declare openly; admit. —**a·vow′al**, n.

a·wait′, v. wait for.

a·wake′, v. [pt. & alt. pp. AWOKE] rouse from sleep. —a. 1. not asleep. 2. alert.

a·wak′en, v. rouse; awake. —**a·wak′en·ing**, n. & a.

a·ward′, v. give after judging. —n. 1. decision, as by judges. 2. prize.

a·ware′, a. conscious; knowing. —**a·ware′ness**, n.

a·way′, adv. 1. to another place. 2. aside. 3. from one's keeping. —a. 1. absent. 2. at a distance. —**do away with**, get rid of.

awe, n. reverent fear and wonder. —v. inspire awe in. —**awe′-struck′**, a.

awe′some, a. causing awe.

aw′ful, a. 1. terrifying; dreadful. 2. [Col.] bad. —adv. [Col.] very. —**aw′ful·ly**, adv.

a·while′, adv. for a short time.

awk′ward, a. 1. clumsy. 2. uncomfortable. 3. embarrassing. —**awk′ward·ly**, adv.

awl, n. pointed tool for making holes in wood, etc.

awn, n. bristly fibers on a head of barley, oats, etc.

awn′ing, n. overhanging shade of canvas, metal, etc.

a·wry (ə-rī′) adv. & a. 1. with a twist to a side. 2. amiss.

ax, **axe**, n. [pl. AXES] tool for chopping wood, etc.

ax′i·om, n. an evident truth. —**ax′i·o·mat′ic**, a.

ax′is, n. [pl. AXES (-ēz)] straight line around which a thing rotates. —**ax′i·al**, a.

ax′le, n. rod on which a wheel revolves.

aye, **ay** (ā) adv. [Ar.] always.

aye, **ay** (ī) adv. & n. yes.

a·zal′ea (-zāl′ya) n. shrub with brightly colored flowers.

az′ure (azh′-) a. & n. sky blue.

B

baa (bä) v. & n. bleat.

bab′ble, v. 1. talk in a foolish or jumbled way. 2. murmur. —n. babbling talk or sound. —**bab′bler**, n.

babe, n. baby.

ba'bel (bā'-) *n.* tumult.

ba·boon', *n.* ape with dog-like snout.

ba·bush'ka (-boosh'-) *n.* scarf worn on the head.

ba'by, *n.* [*pl.* -BIES] very young child; infant. —*a.* 1. of, for, or like a baby. 2. small or young. —*v.* [-BIED, -BYING] pamper. —**ba'by·hood'**, *n.* —**ba'by·ish'**, *a.*

ba'by-sit', *v.* [-SAT, -SITTING] take care of children when parents are away. —**baby sitter.**

bac·ca·lau·re·ate (-lô'ri-it) *n.* 1. bachelor's degree. 2. a talk to graduating class.

bac'cha·nal (bak'ə-) *n.* drunken orgy. —**bac'cha·na'li·an** (-nā'-) *a.*

bach'e·lor, *n.* unmarried man. —**bach'e·lor·hood**, *n.*

Bachelor of Arts (or **Science**, etc.) college degree.

ba·cil'lus (-sil'-) *n.* [*pl.* -LI (-lī)] kind of bacteria.

back, *n.* 1. rear or hind part. 2. backbone. 3. the reverse. 4. football player behind the line. —*a.* 1. at the rear. 2. of the past. 3. backward. —*adv.* 1. at or to the rear. 2. to a former time, etc. 3. in return. —*v.* 1. move backward. 2. support. 3. provide a back for. —**back down**, retract an opinion, etc.

back'er, *n.* —**back'ing**, *n.*

back'bite, *v.* to slander.

back'bone, *n.* 1. spinal column. 2. courage; firmness.

back'drop, *n.* curtain at the back of a stage.

back'fire, *n.* faulty ignition, as in the exhaust pipe of an engine. —*v.* 1. have a backfire. 2. go awry.

back·gam'mon, *n.* game played on a special board.

back'ground, *n.* 1. the part behind, more distant, etc. 2. past events, causes, etc.

back'hand, *n.* backhanded stroke, as in tennis.

back'hand·ed, *a.* 1. with the back of the hand forward. 2. insincere.

back'log, *n.* piling up, as of work to be done.

back'pack, *n.* knapsack. —*v.* hike wearing a backpack.

back'slide, *v.* to fall back in morals, religious faith, etc.

back'stage', *adv.* in theater dressing rooms, etc.

back talk, [Col.] insolence.

back'track, *v.* to retreat.

back'ward, *adv.* 1. toward the back. 2. with the back

foremost. 3. into the past. Also **back'wards**. —*a.* 1. turned to the rear or away. 2. shy. 3. retarded. —**back'ward·ness**, *n.*

back'woods', *n.pl.* remote, wooded areas. —**back'woods'man** [*pl.* -MEN] *n.*

ba'con, *n.* cured meat from hog's back or sides.

bac·te'ri·a, *n.pl.* [*sing.* -RIUM] microorganisms causing diseases, fermentation, etc. —**bac·te'ri·al**, *a.*

bac·te'ri·ol'o·gy, *n.* study of bacteria.

bad, *a.* [WORSE, WORST] 1. not good. 2. spoiled. 3. incorrect. 4. wicked. 5. severe. —*adv.* [Col.] badly. —*n.* anything bad. —**in bad**, [Col.] in trouble. —**bad'ly**, *adv.* —**bad'ness**, *n.*

bade (bad) *pt.* of **bid**.

badge, *n.* pin or emblem worn to show rank, membership, etc.

badg'er, *n.* burrowing animal. —*v.* to nag; pester.

bad'min·ton, *n.* game using rackets & a feathered cork.

baf'fle, *v.* puzzle; bewilder. —*n.* deflecting screen. —**baf'fling**, *a.*

bag, *n.* 1. container made of fabric, paper, etc. 2. suitcase. 3. purse. —*v.* [BAGGED, BAGGING] 1. hang loosely. 2. kill or capture. —**in the bag**, [Col.] certain. —**bag'gy**, *a.*

bag·a·telle', *n.* a trifle.

bag'gage, *n.* luggage.

bag'pipe(s), *n.* musical instrument with a bag from which air is forced into pipes.

bah (bä) *int.* shout of scorn.

bail, *n.* money left as security to free a prisoner until trial. —*v.* 1. get freed by giving bail. 2. dip out (water) from (a boat). —**bail out**, to parachute.

bail'iff, *n.* 1. court officer guarding prisoners and jurors. 2. sheriff's assistant.

bail'i·wick, *n.* one's field of interest or authority.

bait, *v.* 1. torment, as by insults. 2. put food on (a hook, etc.) as a lure. —*n.* anything used as a lure.

bake, *v.* 1. cook by dry heat in an oven. 2. harden by heat. —**bak'er**, *n.*

bak'er·y, *n.* [*pl.* -IES] place where bread, etc. is baked.

baking powder, leavening powder.

baking soda, sodium bicarbonate, powder used as leav-

bal'ance, *n.* 1. instrument for weighing, with two pans. 2. equilibrium. 3. harmonious proportion. 4. equality of or difference between credits and debits. 5. [Col.] remainder. —*v.* 1. compare. 2. offset; counteract. 3. put, keep, or be in equilibrium. 4. be equal. 5. sum up or equalize the debits and credits of (an account). —**in the balance,** not yet settled.

bal'co·ny, *n.* [*pl.* -NIES] 1. platform projecting from an upper story. 2. tier of theater seats above main floor.

bald, *a.* 1. lacking hair on the head. 2. plain and frank. —**bald'ness,** *n.*

bal'der·dash (bôl'-) *n.* nonsense.

bale, *n.* large bundle, as of raw cotton. —*v.* make into bales.

bale'ful, *a.* harmful; evil.

balk (bôk) *v.* 1. stop and refuse to move. 2. obstruct. —*n.* obstruction; hindrance. —**balk'y,** *a.*

ball, *n.* 1. round object; sphere. 2. round or oval object used in games. 3. formal social dance. —*v.* form into a ball. —**on the ball,** [Sl.] alert.

bal'lad, *n.* 1. popular love song. 2. folk song or poem telling a story.

bal'last (-əst) *n.* heavy matter put in a ship, etc. to keep it steady. —*v.* to furnish with ballast.

ball bearing, 1. bearing in which the parts turn on rolling metal balls. 2. one of these balls.

bal'le·ri'na (-rē'-) *n.* woman ballet dancer.

bal'let (-ā) *n.* intricate, formalized group dance.

bal·lis'tics, *n.* science of the motion of projectiles.

bal·loon', *n.* bag that rises when filled with light gas. —*v.* swell; expand.

bal'lot, *n.* 1. paper marked in voting. 2. voting. —*v.* to vote.

ball'room, *n.* large room for social dances.

bal'ly·hoo', *n.* [Col.] loud, exaggerated talk, etc.

balm (bäm) *n.* fragrant healing ointment or oil.

balm'y, *a.* [-IER, -IEST] soothing, mild, etc.

ba·lo'ney, *n.* 1. bologna. 2. [Sl.] nonsense.

bal'sa (bôl'-) *n.* lightweight wood of a tropical tree.

bal'sam (bôl'-) *n.* 1. aromatic resin. 2. tree yielding it.

bal'us·ter, *n.* railing post.

bal·us·trade', *n.* row of balusters supporting a rail.

bam·boo', *n.* tropical grass with hollow, treelike stems.

bam·boo'zle, *v.* [Col.] 1. trick. 2. confuse.

ban, *v.* [BANNED, BANNING] forbid. —*n.* formal forbidding by authorities.

ba'nal (bā'-) *a.* trite. —**ba·nal'i·ty** (-TIES) *n.*

ba·nan'a, *n.* long tropical fruit with creamy flesh.

band, *n.* 1. strip of cloth, etc. as for binding. 2. stripe. 3. range of radio wave lengths. 4. group of people. 5. group of performing musicians. —*v.* 1. mark or tie with a band. 2. join.

band'age (-ij) *n.* cloth strip to bind an injury. —*v.* bind with a bandage.

ban·dan'na, ban·dan'a, *n.* large, colored handkerchief.

band'box, *n.* light pasteboard box for hats, etc.

ban'dit, *n.* robber; brigand. —**ban'dit·ry,** *n.*

band'stand, *n.* (outdoor) platform for an orchestra.

band'wag'on, *n.* winning or popular side.

ban'dy, *v.* [-DIED, -DYING] toss or pass back and forth. —*a.* curved outward. —**ban'dy-leg'ged,** *a.*

bane, *n.* cause of harm or ruin. —**bane'ful,** *a.*

bang, *v. & n.* (make, or hit with) a loud noise.

ban'gle, *n.* bracelet.

bangs, *n.pl.* short hair worn across the forehead.

ban'ish, *v.* 1. to exile. 2. dismiss. —**ban'ish·ment,** *n.*

ban'is·ter, *n.* 1. baluster. 2. *pl.* balustrade.

ban'jo, *n.* [*pl.* -JOS, -JOES] stringed musical instrument with a circular body. —**ban'jo·ist,** *n.*

bank, *n.* 1. mound; heap. 2. steep slope, as beside a river. 3. row; tier. 4. business handling savings, loans, etc. —*v.* 1. form a bank. 2. put (money) in a bank. 3. cover (a fire) to make last. —**bank on,** [Col.] rely on. —**bank'er,** *n.*

bank'rupt, *a.* 1. legally declared unable to pay one's debts. 2. lacking. —*n.*

bankrupt person. —v. make bankrupt. —**bank'rupt·cy,** n.

ban'ner, n. flag. —a. foremost; leading.

banns, bans, n.pl. church notice of coming marriage.

ban'quet, n. formal dinner.

ban'shee, n. Folklore female spirit warning of death.

ban'tam, n. [B-] breed of small chickens. —a. small.

ban'ter, v. tease playfully. —n. genial teasing.

ban'yan, n. Asian fig tree with many trunks.

bap'tism, n. rite of admission into a Christian church by dipping in or sprinkling with water. —**bap·tis'mal,** a. —**bap'tize,** v.

bar, n. 1. long, narrow piece of wood, metal, etc. 2. oblong piece, as of soap. 3. obstruction. 4. band or strip. 5. law court. 6. legal profession. 7. counter or place for serving liquor. 8. Music a measure or vertical line marking it off. —v. [BARRED, BARRING] 1. obstruct; close. 2. oppose. 3. exclude. —prep. excluding.

barb, n. sharp, back-curving point. —**barbed,** a.

bar·bar'i·an (-bâr'-) n. uncivilized person; savage. —a. uncivilized. —**bar·bar'ic,** a. —**bar·bar'i·ty,** n.

bar'ba·rous, a. 1. uncivilized. 2. crude; coarse. 3. brutal. —**bar'ba·rism,** n.

bar'be·cue, n. 1. animal roasted whole over open fire. 2. picnic at which such meat is served. —v. 1. roast whole. 2. broil in spicy sauce (**barbecue sauce**).

bar'ber, n. one who cuts hair, shaves beards, etc.

bar·bi'tu·rate (-bich'ə-rit) n. drug used as a sedative.

bard, n. poet.

bare, a. 1. naked. 2. exposed. 3. empty. 4. mere. —v. uncover. —**bare'foot(ed),** a. & adv. —**bare'head·ed,** a. & adv.

bare'back, adv. & a. on a horse with no saddle.

bare'faced, a. shameless.

bare'ly, adv. only just.

bar'gain (-g'n) n. 1. agreement or contract. 2. item bought at a favorable price. —v. haggle. —**bargain for,** expect.

barge, n. flat-bottomed freight boat. —v. [Col.] enter abruptly (into).

bar'i·tone (bar'-) n. male voice, or instrument, between tenor and bass.

bar'i·um, n. silver-white metallic chemical element.

bark, n. 1. outside covering of trees. 2. sharp cry of a dog. 3. sailing vessel. —v. 1. utter a bark. 2. scrape off the skin of.

bark'er, n. announcer at a carnival side show.

bar'ley (-li) n. cereal grain.

barn, n. farm building for livestock, storage, etc. —**barn'yard,** n.

bar'na·cle, n. shellfish that clings to ships, etc.

barn'storm, v. tour small towns, acting plays, etc.

ba·rom'e·ter, n. instrument to measure atmospheric pressure. —**bar'o·met'ric,** a.

bar'on, n. nobleman of lowest rank. —**bar'on·ess,** n.fem. —**ba·ro'ni·al** (-rō'-) a.

bar'o·net, n. Br. man with hereditary rank of honor.

ba·roque' (-rōk') a. having elaborate decoration.

bar'racks, n.pl. building(s) for housing soldiers.

bar·ra·cu'da (-kōō'-) n. [pl. -DA, -DAS] fierce tropical fish.

bar·rage (bə-räzh') n. curtain of artillery fire.

bar'rel, n. 1. round, wooden container with bulging sides. 2. tube of a gun.

bar'ren, a. 1. sterile. 2. unproductive.

bar·rette (bə-ret') n. clasp for a girl's hair.

bar'ri·cade, n. barrier for defense. —v. block with a barricade.

bar'ri·er (bar'-) n. fence, wall, or other obstruction.

bar'ring, prep. excepting.

bar'ris·ter (bar'-) n. Br. courtroom lawyer.

bar'room, n. room with a bar (n. 7).

bar'row (bar'ō) n. traylike frame for carrying loads.

bar'tend'er, n. man serving drinks at a bar (n. 7).

bar'ter, v. exchange (goods). —n. a bartering.

bas'al (bā's'l) a. basic.

ba·salt' (bə-sôlt') n. dark volcanic rock.

base, n. 1. part that a thing rests on. 2. basis. 3. goal in some games. 4. headquarters. 5. substance reacting with an acid to form a salt. —v. put on a base. —a. 1. morally low. 2. inferior. —**base'ly,** adv.

base′ball, n. 1. team game played with bat and ball. 2. the ball used.

base′less, a. unfounded.

base′ment, n. story just below the main floor.

bash, v. [Col.] hit hard.

bash′ful, a. socially timid; shy. —**bash′ful·ly,** adv.

bas′ic, a. of or at the base; fundamental. —**bas′i·cal·ly,** adv.

bas·il (baz′l) n. an herb.

ba·sil′i·ca, n. ancient kind of church building.

ba′sin, n. 1. wide, shallow container for liquid. 2. a sink. 3. bay, cove, etc. 4. area drained by a river.

ba′sis, n. [pl. -SES (-sēz)] 1. base or foundation. 2. main constituent.

bask, v. warm oneself.

bas′ket, n. 1. container made of interwoven strips. 2. goal in basketball.

bas′ket·ball, n. 1. team game with raised open nets through which a large ball must be tossed. 2. this ball.

bass (bās) n. 1. lowest male singing voice. 2. singer or instrument with low range.

bass (bas) n. perchlike fish.

bas′set, n. short-legged hound.

bas·si·net′, n. baby's bed like a large basket.

bas·soon′, n. double-reed, bass wood-wind instrument.

bass viol, huge, deep-toned violinlike instrument.

bast, n. plant fiber used for ropes, mats, etc.

bas′tard, n. illegitimate child. —a. 1. illegitimate. 2. sham, not standard, etc.

baste, v. 1. sew with loose, temporary stitches. 2. moisten (a roast) with drippings, etc. —**bast′ing,** n.

bas·tion (bas′chan) n. 1. part of a fort that juts out. 2. any strong defense.

bat, n. 1. a club to hit a ball, as in baseball. 2. nocturnal, mouselike, flying mammal. —v. [BATTED, BATTING] 1. hit as with a bat. 2. [Col.] blink.

batch, n. quantity taken, made, etc. in one lot.

bat′ed (bāt′-) a. held in, as the breath in fear.

bath, n. 1. a washing of the body. 2. water, etc. for bathing or soaking something. 3. bathtub. 4. bathroom.

bathe (bāth) v. 1. give a bath to, or take a bath. 2. put into a liquid. 3. cover as with liquid. —**bath′er,** n.

ba′thos (bā′-) n. a shift from noble to trivial.

bath′robe, n. loose robe worn to and from the bath.

bath′room, n. room with a bathtub, toilet, etc.

bath′tub, n. tub to bathe in.

ba·tiste′ (-tēst′) n. fine, thin cotton fabric.

ba·ton′ (-ton′) n. 1. stick used in leading an orchestra, etc. 2. staff serving as a symbol of office.

bat·tal′ion, n. subdivision of a regiment.

bat′ten, n. strip of wood. —v. 1. fasten with battens. 2. fatten; thrive.

bat′ter, v. 1. strike repeatedly. 2. injure by hard use. —n. 1. player at bat in baseball. 2. mixture of flour, milk, etc. for making cakes.

bat′ter·y, n. [pl. -IES] 1. cell or cells providing electric current. 2. set of artillery guns. 3. pitcher and catcher in baseball. 4. illegal beating of a person.

bat′ting, n. wadded fiber.

bat′tle, n. & v. fight, esp. between armies. —**bat′tler,** n.

bat′tle-ax(e)′, n. heavy ax formerly used as a weapon.

bat′tle·dore, n. racket for a game like badminton.

bat′tle·field, n. place of battle: also **bat′tle·ground.**

bat′tle·ment, n. low wall on a tower with open spaces for shooting.

bat′tle·ship, n. large warship with big guns.

bat′ty, a. [-TIER, -TIEST] [Sl.] crazy, odd, queer, etc.

bau′ble (bô′-) n. trinket.

baux·ite (bôks′īt, bô′zīt) n. claylike aluminum ore.

bawd′y, a. [-IER, -IEST] obscene. —**bawd′i·ness,** n.

bawl, v. 1. to shout. 2. [Col.] weep noisily. —**bawl out** [Sl.] scold angrily.

bay, n. 1. wide inlet of a sea or lake. 2. alcove. 3. recess in a wall, as for a window (**bay window**). 4. laurel tree. 5. a) reddish brown. b) horse of this color. —n. bark in long, deep tones. —v. at bay. 1. with escape cut off. 2. held off. —**bring to bay,** cut off escape of.

bay′ber·ry, n. [pl. -RIES] 1. wax myrtle. 2. its berry.

bay′o·net, n. blade attached to a rifle barrel. —v. stab with a bayonet.

bay·ou (bī'ōō) *n.* marshy inlet or outlet, as of a lake.

ba·zaar′, ba·zar′ (-zär′) *n.* 1. Oriental market place. 2. benefit sale for a club, etc.

ba·zoo′ka, *n.* portable rocket-firing weapon.

BB (shot), tiny metal shot for an air rifle (**BB gun**).

B.C., before Christ.

be, *v.* [WAS or WERE, BEEN, BEING] 1. exist; live. 2. occur. 3. remain; continue. *Be* is an important helping verb.

be-, *pref.* 1. around. 2. completely. 3. away. 4. about.

beach, *n.* stretch of sandy shore. —*v.* ground (a boat).

beach′comb′er, *n.* hobo living on a beach.

beach′head′, *n.* shore area taken by invading troops.

bea′con, *n.* guiding light.

bead, *n.* 1. small ball of glass, etc., pierced for stringing. 2. *pl.* string of beads. 3. drop or bubble. —**bead′ed,** *a.* —**bead′y,** *a.*

bea′gle, *n.* small, short-legged hound.

beak, *n.* 1. bird's bill. 2. any beaklike mouth part.

beak′er, *n.* broad glass container.

beam, *n.* 1. long, thick piece of timber. 2. ship's greatest breadth. 3. shaft of light. 4. radiant look or smile. 5. guiding radio signal. —*v.* radiate in a beam.

bean, *n.* 1. edible seed of some plants. 2. pod of these.

bear (bâr) *n.* 1. large, heavy mammal with shaggy fur. 2. rough, rude person. —*v.* [BORE, BORNE or BORN, BEARING] 1. carry. 2. have or show. 3. give birth to. 4. produce. 5. permit of. 6. endure. —**bear down,** exert pressure. —**bear on,** relate to. —**bear out,** confirm. —**bear up,** endure. —**bear with,** tolerate. —**bear′a·ble,** *a.* —**bear′er,** *n.*

beard (bērd) *n.* 1. hair on a man's face. 2. awn. —*v.* defy face to face. —**beard′ed,** *a.* —**beard′less,** *a.*

bear′ing (bâr′-) *n.* 1. way one carries oneself. 2. *often in pl.* relative position or direction. 3. relation. 4. ball, roller, etc. on which something turns or slides.

beast, *n.* 1. any large four-footed animal. 2. brutal, gross person. —**beast′ly,** *a.*

beat, *v.* [BEAT, BEATEN, BEATING] 1. strike repeatedly. 2.

punish by striking. 3. mix by stirring. 4. defeat. 5. throb. 6. flap (wings). 7. make (a path) by tramping. —*n.* 1. a throbbing. 2. habitual route. 3. unit of musical rhythm. —*a.* [Sl.] tired. —**beat back** (or **off**), drive back. —**beat′er,** *n.*

be·at′if·ic, *a.* blissful.

be·at′i·fy, *v.* [-FIED, -FYING] R.C.Ch. declare one who has died to be among the blessed in heaven.

be·at′i·tude, *n.* bliss.

beau (bō) *n.* [*pl.* BEAUS, BEAUX (bōz)] woman's lover.

beau′ti·ful (bū′-) *a.* having beauty: also **beau′te·ous.** —**beau′ti·ful·ly,** *adv.*

beau′ti·fy, *v.* [-FIED, -FYING] make beautiful.

beau′ty, *n.* [*pl.* -TIES] 1. pleasing quality as in looks, sound, etc. 2. person or thing of beauty.

bea′ver (bē′-) *n.* 1. amphibious animal with webbed rear feet. 2. its brown fur.

be·cause′, *con.* for the reason that. —**because of,** on account of.

beck, *n.* beckoning gesture.

beck′on, *v.* call by gesture.

be·cloud′, *v.* to obscure.

be·come′, *v.* [CAME, -COME, -COMING] 1. come to be. 2. suit. —**become of,** happen to.

be·com′ing, *a.* right or suitable; attractive.

bed, *n.* 1. piece of furniture to sleep on. 2. plot of soil for plants. 3. flat bottom or foundation. 4. layer. —*v.* [BEDDED, BEDDING] put or go to bed.

bed′bug, *n.* small, wingless, biting insect.

bed′clothes, *n.pl.* bed sheets, blankets, etc.

bed′ding, *n.* mattresses and bedclothes.

be·deck′, *v.* adorn.

be·dev′il, *v.* to torment or worry.—**be·dev′il·ment,** *n.*

bed′lam, *n.* noisy confusion.

bed′ou·in (-ōō-) *n.* Arab nomad.

be·drag′gled, *a.* wet and dirty; messy.

bed′rid·den, *a.* confined to bed, as by long illness.

bed′room, *n.* sleeping room.

bed′sore, *n.* sore on a bedridden person.

bed′spread, *n.* ornamental cover for a bed.

bed′spring, *n.* framework of springs under a mattress.

bed'stead, n. frame of a bed.

bee, n. 1. winged insect that makes honey. 2. meeting of group, as to work together.

beech, n. tree with gray bark and edible nuts.

beef, n. [pl. BEEVES, BEEFS] 1. cow, bull, or steer. 2. its meat. —v. [Sl.] complain.

bee'hive, n. hive for bees.

bee'line, n. straight course.

been, pp. of be.

beer, n. mildly alcoholic drink brewed from malt, hops, etc.

bees'wax, n. wax from bees, used in their honeycombs.

beet, n. plant with edible red or white root.

bee'tle, n. insect with hard front wings. —v. jut out.

be·fall', v. [-FELL, -FALLEN, -FALLING] happen (to).

be·fit', v. [-FITTED, -FITTING] be fitting for.

be·fore', adv. 1. in front. 2. till now. 3. earlier. —prep. 1. ahead of. 2. in sight of. 3. earlier than. 4. rather than. —con. earlier or sooner than.

be·fore'hand', adv. & a. ahead of time.

be·friend', v. be a friend to.

be·fud'dle, v. confuse.

beg, v. [BEGGED, BEGGING] 1. ask for (alms). 2. entreat. —go begging, be unwanted.

be·get', v. [-GOT or Ar. -GAT, -GOTTEN or -GOT, -GETTING] 1. to father. 2. to cause.

beg'gar, n. 1. one who lives by begging. 2. very poor person. —v. 1. make a beggar of. 2. make seem useless.

beg'gar·ly, a. poor; mean.

be·gin', v. [-GAN, -GUN, -GINNING] 1. start. 2. originate. —be·gin'ner, n.

be·gin'ning, n. 1. start. 2. origin. 3. first part.

be·gone', int. & v. go away.

be·go'nia (-gōn'yə) n. plant with showy flowers.

be·grudge', v. 1. envy the possession of. 2. give reluctantly.

be·guile' (-gīl') v. 1. deceive or trick. 2. charm. 3. pass (time) pleasantly.

be·half' (-haf') n. support, side, etc. —in (or on) behalf of, in the interest of.

be·have', v. 1. conduct (oneself), esp. properly. 2. act.

be·hav'ior, n. conduct.

be·head', v. cut off the head of.

be·he'moth (bi-hē'-, bē'ə-) n. huge animal.

be·hest', n. a command.

be·hind', adv. 1. in the rear. 2. slow; late. 3. to the back. —prep. 1. in back of. 2. later or slower than. 3. supporting. —a. 1. that follows. 2. in arrears.

be·hold', v. [-HELD, -HOLDING] see. —int. look! see!

be·hold'en, a. indebted.

be·hoove' (-hōōv') v. be necessary or fitting (for).

beige (bāzh) n. grayish tan.

be'ing, n. 1. existence; life. 2. one that lives.

be·la'bor, v. 1. beat; attack.

be·lat'ed (-lāt'-) a. too late.

belch, v. 1. expel stomach gas orally. 2. eject with force. —n. a belching.

be·lea'guer (-lē'gēr) v. 1. besiege. 2. beset.

bel'fry, n. [pl. -FRIES] bell tower.

be·lie', v. [-LIED, -LYING] 1. misrepresent. 2. prove false.

be·lief', n. 1. conviction; faith. 2. trust. 3. opinion.

be·lieve', v. 1. take as true. 2. have faith (in). 3. suppose; guess. —be·liev'a·ble, a. —be·liev'er, n.

be·lit'tle, v. make seem little or unimportant.

bell, n. 1. hollow metal object that rings when struck. 2. sound of a bell.

bel·la·don'na, n. 1. poisonous plant yielding a drug that relieves spasms. 2. the drug.

bell'boy, n. one who does errands at a hotel: also [Sl.] **bell'hop.**

belle (bel) n. pretty girl.

bel'li·cose, a. quarrelsome. —bel·li·cos'i·ty (-kos'-) n.

bel·lig'er·ent (-lij'-) a. warlike. —n. nation or person at war. —bel·lig'er·ence, n.

bel'low, v. 1. roar or shout. 2. utter loudly. —n. this sound.

bel'lows, n. sing. & pl. collapsible device for producing a stream of air.

bell'weth'er, n. male sheep that leads a flock.

bel'ly, n. [pl. -LIES] 1. abdomen. 2. stomach. —v. [-LIED, -LYING] to bulge.

bel'ly·ache', n. [Col.] pain in the belly. —v. [Sl.] complain.

be·long', v. 1. have a proper place. —belong to, 1. be a part of. 2. be owned by. 3. be a member of.

be·long'ings, n.pl. possessions.

be·lov'ed, a. & n. dearly loved (person).

be·low', adv. & a. in or to a lower place; beneath. —prep. lower than; beneath

belt, *n.* 1. encircling band, as around the waist. 2. distinct area. —*v.* strike as with a belt.

be·moan′, *v.* lament.

be·mused′, *a.* preoccupied.

bench, *n.* 1. long seat. 2. worktable. 3. seat for judges. 4. status of a judge. —*v.* remove (a player) from a game.

bend, *v.* [BENT, BENDING] 1. to curve, as by pressure. 2. (make) yield. 3. stoop. —*n.* 1. a bending. 2. bent part.

be·neath′, *adv. & a.* below; underneath. —*prep.* 1. below; under. 2. unworthy of.

ben′e·dic′tion, *n.* blessing.

ben′e·fac′tor, *n.* one who has given money or aid. —**ben′e·fac′tion,** *n.* —**ben′e·fac′tress,** *n.fem.*

ben′e·fice (-fis) *n.* endowed church position.

be·nef′i·cence, *n.* 1. kindness. 2. kindly act or gift. —**be·nef′i·cent,** *a.*

ben′e·fi′cial (-fish′əl) *a.* producing benefits.

ben′e·fi′ci·ar·y (-fish′ēr-i) *n.* [*pl.* -IES] one receiving benefits, as from insurance.

ben′e·fit, *n.* 1. help or advantage. 2. a show, etc. to raise money for a cause. —*v.* 1. to help. 2. profit.

be·nev′o·lence, *n.* the wish to do good; kindness; generosity. —**be·nev′o·lent,** *a.*

be·night′ed, *a.* ignorant.

be·nign′ (-nīn′) *a.* 1. kindly. 2. favorable. 3. not malignant.

be·nig′nant (-nig′-) *a.* benign.

bent, *a.* 1. curved. 2. determined (on). —*n.* inclination.

be·numb′, *v.* make numb.

ben′zene, *n.* coal-tar derivative used as a solvent.

ben′zine (-zēn) *n.* petroleum derivative used as a motor fuel, in dry cleaning, etc.

ben′zo·ate, *n.* chemical used to preserve food.

be·queath′ (-kwēth′, -kwēth′) *v.* 1. leave (property) by a will. 2. hand down. —**be·quest′,** *n.*

be·rate′, *v.* scold severely.

be·reave′, *v.* [alt. pp. -REFT] 1. deprive. 2. leave forlorn as by death. —**be·reave′ment,** *n.* —**be·reft′,** *a.*

be·ret′ (-rā′) *n.* flat, round, soft cap.

ber′i·ber′i, *n.* disease caused by lack of vitamin B₁.

ber′ry, *n.* [*pl.* -RIES] small, fleshy fruit with seeds.

ber·serk′ (bûr′sûrk′) *a. & adv.* in(to) a violent rage.

berth, *n.* 1. ship's place of anchorage. 2. built-in bed. 3. position or job.

ber′yl (ber′il) *n.* hard, bright mineral, as the emerald.

be·seech′, *v.* [-SOUGHT or -SEECHED, -SEECHING] ask (for) earnestly; entreat. —**be·seech′ing·ly,** *adv.*

be·set′, *v.* [-SET, -SETTING] 1. attack from all sides. 2. surround.

be·side′, *prep.* 1. at the side of; near. 2. as compared with. 3. besides. 4. aside from. —*adv.* besides. —**beside oneself,** wild, as with fear.

be·sides′, *adv.* 1. in addition. 2. else. 3. moreover. —*prep.* in addition to.

be·siege′, *v.* 1. lay siege to; hem in. 2. overwhelm.

be·smirch′, *v.* to soil; sully.

be·sot′ted, *a.* stupefied, as with liquor.

be·speak′, *v.* 1. speak for; reserve. 2. indicate.

best, *a.* 1. most excellent. 2. most suitable. —*adv.* 1. in the best way. 2. most. —*n.* 1. best person, thing, etc. 2. the utmost. —*v.* 1. outdo; beat. —**get** (or **have**) **the best of,** defeat or outwit. —**had best,** should. —**make the best of,** adjust to.

bes′tial (-chəl) *a.* like a beast; brutal.

be·stir′, *v.* stir up; busy.

best man, main attendant of a bridegroom.

be·stow′ (-stō′) *v.* present as a gift (*on* or *upon*).

bet, *n.* 1. agreement that the one proved wrong will pay something. 2. thing so staked. —*v.* [BET or BETTED, BETTING] 1. make a bet. 2. stake in a bet. —**bet′tor,** *n.*

be·ta (bā′tə) *n.* second letter of the Greek alphabet.

be·take′, *v.* take (oneself); go.

be·think′, *v.* think of; remind (oneself).

be·tide′, *v.* happen (to).

be·to′ken, *v.* be a sign of.

be·tray′, *v.* 1. be disloyal to. 2. deceive. 3. seduce. 4. reveal. —**be·tray′al,** *n.*

be·troth′ (-trōth′, -trōth′) *v.* promise in marriage. —**be·troth′al,** *n.* —**be·trothed′,** *a. & n.*

bet′ter, *a.* 1. more excellent. 2. more suitable. 3. improved. —*adv.* 1. in a better way. 2. more. —*n.* 1. a superior. 2. better thing, etc. —*v.* surpass or improve.

better off, in better circumstances. —**get** (or **have**) **the better of,** defeat or outwit. —**had better,** should. —**think better of,** reconsider.

bet'ter·ment, *n.* improvement.

be·tween', *prep.* 1. in the space or time separating. 2. involving. 3. joining. 4. in the common possession of. 5. one of. —*adv.* in the middle.

be·twixt', *prep. & adv.* [Ar.] between.

bev'el, *n.* 1. angled part or surface. 2. tool for marking angles. —*v.* cut or slope at an angle.

bev'er·age (-ij) *n.* drink.

bev'y, *n.* [*pl.* -IES] 1. group, as of girls. 2. flock of quail.

be·wail', *v.* wail over.

be·ware', *v.* guard against.

be·wil'der, *v.* confuse. —**be·wil'der·ment,** *n.*

be·witch', *v.* enchant.

be·yond', *prep.* 1. farther or later than; past. 2. more than. —*adv.* farther away. —**the (great) beyond,** whatever follows death.

bi- (bī) *pref.* two or twice.

bi·an'nu·al, *a.* twice a year.

bi·as (bī'əs) *n.* 1. diagonal or slanting line. 2. prejudice. —*v.* to prejudice. —**on the bias,** diagonally.

bib, *n.* cloth tied under a child's chin at meals.

Bi'ble, *n.* sacred book of Christians or of Jews. —**Bib'li·cal, bib'li·cal,** *a.*

bib'li·og'ra·phy, *n.* [*pl.* -PHIES] list of writings on one subject or by one author.

bi·cam'er·al, *a.* having two legislative branches.

bi·cen·ten'ni·al (-sen-) *n.* 200th anniversary.

bi'ceps (-seps) *n.* large front muscle of the upper arm.

bick'er, *v. & n.* quarrel.

bi·cus'pid (-kus'-) *n.* tooth with two-pointed crown.

bi'cy·cle (-si·k'l) *n.* two-wheeled vehicle. —*v.* ride a bicycle. —**bi'cy·clist,** *n.*

bid (bid), *v.* [BADE or BID, BIDDEN or BID, BIDDING] 1. command or ask. 2. tell. 3. [*pt. & pp.* BID] offer as a price. —*n.* 1. amount bid. 2. attempt. —**bid'der,** *n.*

bide (bīd), *v.* [BODE or BIDED

or BADE, BIDED, BIDING] [Ar.] 1. stay. 2. dwell. 3. wait. —**bide one's time,** wait patiently for a chance.

bi·en'ni·al, *a.* 1. every two years. 2. lasting two years. —*n.* plant living two years.

bier (bēr) *n.* frame on which a coffin is put.

bi·fo'cals, *n.pl.* eyeglasses with lenses having two parts, for close and far focus.

big, *a.* [BIGGER, BIGGEST] 1. of great size. 2. loud. 3. important. 4. noble. —*adv.* [Col.] 1. boastfully. 2. impressively. —**big'ness,** *n.*

big'a·my (-mi) *n.* crime of marrying again while still married. —**big'a·mist,** *n.*

big'horn, *n.* horned, wild sheep of Rocky Mountains.

bight (bit) *n.* 1. loop in a rope. 2. a bay.

big'ot, *n.* narrow-minded, intolerant person. —**big'ot·ed,** *a.* —**big'ot·ry,** *n.*

bike, *n. & v.* [Col.] bicycle.

bi·lat'er·al, *a.* on, by, or having two sides.

bile (bīl) *n.* 1. bitter liver secretion. 2. bad temper.

bilge (bilj) *n.* 1. lower part of a ship's hold. 2. stale water that gathers there. 3. [Sl.] nonsense.

bil'ious (-yəs) *a.* 1. having a disorder of the bile or liver. 2. bad-tempered.

bilk, *v.* to swindle.

bill, *n.* 1. statement of charges, as for goods. 2. list of things offered. 3. proposed law. 4. piece of paper money. 5. bird's beak. —*v.* present a bill of charges to. —**bill and coo,** act in a loving way.

bill'board, *n.* signboard.

bil'let, *n.* lodging, as for soldiers. —*v.* assign to lodging.

bill'fold, *n.* wallet.

bil'liards (-yĕrdz) *n.* game played with cue and balls on a table with raised edges.

bil'lion, *n.* thousand millions. —**bil'lionth,** *a. & n.*

bill of fare, menu.

bill of sale, paper transferring ownership by sale.

bil'low, *n.* 1. large wave. 2. swelling mass, as of smoke. —*v.* surge or swell. —**bil'low·y** [-IER, -IEST] *a.*

billy goat [Col.] male goat.

bin, *n.* box or enclosed space for storage.

bi'na·ry (bī'-) *a.* twofold.

bind, *v.* [BOUND, BINDING] 1. tie together. 2. hold; restrain. 3. encircle with (belt, etc.). 4. bandage. 5. put round (a book) with a cover. 6. obligate. —**bind′er,** n.

bind′er·y, n. [pl. -IES] place where books are bound.

bind′ing, n. 1. anything that binds. 2. covers and backing of a book.

binge (binj) n. [Sl.] spree.

bin′go, n. game played on cards with numbered squares.

bin·oc′u·lars (bĭ-nok′-) n. pl. field glasses.

bi′o·chem′is·try, n. chemistry of living organisms.

bi′o·de·grad′a·ble, a. readily decomposed by bacteria.

bi·og′ra·phy, n. [pl. -PHIES] one's life story written by another. —**bi·og′ra·pher,** n. —**bi′o·graph′i·cal,** a.

bi·ol′o·gy, n. science of plants and animals. —**bi′o·log′i·cal,** a. —**bi·ol′o·gist,** n.

bi·par′ti·san (-pär′-) a. representing two parties.

bi′ped, n. two-footed animal.

birch, n. 1. tree with smooth bark. 2. its hard wood.

bird, n. warm-blooded vertebrate with feathers & wings.

bird′ie, n. Golf score of one under par for a hole.

bird's′-eye′, a. seen from above; general.

birth, n. 1. a being born. 2. descent or origin. 3. beginning. —**give birth to,** bring into being. —**birth′place,** n.

birth′day, n. day of birth or its anniversary.

birth′mark, n. skin blemish present at birth.

birth′right, n. rights a person has by birth.

bis′cuit (-kit) n. 1. small bread roll. 2. [Br.] cracker.

bi·sect′, v. divide into two equal parts. —**bi·sec′tor,** n.

bish′op, n. 1. clergyman heading a diocese. 2. chessman moving diagonally.

bish′op·ric, n. diocese, rank, etc. of a bishop.

bis′muth (biz′-) n. metallic chemical element whose salts are used in medicine.

bi′son, n. [pl. BISON] shaggy, oxlike animal of N. America.

bis′tro, n. [Fr.] small café.

bit, n. 1. mouthpiece on a bridle, for control. 2. cutting part of a drill. 3. small piece or amount. 4. [Col.] short time. —**bit by bit,** gradually. —**do one's bit,** do one's share.

bitch, n. female dog, fox,

etc. —v. [Sl.] complain.

bite, v. [BIT, BITTEN or BIT, BITING] 1. seize or cut as with the teeth. 2. sting, as a bee. 3. cause to smart. 4. swallow a bait. —n. 1. a biting. 2. biting quality; smart. 3. wound from biting. 4. mouthful. 5. [Col.] light meal. —**bit′er,** n.

bit′ing, a. 1. cutting; sharp. 2. sarcastic.

bit′ter, a. 1. sharp to the taste. 2. sorrowful, painful, resentful, etc. 3. harsh. —**bit′ter·ly,** adv.

bit′tern, n. heronlike bird.

bi·tu′men, n. natural asphalt or similar substance made from coal, etc.

bi·tu′mi·nous coal, soft coal, easy to burn but smoky.

bi′valve, n. mollusk with two shells, as a clam.

biv′ouac (-wak) n. temporary camp (of soldiers). —v. [-OUACKED, -OUACKING] make such a camp.

bi·zarre (bi·zär′) a. odd; fantastic.

blab, v. [BLABBED, BLABBING] to tattle, gossip, etc.

black, a. 1. of the color of coal; opposite to white. 2. having dark skin. 3. without light; dark. 4. dirty. 5. evil. 6. sad. —n. 1. black pigment. 2. Negro. —v. blacken. —**black out,** lose consciousness. —**black′ness,** n.

black-and-blue a. discolored by a bruise.

black′ball, n. & v. vote against.

black′ber′ry, n. [pl. -RIES] 1. small, edible, dark fruit. 2. bramble it grows on.

black′bird, n. bird the male of which is all black.

black′board, n. smooth surface for writing with chalk.

black′en, v. 1. make or become black. 2. slander.

black′guard (blag′ẽrd) n. scoundrel; villain.

black′head, n. plug of dirt in a pore of the skin.

black′jack, n. 1. small bludgeon. 2. a card game.

black list, list of those to be punished, refused jobs, etc.

black′mail, n. money extorted on threat of disclosing something disgracing. —v. get or try to get blackmail from. —**black′mail·er,** n.

black market, system for selling goods illegally during rationing, etc.

black'out, n. 1. concealing of light, facts, etc. 2. a faint.

black sheep, disgraceful member of a family, etc.

black'smith, n. man who forges iron and shoes horses.

black widow, small, poisonous spider.

blad'der, n. sac that collects urine from the kidneys.

blade, n. 1. leaf of grass. 2. cutting part of a knife, tool, etc. 3. flat surface, as of an oar. 4. gay young man.

blame, v. 1. accuse or find at fault. 2. put the responsibility of (on). —n. 1. a blaming. 2. responsibility for a fault. —**to be blamed, deserve blame. —blame'less,** a. —**blame'wor'thy,** a.

blanch, v. 1. bleach. 2. make or turn pale.

bland, a. mild; soothing.

blan'dish, v. flatter; coax. —**blan'dish·ment,** n.

blank, a. 1. not written on. 2. empty. 3. utter. —n. 1. (printed form with) space to be filled in. 2. cartridge without a bullet.

blan'ket, n. 1. woo spread used as bed cover, etc. 2. a covering, as of snow. —a. all-inclusive. —v. to cover.

blare, v. sound loudly. —n. loud, trumpetlike sound.

blar'ney (blär'-) n. flattery.

bla·sé (blä-zä') a. bored.

blas'phe·my (-fə-mi) n. [pl. -MIES] profane abuse of God. —**blas·pheme'** (-fēm') v. —**blas'phe·mous,** a.

blast, n. 1. strong rush of air. 2. loud sound of horn, etc. 3. explosion. —v. 1. explode. 2. blight; wither.

blast furnace, furnace for smelting iron ore.

bla'tant (blā'-) a. loud and vulgar. —**bla'tan·cy,** n.

blaze, n. 1. burst of flame. 2. bright light. 3. vivid display. 4. outburst. 5. white spot on an animal's face. —v. 1. burn or shine brightly. 2. mark (a trail).

bla'zon (-z'n) n. coat of arms. —v. proclaim.

bleach, v. whiten. —n. chemical that bleaches.

bleach'ers, n.pl. roofless stand where spectators sit.

bleak, a. 1. unsheltered; bare. 2. cheerless; gloomy.

blear, v. to dim or blur, as with tears. —**blear'y,** a.

bleat, n. cry of a sheep or goat. —v. make this cry.

bleed, v. [BLED, BLEEDING] 1. lose blood. 2. draw blood from. 3. [Col.] extort from.

blem'ish, v. mar; injure. —n. defect; fault.

blend, v. 1. mix. 2. shade into each other. —n. 1. a blending. 2. mixture.

bless, v. [alt. pt. & pp. BLEST] 1. make holy. 2. ask divine favor for. 3. make happy. —**bless'ed,** a. —**bless'ing,** n.

blew (bloō) pt. of **blow.**

blight (blīt) n. 1. insect, disease, etc. that destroys plants. 2. anything that destroys. —v. destroy; ruin.

blimp, n. small airship like a dirigible.

blind, a. 1. without sight. 2. lacking insight. 3. having no outlet. 4. not controlled by reason. —n. 1. window shade. 2. a decoy. —**blind'ly,** adv. —**blind'ness,** n.

blind'fold, v. cover the eyes of. —n. cloth used for this.

blink, v. 1. wink rapidly. 2. flash on and off. —n. 1. a blinking. 2. glimmer. —**blink at,** ignore. —**on the blink,** [Sl.] out of order.

blink'er, n. flashing light.

bliss, n. great happiness. —**bliss'ful,** a.

blis'ter, n. fluid-filled skin swelling caused by a burn, etc. —v. form blisters.

blithe (blīth) a. gay.

bliz'zard, n. severe snowstorm with high wind.

bloat, v. swell up.

blob, n. small drop or mass.

bloc, n. group united for a common purpose.

block, n. 1. solid piece. 2. auction platform. 3. obstruction. 4. city square or street section. 5. pulley in a frame. 6. part taken as a unit. —v. 1. obstruct. 2. shape. —**block in** (or **out**), sketch roughly.

block·ade', n. shutting off of a place by warships, etc. —v. subject to a blockade.

block'head, n. stupid person.

block'house, n. wooden fort.

blond, a. 1. having light-colored hair and skin. 2. light-colored. Also **blonde.** —n. blond man or boy.

blonde, n. fem.

blood, n. 1. red fluid in the arteries and veins. 2. lineage. 3. kinship. —**bad blood,** hatred. —**in cold blood,** deliberately. —**blood'less,** a.

blood'cur·dling, a. very frightening; terrifying.

blood'hound, n. large, keen-scented tracking dog.

blood'shed, n. killing.

blood'shot, a. tinged with blood: said of the eyes.

blood'thirst·y, a. murderous.

blood'y, a. [-IER, -IEST] 1. of or covered with blood. 2. involving bloodshed 3. bloodthirsty. —v. [-IED, -YING] stain with blood.

bloom, n. 1. a flower. 2. time of flowering. 3. healthy glow. —v. be in bloom.

bloom'ers, n.pl. women's baggy underpants.

blos'som, n. & v. flower.

blot, n. spot or stain. —v. [BLOTTED, BLOTTING] 1. spot, as with ink. 2. erase or cancel (out). 3. dry with soft paper, etc. —**blot'ter**, n.

blotch, n. discolored spot. —v. mark with blotches. —**blotch'y**, a.

blouse, n. shirtlike garment for girls.

blow, v. [BLEW, BLOWN, BLOWING] 1. move, as (by) wind. 2. force air out, as with the mouth. 3. sound by blowing. —n. 1. a blowing. 2. gale. 3. a hit. 4. shock. —**blow out**, 1. extinguish. 2. burst. —**blow up**, 1. inflate. 2. explode. —**blow'er**, n.

blow'out, n. 1. bursting of a tire. 2. [Sl.] party.

blow'torch, n. small, hot-flamed torch for welding. —v. weep loudly.

blub'ber, n. whale fat. —v. weep loudly.

bludg·eon (bluj'ən), n. short, heavy club. —v. to club.

blue, a. 1. of the color of the clear sky. 2. gloomy. —n. color of the clear sky. —v. use bluing on. —**the blues**, 1. [Col.] depressed feeling. 2. slow, sad jazz song. —**blu'ish**, a.

blue'bell, n. plant with blue, bell-shaped flowers.

blue'ber·ry, n. pl. -RIES] small, edible, bluish berry.

blue'bird, n. small bird with blue back and wings.

blue'fish, n. silvery-blue Atlantic food fish.

blue'jay, n. crested bird with a blue back.

blue'-pen'cil, v. edit.

blue'print, n. 1. photographic copy, white on blue, of architectural plans, etc. 2. any detailed plan. —v. make a blueprint of.

bluff, v. mislead by a fake, bold front. —a. rough and

frank. —n. 1. a bluffing. 2. one who bluffs. 3. steep bank.

blu'ing, blue'ing, n. blue rinse for white fabrics.

blun'der, n. foolish mistake. —v. 1. make a blunder. 2. move clumsily.

blun'der·buss, n. obsolete gun with a broad muzzle.

blunt, a. 1. dull-edged. 2. plain-spoken. —v. make dull.

blur, v. [BLURRED, BLURRING] 1. smudge. 2. make or become indistinct. —n. indistinct thing. —**blur'ry**, a.

blurb, n. [Col.] exaggerated advertisement.

blurt, v. say impulsively.

blush, v. redden, as from shame. —n. a blushing.

blus'ter, v. 1. blow stormily. 2. speak noisily or boastfully. —n. swaggering talk. —**blus'ter·y**, a.

bo·a (bō'ə), n. 1. large snake that crushes its prey in its coils. 2. scarf of feathers.

boar, n. wild hog.

board, n. 1. broad, flat piece of wood, etc. 2. meals provided regularly for pay. 3. council. —v. 1. cover (up) with boards. 2. get on (a ship, train, etc.). 3. get board (n. 2). —**on board**, on a ship, etc. —**board'er**, n.

board'walk, n. wooden walk along a beach.

boast, v. 1. talk with too much pride. 2. take pride in. —n. thing boasted of. —**boast'er**, n. —**boast'ful**, a.

boat, n. water craft, esp. a small one. —**in the same boat**, in the same situation. —**boat'man** [pl. -MEN] n.

boat'ing, n. rowing, sailing, etc.

boat'swain (bō's'n) n. petty officer directing deck work.

bob, n. 1. small hanging weight. 2. float on a fishing line. —v. [BOBBED, BOBBING] 1. move jerkily. 2. cut short, as hair. —**bob up**, appear unexpectedly.

bob'bin, n. spool for thread.

bob'by pin, tight hairpin.

bobby socks [Col.] girls' short socks. —**bobby sox'er.**

bob'cat, n. American lynx.

bob'o·link, n. songbird with a call like its name.

bob'sled, n. racing sled.

bob'white', n. small quail.

bock (beer), a dark beer.

bode (bōd) v. be an omen of.

bode, pt. of **bide**.

bod·ice (bod'is) n. snug upper part of a dress.

bod'y, *n.* 1. whole physical structure. 2. trunk of a man or animal. 3. main part. 4. distinct mass or group. 5. [Col.] person. —**bod'i·ly**, *a. & adv.*

bod'y·guard, *n.* guard to protect a person.

bog, *n.* small swamp. —*v.* [BOGGED, BOGGING] sink (down) as in a bog. —**bog'gy**, *a.*

bo'gus (bō'-) *a.* not genuine.

bo'gy (bō'-) *n.* [*pl.* -GIES] imaginary evil spirit; goblin: also sp. bogey, bogie.

Bo·he'mi·an, *n.* one who lives unconventionally.

boil, *v.* 1. bubble up into vapor by heating. 2. be agitated. 3. cook by boiling. —*n.* 1. boiling state. 2. pus-filled pimple. —**boil down**, condense.

boil'er, *n.* tank for making steam or storing hot water.

bois'ter·ous, *a.* rough, noisy, lively, etc.

bold, *a.* 1. daring; fearless. 2. impudent. 3. sharp and clear. —**bold'ly**, *adv.*

bo·le'ro, (-lâr'ō) *n.* [*pl.* -ROS] 1. Spanish dance. 2. short, open vest.

boll weevil, (bōl) beetle that harms cotton pods (bolls).

bo·lo'gna, (-lō'nə, -ni) *n.* type of smoked sausage.

bol'ster (bōl'-) *n.* long pillow. —*v.* prop (up).

bolt, *n.* 1. flash of lightning. 2. sliding bar that locks. 3. threaded metal rod used with a nut. 4. roll of cloth. —*v.* 1. gulp (food). 2. rush out. 3. fasten with a bolt. 4. sift. —**bolt upright**, straight upright.

bomb (bom) *n.* explosive device or missile. —*v.* attack with bombs.

bom·bard', *v.* attack as with artillery or bombs. —**bom·bard'ier'** (-bâr-dêr') *n.* —**bom·bard'ment**, *n.*

bom'bast, *n.* pompous speech. —**bom·bas'tic**, *a.*

bomb'er, *n.* airplane designed for dropping bombs.

bomb'shell, *n.* 1. bomb. 2. shocking surprise.

bo·na fi·da (bō'nə fī'di or fid) in good faith; sincere.

bo·nan'za, *n.* 1. rich vein of ore. 2. any rich source.

bon'bon, *n.* piece of candy.

bond, *n.* 1. thing that binds or unites. 2. binding agreement. 3. interest-bearing certificate. 4. surety against

theft, etc. —*v.* 1. bind. 2. furnish a bond (*n.* 4) for.

bond'age (-ij) *n.* slavery.

bond'man [*pl.* -MEN] *n.* —**bond'wom·an** [*pl.* -WOMEN] *n.*

bonds'man, *n.* [*pl.* -MEN] one furnishing bond (*n.* 4).

bone, *n.* material of the skeleton or piece of this. —*v.* 1. remove the bones from. 2. [Sl.] study hard (with *up*). —**make no bones about**, admit freely. —**bone'less**, *a.*

bon'er, (bōn'-) *n.* [Sl.] a blunder.

bon'fire, *n.* outdoor fire.

bo·ni'to (-nē'tō) *n.* [*pl.* -TOS, -TOES] kind of tuna.

bon'net, *n.* hat.

bon'ny, *a.* [-NIER, -NIEST] handsome; pretty.

bo'nus, *n.* payment over the usual or required amount.

bon·y (bōn'i) *a.* [-IER, -IEST] 1. (full of) bones. 2. lean; thin. —**bon'i·ness**, *n.*

boo (bōō) *int. & n.* [*pl.* BOOS] sound made to show disapproval or to startle. —*v.* shout "boo" at.

boo'by, *n.* [*pl.* -BIES] a fool.

book, *n.* 1. a bound, printed work. 2. a division of a long literary work. 3. ledger. —*v.* 1. to list in a book. 2. to reserve, as rooms. —**book'case**, *n.*

book end, end piece to hold a row of books upright.

book'ie, *n.* [Sl.] bookmaker.

book'ish, *a.* 1. inclined to read or study. 2. pedantic.

book'keep'ing, *n.* work of recording business transactions. —**book'keep'er**, *n.*

book'let, *n.* small book.

book'mak'er, *n.* one who takes bets, esp. on horses.

book'mark, *n.* slip, etc. for marking a place in a book.

book'worm, *n.* one who reads or studies much.

boom, *v.* 1. make a deep, hollow sound. 2. grow rapidly. 3. promote. —*n.* 1. deep sound. 2. long beam on a derrick. 3. spar at the foot of a sail. 4. period of prosperity.

boom'er·ang, *n.* 1. Australian curved stick that returns to the thrower. 2. scheme that backfires.

boon (bōōn) *n.* benefit.

boor (boor) *n.* rude person.

boost, *v. & n.* [Col.] 1. push upward; raise. 2. support. —**boost'er**, *n.*

boot, n. outer covering for the foot and leg. —v. 1. to kick. 2. [Sl.] dismiss.

booth, n. small stall or enclosure.

boot'leg, v. [-LEGGED, -LEGGING] sell (liquor) illegally. —a. sold illegally. —**boot'leg·ger,** n.

boot'less, a. useless.

boo'ty, n. plunder; spoils.

booze, n. [Col.] liquor.

bo'rax, n. a white salt used in glass, soaps, etc.

bor'der, n. 1. edge; margin. 2. boundary. —v. put or be a border on. —a. near a border. —**border on** (or **upon**), be next to. —**bor'der·land,** n. —**bor'der·line,** n.

bore, v. 1. drill a hole (in). 2. weary by being dull. —n. 1. inside or diameter of a tube. 2. dull person or thing. —**bore'dom,** n.

bore, pt. of **bear**.

bo'ric acid, powder used in solution as an antiseptic.

born, pp. of **bear** (give birth). —a. 1. brought into life. 2. by nature.

borne, pp. of **bear** (carry).

bo'ron, n. nonmetallic chemical element.

bor'ough (bûr'ō) n. 1. self-governing town. 2. division of New York City.

bor'row (bor'-) v. 1. take on loan. 2. adopt (an idea).

bos'om (booz'-) n. breast. —a. intimate, as a friend.

boss, n. [Col.] 1. employer or supervisor. 2. head politician. —v. [Col.] 1. supervise. 2. be domineering. —**boss'y** [-IER, -IEST] a.

bot'a·ny, n. science of plants. —**bo·tan'i·cal,** a. —**bot'a·nist,** n.

botch, v. spoil; bungle. —n. bungled work.

both, a. & pron. the two. —con. & adv. equally.

both'er (both'-) v. 1. annoy; worry. 2. trouble (oneself). —n. trouble. —**both'er·some,** a.

bot'tle, n. glass container for liquids. —v. 1. put into a bottle. 2. stop (up).

bot'tle·neck, n. 1. narrow passage. 2. any hindrance.

bot'tom, n. 1. lowest part; base; underside. 2. basis or cause; origin.

bou·doir (bōō'dwär) n. woman's private room.

bouf·fant (bōō-fänt') a. [Fr.] puffed out; full.

bough (bou) n. tree branch.

bought (bôt) pt. & pp. of **buy**.

bouil·lon (bool'yon) n. clear broth.

boul'der (bōl'-) n. large rock.

boul'e·vard (bool'-) n. broad, tree-lined street.

bounce (bouns) v. 1. spring back on impact. 2. make bounce. 3. leap. —n. a bouncing.

bounc'ing, a. healthy.

bound, pt. & pp. of **bind**. —a. 1. tied. 2. certain (to). 3. obliged. 4. with a binding. 5. headed (for). 6. [Col.] determined. —v. 1. leap or bounce. 2. be a limit or boundary to. —n. 1. a leap or bounce. 2. boundary. —**out of bounds,** prohibited. —**bound'less,** a.

bound'a·ry, n. [pl. -RIES] anything marking a limit.

bound'er, n. [Col.] cad.

boun'te·ous, a. 1. generous. 2. abundant.

boun'ti·ful, a. bounteous.

boun'ty, n. [pl. -TIES] 1. generosity. 2. gift or reward.

bou·quet (bō-kā', bōō-) n. 1. bunch of flowers. 2. aroma.

bour·bon (bûr'bən) n. corn whisky.

bour·geoi·sie (boor-zhwä-zē') n. social middle class. —**bour·geois'** (-zhwä') a. & n.

bout (bout) n. 1. struggle; contest. 2. spell or term.

bo·vine (bō'vīn) a. cowlike.

bow (bou) v. 1. bend down in respect. 2. submit. 3. weigh (down). —n. 1. bending of the head or body. 2. front part of a ship. —**take a bow,** acknowledge applause.

bow (bō) n. 1. curved stick strung with cord for shooting arrows. 2. stick strung with horsehairs, for playing a violin, etc. 3. knot with broad loops. —a. curved. —v. play (a violin) with a bow.

bow'els (bou'-) n.pl. 1. intestines. 2. depths.

bow'er (bou'-) n. arbor.

bowl (bōl) n. 1. hollow, rounded dish or part. 2. amphitheater. 3. ball for bowling. —v. 1. roll (a ball) in bowling. 2. move fast. —**bowl over,** knock over.

bow'leg·ged (bō'-) a. with the legs curved out.

bowl'ing, n. game in which a ball is rolled at ten pins.

bow'man (bō'-) *n.* [*pl.* -MEN] archer.

box, *n.* 1. container made of wood, cardboard, etc. 2. enclosed group of seats. 3. blow with the hand. 4. evergreen shrub: also **boxwood.** —*v.* 1. put (in) or shut (up) as in a box. 2. fight with the fists. —**box'er,** *n.* —**box'ing,** *n.*

box'car, *n.* enclosed railroad freight car.

box office, place in a theater to buy tickets.

boy, *n.* male child. —**boy'hood,** *n.* —**boy'ish,** *a.*

boy'cott, *v.* refuse to deal with. —*n.* a boycotting.

brace, *v.* 1. strengthen with supports. 2. prepare for a shock. 3. stimulate. —*n.* 1. pair. 2. clamp. 3. supporting device. 4. handle of a drilling tool (**brace and bit**). 5. either of the signs { }, for connecting lines, etc.

brace'let, *n.* decorative band for the arm.

brack'et, *n.* 1. projecting support. 2. either of the signs [ ], for enclosing words. 3. classification. —*v.* 1. support with brackets. 2. enclose in brackets. 3. classify together.

brack'ish, *a.* salty or rank.

brad, *n.* thin wire nail.

brag, *n. & v.* [BRAGGED, BRAGGING] boast.

brag'gart, *n.* boaster.

braid, *v.* 1. interweave strands of. 2. trim with braid. —*n.* braided strip.

Braille, braille (brāl) *n.* system of printing for the blind, using raised dots.

brain, *n.* 1. mass of nerve tissue in the head. 2. *pl.* intelligence. —*v.* smash the brains of. —**brain'y,** *a.*

brain'wash, *v.* [Col.] indoctrinate thoroughly.

braise (brāz) *v.* brown (meat), then simmer it.

brake, *n.* 1. thicket. 2. device to stop or slow a machine, etc. —*v.* stop or slow as with a brake.

brake'man, *n.* [*pl.* -MEN] train conductor's assistant.

bram'ble, *n.* prickly shrub.

bran, *n.* husks separated from grains of wheat, etc.

branch, *n.* 1. limb of a tree. 2. offshoot or division. 3. tributary stream. 4. local unit of an organization. —*v.* put forth branches. — **branch off,** diverge. —

branch out, broaden one's interests.

brand, *n.* 1. burning stick. 2. owner's mark burned on cattle. 3. iron used to brand. 4. stigma. 5. trademark. 6. make or kind. —*v.* mark with a brand.

bran'dish, *v.* wave about.

brand'-new', *a.* fully new.

bran'dy, *n.* [*pl.* -DIES] liquor distilled from wine or fruit juice.

brash, *a.* rash or insolent.

brass, *n.* 1. alloy of copper and zinc. 2. *pl.* brass winds. 3. [Col.] rude boldness. 4. [Sl.] military officers. —**brass'y,** [-IER, -IEST] *a.*

bras·siere (bra-zēr') *n.* woman's undergarment for supporting the breasts.

brass winds, coiled musical instruments, as the trumpet, tuba, etc. —**brass'wind',** *a.*

brat, *n.* unruly child.

bra·va'do (-vä'-, -vā'-) *n.* pretended courage.

brave, *a.* full of courage. —*n.* American Indian warrior. —*v.* 1. defy. 2. meet with courage. —**brav'er·y,** *n.*

bra'vo (brä'-) *int. & n.* [*pl.* -VOS] shout of approval.

brawl, *v.* quarrel or fight noisily. —*n.* noisy fight.

brawn, *n.* muscular strength. —**brawn'y** [-IER, -IEST] *a.*

bray, *n.* sound a donkey makes. —*v.* make this sound.

bra'zen, *a.* 1. of or like brass. 2. shameless. —**brazen out,** act unashamed of.

bra·zier (brā'zhēr) *n.* pan for holding burning coals.

Bra·zil' nut, edible, threesided, tropical nut.

breach, *n.* 1. break in something; gap. 2. violation of a promise, friendship, etc. —*v.* make a breach in.

bread, *n.* 1. baked food of flour dough. 2. livelihood. —*v.* cover with bread crumbs.

breadth, *n.* width or scope.

break, *v.* [BROKE, BROKEN, BREAKING] 1. split apart; smash. 2. make or become unusable. 3. tame by force. 4. make penniless. 5. surpass (a record). 6. violate (a law). 7. interrupt. 8. stop. 9. make or become known. —*n.* 1. a breaking. 2. broken place. 3. interruption. 4. beginning (of day). 5. sudden change. 6. [Sl.] a chance. —**break in,** 1. enter forcibly. 2. interrupt. 3. train. —**break out,** develop pimples. —**break′a·ble,** a.

break′age, n. 1. a breaking. 2. loss due to breaking.

break′down, n. 1. mechanical failure. 2. physical or mental collapse. 3. analysis.

break′er, n. breaking wave.

break′fast (brek′fəst) n. first meal of the day. —v. eat breakfast.

break′up, n. a going apart.

break′wa′ter, n. barrier to break the impact of waves.

breast (brest) n. 1. milk-secreting gland on a woman's body. 2. upper front of the body. 3. the emotions. —v. face bravely. —**make a clean breast of,** confess.

breast′bone, n. sternum.

breast′work, n. low barrier to protect gunners.

breath (breth) n. 1. air taken into and let out of the lungs. 2. easy breathing. 3. life. 4. slight breeze.

breathe (brē*th*) v. 1. inhale and exhale. 2. live. 3. whisper. 4. rest.

breath′less, a. exciting.

breath′tak′ing, a. exciting.

breech, n. 1. back part. 2. gun part behind the barrel.

breech′es (brich′-) n.pl. knickers or trousers.

breed, v. [BRED, BREEDING] 1. bring forth (offspring). 2. produce. 3. raise (animals). —n. 1. race; stock. 2. type.

breeze, n. gentle wind. —v. [Sl.] move briskly. —**breez′y** [-IER, -IEST] a.

breth′ren, n.pl. [Ar.] brothers.

bre′vi·ar′y (brē′-) n. R.C.Ch. book of daily prayers.

brev′i·ty, n. briefness.

brew, v. 1. make (beer, etc.). 2. steep (tea, etc.). 3. plot. 4. form. —n. beverage brewed. —**brew′er,** n.

brew′er·y n. [pl. -IES] place where beer is brewed.

bribe, n. thing given or promised as an inducement, esp. to wrongdoing. —v. offer or give a bribe to.

bric-a-brac (brik′ə-brak′) n. figurines, curios, etc.

brick, n. 1. building block of baked clay. 2. any oblong piece. —a. built of brick. —v. cover with bricks.

brick′lay′ing, n. work of building with bricks.

bride, n. woman just married or about to be married. —**brid′al,** a.

bride′groom, n. man just married or being married.

brides′maid, n. any of the bride's wedding attendants.

bridge, n. 1. structure for crossing or crossing a river, etc. 2. thing like a bridge in shape, etc. 3. mounting for false teeth. 4. card game for two pairs of players. —v. build or be a bridge over.

bri′dle (brī′-) n. 1. head harness for a horse. 2. thing that restrains. —v. 1. put a bridle on. 2. curb.

brief, a. short; concise. —n. summary, as of a law case. —v. summarize the facts for.

brief case, small case for carrying papers, books, etc.

bri′er (brī′-) n. 1. thorny bush. 2. heath root for making tobacco pipes.

brig, n. 1. two-masted ship with square sails. 2. ship's prison.

bri·gade′, n. 1. military unit of several regiments. 2. group organized for a task.

brig·a·dier′ general (-dêr′) officer just above a colonel.

brig′and, n. roving bandit.

bright, a. 1. shining; full of light. 2. vivid. 3. cheerful. 4. mentally quick. —**bright′en,** v. —**bright′ly,** adv. —**bright′ness,** n.

bril′liant, a. 1. shining brightly. 2. splendid. 3. keenly intelligent. —**bril′liance,** n. —**bril′liant·ly,** adv.

brim, n. 1. top edge of a cup, etc. 2. projecting rim of a hat. —v. [BRIMMED, BRIMMING] fill or be full to the brim. —**brim′ful,** a.

brim′stone, n. sulfur.

brin′dle, brin′dled, a. having dark streaks, as a cow.

brine (brīn) n. 1. water full of salt. 2. ocean. —**brin′y** [-IER, -IEST] a.

bring, v. [BROUGHT, BRINGING] cause to come or happen; fetch, get, lead to, etc. —**bring forth,** give birth to; produce. —**bring off,** accomplish. —**bring to,** revive. —**bring up,** 1. rear (children). 2. mention.

brink, n. edge, as of a cliff.

brisk, a. 1. quick; energetic. 2. invigorating.

bris′ket, n. breast meat.

bris′tle (bris′'l) n. short, stiff hair. —v. 1. stiffen like bristles. 2. stiffen with anger. —**bris′tly,** a.

Brit′ish, a. of Great Britain or its people.

brit'tle, *a.* hard but easily broken. **—brit'tle·ness,** *n.*

broach (brōch) *n.* tapered bit for reaming out holes. *—v.* 1. make a hole in. 2. start a discussion of.

broad, *a.* 1. wide. 2. obvious. 3. tolerant. 4. extensive; general. **—broad'en,** *v.*

broad'cast, *v.* [-CAST or -CASTED, -CASTING] 1. spread widely. 2. send by radio. —n. radio program. **—broad'cast'er,** *n.*

broad'cloth, *n.* a fine cloth.

broad jump, jump for distance.

broad'loom, *a.* woven on a wide loom, as a carpet.

broad'-mind'ed, *a.* liberal.

broad'side, *n.* 1. firing of all guns on a ship's side. 2. large sheet with advertising. *—adv.* with the side facing.

bro·cade', *n.* cloth of a richly patterned weave. *—v.* weave a raised design in.

broc'co·li (brok'ə-) *n.* green-headed cauliflower.

bro·chure' (brō-shoor') *n.* pamphlet.

brogue (brōg) *n.* 1. Irish accent. 2. heavy oxford shoe.

broil, *v.* cook by direct heat.

broil'er, *n.* 1. pan or stove section for broiling. 2. chicken fit for broiling.

broke, pt. of **break.** —*a.* [Sl.] without money.

bro'ken, pp. of **break.** —*a.* 1. fractured. 2. violated, as a vow. 3. interrupted. 4. imperfectly spoken.

bro'ken·heart'ed, *a.* crushed by grief.

bro'ker, *n.* agent hired to buy and sell. **—bro'ker·age,** *n.*

bro'mide (-mīd) *n.* 1. sedative. 2. trite saying.

bro'mine (-mēn) *n.* fuming liquid, a chemical element.

bron'chi·al (-ki-) *a.* of the branches of the windpipe.

bron·chi'tis (-kī'-) *n.* inflammation of the bronchial tubes.

bron'co, *n.* [*pl.* -COS] small, wild horse of the West.

bronze, *n.* 1. alloy of copper and tin. 2. reddish brown. *—v.* make bronze in color.

brooch (brōch) *n.* large ornamental pin with a clasp.

brood, *n.* 1. birds hatched at one time. 2. offspring. *—v.* dwell on moodily.

brook (brook) *n.* small stream. *—v.* endure or tolerate.

broom (brōōm) *n.* 1. long-handled brush for sweeping. 2. kind of shrub.

broom'stick, *n.* broom handle.

broth (brôth) *n.* clear soup.

broth'el, *n.* house of prostitution.

broth'er, *n.* 1. male related to one by having the same parents. 2. fellow member. **—broth'er·hood,** *n.* **—broth'er·ly,** *a.*

broth'er-in-law', *n.* [*pl.* BROTHERS-IN-LAW] 1. brother of one's spouse. 2. sister's husband.

brought, pt. & pp. of **bring.**

brow (brou) *n.* 1. eyebrow. 2. forehead. 3. edge of a cliff.

brow'beat, *v.* [-BEAT, -BEAT-EN, -BEATING] to bully.

brown, *a.* 1. chocolate-colored. 2. tanned; dark-skinned. —n. brown color. *—v.* make or become brown.

browse, *v.* 1. feed on grass, etc. 2. glance through books. **—brows'er,** *n.*

bru'in (brōō'-) *n.* a bear.

bruise (brōōz) *v.* injure and discolor (the skin) without breaking it. *—n.* discolored injury of the skin.

bruis'er, *n.* pugnacious man.

bruit (brōōt) *n.* & *v.* rumor.

bru·nette' (-net') *a.* having dark hair and complexion. —n. brunette woman or girl. **—bru·net',** *a.* & *n. masc.*

brunt, *n.* main impact.

brush, *n.* 1. device with bristles, wires, etc. for cleaning, painting, etc. 2. a brushing. 3. skirmish. 4. underbrush. 5. sparsely settled land. *—v.* 1. use a brush on. 2. touch lightly. 3. remove as with a brush. **—brush off,** dismiss. **—brush up,** refresh one's memory.

brusque (brusk) *a.* abrupt in manner. **—brusque'ly,** *adv.*

bru'tal, *a.* savage, cruel, etc. **—bru·tal'i·ty** [*pl.* -TIES] *n.* **—bru'tal·ly,** *adv.*

brute, *a.* of or like an animal; cruel, stupid, etc. —n. 1. animal. 2. brutal person. **—brut'ish,** *a.*

bub'ble, *n.* globule of air or gas in a liquid. *—v.* 1. rise in bubbles. 2. gurgle. **—bub'bly,** *a.*

bu·bon'ic plague (bū-) deadly contagious disease.

buc·ca·neer' (buk-ə-) *n.* pirate.

buck, *n.* 1. male deer, goat, etc. 2. a bucking. 3. [Sl.] dollar. *—v.* 1. rear up, as to throw off (a rider). 2. [Col.]

resist. —**buck up** [Col.] cheer up. —**pass the buck** [Col.] shift the blame.

buck'et, *n.* container with a handle, for water, etc.; pail. —**buck'et-ful,** *n.*

buck'le, *n.* clasp for fastening a belt, etc. —*v.* 1. fasten with a buckle. 2. bend or crumple. —**buckle down,** apply oneself.

buck'ler, *n.* round shield.

buck'ram, *n.* stiff cloth.

buck'shot, *n.* large lead shot for a gun.

buck'skin, *n.* leather from skins of deer or sheep.

buck'tooth, *n.* [*pl.* -TEETH] projecting tooth.

buck'wheat, *n.* plant with seeds ground into dark flour.

bu·col'ic (bū-kol'-) *a.* rustic.

bud, *n.* small swelling on a plant, start of a leaf, shoot, or flower. —*v.* [BUDDED, BUDDING] 1. put forth buds. 2. begin to develop.

Bud·dhism (bood'iz'm) *n.* a religion of Asia. —**Bud'dhist,** *n. & a.*

bud'dy, *n.* [*pl.* -DIES] [Col.] comrade.

budge, *v.* move slightly.

budg'et, *n.* 1. plan adjusting expenses to income. 2. estimated cost of operating, etc. —*v.* 1. put on a budget. 2. schedule.

buff, *v.* polish, as with soft leather. —**buff'er,** *n.*

buf'fa·lo, *n.* [*pl.* -LOES, -LOS] 1. wild ox. 2. American bison. —*v.* [Sl.] to bluff.

buff'er, *n.* anything that lessens shock.

buff'et, *n. & v.* blow; slap.

buf·fet' (-fā') *n.* 1. cabinet for dishes, silver, etc. 2. food which guests serve themselves as from a buffet.

buf·foon', *n.* a clown. —**buf·foon'er·y,** *n.*

bug, *n.* 1. crawling insect, esp. when a pest. 2. [Col.] germ. 3. [Sl.] defect.

bug'bear, *n.* imaginary terror: also **bug'a·boo** [*pl.* -BOOS].

bug'gy, *n.* [*pl.* -GIES] 1. light, one-horse carriage. 2. carriage for a baby.

bu'gle, *n.* small, valveless trumpet. —**bu'gler,** *n.*

build, *v.* [BUILT, BUILDING] 1. make by putting together parts. 2. create, develop, etc. —*n.* form or structure. —**build'er,** *n.*

build'ing, *n.* a structure.

bulb, *n.* 1. underground bud,

as the onion. 2. bulblike electric lamp. 3. outward swelling. —*v.* swell out. —**bulg'y,** *a.*

bulge, *n.* outward swelling. —*v.* swell out. —**bulg'y,** *a.*

bulk, *n.* 1. size or mass, esp. if great. 2. main part. —*v.* have, or gain in, size or importance. —*a.* not packaged. —**bulk'y** [-IER, -IEST] *a.*

bulk'head, *n.* vertical partition, as in a ship.

bull, *n.* 1. male bovine animal, or male seal, elephant, etc. 2. edict of the Pope. —*a.* male.

bull'dog, *n.* heavily built dog with a stubborn grip.

bull'doze, *v.* [Col.] to bully.

bull'doz'er, *n.* tractor with large shovellike blade.

bul'let, *n.* shaped metal piece to be shot from a gun.

bul'le·tin, *n.* 1. brief news item. 2. regular publication of a group.

bull'fight, *n.* spectacle in which a bull is goaded to fury, then killed. —**bull'fight'er,** *n.*

bull'finch, *n.* small European songbird.

bull'frog, *n.* large frog.

bull'head·ed, *a.* stubborn.

bul·lion (bool'yən) *n.* gold or silver ingots.

bull'ock, *n.* castrated bull.

bull's'-eye', *n.* target center.

bul'ly, *n.* [*pl.* -LIES] one who hurts or threatens weaker people. —*v.* [-LIED, -LYING] act the bully (toward).

bul'rush, *n.* tall grasslike plant, in marshes, etc.

bul'wark, *n.* rampart; defense.

bum, *n.* [Col.] vagrant. —*v.* [BUMMED, BUMMING] [Col.] 1. beg. 2. loaf. —*a.* [Sl.] poor in quality.

bum'ble·bee', *n.* large bee.

bump, *v.* collide (with). —*n.* 1. light collision. 2. swelling. —**bump'y** [-IER, -IEST] *a.*

bump'er, *n.* device, as on a car, for easing collisions. —*a.* unusually abundant.

bun, *n.* small bread roll.

bunch, *n.* cluster of similar things. —*v.* gather; group.

bun'dle, *n.* 1. number of things bound together. 2. package. —*v.* 1. make into a bundle. 2. hustle (*off*).

bun'ga·low, *n.* small house.

bun'gle, *v.* do clumsily; spoil —**bun'gler,** *n.*

bun'ion, *n.* swelling at the base of the big toe.

bunk, *n.* 1. built-in bed. 2. any narrow bed. 3. [Sl.] emp-

ty talk. —v. sleep in a bunk.
bunk′er, n. 1. large bin. 2. obstacle on a golf course.
bunt′ing, n. 1. thin cloth for flags, etc. 2. baby's hooded blanket. 3. small finch.
buoy (boi, bōō′i) n. floating marker. —v. 1. keep afloat. 2. lift up in spirits.
buoy′an·cy, n. 1. ability to float. 2. cheerfulness. —**buoy′ant,** a.
bur, n. prickly seedcase.
bur′den, n. 1. load carried. 2. thing hard to bear. —v. weigh down. —**bur′den·some,** a.
bur′dock, n. plant with prickly burs.
bu·reau (byoo′rō) n. [pl. -REAUS, -REAUX (-rōz)] 1. chest of drawers. 2. government department. 3. office.
bu·reauc′ra·cy (-rok′-) n. [pl. -CIES] 1. government by officials following rigid rules. 2. such officials. —**bu′reau·crat,** n. —**bu′reau·crat′ic,** a.
burg, n. [Col.] city or town.
bur′geon (-jən) n. sprout.
bur′glar, n. one who breaks into a building to steal. —**bur′gla·ry** [pl. -RIES] n.
bur′i·al (ber′-) n. burying of a dead body.
bur′lap, n. coarse cloth of hemp, etc., used for bags.
bur·lesque′ (-lesk′) n. 1. broadly comic satire. 2. type of vaudeville. —v. imitate comically.
bur′ly, a. [-LIER, -LIEST] big and strong.
burn, v. [BURNED or BURNT] 1. be or set on fire. 2. destroy or be destroyed by fire. 3. hurt or be hurt by acid, friction, etc. 4. feel or make feel hot. 5. be excited. —n. injury from fire, acid, etc.
burn′er, n. part of a stove, etc. producing the flame.
bur′nish, v. & n. polish.
burp, v. & n. [Sl.] belch.
burr, n. 1. rough edge left on metal. 2. dentist's drill. 3. trilling of r. 4. bur.
bur′ro, n. [pl. -ROS] donkey.
bur′row, n. hole dug by an animal. —v. make a burrow.
bur′sar, n. college treasurer.
bur·si′tis, n. inflammation of a sac between bone joints.
burst, v. [BURST, BURSTING] 1. come apart suddenly; explode. 2. appear, enter, etc. suddenly. 3. be too full. —n. a bursting.
bur·y (ber′i) v. -IED, -YING]

1. put in a grave, tomb, etc. 2. cover; hide.
bus, n. [pl. BUSES, BUSSES] large motor coach.
bus boy, waiter's assistant.
bush, n. 1. low, woody plant. 2. uncleared land. —**bush′y** [-IER, -IEST] a.
bush′el, n. a dry measure equal to 4 pecks.
bush′ing, n. removable metal lining to reduce friction.
busi·ness (biz′nis) n. 1. commerce. 2. commercial or industrial establishment. 3. occupation. 4. rightful concern. 5. matter; affair. —**busi′ness·man** [pl.-MEN] n.
busi′ness·like, a. efficient.
bus′ing, bus′sing, n. a taking children by bus to a school so as to achieve racial balance.
bust, n. 1. sculpture of head and shoulders. 2. woman's bosom. —v. [Sl.] break.
bus·tle (bus′'l) v. hurry busily. —n. 1. a bustling. 2. skirt padding in back.
bus′y, a. [-IER, -IEST] 1. active; at work. 2. full of activity. —v. [-IED, -YING] make busy. —**bus′i·ly,** adv.
bus′y·bod′y, n. [pl. -IES] meddler.
but, prep. except. —con. 1. yet. 2. on the contrary. 3. unless. —adv. 1. only. 2. merely. —**all but,** almost. —**but for,** if it were not for.
butch′er, n. 1. one who kills and dresses animals for meat. 2. one who sells meat. 3. killer. —v. 1. slaughter. 2. botch. —**butch′er·y,** n.
but′ler, n. head manservant.
butt, n. 1. thick end. 2. stub. 3. object of ridicule. 4. large cask. —v. 1. join end to end. 2. ram with the head. —**butt in(to),** [Sl.] meddle (in).
butte (būt) n. small mesa.
but′ter, n. yellow fat churned from cream. —v. spread with butter. —**but′ter·y,** a.
but′ter·cup, n. yellow, cup-shaped flower.
but′ter·fat, n. fatty part of milk.
but′ter·fly, n. [pl. -FLIES] insect with 4 broad wings.
but′ter·milk, n. sour milk left after churning butter.
but′ter·nut, n. white walnut tree or its edible nut.
but′ter·scotch, n. hard candy made with butter.
but′tocks, n.pl. fleshy,

rounded parts of the hips.

but′ton, n. 1. small disk for fastening a garment, etc. 2. buttonlike part. —v. fasten with buttons.

but′ton·hole, n. slit for a button. —v. detain in talk.

but′tress, n. 1. outer structure supporting a wall. 2. a prop. —v. prop up.

bux·om (buk′səm) a. comely, plump, etc.: said of women.

buy, v. [BOUGHT, BUYING] 1. get by paying money, etc. 2. to bribe. —n. [Col.] something worth its price. —**buy′er**, n.

buzz, v. hum like a bee. —n. buzzing sound.

buz′zard, n. 1. kind of large hawk. 2. kind of vulture.

buzz′er, n. electrical device signaling with a buzz.

by, prep. 1. near; beside. 2. during. 3. not later than. 4. through. 5. past. 6. for. 7. according to. —adv. 1. near. 2. past. —**by and by**, after a while. —**by and large**, in most respects. —**by the by**, incidentally.

by′gone, a. past. —n. anything past.

by′law, n. local law or rule.

by′-line′, n. writer's name heading a newspaper article.

by′-pass′, n. road, pipe, etc. that goes around the main way. —v. 1. to detour around. 2. ignore.

by′path, n. side path.

by′-prod′uct, n. secondary product or result.

by′stand′er, n. one standing near but not taking part.

by′way, n. side road.

by′word, n. 1. proverb. 2. thing proverbially bad.

C

cab, n. 1. taxicab. 2. place in a truck, etc. where the operator sits.

ca·bal (kə-bal′) n. 1. group of conspirators. 2. plot.

ca·ba′na, n. 1. cabin. 2. small bathhouse.

cab·a·ret′ (-rā′) n. café with entertainment.

cab′bage, n. vegetable with round head of thick leaves.

cab′in, n. 1. hut. 2. a room on a ship, etc.

cab′i·net, n. 1. case with drawers or shelves. 2. [C-] body of official advisers.

ca′ble, n. 1. thick rope, often of wire. 2. cablegram. —v. send a cablegram (to).

ca′ble·gram, n. telegram sent overseas by wire.

ca·boose′ (-bōōs′) n. crew's car on a freight train.

ca·ca·o (**bean**) (kə-kā′ō) seed of a tropical Am. tree: source of chocolate.

cache (kash) n. 1. place for hiding food, supplies, etc. 2. anything so hidden. —v. place in a cache.

cack′le, v. & n. (make) the shrill sound of a hen.

ca·coph′o·ny (-kof′-) n. harsh, jarring sound.

cac′tus, n. [pl. -TUSES, -TI (-tī)] spiny desert plant.

cad, n. ungentlemanly man.

ca·dav′er (kə-dav′-) n. corpse. —**ca·dav′er·ous**, a.

cad′die, cad′dy [pl. -DIES] n. attendant to a golfer. — v. [-DIED, -DYING] be a caddy.

cad′dy, n. [pl. -DIES] small container, as for tea.

ca′dence (kā′-) n. 1. fall of the voice in speaking. 2. rhythm; measured movement.

ca·det′ (kə-) n. student at a military or naval school.

cadge, v. [Col.] beg. — **cadg′er**, n.

ca·dre (kad′ri) n. nucleus for a larger organization.

ca·fé (ka-fā′) n. 1. restaurant. 2. barroom.

caf′e·te′ri·a (-tēr′i-ə) n. self-service restaurant.

caf·feine, caf·fein (kaf′ēn) n. alkaloid in coffee, tea, etc.: a stimulant.

cage, n. openwork structure, esp. for confining animals. —v. put in a cage.

cag′ey, cag′y, a. [Col.] sly; cunning. —**cag′i·ly**, adv.

ca·hoots′, n. [Sl.] scheming partnership.

cais′son (kā′-) n. 1. ammunition wagon. 2. watertight box for underwater construction work.

ca·jole′ (-jōl′) v. coax or wheedle. —**ca·jol′er·y**, n.

cake, n. 1. baked dough or batter of flour, eggs, sugar, etc. 2. solid, formed, usually flat mass. —v. form into a hard mass.

cal′a·bash′, n. gourdlike fruit of a tropical tree.

cal′a·mine, n. zinc compound used in lotions, etc.

ca·lam′i·ty, n. [pl. -TIES] disaster. —**ca·lam′i·tous**, a.

cal′ci·fy′ (-sə-) v. [-FIED, -FY-ING] change into stony matter. —**cal′ci·fi·ca′tion**, n.

cal′ci·mine, n. thin, watery

paint for covering plaster. —v. cover with calcimine.

cal′ci·um, n. chemical element in bone, limestone, etc.

cal′cu·late (-kyoo-) v. 1. figure by arithmetic. 2. estimate. 3. intend. —**cal′cu·la·ble,** a. —**cal′cu·la′tion,** n. —**cal′cu·la′tor,** n.

cal′cu·lat′ing, a. 1. scheming. 2. shrewd; cautious.

cal′cu·lus (-kyoo-) n. branch of higher mathematics.

cal′dron (kôl′-) n. large kettle or boiler.

cal′en·dar, n. 1. table showing the days, weeks, and months of a year. 2. schedule.

calf, n. [pl. **CALVES**] 1. young cow or bull. 2. young elephant, seal, etc. 3. fleshy part of leg below the knee.

cal′i·ber, cal′i·bre, n. 1. diameter of a bullet, bore of a gun, etc. 2. quality.

cal′i·brate, v. mark or fix the graduations of (a measuring device). —**cal′i·bra′tion,** n. —**cal′i·bra′tor,** n.

cal′i·co, n. cotton cloth, usually printed.

cal′i·pers, n.pl. instrument for measuring diameter.

ca′liph, ca′lif (kā′lif) n. old title of Moslem rulers.

cal′is·then′ics, n.pl. athletic exercises.

calk (kôk) v. make watertight by stopping up cracks with a filler.

call, v. 1. say loudly; shout. 2. summon. 3. name. 4. telephone. 5. stop (a game). —n. 1. shout or cry. 2. summons. 3. demand. 4. need. 5. short visit. —**call for,** 1. demand. 2. come and get. —**call off,** [Col.] cancel. —**call on,** 1. visit briefly. 2. ask (one) to speak. —**on call,** available when called. —**call′er,** n.

call′ing, n. vocation; trade.

cal·li′o·pe (-lī′ə-pē) n. organlike musical instrument with steam whistles.

cal′lous (kal′əs) a. 1. hardened. 2. unfeeling. —**cal′lous·ly,** adv.

cal′low, a. inexperienced.

cal′lus, n. hard, thickened place on the skin.

calm (käm) n. stillness. —a. still; tranquil. —v. make or become calm. —**calm′ly,** adv. —**calm′ness,** n.

ca·lor′ic, a. of heat.

cal′o·rie, cal′o·ry (-ri) n. [pl. **-RIES**] unit of heat or of

the energy got from food.

ca·lum′ni·ate, v. to slander. —**ca·lum′ni·a′tion,** n.

cal·um′ny, n. [pl. **-NIES**] slander.

calve (kav) v. give birth to (a calf).

ca·lyp′so (-lip′sō) n. improvised ballad sung in the West Indies.

ca·lyx (kā′liks) n. [pl. **-LYXES**] sepals of a flower.

cam, n. projection on a wheel to give irregular motion, as to a shaft.

ca·ma·ra′de·rie (kä′mə·rä′dēr-i) n. comradeship.

cam′ber, n. slight convexity.

cam′bric (kām′-) n. fine linen or cotton cloth.

came, pt. of **come.**

cam′el, n. beast of burden with a humped back.

ca·mel′li·a (-mēl′yə) n. large, roselike flower.

cam′e·o, n. [pl. **-os**] gem with figure carved on it.

cam′er·a, n. 1. device for taking photographs. 2. TV device that first receives the images for transmission.

cam′ou·flage (-ə-fläzh) n. a disguising of potential targets in wartime. —v. conceal by disguising.

camp, n. 1. place with tents, huts, etc., as for vacationers or soldiers. 2. supporters of a cause. —v. set up a camp. —**camp′er,** n.

cam·paign′ (-pān′) n. series of planned actions, as in war, an election, etc. —v. wage a campaign.

cam·pa·ni′le (-nē′li) n. bell tower.

cam′phor, n. strong-smelling crystalline substance used in moth balls, medicine, etc.

cam′pus, n. school or college grounds. —a. of students.

can, v. [pt. **COULD**] 1. know how or be able to. 2. may.

can, n. metal container, as for foods. —v. [**CANNED, CAN NING**] preserve (food) in cans or jars. —**can′ner,** n.

Ca·na′di·an, n. & a. (native) of Canada.

ca·nal′, n. 1. artificial waterway. 2. body duct.

ca·na·pé (-pi, -pā) n. appetizer on a cracker, etc.

ca·nard′, n. false rumor.

ca·nar′y, n. [pl. **-IES**] yellow songbird kept in a cage.

can′cel (-s′l) v. 1. cross out. 2. make invalid. 3. abolish. —**can′cel·la′tion,** n.

can'cer (-sĕr) *n.* 1. malignant tumor. 2. a spreading evil. 3. [C-] 4th sign of the zodiac; Crab. —**can'cer·ous,** *a.*

can'de·la'brum, *n.* [*pl.* -BRA, -BRUMS] large, branched candlestick: also **can'de·la'bra** [*pl.* -BRAS].

can'did, *a.* frank; honest.

can'di·date, *n.* one seeking office, etc.—**can'di·da·cy,** *n.*

can'dle, *n.* wax taper with a wick, burned for light.

candle power, unit for measuring light.

can'dle·stick, *n.* holder for a candle or candles.

can'dor, *n.* frankness.

can'dy, *n.* [*pl.* -DIES] confection of sugar or sirup. —*v.* [-DIED, -DYING] cook or preserve in sugar.

cane, *n.* 1. hollow, jointed stem, as of bamboo. 2. walking stick. 3. split rattan. —*v.* beat with a cane.

ca'nine (kā'-) *a.* of or like a dog. —*n.* dog.

canine tooth, any of the four sharp-pointed teeth.

can'is·ter, *n.* box or can for coffee, tea, etc.

can'ker, *n.* a sore, esp. in the mouth. —**can'ker·ous,** *a.*

can'ner·y, *n.* [*pl.* -IES] factory for canning foods.

can'ni·bal, *n.* person who eats human flesh. —**can'ni·bal·ism,** *n.* —**can'ni·bal·is'tic,** *a.*

can'non, *n.* [*pl.* -NONS, -NON] large mounted gun.

can'not, can not.

can'ny, *a.* [-NIER, -NIEST] 1. cautious. 2. shrewd.

ca·noe' (-nōō') *n.* narrow, light boat moved with paddles. —*v.* paddle a canoe.

can'on, *n.* 1. body of church laws. 2. any law. 3. official list. 4. clergyman serving in a cathedral. 5. musical round. —**ca·non'i·cal,** *a.*

can'on·ize, *v.* name as a saint.—**can'on·i·za'tion,** *n.*

can'o·py, *n.* [*pl.* -PIES] covering hung over a bed, throne, etc. —**can'o·pied,** *a.*

cant, *n.* 1. special talk of a class; jargon. 2. hypocritical talk. —*v.* use cant.

cant, *n.* & *v.* tilt; slant.

can't, cannot.

can'ta·loupe, can'ta·loup (-lōp) *n.* sweet, juicy melon.

can·tan'ker·ous, *a.* bad-tempered; quarrelsome.

can·ta'ta (-tä'-) *n.* dramatic choral composition.

can·teen', *n.* 1. general store at an army post. 2. soldier's water flask.

can'ter, *n.* easy gallop. —*v.* go at this pace.

can'ti·cle (-k'l) *n.* hymn.

can'ti·le'ver, *n.* structure anchored at only one end.

can'to, *n.* [*pl.* -TOS] division of a long poem.

can'tor, *n.* liturgical singer in a synagogue.

can'vas, *n.* coarse cloth used for tents, sails, oil paintings, etc.

can'vass (-vəs) *v.* seek votes, opinions, etc. from. —*n.* a canvassing.

can'yon, *n.* narrow valley between high cliffs.

cap, *n.* 1. brimless hat, often with a visor. 2. caplike cover. —*v.* [CAPPED, CAPPING] 1. put a cap on. 2. surpass.

ca'pa·ble, *a.* able; skilled. —**capable of,** able or likely to. —**ca'pa·bil'i·ty** [*pl.* -TIES] *n.* —**ca'pa·bly,** *adv.*

ca·pa'cious, *a.* roomy; wide.

ca·pac'i·ty, *n.* 1. ability to contain or hold. 2. volume. 3. ability. 4. position.

cape, *n.* 1. sleeveless coat fastened about the neck. 2. land jutting into water.

ca'per, *v.* skip about playfully. —*n.* gay leap. —**cut a caper,** play a silly trick.

ca'pers, *n.pl.* tiny pickled buds used as seasoning.

cap'il·lar'y, *a.* having a tiny bore, as a tube. —*n.* [*pl.* -IES] tiny blood vessel.

cap'i·tal, *a.* 1. bringing or punishable by death. 2. chief; main. 3. excellent. —*n.* 1. see **capital letter.** 2. city from which a state is governed. 3. money or property owned or used in business. 4. capitalists collectively. 5. top of a column. —**make capital of,** use to advantage.

cap'i·tal·ism, *n.* economic system in which the means of production and distribution are privately owned by capitalists in business. —**cap'i·tal·ist,** *n.* owner of wealth used in business. —**cap'i·tal·is'tic,** *a.*

cap'i·tal·ize, *v.* 1. convert into capital. 2. use to advantage (with *on*). 3. supply capital for. 4. write with a capital letter. —**cap'i·tal·i·za'tion,** *n.*

capital letter, large letter used to begin a sentence, name, etc.

cap'i·tol, *n.* building where a legislature meets.

ca·pit'u·late (-pich′ə-) *v.* surrender. **—ca·pit'u·la'tion,** *n.*

ca'pon, *n.* castrated rooster.

ca·price' (-prēs′) *n.* whim.

ca·pri'cious (-prish′əs) *a.* unpredictable.

cap·size', *v.* upset; overturn.

cap'stan, *n.* device around which cables are wound.

cap'sule, *n.* small case, as for a dose of medicine.

cap'tain, *n.* 1. leader. 2. army officer above lieutenant. 3. navy officer above commander. 4. master of a ship. **—v.** to head. **—cap'tain·cy,** *n.*

cap'tion, *n.* title, as of a newspaper picture.

cap'ti·vate, *v.* fascinate.

cap'tive, *a.* & *n.* (held) prisoner. **—cap·tiv'i·ty,** *n.*

cap'tor, *n.* one who captures.

cap'ture, *v.* take by force, surprise, etc. **—n.** a capturing or the thing captured.

car, *n.* 1. wheeled vehicle, esp. an automobile. 2. elevator.

car'a·mel, *n.* 1. burnt sugar used to flavor. 2. chewy candy.

car'at (kar′-) *n.* 1. unit of weight for jewels. 2. one 24th part (of pure gold).

car'a·van, *n.* group traveling together for safety.

car'a·way (kar′-) *n.* spicy seeds used as flavoring.

car'bine (-bīn, -bēn) *n.* light, short-barreled rifle.

car'bo·hy'drate, *n.* compound of carbon, hydrogen, and oxygen, as sugar or starch.

car·bol'ic acid, an acid used as an antiseptic, etc.

car'bon, *n.* nonmetallic chemical element in all organic compounds: diamond & graphite are pure carbon.

car'bon·ate, *v.* charge with carbon dioxide.

carbon dioxide, odorless gas given off in breathing.

car'bon·if'er·ous, *a.* containing carbon or coal.

carbon monoxide, colorless, odorless, poisonous gas.

carbon paper, paper coated with a carbon preparation, used to make copies (**carbon copies**) of letters, etc.

car·bon·tet'ra·chlo'ride (-klôr′-) cleaning fluid.

car'bun·cle, *n.* painful inflammation below the skin.

car'bu·re'tor (-bə-rā′-) *n.* device in an engine for mixing air with gasoline.

car'cass, car'case (-kəs) *n.* dead body of an animal.

card, *n.* 1. flat piece of stiff paper. 2. post card. 3. playing card. 4. *pl.* game played with cards. 5. metal comb for wool, etc. **—v.** comb with a card.

card'board, *n.* stiff paper.

car'di·ac, *a.* of the heart.

car'di·gan, *n.* knitted jacketlike sweater.

car'di·nal, *a.* 1. chief; main. 2. bright-red. **—n.** 1. high R.C. Ch. official. 2. red American songbird.

cardinal number, number used in counting, as 7, 42, etc.

car'di·o·graph', *n.* an electrocardiograph.

care, *n.* 1. worry. 2. watchfulness; heed. 3. charge; keeping. **—v.** 1. be concerned. 2. wish (*to do*). **—care for,** 1. love or like. 2. look after. **—care of,** at the address of. **—care'free',** *a.* **—care'ful,** *a.* **—care'less,** *a.*

ca·reen', *v.* tilt; lurch.

ca·reer', *n.* 1. full speed. 2. progress through life. 3. profession or occupation.

ca·ress', *v.* touch lovingly. **—n.** affectionate touch.

car'et (kar′-) *n.* mark (^) to show where addition is to be made in a printed line.

care'tak'er, *n.* one who takes care of a building, etc.

care'worn, *a.* weary with care.

car'go, *n.* [*pl.* -GOES, -GOS] load carried by a ship, etc.

car'i·bou (kar′ə-boō) *n.* N. American reindeer.

car'i·ca·ture (kar′i·kə·chẽr) *n.* distorted imitation or picture for satire. **—v.** do a caricature of.

car·ies (kâr′ēz) *n.* decay of teeth, bones, etc.

car·il·lon (kar′-) *n.* set of tuned bells.

car'mine (-min, -mīn) *n.* red or purplish red.

car'nage (-nij) *n.* slaughter.

car'nal, *a.* bodily; sensual.

car·na'tion, *n.* 1. variety of the pink. 2. its flower.

car'ni·val, *n.* 1. festivity. 2. kind of fair, with rides, etc.

car·niv'o·rous, *a.* flesh-eating. **—car'ni·vore,** *n.*

car'ol (kar′-) *n.* (Christmas) song of joy. **—v.** sing. **—car'ol·er, car'ol·ler,** *n.*

car'om (kar′-) *n.* & *v.* hit and rebound.

ca·rot′id, *n.* either of two main arteries in the neck.

ca·rouse′ (-rouz′) *v.* & *n.* (join in) a drinking party.

carp, *n.* fresh-water fish. — *v.* find fault pettily.

car′pel, *n.* modified leaf forming a pistil.

car′pen·ter, *n.* construction worker who makes wooden parts. —**car′pen·try,** *n.*

car′pet, *n.* heavy fabric for covering a floor. —*v.* to cover as with a carpet.

car′port, *n.* roofed shelter for an automobile.

car′riage (kar′ij) *n.* 1. horse-drawn vehicle. 2. posture. 3. moving part that holds and shifts something.

car′ri·er, *n.* one that carries.

car′ri·on (kar′-) *n.* decaying flesh of a dead body.

car′rot, *n.* plant with an edible, orange-red root.

car′rou·sel, car′ou·sel (-rə-) *n.* merry-go-round.

car′ry, *v.* [-RIED, -RYING] 1. take to another place. 2. lead, transmit, etc. 3. win (an election, etc.). 4. hold; support. 5. bear (oneself). 6. keep in stock. 7. cover a range. —**carry away,** excite emotion in. —**carry on,** 1. do or continue. 2. [Col.] behave wildly. —**carry out,** accomplish. —**carry over,** postpone.

cart, *n.* small wagon. —*v.* carry in a vehicle.

cart′age (-ij) *n.* 1. a carting. 2. charge for this.

carte blanche (blänsh) [Fr.] full authority.

car·tel′, *n.* international monopoly.

car′ti·lage (-lij) *n.* tough, elastic skeletal tissue.

car·tog′ra·phy, *n.* map-making. —**car·tog′ra·pher,** *n.*

car′ton, *n.* cardboard box.

car·toon′, *n.* 1. drawing that is a caricature. 2. comic strip. —**car·toon′ist,** *n.*

car′tridge (-trij) *n.* cylinder holding the charge and bullet or shot for a firearm.

carve, *v.* 1. make or shape by cutting. 2. slice. —**carv′er,** *n.* —**carv′ing,** *n.*

cas·cade′, *n.* 1. waterfall. 2. shower. —*v.* fall in a cascade.

case, *n.* 1. example or instance. 2. situation. 3. lawsuit. 4. form of a noun, etc. showing its relation to neighboring words. 5. container. 6. protective cover. —*v.* 1.

put in a case. 2. [Sl.] examine carefully. —**in case,** if. —**in case of,** in the event of.

ca·se′in (kā′si-in) *n.* protein constituent of milk.

case′ment, *n.* hinged window that opens outward.

cash, *n.* money on hand. —*v.* give or get cash for.

cash′ew, *n.* kidney-shaped, edible nut.

cash·ier′ (-êr′) *n.* one in charge of cash transactions. —*v.* dismiss in disgrace.

cash′mere, *n.* soft, fine goat's wool, or a cloth of this.

cas′ing (kās′-) *n.* 1. outer covering. 2. door frame.

ca·si′no (-sē′-) *n.* [pl. -NOS] hall for dancing, gaming, etc.

cask, *n.* barrel for liquids.

cas′ket, *n.* coffin.

cas·sa′va (-sä′-) *n.* tropical plant with starchy roots.

cas′se·role, *n.* covered dish for baking and serving.

cas·sette′ (-set′), *n.* case with film or tape for a camera or tape recorder.

cas·si′no (-sē′-) *n.* card game.

cas′sock, *n.* long vestment worn by clergymen.

cast, *v.* [CAST, CASTING] 1. throw. 2. deposit (a vote). 3. mold. 4. select (an actor). —*n.* 1. a throw. 2. plaster form for broken limb. 3. the actors in a play. 4. type or quality. 5. tinge. —**cast about,** search. —**cast aside** (or away), discard.

cas·ta·nets′, *n.pl.* two hollow pieces clicked together in one hand in rhythm.

cast′a·way, *n.* shipwrecked person.

caste (kast) *n.* class distinction based on birth, etc.

cast′er, *n.* small swiveled wheel as on a table leg.

cas′ti·gate, *v.* criticize severely. —**cas′ti·ga′tion,** *n.* —**cas′ti·ga′tor,** *n.*

cast iron, hard, brittle pig iron. —**cast′-i′ron,** *a.*

cas·tle (kas′l) *n.* 1. large, fortified dwelling. 2. chessman moving horizontally or vertically.

cast′off, *a.* discarded. —*n.* person or thing abandoned.

cas′tor-oil′ plant, plant with large seeds yielding a cathartic oil (**castor oil**).

cas′trate, *v.* remove the testicles of. —**cas·tra′tion,** *n.*

cas·u·al (kazh′ōō-əl) *a.* 1. by chance. 2. careless. 3.

nonchalant. 4. informal.

cas'u·al·ty, n. [pl. -TIES] one hurt or killed in an accident or in war.

cas'u·ist·ry (kazh'oo-) n. subtle but false reasoning. —**cas'u·ist**, n.

cat, n. 1. small, soft-furred animal kept as a pet. 2. any related mammal, as the lion. 3. spiteful woman.

cat'a·clysm (-kliz'm) n. sudden, violent change. —**cat'a·clys'mic**, a.

cat'a·comb (-kōm) n. tunnellike burial place.

cat'a·lep'sy, n. loss of consciousness, with body rigidity. —**cat'a·lep'tic**, a. & n.

cat'a·logue (-log) n. complete list, as of library books. —v. list.

ca·tal'pa (-tal'-) n. tree with heart-shaped leaves.

cat'a·lyst (-list) a. substance that affects a chemical reaction but itself remains unchanged. —**cat'a·lyt'ic**, a.

cat'a·pult', n. device for throwing or launching. —v. shoot as from a catapult.

cat'a·ract, n. 1. large waterfall. 2. condition of opaque lens in the eye.

ca·tarrh' (-tär') n. inflammation of the respiratory passages.

ca·tas'tro·phe (-tra-fi) n. great disaster. —**cat'a·stroph'ic** (-strof'-) a.

cat'bird, n. songbird with a call like a cat's.

cat'call, n. derisive call.

catch, v. [CAUGHT, CATCHING] 1. capture. 2. deceive. 3. surprise. 4. get. 5. grab. 6. understand. 7. take or keep hold. —n. 1. a catching. 2. thing that catches or is caught. 3. [Col.] trick. —catch on, [Col.] 1. understand. 2. become popular. —catch up, 1. prove wrong. 2. overtake. —**catch'er**, n.

catch'ing, a. contagious.

catch'up, n. ketchup.

catch'y, a. [-IER, -IEST] 1. easily remembered. 2. tricky.

cat'e·chism (-kiz'm) n. list of questions and answers to teach religious beliefs.

cat'e·gor'i·cal, a. 1. of or in a category. 2. positive.

cat'e·go·ry, n. [pl. -RIES] any of a system of classes.

ca'ter, v. provide food, etc. for a party. —**ca'ter·er**, n.

cat'er·cor'nered, a. diagonal. —adv. diagonally.

cat'er·pil'lar, n. larva of a butterfly, moth, etc.

cat'er·waul, v. & n. wail.

cat'fish, n. fish with long feelers about the mouth.

cat'gut, n. tough thread made from animal intestines.

ca·thar'sis, n. a relieving of the emotions.

ca·thar'tic, n. purging. —a. laxative.

ca·the'dral, n. large church.

cath'e·ter, n. tube put in the bladder to remove urine.

cath'ode, n. negatively charged electrode.

cath'o·lic, a. 1. universal. 2. liberal. 3. [C-] Roman Catholic. —n. [C-] member of the R.C. Church. —**ca·thol'i·cism**, n. —**cath'o·lic'i·ty**, n.

cat'kin, n. spike of clustered small flowers.

cat nap, short sleep; doze. —**cat'-nap'**, v.

cat'nip, n. plant like mint.

cat's'-paw', n. a dupe.

cat·sup (kech'əp) n. ketchup.

cat'tail, n. marsh plant with long, brown spikes.

cat'tle, n. 1. livestock. 2. cows, bulls, steers, or oxen. —**cat'tle·man** [pl. -MEN] n.

cat'ty, a. [-TIER, -TIEST] spiteful; mean.

cat'walk, n. high narrow walk.

Cau·ca'sian (kô-) n. & a. (person) of the white race.

cau'cus, n. political meeting to choose party candidates, etc. —v. hold a caucus.

cau'dal, a. of the tail.

caul'dron, n. caldron.

cau'li·flow'er, n. hard, white head of a cabbagelike plant.

caulk (kôk) v. calk.

caus'al, a. of a cause or causes. —**cau·sal'i·ty**, n.

cause, n. 1. thing bringing a result. 2. motive. 3. group movement with an aim. 4. lawsuit. —v. bring about.

cause'way, n. raised road, as across a marsh.

caus'tic, a. 1. corrosive. 2. sarcastic. —n. caustic substance. —**caus'ti·cal·ly**, adv.

cau'ter·ize, v. burn dead tissue off, as with a hot iron.

cau'tion, n. 1. warning. 2. prudence. —v. warn. —**cau'tious**, a.

cav'al·cade', n. procession.

cav·a·lier' (-lēr') n. 1. knight. 2. gallant gentleman. —a. 1. gay. 2. arrogant. —**cav·a·lier'ly**, adv.

cav'al·ry, n. [pl. -RIES] army

troops on horses or in motorized vehicles.—**cav´al·ry·man** [*pl.* **-MEN**]

cave, *n.* hollow place in the earth. —*v.* collapse (*in*).

cav´ern, *n.* large cave. —**cav´ern·ous**, *a.*

cav´i·ar, **cav´i·are** (-är) *n.* fish eggs eaten as a relish.

cav´il, *v.* quibble.

cav´i·ty, *n.* [*pl.* **-TIES**] hole or hollow place.

ca·vort´, *v.* prance; caper.

caw, *n.* crow's harsh cry. —*v.* make this sound.

cay·enne´ (kī-, kā-) *n.* ground hot red pepper.

cease, *v.* to end; stop.

cease´less, *a.* unceasing.

ce´dar, *n.* evergreen tree with fragrant wood.

code, *v.* give up; transfer.

ceil´ing, *n.* **1.** inner roof of a room. **2.** upper limit.

cel´e·brate, *v.* **1.** perform (a ritual). **2.** commemorate with festivity. **3.** honor; praise. —**cel´e·bra´tion**, *n.*

cel´e·brat´ed, *a.* famous.

ce·leb´ri·ty, *n.* [*pl.* **-TIES**] **1.** famous person.

ce·ler´i·ty, *n.* speed.

cel´er·y, *n.* plant with edible crisp stalks.

ce·les´tial (-chəl) *a.* **1.** of the heavens. **2.** divine.

cel´i·ba·cy (-sē), *n.* unmarried state. —**cel´i·bate** (-bit) *a.* & *n.*

cell, *n.* **1.** small room as in a prison. **2.** small unit of protoplasm. **3.** device for generating electricity chemically. **4.** unit of an organization.—**cel´lu·lar**, *a.*

cel´lar, *n.* room(s) below ground under a building.

cel·lo, **´cel·lo** (chel´ō) *n.* [*pl.* **-LOS**] instrument like a large violin, held between the knees in playing.—**cel´list**, **´cel·list**, *n.*

cel´lo·phane (sel´ə-) *n.* thin transparent cellulose material, used as a wrapping.

cel´lu·loid, *n.* brittle, flexible cellulose substance: trademark (**C-**).

cel´lu·lose (-lōs) *n.* substance in plant cell walls, used in making paper, etc.

Cel´si·us, *a.* of a thermometer on which 0° is the freezing point and 100° the boiling point of water.

ce·ment´, *n.* **1.** mixture of lime, clay, and water, used for paving, in mortar, etc. **2.** any adhesive. —*v.* join as with cement.

cem´e·ter·y, *n.* [*pl.* **-IES**] place for burying the dead.

cen´ser, *n.* container in which incense is burned.

cen´sor, *n.* one who examines books, mail, etc. to remove things considered unsuitable. —*v.* act as a censor of. —**cen´sor·ship**, *n.*

cen·so´ri·ous, *a.* critical.

cen´sure, *n.* & *v.* blame.

cen´sus, *n.* official count of population.

cent, *n.* 100th part of a dollar; penny.

cen´taur (-tôr) *n.* *Gr. myth.* monster with a man's head and trunk and a horse's body.

cen·ten´ni·al, *a.* 100th anniversary. —*a.* of a centennial. Also **cen´te·nar´y**.

cen´ter, *n.* **1.** middle point, esp. of a circle or sphere. **2.** any central place, thing, or person. —*v.* **1.** put or be at the center. **2.** gather.

cen´ter·piece, *n.* ornament for the center of a table.

cen´ti·grade, *a.* Celsius.

cen´ti·gram, *n.* 1/100 gram.

cen´ti·me´ter, *n.* 1/100 meter.

cen´ti·pede, *n.* wormlike animal with many pairs of legs.

cen´tral, *a.* **1.** in or near the center. **2.** main; chief. —**cen´tral·ly**, *adv.*

cen´tral·ize, *v.* **1.** bring to a center. **2.** organize under one control. —**cen´tral·i·za´tion**, *n.*

cen´tre, *n.* & *v.* center: Br. sp.

cen·trif´u·gal, *force* force that makes rotating bodies move away from the center.

cen·trip´e·tal, *force* force that makes rotating bodies move toward the center.

cen·tu´ri·on, *n.* military commander in ancient Rome.

cen´tu·ry, *n.* [*pl.* **-RIES**] period of 100 years.

ce·ram´ics, *n.* (the making of) pottery, porcelain, etc. —**ce·ram´ic**, *a.*

ce´re·al, *n.* **1.** grain used for food, as wheat, oats, etc. **2.** food made from grain.

cer´e·bel´lum (ser´-) *n.* lower rear part of the brain.

cer´e·bral, *a.* of the brain.

cerebral palsy, paralysis due to a lesion of the cerebrum.

cer´e·brum, *n.* upper main part of the brain.

cer´e·mo´ni·al, *a.* ritual; formal. —*n.* system of rites.

cer´e·mo´ny, *n.* [*pl.* **-NIES**] **1.** set of formal acts; rite.

2. rigid etiquette; formality.
—**cer'e·mo'ni·ous,** a.

ce·rise' (-rēs') a. clear red.

cer'tain, a. 1. fixed; settled. 2. sure; positive. 3. specific, but unnamed. —**for certain,** surely. —**cer'tain·ly,** adv. —**cer'tain·ty,** n.

cer·tif'i·cate (-kit) n. written statement testifying to a fact, promise, etc.

cer'ti·fy, v. [-FIED, -FYING] 1. formally declare to be true, etc. 2. guarantee. —**cer'ti·fi·ca'tion,** n.

cer'ti·tude, n. assurance.

ce·ru'le·an, a. sky-blue.

cer'vix, n. necklike part. —**cer'vi·cal,** a.

ces·sa'tion, n. stop; pause.

ces'sion, n. a ceding.

cess'pool, n. deep hole in the ground for sewage, etc.

chafe, v. 1. make warm or sore by rubbing. 2. be angry.

chaff, n. 1. threshed husks of grain. 2. worthless stuff. —v. tease; banter.

chafing dish (chāf'-) pan for cooking food at the table.

cha·grin' (sha-) n. disappointment, humiliation, etc. —v. make feel chagrin.

chain, n. 1. flexible series of joined links. 2. pl. fetters. 3. connected series. —v. restrain as with chains.

chain reaction, series of (nuclear) reactions whose products cause new reactions.

chain store, any of a group of retail stores owned by one company.

chair, n. 1. seat with a back. 2. office of authority.

chair'man, n. [pl. -MEN] one who presides at a meeting. —**chair'man·ship,** n.

chaise longue (shāz' lông') [pl. CHAISE LONGUES] couch-like chair with a long seat.

cha·let (sha-lā') n. cottage with overhanging eaves.

chal·ice (chal'is) n. cup.

chalk (chôk) n. soft limestone for writing on a blackboard. —**chalk up,** to record. —**chalk'y** [-IER, -IEST] a.

chal'lenge, n. 1. demand for identification. 2. a calling into question. 3. call to a contest, etc. —v. put a challenge to. —**chal'leng·er,** n.

cham'ber (chām'-) n. 1. room. 2. pl. judge's office. 3. assembly or council. 4. part of a gun for the cartridge.

cham'ber·maid, n. maid who keeps bedrooms neat.

cham'bray (sham'-) n. kind of gingham.

cha·me'le·on (kə-mēl'-) n. lizard able to change its color.

cham·ois (sham'i) n. [pl. CHAMOIS] 1. small antelope. 2. soft kind of leather.

champ, v. chew or bite noisily. —n. [Sl.] champion.

cham·pagne (sham-pān') n. effervescent white wine.

cham'pi·on, n. 1. one who fights for a cause. 2. winner of first place. —a. best. —v. defend; support. —**cham'pi·on·ship',** n.

chance, n. 1. luck; fortune. 2. risk. 3. opportunity. 4. possibility. —a. accidental. —v. 1. happen. 2. risk.

chan'cel, n. place around an altar for clergy and choir.

chan'cel·lor, n. 1. high state or church official. 2. university head. —**chan'cel·ler·y** [pl. -IES] n.

chan·cre (shan'kẽr) n. sore or ulcer of syphilis.

chanc'y, a. risky.

chan·de·lier (shan'də-lêr') n. hanging lighting fixture.

chan'dler, n. 1. candle maker. 2. dealer in groceries, etc.

change, v. 1. substitute. 2. exchange. 3. alter; vary. —n. 1. alteration or variation. 2. variety. 3. money returned as overpayment. 4. small coins. —**change'a·ble,** a. —**change'less,** a.

chan'nel, n. 1. bed of a river, etc. 2. wide strait joining two seas. 3. any passage. 4. official course of action. 5. assigned frequency band, esp. in TV. —v. make, or send through, a channel.

chant, n. song with several words to each tone. —v. utter in a chant.

chant·ey (shan'ti, chan'-) n. sailors' work song.

cha'os (kā'-) n. complete disorder. —**cha·ot'ic,** a.

chap, n. 1. jaw. 2. cheek. 3. [Col.] fellow. —v. [CHAPPED, CHAPPING] become rough and red as from the cold.

chap'el, n. small church.

chap·er·on (shap'ə-rōn) n. older person in charge of unmarried people at social affairs. —v. be a chaperon to.

chap'lain (-lin) n. clergyman in the armed forces.

chap'let, n. garland.

chap'ter, n. 1. main division of a book. 2. branch of an organization.

char, v. [CHARRED, CHARRING] scorch.

char·ac·ter (kar'-) n. 1. letter or symbol. 2. trait. 3. kind or sort. 4. personality. 5. moral strength. 6. person in a play, novel, etc. 7. [Col.] eccentric person.

char·ac·ter·is·tic, a. typical; distinctive. —n. distinguishing quality.

char·ac·ter·ize, v. 1. describe. 2. be a quality of.

cha·rade' (shə-) n. word game in pantomime.

char·coal, n. pieces of incompletely burned wood.

chard, n. beet with edible leaves and stalks.

charge, v. 1. fill (with). 2. add electricity to. 3. command. 4. accuse. 5. ask payment (for). 6. put as a debt. 7. attack. —n. 1. load. 2. responsibility or care. 3. command. 4. accusation. 5. cost. 6. attack. —in charge, in control. —charge'a·ble, a.

charg'er, n. war horse.

char·i·ot (char'-) n. ancient, horse-drawn, two-wheeled cart. —char'i·ot·eer', n.

char·i·ty, n. [pl. -TIES] 1. leniency in judging others. 2. a helping those in need. 3. institution for so helping. —char'i·ta·ble, a.

char·la·tan (shär'-) n. quack; impostor.

charm, n. 1. words or thing supposed to have magic power. 2. trinket on a bracelet, etc. 3. fascination; allure. —v. 1. use a magical charm on. 2. fascinate; delight. —charm'ing, a.

char'nel (house), place where there are corpses.

chart, n. 1. map, esp. for navigation. 2. graph, table, etc. —v. make a chart of.

char'ter, n. official paper licensing a new company, society, chapter, etc. —v. 1. grant a charter to. 2. hire.

char·treuse (shär-trooz') n. & a. pale, yellowish green.

char'wom·an, n. [pl. -WOMEN] cleaning woman.

char·y (chãr'ĭ) a. [-IER, -IEST] careful. —char'i·ly, adv.

chase, v. 1. follow in order to catch. 2. drive away. 3. [Col.] rush. 4. decorate (metal) as by engraving. —n. a chasing. —give chase, pursue.

chas'er, n. [Col.] water, etc. taken after liquor.

chasm (kaz'm) n. deep crack in the earth's surface.

chas·sis (chas'i, shas'i) n. [pl. -SIS (-iz)] 1. frame, wheels, and motor of a car. 2. frame, tubes, etc. of a radio or TV.

chaste, a. 1. sexually virtuous. 2. decent; modest. 3. simple in style. —chas'ti·ty (chas'-) n.

chas·ten (chãs'n) v. 1. punish so as to correct. 2. subdue.

chas·tise, v. punish as by beating. —chas·tise'ment, n.

chat, v. [CHATTED, CHATTING] & n. talk in a light, informal way. —chat'ty, a.

cha·teau (sha-tō') n. [pl. -TEAUX (-tōz')] mansion.

chat'tel, n. piece of movable property.

chat·ter, v. 1. talk much and foolishly. 2. click together rapidly. —n. a chattering.

chauf·feur (shō'fēr) n. man hired to drive one's car. —v. act as chauffeur to.

chau·vin·ism (shō'-) n. fanatical patriotism. —chau'vin·ist, a. & n.

cheap, a. 1. low in price. 2. of little value. —adv. at a low cost. —cheap'ly, adv.

cheap'en, v. make cheaper.

cheat, n. 1. fraud. 2. swindler. —v. 1. deceive or practice fraud. 2. escape.

check, n. 1. sudden stop. 2. restraint or restrainer. 3. test of accuracy, etc. 4. mark (√) used to verify. 5. token to show ownership. 6. bill, as at a restaurant. 7. written order to a bank to pay money. 8. pattern of squares. 9. Chess threat to the king. —int. [Col.] right! —v. 1. stop or restrain. 2. test, verify, etc. 3. mark with a check. 4. deposit temporarily. —check in, register at a hotel, etc.—check'er, n.

check'er, n. flat, round piece used in checkers.

check'er·board, n. board for checkers, with 64 squares.

check'ered, a. 1. having a pattern of squares. 2. varied.

check'ers, n. game like chess, for two players.

check'mate, n. Chess position from which king cannot escape, ending the game. —v. put in checkmate.

cheek, n. 1. side of face below eye. 2. [Col.] impudence.

cheer, *n.* 1. joy; gladness. 2. shout of excitement, welcome, etc. —*v.* 1. fill with cheer. 2. urge on, praise, etc. with cheers. —**cheer up,** make or become glad.

cheer'ful, *a.* 1. gay. 2. bright and attractive. Also **cheer'y** (-IER, -IEST). —**cheer'ful·ly,** *adv.*

cheer'less, *a.* not cheerful.

cheese, *n.* solid food made from milk curds.

cheese'cloth, *n.* cotton cloth with a loose weave.

chee'tah, *n.* animal like the leopard.

chef (shef) *n.* cook.

chem'i·cal (kem'-) *a.* of, in, or by chemistry. —*n.* substance used in or got by chemistry. —**chem'i·cal·ly,** *adv.*

che·mise (shə-mēz') *n.* woman's undergarment.

chem'is·try, *n.* science dealing with the composition, reactions, etc. of substances. —**chem'ist,** *n.*

che·nille (shə-nēl') *n.* fabric woven with tufted cord.

cheque (chek) *n.* check (*n.*7): Br. sp.

cher'ish, *v.* 1. hold or treat tenderly. 2. keep in mind.

cher'ry, *n.* [*pl.* -RIES] red fruit with small, red fruit.

cher'ub, *n.* [*pl.* -UBIM, -UBS] angel, pictured as a chubby, winged child. —**che·ru'bic** (-rōō'-) *a.*

chess, *n.* checkerboard game for two players using various pieces (**chess'men**).

chest, *n.* 1. box with a lid. 2. piece of furniture with drawers. 3. front part of the body above the abdomen.

chest'nut, *n.* 1. edible nut of a kind of beech. 2. [Col.] trite joke. —*a.* reddish-brown.

chev·i·ot (shev'i-ət) *n.* twilled wool fabric.

chev'ron (shev'-) *n.* V-shaped sleeve insigne of rank.

chew, *v.* grind with the teeth. —*n.* something for chewing.

chewing gum, flavored chicle, etc. for chewing.

chic (shēk) *a.* [CHICQUER, CHICQUEST] smartly stylish.

chi·can'er·y (shi-kān'-) *n.* [*pl.* -IES] 1. trickery. 2. trick.

Chi·ca·no (chi kä'nō) *n.* [*pl.* -NOS] Mexican-American.

chick, *n.* young chicken.

chick'a·dee, *n.* small bird of the titmouse family.

chick'en, *n.* hen or rooster, or its edible flesh.

chicken pox, infectious disease with skin eruption.

chi'cle ('-l) *n.* gummy substance from a tropical tree.

chic'o·ry, *n.* plant with leaf used in salads and root used as a coffee substitute.

chide, *v.* scold; rebuke.

chief, *n.* leader. —*a.* main; most important. —**chief'ly,** *adv.*

chief'tain (-tən) *n.* chief of a clan or tribe.

chif'fon (shi-fon') *n.* sheer silk cloth.

chig'ger, *n.* mite larva that causes itching.

chi·gnon (shēn'yon) *n.* coil of hair worn by women.

chil'blain, *n.* inflamed sore caused by exposure to cold.

child, *n.* [*pl.* CHILDREN] 1. infant. 2. boy or girl before puberty. 3. son or daughter. —**with child,** pregnant. —**child'hood,** *n.*

child'ish, *a.* silly.

chil'i, *n.* hot red pepper.

chill, *n.* 1. moderate coldness. 2. body coldness, with shivering. 3. sudden fear. —*a.* uncomfortably cool. —*v.* make or become cold. —**chill'y** [-LIER, -LIEST] *a.*

chime (chīm) *n.* usually pl. set of tuned bells. —*v.* sound as a chime.

chim'ney, *n.* passage for smoke from a furnace, etc.

chim·pan·zee', *n.* medium-sized African ape.

chin, *n.* face below the lips.

chi'na, *n.* dishes, etc. of fine porcelain.

chin·chil'la, *n.* 1. small S. American rodent. 2. its costly fur.

Chi·nese', *n.* [*pl.* -NESE] & *a.* (native or language) of China.

chink, *n.* 1. crack. 2. clinking sound. —*v.* to clink.

chintz, *n.* glazed, printed cotton cloth.

chip, *v.* [CHIPPED, CHIPPING] break or cut off bits from. —*n.* 1. fragment. 2. place where bit is chipped off. 3. small disk used in gambling. 4. thin slice of food. —**chip in,** [Col.] contribute.

chip'munk, *n.* small striped squirrel.

chip'per, *a.* [Col.] lively.

chi·rop'o·dist (ki-rop'-) *n.* podiatrist.

chi'ro·prac'tic (kī'rə-) *n.* method of treatment by

manipulation of body joints, etc. —**chi'ro·prac'tor,** n.

chirp, v. make short, shrill sounds. —n. such a sound.

chir'rup, v. & n. chirp.

chis'el (chiz'-) n. tool for chipping wood, stone, etc. —v. 1. chip with a chisel. 2. [Col.] swindle. —**chis'el·er,** n.

chit'chat, n. small talk.

chi'tin (ki'-) n. horny covering of insects, etc.

chiv'al·ry (shiv'-) n. 1. medieval system of knighthood. 2. courtesy, fairness, etc. —**chiv'al·rous,** a.

chive, n. plant like the onion with fine leaves used to flavor.

chlo'ride (klôr'-) n. compound of chlorine.

chlo'rin·ate, v. purify (water) with chlorine.

chlo'rine (-rēn) n. greenish gas, a chemical element.

chlo'ro·form, n. colorless liquid anesthetic. —v. anesthetize or kill with this.

chlo'ro·phyll (-fil) n. green coloring in plants.

chock, n. & n. block; wedge. —adv. completely.

choc'o·late (-lit) n. 1. ground cacao seeds. 2. drink or candy made with this. 3. reddish brown.

choice, n. 1. selection. 2. right to choose. 3. the one chosen. —a. excellent.

choir (kwir) n. group of singers, esp. in a church.

choke, v. 1. stop the breathing of; suffocate. 2. obstruct; clog. —n. a choking. —**choke** back, hold back (sobs, etc.).

chol'er (käl'-) n. anger. —**chol'er·ic,** a.

chol'er·a (kol'-) n. infectious, often fatal, disease.

cho·les'ter·ol (kə-) n. substance in animal fats, etc.

choose, v. [CHOSE, CHOSEN, CHOOSING] 1. take; select. 2. prefer; decide.

choos'y, a. [Col.] fussy.

chop, v. [CHOPPED, CHOPPING] 1. cut by blows of a sharp tool. 2. cut in bits. —n. 1. sharp blow. 2. slice from rib or loin. —**chop'per,** n.

chop'py, a. with rough, abrupt waves or motions.

chops, n.pl. 1. jaws. 2. flesh about the mouth.

chop'sticks, n.pl. two sticks used by Chinese and Japanese to eat with.

chop su·ey (sōō'i) Am.-Chinese stew served with rice.

cho'ral (kôr'-) a. of or for a choir or chorus.

cho·rale', cho·rale', n. simple hymn tune.

chord, n. 1. straight line joining two points on an arc. 2. three or more tones together in harmony.

chore (chôr) n. daily task.

chor'e·og'ra·phy (kôr'-) n. the devising of ballets. —**chor'e·og'ra·pher,** n.

chor'is·ter, n. choir member.

chor'tle (chôr'-) v. & n. chuckle or snort.

cho'rus, n. 1. group of singers or of singers and dancers. 2. music for group singing. 3. refrain of a song. —v. sing or recite in unison.

chose, pt. of choose.

cho'sen, pp. of choose. —a. selected; choice.

chow, n. 1. medium-sized Chinese dog. 2. [Sl.] food.

chow'der, n. fish or clam soup with vegetables.

chow mein (mān) Am.-Chinese stew served on fried noodles.

Christ, n. Jesus as the Messiah.

chris'ten, v. 1. baptize. 2. name. —**chris'ten·ing,** n.

Chris'ten·dom, n. Christians collectively.

Chris'tian·i·ty, n. religion based on teachings of Jesus. —**Chris'tian,** a. & n.

Christian Science, religion and system of healing.

Christ'mas, n. celebration of Jesus' birth; Dec. 25.

chro·mat'ic, a. 1. of color. 2. Music in half tones.

chrome, n. chromium.

chro'mi·um, n. hard metal in alloys, a chemical element.

chro'mo·some, n. any of the microscopic bodies carrying the genes of heredity.

chron'ic, a. long-lasting or recurring. —**chron'i·cal·ly,** adv.

chron'i·cle, n. historical record. —v. tell the history of. —**chron'i·cler,** n.

chron'o·log'i·cal, a. in order of occurrence. —**chron'o·log'i·cal·ly,** adv. —**chro·nol'o·gy,** n.

chro·nom'e·ter, n. very accurate clock or watch.

chrys'a·lis (kris'-) n. pupa or its cocoon.

chrys·an'the·mum, n. plant with ball-shaped flowers.

chub'by, a. plump.

chuck, v. 1. tap playfully.

2. toss. —n. 1. tap. 2. toss. 3. shoulder cut of beef. 4. clamplike device as on a lathe.

chuck'le, v. laugh softly. —n. soft laugh.

chug, n. explosive sound, as of an engine. —v. [CHUGGED, CHUGGING] make this sound.

chum, n. close friend. —v. [CHUMMED, CHUMMING] be chums. —**chum'my,** a.

chump, n. [Col.] fool.

chunk, n. thick piece.

chunk'y, a. [-IER, -IEST] [Col.] short and thickset.

church, n. 1. building for public worship. 2. religion or religious sect.

church'yard, n. yard beside a church, often a cemetery.

churl, n. rude, surly person. —**churl'ish,** a.

churn, n. device for making butter. —v. 1. shake (cream) in a churn to make butter. 2. stir about vigorously.

chute (sho͞ot) n. inclined passage for sliding things.

ci·ca'da (si-kā'-) n. large locust making a shrill sound.

ci'der, n. juice from apples.

ci·gar', n. roll of tobacco leaves for smoking.

cig·a·rette', cig·a·ret', n. tobacco cut and rolled in paper for smoking.

cil'i·a (sil'-) n.pl. small hairlike growths.

cinch, n. 1. saddle girth. 2. [Sl.] thing easy to do. —v. [Sl.] make sure of.

cin·cho'na (sin-kō'-) n. tree whose bark yields quinine.

cinc'ture (sink'-) n. belt or girdle. —v. gird.

cin'der, n. 1. tiny charred piece of wood, etc. 2. pl. ashes.

cin'e·ma, n. motion picture or motion picture theater.

cin'na·mon, n. brown spice from East Indian tree bark.

ci'pher, n. 1. zero; 0. 2. code. 3. key to a code.

cir·ca (sûr'kə) prep. about; approximately.

cir'cle, n. 1. closed, curved line always equidistant from the center. 2. cycle. 3. group with interests in common. 4. extent; scope. —v. form or go in a circle around.

cir'cuit (-kit) n. 1. boundary. 2. regular, routine journey. 3. theater chain. 4. path for electric current. —**cir·cu'i·tous** (-kū'-) a. roundabout; indirect.

cir'cu·lar, a. 1. round. 2.

roundabout. —n. advertisement sent to many people.

cir'cu·late, v. move or spread about. —**cir·cu·la·to'ry,** a.

cir·cu·la'tion, n. 1. movement, as of blood through the body. 2. distribution.

cir'cum·cise, v. cut off the foreskin of. —**cir'cum·ci'sion** (-sizh'ən) n.

cir·cum'fer·ence, n. distance around a circle, etc.

cir'cum·flex, n. pronunciation mark (^).

cir·cum·lo·cu'tion, n. roundabout way of talking.

cir·cum·nav'i·gate, v. sail around (the earth, etc.).

cir'cum·scribe, v. 1. encircle. 2. limit; confine.

cir'cum·spect, a. cautious; discreet. —**cir'cum·spec'tion,** n.

cir'cum·stance', n. 1. connected fact or event. 2. pl. financial condition. 3. ceremony. —**under no circumstances,** never. —**cir'cum·stan'tial** (-shəl) a.

cir'cum·vent', v. outwit or prevent by cleverness.

cir'cus, n. a show with acrobats, animals, clowns, etc.

cir·rho'sis (si-rō'-) n. disease, esp. of the liver.

cir'rus (sir'-) n. fleecy, white cloud formation.

cis'tern, n. large storage tank, esp. for rain water.

cit'a·del, n. fortress.

cite, v. 1. summon by law. 2. quote. 3. mention as an example. 4. mention in praise. —**ci·ta'tion,** n.

cit'i·zen, n. member of a nation by birth or naturalization. —**cit'i·zen·ry,** a. —**cit'i·zen·ship,** n.

cit'ric acid, weak acid in citrus fruits.

cit'ron, n. lemonlike fruit.

cit·ron·el'la, n. pungent oil that repels insects.

cit'rus, n. orange, lemon, etc. —a. of these trees or fruits.

cit'y, n. [pl. -IES] large town.

civ'et, n. fatty secretion of an animal (civet cat): used in perfume.

civ'ic, a. of a city or citizens.

civ'ics, n. study of civic affairs and duties.

civ'il, a. 1. of citizens. 2. polite. 3. not military or religious. —**civ'il·ly,** adv.

ci·vil'ian, a. & n. (of a) person not in armed forces.

ci·vil'i·ty, n. 1. courtesy. 2. [pl. -TIES] polite act.

civ·i·li·za'tion, n. 1. high social and cultural development. 2. culture of a certain time or place.

civ·i·lize, v. bring out of savagery or barbarism.

civil liberties, rights of free speech, assembly, etc.

civil rights, rights of all people to equal treatment.

civil service, government employees except soldiers, etc.

civil war, war between factions of the same nation.

clack, v. make an abrupt, sharp sound. —n. this sound.

clad, alt. pt. & pp. of **clothe.**

claim, v. 1. demand as rightfully one's own. 2. assert. —n. 1. a claiming. 2. right to something. 3. something claimed. —**claim'ant**, n.

clair·voy'ance (klâr-voi'-) n. supposed ability to perceive things not in sight. —**clair·voy'ant**, a. & n.

clam, n. hard-shelled, often edible, bivalve mollusk.

clam'ber, v. climb clumsily.

clam'my, a. [-MIER, -MIEST] moist, cold, and sticky.

clam'or, n. 1. uproar. 2. noisy demand. —v. make a clamor. —**clam'or·ous**, a.

clamp, n. device for clasping things together. —v. fasten with a clamp.

clan, n. 1. group of related families. 2. group with interests in common.

clan·des'tine (-tin) a. secret.

clang, v. make a loud ringing sound. —n. this sound.

clan'gor, n. series of clangs.

clank, n. make a sharp metallic sound. —n. this sound.

clap, v. [CLAPPED, CLAPPING] 1. make the sound of flat surfaces struck together. 2. strike together briskly. —n. sound or act of clapping.

clap·board (klab'ērd) n. tapered board for siding.

claque (klak) n. group paid to applaud.

clar'et, n. dry red wine.

clar'i·fy, v. [-FIED, -FYING] make or become clear. —**clar'i·fi·ca'tion**, n.

clar·i·net', n. single-reed, wood-wind instrument.

clar'i·on, a. clear and shrill.

clar'i·ty, n. clearness.

clash, v. 1. collide noisily. 2. disagree. —n. a clashing.

clasp, n. 1. device to fasten things. 2. embrace. 3. grip of the hand. —v. 1. fasten. 2. hold tightly.

class, n. 1. group of like people or things; sort. 2. social rank. 3. group of students in school. 4. quality. —v. classify. —**class'mate**, n. —**class'room**, n.

clas'sic, a. 1. most excellent. 2. in the style of ancient Greece or Rome. —n. a book, work of art, etc. of highest excellence. —**the classics**, writings of Greece and Rome.

clas'si·cal, a. 1. classic. 2. of such music as symphonies, concertos, etc.

clas'si·fy, v. [-FIED, -FYING] 1. arrange in classes. 2. designate as secret. —**clas'si·fi·ca'tion**, n.

clat'ter, n. series of sharp noises. —v. make a clatter.

clause, n. 1. part of a sentence, with a subject and verb. 2. provision in a document.

claus·tro·pho'bi·a, n. fear of enclosed places.

clav'i·chord (-kôrd) n. early kind of piano.

claw, n. sharp nail of an animal's or bird's foot. —v. scratch as with claws.

clay, n. firm, plastic earth, used for pottery, etc.

clean, a. 1. free from dirt. 2. sinless. 3. free from flaws. 4. complete. —adv. completely. —v. make clean. —**clean'er**, n. —**clean'ly** (klen'-) a. **clean'li·ness**, n.

cleanse (klenz) v. make clean or pure. —**cleans'er**, n.

clear, a. 1. free from clouds. 2. transparent. 3. distinct. 4. obvious. 5. free from charges, guilt, obstruction, debt, etc. —v. 1. make or become clear. 2. pass or leap over. 3. make as profit. —**clear away** (or **off**), remove. —**clear out**, [Col.] depart. —**in the clear**, in the open. —**clear'ly**, adv. —**clear'ness**, n.

clear'ance, n. clear space between two objects.

clear'ing, n. plot of land cleared of trees.

cleat, n. piece used to give firmness or secure footing.

cleave, v. [CLEFT OR CLEAVED, CLEAVING] split; sever.

cleave, v. adhere; cling.

cleav'er, n. butcher's tool.

clef, n. musical symbol to indicate pitch.

cleft, a. & n. split.

clem'ent, a. 1. lenient. 2. mild. —**clem'en·cy**, n.

clench, v. close tightly.

cler'gy, *n.* [*pl.* -GIES] ministers, priests, etc. collectively.

cler'gy·man, *n.* [*pl.* -MEN] minister, priest, etc.

cler'i·cal (kler'-) *a.* 1. of the clergy. 2. of clerks.

clerk, *n.* 1. office worker who keeps records, etc. 2. salesperson in a store. —*v.* work as a clerk.

clev'er, *a.* 1. skillful. 2. intelligent. —**clev'er·ness,** *n.*

clew, *n.* 1. ball of thread, etc. 2. clue.

cli·ché (klē-shā') *n.* trite expression or idea.

click, *n.* slight, sharp sound. —*v.* make a click.

cli'ent, *n.* 1. person or company for whom a lawyer, etc. acts. 2. customer.

cli·en·tele' (-tel') *n.* clients.

cliff, *n.* high, steep rock.

cli'mate, *n.* average weather conditions. —**cli·mat'ic,** *a.*

cli'max, *n.* highest point, as of interest; culmination. —**cli·mac'tic,** *a.*

climb, *v.* go up; ascend. —*n.* a climbing. —**climb down,** descend.

clinch, *v.* 1. fasten (a nail) by bending the end. 2. settle (an argument, etc.). 3. *Boxing* grip with the arms. —*n.* a clinching in boxing.

cling, *v.* [CLUNG, CLINGING] 1. hold fast. 2. stay near.

clin'ic, *n.* 1. place where medical specialists practice as a group. 2. outpatient department. —**clin'i·cal,** *a.*

clink, *n.* short, tinkling sound. —*v.* make this sound.

clink'er, *n.* fused mass left in burning coal.

clip, *v.* [CLIPPED, CLIPPING] 1. cut short. 2. cut the hair of. 3. [Col.] hit sharply. 4. fasten together. —*n.* 1. a clipping. 2. [Col.] rapid pace. 3. fastening device.

clip'per, *n.* 1. clipping tool. 2. fast sailing ship.

clique (klēk) *n.* small, exclusive circle of people.

cloak, *n.* 1. loose, sleeveless outer garment. 2. thing that conceals. —*v.* conceal; hide.

clock, *n.* device for measuring and showing time.

clock'wise, *adv.* & *a.* in the direction in which the hands of a clock rotate.

clod, *n.* lump of earth.

clog, *n.* 1. thing that hinders. 2. heavy shoe. —*v.* [CLOGGED, CLOGGING] 1. hinder. 2. block up.

clois'ter, *n.* 1. monastery or convent. 2. covered walk along a wall. —*v.* seclude.

close (klōs) *a.* 1. confined. 2. secretive. 3. stingy. 4. humid; stuffy. 5. near together. 6. intimate. 7. thorough. 8. nearly alike; nearly equal. —*adv.* in a close way or position. —*n.* enclosed place. —**close'ly,** *adv.*

close (klōz) *v.* 1. shut or stop up. 2. end. 3. come close, as to attack. —*n.* end. —**close down** (or **up**), stop entirely. —**close in,** surround.

clos'et (kloz'-) *n.* small room for clothes, etc. —*v.* shut in a room for private talk.

clot, *n.* coagulated mass, as of blood. —*v.* [CLOTTED, CLOTTING] coagulate.

cloth (klôth) *n.* 1. fabric of cotton, wool, synthetics, etc. 2. tablecloth, dustcloth, etc.

clothe (klōth) *v.* [alt. *pt.* & *pp.* CLAD] to dress.

clothes (klōz, klōthz) *n.* 1. clothing. 2. bedclothes.

cloth'ing (klōth'-) *n.* wearing apparel; garments.

cloud, *n.* 1. mass of vapor in the sky. 2. mass of smoke, dust, etc. 3. thing that darkens, etc. —*v.* darken as with clouds, gloom, etc. —**cloud'y** [-IER, -IEST] *a.*

cloud'burst, *n.* sudden heavy rain.

clout, *n.* & *v.* [Col.] hit.

clove, *n.* 1. pungent spice. 2. segment of a bulb.

clo'ven, *a.* split.

clo'ver, *n.* small forage plant with triple leaves.

clo'ver·leaf, *n.* highway intersection with curving ramps to ease traffic.

clown, *n.* comic entertainer as in a circus. —*v.* act like a clown.

cloy, *v.* surfeit by excess.

club, *n.* 1. stick used as a weapon, or in games. 2. social group. 3. playing card marked with a ♣. —*v.* [CLUBBED, CLUBBING] strike with a club.

cluck, *n.* low, clicking sound made by a hen. —*v.* make this sound.

clue, *n.* hint or fact that helps solve a mystery.

clump, *n.* 1. lump. 2. cluster. —*v.* tramp heavily.

clum'sy, *a.* [-SIER, -SIEST] awkward. —**clum'si·ly,** *adv.*

clung, *pt.* & *pp.* of **cling.**

clus'ter, *n.* & *v.* group; bunch.

clutch, *v.* 1. snatch (at). 2.

hold tightly. —n. 1. pl. control. 2. grip. 3. device for engaging and disengaging an engine.

clut'ter, n. & v. disorder.

co-, pref. 1. together. 2. joint. 3. equally.

coach, n. 1. big, four-wheeled carriage. 2. railroad passenger car. 3. bus. 4. trainer of athletes. —v. be a coach.

co·ag'u·late, v. thicken to a semisolid; clot. —co·ag'u·la'tion, n.

coal, n. 1. black mineral used as fuel. 2. ember.

co·a·lesce' (kō-ə-les') v. unite into a single body. —co'a·les'cence, n.

coarse, a. 1. made up of large particles. 2. rough. 3. vulgar. —coars'en, n.

coast, n. seashore. —v. 1. slide down an incline. 2. continue moving on momentum. —coast'al, a.

coast'er, n. small tray put under a glass.

coast guard, group defending a nation's coasts, aiding ships in distress, etc.

coat, n. 1. sleeved outer garment. 2. natural covering. 3. layer, as of paint. —v. cover with a layer.

coax, v. urge or get by soothing words, etc.

co·ax'i·al cable, cable for sending telephone, telegraph, and television impulses.

cob, n. corncob.

co·balt (kō'bôlt) n. gray metallic chemical element.

cob'ble, v. mend (shoes). —cob'bler, n.

cob'ble·stone, n. rounded stone once used for paving.

co'bra, n. poisonous snake of Asia and Africa.

cob'web, n. spider web.

co·caine', n. drug used as a narcotic or anesthetic.

coch·i·ne'al (koch-ə-nēl') n. red dye from tropical insect.

coch'le·a (kok'li-ə) n. spiral part of the inner ear.

cock, n. 1. rooster. 2. any male bird. 3. faucet. 4. cone-shaped pile. —v. 1. tilt. 2. turn alertly. 3. set hammer of (a gun) to fire.

cock·ade', n. badge on a hat.

cock·a·too', n. crested Australian parrot.

cock'er (spaniel), small spaniel with drooping ears.

cock'eyed, a. 1. cross-eyed.

2. [Sl.] a) awry. b) absurd.

cock'le, n. edible shellfish. —cockles of one's heart, one's deepest feelings.

cock'pit, n. space for pilot in a small airplane.

cock'roach, n. flat-bodied, dark insect, a kitchen pest.

cocks'comb, n. red, fleshy growth on a rooster's head.

cock'sure', a. self-confident.

cock'tail, n. 1. mixed alcoholic drink. 2. appetizer.

cock'y, a. [Col.] conceited.

co·co (kō'kō) n. [pl. -cos] coconut palm or coconut.

co'coa (-kō) n. 1. powder made from roasted cacao seeds. 2. drink made of this.

co'co·nut, co'coa·nut, n. hard-shelled fruit of a palm tree, with edible white meat.

co·coon', n. silky case of certain insect larvae.

cod, n. N. Atlantic food fish: also **cod'fish.**

co'da, n. Mus. end passage.

cod'dle, v. pamper.

code, n. 1. body of laws. 2. set of principles. 3. set of signals or symbols for messages. —v. put in a code.

co'deine (-dēn) n. sedative drug derived from opium.

codg'er, n. [Col.] odd person.

cod'i·cil (-s'l) n. addition to a will.

cod'i·fy, v. [-FIED, -FYING] arrange (laws) in a code.

co·ed', co·ed', n. [Col.] girl at a coeducational college.

co'ed·u·ca'tion, n. education of both sexes in the same classes. —co·ed·u·ca'tion·al, a.

co·erce' (-ûrs') v. force; compel. —co·er'cion, n. —co·er'cive, a.

co·ex·ist', v. exist together. —co·ex·ist'ence, n.

cof'fee, n. 1. drink made from roasted seeds of a tropical shrub. 2. the seeds.

cof'fer, n. 1. chest for money. 2. pl. treasury.

cof'fin, n. case in which to bury a dead person.

cog, n. tooth on a cogwheel.

co'gent (-jənt) a. convincing. —co'gen·cy, n.

cog'i·tate (koj'-) v. think (about). —cog'i·ta'tion, n.

co'gnac (-nyak) n. brandy.

cog'nate, a. related; kindred.

cog·ni'tion, n. knowledge.

cog'ni·zance, n. awareness; notice. —cog'ni·zant, a.

cog·no'men, n. surname.

cog'wheel, n. wheel rimmed with teeth, as in a gear.

co·hab·it, v. live together as if husband and wife.

co·here′, v. 1. stick together. 2. be connected logically.

co·her′ent, a. clear and intelligible. —**co·her′ence,** n.

co·he′sion, n. a sticking together. —**col·he′sive,** a.

co′hort, n. 1. group, esp. of soldiers. 2. an associate.

coif·fure (kwä-fyoor′) n. 1. headdress. 2. hair style.

coil, v. to wind in a spiral. —n. anything coiled.

coin, n. stamped metal piece, issued as money. —v. 1. make into coins. 2. make up (new word). —**coin′age,** n.

co·in·cide′, v. 1. occur at the same time. 2. agree; match. —**co·in′ci·dent,** a.

co·in′ci·dence, n. 1. a coinciding. 2. accidental occurrence together of events. —**co·in′ci·den′tal,** a.—**co·in′ci·den′tal·ly,** adv.

co′i·tus, n. sexual intercourse: also **co·i′tion.**

coke, n. fuel made by removing gases from coal.

col′an·der (kul′-) n. perforated bowl used as a strainer.

cold, a. 1. low in temperature. 2. feeling chilled. 3. without feeling. 4. [Sl.] unconscious. —n. 1. absence of heat. 2. common virus disease with sneezing, coughing, etc. —**catch cold,** become ill with a cold. —**cold′ly,** adv.

cold′-blood′ed, a. callous.

cold cream, creamy cleanser for the skin.

cold war, conflict between nations without actual war.

cole′slaw, n. salad made of shredded raw cabbage.

col′ic, n. sharp bowel pain.

col·i·se′um, n. large stadium.

co·li′tis (kō-lī′-) n. inflammation of the colon.

col·lab′o·rate, v. 1. work together. 2. help the enemy. —**col·lab′o·ra′tion,** n. —**col·lab′o·ra′tor,** n.

col·lapse′, v. 1. fall in or shrink in. 2. break down; fail. 3. fold together. —n. a collapsing. —**col·laps′i·ble,** a.

col′lar, n. a band, or the part of a garment, about the neck. —v. 1. put a collar on. 2. seize by the collar.

col·late′, v. compare (texts).

col·lat′er·al, a. 1. of the same descent but in a different line. 2. secondary. —n.

thing pledged as security for a loan.

col′league (-lēg) n. fellow worker; associate.

col·lect′, v. 1. gather together. 2. get payment for. 3. regain control of (oneself). —a. & adv. with the receiver paying. —**col·lec′tion,** n. —**col·lec′tor,** n.

col·lec′tive, a. 1. of or as a group. 2. singular in form, but referring to a group. —n. 1. a collective enterprise. 2. collective noun.

col′lege, n. 1. school of higher learning or special instruction. 2. group with certain powers. —**col·le′gian** (-jan) n. —**col·le′giate** (-jit) a.

col·lide′, v. crash or clash.

col·lie, n. large, long-haired sheep dog.

col·li′sion (-lizh′ən) n. 1. a colliding. 2. conflict.

col′loid, n. substance of insoluble particles suspended in a fluid. —**col·loi′dal,** a.

col·lo·qui·al (-kwi-) a. used in informal talk and writing. —**col·lo′qui·al·ism,** n.

col′lo·quy (-kwi) n. [pl. -QUIES] conversation.

col·lu′sion, n. secret agreement for a wrong purpose.

co·logne′ (-lōn′) n. scented liquid like diluted perfume.

co′lon, n. 1. mark of punctuation (:). 2. lower part of the large intestine.

colo·nel (kûr′n'l) n. officer above lieutenant colonel.

col·on·nade′, n. row of evenly spaced columns.

col′o·ny, n. [pl. -NIES] 1. group of settlers from another, distant land. 2. land ruled by a distant country. 3. community with common interests. —**co·lo′ni·al,** a. —**col′o·nist,** n. —**col′o·nize,** v.

col′or, n. 1. effect on the eyes of light waves of different wave lengths. 2. pigment. 3. complexion. 4. pl. a flag. 5. outward appearance. 6. picturesque quality. —v. 1. paint or dye. 2. alter or distort. 3. blush. —**with flying colors,** with great success. —**col′or·a′tion,** n. —**col′or·ful,** a. —**col′or·ing,** n. —**col′or·less,** a.

col·o·ra·tu′ra (soprano) (-tyoor′ə) soprano with high, flexible voice.

col′or-blind, a. unable to distinguish (certain) colors.

col′ored, a. Negro.

co·los'sal, *a.* huge; immense.

co·los'sus, *n.* huge or important person or thing.

col'our, *n. & v.* color: Br. sp.

colt, *n.* young male horse.

col'um·bine, *n.* plant with showy, spurred flowers.

col'umn (-əm) *n.* 1. slender upright structure. 2. vertical section of printed matter. 3. line of troops, etc. —**col'um·nist,** *n.*

com-, *pref.* with; together.

co'ma (kō'-) *n.* deep unconsciousness, as from injury. —**com·a·tose** (kom'ə-tōs) *a.*

comb (kōm) *n.* 1. flat, toothed object for grooming the hair. 2. cockscomb. 3. honeycomb. —*v.* 1. groom with a comb. 2. search.

com'bat, (käm-bat') *& n.* fight; struggle. —**com'bat·ant,** *a. & n.*

com·bat'ive, *a.* ready or eager to fight.

com'bi·na'tion, *n.* 1. a combining. 2. combined things, groups, etc. 3. series of numbers dialed to open a lock.

com·bine' *v.* join; unite. —*n.* (kom'bīn) 1. machine for harvesting and threshing grain. 2. [Col.] commercial or political alliance.

com·bus'ti·ble, *a. & n.* inflammable (thing).

com·bus'tion, *n.* a burning.

come, *v.* [CAME, COME, COMING] 1. move from "there" to "here." 2. arrive or appear. 3. happen. 4. result. 5. become. 6. amount. 7. extend. —**come off,** *v.* get. —**come off,** *v.* occur. —**come to,** gain consciousness. —**come to,** **up,** arise in discussion.

come'back, *n.* 1. [Col.] a return. 2. to power. 2. [Sl.] witty answer.

co·me'di·an, *n.* actor who plays comic parts. —**co·me'di·enne'** (-en') *n.fem.*

com'e·dy, *n.* [*pl.* -DIES] a humorous play.

come'ly (kum'li) *a.* [-LIER -LIEST] attractive. —**come'li·ness,** *n.*

come'-on', *n.* [Sl.] inducement.

com'et, *n.* starlike body with a luminous tail.

com'fort (kum'-) *v.* soothe in distress; console. —*n.* 1. relief from distress. 2. one that comforts. 3. ease. —**com'fort·a·ble,** *a.*

com'fort·er, *n.* 1. one that comforts. 2. a quilt.

com'ic (kom'-) *a.* 1. of comedy. 2. funny: also **comical.** —*n.* 1. comedian. 2. *pl.* [Col.] comic strips.

comic strip, cartoon series, as in a newspaper.

com'ma, *n.* mark of punctuation (,).

com·mand', *v.* 1. to order. 2. to control. 3. deserve and get. —*n.* 1. an order. 2. control. 3. military force, etc. under someone's control.

com'man·dant', *n.* commanding officer.

com·man·deer', *v.* seize for military or government use.

com·mand'er, *n.* 1. leader; officer. 2. naval officer below a captain.

commander in chief, top commander of a nation's armed forces.

com·mand'ment, *n.* command; law.

com·man'do, *n.* [*pl.* -DOS, -DOES] member of a small force for raiding enemy territory.

com·mem'o·rate', *v.* honor the memory of. —**com·mem'o·ra'tion,** *n.*

com·mence', *v.* begin.

com·mence'ment, *n.* 1. beginning. 2. graduation ceremony of a school, etc.

com·mend', *v.* 1. entrust. 2. recommend. 3. praise. —**com·mend'a·ble,** *a.* —**com'men·da'tion,** *n.*

com·men'su·rate (-shoor-it) *a.* equal or proportionate.

com'ment, *n.* 1. explanatory note. 2. remark. 3. talk. —*v.* make comments.

com'men·tar'y (-ter'-) *n.* [*pl.* -IES] series of explanatory notes or remarks.

com'men·ta'tor *n.* news analyst, as on the radio.

com'merce, *n.* trade on a large scale.

com·mer'cial (-shəl) *a.* 1. connected with commerce. 2. done for profit. —*n. Radio & TV* paid advertisement. —**com·mer'cial·ize,** *v.*

com·min'gle, *v.* mix; blend.

com·mis'er·ate (-miz'-) *v.* sympathize (with).

com·mis·sar', *n.* formerly, government department head in the Soviet Union.

com'mis·sar'y (-sâr'-) *n.* store in an army camp for the sale of food, etc.

com·mis'sion, *n.* 1. authority to act. 2. group chosen to do something. 3. percentage of a sale allotted to the agent. 4. military officer's certificate of rank. —*v.* 1. give a commission to. 2. authorize. —**in** (not **out of**) **commission,** (not) usable.

com·mis'sion·er, *n.* governmental department head.

com·mit', *v.* [-MITTED, -MITTING] 1. put in custody. 2. do. 3. pledge; bind.

com·mit'tee, *n.* group chosen to do something.

com·mo'di·ous, *a.* spacious.

com·mod'i·ty, *n.* [*pl.* -TIES] anything bought and sold.

com'mo·dore, *n.* former naval rank.

com'mon, *a.* 1. shared by all. 2. general. 3. usual; ordinary. 4. vulgar. 5. designating a noun that refers to any of a group. —*n. also pl.* town's public land. — **com'mon·ly,** *adv.*

com'mon·er, *n.* person not of the nobility.

common law, unwritten law based on custom, usage, etc.

com'mon·place, *n.* 1. trite remark. 2. anything ordinary. —*a.* ordinary.

com'mon·weal (-wēl) *n.* public welfare.

com'mon·wealth, *n.* 1. people of a state. 2. democracy or republic.

com·mo'tion, *n.* turmoil.

com·mu'nal (or kə-mū'-) *a.* of a community; public.

com·mune', *v.* talk intimately.

com·mu'ni·cate, *v.* 1. transmit. 2. give or exchange (information). 3. be connected. —**com·mu'nica·ble,** *a.* —**com·mu'nica'tive,** *a.*

com·mu'ni·ca'tion, *n.* 1. a communicating or means of doing this. 2. message, etc.

com·mun'ion, *n.* 1. a sharing or being close. 2. group of the same religious faith. 3. [C-] see **Holy Communion.**

com·mu'ni·qué' (-kā') *n.* official communication.

com'mu·nism, *n.* theory or system of ownership or production by the community. —**com'munist,** *n.*

com·mu'ni·ty, *n.* [*pl.* -TIES] 1. body of people living in the same place. 2. a sharing in common.

com·mute', *v.* 1. lessen (a punishment, etc.). 2. travel by train, etc. to and from work. —**com·mut'er,** *n.*

com·pact', *a.* 1. firmly packed. 2. terse. —*n.*

(kom'-) 1. small case for face powder, etc. 2. agreement.

com·pac'tor, *n.* device that compresses trash.

com·pan'ion, *n.* 1. comrade; associate. 2. thing that matches another. —**compan'ion·a·ble,** *a.* —**compan'ion·ship,** *n.*

com'pa·ny, *n.* [*pl.* -NIES] 1. group of people associated for some purpose. 2. [Col.] guest(s). 3. military unit.

com·par'a·tive, *a.* by comparison. —*n.* the second degree of comparison of adjectives and adverbs.

com·pare', *v.* 1. liken (*to*). 2. examine for similarities or differences. 3. show 3 degrees in form, as *long, longer, longest.* —**beyond compare,** without equal. —**com'para·ble,** *a.* —**com·par'ison,** *n.*

com·part'ment, *n.* section partitioned off.

com'pass (kum'-) *n.* 1. instrument for drawing circles, etc. 2. range; extent. 3. instrument for showing direction.

com·pas'sion, *n.* pity. — **com·pas'sion·ate** (-it) *a.*

com·pat'i·ble, *a.* in agreement.

com·pa'tri·ot, *n.* fellow countryman.

com·pel', *v.* [-PELLED, -PELLING] to force.

com·pen'di·um, *n.* [*pl.* -UMS, -A] comprehensive summary.

com'pen·sate, *v.* make up for; pay. —**com'pen·sa'tion,** *n.*

com·pete', *v.* 1. vie; rival. 2. take part (*in* a contest).

com'pe·tent, *a.* 1. capable; able. 2. adequate. —**com'pe·tence,** *n.*

com'pe·ti'tion (-tish'ən) *n.* 1. a competing; rivalry. 2. contest. —**com·pet'i·tive,** *a.* —**com·pet'i·tor,** *n.*

com·pile', *v.* compose by collecting from various sources. —**com·pi·la'tion,** *n.*

com·pla'cen·cy, *n.* 1. contentment. 2. smugness. —**com·pla'cent,** *a.*

com·plain', *v.* 1. express pain, dissatisfaction, etc. 2. make an accusation. —**complaint',** *n.*

com'ple·ment (-mənt) *n.* 1. that which completes. 2. entirety. —*v.* (-ment') make complete.—**com'ple·men'-ta·ry,** a.

com·plete', a. 1. lacking no parts. 2. finished. 3. thorough; perfect,—v. make complete. —**com·ple'tion,** n.

com·plex' (or kom'pleks) a. 1. having two or more parts. 2. complicated. —n. (kom'-) 1. complex whole. 2. mixed-up feeling about a thing. —**com·plex'i·ty** [pl. -TIES] n.

com·plex'ion (-plek'shən) n. 1. color or texture of the skin. 2. character; aspect.

com'pli·cate, v. make difficult or involved. —**com'-pli·cat'ed,** a. —**com'pli-ca'tion,** n.

com·plic'i·ty (-plis'-) n. partnership in wrongdoing.

com'pli·ment, n. 1. something said in praise. 2. pl. respects. —v. (-ment') pay a compliment to.

com'pli·men'ta·ry, a. 1. giving praise. 2. given free.

com·ply', v. [-PLIED, -PLY-ING] conform (with rules). —**com·pli'ance,** n. —**com-pli'ant,** a.

com·po'nent, a. & n. (being) part of a whole.

com·port', v. 1. conduct (oneself). 2. accord (with). —**com·port'ment,** n.

com·pose', v. 1. make by combining. 2. put into proper form. 3. write (a song, poem, etc.). 4. make calm. —**com-posed',** a. —**com'po·si'-tion** (-zish'ən) n.

com·pos'ite (-poz'-) n. & a. (thing) formed of distinct parts.

com'post, n. rotting vegetation used as fertilizer.

com·po'sure (-zhēr) n. calmness; self-possession.

com'pote (-pōt) n. 1. stewed fruit. 2. stemmed dish.

com'pound, v. combine.—n. (kom'pound) 1. substance with combined elements. 2. enclosed place.—a. with two or more parts.

com'pre·hend', v. 1. understand. 2. include. —**com'pre·hen'si·ble,** a. —**com'pre·hen'sion,** n. —**com'pre·hen'sive,** a.

com·press', v. press tight.—n. (kom'pres) wet pad.—**com·pres'sion,** n. —**com·pres'sor,** n.

com·prise', v. consist of.

com'pro·mise, n. settlement made with concessions.—v. 1. settle by compromise. 2. make suspect.

comp·trol'ler (kən-) n. one who controls (sense 1).

com·pul'sion, n. a forcing or being forced. —**com-pul'sive,** a. —**com·pul'so·ry,** a.

com·punc'tion, n. slight regret for wrongdoing.

com·pute', v. calculate; figure. —**com'pu·ta'tion,** n.

com·put'er, n. (electronic) computing machine.

com'rade (-rad) n. 1. close friend. 2. associate. —**com'rade·ship',** n.

con, adv. against. —v. [CONNED, CONNING] 1. study carefully. 2. [Sl.] swindle.

con·cave', a. curved like the inside of a sphere.

con·ceal', v. hide. —**con-ceal'ment,** n.

con·cede', v. 1. admit as true. 2. grant as a right.

con·ceit', n. 1. vanity; pride. 2. fanciful notion. —**con·ceit'ed,** a.

con·ceive', v. 1. become pregnant. 2. think of. 3. understand. —**con·ceiv'-a·ble,** a.

con·cen·trate, v. 1. fix one's attention, etc. (on). 2. increase, as in density. —n. concentrated substance. —**con'cen·tra'tion,** n.

con·cen'tric, a. having a common center, as circles.

con'cept, n. idea; notion.

con·cep'tion, n. 1. a conceiving. 2. concept.

con·cern', v. be related to; involve. —n. 1. business. 2. regard. 3. worry.

con·cerned', a. 1. involved or interested. 2. anxious.

con·cern'ing, prep. relating to.

con'cert, n. 1. agreement. 2. musical performance.

con·cert'ed, a. combined.

con'cer·ti'na (-tē'-) n. small accordion.

con·cer'to (-cher'-) n. [pl. -TOS] composition for solo instrument(s) and orchestra.

con·ces'sion, n. 1. a conceding. 2. thing conceded. 3. franchise, as for selling food.

conch (koŋk, konch) n. large, spiral sea shell.

con·cil'i·ate, v. make friendly. —**con·cil'i·a'tion,** n. —**con·cil'i·a'tor,** n. —**con·cil'i·a·to'ry,** a.

con·cise', a. short and clear; terse. —**con·cise'ly,** adv.

con'clave, n. private meeting.

con·clude′, v. 1. finish. 2. decide. 3. arrange. **—con·clu′sion,** n.

con·clu′sive, a. decisive.

con·coct′, v. prepare or plan. **—con·coc′tion,** n.

con·com′i·tant, a. accompanying. **—n.** concomitant thing.

con′cord, n. 1. agreement. 2. peaceful relations.

con·cord′ance, n. 1. agreement. 2. complete list of the words used in a book.

con·cor′dat, n. agreement.

con′course, n. 1. a crowd. 2. open space for crowds.

con′crete, a. 1. real; actual. 2. specific. **—n.** hard material made of sand, gravel, and cement. **—con·crete′ly,** adv. **—con·cre′tion,** n.

con′cu·bine, n. wife of lesser status.

con·cu′pis·cence, n. lust. **—con·cu′pis·cent,** a.

con·cur′, v. [CURRED, -CURRING] 1. occur together. 2. agree. **—con·cur′rence,** n. **—con·cur′rent,** a.

con·cus′sion, n. 1. jarring shock. 2. brain injury from a blow.

con·demn′, v. 1. disapprove of. 2. declare guilty. 3. doom. 4. take for public use. 5. declare unfit. **—con′·dem·na′tion,** n.

con·dense′, v. 1. make or become denser. 2. express concisely. **—con·den·sa′tion,** n. **—con·dens′er,** n.

con·de·scend′ (-send′) v. stoop; deign. **—con′de·scen′sion,** n.

con′di·ment, n. seasoning.

con·di′tion, n. 1. prerequisite. 2. state of being. 3. healthy state. 4. rank. **—** v. 1. make healthy. 2. make accustomed (to). **—on condition that,** provided that. **—con·di′tion·al,** a. qualified. **—con·di′tion·al·ly,** adv.

con·dole′, v. show sympathy. **—con·do′lence,** n.

con·do·min′i·um, n. separately owned unit in a multiple-unit dwelling.

con·done′ (-dōn′) v. forgive or overlook.

con′dor, n. large vulture.

con·duce′, v. tend; lead (to). **—con·du′cive,** a.

con·duct′, v. 1. management. 2. behavior. **—v.** (kən-dukt′) 1. lead. 2. manage. 3. direct. 4. behave (oneself). 5. transmit, as electricity. **—con·duc′tion,** n.

con·duc′tor, n. 1. orchestra leader. 2. one in charge of passengers, etc. 3. thing that conducts heat, etc.

con′duit (-dit) n. pipe, tube, etc. for fluids or wires.

cone, n. 1. pointed, tapered figure with circular base. 2. woody fruit of evergreens.

con·fec′tion, n. candy, ice cream, etc.

con·fec′tion·er·y, n. [pl. -IES] confectioner's shop.

con·fed′er·a·cy, n. [pl. -CIES] 1. league. 2. [C-] South in the Civil War.

con·fed′er·ate (-it) a. united; allied. **—n.** 1. ally. 2. accomplice. **—v.** (-āt) unite; ally. **—con·fed′er·a′tion,** n.

con·fer′, v. [-FERRED, -FERRING] 1. give. 2. meet to discuss. **—con′fer·ence,** n.

con·fess′, v. 1. admit (a crime). 2. affirm (a faith). 3. tell (one's sins). **—con·fes′sion,** n.

con·fes′sion·al, n. box where a priest hears confessions.

con·fes′sor, n. priest who hears confessions.

con·fet′ti, n. bits of colored paper thrown at carnivals.

con·fi·dant′, n. trusted friend. **—con·fi·dante′,** n. fem.

con·fide′, v. 1. trust (in). 2. share a secret.

con′fi·dence, n. 1. trust. 2. assurance. 3. self-reliance. 4. a sharing of a secret. **—con′fi·dent,** a.

con′fi·den′tial (-shal) a. 1. secret. 2. entrusted with private matters.

con·fig·u·ra′tion, n. form.

con·fine′, n. usually in pl. limit. **—v.** (kən-fīn′) 1. restrict. 2. shut up, as in prison. **—con·fine′ment,** n.

con·firm′, v. 1. strengthen. 2. approve formally. 3. prove to be true. 4. admit to membership in a church. **—con′fir·ma′tion,** n.

con·firmed′, a. firmly established; habitual.

con′fis·cate, v. seize legally. **—con′fis·ca′tion,** n.

con′fla·gra′tion, n. big, destructive fire.

con·flict′, v. be in opposition. **—n.** (kon′flikt) 1. a fight. 2. sharp disagreement.

con·form′, v. 1. be in accord. 2. act according to rules, customs, etc. **—con·form′ist,** n. **—con·form′i·ty,** n.

con·found′, v. confuse.

con·found'ed, a. 1. confused. 2. damned.

con·front', v. 1. face boldly. 2. bring face to face. —**con·fron·ta'tion,** n.

con·fuse', v. 1. mix up. 2. bewilder. —**con·fu'sion,** n.

con·fute', v. prove wrong.

con·geal' (-jēl') v. 1. freeze. 2. thicken; jell.

con·gen'ial (-jēn'yəl) a. friendly; agreeable. —**con·ge'ni·al·i·ty,** n.

con·gen'i·tal (-jen'-) a. existing from birth. —**con·gen'i·tal·ly,** adv.

con·gest' (-jest') v. fill too full, as with blood. —**con·ges'tion,** n.

con·glom'er·ate (-it) a. collected into a compact mass. —n. large corporation formed by merging many companies. —**con·glom·er·a'tion,** n.

con·grat'u·late, v. rejoice with (a fortunate person). —**con·grat'u·la·to·ry,** a.

con·grat·u·la'tions, n.pl. expressions of pleasure over another's good luck, etc.

con'gre·gate, v. gather into a crowd.

con·gre·ga'tion, n. assembly of people, esp. for worship.

con'gress, n. 1. assembly. 2. legislature, esp. [C-] of the U.S. —**con·gres'sion·al** (-gresh'ən-) a. —**con'gress·man** [pl. -MEN], n.

con'gru·ent, a. agreeing; corresponding.

con·gru'ous, a. suitable. —**con·gru'i·ty,** n.

con'i·cal, a. of or like a cone: also **con'ic.**

co'ni·fer (kō'nə-, kon'ə-) n. cone-bearing tree.

con·jec'ture (-chēr) n. & v. guess. —**con·jec'tur·al,** a.

con·join', v. join together.

con'ju·gal, a. of marriage.

con'ju·gate, v. give the inflectional forms of (a verb). —**con·ju·ga'tion,** n.

con·junc'tion, n. 1. a joining together. 2. an occurring together. 3. word used to join words, clauses, etc. —**con·junc'tive,** a.

con'jure, v. 1. practice magic. 2. entreat. 3. cause to appear, etc. as by magic. —**con'jur·er, con'jur·or,** n.

con·nect', v. 1. join; link. 2. show or think of as related. —**con·nec'tive,** a.

con·nec'tion, n. 1. a connecting or being connected.

2. thing that connects. 3. relation. Br.sp., **connexion.**

con·nive', v. 1. pretend not to look (at crime, etc.). 2. cooperate secretly in wrongdoing. —**con·niv'ance,** n.

con·nois·seur (kon-ə-sûr') n. expert, esp. in the fine arts.

con·note', v. suggest in addition to the explicit meaning. —**con·no·ta'tion,** n.

con·nu'bi·al, a. of marriage.

con'quer (-kēr) v. defeat; overcome. —**con'quer·or,** n. —**con'quest** (-kwest) n.

con'science (-shəns) n. sense of right and wrong.

con·sci·en'tious (-shi-) a. scrupulous; honest.

con'scious (-shəs) a. 1. aware (of or that). 2. able to feel and think; awake. 3. intentional. —**con'scious·ness,** n.

con·script', v. draft (into the armed forces). —**con·scrip'tion,** n.

con'se·crate, v. 1. set apart as holy. 2. devote. —**con'se·cra'tion,** n.

con·sec'u·tive, a. following in order without a break. —**con·sec'u·tive·ly,** adv.

con·sen'sus, n. general opinion.

con·sent', v. agree. —n. agreement or approval.

con'se·quence, n. 1. a result. 2. importance.

con'se·quent, a. resulting.

con·se·quen'tial, a. 1. consequent. 2. self-important.

con'se·quent·ly, adv. as a result; therefore.

con·serv'a·tive, a. 1. opposed to change. 2. cautious. —n. conservative person.

con·serv'a·to·ry, n. school of music, art, etc.

con·serve', v. keep from being damaged, lost, etc. —**con·ser·va'tion,** n.

con·sid'er, v. 1. think over. 2. keep in mind. 3. have regard for. 4. believe to be. —**con·sid'er·ate** (-it) a. —**con·sid·er·a'tion,** n.

con·sid'er·a·ble, a. large or important. —**con·sid'er·a·bly,** adv.

con·sid'er·ing, prep. taking into account.

con·sign', v. 1. entrust. 2. assign. 3. deliver (goods). —**con·sign'ment,** n.

con·sist', v. be made up (of).

con·sist'en·cy, n. [pl. -CIES] 1. thickness, as of a liquid. 2. agreement. 3. uniformity of action. —**con·sist'ent,** a.

con·sole′, *v.* comfort; cheer up. —**con·so·la′tion,** *n.*

con·sole, *n.* floor cabinet of an organ, radio, TV, etc.

con·sol′i·date, *v.* unite. —**con·sol′i·da′tion,** *n.*

con·som·mé′ (-mā′) *n.* clear meat soup.

con′so·nant, *n.* letter for a breath-blocked sound, as *p, t, l,* etc. —*a.* in harmony. —**con′so·nance,** *n.*

con·sort′, *n.* spouse, esp. of a monarch. —*v.* (kən-sôrt′) to associate.

con·spic′u·ous, *a.* 1. easy to see. 2. outstanding. —**con·spic′u·ous·ly,** *adv.*

con·spire′, *v.* join in a plot. —**con·spir′a·cy** (-spir′-) *n.* —**con·spir′a·tor,** *n.*

con′sta·ble, *n.* policeman.

con′stant, *a.* 1. not changing; fixed. 2. faithful. 3. continual. —*n.* unchanging thing. —**con′stan·cy,** *n.* —**con′stant·ly,** *adv.*

con′stel·la′tion, *n.* group of fixed stars.

con′ster·na′tion, *n.* great alarm or dismay.

con′sti·pate, *v.* make it difficult to move the bowels. —**con′sti·pa′tion,** *n.*

con·stit′u·en·cy, *n.* voters in a district.

con·stit′u·ent, *n.* 1. necessary part. 2. voter. —*a.* needed to form a whole.

con′sti·tute, *v.* form; set up.

con′sti·tu′tion, *n.* 1. structure; make-up. 2. basic laws of a government, race, etc., esp. [C-] of the U.S. —**con′sti·tu′tion·al,** *a.*

con·strain′, *v.* force or restrain. —**con·straint′,** *n.*

con·strict′, *v.* make smaller by squeezing, etc.; contract. —**con·stric′tion,** *n.*

con·struct′, *v.* build; devise. —**con·struc′tion,** *n.* 1. a constructing. 2. structure. 3. explanation. 4. arrangement of words. —**con·struc′tive,** *a.*

con·strue′, *v.* interpret.

con′sul, *n.* government official in a foreign city looking after his country's business there. —**con′su·lar,** *a.* —**con′su·late,** *n.*

con·sult′, *v.* 1. confer. 2. ask the advice of. 3. consider. —**con·sult′ant,** *n.* —**con′sul·ta′tion,** *n.*

con·sume′, *v.* 1. destroy. 2. use up. 3. eat or drink up. —**con·sum′er,** *n.*

con′sum·mate, *v.* complete.

—*a.* (kən-sum′it) complete.

con·sump′tion, *n.* 1. a consuming. 2. using up of goods. 3. amount used up. 4. tuberculosis of the lungs.

con′tact, *n.* 1. a touching. 2. being in touch (*with*). 3. connection. —*v.* 1. place in contact. 2. [Col.] get in touch with.

con·ta′gion, *n.* a spreading of disease, an idea, etc. —**con·ta′gious,** *a.*

con·tain′, *v.* 1. have in it. 2. be able to hold. 3. restrain. —**con·tain′er,** *n.*

con·tam′i·nate, *v.* make impure; pollute. —**con·tam′i·na′tion,** *n.*

con′tem·plate, *v.* 1. watch intently. 2. meditate. 3. intend. —**con′tem·pla′tion,** *n.* —**con′tem·pla′tive,** *a.*

con·tem′po·ra′ry, *n.,* [*pl.* -RIES] *& a.* (one) living in the same period. —**con·tem′po·ra′ne·ous,** *a.*

con·tempt′, *n.* 1. scorn. 2. disgrace. 3. disrespect shown for a judge, etc.

con·tempt′i·ble, *a.* deserving contempt.

con·temp′tu·ous, *a.* scornful; disdainful.

con·tend′, *v.* 1. struggle. 2. compete. 3. assert.

con·tent′, *a.* satisfied: also **con·tent′ed.** —*n.* satisfaction. —**con·tent′ment,** *n.*

con′tent, *n.* 1. *pl.* all that is contained. 2. meaning. 3. capacity.

con·ten′tion, *n.* argument or struggle. —**con·ten′tious,** *a.*

con·test′, *v.* 1. to dispute; question. 2. fight for. —*n.* (kon′test) 1. struggle. 2. race, game, etc. with competition. —**con·test′ant,** *n.*

con′text, *n.* words surrounding a word or phrase that fix its meaning.

con·tig′u·ous, *a.* in contact.

con′ti·nence, *n.* self-restraint, esp. sexually. —**con′ti·nent,** *a.*

con′ti·nent, *n.* large land mass. —**the Continent,** Europe. —**con′ti·nen′tal,** *a.*

con·tin′gen·cy (-jən) *n.* [*pl.* -CIES] uncertain event.

con·tin′gent, *a.* dependent (*on*); conditional. —*n.* quota, as of troops.

con·tin′u·al, *a.* 1. repeated often. 2. continuous.

con·tin′ue, *v.* 1. keep on; go on. 2. endure; last. 3. resume. 4. extend. 5. postpone. —con·tin'u·ance, n.

con·tin'u·a'tion, n.

con·ti·nu'i·ty, n. [pl. -TIES]
1. continuous state or thing.
2. radio script, etc.

con·tin'u·ous, a. without interruption; unbroken.

con·tort', v. twist out of shape. —con·tor'tion, n.

con'tour (-toor) n. outline of a figure, land, etc.

contra-, pref. against.

con'tra·band, n. smuggled goods. —a. prohibited.

con'tra·cep'tion, n. prevention of human conception. —con'tra·cep'tive, a. & n.

con'tract, n. legally valid agreement. —v. (kən·trakt')
1. undertake by contract. 2. get; incur. 3. shrink. —con'trac·tor, n. —con·trac'tu·al, a.

con·trac'tion, n. 1. a contracting. 2. shortened form, as don't for do not.

con·tra·dict', v. say or be the opposite of. —con·tra·dic'tion, n. —con·tra·dic'to·ry, a.

con·tral'to, n. [pl. -TOS] lowest female voice.

con·trap'tion, n. [Col.] contrivance; gadget.

con'tra·ry, a. 1. opposed; different. 2. (kən·trâr'i) perverse. —n. the opposite. —on the contrary, as opposed to what has been said. —con'tra·ri·ly, adv. —con'tra·ri·wise', adv.

con·trast', v. 1. compare. 2. show differences. —n. (kon'trast) striking difference when compared.

con'tra·vene', v. go against.

con·trib'ute, v. 1. give, esp. to a common fund. 2. furnish (an idea, article, etc.). —contribute to, help bring about. —con'tri·bu'tion, n. —con·trib'u·tor, n.

con·trite', a. remorseful. —con·tri'tion (-trish'-) n.

con·trive', v. 1. devise; invent. 2. manage; bring about. —con·triv'ance, n.

con·trol', v. [-TROLLED, -TROLLING] 1. regulate (finances). 2. direct. 3. restrain. —n. 1. authority. 2. means of restraint. 3. pl. regulating mechanism. —con·trol'ler, n.

con'tro·ver'sy, n. debate or dispute. —con'tro·ver'sial (-shəl) a.

con'tro·vert', v. to dispute. —con'tro·vert'i·ble, a.

con·tu'ma·cy, n. disobedience. —con·tu·ma'cious (-shəs) a.

con·tu·me·ly (-too-mə-li) n. haughty rudeness.

con·tu'sion, n. a bruise.

co·nun'drum, n. a puzzle.

con·va·les'cence, n. (period of) recovery after illness. —con'va·lesce', v. —con'va·les'cent, a. & n.

con·vec'tion, n. transmission of heat in currents.

con·vene', v. assemble; meet.

con·ven'ience, n. 1. a being convenient. 2. comfort. 3. thing that saves work, etc.

con·ven'ient, a. easy to do, use, or get to; handy.

con'vent, n. community of nuns or their living place.

con·ven'tion, n. 1. an assembly. 2. custom; usage.

con·ven'tion·al, a. 1. customary. 2. conforming.

con·verge', v. come together. —con·ver'gence, n. —con·ver'gent, a.

con·ver'sant, a. familiar (with).

con'ver·sa'tion, n. informal talk. —con'ver·sa'tion·al, a.

con·verse', v. to talk. —a. opposite. —n. (kon'vêrs) 1. conversation. 2. the opposite. —con·verse'ly, adv.

con·vert', v. change in form, use, etc. or in religion. —n. (kon'vêrt) person converted. —con·ver'sion, n.

con·vert'i·ble, a. that can be converted. —n. automobile with a folding top.

con'vex', a. curved like the outside of a sphere.

con·vey' (-vā') v. 1. carry. 2. transmit. —con·vey'er, con·vey'or, n.

con·vey'ance, n. 1. a conveying. 2. vehicle.

con·vict', v. prove or find guilty. —n. (kon'vikt) prisoner serving a sentence.

con·vic'tion, n. 1. a being convicted. 2. strong belief.

con·vince', v. make feel sure. —con·vinc'ing, a.

con·viv'i·al, a. sociable; gay. —con·viv'i·al'i·ty, n.

con·voke', v. call together. —con'vo·ca'tion, n.

con'vo·lu'tion, n. a twist or twisting.

con'voy, v. escort. —n. ships, etc. being escorted.

con·vulse', v. shake as with violent spasms. —con·vul'sion, n. —con·vul'sive, a.

co'ny, n. [pl. -NIES] 1. rabbit. 2. rabbit fur.

coo, v. make the soft sound of a pigeon or dove. —n. this sound.

cook, v. boil, bake, fry, etc. (food). —n. one who cooks. —**cook'er·y,** n.

cook'ie, cook'y, n. [pl. -IES] small, sweet, flat cake.

cool, a. 1. moderately cold. 2. not excited. 3. unfriendly. —v. make or become cool. —**cool'ly,** adv.—**cool'ness,** n.

cool'er, n. refrigerator.

coo'lie, coo'ly, n. [pl. -LIES] Oriental laborer.

coop, n. pen for poultry. — v. confine in a coop.

co-op'er·ate, v. to work together: also **coöperate, cooperate.** —**co-op'er·a'tion,** n.

co-op'er·a'tive, a. co-operating. —n. collective, profit-sharing enterprise. Also **coöperative, cooperative.**

co-opt', v. get (an opponent) to join one's side. —v. —**co-op'tion,** n.

co·or'di·nate (-nit) a. equally important. —v. (-nāt) harmonize; adjust. Also **coördinate, coordi-nate.**—**co·or'di·na'tion,** n.

coot, n. water bird.

cop, n. [Sl.] policeman.

cope, v. deal (with) successfully. —n. priest's vestment.

co'pi'lot, n. assistant pilot of an aircraft.

cop'ing (kōp'-) n. top of masonry wall.

co'pi·ous, a. abundant.

cop'per, n. reddish-brown metal, a chemical element.

cop'per·head, n. poisonous snake.

cop'ra (kop'-) n. dried coconut meat.

copse (kops) n. thicket.

cop'u·late, v. have sexual intercourse. —**cop'u·la'tion,** n.

cop'y, n. [pl. -IES] 1. thing made just like another. 2. one of many books, etc. all alike. —v. [-IED, -YING] 1. make a copy of. 2. imitate.

cop'y·right, n. exclusive rights over a book, song, etc. —v. protect by copyright.

co·quette' (-ket') n. & v. [-QUETTED, -QUETTING] flirt. —**co·quet'tish,** a.

cor'al, n. 1. hard mass of sea animal skeletons. 2. yellowish red.

cord, n. 1. thick string. 2. wood pile of 128 cu. ft. 3. insulated electric wire.

cor'dial (-jəl) a. friendly.— n. sirupy alcoholic drink. —**cor·dial'i·ty** (-jal'-) n. —**cor'dial·ly,** adv.

cor'don, n. a guarding force in a line.

cor'do·van, n. soft leather.

cor'du·roy, n. ribbed cotton fabric.

core, n. 1. central part, as of an apple. 2. most important part. —v. remove the core of.

cork, n. 1. light, thick bark of a certain oak. 2. stopper. —v. stop with a cork.

cork'screw, n. spiral device for uncorking bottles.

corm, n. bulblike underground stem of certain plants.

cor'mo·rant, n. 1. voracious sea bird. 2. glutton.

corn, n. 1. grain. 2. grain that grows on large ears; maize. 3. [Sl.] trite humor. 4. horny thickening of the skin. —v. pickle (meat, etc.).

cor'ne·a (-ni-ə) n. clear, outer layer of the eyeball.

cor'ner, n. 1. place where lines or surfaces meet. 2. region. 3. monopoly. —v. 1. put into a difficult position. 2. get a monopoly in.

cor'ner·stone, n. stone at a corner of a building.

cor·net', n. brass-wind instrument like a trumpet.

corn'flow'er, n. plant with showy disk flowers.

cor'nice (-nis) n. molding along the top of a wall, etc.

corn'starch, n. starchy flour used in cooking.

cor'nu·co'pi·a, n. horn-shaped container overflowing with fruits, flowers, etc.

co·rol'la (-rol'-) n. petals of a flower.

cor'ol·lar'y, n. [pl. -IES] proposition following from one already proved.

co·ro'na, n. ring of light around the sun or moon.

cor'o·nar'y, a. of the arteries supplying the heart.

cor'o·na'tion, n. crowning of a sovereign.

cor'o·ner, n. official who investigates unnatural deaths.

cor'po·ral, n. lowest ranking noncommissioned officer. — a. of the body.

cor'po·ra'tion, n. group given legal status of an individual. —**cor'po·rate** (-rit) a.

cor·po're·al (-pôr'i-) a. 1. of the body. 2. material.

corps (kôr) *n.* 1. organized group. 2. large military unit.

corpse (kôrps) *n.* dead body.

cor'pu·lent (-pyoo-) *a.* fat; fleshy. —**cor'pu·lence**, *n.*

cor'pus, *n.* body, as of laws.

cor'pus·cle (-pəs-'l) *n.* cell in the blood, lymph, etc.

cor·ral', *n.* pen for horses, etc. —*v.* [-RALLED, -RAL-LING] confine in a corral.

cor·rect', *v.* 1. make right. 2. mark errors of. 3. punish. —*a.* right, true, etc. —**cor·rec'tion**, *n.* —**cor·rec'tive**, *a.* & *n.* —**cor·rect'ly**, *adv.*

cor're·late, *v.* bring into mutual relation. —**cor're·la'tion**, *n.*

cor'rel·a'tive, *n.* & *a.* (conjunction) showing mutual relation, as *either . . . or.*

cor're·spond', *v.* 1. be similar or equal to. 2. communicate as by letters. —**cor·re·spond'ence**, *n.*—**cor·re·spond'ent**, *n.*

cor'ri·dor, *n.* long hall.

cor·rob'o·rate, *v.* confirm. —**cor·rob'o·ra'tion**, *n.* —**cor·rob'o·ra'tive**, *a.*

cor·rode', *v.* wear away; rust. —**cor·ro'sion**, *n.* —**cor·ro'sive**, *a.* & *n.*

cor'ru·gate, *v.* make folds or wrinkles in.

cor·rupt', *a.* 1. rotten. 2. evil. 3. taking bribes. —*v.* make or become corrupt. —**cor·rupt'i·ble**, *a.* —**cor·rup'tion**, *n.*

cor·sage' (-säzh') *n.* small bouquet worn by a woman.

cor'set, *n.* tight undergarment to support the torso.

cor·tege' (-tezh') *n.* ceremonial procession.

cor'tex, *n.* outer layer of a body organ. —**cor'ti·cal**, *a.*

cor'ti·sone, *n.* hormone used to treat arthritis, etc.

co·run'dum, *n.* mineral used for grinding wheels, etc.

cos·met'ic, *n.* & *a.* (preparation) for enhancing beauty.

cos'mic, *a.* of the cosmos; orderly. 2. vast; huge.

cos'mo·pol'i·tan, *a.* at home all over the world; worldly. —*n.* a worldly person: also **cos·mop'o·lite** (-līt).

cos'mos, *n.* the universe seen as an orderly system.

cost, *v.* [COST, COSTING] require the payment, etc. of. —*n.* 1. price. 2. loss; sacrifice. —**at all costs**, by any means whatever.

cost'ly, *a.* [-LIER, -LIEST] expensive. —**cost'li·ness**, *n.*

cos'tume, *n.* 1. the dress of a people, period, etc. 2. set of outer clothes.

co'sy (-zi) *a.* [-SIER, -SIEST] cozy. —**co'si·ly**, *adv.*

cot, *n.* folding bed.

cote (kōt) *n.* small shelter for birds, sheep, etc.

co·te·rie (kō'tēr-i) *n.* social set; clique.

co·til'lion, *n.* formal dance.

cot'tage, *n.* small house.

cot'ter pin, pin with 2 stems that can be spread apart.

cot'ton, *n.* 1. plant with heads of soft, white fibers. 2. thread or cloth from this. —**cot'ton·seed**, *n.*

couch, *n.* piece of furniture to lie on. —*v.* put in words.

cou'gar (koo'gər) *n.* large American wild cat.

cough (kôf) *v.* expel lung air in a loud burst. —*n.* 1. a coughing. 2. condition of coughing frequently.

could, *pt.* of can.

couldn't, could not.

coun'cil (koun'-) *n.* advisory or legislative body. —**coun'cil·man** [*pl.* -MEN] *n.* —**coun'ci·lor**, **coun'cil·lor**, *n.*

coun'sel, *n.* 1. advice. 2. lawyer(s). —*v.* advise. —**coun'se·lor**, **coun'sel·lor**, *n.*

count, *v.* 1. add up to get a total. 2. name numbers in order. 3. include or be included. 4. consider. 5. be important. —*n.* 1. a counting. 2. total number. 3. each charge in an indictment. 4. nobleman. —**count on** (or **upon**), rely on.

coun'te·nance, *n.* 1. facial expression. 2. face. —*v.* to sanction.

count'er, *n.* long table for displaying goods, serving food, etc. —*adv.* & *a.* contrary. —*v.* oppose.

counter-, *pref.* 1. opposite. 2. against. 3. in return.

coun'ter·act', *v.* act against.

coun'ter·at·tack', *n.* & *v.* attack in return.

coun'ter·bal'ance, *n.* weight or influence that balances another. —*v.* offset.

coun'ter·feit (-fit) *a.* made in imitation with intent to defraud. —*n.* fraudulent imitation. —*v.* 1. make counterfeits. 2. pretend.

coun'ter·mand', *v.* cancel (a command).

coun'ter·part, *n.* matching or corresponding thing.

coun'ter·point, *n.* harmonic interweaving of melodies.

coun'ter·sign, *n.* password. —*v.* confirm another's signature by signing.

count'ess, *n.* wife or widow of a count or earl.

count'less, *a.* too many to count.

coun'try, *n.* [*pl.* -TRIES] 1. region. 2. nation. 3. rural area.—*a.* rural.—**coun'try·man** [*pl.* -MEN] *n.* —**coun'try·side,** *n.*

coun'ty, *n.* [*pl.* -TIES] subdivision of a State.

coup (kōō) *n.* [*pl.* COUPS] bold, successful stroke.

cou'ple, *n.* 1. a pair. 2. engaged, married, etc. man and woman. 3. [Col.] a few. —*v.* join together.

cou'pling, *n.* device for joining things together.

cou'pon (kōō'-, kū'-) *n.* certificate, ticket, etc. redeemable for cash or gifts.

cour'age, *n.* fearless or brave quality. —**cou·ra'geous,** *a.*

cou'ri·er (koor'i-, kūr'i-) *n.* messenger.

course, *n.* 1. path or channel. 2. direction taken. 3. regular mode of action. 4. series. 5. separate part of a meal. 6. a study or series of studies. —*v.* run. —**in the course of,** during. —**of course,** 1. naturally. 2. certainly.

court, *n.* 1. open space surrounded by buildings or walls: also **court'yard.** 2. playing area. 3. royal palace. 4. family, advisers, etc. of a sovereign. 5. courtship. 6. *Law* a) judge(s). b) place where trials are held: also **court'room.** —*v.* woo.

cour'te·san, *n.* prostitute.

cour'te·sy (kūr'-) *n.* [*pl.* -SIES] polite behavior or act. —**cour'te·ous,** *a.*

court'house, *n.* building housing the offices and courtrooms of a county.

cour'ti·er (kôr'-) *n.* attendant at a royal court.

court'ly, *a.* dignified.

court'-mar'tial, *n.* [*pl.* COURTS-MARTIAL] trial by a military or naval court. —*v.* try by such a court.

court'ship, *n.* period or act of courting a woman.

cous'in (kuz'-) *n.* child of one's uncle or aunt.

cove (kōv) *n.* small bay.

cov'e·nant (kuv'-) *n.* agreement; compact.

cov'er, *v.* 1. place something over. 2. extend over. 3. conceal. 4. protect. 5. include; deal with. —*n.* anything that covers. —**take cover,** seek shelter. —**cov'er·ing,** *n.*

cov'er·age (-ij) *n.* amount covered by something.

cov'er·alls, *n.pl.* one-piece work garment with legs.

cov'er·let, *n.* bedspread.

cov'ert (kuv'-) *a.* hidden.

cov'et, *v.* desire ardently (what belongs to another).

cov'et·ous, *a.* greedy.

cov'ey (kuv'i) *n.* small flock of birds, esp. quail.

cow, *n.* mature female of the ox, or the elephant, seal, etc. —*v.* make timid.

cow'ard, *n.* one lacking courage. —**cow'ard·ice** (-is) *n.* —**cow'ard·ly,** *a.* & *adv.*

cow'boy, *n.* worker who herds cattle: also **cow'hand.**

cow'er, *v.* cringe as in fear.

cow'hide, *n.* leather made from the hide of a cow.

cowl, *n.* monk's hood.

cow'lick, *n.* tuft of hair difficult to comb flat.

cowl'ing, *n.* metal covering for an airplane engine.

cow'slip, *n.* 1. swamp plant with yellow flowers. 2. English primrose.

cox'comb (-kŏm) *n.* fop.

cox'swain (-s'n, -swān) *n.* one who steers a boat.

coy, *a.* shy or pretending to be shy. —**coy'ly,** *adv.*

coy·ote (kī'ōt, kī-ō'ti) *n.* small prairie wolf.

coz'en (kuz'-) *v.* cheat.

co'zy, *a.* [-ZIER, -ZIEST] warm and comfortable; snug.

crab, *n.* 1. shellfish with 8 legs and 2 pincers. 2. complainer. —*v.* [CRABBED, CRAB-BING] [Col.] complain.

crab apple, small, sour apple.

crab'by, *a.* [-BIER, -BIEST] peevish. —**crab'bi·ness,** *n.*

crack, *v.* 1. make a sudden, sharp breaking noise. 2. break without separation of parts. 3. [Sl.] make (a joke). 4. [Col.] solve. —*n.* 1. sudden, sharp noise. 2. incomplete break. 3. sharp blow. 4. [Sl.] try. 5. [Sl.] gibe. —*a.* [Col.] first-rate. —**crack down** (on), [Col.] become strict with —**crack up,** [Col.] 1. crash. 2. have a mental breakdown.

crack'er, *n.* thin, crisp wafer.

crack'le, *v.* & *n.* (make) a series of slight, sharp sounds.

crack'pot, *n.* [Col.] fanatic.

cra'dle, *n.* baby's bed on rockers. —*v.* put as in a cradle.

craft, *n.* 1. skill; art. 2. slyness. 3. boat or aircraft.

crafts'man, *n.* [*pl.* -MEN] skilled workman. —**crafts'man·ship,** *n.*

craft'y, *a.* [-IER, -IEST] sly; cunning. —**craft'i·ly,** *adv.*

crag, *n.* steep, projecting rock. —**crag'gy,** *a.*

cram, *v.* [CRAMMED, CRAM-MING] 1. stuff. 2. [Col.] study hurriedly for a test.

cramp, *n.* 1. painful contraction of a muscle. 2. *pl.* intestinal pain. —*v.* hamper.

cran'ber·ry, *n.* [*pl.* -RIES] sour, edible, red berry.

crane, *n.* 1. long-legged wading bird. 2. machine for lifting heavy weights. —*v.* stretch (the neck).

cra'ni·um (krā'-) *n.* the skull. —**cra'ni·al,** *a.*

crank, *n.* 1. handle for turning a shaft. 2. [Col.] an eccentric. —*v.* start or work by a crank.

crank'y, *a.* [-IER, -IEST] irritable; cross.

cran'ny, *n.* [*pl.* -NIES] chink.

crape, *n.* crepe.

craps, *n.pl.* dice game.

crash, *v.* 1. fall, break, drop etc. with a loud noise. 2. fail. —*n.* 1. loud noise. 2. a crashing. 3. failure, as of business. 4. coarse linen.

crass, *a.* grossly dull.

crate, *n.* wooden packing case. —*v.* pack in a crate.

cra'ter, *n.* bowl-shaped cavity or pit, as of a volcano.

cra·vat', *n.* necktie.

crave, *v.* ask or long for.

cra'ven, *a.* cowardly. —*n.* coward.

crav'ing, *n.* intense desire.

craw, *n.* bird's crop.

crawl, *v.* 1. move slowly, as while flat on the ground. 2. swarm with crawling things. —*n.* 1. a crawling. 2. swimming stroke.

cray'fish or **craw'fish,** *n.* shellfish like a small lobster.

cray'on, *n.* small stick of chalk, wax, etc. for drawing.

craze, *v.* make or become insane. —*n.* fad.

cra'zy, *a.* [-ZIER, -ZIEST] insane, mad, etc. —**cra'zi·ly,** *adv.* —**cra'zi·ness,** *n.*

creak, *v. & n.* squeak.

cream, *n.* 1. oily part of milk. 2. creamy cosmetic. 3. best part. —*v.* beat till smooth as cream. —**cream of,** purée of. —**cream'y** [-IER, -IEST] *a.*

cream'er, *n.* cream pitcher.

cream'er·y, *n.* [*pl.* -IES] place where dairy products are made or sold.

crease, *n.* line made by folding. —*v.* make a crease in.

cre·ate', *v.* make; bring about. —**cre·a'tion,** *n.* —**cre·a'tive,** *a.* —**cre·a'tor,** *n.*

crea'ture (-cher) *n.* living being, animal or human.

cre'dence, *n.* belief; trust.

cre·den'tials (-shalz) *n.pl.* papers showing one's right to a certain position, etc.

cred'i·ble, *a.* believable. —**cred·i·bil'i·ty,** *n.*

cred'it, *n.* 1. belief; trust. 2. reputation. 3. praise or source of praise. 4. trust that one will pay later. 5. completed unit of study. —*v.* 1. believe; trust. 2. give credit for. —**cred'it·a·ble,** *a.* —**cred'it·a·bly,** *adv.*

cred'i·tor, *n.* one to whom another owes a debt.

cre'do, *n.* [*pl.* -DOS] creed.

cred'u·lous, *a.* believing too readily. —**cre·du'li·ty,** *n.*

creed, *n.* statement of belief.

creek, *n.* small stream.

creel, *n.* basket for fish.

creep, *v.* [CREPT, CREEPING] 1. go on hands and knees. 2. go slowly or stealthily. 3. grow along the ground, etc.

cre'mate, *v.* burn (a dead body). —**cre·ma'tion,** *n.* —**cre'ma·to'ry** (-tôr-) *n.* [*pl.* -RIES] *n.*

cre'o·sote, *n.* oily preservative distilled from tar.

crepe, crêpe (krāp) *n.* thin, crinkled silk, rayon, etc.

crept, *pt. & pp.* of **creep.**

cre·scen'do (-shen'-) *n.* [*pl.* -DOS] *Mus.* a growing louder.

cres'cent, *n.* shape of a quarter moon.

crest, *n.* 1. tuft on an animal's head. 2. heraldic device. 3. top; summit.

crest'fall·en, *a.* dejected.

cre'tin, *n.* deformed idiot.

cre·tonne' (-ton') *n.* printed linen or cotton cloth.

cre·vasse' (-vas') *n.* deep crack, as in a glacier.

crev'ice (-is) *n.* narrow crack.

crew, *n.* group of workers, as the seamen on a ship.

crew, *alt. pt.* of **crow.**

crib, *n.* 1. box for fodder. 2. baby's small bed. 3. wood shed for grain. —*v.* [CRIBBED, CRIBBING] 1. confine. 2. [Col.] plagiarize.

crib'bage, n. card game.

crick, n. painful cramp.

crick'et, n. 1. leaping insect. 2. ball game played with bats and wickets.

cried, pt. & pp. of **cry**.

cri'er, n. shouter of news.

crime, n. 1. an act in violation of a law. 2. sin.

crim'i·nal, a. of crime. —n. person guilty of crime.

crim'i·nol'o·gy, n. study of crime and criminals.

crimp, v. & n. pleat or curl.

crim'son, n. deep red. —v. 1. make or become crimson.

cringe (krinj) v. 1. shrink back as in fear. 2. to fawn.

crin'kle, v. to wrinkle or rustle. —**crin'kly**, a.

crin'o·line (-lin) n. 1. stiff cloth. 2. hoop skirt.

crip'ple, n. disabled person. —v. disable.

cri'sis, n. [pl. **-SES** (-sēz)] 1. turning point. 2. crucial situation.

crisp, a. 1. brittle. 2. clear. 3. fresh; bracing.

criss'cross, n. crossed lines. —v. mark with crisscross.

cri·ter'i·on (krī-tēr'-) n. [pl. **-IA**, **-IONS**] standard; rule.

crit'ic, n. 1. judge of books, art, etc. 2. faultfinder.

crit'i·cal, a. 1. finding fault. 2. of critics or their work. 3. being a crisis. —**crit'i·cal·ly**, adv.

crit'i·cize, v. 1. judge as a critic. 2. find fault (with). Br. sp. **criticise**. —**crit'i·cism**, n.

cri·tique' (-tēk') n. critical analysis or review.

croak (krōk) v. & n. (make) a deep, hoarse sound.

cro·chet' (krō-shā') v. knit with one hooked needle.

crock, n. earthenware jar.

crock'er·y, n. earthenware.

croc'o·dile', n. large reptile of tropical streams.

cro'cus, n. small plant of the iris family.

crone, n. old hag.

cro'ny, n. [pl. **-NIES**] close friend.

crook (krook) n. 1. bend or curve. 2. [Col.] swindler.

crook'ed, a. 1. not straight. 2. dishonest.

croon (krōon) v. sing in a soft tone. —**croon'er**, n.

crop, n. 1. saclike part of a bird's gullet. 2. farm product, growing or harvested. 3. group. 4. riding whip. v. [CROPPED, CROPPING] cut or bite off the ends of.

—**crop out** (or **up**), appear suddenly. —**crop'per**, n.

cro·quet' (krō-kā') n. game with hoops in the ground through which balls are hit.

cro·quette' (krō-ket') n. small mass of meat, fish, etc. fried in deep fat.

cross, n. 1. upright post with another across it. 2. figure of this, symbolic of Christianity. 3. any affliction. 4. mark made by intersecting lines, bars, etc. —v. 1. place, go, or lie across. 2. intersect. 3. draw a line across. 4. thwart. 5. interbreed. —a. 1. lying or passing across. 2. irritable. —**cross off** (or **out**), cancel as by drawing lines across. —**cross'ing**, n. —**cross'ness**, n.

cross'breed, v. hybrid. —v. to breed as a hybrid.

cross'-ex·am'ine, v. Law question (an opposition witness). —**cross'-ex·am'i·na'tion**, n.

cross'-eyed', a. having the eyes turned toward the nose.

cross'road, n. 1. road that crosses another. 2. pl. road intersection.

cross section, 1. part cut straight across. 2. broad sample.

cross'walk, n. pedestrians' lane across a street.

cross'wise, adv. across: also **cross'ways**.

crotch, n. place where branches or legs fork.

crotch'et, n. whim. —**crotch'et·y**, a.

crouch, v. & n. stoop with legs bent low.

croup (krōop) n. disease with cough and hard breathing.

crou'ton (krōo'ton) n. bit of toast served in soup.

crow, n. 1. large, black bird with a harsh call. 2. roost'er's cry. —v. 1. make a rooster's cry. 2. exult.

crow'bar, n. long, metal bar for prying, etc.

crowd, v. to throng, press, cram, etc. —n. mass of people. —**crowd'ed**, a.

crown, n. 1. head covering of a monarch. 2. power of a monarch. 3. top part, position, quality, etc. —v. 1. make a monarch of. 2. honor. 3. be atop. 4. climax.

cru'cial (krōo'shəl) a. 1. decisive. 2. trying.

cru'ci·ble, n. container for melting metals.

cru·ci·fix, *n.* representation of Jesus on the cross.

cru·ci·fy, *v.* [-FIED, -FYING] execute by suspending from a cross. —**cru·ci·fix'ion** (-fĭk'shən) *n.*

crude, *a.* 1. raw; unprocessed. 2. rough or clumsy. —**cru'di·ty, crude'ness,** *n.*

cru'el, *a.* causing suffering; pitiless. —**cru'el·ty,** *n.*

cru'et, *n.* small bottle for vinegar, oil, etc.

cruise (krōōz) *v.* travel about, as by ship. —*n.* voyage.

cruis'er, *n.* 1. police car. 2. large, fast warship.

crumb (krum) *n.* small piece, as of bread; bit. —**crumb'y** [-IER, -IEST] *a.*

crum'ble, *v.* break into crumbs. —**crum'bly** [-BLIER, -BLIEST] *a.*

crum'ple, *v.* to crush into wrinkles.

crunch, *v.* chew or crush with a crackling sound.

cru·sade', *v. & n.* (engage in) united action against an abuse. —**cru·sad'er,** *n.*

crush, *v.* 1. press out of shape. 2. pound into bits. 3. subdue. —*n.* 1. a crushing. 2. crowded mass. 3. [Col.] infatuation.

crust, *n.* 1. hard outer part of bread, earth, etc. 2. dry piece of bread. —**crust'y,** *a.*

crus·ta'cean (-shən) *n.* hard-shelled invertebrate, as a shrimp, lobster, etc.

crutch, *n.* support held under the arm to aid in walking.

crux, *n.* essential point.

cry, *v.* [CRIED, CRYING] 1. utter loudly. 2. sob; weep. —*n.* [*pl.* CRIES] 1. a shout. 2. entreaty. 3. call of a bird, etc. —**a far cry**, a great difference.

crypt (kript) *n.* underground (burial) vault.

cryp'tic, *a.* secret; mysterious. —**cryp'ti·cal·ly,** *adv.*

cryp·tog'ra·phy, *n.* secret-code writing or deciphering. —**cryp·tog'ra·pher,** *n.*

crys'tal, *n.* 1. clear quartz. 2. clear, brilliant glass. 3. solidified substance with symmetrical plane faces. —**crys'tal·line,** *a.*

crys'tal·lize, *v.* 1. form crystals. 2. take on or give definite form. —**crys'tal·li·za'tion,** *n.*

cub, *n.* young bear, lion, etc.

cub'by·hole, *n.* small, enclosed space.

cube (kūb) *n.* 1. a solid with six equal, square sides. 2. product obtained by multiplying a number by its square. —*v.* get the cube (*n.* 2) of. 2. cut into cubes. —**cu'bic, cu'bi·cal,** *a.*

cu'bi·cle, *n.* small room.

cuck'old, *n.* man whose wife is unfaithful.

cuck·oo (kōō'kōō) *n.* brown, slender bird. —*a.* [Sl.] crazy.

cu'cum·ber, *n.* long, green-skinned, fleshy vegetable.

cud, *n.* food regurgitated by cattle and chewed again.

cud'dle, *v.* hold or lie close and snug.

cudg'el (kuj'-) *v. & n.* (beat with) a short club.

cue (kū) *n.* 1. signal to begin. 2. hint. 3. rod for striking a billiard ball. —*v.* [Col.] to signal.

cuff, *n.* 1. band or fold at the wrist of a sleeve or the bottom of a trouser leg. 2. a slap. —*v.* to slap.

cui·sine (kwi-zēn') *n.* 1. style of cooking. 2. food cooked.

cu'li·nar'y (kū'-) *a.* of cookery.

cull, *v.* pick over; select.

cul'mi·nate, *v.* reach its highest point. —**cul'mi·na'tion,** *n.*

cul'pa·ble, *a.* deserving blame. —**cul'pa·bil'i·ty,** *n.*

cul'prit, *n.* one accused, or found guilty, of a crime.

cult, *n.* system of worship or group of worshipers.

cul'ti·vate, *v.* 1. prepare (land) for crops. 2. grow (plants). 3. develop, as the mind. —**cul'ti·va'tion,** *n.*

cul'ture (-chēr) *n.* 1. animal or plant breeding. 2. training of the mind, taste, etc. 3. civilization of a people or period. —**cul'tur·al,** *a.*

cul'vert, *n.* drain or waterway under a road, etc.

cum'ber·some, *a.* unwieldy.

cu'mu·la'tive (kūm'yə-) *a.* increasing by additions.

cu'mu·lus, *n.* cloud having rounded masses piled up.

cun'ning, *a.* 1. sly; crafty. 2. pretty. —*n.* craft.

cup, *n.* small bowl with handle, for beverages. —*v.* [CUPPED, CUPPING] shape like a cup. —**cup'ful** [*pl.* -FULS] *n.*

cup'board (kub'ērd) *n.* cabinet for dishes, food, etc.

cup'cake, *n.* small cake.

cu·pid'i·ty (kū-) *n.* greed.

cu'po·la (kū'-) *n.* small dome.

cur, *n.* **1.** mongrel dog. **2.** contemptible person.

cu·rate (kyoor'it) *n.* clergyman helping a vicar or rector.

cu·ra'tor (kyoo-rā'-) *n.* one in charge, as of a museum.

curb, *n.* **1.** chain or strap on a horse's bit for checking the horse. **2.** thing that restrains. **3.** edging along a street. —*v.* restrain.

curd, *n.* coagulated part of soured milk.

cur'dle, *v.* form curd.

cure, *n.* **1.** a healing. **2.** remedy. —*v.* **1.** make well; heal. **2.** remedy. **3.** preserve (meat). —**cur'a·ble,** *a.*

cur'few, *n.* evening deadline for being off the streets.

cu'ri·o (kyoo'-) *n.* [*pl.* -os] odd art object.

cu·ri·os'i·ty, *n.* **1.** desire to know. **2.** [*pl.* -TIES] oddity.

cu'ri·ous, *a.* **1.** eager to know; inquisitive. **2.** strange.

curl, *v.* **1.** twist (hair, etc.) into ringlets. **2.** curve around; coil. —*n.* **1.** ringlet of hair. **2.** any curling. —**curl'y** [-IER, -IEST] *a.*

cur'lew, *n.* wading bird.

curl'i·cue, *n.* fancy curve.

cur'rant, *n.* **1.** small, seedless raisin. **2.** sour berry.

cur'ren·cy, *n.* [*pl.* -CIES] **1.** money circulated in a country. **2.** general use; prevalence.

cur'rent, *a.* **1.** of this day, week, etc. **2.** commonly accepted or known. —*n.* flow of air, water, electricity, etc.

cur·ric'u·lum, *n.* [*pl.* -LUMS, -LA] course of study.

cur'ry, *n.* spicy powder or sauce. —*v.* [-RIED, -RYING] brush the coat of (a horse, etc.). —**curry favor,** try to win favor, as by flattery.

curse, *v.* **1.** call or bring evil down on. **2.** swear (at). —*n.* **1.** a cursing. **2.** evil or injury. —**curs'ed,** *a.*

cur'so·ry, *a.* hastily done.

curt, *a.* so brief as to be rude. —**curt'ness,** *n.*

cur·tail', *v.* cut short. —**cur·tail'ment,** *n.*

cur'tain (-t'n) *n.* piece of cloth hung, as at a window, to decorate or conceal. —*v.* furnish as with a curtain.

curt'sy, *n.* [*pl.* -SIES] graceful bow that women make by bending the knees. —*v.* [-SIED, -SYING] make a curtsy.

curve, *n.* line, surface, etc. having no straight part. —

v. form or move in a curve. —**curv'a·ture** (-chēr) *n.*

cush'ion, *n.* **1.** pillow or pad. **2.** something absorbing shock. —*v.* provide with a cushion.

cusp, *n.* arched, pointed end.

cus'pi·dor, *n.* spittoon.

cuss, *n.* & *v.* [Col.] curse.

cus'tard, *n.* pudding made with eggs, milk, and sugar.

cus·to'di·an, *n.* **1.** one having custody. **2.** janitor.

cus'to·dy, *n.* **1.** guarding; care. **2.** imprisonment.

cus'tom, *n.* **1.** usual or traditional practice; usage. **2.** *pl.* duties on imported goods. —*a.* made to order: also **custom-made.**

cus'tom·ar·y, *a.* usual. —**cus'tom·ar'i·ly,** *adv.*

cus'tom·er, *n.* one who buys.

cut, *v.* [CUT, CUTTING] **1.** gash. **2.** pierce. **3.** sever. **4.** hew. **5.** reap. **6.** trim. **7.** pass across. **8.** reduce. **9.** [Col.] snub. —*n.* **1.** a cutting. **2.** part cut open or off. **3.** reduction. **4.** style. **5.** plate engraved for printing. **6.** insult. **7.** [Sl.] share, as of profits. —**cut and dried,** dull; boring. —**cut out for,** suited for.

cute, *a.* [Col.] **1.** clever. **2.** pretty or pleasing.

cu'ti·cle (kū'-) *n.* hardened skin, as at the base and sides of a fingernail.

cut'lass, cut'las, *n.* short, thick, curved sword.

cut'ler·y, *n.* cutting tools, as knives, scissors, etc.

cut'let, *n.* small slice of meat from the ribs or leg.

cut'-rate', *a.* selling or on sale at a lower price.

cut'ter, *n.* small, swift ship.

cut'throat, *n.* murderer. —*a.* merciless.

cut'tle·fish, *n.* mollusk with ten arms.

-cy, *suf.* **1.** quality or state of being. **2.** position, rank, or office of.

cy·a·nide (sī'ə-nīd) *n.* poisonous white compound.

cy'cla·mate, *n.* artificial sweetener.

cy'cle (sī'-) *n.* **1.** complete round of regularly recurring events, or period for this. **2.** bicycle, tricycle, etc. —*v.* ride a bicycle, etc. —**cy'clic, cy'cli·cal,** *a.* —**cy'clist,** *n.*

cy'clone, *n.* storm with heavy rain and whirling winds.

cy·clo·pe'di·a, *n.* encyclopedia.

cy′clo·tron, *n.* apparatus that speeds up particles, as to split atomic nuclei.

cyg′net (sig′-) *n.* young swan.

cyl′in·der, *n.* round figure with two flat ends that are parallel circles. —**cy·lin′-dri·cal,** *a.*

cym′bals, *n.pl.* pair of round brass plates struck together for a ringing sound.

cyn′ic, *n.* one inclined to question goodness, sincerity, etc. —**cyn′i·cal,** *a.* —**cyn′i·cism,** *n.*

cy′no·sure, *n.* center of attention.

cy′press, *n.* evergreen tree.

cyst (sist) *n.* sac containing fluid or hard matter.

czar (zär) *n.* 1. Russian emperor. 2. an autocrat.

D

′d, *had* or *would,* as in I′d.

dab, *v.* [DABBED, DABBING] pat or put on with light, quick strokes. —*n.* soft or moist bit. —**dab′ber,** *n.*

dab′ble, *v.* 1. splash the hands in water. 2. do something superficially (with *in* or *at*). —**dab′bler,** *n.*

dachs·hund (däks′hoond) *n.* small dog with a long body.

da′cron (dā′-) *n.* synthetic fabric: trademark (**D-**).

dad, *n.* [Col.] father: also **dad′dy** [*pl.* -DIES].

dad′dy-long′legs, *n.* [*sing.* & *pl.*] long-legged arachnid.

daf′fo·dil, *n.* yellow flower.

daf′fy, *a.* [-FIER, -FIEST] [Col.] crazy; silly.

daft, *a.* 1. silly. 2. insane.

dag′ger *n.* 1. short, sharp-pointed weapon. 2. printed reference mark (†).

dahl·ia (dal′ya) *n.* plant with large, showy flowers.

dai′ly, *a.* & *adv.* (done or happening) every day. —*n.* daily newspaper.

daily dozen [Col.] daily gymnastic exercises.

dain′ty, *a.* [-TIER, -TIEST] 1. delicately pretty. 2. fastidious. —*n.* [*pl.* -TIES] a delicacy. —**dain′ti·ly,** *adv.* —**dain′ti·ness,** *n.*

dair′y, *n.* [*pl.* -IES] place where milk, butter, etc. are made or sold. —**dair′y·man** [*pl.* -MEN] *n.*

da·is (dā′is) *n.* platform.

dai′sy (-zi) *n.* [*pl.* -SIES] flower with white rays around a yellow disk.

dale, *n.* small valley.

dal′ly, *v.* [-LIED, -LYING] 1. to toy or flirt. 2. loiter.

Dal·ma′tian (-shən) *n.* large, black-and-white dog.

dam, *n.* 1. barrier to hold back flowing water. 2. female parent of a horse, cow, etc. —*v.* [DAMMED, DAMMING] keep back; confine.

dam′age, *n.* 1. injury; harm. 2. *pl.* money paid for harm done. —*v.* do damage to.

dam′ask, *n.* fabric with figured weave. —*a.* deep-pink.

dame, *n.* 1. lady. 2. [D-] woman′s title of honor in Britain. 3. [Sl.] any woman.

damn (dam) *v.* [DAMNED, DAMNING] condemn; declare bad, doomed, etc. —*a.* & *adv.* [Col.] damned. —**dam′na·ble,** *a.* —**dam·na′tion,** *n.*

damp, *n.* 1. moisture. 2. mine gas. —*a.* slightly wet; moist. —*v.* 1. moisten. 2. check or deaden. Also **damp′en.**

damp′er, *n.* 1. one that depresses. 2. valve in a flue to control the draft.

dam′sel, *n.* [Ar.] girl.

dance, *v.* move in rhythm to music. —*n.* 1. rhythmic movement to music. 2. party or piece of music for dancing. —**danc′er,** *n.*

dan′de·li·on, *n.* common weed with yellow flowers.

dan′der, *n.* [Col.] anger.

dan′dle, *v.* dance (a child) up and down on the knee.

dan′druff, *n.* little scales of dead skin on the scalp.

dan′dy, *n.* [*pl.* -DIES] vain man. —*a.* [Sl.] very good.

dan′ger, *n.* 1. liability to injury, loss, etc.; peril. 2. thing that may cause injury, etc. —**dan′ger·ous,** *a.*

dan′gle, *v.* hang loosely.

dank, *a.* disagreeably damp. —**dank′ness,** *n.*

dap′per, *a.* trim; spruce.

dap′ple, *a.* spotted; mottled: also **dap′pled.** —*v.* mottle.

dare, *v.* 1. have the courage (*to*). 2. challenge. —*n.* a challenge. —**dare say,** think probable. —**dar′ing,** *a.* & *n.*

dare′dev′il, *n.* & *a.* (one who is) bold and reckless.

dark, *a.* 1. with little or no light. 2. not light in color. 3. gloomy. 4. ignorant. —*n.* a being dark. —**dark′en,** *v.* —**dark′ness,** *n.*

dark horse [Col.] one who wins or may win unexpectedly.

dar'ling, n. & a. beloved.

darn, v. mend by sewing.

dart, n. 1. small pointed weapon for throwing. 2. sudden movement. —v. throw or move quickly.

dash, v. 1. smash. 2. strike violently against. 3. do hastily (with *off*). 4. rush. —n. 1. bit of something. 2. short race. 3. vigor. 4. mark of punctuation (—).

dash'board, n. instrument panel in an automobile.

dash'ing, a. lively.

das'tard, n. mean coward. —**das'tard·ly,** a.

da'ta, n.pl. [often construed as sing.] facts.

date, n. 1. time of an event. 2. day of the month. 3. [Col.] social engagement. 4. fruit of a tall palm. —v. 1. mark with a date. 2. belong to a particular time. —**out of date,** old-fashioned. —**up to date,** modern.

daub (dôb) v. 1. smear with sticky stuff. 2. paint badly.

daugh'ter (dô'-) n. female in relation to her parents.

daugh'ter-in-law', n. [pl. DAUGHTERS-IN-LAW] wife of one's son.

daunt, v. 1. frighten. 2. dishearten. —**daunt'less,** a.

dav'en·port, n. large sofa.

daw'dle, v. waste time.

dawn, v. 1. begin to be day. 2. begin to be understood. —n. 1. daybreak. 2. beginning.

day, n. 1. period from sunrise to sunset. 2. period of 24 hours, esp. from midnight to midnight. 3. *also pl.* era. —**day'light,** n. —**day'-time,** n.

day'break, n. time of the first light in the morning.

day'dream, n. pleasant, dreamy thinking or wishing. —v. have daydreams.

day'light-sav'ing time, time 1 hour later than standard.

daze, v. 1. stun. 2. dazzle. —n. dazed condition.

daz'zle, v. overpower with light or brilliance.

DDT, powerful insecticide.

de-, *pref.* 1. away from; off. 2. reverse the action of.

dea'con (dē'-) n. one who assists a minister.

dead (ded) a. 1. not living. 2. dull; inactive. 3. complete. —n. time of most cold, darkness, etc. —adv. completely.

dead'beat, n. [Sl.] one who avoids paying for things.

dead'en, v. to dull.

dead end, street closed at one end. —**dead'-end',** a.

dead heat, a tie in a race.

dead'line, n. time limit.

dead'lock, n. standstill with equal forces opposed.

dead'ly, a. [-LIER, -LIEST] 1. fatal. 2. as or until death. —adv. extremely.

dead'pan', a. & adv. [Sl.] without expression.

dead'wood, n. useless thing.

deaf (def) a. 1. unable to hear. 2. unwilling to respond. —**deaf'en,** v.

deaf'-mute', n. deaf person who has not learned speech.

deal (dēl) v. [DEALT (delt), DEALING] 1. distribute. 2. have to do (with). 3. do business. —n. [Col.] transaction or agreement. —**a good (or great) deal,** 1. large amount. 2. very much. —**deal'er,** n. —**deal'ing,** n.

dean (dēn) n. 1. church or college official. 2. senior member of a group.

dear (dēr) a. 1. much loved. 2. esteemed. 3. costly. 4. earnest. —n. darling.

dearth (dûrth) n. scarcity.

death (deth) n. 1. a dying or being dead. 2. cause of death. —**death'less,** a.

death'ly, a. characteristic of death. —adv. extremely.

de·ba'cle (dā-bä'k'l) n. sudden disaster.

de·bar', v. [-BARRED, -BARRING] exclude (from).

de·base', v. to lower in quality, etc. —**de·base'ment,** n.

de·bate', v. argue in a formal way. —n. formal argument. —**de·bat'a·ble,** a. —**de·bat'er,** n.

de·bauch' (-bôch') v. to corrupt. —n. orgy. —**de·bauch'er·y** [pl. -IES] n.

de·bil'i·tate, v. make weak. —**de·bil'i·ta'tion,** n.

de·bil'i·ty, n. weakness.

deb'it, n. entry in an account of money owed. —v. enter as a debt.

deb·o·nair', deb·o·naire' (-nâr') a. affable and gay.

de·bris (də-brē') n. broken, scattered remains; rubbish.

debt, n. 1. something owed. 2. state of owing.

debt'or, n. one owing a debt.

de·bunk', v. [Col.] expose false claims, etc. of.

de·but (di-bū') n. 1. first public appearance, as of an

actor. 2. formal introduction into society.

deb·u·tante′ (-tänt′) n. girl making a social debut.

dec′ade, n. ten-year period.

dec′a·dence, n. a declining, as in morals, art, etc.—**dec′a·dent**, a. & n.

de·cal′co·ma′ni·a, n. picture for transfer from prepared paper: also **de·cal′**.

Dec′a·logue (-lôg), **Dec′a·log**, n. Ten Commandments.

de·camp′, v. leave secretly.

de·cant′, v. pour off gently.

de·cant′er, n. decorative bottle for serving wine.

de·cap′i·tate, v. behead.—**de·cap′i·ta′tion**, n.

dec′ath·lon, n. contest of ten track and field events.

de·cay′, v. 1. fall into ruin. 2. rot.—n. a decaying; rot.

de·cease′, n. death.

de·ceased′, a. dead.—**the deceased**, dead person(s).

de·ceit′ (-sēt′) n. 1. act of deceiving. 2. deceitful quality.—**de·ceit′ful**, a.

de·ceive′, v. make believe what is not true; mislead.

de·cel′er·ate (-sel′-) v. slow down.

De·cem′ber, n. 12th month.

de′cent, a. 1. proper. 2. respectable. 3. adequate.—**de′cen·cy** [pl. -CIES] n.

de·cep′tion, n. 1. a deceiving. 2. illusion or fraud.—**de·cep′tive**, a.

de·cide′, v. 1. settle by passing judgment. 2. make up one's mind.

de·cid′ed, a. definite.—**de·cid′ed·ly**, adv.

de·cid′u·ous (-sij′ōō-) a. shedding leaves annually.

dec′i·mal (des′-) a. based on the number ten.—n. fraction with a denominator of ten or a power of ten, shown by a point (**decimal point**) before the numerator.

de·ci′pher, v. translate from code or illegibility.

de·ci′sion, n. 1. a deciding. 2. judgment. 3. determination.

de·ci′sive (-sī′-) a. 1. conclusive. 2. showing decision.

deck, n. 1. floor of a ship. 2. pack of playing cards.—v. adorn; trim.

de·claim′, v. speak in a loud, rhetorical way.—**dec′la·ma′tion**, n.

de·clare′, v. 1. announce formally. 2. say emphatically.—**dec′la·ra′tion**, n.—**de·clar′a·tive**, a.

de·clen′sion, n. grammatical inflection of nouns, etc.

de·cline′, v. 1. slope downward. 2. lessen, as in force. 3. refuse politely. 4. Gram. give inflected forms of.—n. 1. a failing, decay, etc. 2. downward slope.

de·cliv′i·ty, n. downward slope.

de·coct′, v. extract by boiling.—**de·coc′tion**, n.

dé·colle·té (dā-kol-tā′) a. [Fr.] cut low at the neck.

de·com·pose′, v. 1. break up into basic parts. 2. rot.—**de′com·po·si′tion**, n.

de·con′gest·ant, n. medicinal relief for congestion, as of nasal passages.

dé·cor (dā-kôr′) n. [Fr.] decorative scheme.

dec′o·rate, v. 1. adorn; ornament. 2. give a medal to.—**dec′o·ra′tive**, a.—**dec′o·ra′tor**, n.—**dec′o·ra′tion**, n.

de·co′rum, n. proper behavior, speech, etc.—**dec′o·rous**, a.—**dec′o·rous·ly**, adv.

de·coy′, n. artificial bird, etc. used as a lure.—v. lure.

de·crease′, v. grow or make less or smaller.—n. (dē′-krēs) a decreasing.

de·cree′, n. official order; edict.—v. [-CREED, -CREE-ING] order by decree.

de·crep′it, a. old and worn out.—**de·crep′i·tude**, n.

de·cry′, v. [-CRIED, -CRYING] denounce; censure.

ded′i·cate, v. 1. set apart formally. 2. devote. 3. inscribe.—**ded′i·ca′tion**, n.

de·duce′, v. conclude by reasoning; infer.

de·duct′, v. subtract.

de·duc′tion, n. 1. a deducing or deducting. 2. amount deducted. 3. conclusion.

deed, n. 1. act. 2. feat of courage, etc. 3. legal document transferring property.—v. transfer by deed.

deem, v. think; believe.

deep, a. 1. extending far down, in, or back. 2. hard to understand. 3. involved (in). 4. of low pitch. 5. intense.—n. deep place or part.—adv. far down, etc.—**deep′en**, v.

deep′-seat′ed, a. firmly fixed: also **deep′-root′ed**.

deer, n. [pl. DEER] hoofed, cud-chewing animal, the male of which bears antlers

de·face′, v. mar.

de·fame', v. slander. **—def'·a·ma'tion**, n.

de·fault', v. & n. fail(ure) to do or pay as required.

de·feat', v. 1. win victory over. 2. frustrate. —n. a defeating or being defeated.

de·feat'ist, n. & a. (one) too readily accepting defeat.

def'e·cate, v. excrete waste matter from bowels.

de·fect' (or dē'fekt) n. imperfection; fault. —v. (dĭfekt') to desert. **—de·fec'tion**, n. **—de·fec'tive**, a.

de·fend', v. 1. protect. 2. support by speech or act. 3. Law act for (an accused). **—de·fend'er**, n.

de·fend'ant, n. Law person sued or accused.

de·fense', n. 1. a defending against attack. 2. something that defends. 3. defendant and his counsel. **—de·fense'less**, a. **—de·fen'sive**, a. & n.

de·fer' (-fûr') v. [-FERRED, -FERRING] 1. postpone. 2. yield in opinion, etc.

def'er·ence, n. 1. a yielding in opinion, etc. 2. respect. **—def'er·en'tial**, a.

de·fi'ance (-fī'-) n. open resistance to authority. **—de·fi'ant**, a.

de·fi'cien·cy (-fĭsh'ən-) n. [pl. -CIES] shortage; lack. **—de·fi'cient**, a.

def'i·cit (-sĭt) n. amount by which a sum of money is less than expected, etc.

de·file', v. dirty; sully. —n. narrow pass.

de·fine', v. 1. mark the limits of. 2. state the meaning of. **—def'i·ni'tion**, n.

def'i·nite (-nĭt) a. 1. having exact limits. 2. explicit. 3. certain.

de·fin'i·tive, a. 1. conclusive. 2. most nearly complete.

de·flate', v. 1. collapse by letting out air. 2. lessen in amount, importance, etc. **de·fla'tion**, n. fall in prices.

de·flect', v. turn to one side.

de·fo'li·ant, n. chemical that strips plants of leaves.

de·form', v. mar the form of. **—de·form'i·ty** [pl. -TIES] n.

de·fraud', v. cheat.

de·fray', v. pay (the cost).

de·frost', v. rid or become rid of frost or ice.

deft, a. quick and skillful.

de·funct', a. no longer existing.

de·fy', v. [-FIED, -FYING] 1. resist openly. 2. dare.

de·gen'er·ate, v. lose normal or good qualities. —a. (-ĭt) deteriorated. —n. (-ĭt) a degenerate person. **—de·gen'er·a·cy**, n. **—de·gen'er·a'tion**, n.

de·grade', v. lower in rank, moral character, etc. **—deg'ra·da'tion**, n.

de·gree', n. 1. successive step in a series. 2. intensity, extent, etc. 3. rank given to a college graduate. 4. unit of measure, as for angles, temperature, etc.

de·hy'drate (-hī'-) v. remove water from; dry (up).

de·i'fy (dē'ə-) v. [-FIED, -FYING] make a god of.

deign (dān) v. condescend.

de'i·ty, n. [pl. -TIES] god or goddess. **—the Deity**, God.

de·ject'ed, a. sad; depressed. **—de·jec'tion**, n.

de·lay', v. 1. put off; postpone. 2. make late; detain. —n. a delaying.

de·lec'ta·ble, a. delightful.

del'e·gate (or -gĭt) n. representative. —v. (-gāt) 1. appoint as delegate. 2. entrust to another.

del'e·ga'tion, n. group of delegates.

de·lete' (-lēt') v. take out (a word, etc.). **—de·le'tion**, n.

del'e·te'ri·ous (-tēr'ĭ-) a. harmful to health, etc.

del'i, n. [Col.] delicatessen.

de·lib'er·ate, v. consider carefully. —a. (-ĭt) 1. done on purpose. 2. not rash or hasty. 3. unhurried. **—de·lib'er·a'tion**, n.

del'i·ca·cy, n. 1. delicate quality. 2. [pl. -CIES] a choice food; dainty.

del'i·cate, a. 1. fine and lovely. 2. fragile or frail. 3. needing care. 4. sensitive. 5. considerate and tactful. **—del'i·cate·ly**, adv.

del'i·ca·tes'sen, n. 1. prepared meats, fish, cheeses, etc. 2. shop selling these.

de·li'cious, a. very pleasing, esp. to taste or smell.

de·light', v. please greatly. —n. great pleasure. **—de·light'ful**, a.

de·lin'e·ate, v. 1. draw; sketch. 2. describe.

de·lin'quent, a. 1. not obeying duty or law. 2. overdue. —n. one guilty of minor crimes. **—de·lin'quen·cy**, n.

de·lir'i·um, n. 1. temporary mental illness. 2. wild excitement. **—de·lir'i·ous**, a.

de·liv'er, v. 1. set free; rescue. 2. assist in birth.

3. utter. 4. hand over. 5. distribute. 6. strike or throw. —**de·liv'er·ance**, n.

de·liv'er·y, n. [pl. -IES] a delivering or something delivered.

dell, n. small valley.

del·phin'i·um, n. tall plant with flower spikes.

del'ta, n. 1. letter of Greek alphabet. 2. soil deposit at a river mouth.

de·lude', v. mislead.

del'uge (-ūj) n. 1. great flood. 2. heavy rainfall. —v. 1. flood. 2. overwhelm.

de·lu'sion, n. false, esp. psychotic, belief. —**de·lu'sive,** a.

de luxe, very good; elegant.

delve, v. investigate.

dem'a·gogue (gŏg) **dem'a·gog,** n. one who appeals to prejudices, etc. to win power. —**dem'a·gog'uer·y,** n.

de·mand', v. 1. ask for boldly. 2. require. —n. 1. strong request. 2. requirement. —**on demand,** when presented for payment.

de'mar·ca'tion, de'mar·ka'tion, n. boundary line.

de·mean', v. degrade.

de·mean'or, n. behavior.

de·ment'ed, a. mentally ill.

de·men'tia (-shə) n. loss of mental powers.

de·mer'it, n. 1. fault. 2. mark for poor work, etc.

demi-, pref. half.

dem'i·god, n. minor deity.

dem'i·john, n. large, wicker-covered bottle.

de·mise' (-mīz') n. death.

dem'i·tasse (-tas) n. small cup of coffee.

de·moc'ra·cy, n. [pl. -CIES] 1. government in which the power is vested in all the people. 2. equality of rights, etc. —**dem'o·crat,** n. —**dem'o·crat'ic,** a.

de·mol'ish, v. destroy; ruin. —**dem'o·li'tion,** n.

de'mon, n. devil; evil spirit. —**de·mon'ic,** a.

dem'on·strate, v. 1. prove. 2. explain with examples. 3. show the working of. 4. show feelings publicly. —**de·mon'stra·ble,** a. —**dem'on·stra'tion,** n. —**dem'on·stra'tor,** n.

de·mon'stra·tive, a. 1. showing clearly. 2. giving proof (of). 3. showing feelings openly.

de·mor'al·ize, v. 1. to corrupt in morals. 2. to lower in morale. —**de·mor'al·i·za'tion,** n.

de·mote', v. reduce in rank. —**de·mo'tion,** n.

de·mur' (-mûr') v. [-MURRED, -MURRING] to scruple (at). —n. objection.

de·mure' (-myoor') a. coy.

de·mur'rage (-mûr'ij) n. 1. delay in shipping. 2. compensation paid for this.

den, n. 1. animal's lair. 2. haunt of thieves, etc. 3. small, cozy room.

de·na'ture (-chēr) v. make (alcohol) unfit to drink.

de·ni'al, n. 1. a denying. 2. contradiction.

den'im, n. coarse, twilled cotton cloth.

den'i·zen, n. inhabitant.

de·nom'i·nate, v. to name.

de·nom'i·na'tion, n. 1. a name. 2. specific class or kind. 3. religious sect.

de·nom'i·na'tor, n. term below the line in a fraction.

de·note', v. 1. indicate. 2. mean explicitly. —**de'no·ta'tion,** n.

de·noue'ment (dā-nōō'mäN) n. [Fr.] unraveling of a plot.

de·nounce', v. 1. accuse publicly. 2. condemn strongly.

dense, a. [DENSER, DENSEST] 1. packed tightly. 2. thick. 3. stupid. —**dense'ly,** adv.

den'si·ty, n. 1. number per unit. 2. ratio of the mass of an object to its volume.

dent, n. slight hollow made in a surface by a blow. —v. make a dent in.

den'tal, a. of the teeth.

den'ti·frice (-fris) n. substance for cleaning teeth.

den'tine (-tēn) n. tissue under the enamel of teeth.

den'tist, n. one who cares for and repairs teeth.

den'ture (-chēr) n. set of artificial teeth.

de·nude', v. make bare.

de·nun'ci·a'tion, n. a denouncing.

de·ny', v. 1. declare untrue. 2. refuse to give, accept, etc. —**deny oneself,** do without.

de·o'dor·ant, n. & a. (substance) that masks odors.

de·part', v. 1. leave. 2. die. 3. deviate (from). —**de·par'ture** (-chēr) n.

de·part'ment, n. 1. division. 2. field of knowledge. —**de'part·men'tal,** a.

de·pend', v. 1. be determined by something else. 2. rely, as for support. —**de·pend'ence,** n. —**de·pend'ent,** a. & n.

de·pend′a·ble, *a.* reliable.
— **de·pend′a·bil′i·ty**, *n.*

de·pict′, *v.* 1. represent by drawing, etc. 2. describe.

de·plete′, *v.* 1. empty wholly or partly. 2. exhaust. — **de·ple′tion**, *n.*

de·plore′, *v.* be sorry about. — **de·plor′a·ble**, *a.*

de·ploy′, *v. Mil.* spread out.

de·pop′u·late, *v.* reduce the population of.

de·port′, *v.* 1. behave (oneself). 2. banish.

de·port′ment, *n.* behavior.

de·pose′, *v.* 1. remove from office. 2. testify. — **dep·o·si′tion**, *n.*

de·pos′it, *v.* 1. place for safe-keeping. 2. give as partial payment. 3. set down. — *n.* something deposited. — **de·pos′i·tor**, *n.*

de·pos′i·to·ry, *n.* place to put things for safekeeping. warehouse. 2. train station.

de·prave′, *v.* make morally bad. — **de·praved′**, *a.* — **de·prav′i·ty** [*pl.* -TIES] *n.*

dep′re·cate, *v.* express disapproval of. — **dep′re·ca′tion**, *n.* — **dep′re·ca′to·ry**, *a.*

de·pre·ci·ate (-prē′shi·) *v.* 1. lessen in value. 2. belittle. — **de·pre′ci·a′tion**, *n.*

dep·re·da′tion, *n.* a looting.

de·press′, *v.* 1. press down. 2. sadden. 3. lower in value, etc. — **de·pressed′**, *a.*

de·pres′sion, *n.* 1. a depressing. 2. hollow place. 3. dejection. 4. period of reduced business and prosperity.

de·prive′, *v.* 1. take away from. 2. withhold from. — **dep′ri·va′tion**, *n.*

depth, *n.* 1. distance from the top or back. 2. deepness. 3. profundity. 4. *pl.* deepest part.

dep·u·ta′tion, *n.* delegation.

dep′u·tize, *v.* make a deputy.

dep′u·ty, *n.* [*pl.* -TIES] substitute of person.

de·rail′, *v.* run off the rails.

de·range′, *v.* 1. upset or disturb. 2. make insane.

der·by (dûr′bi) *n.* stiff felt hat with a round crown.

der·e·lict, *a.* 1. abandoned. 2. negligent. — *n.* thing or person abandoned as worthless. — **der′e·lic′tion**, *n.*

de·ride′, *v.* ridicule. — **de·ri′sion** (-rizh′ən) *n.* — **de·ri′sive** (-rī′-) *a.*

de·rive′, *v.* 1. take or get (*from*). 2. deduce. 3. origi-

nate. 4. trace to a source. — **der·i·va′tion**, *n.* — **de·riv′a·tive** (-riv′-) *n.*

der′ma·tol′o·gy, *n.* study of the skin and its diseases.

de·rog′a·to·ry, *a.* disparaging. — **der′o·ga′tion**, *n.*

der′rick, *n.* machine for moving heavy objects.

de·scend′ (-send′) *v.* 1. move down. 2. come from earlier times. 3. derive. 4. make a sudden attack (*on*). — **de·scent′**, *n.*

de·scend′ant, *n.* offspring of a certain ancestor.

de·scribe′, *v.* 1. picture in words; tell about. 2. trace the outline of. — **de·scrip′tion**, *n.* — **de·scrip′tive**, *a.*

de·scry′ (-skrī′) *v.* [-SCRIED, -SCRYING] catch sight of.

des′e·crate, *v.* violate the sacredness of; profane. — **des′e·cra′tion**, *n.*

de·seg′re·gate, *v.* end racial segregation (in). — **de·seg′re·ga′tion**, *n.*

de·sert′ (-zûrt′) *v.* abandon. — *n.* [in *pl.*] reward or punishment. — **de·ser′tion**, *n.*

des′ert (dez′-) *n.* arid, sandy region.

de·serve′, *v.* be worthy of. — **de·serv′ing**, *a.*

des′ic·cate, *v.* dry up. — **des′ic·ca′tion**, *n.*

de·sign′, *v.* 1. to plan. 2. contrive. — *n.* 1. plan; scheme. 2. purpose. 3. pattern. — **de·sign′ing**, *a. & n.*

des′ig·nate, *v.* 1. point out; specify. 2. appoint. — **des′ig·na′tion**, *n.*

de·sire′, *v.* wish or long for; want. — *n.* 1. a wish. 2. thing wished for. 3. sexual appetite. — **de·sir′a·ble**, *a.* — **de·sir′ous**, *a.*

de·sist′, *v.* stop; cease.

desk, *n.* writing table.

des′o·late (-lit) *a.* 1. lonely; orlorn. 2. uninhabited. 3. laid waste. — *v.* (-lāt) make desolate. — **des′o·la′tion**, *n.*

de·spair′, *v.* lose hope. — *n.* loss of hope.

des·per·a′do, *n.* [*pl.* -DOES, -DOS] reckless outlaw.

des′per·ate (-it) *a.* 1. reckless from despair. 2. serious. — **des′per·a′tion**, *n.*

des′pi·ca·ble, *a.* deserving scorn; contemptible.

de·spise′, *v.* to scorn.

de·spite′, *prep.* in spite of.

de·spoil′, *v.* rob; plunder.

de·spond′en·cy, *n.* **de·spond′ence**, *n.* loss of hope; dejection. — **de·spond′ent**, *a.*

des'pot, n. tyrant. —**des'pot'ic**, a. —**des'pot·ism**, n.

des·sert (di-zûrt') n. sweet dish ending a meal.

des'ti·na'tion, n. place to which one is going.

des'tine, v. head for, as by fate. —**destined for**, bound or intended for.

des'tin·y, n. [pl. -IES] (one's) fate.

des'ti·tute, a. needy. —**destitute of**, lacking.

des'ti·tu'tion, n.

de·stroy', v. 1. tear down; demolish. 2. ruin. 3. kill.

de·stroy'er, n. fast warship.

de·struc'tion, n. ruin. —**de·struc'tive**, a.

des'ul·to·ry, a. 1. not methodical. 2. random.

de·tach', v. unfasten and remove. —**de·tach'a·ble**, a.

de·tach'ment, n. 1. separation. 2. troops on special task. 3. aloofness

de·tail', v. 1. tell minutely. 2. Mil. choose for a special task. —n. (also dē'tāl) 1. minute account. 2. small part. 3. Mil. special task.

de·tain', v. 1. keep in custody. 2. delay. —**de·ten'tion**, n.

de·tect', v. discover (thing hidden, etc.). —**de·tec'tion**, n. —**de·tec'tor**, n.

de·tec'tive, n. one who investigates crimes, etc.

de·ter', v. [-TERRED, -TER-RING] keep someone from an action. —**de·ter'ment**, n. **de·ter'rent**, a. & n.

de·ter'gent, a. & n. cleansing (substance).

de·te'ri·o·rate' (-tēr'-) v. make or become worse. —**de·te'ri·o·ra'tion**, n.

de·ter'mine, v. 1. set limits to. 2. decide; resolve. 3. find out exactly. —**de·ter'mi·na'tion**, n.

de·test', v. hate. —**de·test'a·ble**, a. —**de'tes·ta'tion**, n.

det'o·nate', v. explode. —**det'o·na'tor**, n.

de'tour, v. & n. (use) an indirect or alternate road.

de·tract', v. take something desirable (from).

det'ri·ment, n. damage; harm. —**det'ri·men'tal**, a.

deuce (dōos, dūs) n. 1. playing card with 2 spots. 2. the devil: a mild curse.

de·val'u·ate, v. lessen the value of.

dev'as·tate, v. destroy; ravage. —**dev'as·ta'tion**, n.

de·vel'op, v. 1. grow, im-prove, expand, etc. 2. work out by degrees. —**de·vel'op·ment**, n.

de'vi·ate, v. turn aside; diverge. —**de'vi·a'tion**, n.

de·vice', n. 1. a plan or scheme. 2. mechanical contrivance. 3. a design.

dev'il, n. 1. [also D-] evil spirit, esp. Satan. 2. wicked or reckless person. —v. 1. season (food) highly. 2. tease. —**dev'il·try** [pl. -TRIES] —**dev'il·ish**, a.

dev'il·may-care', a. reckless; careless.

de'vi·ous, a. roundabout.

de·vise' (-vīz') v. 1. to plan. 2. bequeath by will.

de·void', a. empty (of).

de·volve', v. pass (on) to another, as a duty.

de·vote', v. 1. dedicate. 2. apply to a purpose.

de·vot'ed, a. 1. dedicated. 2. loyal. —**de·vot'ed·ly**, adv.

dev·o·tee', n. one devoted to something or someone.

de·vo'tion, n. 1. a devoting. 2. pl. prayers. 3. loyalty.

de·vour', v. 1. eat up hungrily. 2. take in eagerly.

de·vout', a. pious or sincere.

dew, n. atmospheric moisture condensing on cool surfaces at night. —**dew'y**, a.

dex'ter·ous, a. skillful in using one's hands, mind, etc. —**dex·ter'i·ty**, n.

dex'trose, n. sugar found in plants and animals.

di-, pref. twice; double.

di·a·be·tes (dī'ə-bē'tis) n. disease marked by excess sugar in the blood and urine. —**di'a·bet'ic**, a. & n.

di'a·bol'ic, a. devilish.

di'a·crit'ic, n. a mark to show pronunciation. —**di'a·crit'i·cal**, a.

di'a·dem, n. a crown.

di'ag·no'sis, n. identifying of a disease. —**di·ag·nose'**, v.

di·ag'o·nal, a. slanting between opposite corners. —n. diagonal line.

di'a·gram, n. & v. sketch, plan, etc. to help explain. —**di'a·gram·mat'ic**, a.

di'al, n. 1. face of a clock, meter, etc. for indicating some variable. 2. rotating disk on a telephone. —v. 1. tune in on a radio dial. 2. call by using a telephone dial.

di'a·lect, n. form of speech peculiar to a region, group, etc. —**di'a·lec'tal**, a.

di'a·logue (-lôg), **di'a·log**, n. conversation.

di·am'e·ter, n. 1. straight line through the center of a circle, etc. 2. its length. — **di·a·met'ri·cal,** a.

di'a·mond, n. 1. precious gem of great brilliance. 2. figure shaped like ◆. 3. baseball field.

di'a·per, n. cloth worn about a baby's crotch. —v. to put a diaper on.

di·aph'a·nous, a. gauzy.

di'a·phragm (-fram) n. 1. wall of muscle between chest and abdomen. 2. vibrating disk, as in an earphone.

di·ar·rhe'a (dī'a-rē'a) n. very loose bowel movements.

di'a·ry, n. [pl. -RIES] daily record of personal notes.

di'a·tribe, n. denunciation.

dice, n.pl. [sing. DIE] small, spotted cubes, used in gambling. —v. cut into cubes.

dick'er, v. barter; haggle.

dick'ey, n. detachable collar or shirt front.

dic'tate, v. 1. speak (something) for another to write down. 2. command. —n. an order. —**dic·ta'tion,** n.

dic·ta'tor, n. absolute ruler; tyrant. —**dic·ta·to'ri·al,** a. —**dic·ta'tor·ship',** n.

dic'tion, n. 1. choice of words. 2. enunciation.

dic'tion·ar'y, n. [pl. -IES] book of words alphabetically listed and defined.

dic'tum, n. judicial opinion.

did, pt. of **do.**

di·dac'tic (dī-) a. meant to teach; instructive.

did'n't, did not.

die, v. [DIED, DYING] 1. stop living. 2. to end. 3. [Col.] wish very much. —n. 1. sing. of **dice.** 2. device for molding, stamping, etc. — **die away** (or **down**), cease gradually. —**die out,** go out of existence.

die'-hard', die'hard', n. stubborn, resistant person.

Die·sel, die'sel (dē'z'l) n. internal-combustion engine that burns fuel oil.

di'et, n. 1. one's usual food. 2. special food taken as for health. —v. follow a diet, as to lose weight. —**di'e·tar'y,** a.

di'e·ti'tian, di'e·ti'cian (-tish'en) n. planner of diets. —**di·e·tet'ics,** n.

dif'fer, v. 1. to be different or unlike. 2. disagree.

dif'fer·ence, n. 1. a being unlike. 2. distinguishing characteristic. 3. disagreement. 4. amount by which two quantities differ. — **dif'fer·en'tial,** a & n.

dif'fer·ent, a. 1. not alike. 2. distinct. 3. unusual.

dif'fer·en'ti·ate (-en'shi-) v. 1. be or make different. 2. distinguish between.

dif'fi·cult, a. hard to do, learn, deal with, etc. — **dif'fi·cul'ty** [pl. -TIES] n.

dif'fi·dent, a. shy. —**dif'fi·dence,** n.

dif·frac'tion, n. a breaking up of light as into the colors of the spectrum.

dif·fuse' (-fūs') a. 1. spread out. 2. wordy. —v. (-fūz') spread widely. —**dif·fu'sion,** n.

dig, v. [DUG, DIGGING] 1. turn up (soil), as with a spade. 2. make or get by digging. — n. [Col.] sarcastic remark.

di·gest' (-jest') v. 1. summary. 2. change (food) in the stomach, etc. so that it can be absorbed. 2. absorb mentally. —**di·gest'i·ble,** a. — **di·ges'tion,** n.

dig'it (dij'-) n. 1. any number from 0 to 9. 2. a finger or toe.

dig'ni·fy (-fī) v. [-FIED, -FYING] give dignity to.

dig'ni·tar'y, n. [pl. -IES] person of high position.

dig'ni·ty, n. 1. worthiness. 2. high repute; honor. 3. calm stateliness.

di·gress', v. wander from the subject, as in talking. — **di·gres'sion,** n.

dike, n. embankment to hold back the sea, etc.

di·lap'i·dat·ed (-dăt'-) a. falling to pieces.

di·late', v. make or become wider. —**di·la'tion,** n.

dil'a·to'ry, a. 1. causing delay. 2. slow.

di·lem'ma, n. perplexing situation.

dil'et·tan'te (-tan'ti, -tänt') n. dabbler in the arts.

dil'i·gent, a. careful and industrious. —**dil'i·gence,** n.

dill, n. plant with aromatic seeds.

dil'ly·dal'ly, v. [-LIED, -LYING] waste time.

di·lute', v. weaken as by mixing with water. —a. diluted. —**di·lu'tion,** n.

dim, a. [DIMMER, DIMMEST] not bright or clear. —v. [DIMMED, DIMMING] make or grow dim. —**dim'ly,** adv.

dime, n. silver coin equal to ten cents.

di·men'sion, n. 1. any measurable extent. 2. pl. measurement in length, breadth, and, often, height.

di·min'ish, v. lessen.

di·min'u·tive, a. tiny.

dim'i·ty, n. a thin cotton cloth.

dim'ple, n. small, natural hollow, as on the cheek. —v. [DINNED, DINNING] 1. make a din. 2. keep repeating.

din, n. confused clamor. —v. [DINNED, DINNING] 1. make a din. 2. keep repeating.

dine, v. 1. eat dinner. 2. give dinner to.

din'er (dīn'-)? n. 1. railroad car for serving meals. 2. restaurant built like this.

di·nette (dī-net')? n. small dining room or alcove.

din'gy (-ji) a. [-GIER, -GIEST] dirty; shabby.

din'ner, n. chief daily meal.

di'no·saur (-sôr) n. huge extinct reptile.

dint, n. force.

di'o·cese (-sēs) n. district headed by a bishop. —**di·oc'e·san** (-os'ə-s'n) a.

di·ox'ide, n. oxide with two oxygen atoms per molecule.

dip, v. [DIPPED, DIPPING] 1. plunge into liquid for a moment. 2. scoop up. 3. sink or slope down. —n. 1. a dipping. 2. downward slope.

diph·the'ri·a (dif-thēr'i-, dip-)? n. acute infectious disease of throat.

diph'thong, n. sound made by two glided vowels.

di·plo'ma, n. certificate of graduation from a school.

di·plo'ma·cy, n. 1. the conducting of relations between nations. 2. tact. —**dip'lo·mat**, n. —**dip'lo·mat'ic**, a.

dip'per, n. long-handled cup, etc. for dipping.

dip·so·ma'ni·a, n. insatiable desire for alcoholic drink. —**dip·so·ma'ni·ac**, n.

dire, a. dreadful; terrible.

di·rect', a. 1. straight. 2. immediate. 3. complete. —v. 1. manage; guide. 2. order. 3. aim. —adv. directly. —**di·rect'ly**, adv. —**di·rec'tor**, n.

di·rec'tion, n. 1. management; guidance. 2. pl. instructions. 3. an order. 4. the point one faces or moves toward. —**di·rec'tion·al**, a.

di·rec'tive, n. an order.

di·rec'to·ry, n. [pl. -RIES] book of names and addresses of a specific group.

dire'ful, a. dire.

dirge, n. song of mourning.

dir'i·gi·ble, n. cigar-shaped balloon that can be steered.

dirt, n. 1. dust, filth, etc. 2. earth; soil.

dirt'y, a. [-IER, -IEST] 1. soiled. 2. obscene. 3. mean. 4. rough. —v. [-IED, -YING] to soil. —**dirt'i·ness**, n.

dis-, pref. 1. the opposite of. 2. reverse the action of.

dis·a'ble, v. make unable or unfit; cripple. —**dis·a·bil'i·ty** [pl. -TIES] n.

dis·a·buse', v. rid of false ideas.

dis·ad·van'tage, n. drawback; handicap; detriment. —**dis·ad·van·ta'geous**, a.

dis·af·fect', v. make hostile. —**dis·af·fec'tion**, n.

dis·a·gree', v. 1. differ. 2. quarrel. 3. be harmful. —**dis·a·gree'ment**, n.

dis·a·gree'a·ble, a. 1. unpleasant. 2. quarrelsome.

dis·ap·pear', v. 1. go out of sight. 2. cease being. —**dis·ap·pear'ance**, n.

dis·ap·point', v. spoil the hopes of. —**dis·ap·point'ment**, n.

dis·ap·prove', v. 1. have an unfavorable opinion. 2. reject. —**dis·ap·prov'al**, n.

dis·arm', v. 1. remove weapons from. 2. make friendly. 3. reduce armed forces. —**dis·ar'ma·ment**, n.

dis·ar·range', v. disorder. —**dis·ar·range'ment**, n.

dis·ar·ray', n. & v. disorder.

dis·as'ter, n. sudden misfortune; calamity. —**dis·as'trous**, a.

dis·a·vow', v. deny knowing or approving. —**dis·a·vow'al**, n.

dis·band', v. break up.

dis·bar', v. [-BARRED, -BARRING] deprive of the right to practice law.

dis·be·lieve', v. fail to believe (in). —**dis·be·lief'**, n.

dis·burse', v. pay out.

disc, n. disk.

dis·card', v. throw away. —n. (dis'kärd) thing discarded.

dis·cern' (di-zürn') v. perceive. —**dis·cern'i·ble**, a.

dis·charge', v. 1. dismiss. 2. unload. 3. shoot. 4. emit. 5. do (a duty). —n. a discharging or thing discharged.

dis·ci'ple, n. follower; pupil.

dis'ci·pli·nar'i·an, n. enforcer of discipline.

dis'ci·pline (-plin) n. 1. orderly training or conduct. 2. punishment. —v. 1. train; control. 2. punish. —**dis'ci·pli·nar'y**, a.

dis·claim′, v. disown; deny.

dis·close′ (-klōz′) v. reveal. —**dis·clos′ure**, n.

dis·col′or, v. to stain; tarnish. —**dis·col′or·a′tion**, n.

dis·com′fit, v. upset; embarrass. —**dis·com′fi·ture**, n.

dis·com′fort, n. lack of comfort or cause of this.

dis·com·mode′, v. to inconvenience.

dis·con·cert′, v. confuse.

dis·con·nect′, v. to separate.

dis·con′so·late (-lit) a. very unhappy.

dis·con·tent′, adj. not contented: also **dis′con·tent′ed**. —n. dissatisfaction.

dis·con·tin′ue, v. to stop.

dis′cord, n. 1. disagreement. 2. dissonance; harsh sound. —**dis·cord′ant**, a.

dis′count, v. 1. deduct, as from a price. 2. disregard in part or entirely. —n. deduction.

dis·cour′age, v. 1. deprive of hope or confidence. 2. dissuade. 3. work against. —n.

dis′course, n. talk or formal lecture. —v. to talk.

dis·cour′te·ous, a. impolite. —**dis·cour′te·sy**, n.

dis·cov′er, v. 1. be the first to find, see, etc. 2. find out. —**dis·cov′er·y** [pl. -IES] n.

dis·cred′it, v. 1. disbelieve. 2. cast doubt on. 3. disgrace. —n. 1. doubt. 2. disgrace.

dis·creet′, a. careful; prudent. —**dis·creet′ly**, adv.

dis·crep′an·cy [pl. -CIES] n. inconsistency.

dis·cre′tion (-kresh′ən) n. 1. freedom to decide. 2. prudence.

dis·crim′i·nate, v. 1. distinguish. 2. show partiality. —**dis·crim′i·na′tion**, n. —**dis·crim′i·na·to′ry**, a.

dis·cur′sive, a. rambling.

dis′cus, n. heavy disk thrown in a contest.

dis·cuss′, v. talk or write about. —**dis·cus′sion**, n.

dis·dain′, v. & n. scorn. —**dis·dain′ful**, a.

dis·ease′ (di-zēz′) n. (an) illness. —**dis·eased′**, a.

dis·em·bark′, v. go ashore.

dis·em·bod′y, v. [-BODIED, -BODYING] to free from bodily existence.

dis·en·chant′, v. to free from a false idea.

dis·en·gage′, v. disconnect.

dis·fa′vor, n. 1. dislike. 2. a being disliked.

dis·fig′ure, v. spoil the looks of; mar.

dis·gorge′, v. 1. to vomit. 2. pour forth.

dis·grace′, n. shame; dishonor. —v. bring shame upon. —**dis·grace′ful**, a.

dis·grun′tle, v. make sulky.

dis·guise′ (-gīz′) v. make unrecognizable. —n. thing used for disguising.

dis·gust′, n. sickening dislike; loathing. —v. cause disgust in. —**dis·gust′ed**, a.

dish, n. 1. plate, etc. for food. 2. kind of food.

dis·heart′en, v. discourage.

dis·shev′el, v. muss up (hair, etc.); rumple.

dis·hon′est, a. not honest. —**dis·hon′es·ty**, n.

dis·hon′or, n. & v. shame; disgrace. —**dis·hon′or·a·ble**, a.

dis·il·lu′sion, v. to free from illusion.

dis·in·fect′, v. kill bacteria in. —**dis·in·fect′ant**, n.

dis·in·her′it, v. deprive of an inheritance.

dis·in′te·grate, v. separate into parts; break up. —**dis·in′te·gra′tion**, n.

dis·in′ter·est·ed, a. 1. impartial. 2. [Col.] indifferent.

dis·joint′, v. 1. put out of joint. 2. dismember.

disk, n. 1. thin, flat, circular thing. 2. phonograph record. Also sp. **disc**.

disk jockey, one who conducts a radio record program.

dis·like′, v. & n. (have) a feeling of not liking.

dis·lo·cate′, v. 1. put out of joint. 2. disarrange. —**dis′lo·ca′tion**, n.

dis·lodge′, v. force from its place.

dis·loy′al, a. not loyal. —**dis·loy′al·ty**, n.

dis′mal (diz′-) a. dreary.

dis·man′tle, v. take apart.

dis·may′, v. make afraid; daunt. —n. loss of courage.

dis·mem′ber, v. tear apart.

dis·miss′, v. 1. request or allow to leave. 2. discharge. 3. set aside. —**dis·miss′al**, n.

dis·mount′, v. 1. get off. 2. take from its mounting.

dis·o·bey′, v. refuse or fail to obey. —**dis·o·be′di·ence**, n. —**dis·o·be′di·ent**, a.

dis·or′der, n. 1. confusion. 2. commotion; riot. 3. ailment. —v. cause disorder in. —**dis·or′der·ly**, a.

dis·or′gan·ize, v. throw into confusion. —**dis·or′gan·i·za′tion**, n.

dis·own′, v. refuse to acknowledge as one's own.

dis·par′age, v. belittle.

dis·par′i·ty, n. [pl. -TIES] difference; unlikeness.

dis·pas′sion·ate (-it) a. free from emotion or bias.

dis·patch′, v. 1. send. 2. finish quickly. 3. kill. —n. 1. speed. 2. message. 3. news story. —**dis·patch′er**, n.

dis·pel′, v. [-PELLED, -PELLING] drive away.

dis·pen′sa·ry, n. [pl. -RIES] place in a school, etc. for getting medicines or first aid.

dis·pense′, v. 1. deal out. 2. prepare and give out. —dispense with, do without. —**dis·pen·sa′tion**, n.

dis·perse′, v. scatter. —**dis·pers′al**, n. —**dis·per′sion**, n.

dis·pir′it·ed, a. dejected.

dis·place′, v. 1. move from its usual place. 2. replace. —**dis·place′ment**, n.

dis·play′, v. to show; exhibit. —n. exhibition.

dis·please′, v. annoy; offend. —**dis·pleas′ure**, n.

dis·port′, v. 1. to play. 2. amuse (oneself).

dis·pose′, v. 1. arrange. 2. incline mentally. —dispose of, 1. settle. 2. get rid of. —**dis·pos′a·ble**, a. —**dis·pos′al**, n. —**dis·po·si′tion**, n.

dis·pos·sess′, v. force to give up property; oust.

dis·pro·por′tion, n. lack of proportion.

dis·prove′, v. prove false.

dis·pute′, v. & n. 1. debate. 2. quarrel. —in dispute, not settled. —**dis·pu′ta·ble**, a. —**dis·pu·ta′tion**, n.

dis·qual′i·fy, v. [-FIED, -FYING] make ineligible.

dis·qui′et, v. make uneasy.

dis·re·gard′, v. ignore. —n. lack of attention.

dis·re·pair′, n. worn state.

dis·re·pute′, n. bad reputation. —**dis·rep′u·ta·ble**, a.

dis·re·spect′, n. lack of respect. —**dis·re·spect′ful**, a.

dis·robe′, v. undress.

dis·rupt′, v. 1. break up; disorder. —**dis·rup′tion**, n.

dis·sat·is·fy′, v. [-FIED, -FYING] make discontented. —**dis·sat·is·fac′tion**, n.

dis·sect′, v. 1. cut apart so as to examine. 2. analyze closely. —**dis·sec′tion**, n.

dis·sem′ble, v. feign; pretend.

dis·sem′i·nate, v. spread widely. —**dis·sem′i·na′tion**, n.

dis·sen′sion, n. strife.

dis·sent′, v. disagree. —n. difference of opinion.

dis·ser·ta′tion, n. formal discourse; thesis.

dis·serv′ice, n. harm.

dis·si′dence, n. disagreement. —**dis′si·dent**, a. & n.

dis·sim′i·lar, a. not alike.

dis′si·pate, v. 1. vanish or dispel. 2. squander. 3. indulge in wild, harmful pleasure. —**dis′si·pa′tion**, n.

dis·so′ci·ate (-sō′shi-) v. sever association (with).

dis′so·lute, a. dissipated and immoral.

dis·so·lu′tion, n. a dissolving or breaking up.

dis·solve′, v. 1. melt. 2. pass or make pass into solution. 3. break up. 4. end. 5. disappear or make disappear.

dis′so·nance, n. lack of harmony, esp. in sound; discord. —**dis′so·nant**, a.

dis·suade′ (-swād′) v. cause to turn from a purpose.

dis′taff, n. staff for holding flax, wool, etc. in spinning.

dis′tance, n. 1. length between two points. 2. aloofness. 3. faraway place.

dis′tant, a. 1. far apart; remote. 2. away. 3. aloof.

dis·taste′, n. dislike.

dis·tend′, v. swell.

dis·till′, v. subject to or obtain by distillation.

dis·til·la′tion, n. process of purifying a mixture by heating it and condensing the resulting vapor.

dis·till′er·y, n. [pl. -IES] place for distilling alcoholic liquors. —**dis·till′er**, n.

dis·tinct′, a. 1. not alike. 2. separate. 3. definite.

dis·tinc′tion, n. 1. a keeping distinct. 2. quality that differentiates. 3. fame; eminence.

dis·tinc′tive, a. making distinct.

dis·tin′guish (-tiŋ′gwish) v. 1. perceive or show a difference. 2. classify. 3. make famous. —**dis·tin′guish·a·ble**, a. —**dis·tin′guished**, a.

dis·tort′, v. 1. twist out of shape. 2. misrepresent.

dis·tract′, v. 1. divert (the mind, etc.). 2. confuse. 3. derange. —**dis·trac′tion**, n.

dis·traught′ (-strôt′) a. 1. harassed. 2. crazed.

dis·tress', *v. & n.* pain, trouble, worry, etc.

dis·trib'ute, *v.* 1. deal out. 2. spread out. 3. arrange. —**dis'tri·bu'tion**, *n.*

dis·trib'u·tor, *n.* 1. one who distributes, deals in a product, etc. 2. device distributing electricity to spark plugs in a gasoline engine.

dis'trict, *n.* 1. division of a state, etc. 2. region.

district attorney, prosecuting attorney of a district.

dis·trust', *v.* 1. lack of trust. —*v.* to doubt; mistrust.

dis·turb', *v.* 1. break up the quiet or settled order of. 2. make uneasy. 3. interrupt. —**dis·turb'ance**, *n.*

dis·use' (-ūs') *n.* lack of use.

ditch, *n.* channel dug out for drainage, etc. —*v.* [Sl.] get rid of.

dith'er, *n.* excited state.

ditto mark, mark (") in lists showing the item above is to be repeated.

dit'ty, *n.* [*pl.* **-TIES**] short, simple song.

di·ur'nal, *a.* daily.

dive, *v.* [alt. pt. **DOVE**] 1. plunge head first into water. 2. submerge. 3. plunge suddenly or deeply. —*n.* 1. sudden plunge. 2. [Col.] cheap saloon.

di·verge' (-vûrj') *v.* 1. branch off. 2. deviate.

di'vers (-vērz) *a.* various.

di·verse', *a.* 1. different. 2. varied.

di·ver'si·fy, *v.* [**-FIED, -FY-ING**] vary.

di·ver'sion, *n.* 1. a diverting. 2. pastime; amusement.

di·ver'si·ty, *n.* variety.

di·vert', *v.* 1. turn aside (*from*). 2. amuse.

di·vest', *v.* strip (*of*).

di·vide', *v.* 1. separate into parts. 2. apportion. 3. *Math.* separate into equal parts by a divisor. —*n.* ridge. —**di·vis'i·ble**, *a.*

div'i·dend, *n.* 1. number to be divided. 2. sum divided among stockholders, etc.

di·vine', *a.* 1. of God or a god. 2. supremely good. —*n.* clergyman. —*v.* 1. prophesy. 2. guess.

di·vin'i·ty (-vin'-) *n.* 1. a being divine. 2. a god.

di·vi'sion, *n.* 1. a dividing. 2. thing that divides. 3. segment, group, etc. 4. section of an army corps.

di·vi'sor, *n.* number by which the dividend is divided.

di·vorce', *n.* 1. legal dissolution of a marriage. 2. separation. —*v.* separate from, as by divorce.

di·vor·cée' (-sā') *n.* divorced woman.

div'ot (div'-) *n.* turf dislodged by a golf club.

di·vulge', *v.* make known.

diz'zy, *a.* [**-ZIER, -ZIEST**] 1. giddy; confused. 2. causing dizziness. —**diz'zi·ly**, *adv.* —**diz'zi·ness**, *n.*

do, *v.* [**DID, DONE, DOING**] 1. perform (an action). 2. finish. 3. cause. 4. deal with as required. 5. have to do with one's work. 6. get along. 7. be adequate. —**do away with**, 1. get rid of. 2. kill. —**do without**, get along without. —**have to do with**, relate to. —**do'er**, *n.*

do'cile (dos'l) *a.* easy to train. —**do·cil'i·ty**, *n.*

dock, *n.* 1. landing pier; wharf. 2. water between piers. 3. place for the accused in a courtroom. —*v.* 1. bring or come to a dock. 2. cut short. 3. deduct from.

dock'et, *n.* list of cases to be tried by a law court.

doc'tor, *n.* 1. person with the highest degree from a university. 2. physician or surgeon. —*v.* [Col.] 1. try to heal. 2. tamper with.

doc'trine (-trin) *n.* something taught, as a religious tenet.

doc'u·ment, *n.* written record relied on as evidence.

doc'u·men'ta·ry, *a.* 1. of or supported by documents. 2. recording news events dramatically. —*n.* [*pl.* **-RIES**] documentary film, etc.

dod'der, *v.* shake as from old age.

dodge, *v.* 1. move quickly aside. 2. avoid; evade. —*n.* 1. a dodging. 2. trick.

do'do, *n.* large extinct bird.

doe (dō) *n.* female deer, etc. —**doe'skin**, *n.*

does (duz) pres. t. of **do**: used with *he, she,* or *it.*

does'n't, does not.

doff, *v.* take off; remove.

dog, *n.* 1. domesticated animal of the wolf family. 2. mean fellow. —*v.* [**DOGGED, DOGGING**] follow like a dog.

dog'-eared', *n.* turned-down corner of a page. —**dog'-eared'**, *a.*

dog'ged, *a.* stubborn.

dog'ger·el, *n.* trivial verse.

do·gie (dō'gi) *n.* stray calf.

dog′ma, _n._ strict doctrine.

dog·mat′ic, _a._ 1. of a dogma. 2. positive in stating opinion; arrogant. —**dog·mat′i·cal·ly,** _adv._ —**dog′ma·tism,** _n._

dog′wood, _n._ tree with pink or white flowers.

doi′ly, _n._ [_pl._ -LIES] small mat to protect a table, etc.

do′ings, _n.pl._ actions.

dol′drums, _n.pl._ low spirits.

dole, _n._ money paid to the unemployed by the government. —_v._ give sparingly.

dole′ful, _a._ sad; sorrowful.

doll, _n._ child's toy made to resemble a person.

dol′lar, _n._ U.S. monetary unit, equal to 100 cents.

dol′ly, _n._ [_pl._ -IES] 1. doll. 2. low, wheeled frame for moving heavy objects.

dol′or·ous, _a._ sorrowful.

dol′phin, _n._ sea mammal with a beaklike snout.

dolt (dōlt) _n._ stupid person.

-dom, _suf._ 1. rank or domain of. 2. state of being.

do·main′ (dō-) _n._ 1. territory under one ruler. 2. field of activity.

dome, _n._ large, round roof.

do·mes′tic, _a._ 1. of home or family. 2. of one's country. 3. tame. —_n._ a maid, cook, etc. —**do·mes′ti·cal·ly,**_adv._ —**do·mes·tic′i·ty,** _n._

do·mes′ti·cate, _v._ to tame. —**do·mes·ti·ca′tion,** _n._

dom′i·cile (-sil) _n._ home.

dom′i·nate, _v._ 1. rule or control. 2. rise high above. —**dom′i·nance,** _n._—**dom′i·nant,** _a._ —**dom′i·na′tion,** _n._

dom·i·neer′, _v._ rule harshly.

do·min′ion, _n._ 1. rule; power. 2. governed territory.

dom′i·noes, _n._ game with tiles marked with dots.

don, _v._ [DONNED, DONNING] put on (clothes).

do′nate, _v._ give; contribute. —**do·na′tion,** _n._

done, _pp._ of do.

don′key, _n._ [_pl._ -KEYS] horse-like animal with long ears.

do′nor, _n._ one who donates.

don′t, do not.

doo′dle, _v. & n._ scribble.

doom, _n._ 1. a judgment. 2. fate. 3. ruin. —_v._ 1. condemn. 2. destine; fate.

door, _n._ 1. movable panel for closing an entrance. 2. entrance, with or without a door: also **door′way.** —**out of doors,** outdoors.

dope, _n._ [Sl.] 1. narcotic. 2.

information. 3. stupid person. —_v._ to drug.

dor′mant, _a._ 1. sleeping. 2. quiet; inactive.

dor′mer, _n._ upright window structure in a sloping roof.

dor′mi·to·ry, _n._ [_pl._ -RIES] 1. room with many beds. 2. building with many bedrooms.

dor′mouse, _n._ [_pl._ -MICE] small, squirrellike rodent.

dor′sal, _a._ of the back.

do′ry, _n._ [_pl._ -RIES] small, flat-bottomed fishing boat.

dose, _n._ amount of medicine taken at one time. —_v._ give doses to. —**dos′age,** _n._

dost [Ar.] do: used with _thou._

dot, _n._ tiny mark or round spot. —_v._ [DOTTED, DOTTING] mark with dots.

dot′age (dōt′ij) _n._ feebleness of old age.

dote, _v._ be too fond.

doth, [Ar.] does.

dou′ble, _a._ 1. of or for two. 2. twice as much or as many. —_adv._ twofold or twice. —_n._ 1. twice as much or as many. 2. a duplicate. 3. _Baseball_ hit putting the batter on second. —_v._ 1. make or become double. 2. fold. 3. duplicate. 4. turn backward. 5. serve two purposes, etc.

dou′ble-cross′, _v. & n._ [Sl.] betray(al).

dou′blet (dub′-) _n._ formerly, man's tight jacket.

dou′bly, _adv._ twice.

doubt (dout) _v._ 1. be uncertain about. 2. disbelieve. —_n._ 1. wavering of belief. 2. uncertainty. —**no doubt,** certainly. —**doubt′ful,** _a._

doubt′less, _adv._ certainly.

douche (dōōsh) _n._ liquid jet for cleaning a body part. —_v._ use a douche on.

dough, _n._ 1. thick mixture of flour, liquid, etc. for baking. 2. [Sl.] money.

dough′nut, _n._ small fried cake, usually ring-shaped.

dour (dōōr, dour) _a._ gloomy.

douse (dous) _v._ 1. thrust into liquid. 2. drench. 3. [Col.] extinguish (a light).

dove (duv) _n._ kind of pigeon.

dove′tail, _n._ joint formed by fitting together wedge-shaped parts. —_v._ join closely, as with dovetails.

dow′a·ger (-jēr) _n._ wealthy widow.

dow′dy, _a._ [-DIER, -DIEST] not neat or not stylish.

dow′el, _n._ peg fitted into

holes to join two pieces.

dow'er, *n.* widow's inheritance. —*v.* endow.

down, *adv.* 1. to or in a lower place, state, etc. 2. to a later time. 3. in cash. 4. in writing. —*a.* 1. descending. 2. in a lower place. 3. gone, paid, etc. down. 4. discouraged. —*prep.* down toward, into, etc. —*v.* put down. —*n.* 1. descent. 2. misfortune. 3. soft feathers or hair. 4. *pl.* high, grassy land. —**down with!** overthrow!

down'cast, *a.* 1. directed downward. 2. sad.

down'fall, *n.* sudden fall, as from power.

down'grade, *n.* downward slope. —*adv.* & *a.* down. —*v.* demote.

down'heart'ed, *a.* sad.

down'hill, *adv.* & *a.* down a slope; downward.

down'pour, *n.* heavy rain.

down'right, *adv.* thoroughly. —*a.* 1. utter. 2. plain.

down'trod'den, *a.* oppressed.

down'ward, *adv.* & *a.* toward a lower place, etc.: also **down'wards,** *adv.*

down'y, *a.* soft and fluffy.

dow'ry, *n.* property a bride brings to her husband.

doze, *n.* & *v.* sleep; nap.

doz'en, *n.* set of twelve.

Dr., Doctor.

drab, *a.* [DRABBER, DRABBEST] dull. —**drab'ness,** *n.*

draft, *n.* 1. drink. 2. rough sketch of a writing. 3. plan. 4. current of air. 5. written order for money. 6. selection for compulsory military service. 7. depth of water a ship displaces. —*v.* 1. select to serve. 2. make a plan, outline, etc. for. —*a.* drawn from a cask.

draf·tee', *n.* one drafted for military service.

drafts'man, *n.* [*pl.* -MEN] one who draws plans of structures or machinery.

draft'y, *a.* [-IER, -IEST] open to drafts of air.

drag, *v.* [DRAGGED, DRAGGING] 1. pull or be pulled with effort, esp. along the ground. 2. search (a river bottom, etc.) as with a net. 3. pass slowly. —*n.* 1. hindrance. 2. [Sl.] puff of a cigarette. etc.

drag'net, *n.* 1. net dragged along water bottom. 2. system for catching criminals.

drag'on, *n.* large, mythical reptile breathing out fire.

drag'on·fly, *n.* [*pl.* -FLIES] long insect with four wings.

drain, *v.* 1. draw off (liquid, etc.) gradually. 2. empty. 3. exhaust, as energy. 4. flow off. —*n.* channel; pipe.

drain'age (-ij) *n.* 1. a draining or system for draining. 2. that which is drained off.

drake (drāk) *n.* male duck.

dram, *n.* 1. apothecaries' weight, ⅛ oz. 2. small drink of alcoholic liquor.

dra'ma, *n.* 1. a play. 2. art of writing & staging plays.

dra·mat'ic, *a.* 1. of drama. 2. vivid, exciting, etc.

dra·mat'ics, *n.* performing or producing of plays.

dram'a·tist, *n.* playwright.

dram'a·tize, *v.* 1. make into a drama. 2. regard or show in a dramatic manner.

drank, pt. of **drink.**

drape, *v.* cover or hang as with cloth in loose folds. —*n.* usually in *pl.* curtain.

dra'per·y, *n.* [*pl.* -IES] curtain.

dras'tic, *a.* severe; harsh.

draught (draft) *n.*, *v.*, *a.* draft.

draw, *v.* [DREW, DRAWN, DRAWING] 1. pull. 2. attract. 3. inhale. 4. take out; get. 5. come; move. 6. write (a check). 7. deduce. 8. stretch. 9. make (lines, pictures, etc.) as with a pencil. —*n.* 1. stalemate. 2. thing that attracts.

draw'back, *n.* disadvantage.

draw'bridge, *n.* bridge that can be raised.

drawer (drôr) *n.* 1. sliding box in a table, etc. 2. *pl.* underpants.

draw'ing, *n.* 1. art of sketching. 2. picture sketched.

drawing room, parlor.

drawl, *n.* slow, prolonged manner of speech. —*v.* speak with a drawl.

drawn, *a.* haggard.

dread (dred) *v.* await with fear or distaste. —*n.* fear. —*a.* inspiring fear. —**dread'ful,** *a.*

dream, *n.* 1. images, etc. seen during sleep. 2. reverie. 3. fond hope. —*v.* [alt. pt. & pp. DREAMT (dremt)] have dreams. —**dream'y,** *a.*

drear'y, *a.* [-IER, -IEST] dismal. —**drear'i·ness,** *n.*

dredge, *n.* apparatus for scooping up mud, etc. as in deepening channels. —*v.* 1. enlarge with a dredge. 2.

sprinkle with flour.

dregs, *n.pl.* 1. particles at the bottom in a liquid. 2. most worthless part.

drench, *v.* soak.

dress, *v.* 1. clothe. 2. adorn. 3. treat (a wound, etc.). 4. prepare, as a fowl. —*n.* 1. clothes. 2. woman's garment. —**dress'mak'er,** *n.*

dress'er, *n.* chest of drawers with a mirror.

dress'ing, *n.* 1. bandages, etc. 2. salad sauce. 3. stuffing for roast fowl.

dress'y, *a.* [-IER, -IEST] [Col.] elegant.

drew (drōō) *pt.* of **draw.**

drib'ble, *v.* 1. flow in drops. 2. drool. —*n.* dribbling flow.

drib'let, *n.* small amount.

dried, *pt. & pp.* of **dry.**

dri'er, *n.* device or substance that dries.

drift, *v.* be carried along, as by a current. —*n.* 1. snow, etc. driven into a heap. 2. trend. 3. meaning. —**drift'er,** *n.*

drift'wood, *n.* wood that has drifted ashore.

drill, *n.* 1. tool for boring. 2. systematic training. 3. seeding machine. 4. coarse, twilled cloth. —*v.* 1. bore with a drill. 2. train systematically. —**drill'er,** *n.*

drink, *v.* [DRANK, DRUNK, DRINKING] swallow (liquid). —*n.* 1. liquid for drinking. 2. alcoholic liquor.

drip, *v.* [DRIPPED, DRIPPING] fall or let fall in drops. —*n.* a dripping.

drive, *v.* [DROVE, DRIVEN, DRIVING] 1. force to go, do, pierce, etc. 2. operate, or go in, a vehicle. —*n.* 1. trip in a vehicle. 2. paved road. 3. energy. 4. urge. 5. campaign. —**drive at,** to mean. —**driv'er,** *n.*

drive'-in', *n.* place for eating, etc. in one's car.

driv'el, *v.* to slobber; drool. —*n.* silly talk.

drive'way, *n.* path for cars.

driz'zle, *v. & n.* rain in fine, mistlike drops.

droll, *a.* quaintly amusing.

drom'e·dar'y, *n.* [*pl.* -IES] one-humped camel.

drone, *n.* 1. male honeybee. 2. constant hum. —*v.* 1. to hum. 2. talk monotonously.

drool, *v.* drip saliva.

droop, *v.* 1. sink or bend down. 2. lose vitality. —*n.* a drooping. —**droop'y** [-IER, -IEST] *a.* —**droop'i·ly,** *adv.*

drop, *n.* 1. small, round mass, as of falling liquid. 2. tiny amount. 3. sudden fall. 4. distance down. —*v.* [DROPPED, DROPPING] 1. fall or let fall. 2. to send. 3. utter (a hint, etc.). —**drop in,** visit. —**drop out,** stop taking part. —**drop'per,** *n.*

drop'sy, *n.* abnormal amount of fluid in the body.

dross, *n.* rubbish; refuse.

drought (drout) *n.* spell of dry weather: also **drouth.**

drove, *pt.* of **drive.** —*n.* herd of cattle, etc.

drown, *v.* 1. die or kill by suffocation in water. 2. muffle (sound, etc.).

drowse, *v.* be sleepy; doze. —**drow'sy,** *a.*

drub, *v.* [DRUBBED, DRUBBING] 1. thrash. 2. defeat. —**drub'bing,** *n.*

drudge, *n.* one who does hard or dull work. —*v.* do such work. —**drudg'er·y,** *n.*

drug, *n.* 1. medicinal substance. 2. narcotic. —*v.* [DRUGGED, DRUGGING] add or give a drug to.

drug'gist, *n.* pharmacist. —**drug'store,** *n.*

drum, *n.* 1. hollow form covered with a membrane and used as a percussion instrument. 2. container, as for oil. 3. eardrum. —*v.* [DRUMMED, DRUMMING] beat as on a drum. —**drum up,** solicit (business). —**drum'mer,** *n.*

drum major, one who leads a marching band. —**drum ma'jor·ette'** (-et') *fem.*

drum'stick, *n.* 1. stick for beating a drum. 2. lower leg of a cooked fowl.

drunk, *pp.* of **drink.** —*a.* overcome by alcohol. —*n.* [Sl.] drunken person. —**drunk'ard,** *n.*

drunk'en, *a.* intoxicated. —**drunk'en·ness,** *n.*

dry, *a.* [DRIER, DRIEST] 1. not wet. 2. lacking rain. 3. thirsty. 4. not sweet. 5. matter-of-fact. 6. dull. —*v.* [DRIED, DRYING] make or become dry. —**dry'ly,** *adv.*

dry'-clean', *v.* to clean (garments) with a solvent, as naphtha. —**dry' cleaner.**

dry'er, *n.* a drier.

dry goods, cloth (products).

dry ice, carbon dioxide in a solid state.

du'al, *a.* 1. of two. 2. double.

dub, *v.* [DUBBED, DUBBING] confer a title upon.

du'bi·ous, *a.* doubtful.

du'cal, *a.* of a duke.

duch'ess, *n.* duke's wife.

duch'y, *n.* [*pl.* -IES] land ruled by a duke.

duck, *n.* 1. flat-billed, web-footed swimming bird. 2. cloth like canvas but lighter. —*v.* 1. dip under water briefly. 2. bend suddenly, as to avoid a blow. 3. avoid.

duck'bill, *n.* small, egg-laying water mammal.

duck'ling, *n.* young duck.

duct, *n.* tube or channel for fluid. —**duct'less,** *a.*

duc'tile, *a.* 1. that can be drawn thin. 2. easily led.

dude, *n.* dandy; fop.

dudg'eon (duj'ən) *n.* anger.

due, *a.* 1. owed. 2. suitable. 3. expected to arrive. —*adv.* exactly. —*n.* anything due. —**due to** 1. caused by. 2. [Col.] because of.

du'el, *n.* planned formal fight between two armed persons. —*v.* fight a duel. —**du'el·ist,** *n.*

dues, *n.pl.* 1. fee or tax. 2. money paid for membership.

du·et', *n.* musical composition for two performers.

dug, *pt.* & *pp.* of **dig.**

dug'out, *n.* 1. boat hollowed out of a log. 2. hole dug as a bomb shelter.

duke, *n.* nobleman next to a prince. —**duke'dom,** *n.*

dul'cet, *a.* pleasant to hear.

dull, *a.* 1. stupid. 2. sluggish. 3. boring. 4. not sharp. 5. not bright. —*v.* make or become dull. —**dul'ly,** *adv.*

dull'ard, *n.* stupid person.

du'ly, *adv.* properly.

dumb, *a.* 1. unable to talk. 2. silent. 3. [Col.] stupid. —**dumb'ly,** *adv.*

dumb'bell, *n.* short bar joining two weights, used in exercising.

dum·found', dumb-found', *v.* make speechless; amaze.

dum'my, *n.* [*pl.* -MIES] 1. humanlike figure for displaying clothes. 2. imitation. —*a.* sham.

dump, *v.* 1. unload in a heap. 2. throw away. —*n.* place for dumping rubbish. —**in the dumps,** dejected.

dump'ling, *n.* 1. piece of baked dough. 2. baked crust filled with fruit.

dun, *a.* dull grayish-brown. —*v.* [DUNNED, DUNNING] demand money owed.

dunce, *n.* stupid person.

dune, *n.* hill of drifted sand.

dung, *n.* animal excrement.

dun·ga·ree', *n.pl.* work clothes of coarse cotton.

dun'geon (-jən) *n.* dark underground prison.

du'o, *n.* [*pl.* -OS] performers of a duet.

du'o·de'num (-dē'-) *n.* first section of small intestine.

dupe, *n.* person easily tricked. —*v.* deceive.

du'plex, *n.* house with two separate family units.

du'pli·cate (-kit) *a.* 1. double. 2. exactly alike. —*n.* exact copy. —*v.* (-kāt) 1. make a copy of. 2. make happen again. —**du'pli·ca'-tion,** *n.* —**du'pli·ca'tor,** *n.*

du·plic'i·ty (-plis'-) *n.* [*pl.* -TIES] cunning deception.

du'ra·ble, *a.* lasting a long time. —**du'ra·bil'i·ty,** *n.*

du·ra'tion, *n.* time that a thing continues or lasts.

du·ress', *n.* coercion.

dur'ing, *prep.* 1. throughout. 2. in the course of.

dusk, *n.* evening twilight. —**dusk'y** [-IER, -IEST] *a.*

dust, *n.* 1. finely powdered matter, esp. earth. 2. earth. —*v.* 1. sprinkle with powder. 2. wipe dust from. —**dust'y** [-IER, -IEST] *a.*

dust'pan, *n.* pan into which floor dust is swept.

Dutch, *a.* & *n.* (of) the people or language of the Netherlands.

du'ti·ful, *a.* showing respect; obedient: also **du'te·ous.** —**du'ti·ful·ly,** *adv.*

du'ty, *n.* [*pl.* -TIES] 1. respect owed, as to parents. 2. sense of obligation, justice, etc. 3. thing one must do. 4. tax, as on imports.

dwarf, *n.* unusually small being or thing. —*v.* 1. stunt in growth. 2. make seem small. —*a.* stunted.

dwell, *v.* [DWELT or DWELLED, DWELLING] make one's home. —**dwell on** (or **upon**), talk or think about at length.

dwell'ing (**place**), residence.

dwin'dle, *v.* decrease.

dye, *n.* coloring matter in solution. —*v.* [DYED, DYEING] color with a dye. —**dy'er,** *n.*

dy'ing, *ppr.* of **die.**

dy·nam'ic, *a.* 1. of energy. 2. energetic; forceful. —**dy·nam'i·cal·ly,** *adv.*

dy'na·mite, *n.* powerful explosive. —*v.* blow up with dynamite.

dy'na·mo, n. [pl. -MOS] device that converts mechanical energy into electricity.

dy'nas·ty, n. [pl. -TIES] family line of rulers.

dys·en'ter'y (dis'-) n. disease characterized by bloody diarrhea.

dys·pep'sia, n. indigestion.

E

each, a. & pron. every one of 2 or more. —adv. apiece.

ea'ger, a. keenly desiring.

ea'gle, n. large bird of prey with sharp vision.

ear, n. 1. organ of hearing. 2. sense of hearing. 3. attention. 4. grain-bearing spike of a cereal plant.

ear'drum, n. thin membrane inside the ear.

earl (ûrl) n. Br. nobleman.

ear'ly, adv. & a. [-LIER, -LIEST] 1. near the beginning. 2. before the expected or usual time.

ear'mark (êr'-) v. reserve for a special purpose.

earn, v. 1. receive for one's work. 2. get as deserved. 3. gain as profit.

ear'nest, a. serious or sincere. —in earnest, 1. serious. 2. with determination.

earn'ings, n.pl. 1. wages. 2. profits, interest, etc.

ear'phone, n. receiver as for a telephone, held to the ear.

ear'ring, n. ear ornament.

ear'shot, n. distance within which a sound can be heard.

earth, n. 1. the planet we live on. 2. land. 3. soil.

earth'en·ware, n. dishes, etc. made of baked clay.

earth'ly, a. 1. terrestrial. 2. worldly. 3. conceivable.

earth'quake, n. a shaking of the crust of the earth.

earth'worm, n. common worm in the soil.

earth'y, a. [-IER, -IEST] 1. of or like earth. 2. coarse.

ease, n. 1. comfort. 2. poise. 3. facility. —v. 1. to comfort. 2. relieve. 3. facilitate. 4. shift carefully.

ea·sel (ē'z'l) n. a stand to hold an artist's canvas.

eas'i·ly, adv. 1. with ease. 2. without a doubt.

east, n. 1. direction in which sunrise occurs. 2. region in this direction. 3. [E-] the Orient. —a. & adv. in, toward, or from the east. —east'er·ly, a. & adv. —east'ern, a. —east'ern·er,

n. —east'ward, a. & (also east'wards) adv.

East'er, n. spring Christian festival.

eas'y, a. [-IER, -IEST] 1. not difficult. 2. without worry, pain, etc. 3. comfortable. 4. not stiff. 5. not strict. 6. unhurried.

eas'y·go'ing, a. not worried, rushed, or strict.

eat, v. [ATE, EATEN, EATING] 1. chew and swallow (food). 2. wear away, corrode, etc. 3. make by eating.

eaves (ēvz) n.pl. projecting edge of a roof.

eaves'drop, v. [-DROPPED, -DROPPING] listen secretly.

ebb, n. & v. 1. flow back toward the sea: said of the tide. 2. decline.

eb'on·y, n. [pl. -IES] hard, dark, tropical wood.—a. black.

e·bul'lient, a. bubbling with joy. —e·bul'lience, n.

ec·cen'tric, a. 1. having its axis off center. 2. odd in conduct. —n. eccentric person. —ec'cen·tric'i·ty (-tris'-) [pl. -TIES] n.

ec·cle'si·as'tic, n. clergyman. —a. ecclesiastical.

ec·cle'si·as'ti·cal, a. of the church or clergy.

ech'e·lon (esh'-) n. 1. steplike formation of troops, ships, or planes. 2. level of command.

ech·o (ek'ō) n. [pl. -OES] repetition of a sound by reflection of sound waves. —v. 1. resound. 2. repeat.

ec·lec'tic, a. using various sources.

e·clipse', n. the obscuring of the sun by the moon, or of the moon by the earth's shadow. —v. surpass.

e·clip'tic, n. sun's apparent annual path.

e·col'o·gy, n. science dealing with organisms in their environment.

e'co·nom'ic, a. 1. of the management of income, expenditures, etc. 2. of economics.

e'co·nom'i·cal, a. thrifty. —e'co·nom'i·cal·ly, adv.

e'co·nom'ics, n. science that deals with the production, distribution, and use of wealth. —e·con'o·mist, n.

e·con'o·mize, v. be thrifty.

e·con'o·my, n. [pl. -MIES] 1. management of finances. 2. thrift. 3. system of producing and consuming wealth.

ec'ru (-rōō) *a. & n.* light tan.

ec'sta·sy, *n.* [*pl.* **-SIES**] overpowering joy. **—ec·stat'ic**, *a.*

ec·u·men'i·cal, *a.* of the Christian Church as a whole.

ec'u·men·ism, *n.* movement to unify Christian churches.

ec'ze·ma (*or* eg·zē'-) *n.* itchy, scaly skin disease.

-ed, *suf.* 1. having or being. 2. pt. and pp. ending of many verbs.

ed'dy, *n.* [*pl.* **-DIES**] little whirlpool or whirlwind. —*v.* [-DIED, -DYING] to whirl.

e·de'ma (-dē'-) *n.* dropsy.

E'den, *n. Bible* garden where Adam and Eve first lived.

edge, *n.* 1. blade's cutting side. 2. brink. 3. border. 4. [Col.] advantage. —*v.* 1. put an edge on. 2. move sideways. **—on edge**, tense.

ed'i·ble, *a.* fit to be eaten.

e'dict, *n.* public order.

ed'i·fice (-fis) *n.* large, imposing building.

ed'i·fy, *v.* [-FIED, -FYING] instruct or improve morally. **—ed·i·fi·ca'tion**, *n.*

ed'it, *v.* 1. revise, select, etc. (writing) for publication. 2. be in charge of (a newspaper, etc.). **—ed'i·tor**, *n.*

e·di'tion, *n.* 1. form in which a book is published. 2. total copies of a book, etc. published at one time.

ed·i·to'ri·al, *n.* article in a newspaper, etc. stating the opinions of the editor or publisher. —*a.* of an editor. **—ed·i·to'ri·al·ize'**, *v.*

ed'u·cate, *v.* develop the knowledge, skill, etc. of by schooling. **—ed·u·ca'tion**, *n.* **—ed'u·ca'tor**, *n.*

eel, *n.* snakelike fish.

e'er (âr) *adv.* [Poet.] ever.

ee'rie, ee'ry, *a.* [-RIER, -RIEST] weird; uncanny.

ef·face', *v.* erase; wipe out.

ef·fect', *n.* 1. a result. 2. influence. 3. meaning. 4. *pl.* belongings. —*v.* bring about. **—in effect**, 1. actually. 2. in operation. **—take effect**, begin to act.

ef·fec'tive, *a.* 1. producing a desired result. 2. in operation. **—ef·fec'tive·ly**, *adv.*

ef·fec'tu·al, *a.* effective (*sense* 1). **—ef·fec'tu·al·ly**, *adv.*

ef·fem'i·nate (-nit) *a.* showing womanly traits; unmanly.

ef·fer·vesce', *v.* to bubble. **—ef·fer·ves'cent**, *a.*

ef·fete', *a.* spent & sterile.

ef·fi·ca'cious, *a.* effective.

ef·fi'cient, *a.* effective with a minimum of effort, expense, etc. **—ef·fi'cien·cy**, *n.* **—ef·fi'cient·ly** *adv.*

ef'fi·gy, *n.* [*pl.* **-GIES**] statue or image; esp., a crude figure as for mock hanging.

ef'fort, *n.* 1. use of energy to do something. 2. attempt.

ef·fron'ter·y, *n.* impudence.

ef·fu'sive, *a.* gushing.

e.g., for example.

egg, *n.* 1. oval body from which young of birds, fish, etc. are hatched. 2. ovum. —*v.* to urge (*on*).

egg'head', *n.* [Sl.] intellectual.

egg'nog', *n.* drink made of eggs, milk, sugar, etc.

egg'plant', *n.* large, purple, pear-shaped vegetable.

e'gis (ē'jis) *n.* aegis.

e'go (ē'-) *n.* 1. the self. 2. [Col.] conceit.

e'go·cen'tric, *a.* self-centered.

e'go·tism, *n.* 1. excessive reference to oneself. 2. self-conceit. **—e'go·tist**, *n.* **—e'go·tis'ti·cal**, *a.*

e·gre'gious (-jəs) *a.* flagrant.

e'gress, *n.* an exit.

e'gret, *n.* heron having long, white plumes.

E·gyp'tian, *n. & a.* (native) of Egypt.

eh (ā, e) *int.* sound expressing surprise, doubt, etc.

ei'der (ī'-) *n.* large sea duck with soft, fine down (**eider down**).

eight, *a. & n.* one more than seven. **—eighth**, *a. & n.*

eight'een', *a. & n.* eight more than ten. **—eight'eenth'**, *a. & n.*

eight'y, *a. & n.* [*pl.* **-IES**] eight times ten. **—eight'i·eth**, *a. & n.*

ei'ther (ē'thər *or* ī'-) *a. & pron.* one or the other (of two). —*con.* correlative used with *or*. —*adv.* any more than the other.

e·jac'u·late, *v.* exclaim suddenly. **—e·jac'u·la'tion**, *n.*

e·ject', *v.* throw out; expel.

eke (ēk) *v.* barely manage to make (a living); with *out*.

e·lab'o·rate, *v.* add details. —*a.* (-rit) in great detail.

e·lapse', *v.* pass, as time.

e·las'tic, *a.* springing back to shape. —*n.* band, etc. with rubber in it. **—e·las·tic'i·ty** (-tis'-) *n.*

e·late', *v.* make proud, happy,

etc. —e·la′tion, n.

el′bow, n. joint between the upper and lower arm. —v. shove as with the elbows.

eld′er, a. older. —n. 1. older person. 2. church official. 3. shrub with dark berries.

eld′er·ber′ry, n. [pl. -RIES] 1. the elder. 2. its berry.

eld′er·ly, a. somewhat old.

eld′est, a. oldest.

e·lect′, v. select, esp. by voting. —a. chosen; selected. —e·lec′tion, n.

e·lec′tion·eer′, v. canvass votes in an election.

e·lec′tive, a. 1. filled by election. 2. optional. —n. optional subject in school.

e·lec′tor, n. 1. qualified voter. 2. member of the electoral college.

e·lec′tor·al college, assembly that formally elects the U.S. president.

e·lec′tor·ate (-it) n. the body of qualified voters.

e·lec′tric, e·lec′tri·cal, a. of, charged with, or worked by electricity.

e·lec·tri′cian (-shən) n. one who installs and repairs electrical apparatus.

e·lec·tric′i·ty (-tris′-) n. 1. form of energy with magnetic, chemical, and radiant effects. 2. electric current.

e·lec′tri·fy, v. [-FIED, -FYING] 1. equip for the use of electricity. 2. thrill.

e·lec′tro·car′di·o·gram′, n. tracing showing electrical changes in the heart.

e·lec′tro·car′di·o·graph′, n.

e·lec′tro·cute (-kūt) v. kill by electricity. —e·lec′tro·cu′tion, n.

e·lec′trode, n. terminal of an electric source.

e·lec·trol′y·sis (-trol′ə-) n. breakdown into ions of a chemical compound in solution by electrical current.

e·lec′tro·lyte (-līt) n. substance which in solution conducts electric current. —e·lec′tro·lyt′ic (-lit′-) a.

e·lec′tro·mag′net, n. soft iron core made magnetic by an electric current.

e·lec′tro·mo′tive, a. producing an electric current.

e·lec′tron, n. negatively charged particle in an atom. —e·lec′tron′ic, a.

e·lec·tron′ics, n. science of electronic action.

electron tube, electronic device used in radio, etc.

e·lec′tro·plate, v. coat with metal by electrolysis.

el′e·gant, a. tastefully luxurious. —el′e·gance, n.

el′e·gy (-ji) n. [pl. -GIES] poem lamenting a dead person. —e·le′gi·ac (-jī′-) a.

el′e·ment, n. 1. natural environment. 2. basic part or feature. 3. Chem. substance that cannot be separated into different substances except by nuclear disintegration. —the elements, wind, rain, etc. —el′e·men′tal, a.

el′e·men′ta·ry, a. of fundamentals; introductory.

el′e·phant, n. huge, thick-skinned mammal with a long trunk and ivory tusks.

el′e·vate, v. 1. raise. 2. raise in rank. 3. elate.

el′e·va′tion, n. 1. high place. 2. height, as above sea level.

el′e·va′tor, n. 1. suspended cage for hoisting or lowering goods or people. 2. warehouse for grain.

e·lev′en, a. & n. one more than ten. —e·lev′enth, a. & n.

elf, n. [pl. ELVES] small fairy. —elf′in, a.

e·lic′it (-lis′-) v. draw forth.

e·lide′, v. slur over.

el′i·gi·ble (-ji-) a. qualified. —n. eligible person. —el′i·bil′i·ty, n.

e·lim′i·nate, v. 1. remove. 2. excrete. —e·lim′i·na′tion, n.

e·lite′ (-lēt′) n. best part of a group.

e·lix′ir (-lik′sēr) n. drug in alcoholic solution.

elk, n. large deer.

ell, n. former measure of length (= 45 inches).

e·lipse′, n. closed curve that is a symmetrical oval. —e·lip′ti·cal, a.

e·lip′sis, n. omission of a word or words.

elm, n. tall shade tree.

el′o·cu′tion, n. art of public speaking.

e·lon′gate, v. lengthen. —e′lon·ga′tion, n.

e·lope′, v. run away to marry. —e·lope′ment, n.

el′o·quent, a. vivid or forceful in expression. —el′o·quence, n.

else, a. 1. different; other. 2. in addition. —adv. 1. otherwise. 2. if not.

else′where, adv. in or to some other place.

e·lu′ci·date, v. explain.

e·lude′, v. escape; evade.

e·lu'sive, *a.* hard to grasp; baffling.

elves, *n.* pl. of elf.

e·ma'ci·ate (-shi-) *v.* make thin. —**e·ma'ci·a'tion**, *n.*

em'a·nate, *v.* come or issue. —**em'a·na'tion**, *n.*

e·man'ci·pate, *v.* set free. —**e·man'ci·pa'tion**, *n.* —**e·man'ci·pa'tor**, *n.*

e·mas'cu·late, *v.* castrate.

em·balm' (-bäm') *v.* preserve (a dead body).

em·bank'ment, *n.* bank of earth, etc. as to keep back water.

em·bar'go, *n.* [*pl.* -GOES] legal restriction of commerce or shipping.

em·bark', *v.* 1. go aboard a ship. 2. begin; start. —**em'bar·ka'tion**, *n.*

em·bar'rass, *v.* make feel self-conscious.

em'bas·sy, *n.* [*pl.* -SIES] staff or headquarters of an ambassador.

em·bed', *v.* [-BEDDED, -BEDDING] set firmly (*in*).

em·bel'lish, *v.* 1. decorate. 2. add details, often untrue.

em'ber, *n.* glowing piece of coal or wood.

em·bez'zle, *v.* steal (money entrusted). —**em·bez'zler**, *n.*

em·bit'ter, *v.* make bitter.

em·bla'zon, *v.* 1. decorate. 2. display openly.

em'blem, *n.* visible symbol; sign. —**em'blem·at'ic**, *a.*

em·bod'y, *v.* [-IED, -YING] 1. give form to. 2. include. —**em·bod'i·ment**, *n.*

em'bo·lism, *n.* obstruction of a blood vessel.

em·boss', *v.* decorate with raised designs.

em·brace', *v.* 1. hug lovingly. 2. adopt, as an idea. 3. include. —*n.* an embracing.

em·broi'der, *v.* ornament with needlework. —**em·broi'der·y** [*pl.* -IES] *n.*

em·broil', *v.* get involved.

em'bry·o, *n.* [*pl.* -OS] animal or plant in earliest stages of development. —**em'bry·on'ic**, *a.*

em·cee', *v.* [-CEED, -CEEING] & *n.* [Sl.] (act as) master of ceremonies.

e·mend', *v.* correct, as a text. —**e'men·da'tion**, *n.*

em'er·ald, *n.* green jewel.

e·merge', *v.* come out; appear. —**e·mer'gence**, *n.*

e·mer'gen·cy, *n.* [*pl.* -CIES] sudden occurrence demanding quick action.

e·mer'i·tus, *a.* retired, but keeping his title.

em'er·y, *n.* hard corundum used for grinding, etc.

e·met'ic, *n.* & *a.* (substance) causing vomiting.

em'i·grate, *v.* leave one country to settle in another. —**em'i·grant**, *a.* & *n.* —**em'i·gra'tion**, *n.*

em'i·nent, *a.* prominent or high. —**em'i·nence**, *n.*

em'is·sar·y, *n.* [*pl.* -IES] one sent on a mission.

e·mit', *v.* [EMITTED, EMITTING] 1. send out; discharge. 2. utter. —**e·mis'sion**, *n.*

mol'li·ent, *n.* & *a.* (medicine) for soothing the skin.

e·mol'u·ment (-yoo-) *n.* salary; payment.

e·mote', *v.* [Col.] show emotion dramatically.

e·mo'tion, *n.* strong feeling, as of love, fear, anger, etc. —**e·mo'tion·al**, *a.*

em'per·or, *n.* ruler of an empire. —**em'press**, *n.fem.*

em'pha·sis, *n.* [*pl.* -SES (-sēz)] 1. stress; importance. 2. stress on a syllable.

em'pha·size, *v.* to stress.

em·phat'ic, *a.* 1. using emphasis. 2. forcible. —**em·phat'i·cal·ly**, *adv.*

em'pire, *n.* group of countries under one sovereign.

em·pir'i·cal, *a.* based on experiment or experience.

em·ploy', *v.* 1. use. 2. keep busy. 3. hire or have as workers. —*n.* employment. —**em·ploy·ee**, **em·ploy·e'** (-ē) *n.* person working for another for pay.

em·ploy'er, *n.* one who employs others for pay.

em·ploy'ment, *n.* 1. an employing or being employed. 2. work; occupation.

em·pow'er, *v.* 1. authorize. 2. enable.

emp'ty, *a.* [-TIER, -TIEST] 1. with nothing or no one in it. 2. worthless. —*v.* [-TIED, -TYING] 1. make or become empty. 2. pour out. —*n.* [*pl.* -TIES] empty bottle, etc. —**emp'ti·ness**, *n.*

e'mu, *n.* ostrichlike bird.

em'u·late, *v.* try to equal or surpass. —**em'u·la'tion**, *n.*

e·mul'si·fy, *v.* [-FIED, -FYING] form into an emulsion.

e·mul'sion, *n.* oil suspended in watery liquid.

en-, *pref.* 1. to put on. 2. to make. 3. in or into.

-en, *suf.* 1. make or become.

2. get or give. 3. made of.

en·a'ble, v. make able.

en·act', v. 1. pass, as a law. 2. act out.

en·am'el, n. 1. glassy coating fused to metal. 2. white coating of teeth. 3. hard, glossy paint. —v. coat with enamel. —**en·am'el·ware,** n.

en·am'or, or **en·am'our,** v. fill with love; charm.

en·case', v. enclose.

-ence, suf. act, state, or result: also **-ency.**

en'ceph·a·li'tis, n. inflammation of the brain.

en·chant', v. charm; delight.

en·cir'cle, v. surround.

en'clave, n. foreign land inside another country.

en·close', v. 1. surround; shut in. 2. insert in an envelope. —**en·clo'sure,** n.

en·co'mi·um, n. high praise.

en·com'pass, v. 1. surround. 2. contain.

en'core (än'-) int. again! —n. song, etc. added by demand.

en·coun'ter, v. 1. meet unexpectedly. 2. fight. —n. 1. unexpected meeting. 2. fight.

en·cour'age, v. 1. give courage or hope to. 2. help. —**en·cour'age·ment,** n.

en·croach', v. intrude (on).

en·crust', v. incrust.

en·cum'ber, v. 1. hinder. 2. burden. —**en·cum'brance,** n.

en·cy'cli·cal (-sik'-) n. papal letter to bishops.

en·cy'clo·pe'di·a, or **en·cy'clo·pae'di·a,** n. book or set of books on one or all branches of knowledge. —**en·cy'clo·pe'di·a(a)e'dic,** a.

end, n. 1. last part; finish. 2. destruction. 3. tip. 4. purpose. —v. finish; stop. —a. final. —**end'ing,** n.

en·dan'ger, v. put in danger.

en·dear', v. make beloved. —**en·dear'ment,** n. affection.

en·deav'or, v. try hard. —n. earnest attempt.

en'dive, n. salad plant.

en'do·crine (gland), any of the ductless glands that regulate bodily functions.

en·dorse', v. 1. sign on the back of (a check). 2. approve. —**en·dorse'ment,** n.

en·dow', v. 1. provide with some quality. 2. give money to. —**en·dow'ment,** n.

en·dur'ance, n. ability to last, stand pain, etc.

en·dure', v. 1. stand (pain, etc.). 2. tolerate. 3. last.

en·e·ma, n. therapeutic flushing of the rectum.

en'e·my, n. [pl. -MIES] person or nation hostile to another; foe.

en'er·gize, v. give energy to.

en'er·gy, n. [pl. -GIES] 1. vigor; power. 2. capacity to do work. —**en·er·get'ic,** a.

en'er·vate, v. weaken.

en·fold', v. 1. wrap up. 2. embrace.

en·force', v. 1. impose by force. 2. make people obey (a law). —**en·force'ment,** n.

en·fran'chise, v. 1. free from slavery. 2. give the right to vote.

en·gage', v. 1. bind by a promise of marriage. 2. involve oneself. 3. hire. 4. attract and hold. 5. enter into conflict with. 6. interlock; mesh. —**en·gaged',** a. —**en·gage'ment,** n.

en·gag'ing, a. charming.

en·gen'der (-jen'-) v. cause.

en'gine, n. 1. machine using energy to develop mechanical power. 2. locomotive.

en'gi·neer', n. 1. one trained in engineering. 2. locomotive driver. —v. manage skillfully.

en·gi·neer'ing, n. practical use of sciences in industry, building, etc.

Eng'lish, a. & n. (of) the people or language of England.

en·grave', v. cut (designs) on (a metal plate, etc.), as for printing. —**en·grav'er,** n. —**en·grav'ing,** n.

en·gross', v. take the whole attention of.

en·gulf', v. swallow up.

en·hance', v. make greater.

e·nig'ma, n. baffling matter, person, etc. —**en'ig·mat'ic,** or **en'ig·mat'i·cal,** a.

en·join', v. 1. to command. 2. prohibit by law.

en·joy', v. 1. get pleasure from. 2. have the use of. —**enjoy oneself,** have a good time. —**en·joy'a·ble,** a. —**en·joy'ment,** n.

en·large', v. make larger. —**enlarge on** (or upon), discuss fully. —**en·large'ment,** n.

en·light'en, v. free from ignorance, prejudice, etc.

en·list', v. 1. enroll in an army, etc. 2. engage in a cause. —**en·list'ment,** n.

en·liv'en, v. liven up.

en'mi·ty, n. ill will.

en·no'ble, v. dignify.

en·nui' (än'wē) n. boredom.

e·nor'mi·ty, n. [pl. -IES] 1. great wickedness. 2. outrageous act.

e·nor'mous, a. huge; vast.

e·nough', a. & adv. as much as is needed. —n. amount needed. —int. no more!

en·quire', v. inquire. —en·quir'y [pl. -IES] n.

en·rage', v. put into a rage.

en·rich', v. make rich(er).

en·roll', v. put or be put in a list, as a member, etc. —en·roll'ment, n.

en route (än rŏŏt') on the way.

en·sconce', v. place snugly.

en·sem'ble (än-säm'-) n. 1. total effect. 2. costume of matching parts. 3. group of musicians playing together.

en·shrine', v. hold as sacred.

en·shroud', v. hide.

en·sign' (-sīn) n. 1. flag. 2. (-s'n) lowest-ranking navy officer.

en·slave', v. make a slave of.

en·snare', v. catch as in a snare.

en·sue', v. follow; result.

en·tail', v. make necessary.

en·tan'gle, v. trap; confuse.

en·ter, v. 1. come or go in. 2. put in a list, etc. 3. join. 4. begin. —enter into, 1. take part in. 2. form a part of. —enter upon (or upon) begin.

en'ter·prise (-prīz) n. 1. important undertaking. 2. energy and boldness.

en'ter·pris'ing, a. full of energy and boldness.

en·ter·tain', v. 1. amuse. 2. act as host to. 3. consider, as an idea. —en·ter·tain'er, n. —en·ter·tain'ment, n.

en·thrall', v. fascinate.

en·thu'si·asm, n. eager interest. —en·thu'si·ast, n. —en·thu'si·as'tic, a.

en·tice', v. tempt.

en·tire', a. complete; whole. —en·tire'ly, adv. —en·tire'ty, n.

en·ti'tle, v. 1. give a title to. 2. give a right to.

en'ti·ty, n. [pl. -TIES] thing having real existence.

en'to·mol'o·gy, n. study of insects.

en'trails, n.pl. inner organs; spec., intestines.

en'trance (-trəns) n. 1. act of entering. 2. door, gate, etc. 3. permission to enter. —v. (-trans') to delight.

en·trap', v. catch in a trap.

en·treat', v. ask earnestly.

en·treat'y, n. [pl. -IES] earnest request; prayer.

en·tree, en·trée (än'trā) n. main dish.

en·trench', v. set securely.

en·tre·pre·neur (än'trə-prə-nûr') n. one who organizes and operates a business.

en·trust', v. assign the care of (to).

en'try, n. [pl. -TRIES] 1. entrance. 2. item in a list, etc. 3. contestant.

en·twine' (-twīn') v. twist together or around.

e·nu'mer·ate, v. name one by one. —e·nu'mer·a'tion, n.

e·nun'ci·ate (-si-) v. 1. state. 2. pronounce (words).

en·vel'op, v. 1. wrap up. 2. surround. —en·vel'op·ment, n.

en'velope, n. covering, esp. for a letter.

en·vi'ron·ment, n. surroundings. —en·vi'ron·men'tal, a.

en·vi'ron·men'tal·ist, n. person working to solve environmental problems.

en·vi'rons, n.pl. suburbs.

en·vis'age (-viz'-) v. imagine.

en'voy, n. 1. messenger. 2. diplomatic official.

en'vy, n. 1. discontent and ill will over another's advantages, etc. 2. object of such feeling. —v. feel envy toward. —en'vi·a·ble, a. —en'vi·ous, a.

en'zyme (-zīm) n. catalyst formed in body cells.

e'on (ē'-) n. aeon.

e·pau'let (ep'ə-) n. shoulder ornament on a uniform.

e·phem'er·al, a. short-lived.

ep'ic, n. long poem about a hero's deeds. —a. heroic.

ep'i·cure, n. one with a fine taste for foods and liquors.

ep'i·dem'ic, n. & a. (disease) that spreads rapidly.

ep'i·der'mis, n. outermost layer of the skin.

ep'i·gram, n. witty saying.

ep'i·lep'sy, n. disease marked by convulsive fits, etc. —ep'i·lep'tic, a. & n.

ep'i·logue, ep'i·log (-lôg) n. part added at the end of a novel, play, etc.

e·pis'co·pal, a. of or governed by bishops.

ep'i·sode, n. incident. —ep'·i·sod'ic, a.

e·pis'tle (-pis'l) n. 1. letter. 2. [E-] Bible letter of an Apostle.

ep'i·taph, n. inscription on a tomb.

ep'i·thet, n. word or phrase characterizing a person, etc.

e·pit'o·me (-mi) n. 1. typical part or thing. 2. summary. **—e·pit'o·mize,** v.

ep'och (-ək) n. period marked by certain events, etc.

ep·ox'y, n. resin used in strong glues, enamels, etc.

Ep'som salts (or **salt**), salt used as a cathartic.

eq'ua·ble (ek'wə-) a. even; calm. **—eq'ua·bly,** adv.

e'qual, a. of the same quantity, value, rank, etc. **—n.** person or thing that is equal. **—v.** be, or do something, equal to. **—equal to,** capable of. **—e·qual'i·ty,** n.

e'qual·ize, v. **—e'qual·ly,** adv.

equal mark (or **sign**), sign (=) indicating equality.

e'qua·nim'i·ty, n. composure.

e·quate', v. treat, regard, or express as equal.

e·qua'tion, n. 1. an equating. 2. equality of two quantities as shown by the equal mark.

e·qua'tor, n. imaginary circle around the earth, equally distant from N. & S. poles.

e·ques'tri·an, a. of horses or horsemanship. **—n.** rider or acrobat on horseback.

equi-, pref. equal, equally.

e'qui·lat'er·al, a. having all sides equal.

e'qui·lib'ri·um, n. state of balance.

e'quine, a. of a horse.

e'qui·nox, n. time when the sun crosses the equator, making night and day of equal length everywhere.

e·quip', v. [-QUIPPED, -QUIP-PING] fit out, as for an undertaking. **—e·quip'ment,** n.

eq'ui·ta·ble, a. fair; just.

eq'ui·ty, n. 1. fairness. 2. value of property beyond amount owed on it.

e·quiv'a·lent, a. equal in quantity, meaning, etc. **—n.** equivalent thing.

e·quiv'o·cal, a. 1. purposely ambiguous. 2. doubtful. **—e·quiv'o·cate,** v.

-er, suf. one that.

e'ra, n. period of time.

e·rad'i·cate, v. wipe out. **—e·rad'i·ca'tion,** n.

e·rase', v. rub out, as writing. **—e·ras'er,** n.

e·ra'sure (-shēr) n. place where something was erased.

ere, con. & prep. [Ar. or Poet.] before.

e·rect', a. upright. **—v.** 1. construct; build. 2. set upright. **—e·rec'tion,** n.

erg, n. unit of work.

er·mine (ūr'min) n. weasel with white fur in winter.

e·rode', v. wear away. **—e·ro'sion,** n.

e·rot'ic, a. causing sexual feelings or desires.

err (ūr) v. 1. be wrong. 2. violate a moral code.

er'rand (er'-) n. short trip to do a thing.

er'rant, a. wandering.

er·rat'ic, a. irregular; odd.

er·ro'ne·ous, a. wrong.

er'ror, n. 1. mistake; blunder. 2. mistaken belief.

erst'while, a. former.

er'u·dite, a. learned; scholarly. **—er'u·di'tion,** n.

e·rupt', v. 1. burst forth. 2. break out in a rash. **—e·rup'tion,** n.

-ery, suf. 1. a place to or for. 2. act or product of. 3. condition of.

er'y·sip'e·las (er'i-) n. acute skin disease.

es'ca·la'tor, n. moving stairway on an endless belt.

es·cal'op, es·cal'lop, n. & v. scallop.

es'ca·pade', n. reckless adventure or prank.

es·cape', v. 1. get free. 2. slip away from. **—n.** act or means of escape.

es·cape'ment, n. notched wheel regulating movement in a clock, etc.

es·cap'ism, n. tendency to escape reality by fantasy.

es'ca·role, n. plant with leaves used in salads.

es·carp'ment, n. cliff.

es·chew', v. shun.

es'cort, n. person(s) accompanying another to protect, honor, etc. **—v.** (i-skôrt') go with as an escort.

es'crow, n. state of a deed held by a third party until conditions are fulfilled.

es·cutch'eon (-ən) n. shield bearing a coat of arms.

Es'ki·mo, n. & a. (member) of a people living in Greenland, arctic N. America, etc.

e·soph'a·gus (-sof'-) n. [pl. -GI (-ji)] passage between the pharynx and stomach.

es·o·ter'ic, a. known by few.

es·pe'cial, a. special; chief. **—es·pe'cial·ly,** adv.

es'pi·o·nage (-nij) n. a spying.

es·pouse' (-spouz') v. 1. marry. 2. support (an idea or cause). —**es·pous'al**, n.

es·py' (-pī') v. [-PIED, -PYING] catch sight of; see.

Es·quire' (-kwīr') n. title of courtesy put after a man's surname: abbrev. Esq.

es·say', v. to try. —n. 1. a try. 2. short personal writing on one subject. 1. a try. **es'say·ist**, n.

es'sence, n. 1. basic nature. 2. substance in concentrated form. 3. perfume.

es·sen'tial (-shəl) n. & a. (something) necessary.

es·tab'lish, v. 1. set up; fix. 2. to found. 3. prove. —**es·tab'lish·ment**, n.

es·tate', n. 1. one's possessions. 2. piece of land with a residence.

es·teem', v. 1. value highly. —n. high regard.

es'ter, n. organic salt.

es·thete', n. aesthete. —**es·thet'ic**, a.

es'ti·ma·ble, a. worthy of esteem.

es'ti·mate, v. figure roughly, as size or cost. —n. (-mit) 1. rough calculation. 2. opinion. —**es'ti·ma'tion**, n.

es·trange', v. make unfriendly.

es'tu·ar'y, n. [pl. -IES] wide mouth of a river.

et cet'er·a (set'-) and so forth: abbrev. etc.

etch, v. put a design on metal plates or glass with acid, often for making prints. —**etch'ing**, n.

e·ter'nal, a. 1. everlasting. 2. forever the same.

e·ter'ni·ty, n. 1. a being eternal. 2. endless time.

e'ther, n. an anesthetic.

e·the're·al, a. 1. light; delicate. 2. heavenly.

eth'i·cal, a. 1. of ethics. 2. proper; right.

eth'ics, n.pl. moral standards; system of morals.

eth'nic, a. of any of the many peoples of mankind. n. member of a nationality group in a larger community.

eth·nol'o·gy, n. study of the world's peoples and cultures. —**eth'no·log'i·cal**, a.

eth'yl, n. carbon-hydrogen radical of common alcohol, etc.

et'i·quette (-ket) n. social forms; good manners.

é'tude (ā'-) n. Mus. instrumental piece stressing a technique.

et'y·mol'o·gy, n. [pl. -GIES] 1. origin of a word. 2. study of word origins.

eu'ca·lyp'tus (ū'-) n. a subtropical evergreen.

Eu'cha·rist (-kə-) n. Holy Communion.

eu·gen'ics, n. science of improving the human race by heredity control. —**eu·gen'ic**, a.

eu'lo·gy, n. [pl. -GIES] praise. —**eu'lo·gize**, v.

eu'nuch, n. castrated man.

eu'phe·mism, n. mild word replacing an offensive one.

eu·pho'ni·ous, a. pleasant sounding. —**eu'pho·ny**, n.

eu·pho'ri·a, n. feeling of wellbeing. —**eu·phor'ic**, a.

Eu·ro·pe'an, n. & a. (native) of Europe.

eu'tha·na'sia (-zhə) n. painless death to end suffering.

e·vac'u·ate, v. 1. make empty. 2. discharge (excrement). 3. remove. 4. withdraw (from). —**e·vac'u·a'tion**, n.

e·vade', v. avoid by deceit, indirect answer, etc. —**e·va'sion**, n. —**e·va'sive**, a.

e·val'u·ate, v. find the value of. —**e·val'u·a'tion**, n.

e·va·nes'cent, a. fleeting.

e'van·gel'i·cal, a. of the Gospels or New Testament.

e·van'gel·ist, n. 1. [E-] Gospel writer. 2. revivalist preacher. —**e·van'gel·ism**, n.

e·vap'o·rate, v. 1. change into vapor. 2. condense by heating. 3. vanish. —**e·vap'o·ra'tion**, n.

eve, n. 1. [Poet.] evening. 2. evening before a holiday. 3. time just before.

e'ven, a. 1. flat; level. 2. constant; uniform. 3. calm. 4. equal. 5. divisible by two. 6. exact. —adv. 1. indeed. 2. exactly. 3. still. —v. make or become even. —**even if**, though. —**e'ven·ly**, adv.

eve'ning, n. end of day and beginning of night.

e·vent', n. 1. an occurrence. 2. sports contest in a series. —**in the event of**, in case of.

e·vent'ful, a. full of events; important.

e·ven'tu·al (-choo-) a. final. —**e·ven'tu·al·ly**, adv.

e·ven'tu·al'i·ty, n. [pl. -TIES] possible outcome.

ev'er, adv. 1. always. 2. at any time. 3. at all.

ev'er·green, n. & a. (tree or plant) having green leaves all year.

ev·er·last'ing, a. eternal.

ev'er·y, a. 1. each of a group. 2. all possible. —**every other,** each alternate. —**ev'er·y·bod'y, ev'er·y·one',** pron. —**ev'er·y·thing',** pron. —**ev'er·y·where',** adv.

e·vict', v. put (a tenant) out by law. —**e·vic'tion,** n.

ev'i·dence, n. 1. sign; indication. 2. proof. —v. make evident.

ev'i·dent, a. easy to see; clear. —**ev'i·dent·ly,** adv.

e'vil, a. 1. morally bad. 2. harmful. —n. wickedness. —**e'vil·do'er,** n. —**e'vil·ly,** adv.

e·vince', v. show plainly (a quality, feeling, etc.).

e·vis'cer·ate, v. remove the entrails from.

e·voke', v. call forth; produce. —**ev'o·ca'tion,** n.

ev·o·lu'tion, n. 1. an evolving. 2. theory that all species developed from earlier forms. —**ev'o·lu'tion·ar·y,** a.

e·volve', v. develop gradually; unfold.

ewe (ū) n. female sheep.

ew'er (ū'-) n. large, wide-mouthed water pitcher.

ex-, pref. former.

ex·act', a. strictly correct; precise. —v. demand and get. —**ex·act'i·tude,** n. —**ex·act'ly,** adv.

ex·act'ing, a. strict; hard.

ex·ag'ger·ate (-aj'ēr-) v. make seem greater than it really is; overstate. —**ex·ag'ger·a'tion,** n.

ex·alt', v. 1. raise in dignity. 2. praise. 3. fill with joy. —**ex'al·ta'tion,** n.

ex·am', n. [Col.] examination.

ex·am'ine, v. 1. inspect. 2. test by questioning. —**ex·am'i·na'tion,** n.

ex·am'ple, n. 1. sample. 2. illustration. 3. model.

ex·as'per·ate, v. annoy; vex. —**ex·as'per·a'tion,** n.

ex'ca·vate, v. 1. make a hole in. 2. unearth. 3. dig out. —**ex'ca·va'tion,** n. —**ex'ca·va'tor,** n.

ex·ceed', v. 1. go beyond (a limit). 2. surpass.

ex·ceed'ing, a. extreme. —**ex·ceed'ing·ly,** adv.

ex·cel', v. (-CELLED, -CEL-LING) be better than.

Ex'cel·len·cy, n. [pl. -CIES] title of honor.

ex'cel·lent, a. unusually good. —**ex'cel·lence,** n.

ex·cel'si·or, n. wood shavings used for packing.

ex·cept', prep. leaving out; but. —v. exclude.

ex·cept'ing, prep. except.

ex·cep'tion, n. 1. person or thing excluded. 2. case to which a rule does not apply. 3. objection.

ex·cep'tion·al, a. unusual.

ex'cerpt, n. passage selected from a book, etc. —v. (ik-sûrpt') select; extract.

ex·cess', n. 1. more than is needed. 2. surplus. —a. (ek'ses) extra. —**ex·ces'sive,** a. —**ex·ces'sive·ly,** adv.

ex·change', v. 1. to trade; barter. 2. interchange. —n. 1. an exchanging. 2. thing exchanged. 3. place for exchanging. —**ex·change'a·ble,** a.

ex·cheq'uer (-chek'ēr) n. 1. treasury. 2. funds.

ex'cise, n. tax on certain goods within a country: also **excise tax.** —v. (ik-sīz') cut out. —**ex·ci'sion,** n.

ex·cite', v. 1. make active. 2. arouse; stir the feelings of. —**ex·cit'a·ble,** a. —**ex·cite'ment,** n.

ex·claim', v. utter sharply. —**ex'cla·ma'tion,** n.

ex·clude', v. keep out or shut out. —**ex·clu'sion,** n.

ex·clu'sive, a. 1. not shared. 2. snobbish. —**exclusive of,** not including. —**ex·clu'sive·ly,** adv.

ex·com·mu'ni·cate, v. expel from communion with a church. —**ex'com·mu'ni·ca'tion,** n.

ex'cre·ment, n. waste matter from the bowels.

ex·cres'cence, n. outgrowth, esp. an abnormal one.

ex'crete, v. eliminate (waste) from the body. —**ex·cre'tion,** n. —**ex'cre·to'ry,** a.

ex·cru'ci·at'ing (-shi-āt'-) a. very painful; agonizing.

ex·cul'pate, v. exonerate.

ex·cur'sion, n. short trip, esp. for pleasure.

ex·cuse' (-skūz') v. 1. apologize for. 2. overlook (a fault). 3. release from a duty. 4. let leave. 5. justify. —n. (-skūs') 1. apology. 2. something that excuses. 3. pretext. —**ex·cus'a·ble,** a.

ex'e·cra·ble, a. detestable.

ex'e·cute, v. 1. carry out; do. 2. put to death legally. —**ex'e·cu'tion,** n.

ex'e·cu'tion·er, n. official who executes (v. 2).

ex·ec′u·tive, a. 1. having to do with managing. 2. administering laws, etc. —n. one who administers affairs.

ex·ec′u·tor, n. one who carries out the provisions of another's will.

ex·em′pla·ry, a. serving as a model or example.

ex·em′pli·fy, v. [-FIED, -FY-ING] show by example.

ex·empt′, v. & a. free(d) from a rule or obligation. —**ex·emp′tion**, n.

ex′er·cise, n. 1. active use. 2. activity to develop the body, a skill, etc. 3. pl. program, as at a graduation ceremony. —v. 1. use. 2. do or give exercises.

ex·ert′, v. put into action.

ex·er′tion, n. 1. act of exerting. 2. effort.

ex·hale′, v. breathe forth. —**ex′ha·la′tion**, n.

ex·haust′ (ig-zôst′) v. 1. use up. 2. drain. 3. tire out. —n. discharge from an engine. —**ex·haust′i·ble**, a. —**ex·haus′tion**, n.

ex·haus′tive, a. thorough.

ex·hib′it (ig-zib′-) v. 1. show; display. —**ex·hib′i·tor**, n.

ex′hi·bi′tion (ek′sə-bi′-) n. 1. a (public) showing. 2. that which is shown.

ex′hi·bi′tion·ist, n. one who likes to show off.

ex·hil′a·rate (ig-zil′-) v. stimulate. —**ex·hil′a·ra′tion**, n.

ex·hort′ (ig-zôrt′) v. urge earnestly.

ex′i·gen·cy, n. [pl. -CIES] urgency.

ex·ile (eg′zil) n. 1. a prolonged, often enforced, living away from one's country. 2. person in exile. —v. send into exile.

ex·ist′, v. 1. be. 2. occur. 3. live. —**ex·ist′ence**, n.

ex′it, n. a (way of) leaving. 2. departure.

ex′o·dus, n. departure.

ex of·fi′ci·o [L.] by virtue of one's position.

ex·on′er·ate, v. to free from blame.

ex·or′bi·tant, a. excessive. —**ex·or′bi·tance**, n.

ex′or·cise, **ex′or·cize**, v. drive out (an evil spirit), as by magic. —**ex′or·cism**, n.

ex·ot′ic, a. 1. foreign. 2. strangely beautiful, etc.

ex·pand′, v. 1. spread out. 2. enlarge. —**ex·pan′sion**, n.

ex·panse′, n. wide extent.

ex·pan′sive, a. 1. broad. 2.

warm and open in talk, etc.

ex·pa′ti·ate (-pā′shi-) v. speak or write at length.

ex·pa′tri·ate, n. & v. exile.

ex·pect′, v. 1. look for as likely or due. 2. [Col.] suppose. —**ex·pect′an·cy**, n. —**ex·pect′ant**, a. —**ex·pec·ta′tion**, n.

ex·pec′to·rate, v. to spit.

ex·pe′di·ent, a. 1. useful for the purpose. 2. based on self-interest. —n. a means to an end. —**ex·pe′di·en·cy**, n.

ex′pe·dite, v. speed up; facilitate. —**ex′pe·dit·er**, n.

ex′pe·di′tion, n. 1. a journey, as for exploration. 2. those on such a journey.

ex·pel′, v. [-PELLED, -PELL-ING] 1. force out. 2. dismiss by authority.

ex·pend′, v. spend; use up.

ex·pend′i·ture (-chēr) n. 1. spending of money, time, etc. 2. amount spent.

ex·pense′, n. 1. cost. 2. pl. charges met with in one's work, etc.

ex·pen′sive, a. high-priced.

ex·pe′ri·ence, n. 1. a living through an event. 2. thing one has done or lived through. 3. skill gotten by training, work, etc. —v. have experience of.

ex·per′i·ment, n. & v. test to discover or prove something. —**ex·per′i·men′tal**, a.

ex′pert, a. very skillful. —n. one with great skill or knowledge in a field.

ex·per·tise′ (-tēz′), n. skill or knowledge of an expert.

ex′pi·ate, v. atone for.

ex·pire′, v. 1. die. 2. end. 3. exhale. —**ex′pi·ra′tion**, n.

ex·plain′, v. 1. make plain or understandable. 2. account for. —**ex′pla·na′tion**, n. —**ex·plan′a·to′ry**, a.

ex′ple·tive, n. oath or exclamation.

ex·plic′it (-plis′-) a. clearly stated; definite.

ex·plode′, v. 1. burst noisily. 2. discredit. —**ex·plo′sion**, n.

ex′ploit, n. bold deed. —v. (iks-ploit′) use to advantage. —**ex′ploi·ta′tion**, n.

ex·plore′, v. 1. investigate. 2. travel in (a region) for discovery. —**ex′plo·ra′tion**, n.

ex·plo′sive, a. of or like an explosion. —n. substance that can explode.

ex·po′nent, n. 1. interpreter. 2. example or symbol.

ex′port, v. send (goods) to

another country for sale. — *n.* something exported. —

ex·por·ta'tion, *n.*

ex·pose', *v.* 1. lay open, as to danger. 2. reveal. —**ex·po'sure**, *n.*

ex·po·sé' (-zā') *n.* disclosure of a scandal.

ex'po·si'tion, *n.* 1. explanation. 2. public exhibition.

ex·pos'i·to'ry, *a.* explaining.

ex·pos'tu·late, *v.* reason with a person in protest.

ex·pound', *v.* explain fully.

ex·press', *v.* 1. put into words. 2. show or symbolize. —*a.* 1. explicit. 2. exact. 3. fast and direct. —*n.* an express train, bus, delivery service, etc.

ex·pres'sion, *n.* 1. an expressing or way of expressing. 2. certain word or phrase. 3. look, etc. that shows how one feels. —**ex·pres'sive**, *a.*

ex·pro'pri·ate, *v.* take (land, etc.) for public use.

ex·pul'sion, *n.* an expelling or being expelled.

ex·punge', *v.* erase.

ex'pur·gate, *v.* delete (from) as a censor.

ex'qui·site, *a.* 1. beautiful, delicate, etc. 2. very keen.

ex'tant, *a.* still existing.

ex·tem'po·re, *adv. & a.* without preparation: also **ex·tem'po·ra'ne·ous**, *a.*

ex·tem'po·rize, *v.* speak, do, etc. extempore.

ex·tend', *v.* 1. prolong. 2. expand. 3. stretch forth. 4. offer.

ex·ten'sion, *n.* 1. an extending. 2. an addition.

ex·ten'sive, *a.* vast; far-reaching.

ex·tent', *n.* 1. size. 2. scope. 3. vast area.

ex·ten'u·ate, *v.* lessen the seriousness of (an offense).

ex·te'ri·or, *a.* on or from the outside. —*n.* the outside.

ex·ter'mi·nate, *v.* destroy entirely. —**ex·ter'mi·na'tion**, *n.* —**ex·ter'mi·na'tor**, *n.*

ex·ter'nal, *a.* 1. on or from the outside. 2. superficial.

ex·tinct', *a.* no longer existing or active.

ex·tinc'tion, *n.* a dying out; annihilation.

ex·tin'guish, *v.* 1. put out (a fire). 2. destroy.

ex'tir·pate, *v.* root out.

ex·tol', ex·toll', *v.* [-TOLLED, -TOLLING] praise highly.

ex·tort', *v.* get (money) by

threats, etc. —**ex·tor'tion**, *n.*

ex'tra, *a.* more than expected; additional. —*n.* extra person or thing. —*adv.* especially.

ex·tract', *v.* 1. pull out. 2. get by pressing, distilling, etc. 3. select. —*n.* (eks'trakt) something extracted. —**ex·trac'tion**, *n.*

ex'tra·dite, *v.* return (a fugitive). —**ex'tra·di'tion**, *n.*

ex·tra'ne·ous, *a.* 1. from outside. 2. not pertinent.

ex·traor'di·nar'y (iks-trôr'-) *a.* very unusual.

ex·trav'a·gant, *a.* 1. excessive. 2. wasteful. —**ex·trav'a·gance**, *n.*

ex·trav'a·gan'za, *n.* spectacular show.

ex·treme', *a.* 1. utmost. 2. final. 3. excessive. 4. radical. —*n.* extreme degree, state, etc. —**ex·treme'ly**, *adv.*

ex·trem'i·ty (-trem'-) *n.* [*pl.* -TIES] 1. end. 2. extreme need, danger, etc. 3. *pl.* hands and feet.

ex'tri·cate, *v.* set free.

ex·trin'sic, *a.* 1. not essential. 2. external.

ex'tro·vert, *n.* one not given to introspection.

ex·trude', *v.* 1. force through a small opening. 2. project. —**ex·tru'sion**, *n.*

ex·u'ber·ant, *a.* 1. very healthy and lively. 2. luxuriant. —**ex·u'ber·ance**, *n.*

ex·ude', *v.* pass out in drops.

ex·ult', *v.* rejoice greatly. —**ex·ult'ant**, *a.* —**ex'ul·ta'tion**, *n.*

eye, *n.* 1. organ of sight. 2. vision. 3. a look. 4. attention. —*v.* [EYED, EYING or EYEING] look at.

eye'ball, *n.* ball-shaped part of the eye.

eye'brow, *n.* bony arch over the eye, or the hair on this.

eye'glass·es, *n.pl.* pair of lenses to help faulty vision.

eye'lash, *n.* hair on the edge of the eyelid.

eye'let, *n.* small hole, as for a hook, cord, etc.

eye'lid, *n.* either of two folds of flesh that cover and uncover the eyeball.

eye'sight, *n.* power of seeing.

eye'sore, *n.* ugly sight.

eye'tooth, *n.* [*pl.* -TEETH] upper canine tooth.

eye'wit'ness, *n.* one who has himself seen the event.

F

fa′ble, n. 1. brief tale having a moral. 2. untrue story.

fab′ric, n. cloth.

fab′ri·cate, v. 1. make. 2. make up (a reason, etc.).

fab′u·lous (-yoo-) a. 1. fictitious. 2. incredible.

fa·çade (fa-säd′) n. main face of a building.

face, n. 1. front of the head. 2. (main) surface. 3. appearance. 4. dignity. —v. 1. turn, or have the face turned, toward. 2. confront. —**fa′cial** (-shal) a.

fac′et (fas′-) n. 1. a surface of a cut gem. 2. aspect.

fa·ce′tious (fa-sē′shəs) a. joking, esp. at the wrong time.

fac·ile (fas′l) a. easy.

fa·cil′i·tate, v. make easier.

fa·cil′i·ty, n. [pl. -TIES] 1. ease or skill. 2. pl. means for doing something easily.

fac·sim′i·le (fak-sim′ə-li) n. exact copy.

fact, n. 1. actual happening. 2. truth. —**in fact**, really.

fac′tion, n. 1. clique. 2. dissension. —**fac′tion·al**, a. —**fac′tious**, a.

fac′tor, n. 1. causal element. 2. *Math.* any of the quantities multiplied together.

fac′to·ry, n. [pl. -RIES] building in which things are manufactured.

fac′tu·al (-choo-) a. of facts; real.

fac′ul·ty, n. [pl. -TIES] 1. natural power or aptitude. 2. staff of teachers.

fad, n. passing fashion.

fade, v. 1. (make) lose color or strength. 2. die out.

fag, v. [FAGGED, FAGGING] make tired.

fag′ot, fag′got, n. bundle of sticks or twigs.

Fahr·en·heit (far′ən-hīt) a. of a thermometer on which the boiling point of water is 212°, the freezing point 32°.

fail, v. 1. fall short. 2. weaken. 3. become bankrupt. 4. not succeed. 5. neglect. 6. not pass a test or course.

fail′ure (-yər) n. 1. act of failing. 2. one that fails.

faint, a. 1. weak, dim, etc. 2. weak and dizzy. —n. state of temporary unconsciousness. —v. fall into a faint. —**faint′ness**, n.

fair, a. 1. beautiful. 2. blond.

3. clear and sunny. 4. just. 5. according to the rules. 6. average. —adv. in a fair way. —n. exposition with exhibits, amusements, etc. —**fair′ly**, adv. —**fair′ness**, n.

fair′y n. [pl. -IES] tiny imaginary being in human form, with magic powers.

faith, n. 1. unquestioning belief, esp. in religion. 2. particular religion. 3. loyalty.

faith′ful, a. 1. loyal. 2. exact. —**faith′ful·ly**, adv.

faith′less, a. disloyal.

fake, v., n., a. [Col.] sham.

fa·kir (fə-kêr′) n. Moslem or Hindu religious mendicant.

fal′con (fôl′-) n. hawk trained to hunt.

fall, v. [FELL, FALLEN, FALLING] 1. to drop or descend. 2. tumble. 3. occur. —n. 1. a falling. 2. autumn. 3. overthrow or ruin. 4. amount of what has fallen. 5. pl. a waterfall. —**fall back**, retreat. —**fall off**, lessen or worsen. —**fall out**, quarrel. —**fall through**, fail. —**fall to**, begin.

fal′la·cy (fal′-) n. [pl. -CIES] 1. false idea; error. 2. false reasoning. —**fal·la′cious**, a.

fal′li·ble, a. liable to error.

fall′out, n. 1. descent to earth of radioactive particles after a nuclear explosion. 2. these particles.

fal·low (fal′ō) a. 1. plowed but unplanted. 2. inactive.

false, a. 1. not true. 2. lying. 3. unfaithful. 4. not real. —**fal′si·fy** [-FIED, -FYING] v. —**fal′si·ty**, n.

false′hood, n. a lie or lying.

fal·set′to, n. artificial, highpitched singing.

fal′ter (fôl′-) v. 1. stumble. 2. stammer. 3. waver.

fame, n. great reputation.

fa·mil′iar (-yər) a. 1. friendly; intimate. 2. too intimate (with). 3. closely acquainted (with). 4. well-known. —**fa·mil′i·ar′i·ty**, n. —**fa·mil′iar·ize′**, v.

fam′i·ly, n. [pl. -LIES] 1. parents and their children. 2. relatives. 3. lineage. 4. group of related things.

fam′ine (-in) n. 1. widespread food shortage. 2. starvation.

fam′ish, v. be hungry; starve.

fa′mous, a. having fame.

fan, n. 1. device to move air for cooling, etc. 2. enthusiastic supporter. —v.

[FANNED, FANNING] 1. blow air toward. 2. stir up. 3. spread (out).

fa·nat'ic, a. too enthusiastic or zealous: also fa·nat'i·cal. —n. fanatic person. —fa·nat'i·cism, n.

fan'ci·er, n. person with a special interest, esp. plant or animal breeding.

fan'cy, n. [pl. -CIES] 1. playful imagination. 2. notion, whim, etc. 3. a liking. —a. [-CIER, -CIEST] 1. extravagant. 2. elaborate. 3. of superior quality. —v. [-CIED, -CYING] 1. imagine. 2. be fond of. 3. suppose. —fan'ci·ful, a.

fan'fare, n. 1. blast of trumpets. 2. showy display.

fang, n. long, pointed tooth.

fan·tas'tic, a. 1. unreal. 2. grotesque. 3. extravagant. —fan·tas'ti·cal·ly, adv.

fan'ta·sy, n. [pl. -SIES] 1. fancy. 2. illusion; reverie. 3. fantastic poem, play, etc.

far, a. [FARTHER, FARTHEST] distant. —adv. 1. very distant. 2. very much.

far'a·way, a. distant.

farce, n. 1. exaggerated comedy. 2. absurd thing. —far'ci·cal, a.

fare, v. get along. —n. 1. transportation charge. 2. paying passenger. 3. food.

fare'well', int. good-by. —a. & n. parting (wishes).

far'fetched', a. not reasonable; strained.

far'flung', a. extensive.

farm, n. land used to raise crops or animals. —v. 1. cultivate (land). 2. let out (work or workers) on contract. —farm'er, n. —farm'house, n. —farm'ing, n.

far'off', a. distant.

far'reach'ing, a. having wide range, influence, etc.

far'sight'ed, a. 1. planning ahead. 2. seeing far objects best.

far'ther, a. 1. more distant. 2. additional. —adv. 1. at or to a greater distance or extent. 2. in addition.

far'thest, a. 1. most distant. 2. longest. —adv. at or to the greatest distance.

fas'ci·nate, v. hold spellbound; captivate.

fas·cism (fash'iz'm) n. militaristic dictatorship. —fas'cist, n. & a.

fash'ion, n. 1. kind; sort. 2. manner. 3. current style. —v. make; form.

fash'ion·a·ble, a. stylish.

fast, a. 1. firm. 2. loyal. 3. unfading. 4. rapid; quick. 5. of loose morals. —adv. 1. firmly. 2. rapidly. —v. abstain from food. —n. period of fasting.

fas·ten (fas'n) v. 1. attach. 2. make secure; fix.

fas'ten·ing, n. thing used to fasten.

fas·tid'i·ous, a. not easy to please; particular.

fat, a. [FATTER, FATTEST] 1. oily; greasy. 2. plump. —n. oily animal substance. —fat'ty, a.

fa'tal, a. causing death.

fa'tal·ist, n. one believing all events are destined.

fa·tal'i·ty, n. [pl. -TIES] death caused by disaster.

fate, n. 1. power supposedly making events inevitable. 2. one's lot in life. 3. outcome. 4. death; ruin. —fate'ful, a.

fat'ed, a. destined.

fa'ther, n. 1. male parent. 2. [F-] God. 3. founder; creator. 4. priest. —v. beget, found, etc. —fa'ther·hood, n. —fa'ther·ly, a.

fa'ther·in·law', n. [pl. FATHERS-IN-LAW] father of one's wife or husband.

fath'om (fath'-) n. Naut. six feet. —v. understand.

fa·tigue' (-tēg') n. weariness. —v. to weary.

fat'ten, v. make or get fat.

fat'u·ous (fach'-) a. foolish.

fau'cet, n. device with valve to draw liquid from a pipe.

fault, n. 1. flaw. 2. error. 3. blame. —find fault (with), criticize. —fault'less, a.

faul'ty, a. [-IER, -IEST] defective.

faun, n. Roman deity, half man and half goat.

fau'na, n. the animals of a certain region.

faux pas (fō'pä') [pl. FAUX PAS (päz')] social blunder.

fa'vor, n. 1. approval. 2. partiality. 3. kind act. 4. small gift. —v. 1. show favor toward. 2. resemble. Also, Br. sp., favour. —in favor of, approving. —fa'vor·a·ble, a.

fa'vor·ite, a. & n. preferred (one). —fa'vor·it·ism, n.

fawn, v. 1. show affection as by licking. 2. flatter servilely. —n. baby deer.

faze, v. [Col.] disturb.

fear, n. 1. anxious anticipa-

tion of danger, pain, etc.
2. awe. —v. 1. be afraid
(of). 2. be in awe (of). —
fear'ful, a. —**fear'less**, a.
fea'si·ble (fē'-) a. 1. possible. 2. probable. 3. suitable. —**fea'si·bil'i·ty**, n.
feast, n. 1. religious festival.
2. banquet. —v. 1. have a
feast (for). 2. delight.
feat, n. bold & daring deed.
feath'er, n. 1. one of the
outgrowths covering a bird.
2. kind. —**feath'er·y**, a.
fea'ture (-chēr) n. 1. pl.
form of the face or its parts.
2. special part, article, etc.
3. main attraction. —v.
make a feature of.
Feb'ru·ar'y, n. 2nd month.
fe'ces (-sēz) n.pl. excrement.
fe'cund, a. fertile.
fed'er·al, a. 1. of a union
of states under a central
government. 2. of the central government, esp. [F-]
of the U.S.
fed'er·ate, v. unite in a
federation.
fed'er·a'tion, n. union of
states or groups; league.
fe·do'ra, n. man's felt hat.
fee, n. charge for some service or right.
fee'ble, a. weak; not strong.
—**fee'bly**, adv.
feed, v. [FED, FEEDING] 1.
give food to. 2. supply as
fuel, material, etc. 3. gratify. 4. eat. —n. fodder.
feel, v. [FELT, FEELING] 1.
touch. 2. have a feeling
(of). 3. be aware of. 4. believe. 5. be or seem to be.
6. grope. —n. 1. sense of
touch. 2. way a thing feels.
—**feel like**, [Col.] have a
desire for. —**feel'er**, n.
feel'ing, n. 1. sense of
touch. 2. sensation. 3. an
emotion. 4. pl. sensitiveness. 5. sympathy. 6.
opinion.
feet, n., pl. of **foot**.
feign (fān) v. 1. make up
(an excuse). 2. pretend.
feint (fānt) n. pretended
attack, as in boxing. —v.
make a feint.
feld'spar, n. hard, crystalline mineral.
fe·lic'i·tate (-lis'-) v. congratulate. —**fe·lic'i·ta'-tion**, n.
fe·lic'i·tous, a. appropriate.
fe·lic'i·ty, n. [pl. -TIES] 1.
happiness. 2. apt and pleasing expression.
fe'line, a. of or like a cat.
—n. a cat.

fell, pt. of **fall**. —v. 1. knock
down. 2. cut down.
fel'low, n. 1. an associate.
2. an equal. 3. a mate. 4.
man or boy. —a. associated.
—**fel'low·ship**, n.
fel'on, n. criminal.
fel'o·ny, n. major crime.
felt, n. fabric made of fibers
pressed together.
fe'male, a. 1. designating or
of the sex that bears offspring. 2. feminine. —n.
female person or animal.
fem'i·nine, a. of or like
women. —**fem'i·nin'i·ty**, n.
fe'mur (fē'-) n. thighbone.
fen, n. swamp; bog.
fence, n. 1. barrier of posts,
wire, etc. 2. dealer in stolen
goods. —v. 1. enclose with a
fence. 2. engage in fencing.
fenc'ing, n. sport of fighting
with foils or swords.
fend, v. ward (off). —**fend
for oneself**, manage by oneself.
fend'er, n. guard over an
automobile wheel.
fer'ment, n. 1. thing causing
fermentation. 2. agitation.
—v. (fēr-ment') undergo or
cause fermentation (in).
fer'men·ta'tion, n. chemical change caused by yeast,
bacteria, etc.
fern, n. nonflowering plant
with fronds.
fe·ro'cious (-shəs) a. savage;
fierce. —**fe·roc'i·ty**, n.
fer'ret, n. kind of weasel.
—v. search out.
fer'ric, fer'rous, a. of iron.
fer'ry, v. [-RIED, -RYING] take
across a river, etc. in a boat.
—n. [pl. -RIES] boat (in full,
ferryboat) used for ferrying.
fer'tile (fūr'-) a. 1. producing
abundantly. 2. able to produce young, fruit, etc. —
fer·til'i·ty, n.
fer'ti·lize, v. 1. make fertile.
2. spread fertilizer on. 3.
make fruitful by introducing
a male germ cell.
fer'ti·liz'er, n. chemicals,
etc. to enrich the soil.
fer'vent, a. intense; ardent.
fer'vid, a. fervent.
fer'vor, n. ardor; zeal.
fes'tal, a. joyous; gay.
fes'ter, v. 1. form pus.
2. rankle.
fes'ti·val, n. time or day of
celebration.
fes'tive, a. joyous; gay.
fes·tiv'i·ty, n. [pl. -TIES]
1. gaiety. 2. pl. festive proceedings.
fes·toon', n. garland, etc.

hanging in loops. —v. adorn with festoons.

fetch, v. 1. go after and bring back; get. 2. sell for.

fetch'ing, a. attractive.

fete, fête (fāt) n. festival; outdoor party. —v. honor with a fete.

fet'id, a. stinking.

fe'tish, n. object thought to have magic power.

fet'ter, n. ankle shackle. —v. restrain as with fetters.

fet'tle, n. condition; trim.

fe'tus (fē'-) n. unborn young.

feud (fūd) n. deadly quarrel, as between families. —v. engage in a feud.

feu'dal·ism (fū'-) n. medieval system with lords, vassals, and serfs. —**feu'dal,** a.

fe'ver, n. abnormally high body temperature. —**fe'ver·ish,** a.

few, a. not many. —pron. & n. a small number.

fi·an·cé (fē'än-sā') n. man to whom one is betrothed. —**fi·an·cée'** (-sā') n.fem.

fi·as·co (fi-as'kō) n. [pl. -COES, -COS] utter failure.

fi'at, n. a decree.

fib, n. petty lie. —v. [FIBBED, FIBBING] tell a fib.

fi'ber, fi'bre (fī'bēr) n. 1. threadlike part forming organic tissue. 2. threadlike part(s) used for weaving, etc. —**fi'brous,** a.

fi'ber·glass, n. material made of fine filaments of glass: also **fiber glass.**

fick'le, a. changeable.

fic'tion, n. literary work(s) with imaginary characters and events. —**fic'tion·al,** a.

fic·ti'tious, a. imaginary.

fid'dle, n. [Col.] violin. —v. 1. [Col.] play a violin. 2. fidget. —**fid'dler,** n.

fi·del'i·ty, n. faithfulness.

fidg'et (fij'-) v. make nervous movements. —**fidg'et·y,** a.

fie (fī) int. shame!

field, n. 1. piece of open land, esp. one for crops, grazing, etc. 2. expanse. 3. playing field. 4. sphere of knowledge or activity. 5. all entrants in a contest.

field glasses, portable, telescopic eyeglasses.

fiend (fēnd) n. 1. devil. 2. [Col.] addict. —**fiend'ish,** a.

fierce, a. 1. savage; wild. 2. violent. —**fierce'ly,** adv.

fi'er·y, a. [-RIER, -RIEST] 1. flaming, hot, etc. 2. ardent.

fi·es'ta, n. festival.

fife, n. small, shrill flute.

fif'teen', a. & n. five more than ten. —**fif'teenth',** a. & n.

fifth, a. preceded by four others. —n. 1. one after the fourth. 2. one of five equal parts. 3. fifth of a gallon.

fif'ti·eth, a. & n.

fif'ty, a. & n. [pl. -TIES] five times ten. —**fif'ti·eth,** a. & n.

fig, n. sweet fruit with seed-filled pulp.

fight, n. & v. [FOUGHT, FIGHTING] struggle; battle; contest. —**fight'er,** n.

fig'ment, n. thing imagined.

fig'ur·a·tive, a. using metaphors, similes, etc.

fig'ure, n. 1. outline; shape. 2. person. 3. likeness of a person or thing. 4. illustration. 5. design. 6. a number. 7. sum of money. —v. 1. compute. 2. be conspicuous. 3. [Col.] predict. —**figure on,** rely on. —**figure out,** solve.

fig'ure·head', n. leader with no real power.

fig'u·rine' (-rēn') n. small statue.

fil'a·ment, n. threadlike part.

fil'bert, n. hazelnut.

filch, v. steal (something trivial).

file, n. 1. container for keeping papers in order. 2. orderly arrangement of papers, etc. 3. line of persons or things. 4. ridged tool for scraping, etc. —v. 1. put papers, etc. in order. 2. move in a file. 3. smooth or grind with a file.

fil'i·bus'ter, n. obstruction of a bill in a legislature, as by a long speech. —v. obstruct a bill in this way.

fil'i·gree, n. lacelike work of fine wire.

fil'ings, n.pl. small pieces scraped off with a file.

fill, v. 1. make or become full. 2. put into or hold (a job or office). 3. supply things ordered. —n. anything that fills. —**fill in,** 1. make complete. 2. substitute. —**fill out,** 1. make or become larger, etc. 2. complete (a blank form).

fi·let' (-lā') n. boneless piece of fish or meat: also **fi·let'.** —v. to bone (fish, etc.).

fill'ing, n. thing used to fill something else.

fil'lip, n. stimulus; tonic.

fil'ly, n. [pl. -LIES] young mare.

film, n. 1. thin coating. 2.

flexible cellulose material used in photography. 3. motion, picture. —v. make a motion picture of.

fil'ter, n. thing used for straining out particles, etc. from a fluid, etc. —v. 1. pass through a filter. 2. remove with a filter. 3. pass slowly. —**fil·tra'tion,** n.

filth, n. 1. foul dirt. 2. obscenity. —**filth'i·ness,** n. —**filth'y** [-IER, -IEST] a.

fin, n. winglike membranous organ on a fish.

fi·na'gle, v. use, or get by, trickery. —**fi·na'gler,** n.

fi'nal, a. 1. last. 2. conclusive. —n.pl. last of a series of contests. —**fi·nal'i·ty,** n. —**fi'nal·ly,** adv. —**fi'nal·ist,** n.

fi·na'le (-nä'li) n. last part of a musical work.

fi·nance' (or fī'nans) n. 1. pl. funds. 2. science of managing money matters. —v. supply money for. —**fi·nan'cial,** a. —**fin'an·cier'** (-sêr') n.

finch, n. small songbird.

find, v. [FOUND, FINDING] 1. come upon; discover. 2. learn. 3. recover (a thing lost). 4. decide. —n. something found.

fine, a. 1. excellent. 2. not heavy or coarse. 3. sharp. 4. discriminating. —adv. [Col.] very well. —n. money paid as a penalty. —v. cause to pay a fine.

fine arts, painting, sculpture, music, etc.

fin'er·y, n. showy clothes.

fi·nesse', n. skill, esp. in handling delicate situations.

fin'ger, n. any of the parts (five with the thumb) at the end of the hand. —v. to handle. —**fin'ger·nail,** n.

fin'ger·print, n. impression of the lines of a finger tip.

fin'ish, v. 1. to end. 2. complete. 3. use up. 4. perfect; polish. —n. 1. last part; end. 2. polish or perfection. 3. way a surface is finished.

fi'nite, a. having limits.

fiord (fyôrd) n. sea inlet bordered by steep cliffs.

fir, n. evergreen tree.

fire, n. 1. flame. 2. thing burning. 3. ardor. —v. 1. make burn. 2. shoot (a gun, etc.). 3. [Col.] discharge from a job. —**on fire,** burning. —**under fire,** under attack. —**fire'proof,** v. & a.

fire'arm, n. rifle, pistol, etc.

fire'crack'er, n. noisy, explosive rolled in paper.

fire engine, truck equipped for fire fighting.

fire'fly, n. winged beetle with a glowing abdomen.

fire'man, n. 1. one who fights fires. 2. stoker.

fire'place, n. place built in a wall for a fire.

fire'plug, n. street hydrant.

fire'works, n.pl. firecrackers, rockets, etc. for noisy or brilliant displays.

firm, a. 1. solid. 2. fixed; stable. 3. strong and steady. —v. make firm. —n. business company. —**firm'ness,** n.

fir'ma·ment, n. [Poet.] sky.

first, a. & adv. before any others. —n. 1. first one. 2. beginning.

first aid, emergency care for injuries. —**first'-aid',** a.

first'-class', a. of the highest quality. —adv. with the best accommodations.

first'hand', a. & adv. from the source; direct.

first'-rate', a. excellent.

fis'cal, a. financial.

fish, n. [pl. FISH; for different kinds, FISHES] cold-blooded animal with gills and fins, living in water. —v. 1. catch fish. 2. angle (for). —**fish'er·man** [pl. -MEN] n. —**fish'er·y** [pl. -IES] n.

fish'y, a. [-IER, -IEST] 1. like a fish. 2. [Col.] questionable.

fis·sion (fish'ən) n. a splitting apart.

fis·sure (fish'ēr) n. a cleft or crack.

fist, n. clenched hand.

fist'i·cuffs, n.pl. boxing.

fit, v. [FITTED, FITTING] 1. be suitable to. 2. be the proper size, etc. (for). 3. adjust to fit. 4. equip. —a. [FITTER, FITTEST] 1. suited. 2. proper. 3. healthy. —n. 1. way of fitting. 2. seizure as of coughing. 3. outburst.

fit'ful, a. not regular.

fit'ting, a. proper. —n. 1. adjustment. 2. pl. fixtures.

five, a. & n. one more than four.

fix, v. 1. fasten or set firmly. 2. determine. 3. repair. 4. prepare (food, etc.). 5. [Col.] influence by bribery, etc. —n. [Col.] predicament. —**fix up,** [Col.] set in order. —**fixed,** a.

fix·a'tion, n. obsession.

fix'ings, n.pl. [Col.] accessories; trimmings.

fix'ture (-chēr) n. usually pl. any of the attached furnishings of a house.

fizz, v. & n. (make) a hissing, bubbling sound.

fiz'zle, v. 1. to fizz. 2. [Col.] fail. —n. 1. fizzing sound. 2. [Col.] failure.

flab'ber·gast, v.[Col.] amaze.

flab'by, a. [-BIER, -BIEST] 1. limp and soft. 2. weak.

flac·cid (flak'sid) a. flabby.

flag, n. 1. cloth with designs, etc. used as a national symbol, etc. 2. iris (flower). —v. [FLAGGED, FLAGGING] 1. signal with flags. 2. grow weak. —**flag'pole**, **flag'staff**, n.

flag'el·late (flaj'-) v. to whip. —**flag·el·la'tion**, n.

flag'on (flag'-) n. container for liquids.

fla'grant, a. glaringly bad. —**fla'gran·cy**, n.

flag'stone, n. a flat, paving stone.

flail, n. implement used to thresh grain by hand. —v. 1. use a flail. 2. beat.

flair, n. aptitude; knack.

flake, n. 1. soft, thin mass. 2. chip or peeling. —v. form into flakes. —**flak'y** [-IER, -IEST] a.

flam·boy'ant, a. showy.

flame, n. tongue(s) of fire; blaze. —v. burst into flame.

fla·min'go, n. pink, long-legged wading bird.

flam'ma·ble, a. easily set on fire.

flange (flanj) n. projecting rim on a wheel, etc.

flank, n. 1. side of an animal between the ribs and the hip. 2. side of anything. —v. be at, or go around, the side of.

flan'nel, n. soft, napped cloth of wool, etc.

flap, n. 1. flat, loose piece. 2. motion or sound of a swinging flap. —v. flutter.

flare, v. 1. blaze up. 2. spread outward. —n. 1. bright, unsteady blaze. 2. brief, dazzling signal light. 3. sudden outburst. 4. a spreading outward.

flash, v. 1. send out a sudden, brief light. 2. sparkle. 3. move suddenly. —n. 1. sudden, brief light. 2. an instant. 3. bit of late news.

flash'-back, n. interruption in a story by a return to some earlier episode.

flash'light, n. portable electric light.

flash'y, a.[-IER, -IEST] gaudy; showy.

flask, n. kind of bottle.

flat, a. [FLATTER, FLATTEST] 1. smooth and level. 2. broad & thin. 3. lying spread out. 4. absolute. 5. tasteless. 6. dull. 7. emptied of air. 8. Mus. below true pitch. —adv. in a flat way. —n. 1. flat surface or part. 2. deflated tire. 3. Mus. note ½ step below another; symbol (♭). 4. apartment. —**flat'ten**, v.

flat'fish, n. fish with a very broad, flat body.

flat'foot, n. foot with the instep arch flattened.

flat'ter, v. 1. praise insincerely. 2. gratify the vanity of. —**flat'ter·y**, n.

flaunt (flônt) v. show off.

fla'vor, n. taste of a substance. —v. give flavor to.

fla'vor·ing, n. added essence, etc. that flavors food.

flaw (flô) n. defect.

flax, n. plant with fibers that are spun into linen thread.

flax'en, a. pale yellow.

flay, v. 1. strip the skin from. 2. criticize harshly.

flea, n. small jumping insect that is parasitic.

fleck, n. & v. spot.

fledg'ling, n. young bird just able to fly.

flee, v. [FLED, FLEEING] escape swiftly, as from danger.

fleece, n. wool covering a sheep. —v. to swindle. —**fleec'y** [-IER, -IEST] a.

fleet, n. 1. group of warships under one command. 2. any similar group, as of trucks, etc. —a. swift.

fleet'ing, a. passing swiftly.

flesh, n. 1. tissue between the skin and bones. 2. pulp of fruits and vegetables. 3. body. —**flesh'ly**, a. —**flesh'y**, a.

flew (flōō) pt. of **fly**.

flex, v. 1. bend, as an arm. 2. contract, as a muscle.

flex'i·ble, a. 1. easily bent; pliable. 2. adaptable.

flick, n. light, quick stroke. —v. strike, throw, etc. with such a stroke.

flick'er, v. 1. move, burn, or shine unsteadily. —n. dart of flame or light.

fli'er, n. aviator.

flight, n. 1. act or power of flying. 2. distance flown. 3. group of things flying together. 4. trip by airplane. 5. set of stairs. 6. a fleeing.

—**flight'less**, *a.*

flight'y, *a.* [-IER, -IEST] unsettled; frivolous.

flim'sy, *a.* [-SIER, -SIEST] 1. easily broken. 2. trivial.

flinch, *v.* draw back, as from a blow.

fling, *v.* throw with force. —*n.* 1. a flinging. 2. brief, wild time.

flint, *n.* a hard quartz.

flip, *v.* [FLIPPED, FLIPPING] toss with a quick jerk.

flip'pant, *a.* saucy.

flip'per, *n.* flat limb adapted for swimming, as in seals.

flirt, *v.* 1. play at love. 2. trifle. —*n.* one who plays at love. —**flir·ta'tion**, *n.*

flit, *v.* [FLITTED, FLITTING] move lightly and rapidly.

float, *n.* 1. thing that stays on the surface of a liquid. 2. flat, decorated vehicle in a parade. —*v.* 1. stay on the surface of a liquid. 2. drift gently in air, etc. 3. put into circulation, as a bond issue.

flock, *n.* group, esp. of animals. —*v.* gather in a flock.

floe (flō) *n.* large sheet of floating ice.

flog, *v.* [FLOGGED, FLOGGING] beat, thrash, or whip.

flood, *n.* 1. overflowing of water on land. 2. great outpouring. —*v.* to overflow.

flood'light, *n.* lamp casting a very bright, broad light.

floor, *n.* 1. bottom surface of a room, etc. 2. story in a building. 3. permission to speak. —*v.* 1. furnish with a floor. 2. knock down.

floor'ing, *n.* material for making a floor.

flop, *v.* [FLOPPED, FLOPPING] 1. move, drop, or flap down clumsily. 2. [Col.] fail. —*n.* a flopping. —**flop'py**, *a.*

flo'ra, *n.* plants of an area.

flo'ral, *a.* of or like flowers.

flor'id, *a.* 1. ruddy. 2. flashy.

flo'rist, *n.* one who grows or sells flowers.

floss, *n.* soft, silky fibers.

flo·til'la, *n.* small fleet.

flot'sam, *n.* floating debris or cargo of a shipwreck.

flounce, *v.* move with quick, flinging motions. —*n.* ruffle.

floun'der, *v.* struggle or speak clumsily. —*n.* kind of edible flatfish.

flour, *n.* powdery substance ground from grain.

flour'ish, (flur'-) *v.* 1. thrive. 2. be in one's prime. 3. brandish. —*n.* 1. sweeping motion or stroke. 2. fanfare.

flout, *v.* mock or scorn.

flow, *v.* 1. move as water does. 2. move smoothly. 3. proceed. 4. hang loose. —*n.* a flowing or thing that flows.

flow'er, *n.* 1. petals and pistil of a plant. 2. plant grown for its blossoms. 3. best part. —*v.* 1. produce blossoms. 2. become its best.

flow'er·y, *a.* [-IER, -IEST] showy in expression.

flown, *pp. of* **fly**.

flu, *n.* influenza.

fluc'tu·ate, *v.* keep changing, as prices.

flue, *n.* shaft in a chimney.

flu'ent, *a.* speaking or writing easily. —**flu'en·cy**, *n.*

fluff, *n.* loose, soft mass. —*v.* 1. make fluffy. 2. bungle. —**fluff'y**, *a.* [-FIER, -FIEST] soft and light.

flu'id, *a.* 1. able to flow. 2. not fixed. —*n.* liquid or gas. —**flu·id'i·ty**, *n.*

fluke, *n.* 1. anchor blade. 2. [Col.] stroke of luck.

flung, *pt. & pp. of* **fling**.

flunk, *v.* [Col.] to fail.

flunk'y, *n.* [*pl.* -IES] low, servile person.

flu'o·res'cent, *a.* giving off cool light. —**flu'o·res'cence**, *n.*

flu'o·ri·da'tion, *n.* addition of fluorides to water.

flu'o·ride, *n.* fluorine salt.

flu'o·rine (-rēn) *n.* yellowish gas, a chemical element.

fluo'ro·scope (floor'ə-) *n.* kind of X-ray machine.

flur'ry, *n.* [*pl.* -RIES] 1. gust of wind, rain, or snow. 2. sudden commotion. —*v.* [-RIED, -RYING] confuse.

flush, *v.* 1. to redden in the face. 2. start up from cover, as a bird. 3. wash out. —*n.* a blush; glow. —*a.* 1. well-supplied. 2. level (*with*). 3. direct.

flus'ter, *v.* make confused.

flute' *n.* tubelike wind instrument.

flut'ter, *v.* wave, move, or beat rapidly and irregularly. —*n.* 1. a fluttering. 2. confusion. —**flut'ter·y**, *a.*

flux, *n.* 1. a flowing. 2. constant change. 3. substance used to help metals fuse.

fly, *v.* [FLEW, FLOWN, FLYING] 1. move through the air by using wings. 2. wave or float in the air. 3. move swiftly. 4. flee. 5. [pt. & pp. FLIED] hit a fly in baseball. 6. travel in or pilot (aircraft). —*n.* [*pl.* FLIES] 1.

flap concealing buttons, etc. in a garment. 2. baseball batted high. 3. winged insect.

fly'er, n. flier.

flying saucer, unidentified flying object.

fly'leaf, n. blank leaf at the front or back of a book.

fly'wheel, n. wheel that regulates a machine's speed.

foal (fōl) n. young horse.

foam, n. bubbly mass on liquids. —v. form foam. —**foam'y** [-IER, -IEST] a.

fob, n. pocket-watch chain or ornament on it.

fo'cus, n. [pl. -CUSES, -CI (-sī)] 1. point where rays of light meet. 2. adjustment of lens distance for clear image. 3. center of activity. —v. 1. bring into focus. 2. concentrate. —**fo'cal,** a.

fod'der, n. coarse food for cattle, horses, etc.

foe, n. enemy.

fog, n. 1. thick mist. 2. mental confusion. —v. [FOGGED, FOGGING] make or become foggy. —**fog'gy** [-GIER, -GIEST] a. —**fog'giness,** n.

fo'gy, n. [pl. -GIES] old-fashioned person.

foi'ble, n. small weakness in character.

foil, v. thwart. —n. 1. thin fencing sword. 2. thin sheet of metal. 3. one that enhances another by contrast.

foist, v. impose by fraud.

fold, v. 1. double (material) over. 2. intertwine. 3. wrap up. —n. 1. folded layer. 2. pen for sheep.

-fold, suf. times as many.

fold'er, n. 1. folded sheet of cardboard to hold papers. 2. booklet of folded sheets.

fo'li·age (-ij) n. plant leaves.

fo'li·o, n. [pl. -OS] largest regular size of book.

folk, n. [pl. FOLK, FOLKS] people. —a. of the common people.

folk'lore', n. beliefs, legends, etc. of a people.

fol'li·cle (-k'l) n. small sac or gland, as in the skin.

fol'low, v. 1. come or go after. 2. go along. 3. take up (a trade). 4. result (from). 5. obey. 6. pay attention to. 7. understand. —**follow out** (or **up**), carry out fully. —**fol'low·er,** n.

fol'low·ing, a. next after. —n. group of followers.

fol'ly, n. [pl. -LIES] foolish

state, action, belief, etc.

fo·ment' (fō-) v. incite.

fond, a. loving; tender. —**fond of,** liking. —**fond'ly,** a.

fon'dle, v. to caress.

font, n. basin for holy water.

food, n. substance taken in by an animal or plant to enable it to live and grow.

fool, n. 1. silly person. 2. dupe. —v. 1. be silly or playful. 2. trick.

fool'har'dy, a. [-DIER, -DIEST] foolishly daring; rash.

fool'ish, a. silly; unwise.

fool'proof, a. simple, safe, etc.

foot, n. [pl. FEET] 1. end part of the leg, on which one stands. 2. bottom; base. 3. measure of length, 12 inches. —v. [Col.] pay (a bill). —**foot it,** [Col.] to walk. —**on foot,** walking.

foot'ball, n. 1. game played on a field with an inflated leather ball. 2. this ball.

foot'hold, n. place for the feet, as in climbing.

foot'ing, n. 1. secure placing of the feet. 2. basis for relationship.

foot'lights, n.pl. lights at the front of a stage floor.

foot'note, n. note at the bottom of a page.

foot'print, n. mark left by a foot.

foot'step, n. 1. sound of a step. 2. footprint.

foot'stool, n. stool for a seated person's feet.

fop, n. vain man fussy about his clothes, etc.

for, prep. 1. in place of. 2. in the interest of. 3. in favor of. 4. with the purpose of. 5. in search of. 6. meant to be received, used, etc. by. 7. with respect to. 8. because of. 9. to the extent or duration of. —con. because.

for'age (-ij) n. fodder. —v. to search for food.

for'ay (-ā) n. & v. raid.

for·bear', v. [-BORE, -BORNE, -BEARING] 1. refrain (from). 2. control oneself. —**for·bear'ance,** n.

for·bid', v. [-BADE (-bad') or -BAD, -BIDDEN, -BIDDING] not permit; prohibit.

for·bid'ding, a. frightening.

force, n. 1. strength; power. 2. coercion. 3. effectiveness. 4. organized group, as an army. —v. 1. make do something; compel. 2. break open. 3. impose, produce, etc. by force.—**force′ful**, a.

for′ceps, n. [pl. -CEPS] small tongs or pincers.

for′ci·ble, a. with force.—**for′ci·bly**, adv.

ford, n. shallow place in a river.—v. cross at a ford.

fore, adv. & a. (in or toward) the front part.

fore-, pref. before; in front.

fore′arm, n. arm between the elbow and wrist.

fore′bode′, v. foretell.

fore′cast, v. [-CAST or -CASTED, -CASTING] predict.—n. prediction.—**fore′cast′er**, n.

fore·cas·tle (fōk′s'l), fōr′kas'l) n. forward deck or front part of a ship.

fore·close′, v. take away the right to redeem (a mortgage).

fore′fa′ther, n. ancestor.

fore′fin′ger, n. finger nearest the thumb.

fore′front, n. extreme front.

fore′go′ing, a. preceding.

fore′gone, a. previous.

fore′ground, n. part of a scene nearest the viewer.

fore′head, n. part of the face above the eyebrows.

for′eign (-in) a. 1. of or from another country. 2. not characteristic.—**for′eign-born′**, a.—**for′eign·er**, n.

fore′man, n. [pl. -MEN] 1. man in charge of workers. 2. chairman of a jury.

fore′most, a. & adv. first.

fore′noon, n. time before noon.

fo·ren′sic, a. of or suitable for public debate.

fore′run′ner, n. person or thing foretelling another.

fore·see′, v. [-SAW, -SEEN, -SEEING] see beforehand.

fore′shad′ow, v. presage.

fore′sight, n. 1. power to foresee. 2. prudence.

fore′skin, n. fold of skin over the end of the penis.

for′est, n. tract of land covered with trees.

fore·stall′, v. prevent by acting beforehand.

for′est·ry, n. science of the care of forests.

fore·tell′, v. [-TOLD, -TELLING] predict.

fore′thought, n. foresight.

for·ev′er, adv. 1. for all time. 2. at all times.

fore′word, n. preface.

for′feit (-fit) n. penalty.—v. lose as a penalty.—**for′fei·ture** (-chẽr) n.

forge, n. 1. furnace for heating metal to be wrought. 2. smith's shop.—v. 1. to

shape by heating and hammering. 2. counterfeit (a signature). 3. advance slowly.—**for′ger·y** [pl. -IES] n.

for·get′, v. [-GOT, -GOTTEN or -GOT, -GETTING] 1. be unable to remember. 2. neglect.—**for·get′ful**, a.

for·get′-me-not′, n. plant with small, blue flowers.

for·give′, v. [-GAVE, -GIVEN, -GIVING] give up wanting to punish; pardon.—**for·give′ness**, n.—**for·giv′ing**, a.

for·go′, v. [-WENT, -GONE, -GOING] do without.

fork, n. 1. pronged instrument for lifting. 2. place of branching.—v. to branch.

for·lorn′, a. 1. deserted. 2. wretched; miserable.

form, n. 1. shape; figure. 2. mold. 3. style; customary behavior. 4. document to be filled in.—v. 1. to shape. 2. develop (habits). 3. constitute.—**form′less**, a.

for′mal, a. 1. according to custom, rule, etc. 2. stiff; prim. 3. for use at ceremonies.—**for′mal·ly**, adv.

form·al′de·hyde (-hīd) n. disinfectant and preservative.

for·mal′i·ty, n. 1. an observing of customs, rules, etc. 2. [pl. -TIES] formal act.

for′mat, n. general arrangement, as of a book.

for·ma′tion, n. 1. a forming. 2. thing formed; structure.—**form′a·tive**, a.

for′mer, a. 1. of the past. 2. being the first mentioned.—**for′mer·ly**, adv.

for′mi·da·ble, a. 1. causing fear. 2. hard to handle.

for′mu·la, n. [pl. -LAS, -LAE (-lē)] 1. fixed expression or rule. 2. set of symbols expressing a mathematical rule, chemical compound, etc.—**for′mu·late**, v.—**for′mu·la′tion**, n.

for′ni·ca′tion, n. sexual intercourse between unmarried people.—**for′ni·cate**, v.

for·sake′, v. [-SOOK, -SAKEN, -SAKING] abandon; desert.

for·swear′, v. 1. swear to give up. 2. commit perjury.

for·syth′i·a (-sith′-) n. shrub with yellow flowers.

fort, n. fortified place for military defense.

for′te (-ti, -tā) a. & adv. Mus. loud.—n. (fôrt) what one does well.

forth, adv. 1. forward. 2. out; into view.

forth·com'ing, *a.* 1. about to appear. 2. ready at hand.

forth'right', *a.* frank.

forth·with', *adv.* at once.

for·ti·fi·ca'tion, *n.* 1. a fortifying. 2. a fort.

for'ti·fy, *v.* strengthen.

for·tis'si·mo, *a. & adv. Mus.* very loud.

for'ti·tude, *n.* calm courage.

fort'night, *n.* two weeks.

for'tress, *n.* fortified place.

for·tu'i·tous, *a.* accidental.

for'tu·nate (-cha-nit) *a.* lucky. —**for'tu·nate·ly,** *adv.*

for'tune, *n.* 1. luck; fate. 2. good luck. 3. wealth.

for'ty, *a. & n.* [*pl.* -TIES] four times ten. —**for'ti·eth,** *a. & n.*

fo'rum, *n.* meeting for public discussion.

for'ward, *a.* 1. at, to, or of the front. 2. advanced. 3. bold. —*adv.* ahead: also **forwards.** —*v.* 1. promote. 2. send on.

fos'sil, *n.* hardened plant or animal remains, as in rock.

fos'ter, *v.* 1. bring up. 2. promote. —*a.* in a family but not by birth or adoption.

fought, *pt. & pp.* of **fight.**

foul, *a.* 1. filthy. 2. stormy. 3. outside the rules or limits. 4. very bad. —*n.* foul hit, blow, etc.—*v.* 1. make filthy. 2. entangle. 3. make a foul.

found, *pt. & pp.* of **find.** —*v.* establish. —**found'er,** *n.*

foun·da'tion, *n.* 1. establishment or basis. 2. base of a wall, house, etc. 3. philanthropic fund or institution.

foun'der, *v.* 1. fall or go lame. 2. fill and sink, as a ship.

found'ling, *n.* deserted child.

found'ry, *n.* [*pl.* -RIES] place where metal is cast.

fount, *n.* fountain.

foun'tain, *n.* 1. spring of water. 2. jet of water or basin for it. 3. source.

foun'tain·head', *n.* source.

four, *a. & n.* one more than three. —**fourth,** *a. & n.*

four'score', *a. & n.* eighty.

four'some, *n.* group of four people.

four'teen', *a. & n.* four more than ten. —**four'teenth',** *a. & n.*

fowl, *n.* 1. any bird. 2. a domestic bird, as the chicken.

fox, *n.* small, wild, doglike animal. —*v.* to trick. —**fox'y** [-IER, -IEST] *a.*

fox'glove, *n.* plant with long spikes of flowers.

fox'hole, *n.* hole dug as protection against gunfire.

fox trot, ballroom dance.

foy'er, *n.* entrance hall.

fra'cas (frā'-) *n.* brawl.

frac'tion, *n.* 1. part of a whole, as ¾, ½, etc. 2. small part.

frac'tious, *a.* unruly.

frac'ture, *n.* a break, esp. in a bone. —*v.* to break; crack.

frag'ile (fraj'-) *a.* easily broken. —**fra·gil'i·ty,** *n.*

frag'ment, *n.* 1. part broken away. 2. incomplete part. —**frag'men·tar'y,** *a.*

fra'grant (frā'-) *a.* sweet-smelling. —**fra'grance,** *n.*

frail, *a.* 1. fragile. 2. delicate or weak. —**frail'ty** [*pl.* -TIES] *n.*

frame, *v.* 1. make, form, build, etc. 2. enclose in a border. 3. [Sl.] make seem guilty by a plot. —*n.* 1. framework. 2. framing border or case. 3. mood.

frame'work, *n.* supporting or basic structure.

franc, *n.* Fr. monetary unit.

fran'chise (-chiz) *n.* 1. special right. 2. right to vote.

fran'gi·ble (-ja-) *a.* breakable.

frank, *a.* outspoken; candid. —*v.* send (mail) free. —**frank'ly,** *adv.* —**frank'-ness,** *n.*

frank'furt·er, *n.* a smoked link sausage; wiener.

frank'in·cense, *n.* gum resin burned as incense.

fran'tic, *a.* wild with anger, worry, etc.—**fran'ti·cal·ly,** *adv.*

fra·ter'nal, *a.* 1. brotherly. 2. of a fellowship society.

fra·ter'ni·ty, *n.* [*pl.* -TIES] 1. brotherliness. 2. college social club for men. 3. group with like interests.

frat'er·nize, *v.* be friendly.

fraud, *n.* 1. a cheating or tricking; dishonesty. 2. [Col.] hypocrite; cheat.

fraud'u·lent, *a.* 1. using fraud. 2. done by fraud.

fraught, *a.* filled (*with*).

fray, *n.* quarrel or fight. —*v.* make or become ragged.

fraz'zle, *v.* [Col.] wear out. —*n.* [Col.] frazzled state.

freak, *n.* abnormal animal or plant. —*a.* abnormal.

freck·le, *n.* small brown spot on the skin.—*v.* to spot with freckles.

free, *a.* [FREER, FREEST] 1. not under another's control.

2. loose, clear, unrestricted, etc. 3. without cost. —*adv.* 1. without cost. 2. in a free way. —*v.* [FREED, FREEING] make free from (or of), without. —**free'dom,** *n.*

free'boot'er, *n.* a pirate.

free'-for-all', *n.* brawl.

free'think'er, *n.* religious skeptic.

free'way, *n.* multiple-lane highway with interchanges.

freeze, *v.* [FROZE, FROZEN] 1. change into, or become covered with, ice. 2. make very cold. 3. kill or damage by cold. 4. fix (prices, etc.) at a set level. —*n.* a freezing.

freeze'-dry', *v.* preserve (food) by freezing quickly and drying.

freez'er, *n.* refrigerator for freezing and storing foods.

freight (frāt) *n.* 1. goods transported. 2. transportation of goods or its cost. 3. train for freight.

freight'er, *n.* ship for freight.

French, *a. & n.* (of) the people or language of France. —**French'man** [*pl.* -MEN] *n.*

French fried, fried in deep fat.

French horn, brass-wind horn with a coiled tube.

fre·net'ic, *a.* frantic.

fren'zy, *n.* [*pl.* -ZIES] wild excitement. —**fren'zied,** *a.*

fre'quen·cy, *n.* [*pl.* -CIES] 1. frequent occurrence. 2. number of times anything recurs in a given period.

fre'quent, *a.* 1. occurring often. 2. constant. —*v.* (fri-kwent') go to habitually.

fres'co, *n.* [*pl.* -COES, -COS] painting done on wet plaster.

fresh, *a.* 1. not spoiled, stale, worn out, etc. 2. new. 3. refreshing. 4. not salt: said of water. —**fresh'en,** *v.*

fresh'et, *n.* flooded stream.

fresh'man, *n.* [*pl.* -MEN] first-year student in high school or college.

fret, *v.* [FRETTED, FRETTING] & *n.* worry. —**fret'ful,** *a.*

fret'work, *n.* ornate openwork.

fri'a·ble, *a.* easily crumbled.

fri'ar, *n.* R.C.Ch. member of a religious order.

fric'as·see' (-sē') *n.* stewed pieces of meat.

fric'tion, *n.* 1. rubbing of one object against another. 2. conflict. —**fric'tion·al,** *a.*

Fri'day, *n.* sixth day of the week.

fried, pt. & pp. of **fry.**

friend, *n.* 1. person one knows and likes. 2. ally —**friend'ship,** *n.*

friend'ly, *a.* [-LIER, -LIEST] kindly; helpful.

frieze (frēz) *n.* decorative band around a wall, etc.

frig·ate (frig'it) *n.* fast sailing warship.

fright, *n.* sudden fear.

fright'en, *v.* 1. make afraid. 2. drive (*away*) with fear.

fright'ful, *a.* 1. causing fright. 2. disgusting.

frig'id (frij'id) *a.* very cold. —**fri·gid'i·ty,** *n.*

frill, *n.* 1. ruffle. 2. [Col.] fancy ornament. —**frill'y,** *a.*

fringe, *n.* 1. border, as of loose threads. —*v.* to edge, as with a fringe.

frip'per·y, *n.* [*pl.* -IES] showy display, clothes, etc.

frisk, *v.* to frolic.

frisk'y, *a.* [-IER, -IEST] lively. —**frisk'i·ness,** *n.*

frit'ter, *v.* waste (money, etc.) by bit by bit.

friv'o·lous, *a.* 1. trivial. 2. silly. —**fri·vol'i·ty** (-vol'-) [*pl.* -IES]

frizz, friz'zle, *v.* form into tight curls. —**friz'zy,** *a.*

fro, *adv.* back: only in *to and fro,* back and forth.

frock, *n.* 1. dress. 2. robe.

frog, *n.* 1. leaping web-footed animal. 2. braided loop.— **frog in the throat,** hoarseness.

frol'ic, *n.* 1. gay party. 2. fun. —*v.* [-ICKED, -ICKING] have fun. —**frol'ic·some,** *a.*

from, *prep.* 1. beginning at. 2. out of. 3. originating with. 4. out of the possibility, reach, etc. of. 5. as not being like. 6. because of.

frond, *n.* fern or palm leaf.

front, *n.* 1. forward part. 2. first part. 3. land along a street, ocean, etc. 4. outward behavior. —*a.* of or at the front. —*v.* to face. —**front'age,** *n.* —**fron'tal,** *a.*

fron·tier' (-tēr') *n.* 1. border of a country. 2. new or unexplored field. —**fron·tiers'man** [*pl.* -MEN] *n.*

fron'tis·piece, *n.* picture facing the title page.

frost, *n.* 1. temperature causing freezing. 2. frozen dew or vapor. —*v.* cover with frost or frosting. —**frost'y** [-IER, -IEST] *a.*

frost'bite, *n.* injury from intense cold. —**frost'bit'ten,** *a.*

frost'ing, n. 1. icing. 2. dull finish on glass.

froth, n. & v. foam. —**froth'y** [-IER, -IEST] a.

fro'ward (frō'-) a. stubborn.

frown, v. 1. contract the brows. 2. look with disapproval (on). —n. a frowning.

frow'zy, a. slovenly.

froze, pt. of freeze.

fro'zen, pp. of freeze.

fru'gal, a. thrifty or sparing. —**fru·gal'i·ty,** n.

fruit, n. 1. pulpy, edible product of a plant or tree. 2. result; product. —**fruit'ful,** a. —**fruit'less,** a.

fru·i'tion (-ish'ən) n. 1. the bearing of fruit. 2. fulfillment.

frump, n. dowdy woman. —**frump'y,** a.

frus'trate, v. thwart; block. —**frus·tra'tion,** n.

fry, v. [FRIED, FRYING] cook in hot fat or oil. —n. young fish.

fuch'sia (fū'shə) n. plant with purplish-red flowers. —a. purplish-red.

fudge, n. soft candy made of butter, sugar, etc.

fu'el, n. thing burned for heat or power. —v. supply with or get fuel.

fu'gi·tive, a. 1. fleeing. 2. fleeting. —n. one who has fled from the law, etc.

-ful, suf. 1. full of. 2. having the qualities of. 3. apt to. 4. quantity that will fill.

ful'crum, n. support on which a lever turns.

ful·fill', ful·fil', v. [-FILLED, -FILLING] carry out or complete, as a promise or duty.

full, a. 1. containing all there is space for. 2. having much in it. 3. complete. 4. ample. —adv. greatest amount, etc. —adv. 1. completely. 2. exactly. —**full'ness,** n. —**full'y,** adv.

full'blown', a. matured.

full dress, formal dress.

full'-fledged', a. fully developed; of full status.

full'-grown', a. fully grown.

ful'mi·nate (ful'-) v. 1. explode. 2. denounce strongly.

ful'some (fool'-) a. sickeningly insincere.

fum'ble, v. grope or handle clumsily. —n. a fumbling.

fume (fūm) n. offensive smoke or vapor. —v. 1. give off fumes. 2. show anger.

fu'mi·gate, v. fill with fumes so as to kill vermin, germs, etc.

fun, n. 1. lively play; gay time. 2. source of gaiety. —**make fun of,** ridicule.

func'tion, n. 1. special or typical action, use, duty, etc. 2. formal ceremony or social affair. —v. do its work. —**func'tion·al,** a.

fund, n. 1. supply; store. 2. money set aside for a purpose. 3. pl. ready money.

fun·da·men'tal, a. & n. basic (thing).

fu'ner·al, n. burial ceremonies.

fu·ne're·al, a. sad; gloomy.

fun'gus, n. [pl. -GI (-jī), -GUSES] any of the mildews, molds, mushrooms, etc. —**fun'gous,** a.

fun'nel, n. 1. slim tube with a cone-shaped mouth. 2. ship's smokestack. —v. pour as through a funnel.

fun'ny, a. [-NIER, -NIEST] 1. amusing. 2. [Col.] odd.

fur, n. soft, thick hair on an animal. —a. of fur. —**fur'ry** [-RIER, -RIEST] a.

fur'be·low (-lō) n. fancy trimming.

fu'ri·ous (fyoor'i-) a. full of fury.

furl (fûrl) v. roll up tightly, as a flag.

fur'long, n. ⅛ of a mile.

fur'lough (-lō) n. a military leave of absence. —v. grant a furlough to.

fur'nace (-nis) n. structure in which heat is produced.

fur'nish, v. 1. put furniture into. 2. supply.

fur'nish·ings, n.pl. 1. furniture and fixtures, as for a house. 2. things to wear.

fur'ni·ture, n. chairs, beds, etc. in a room, etc.

fu·ror (fyoor'ôr) n. 1. widespread enthusiasm. 2. fury.

fur'ri·er, n. one who processes, or deals in, furs.

fur'row, n. 1. groove made in the ground by a plow. 2. deep wrinkle. —v. make furrows in.

fur'ther, a. 1. additional. 2. more distant. —adv. 1. to a greater extent. 2. in addition. 3. at or to a greater distance. —v. promote. —**fur'ther·ance,** n.

fur'ther·more, adv. besides.

fur'thest, a. most distant. —adv. at or to the greatest distance or extent.

fur'tive (-tiv) a. done or acting in a stealthy way.

fu·ry (fyoor'i) n. 1. wild rage. 2. violence.

fuse (fūz) v. melt (together). —n. 1. wick that is lighted to set off an explosive. 2. safety device that breaks an electric circuit when the current is too strong. —**fu′sion,** n.

fu′se·lage (-lij, -läzh) n. body of an airplane.

fu′sil·lade′ n. simultaneous discharge of many guns.

fuss, n. nervous, excited state. —v. bustle about or worry over trifles. —**fuss′y** [-IER, -IEST] a.

fu′tile (-til) a. useless. —**fu·til′i·ty,** n.

fu′ture (-chēr) a. that is to be or come. —n. 1. time that is to come. 2. what is going to be; prospects.

fuzz, n. loose, light particles; fine hairs. —**fuzz′y** [-IER, -IEST] a.

G

gab, n. & v. [GABBED, GAB-BING] [Col.] chatter. —**gab′by** [-BIER, -BIEST] a.

gab′ar·dine (-ēr-dēn) n. cloth with a diagonal weave.

gab′ble, v. & n. jabber.

ga′ble, n. triangular wall enclosed by the sloping ends of a roof. —**ga′bled,** a.

gad, v. [GADDED, GADDING] roam about restlessly. —**gad′a·bout,** n.

gad′fly, n. 1. large, stinging fly. 2. an annoying person.

gadg′et (gaj′-) n. small mechanical device.

gaff, n. large hook on a pole for landing fish.

gag, v. [GAGGED, GAGGING] 1. retch or cause to retch. 2. keep from speaking, as with a gag. —n. 1. something put into the mouth to prevent speech. 2. [Sl.] joke.

gage, n. 1. pledge. 2. challenge. 3. gauge. —v. gauge.

gai′e·ty (gā′-) n. 1. a being gay. 2. merrymaking.

gai′ly, adv. in a gay manner.

gain, v. 1. increase. 2. profit. —v. 1. earn. 2. win. 3. get as an addition or advantage. 4. reach. 5. make progress. —**gain on,** draw nearer to, as in a race.

gain′ful, a. profitable.

gain·say′, v. [-SAID, -SAYING] deny or contradict.

gait, n. manner of walking or running.

ga′la, a. festive. —n. festival.

gal′ax·y, n. [pl. -IES] very large group of stars.

gale, n. 1. strong wind. 2. outburst, as of laughter.

gall (gôl) n. 1. bile. 2. tumor on plant tissue. 3. [Col.] impudence. —v. annoy.

gal′lant, a. 1. brave and noble. 2. polite to women. —**gal′lan·try** [pl. -RIES] n.

gall bladder, sac attached to the liver, in which excess bile is stored.

gal′le·on, n. large Spanish ship of 15th-16th centuries.

gal′ler·y, n. [pl. -IES] 1. covered walk. 2. outside balcony. 3. theater balcony. 4. place for art exhibits.

gal′ley, n. [pl. -LEYS] 1. ancient sailing ship with oars. 2. ship's kitchen.

gal′li·vant, v. gad about for pleasure.

gal′lon, n. 4 quarts.

gal′lop, n. fastest gait of a horse. —v. go or make go at a gallop.

gal′lows, n. [pl. -LOWSES, -LOWS] structure for hanging condemned persons.

gall′stone, n. abnormal stony mass in the gall bladder.

ga·lore′, adv. in great plenty.

ga·losh′es, n.pl. high overshoes.

gal·van′ic, a. of electric current, esp. from a battery.

gal′va·nize, v. 1. startle. 2. plate (metal) with zinc.

gam′bit, n. opening move in chess.

gam′ble, v. 1. play games of chance for money. 2. take a risk. 3. bet. —n. risk; chance. —**gam′bler,** n.

gam′bol, v. & n. frolic.

game, n. 1. amusement or sport with competing players. 2. wild animals hunted for sport. —v. gamble. —a. [Col.] 1. plucky. 2. lame.

gam·ete′ (-ēt) n. reproductive cell.

gam′in, n. homeless child.

gam′ut, n. the entire range, esp. of a musical scale.

gam′y, a. [-IER, -IEST] 1. strongly flavored. 2. slightly tainted.

gan′der, n. male goose.

gang, n. group working or acting together.

gan′gling, a. thin and tall.

gan′gli·on, n. mass of nerve cells.

gang′plank, n. movable ramp from a ship to the dock.

gan′grene, n. decay of body tissue from lack of blood

supply. —**gan′gre·nous,** *a.*

gang′ster, *n.* member of a gang of criminals.

gang′way, *n.* 1. passageway. 2. gangplank. —*int.* clear the way!

gant′let, *n.* punishment of being beaten as one runs between two rows of men.

gaol (jāl) *n.* jail: Br. sp.

gap, *n.* 1. opening or break. 2. blank space.

gape, *v.* 1. open wide. 2. stare with the mouth open.

gar, *n.* long fish with a long snout: also **gar′fish.**

ga·rage′ (-räzh′, -räj′) *n.* shelter or repair shop for automobiles, etc.

garb, *n.* clothing; style of dress. —*v.* clothe.

gar′bage (-bij) *n.* waste parts of food.

gar′ble, *v.* distort (a story, etc.).

gar′den, *n.* 1. plot for flowers, vegetables, etc. 2. fertile area. 3. public park. —*v.* make, or work in, a garden. —**gar′den·er,** *n.*

gar·de′ni·a (-dēn′ya) *n.* waxy white flower.

Gar·gan′tu·an, *a.* huge.

gar′gle, *v.* rinse the throat. —*n.* liquid for gargling.

gar′goyle, *n.* gutter spout in the form of a sculptured grotesque creature.

gar′ish (gâr′-) *a.* gaudy.

gar′land, *n.* wreath of flowers, leaves, etc.

gar′lic, *n.* strong-smelling plant bulb, used to season. —**gar′lick·y,** *a.*

gar′ment, *n.* piece of clothing.

gar′ner, *v.* gather and store.

gar′net, *n.* deep-red gem.

gar′nish, *v.* decorate (food). —*n.* decoration for food.

gar′nish·ee′, *v.* attach (a debtor's wages, etc.) to pay the debts.

gar′ret, *n.* attic.

gar′ri·son, *n.* fort or the troops in it. —*v.* provide with troops.

gar·rote′ (-rot′) *v.* strangle. —*n.* device for strangling.

gar′ru·lous (gar′-) *a.* talking much. —**gar·ru′li·ty,** *n.*

gar′ter, *n.* elastic band to hold up a stocking.

gas, *n.* 1. fluid substance that can expand; vapor: some gases are used as fuel. 2. gasoline. —*v.* [GASSED, GASSING] attack with gas. —**gas′e·ous,** *a.*

gash, *v.* cut deep into. —*n.* deep cut.

gas′ket, *n.* rubber or metal ring sealing a joint, etc.

gas′o·line (-lēn) *n.* liquid fuel from petroleum.

gasp, *v.* catch the breath with effort. —*n.* a gasping.

gas′tric, *a.* of the stomach.

gas·tron′o·my, *n.* art of good eating. —**gas′tro·nom′i·cal,** *a.*

gate, *n.* 1. hinged door in a fence or wall. 2. number of paid admissions.

gate′way, *n.* entrance with a gate.

gath′er, *v.* 1. bring or come together; collect. 2. infer. 3. draw into pleats. —*n.* pleat. —**gath′er·ing,** *n.*

gauche (gōsh) *a.* tactless.

gaud′y (gôd′-) *a.* [-IER, -IEST] showy but tasteless. —**gaud′i·ly,** *adv.*

gauge (gāj) *n.* 1. standard measure. 2. device for measuring. —*v.* 1. to measure. 2. to estimate.

gaunt (gônt) *a.* haggard; thin.

gaunt′let, *n.* 1. long glove with a flaring cuff. 2. gantlet. —**throw down the gauntlet,** challenge.

gauze (gôz) *n.* loosely woven material. —**gauz′y,** *a.*

gave, pt. of **give.**

gav′el (gav′-) *n.* chairman's small mallet.

gawk, *v.* stare stupidly.

gawk′y, *a.* [-IER, -IEST] clumsy; ungainly.

gay, *a.* 1. joyous and lively. 2. bright. 3. [Sl.] homosexual.

gaze, *v.* look steadily; stare. —*n.* steady look.

ga·zelle′ *n.* swift antelope.

ga·zette′, *n.* newspaper.

gaz·et·teer′, *n.* dictionary of geographical names.

gear, *n.* 1. equipment. 2. system of toothed wheels that mesh. 3. such a wheel. —*v.* 1. connect by gears. 2. adjust.

gee (jē) *int.* [Sl.] exclamation of surprise, etc.

geese, *n.* pl. of **goose.**

Gei′ger counter (gī′gēr) instrument for measuring radioactivity.

gei·sha (gā′sha) *n.* Japanese woman entertainer.

gel′a·tin (jel′-) *n.* jellied substance extracted from bones, hoofs, vegetables, etc. —**ge·lat′i·nous,** *a.*

geld, *v.* castrate (a horse, etc.). —**geld′ing,** *n.*

gel′id (jel′-) *a.* frozen.

gem, *n.* precious stone.

Gem′i·ni, *n.* 3rd sign of the zodiac; the twins.

gen'der (jen'-) *n.* classification of words as masculine, feminine, or neuter.

gene (jēn) *n.* unit of heredity in chromosomes.

ge'ne·al'o·gy (jē'-) *n.* history of ancestry. —**ge'ne·a·log'i·cal,** *a.*

gen'er·al, *a.* 1. of or for all. 2. widespread. 3. usual. 4. not specific. —*n.* high-ranking army officer. —**in general,** usually. —**gen'er·al·ly,** *adv.*

gen'er·al'i·ty, *n.* [*pl.* -TIES] nonspecific idea or statement. —**gen'er·al·ize,** *v.*

gen'er·ate, *v.* cause to be; produce. —**gen'er·a'tive,** *a.*

gen'er·a'tion, *n.* 1. production. 2. all persons born about the same time. 3. average time (30 years) between generations.

gen'er·a'tor, *n.* machine for changing mechanical into electrical energy.

ge·ner'ic (jə-) *a.* 1. inclusive; general. 2. of a genus.

gen'er·ous, *a.* 1. giving readily; unselfish. 2. ample. —**gen'er·os'i·ty,** *n.*

gen'e·sis, *n.* 1. origin. 2. [G-] first book of the Bible.

ge·net'ics, *n.* study of heredity. —**ge·net'ic,** *a.*

gen'ial (jēn'-) *a.* kindly; amiable. —**ge'ni·al'i·ty,** *n.*

ge·nie (jē'ni) *n.* magic spirit in Moslem tales.

gen'i·tals, *n.pl.* external sex organs. —**gen'i·tal,** *a.*

gen'i·tive, *a. & n. Gram.* (in) the case showing possession or origin.

gen'ius (jēn'-) *n.* 1. great mental or creative ability. 2. person having this.

gen'o·cide (jen'-) *n.* systematic killing of a whole people.

gen·teel', *a.* 1. (overly) polite, refined, etc.

gen'tile, Gen'tile (-tīl) *a. & n.* non-Jewish (person).

gen·til'i·ty, *n.* politeness.

gen'tle, *a.* 1. mild; moderate. 2. kindly; patient. —**gen'tly,** *adv.*

gen'tle·man, *n.* [*pl.* -MEN] 1. well-bred, courteous man. 2. any man; polite term.

gen'try, *n.* people just below the nobility.

gen'u·flect, *v.* bend the knee, as in worship. —**gen'u·flec'tion,** *n.*

gen'u·ine (-in) *a.* 1. real; true. 2. sincere.

ge'nus (jē'-) *n.* [*pl.* GENERA

(jen'ẽr-ə), GENUSES] class; kind, esp. in biology.

ge·og'ra·phy, *n.* science of the earth's surface, climates, plants, animals, etc. —**ge'o·graph'i·cal, ge'o·graph'ic,** *a.*

ge·ol'o·gy, *n.* science of the earth's crust and fossils. —**ge'o·log'i·cal** (-loj'-) *a.* —**ge·ol'o·gist,** *n.*

ge·om'e·try, *n.* branch of mathematics dealing with plane and solid figures. —**ge'o·met'ric, ge'o·met'ri·cal,** *a.*

ge'o·phys'ics, *n.* science of the effects of weather, tides, etc. on the earth. —**ge'o·phys'i·cal,** *a.*

ge·ra'ni·um (jə-rā'-) *n.* plant with showy flowers.

ger'i·at'rics (jer'-) *n.* branch of medicine dealing with diseases of old age.

germ, *n.* 1. microscopic, disease-causing organism. 2. seed, bud, etc. 3. origin.

Ger'man, *n. & a.* (native or language) of Germany.

ger·mane' (jẽr-) *a.* relevant.

ger'mi·cide, *n.* anything used to destroy germs.

ger'mi·nate, *v.* sprout, as from a seed. —**ger'mi·na'tion,** *n.*

ger'und (jer'-) *n.* verbal noun ending in *-ing.*

ges·ta'tion (jes-) *n.* pregnancy.

ges·tic'u·late (jes-) *v.* to gesture.

ges'ture (-chẽr) *n.* movement of part of the body, to express ideas, feelings, etc. —*v.* make gestures.

get, *v.* [GOT, GOT or GOTTEN, GETTING] 1. come to have; obtain. 2. come, go, or arrive. 3. bring. 4. make or become. 5. [Col.] *a)* be obliged. *b)* possess. *c)* baffle. *d)* understand. —**get along,** manage: also **get by.** —**get around,** circumvent. —**get away,** escape. —**get over,** recover from. —**get through,** 1. finish. 2. survive. —**get together,** 1. assemble. 2. [Col.] reach an agreement. —**get up,** rise (from sleep, etc.).

get'a·way', *n.* 1. a starting, as in a race. 2. an escape.

gew'gaw (gū'gô) *n.* trinket.

gey'ser (gī'zẽr) *n.* gushing hot spring.

ghast'ly (gast'-) *a.* [-LIER, -LIEST] 1. horrible. 2. pale as a ghost.

gher'kin (gûr'-) *n.* small pickle.

ghet·to (get'ō) *n.* section of a city to which Jews, etc. are restricted.

ghost, *n.* supposed disembodied spirit of a dead person. —**ghost'ly,** *a.*

ghoul (gōōl) *n.* supposed evil spirit that feeds on the dead. —**ghoul'ish,** *a.*

GI, G.I. (jē'ī') *n.* [Col.] enlisted soldier.

gi'ant, *n.* person or thing of great size, strength, etc. —*a.* like a giant.

gib'ber (jib'-) *v.* speak incoherently.

gib'ber·ish, *n.* confused talk.

gib'bet, (jib'-) *n.* a gallows.

gib'bon (gib'-) *n.* small, slender, long-armed ape.

gibe (jīb) *v. & n.* taunt.

gib'let (jib'-) *n.* edible internal part of a fowl.

gid'dy (gid'-) *a.* [-DIER, -DIEST] 1. dizzy. 2. frivolous. —**gid'di·ness,** *n.*

gift, *n.* 1. a present. 2. a giving. 3. natural ability.

gift'ed, *a.* talented.

gigan'tic (jī-) *a.* huge.

gig'gle, *v.* laugh in a nervous, silly way. —*n.* such a laugh.

Gi·la monster (hē'lə) stout, poisonous lizard.

gild, *v.* [alt. pt. & pp. GILT] 1. overlay with gold. 2. make better than it is.

gill (gil) *n.* 1. breathing organ of a fish. 2. (jil) ¼ pint.

gilt, *n.* surface layer of gold.

gim'let (gim'-) *n.* small tool for making holes.

gim'mick, *n.* [Sl.] tricky or deceptive device.

gin (jin) *n.* 1. an alcoholic liquor. 2. a machine for separating cotton from the seeds.

gin'ger, *n.* spice from the root of a tropical herb.

ginger ale, nonalcoholic drink flavored with ginger.

gin'ger·bread, *n.* cake flavored with ginger.

gin'ger·ly, *a. & adv.* careful(ly) or timid(ly).

ging·ham (giŋ'əm) *n.* cotton cloth in stripes or checks.

gip'sy, *n.* [*pl.* -SIES] gypsy.

gi·raffe', *n.* large African animal with a very long neck.

gird (gûrd) *v.* [alt. pt. & pp. GIRT] 1. encircle. 2. prepare for action.

gird'er, *n.* large beam for supporting a floor, etc.

gir'dle, *n.* 1. a belt. 2. light, flexible corset.

girl, *n.* female child or young woman. —**girl'ish,** *a.*

girth, *n.* 1. horse's belly band. 2. circumference.

gist (jist) *n.* main point.

give, *v.* [GAVE, GIVEN, GIV-ING] 1. hand over; deliver. 2. cause to have. 3. produce. 4. utter. 5. perform. 6. bend, etc. from pressure. —*n.* a bending, etc. under pressure. —**give away,** [Col.] expose. —**give forth** (or **off**), emit. —**give in,** yield. —**give out,** 1. make public. 2. distribute. 3. become worn out. —**give up,** 1. relinquish. 2. stop.

giv'en, *a.* 1. bestowed. 2. accustomed. 3. stated.

giz'zard, *n.* muscular second stomach of a bird.

gla'cier (-shēr) *n.* large mass of ice moving slowly down a slope. —**gla'cial,** *a.*

glad, *a.* [GLADDER, GLADDEST] 1. happy. 2. causing joy. 3. pleased. —**glad'ly,** *adv.*

glad'den, *v.* make glad.

glade, *n.* clearing in a forest.

glad'i·a'tor, *n.* 1. in ancient Rome, a fighter in public shows. 2. any fighter.

glad·i'o·lus, *n.* plant with tall spikes of funnel-shaped flowers: also **glad'i·o'la.**

glam'our, glam'or, *n.* bewitching charm. —**glam'or·ous, glam'our·ous,** *a.*

glance, *v.* 1. strike and go off at an angle. 2. look briefly. —*n.* a glimpse.

gland, *n.* body organ that secretes a substance. —**glan'du·lar** (-joo-) *a.*

glare, *v.* 1. shine with a dazzling light. 2. stare fiercely. —*n.* 1. dazzling light. 2. fierce stare. 3. glassy surface, as of ice.

glar'ing, *a.* flagrant.

glass, *n.* 1. hard, brittle substance, usually transparent. 2. drinking vessel, mirror, etc. made of this. 3. *pl.* eyeglasses or binoculars.

glass'y, *a.* [-IER, -IEST] 1. like glass. 2. expressionless.

glau·co'ma (glô-) *n.* eye disease.

glaze, *v.* 1. furnish with glass. 2. give a glossy finish to. 3. cover with a sugar coating. —*n.* glassy coating.

gla'zier (-zhēr) *n.* one who fits glass in windows.

gleam, *n.* 1. faint glow of light. 2. brief show, as of hope. —*v.* send out a gleam.

glean, *v.* collect slowly, as grain left by reapers.

glee, *n.* joy. —**glee'ful,** *a.*

glen, *n.* secluded valley.

glib, *a.* [GLIBBER, GLIBBEST] fluent, esp. in a shallow way.

glide, *v.* move or descend smoothly and easily. —*n.* smooth, easy flow or descent.

glid′er, *n.* engineless airplane carried by air currents.

glim′mer, *v. & n.* (give) a faint, flickering light.

glimpse, *n.* brief, quick view. —*v.* catch a glimpse of.

glint, *v. & n.* gleam.

glis·ten (glis′n) *v. & n.* sparkle.

glit′ter, *v. & n.* sparkle.

gloam′ing, *n.* twilight.

gloat, *v.* feel or show malicious pleasure.

globe, *n.* 1. ball-shaped thing. 2. the earth, or a model of it.—**glob′al,** *a.*

glob′u·lar (glob′yoo-) *a.* 1. spherical. 2. of globules.

glob′ule, *n.* small drop.

gloom, *n.* 1. darkness. 2. dark place. 3. sadness. — **gloom′y** [-IER, -IEST] *a.*

glo′ri·fy, *v.* [-FIED, -FYING] 1. give glory to; honor. 2. make seem greater. —**glo′ri·fi·ca′tion,** *n.*

glo′ri·ous, *a.* 1. full of glory. 2. splendid.

glo′ry, *n.* [*pl.* -RIES] 1. great praise or fame. 2. splendor. 3. heavenly bliss. —*v.* [-RIED, -RYING] exult (*in*).

gloss, *n.* 1. surface polish. 2. explanation; footnote. —*v.* smooth (*over*), as an error. —**gloss′y** [-IER, -IEST] *a.*

glos′sa·ry, *n.* [*pl.* -RIES] list of difficult terms with definitions, as for a book.

glot′tis, *n.* opening between the vocal cords.

glove, *n.* 1. covering for the hand with sheaths for the fingers. 2. padded mitt for boxing. —**gloved,** *a.*

glow, *v.* 1. give off burning or steady light. 2. be elated. 3. be bright with color. —*n.* 1. bright or steady light. 2. brightness, warmth, etc.

glow′er (glou′-) *v. & n.* stare with sullen anger.

glow′worm, *n.* phosphorescent insect or larva.

glu′cose, *n.* the sugar in fruits and honey.

glue, *n.* thick, adhesive liquid. —*v.* stick together as with glue. —**glu′ey,** *a.*

glum, *a.* [GLUMMER, GLUMMEST] gloomy.

glut, *v.* [GLUTTED, GLUTTING] feed, fill, or supply to excess. —*n.* excess.

glu′ten (glōō′-) *n.* sticky protein substance in wheat flour.

glu′ti·nous, *a.* sticky.

glut′ton, *n.* one who eats toomuch.—**glut′ton·ous,***a.*

glut′ton·y, *n.* overeating.

glyc′er·in, glyc′er·ine (glis′-) *n.* colorless sirupy liquid used in lotions, etc.

gnarl (närl) *n.* knot on a tree. —*v.* to twist.

gnash (nash) *v.* grind (the teeth) together.

gnat (nat) *n.* small insect.

gnaw (nô) *v.* [alt. pp. GNAWN] 1. wear away by biting. 2. torment.—**gnaw′ing,** *a.*

gnome (nōm) *n.* dwarf.

gnu (nōō) *n.* African antelope.

go, *v.* [WENT, GONE, GOING] 1. move along; pass or proceed. 2. depart. 3. work, as a clock. 4. turn or become. 5. fit or suit. 6. belong in a place. —*n.* 1. a success. 2. [Col.] energy. 3. [Col.] a try.—**go back on,** [Col.] break, as a promise. —**go off,** explode. —**go out,** be extinguished. 2. go to social affairs, etc.—**go over,** 1. examine. 2. do again.—**go through,** 1. endure. 2. search.—**let go,** release one's hold.

goad (gōd) *n.* 1. pointed stick. 2. spur. —*v.* urge on.

goal, *n.* 1. place where a race, trip, etc. ends. 2. place one strives for. 3. place to put the ball or puck to score.

goat, *n.* cud-chewing horned animal.

goat·ee′, *n.* pointed beard on a man's chin.

goat′herd, *n.* herder of goats.

gob, *n.* 1. [Col.] lump or mass. 2. [Sl.] U.S. sailor.

gob′ble, *n.* cry of a male turkey. —*v.* 1. make this cry. 2. eat greedily. —**gob′bler,** *n.*

go′-be·tween′, *n.* one acting between two persons.

gob′let, *n.* stemmed glass.

gob′lin, *n.* evil spirit.

God, *n.* 1. monotheistic creator and ruler of the universe. 2. [g-] any divine being. —**god′dess,** *n.fem.*

god′like, *a.*

god′child, *n.* person (**god′daugh′ter** or **god′son**) that a godparent sponsors.

god′less, *a.* 1. irreligious. 2. wicked.

god′ly, *a.* [-LIER, -LIEST] devoted to God; devout.

god′par′ent, *n.* spiritual

sponsor (god'fa'ther or god'moth'er) of an infant, esp. at baptism.

god'send, n. something unexpected but much needed.

gog'gle, v. stare with bulging eyes. —n. [in pl.] large spectacles to protect the eyes against dust, etc.

go'ing, n. 1. departure. 2. degree of ease in traveling. —a. working.

goi'ter, goi'tre, n. enlargement of the thyroid gland.

gold, n. 1. yellow, precious metal, a chemical element. 2. money; wealth. 3. bright yellow. —gold'en, a.

gold'en·rod, n. plant with long, yellow flower clusters.

gold'finch, n. small, yellow American songbird.

gold'fish, n. small yellowish fish, kept in ponds, etc.

golf, n. outdoor game in which a small ball is driven, with special clubs, into holes.

gon'do·la, n. boat used on canals of Venice. —gon'do·lier' (-lêr') n.

gone, pt. & pp. of **go.**

gong, n. metal disk that resounds loudly when struck.

gon·or·rhe'a (gon'ə-rē'ə) n. venereal disease.

goo'ber, n. peanut.

good, a. [BETTER, BEST] 1. having proper qualities. 2. beneficial. 3. of moral excellence. 4. enjoyable, happy, etc. 5. considerable. —n. 1. worth or virtue. 2. benefit. —good'ness, n.

good'-by', good'-bye', int. & n. farewell: also written goodby, goodbye.

Good Friday, Friday before Easter.

good'-heart'ed, a. kind.

good'-look'ing, a. handsome.

good'ly, a. rather large.

good'-na'tured, a. pleasant.

goods, n.pl. 1. personal property. 2. wares. 3. fabric.

good'y, n. [pl. -IES] [Col.] thing good to eat.

goose, n. [pl. GEESE] 1. long-necked water bird like a large duck. 2. silly person.

goose'ber'ry, n. [pl. -RIES] sour berry used for jam, etc.

go'pher (-fēr) n. burrowing rodent.

gore, n. 1. clotted blood. 2. tapered cloth inserted to add width. —v. 1. pierce as with a tusk. 2. insert gores in. —gor'y [-IER, -IEST] a.

gorge, n. deep, narrow pass.

—v. eat or stuff greedily.

gor'geous, a. magnificent.

go·ril'la, n. largest of the apes, native to Africa.

gosh, int. call of surprise.

gos'ling, n. young goose.

gos'pel, n. 1. teachings of Jesus and the Apostles. 2. belief proclaimed as true.

gos'sa·mer, n. filmy cobweb or cloth. —a. filmy.

gos'sip, n. 1. one who chatters about others. 2. such idle talk. —v. indulge in gossip. —gos'sip·y, a.

got, pt. & pp. of **get.**

got'ten, alt. pp. of **get.**

gouge (gouj) n. 1. chisel for cutting grooves. 2. such a groove. —v. 1. scoop out as with a gouge. 2. [Col.] overcharge. —goug'er, n.

gou'lash (gōō'läsh) n. stew seasoned with paprika.

gourd (gôrd, goord) n. 1. bulb-shaped fruit of a trailing plant. 2. its dried shell hollowed out for use.

gour'mand (goor'mənd) n. one who likes to eat.

gour'met (goor'mā) n. judge of fine foods and drinks.

gout, n. disease with painful swelling of the joints.

gov'ern, v. 1. control. 2. influence; determine.

gov'ern·ess, n. woman hired to teach children at home.

gov'ern·ment, n. 1. control; rule. 2. system of ruling. 3. those who rule. —gov'ern·men'tal, a.

gov'er·nor, n. 1. one who governs; esp., head of a State. 2. device to control engine speed automatically.

gown, n. 1. woman's dress. 2. long robe, as for a judge.

grab, v. [GRABBED, GRABBING] snatch suddenly. —n. a grabbing.

grace, n. 1. beauty of form, movement, etc. 2. favor; good will. 3. delay granted for payment due. 4. prayer of thanks at a meal. 5. God's love for man. —v. [GRACED, GRACING] dignify or adorn. —in the good graces of, in favor with. —grace'ful, a. —grace'ful·ly, adv.

gra'cious, a. kind, polite, charming, pleasing, etc.

grack'le, n. small blackbird.

gra·da'tion, n. 1. arrangement in steps. 2. stage in a series.

grade, n. 1. degree in a scale of rank or quality. 2. slope.

3. any of the school years through the 12th. 4. a mark or rating on a test. —v. 1. classify; sort. 2. give a grade (n. 4) to. 3. make (ground) sloped or level.

grade crossing, place where a road crosses a railroad.

grade school, elementary school.

grad'u·al, a. little by little. **—grad'u·al·ly,** adv.

grad'u·ate (-it) n. one who has completed a course of study at a school or college. —v. (-āt) 1. give a diploma to (a graduate). 2. become a graduate. 3. mark with degrees for measuring. **—grad'u·a'tion,** n.

graft, n. 1. shoot, etc. of one plant inserted in another to grow. 2. transplanting of skin, etc. 3. dishonest gain of money by public officers. —v. insert (as a graft).

gra'ham, a. made of unsifted, whole-wheat flour.

grain, n. 1. seed of wheat, corn, etc. 2. cereal plants. 3. particle, as of salt or sand. 4. smallest unit of weight. 5. natural markings on wood, leather, etc.

gram, n. metric unit of weight (1/28 of an ounce).

-gram, suf. a writing or drawing.

gram'mar, n. system of speaking and writing a language. **—gram·mar'i·an,** n. **—gram·mat'i·cal,** a.

gran'a·ry, n. [pl. -RIES] building for storing grain.

grand, a. great in size, beauty, importance, etc.; splendid, imposing, etc. —n. [Sl.] a thousand dollars.

grand child, n. child (**grand daugh ter** or **grand son**) of one's son or daughter.

gran'deur (-jẽr) n. great size, beauty, etc.; splendor.

gran·dil'o·quent, a. bombastic.

gran'di·ose (-ōs) a. 1. very grand. 2. too grand.

grand jury, jury with power to indict persons for trial.

grand'par'ent, n. parent (**grand'fa'ther** or **grand'-moth'er**) of one's father or mother.

grand piano, large piano with a horizontal case.

grand'stand, n. structure for spectators of outdoor sports.

grange, n. 1. farm. 2. [G-] association of farmers.

gran'ite (-it) n. very hard crystalline rock.

gran·o'la, n. breakfast cereal of oats, honey, nuts, etc.

grant, v. 1. consent to or give. 2. concede. —n. something granted. **—take for granted,** consider as a fact.

gran'u·lar, a. of or like granules.

gran'u·late, v. form into granules. **—gran·u·la'tion,** n.

gran'ule, n. small grain.

grape, n. small, round fruit growing in clusters.

grape'fruit, n. large citrus fruit with a yellow rind.

grape'vine, n. 1. woody vine with grapes. 2. rumor.

graph, n. diagram showing changes in value.

-graph, suf. 1. that writes. 2. thing written.

graph'ic, a. 1. vivid; in lifelike detail. 2. of the arts of drawing, printing, etc. **—graph'i·cal·ly,** adv.

graph'ite, n. soft, black carbon in pencils, etc.

grap'nel, n. device with hooks or claws for grasping.

grap'ple, n. grapnel. —v. 1. grip in wrestling. 2. grip and hold. 2. struggle.

grasp, v. 1. grip; seize. 2. comprehend. —n. 1. a grip. 2. control. 3. power to grasp.

grasp'ing, a. greedy.

grass, n. 1. green plant grown for lawns. 2. cereal plant. 3. pasture. **—grass'y,** a.

grass'hop'per, n. leaping insect with long hind legs.

grate, v. 1. form into particles by scraping. 2. rub with a harsh sound. 3. irritate. —n. 1. frame of bars to hold fuel. 2. framework of bars over an opening.

grate'ful, a. thankful.

grat'i·fy, v. [-FIED, -FYING] 1. please. 2. indulge. **—grat'i·fi·ca'tion,** n.

grat'ing, n. grate (n. 2).

gra'tis, adv. & a. free.

grat'i·tude, n. thankful appreciation.

gra·tu'i·tous, a. 1. free of charge. 2. uncalled-for.

gra·tu'i·ty, n. [pl. -TIES] gift of money for a service.

grave, a. 1. serious. 2. solemn. —n. burial place, esp. a hole in the ground.

grav'el (grav'-) n. bits of rock. —v. cover with gravel.

grav'en (grāv'-) a. carved.

grave'yard, n. cemetery.

grav'i·tate, v. be attracted.

gravi·ta'tion, n. *Physics* force of mutual attraction between masses.

grav'i·ty, n. 1. seriousness. 2. weight. 3. *Physics* gravitation; esp., the pull on bodies toward earth's center.

gra'vy, n. [pl. -VIES] juice from cooking meat.

gray, n. mixture of black and white. —a. 1. of this color. 2. dreary. —**gray'ish,** a.

graze, v. 1. feed on growing grass, etc. 2. rub lightly in passing. —n. a grazing.

grease, n. 1. melted animal fat. 2. thick oily lubricant. —v. put grease on. —**greas'y** [-IER, -IEST] a.

great, a. 1. much bigger, more, or better than average. 2. being one generation removed. —**great'ly,** adv.

greed, n. excessive desire, as for wealth. —**greed'y** [-IER, -IEST] a. —**greed'i·ly,** adv.

Greek, n. & a. (native or language) of Greece.

green, n. 1. color of grass. 2. pl. leafy vegetables. 3. smooth turf. —a. 1. of the color green. 2. unripe. 3. inexperienced. —**green'ness,** n.

green'er·y, n. green foliage.

green'house, n. heated glass building for growing plants.

greet, v. address, meet, or receive in a certain way.

greet'ing, n. act or words of one who greets.

gre·gar'i·ous, a. sociable.

gre·nade', n. small bomb usually thrown by hand.

gren·a·dier' (-dêr') n. Brit. soldier of a special regiment.

grew, pt. of **grow.**

grey, n. & a. gray: Br. sp.

grey'hound, n. swift dog.

grid'dle, n. flat pan for cooking pancakes, etc.

grid'i·ron, n. 1. framework of bars on which to broil. 2. football field.

grief, n. deep sorrow. —**come to grief,** fail.

griev'ance (grēv'-) n. complaint or a basis for it.

grieve, v. be or make sad.

griev'ous, a. 1. causing grief. 2. deplorable. —**griev'ous·ly,** adv.

grif'fin, n. mythical beast, part eagle and part lion.

grill, n. 1. gridiron. 2. restaurant serving grilled foods. —v. 1. broil. 2. question relentlessly.

grille (gril) n. open grating forming a screen.

grim, a. [GRIMMER, GRIMMEST] 1. fierce. 2. hideous; ghastly. —**grim'ly,** adv.

gri·mace (gri-mās') n. twisting of the facial features. —v. make grimaces.

grime, n. sooty dirt. —**grim'y** [-IER, -IEST] a.

grin, v. [GRINNED, GRINNING] smile broadly. —n. such a smile.

grind, v. [GROUND, GRINDING] 1. crush into bits. 2. sharpen, smooth, etc. by friction. 3. rub harshly. 4. work by cranking. —n. hard task.

grind'stone, n. revolving stone for sharpening, etc.

grip, n. 1. firm hold. 2. handclasp. 3. a handle. 4. valise. —v. [GRIPPED, GRIPPING] hold firmly.

gripe, v. 1. cause pain in the bowels of. 2. [Sl.] complain. —n. [Sl.] complaint.

grippe (grip) n. influenza.

gris'ly (griz'-) a. [-LIER, -LIEST] ghastly.

grist, n. grain to be ground.

gris'tle n. cartilage.

grit, n. 1. rough bits of sand, etc. 2. obstinate courage. —v. [GRITTED, GRITTING] grind (the teeth). —**grit'ty** [-TIER, -TIEST] a.

griz'zled or **griz'zly,** a. gray.

grizzly bear, large, ferocious N. American bear.

groan, v. & n. (utter) a deep sound of pain, etc.

gro'cer, n. storekeeper who sells food, etc.

gro'cer·y, n. [pl. -IES] 1. store of a grocer. 2. pl. goods sold by a grocer.

grog'gy, a. [-GIER, -GIEST] [Col.] dizzy.

groin, n. fold where the abdomen joins either thigh.

groom, n. 1. man who tends horses. 2. bridegroom. —v. 1. make neat. 2. train.

groove, n. 1. narrow furrow. 2. channel. 3. routine. —v. make a groove in.

grope, v. feel or search about blindly.

gross, a. 1. flagrant. 2. coarse. 3. total. —n. 1. overall total. 2. [pl. GROSS] 12 dozen. —v. [Col.] earn before deductions.

gro·tesque' (-tesk') a. 1. distorted. 2. absurd.

grot'to, n. [pl. -TOES, -TOS] 1. cave. 2. cavelike shrine, place, etc.

grouch, n. [Col.] 1. one who grumbles. 2. sulky mood.

—**grouch'y** [-IER, -IEST] a.

ground, pt. & pp. of **grind.**
—n. 1. land; earth. 2. pl.
tract of land. 3. distance.
4. also pl. cause or basis.
5. background. 6. pl. dregs.
—a. of or on the ground. —
v. 1. set or keep on the
ground. 2. base. 3. instruct
(in). —**ground'less,** a.

ground hog, woodchuck:
also **ground'hog,** n.

ground'work, n. foundation.

group, n. persons or things
gathered or classed together.
—v. form a group.

grouse, n. game bird.

grove, n. small group of
trees.

grov'el, v. 1. crawl abjectly.
2. behave humbly.

grow, v. [GREW, GROWN,
GROWING] 1. develop. 2.
increase. 3. become. 4.
raise (crops).

growl, n. rumbling sound, as
of an angry dog. —v. make
this sound.

grown'-up', a. & n. adult.

growth, n. 1. a growing. 2.
something that grows.

grub, v. [GRUBBED, GRUB-
BING] 1. dig or dig up. 2.
work hard. —n. 1. wormlike
larva, esp. of a beetle. 2.
[Sl.] food.

grub'by, a. [-BIER, -BIEST]
dirty; untidy.

grudge, v. begrudge. —n. resentment; ill will.

gru'el, n. thin cereal broth.

gru'el·ing, gru'el·ling, a.
very tiring; exhausting.

grue'some, a. causing loathing and horror.

gruff, a. 1. rough or surly.
2. hoarse. —**gruff'ly,** adv.

grum'ble, v. mutter in discontent. —**grum'bler,** n.

grump'y, a. [-IER, -IEST]
peevish; surly.

grunt, v. & n. (utter with)
the deep sound of a hog.

guar·an·tee' (gar-) n. 1.
pledge to replace something
sold if faulty. 2. assurance.
3. pledge or security for another's debt or obligation.
—v. 1. give a guarantee for.
2. assure. Also **guar'an·ty.**
—**guar'an·tor,** n.

guard, v. 1. protect; defend.
2. keep from escape. 3. take
precautions. —n. 1. person
or thing that guards. 2.
careful watch.

guard'house, n. Mil. jail.

guard'i·an, n. 1. one legally
in charge of a minor, etc.
2. custodian.

gu'ber·na·to'ri·al, a. of a
governor or his office.

guer·ril'la, guer·ril'la (gə-
ril'-) n. fighter who makes
raids behind enemy lines.

guess, v. 1. estimate; judge.
2. suppose. —n. surmise.

guess'work, n. 1. a guess-
ing. 2. view based on this.

guest, n. 1. one entertained
at another's home, etc. 2.
paying customer, as at a
hotel. —a. 1. for guests. 2.
performing by invitation.

guf·faw', n. & v. laugh in
a loud, coarse burst.

guide, v. 1. show the way
to. 2. control. —n. person
or thing that guides. —
guid'ance, n.

guided missile, war missile
guided by radio or radar.

guild (gild) n. association to
promote mutual interests.

guile (gīl) n. deceit.

guil·lo·tine (gil'ə-tēn) n. instrument for beheading.

guilt, n. fact of having com-
mitted an offense.

guilt'y, a. [-IER, -IEST] having
or showing guilt. —**guilt'-
i·ly,** adv.

guin·ea (gin'ĭ) n. former
English coin = 21 shillings.

guinea fowl (or **hen**), speck-
led domestic fowl.

guinea pig, small rodent
used in experiments.

guise (gīz) n. assumed or
false appearance.

gui·tar' (gi-) n. musical instrument with six strings.

gulch, n. deep narrow valley.

gulf, n. 1. ocean area partly
enclosed by land. 2. wide
chasm. 3. vast separation.

gull, n. 1. gray and white
sea bird. 2. dupe. —v. cheat.

gul'let, n. esophagus.

gul'li·ble, a. easily tricked.
—**gul'li·bil'i·ty,** n.

gul'ly, n. [pl. -LIES] narrow
ravine.

gulp, v. swallow greedily or
hastily. —n. a gulping.

gum, n. 1. sticky substance
from some plants. 2. an adhesive. 3. flesh around the
teeth. —v. [GUMMED, GUM-
MING] make sticky. —**gum'-
my,** a.

gum'bo, n. [pl. -BOS] soup
made with okra pods.

gum'drop, n. chewy candy.

gun, n. weapon for shooting
projectiles. —v. [GUNNED,
GUNNING] hunt with a gun.
—**gun'man** [pl. -MEN] n.

gun'shot, n.

gun'ner·y, n. the making or

firing of large guns. —
gun'ner, n.

gun'ny, n. [pl. -NIES] sack made of coarse fabric.

gun'pow'der, n. explosive powder used in guns, etc.

gun'smith, n. one who makes or repairs small guns.

gun·wale (gun'l) n. upper edge of a boat's side.

gup'py, n. [pl. -PIES] tiny tropical fish.

gur'gle, n. bubbling sound. —v. make this sound.

gush, v. 1. flow copiously. 2. talk too emotionally. —n. a gushing. —**gush'er,** n.

gus'set, n. triangular piece inserted in a garment.

gust, n. 1. sudden rush of air. 2. sudden outburst.

gus'ta·to'ry, a. of the sense of taste.

gus'to, n. zest; relish.

gut, n. 1. intestine. 2. cord made of intestines. 3. pl. [Sl.] courage. —v. [GUTTED, GUTTING] destroy the interior of.

gut'ta-per'cha, n. rubber-like substance from some trees.

gut'ter, n. channel to carry off rain water, etc.

gut'tur·al, a. sounded in the throat; rasping.

guy (gi) n. 1. guiding rope. 2. [Sl.] boy or man.

guz'zle, v. drink greedily.

gym, n. [Col.] gymnasium.

gym·na'si·um (jim-) n. place for physical training and sports.

gym·nas'tics, n.pl. exercises for the muscles. —**gym'-nast,** n. —**gym·nas'tic,** a.

gyn'e·col'o·gy (jin'-, gin'-) n. medical science of women's diseases. —**gyn'e·col'-o·gist,** n.

gyp (jip) n. & v. [GYPPED, GYPPING] [Sl.] swindle.

gyp'sum, n. calcium sulfate, a white chalky mineral.

gyp'sy, n. [pl. -SIES] one of a wandering people.

gy'rate (ji'-) v. to whirl. —**gy·ra'tion,** n.

gy'ro·scope, n. wheel mounted in a ring and spinning rapidly, used as a stabilizer.

H

ha, int. exclamation of surprise, triumph, etc.

hab'er·dash'er, n. dealer in men's hats, shirts, etc. —**hab'er·dash'er·y** [pl. -IES] n.

hab'it, n. 1. costume. 2. custom. 3. fixed practice.

hab'it·a·ble, a. fit to live in.

hab'i·tat, n. natural living place.

hab'i·ta'tion, n. dwelling.

ha·bit'u·al (-bich'oo) a. 1. done by habit. 2. constant. 3. usual. —**ha·bit'u·al·ly,** adv.

ha·bit'u·ate, v. accustom.

ha·bit'u·é (-ā) n. constant frequenter of a place.

hack, v. 1. chop roughly. 2. cough harshly. —n. 1. gash. 2. harsh cough. 3. vehicle for hire. 4. old worn-out horse. 5. literary drudge.

hack'neyed, a. trite; stale.

hack saw, saw for cutting metal: also **hack'saw,** n.

had, pt. & pp. of **have.**

had'dock, n. small ocean fish used as food.

Ha·des (hā'dēz) n. hell.

had'n't, had not.

haft, n. handle, as of an ax.

hag, n. ugly old woman.

hag'gard, a. having a wasted, worn look; gaunt.

hag'gle, v. argue about terms, price, etc.

hail, n. 1. greeting. 2. frozen raindrops. 3. shower of or like hail. —int. shout of greeting, etc. —v. 1. cheer. 2. shout to. 3. pour down (like) hail.

hail'stone, n. piece of hail.

hair, n. 1. threadlike outgrowth from the skin. 2. growth of these, as on the head. —**split hairs,** quibble. —**hair'y** [-IER, -IEST] a.

hair'breadth, n. very short distance. —a. very narrow.

hair'cut, n. act or style of cutting the hair.

hair'-do', n. hair style.

hair'dress'er, n. one who arranges (women's) hair.

hair'pin, n. wire for keeping hair in place. —a. U-shaped.

hair'-rais'ing, a. [Col.] horrifying.

hal'cy·on (-si-) a. tranquil. —v. drag; haul.

hale, a. healthy; robust. —v. drag; haul.

half, n. [pl. HALVES] either of the two equal parts of a thing. —a. 1. being a half 2. partial. —adv. 1. to the extent of a half. 2. partially. —**one's better half,** [Sl.] one's spouse.

half'-breed', n. one with parents of different races.

half brother (or **sister**), brother (or sister) by one parent only.

half'heart'ed, *a.* with little enthusiasm or interest.

half'way', *a.* 1. midway between points. 2. partial. —*adv.* to the halfway point.

half'-wit'ted, *a.* feebleminded. —**half'-wit',** *n.*

hal'i·but, *n.* large flatfish.

hall, *n.* 1. public building with offices. 2. large room for meetings, shows, etc. 3. vestibule. 4. passageway.

hal'le·lu'jah, hal'le·lu'iah (-ya) *int.* praise the Lord!

hall'mark, *n.* mark of quality.

hal'low, *v.* make or regard as holy. —**hal'lowed,** *a.*

Hal'low·een', Hal'low·e'en', *n.* evening of Oct. 31.

hal·lu·ci·na'tion, *n.* apparent perception of sights, etc. not really present.

hal·lu'ci·no·gen, *n.* drug that produces hallucinations.

hall'way, *n.* corridor.

ha'lo, *n.* ring of light.

halt, *v.* 1. to stop. 2. to limp. 3. hesitate. —*n.* stop. —**halt'ing·ly,** *adv.*

hal'ter, *n.* 1. rope to tie an animal. 2. woman's backless upper garment.

halve (hav) *v.* 1. divide into halves. 2. reduce to half.

halves, *n.* pl. of **half.**

hal'yard (-yêrd) *n.* rope for raising a flag, etc.

ham, *n.* 1. upper part of a hog's hind leg. 2. [Sl.] amateur radio operator.

ham'burg·er, *n.* 1. ground beef. 2. cooked patty of such meat. Also **ham'burg.**

ham'let, *n.* small village.

ham'mer, *n.* tool with a metal head for pounding. —*v.* pound, drive, shape, etc. as with a hammer.

ham'mock, *n.* bed of canvas, etc. swung from ropes.

ham'per, *v.* hinder; impede. —*n.* large basket.

ham'ster, *n.* ratlike animal, used in experiments.

hand, *n.* 1. end of the arm beyond the wrist. 2. side or direction. 3. active part. 4. handwriting. 5. applause. 6. help. 7. hired worker. 8. pointer on a clock. 9. cards held by a player in a card game. —*a.* of, for, or by the hand. —*v.* give as with the hand. —**at hand,** near. —**hand in hand,** together. —**hands down,** easily. —**on hand,** available. —**upper hand,** the advantage. —**hand'ful,** *n.*

hand'bag, *n.* woman's purse.

hand'ball, *n.* game in which players hit a ball against a wall with the hand.

hand'book, *n.* handy book of instructions.

hand'clasp, *n.* clasping of hands in greeting, etc.: also **hand'shake.**

hand'cuff, *n.* one of a pair of shackles for the wrists. —*v.* put handcuffs on.

hand'i·cap, *n.* 1. difficulty or advantage given to some contestants to equalize their chances. 2. hindrance. —*v.* [-CAPPED, -CAPPING] hinder.

hand'i·craft, *n.* work calling for skill with the hands.

hand'i·work, *n.* result of one's actions.

hand'ker·chief, *n.* small cloth for wiping the nose, etc.

han'dle, *n.* part of tool, etc. by which it is held. —*v.* 1. touch, lift, etc. with the hand. 2. manage. 3. deal with. 4. deal in.

hand'made', *a.* made by hand, not by machine.

hand'some, *a.* 1. good-looking in a manly or impressive way. 2. sizable. 3. gracious.

hand'writ'ing, *n.* writing done by hand.

hand'y, *a.* [-IER, -IEST] 1. near-by. 2. easily used. 3. clever with the hands. —**hand'i·ly,** *adv.*

hang, *v.* [HUNG or (for *v.* 3) HANGED, HANGING] 1. attach or be attached from above. 2. attach so as to swing freely. 3. kill by suspending from a rope. 4. attach to walls. 5. droop. —*n.* 1. way a thing hangs. 2. way a thing is done. 3. meaning. —**hang around,** [Col.] loiter around. —**hang back,** hesitate, as from shyness.

hang'ar, *n.* aircraft shelter.

hang'dog, *a.* abject; cowed.

hang'er, *n.* that on which something is hung.

hang'nail, *n.* bit of torn skin next to a fingernail.

hang'o'ver, *n.* sickness resulting from being drunk.

hank, *n.* skein of yarn.

hank'er, *v.* long (for).

hap'haz'ard, *a.* not planned; random. —*adv.* by chance.

hap'less, *a.* unlucky.

hap'pen, *v.* 1. take place. 2. occur by chance. 3. have the luck or occasion.

hap'pen·ing, *n.* event.

hap'py, *a.* [-PIER, -PIEST] 1.

showing pleasure or joy. 2. lucky. 3. apt. —**hap′pi·ly**, adv. —**hap′pi·ness**, n.

ha·rangue′ (-rang′) v. & n. (address in) a noisy speech.

har·ass (har′əs, hə-ras′) v. trouble or attack constantly.

har·bin·ger (här′bin-jẽr) n. forerunner.

har′bor, n. protected inlet for ships. —v. 1. to shelter. 2. hold in the mind.

hard, a. 1. firm or solid. 2. powerful. 3. difficult to do, understand, etc. 4. harsh. —adv. 1. with energy. 2. with strength. 3. firmly. —**hard and fast**, strict. —**hard′en**, v.

hard′-core′, a. absolute.

hard′head′ed, a. 1. shrewd. 2. stubborn.

hard′ly, adv. 1. barely. 2. not likely.

hard′ship, n. thing hard to bear, as poverty, pain, etc.

hard′ware, n. metal articles, as tools, nails, etc.

hard′wood, n. tough timber with a compact texture.

har′dy, a. [-DIER, -DIEST] 1. bold and resolute. 2. robust. —**har′di·ness**, n.

hare (hâr) n. rabbit, esp. one of the larger kind.

hare′brained, a. senseless.

hare′lip, n. congenital cleft of the upper lip.

ha·rem (hâr′əm) n. 1. quarters for the women in a Moslem's house. 2. these women.

hark, v. [Poet.] listen. **hark′en**, v. hearken.

har′lot, n. a prostitute.

harm, n. & v. hurt; damage. —**harm′ful**, a. —**harm′less**, a.

har·mon′i·ca, n. small wind instrument with metal reeds.

har′mo·nize, v. 1. to be, sing, etc. in harmony. 2. bring into harmony.

har′mo·ny, n. 1. pleasing agreement of parts. 2. agreement in ideas, action, etc. 3. pleasing combination of musical tones. —**har·mo′ni·ous**, a.

har′ness, n. straps, etc. for hitching a horse to a wagon, etc. —v. 1. put harness on. 2. control for use.

harp, n. stringed musical instrument played by plucking. —v. keep talking or writing (on). —**harp′ist**, n.

har·poon′, n. barbed shaft for spearing whales. —v. strike with a harpoon.

harp′si·chord, n. early keyboard instrument.

har′ri·dan, n. shrewish old woman.

har′row, n. frame with spikes or disks for breaking up plowed land. —v. 1. draw a harrow over. 2. distress.

har′ry, v. [-RIED, -RYING] harass; torment.

harsh, a. 1. rough to the eye, ear, taste, etc. 2. cruel or severe. —**harsh′ly**, adv. —**harsh′ness**, n.

hart, n. male deer; stag.

har′vest, n. 1. a season's crop or the gathering of it. 2. season for this. —v. reap.

has, pres. t. of **have**: used with he, she, it.

hash, n. cooked mixture of chopped meat, potatoes, etc.

hash′ish (-ēsh) n. narcotic made from Indian hemp.

has′n't, has not.

hasp, n. clasplike fastening for a door, lid, etc.

has′sle, **has′sel**, n. [Sl.] squabble; argument.

has′sock, n. firm cushion used as a footstool, etc.

hast, [Ar.] have: with thou.

haste, n. a hurry or rush.

has′ten, v. to hurry.

hast′y, a. [-IER, -IEST] done with haste. —**hast′i·ly**, adv.

hat, n. head covering, often with a brim.

hatch, v. 1. bring or come forth from (an egg). 2. contrive (a plot). —n. hatchway or its lid.

hatch′er·y, n. [pl. -IES] place for hatching eggs.

hatch′et, n. short ax.

hatch′way, n. opening in a ship's deck, or in a floor.

hate, v. dislike strongly. —n. strong dislike: also **hatred**.

hate′ful, a. deserving hate.

hath, [Ar.] has.

haugh′ty (hô′-) a. [-TIER, -TIEST] scornfully proud. —**haugh′ti·ly**, adv. —**haugh′ti·ness**, n.

haul, v. 1. pull; drag. 2. transport by truck, etc. —n. 1. amount caught. 2. load or distance transported.

haunch, n. hip, rump, and upper thigh.

haunt, v. 1. visit often. 2. recur often to. —n. place often visited.

haunt′ed, a. supposedly frequented by ghosts.

have, v. [HAD, HAVING] 1. hold; possess. 2. experience. 3. hold mentally. 4. get; take. 5. beget. 6. engage in.

7. cause to do, be, etc. 8. permit. 9. be forced. *Have* is an important helping verb. —**have on,** be wearing. —**have to do with,** deal with.

ha'ven, *n.* shelter; refuge.

have'n't, have not.

hav'er·sack, *n.* bag for provisions, worn on the back.

hav'oc, *n.* great destruction. —**play havoc with,** ruin.

hawk, *n.* bird of prey. —*v.* 1. peddle (goods) in the streets. 2. clear the throat.

haw'ser, *n.* cable for anchoring or towing a ship.

haw'thorn, *n.* small tree with red berries.

hay, *n.* grass, clover, etc. cut and dried. —**hay'stack,** *n.*

hay fever, allergy to pollen that affects one like a cold.

hay'wire, *a.* [Sl.] wrong or crazy.

haz'ard, *n.* 1. chance. 2. risk; danger. 3. obstacle on a golf course. —*v.* to risk. —**haz'ard·ous,** *a.*

haze, *n.* 1. mist of fog, smoke, etc. 2. vagueness. —**ha'zy** [-ZIER, -ZIEST] *a.*

ha'zel, *n.* 1. tree bearing small nut (**hazelnut**). 2. reddish brown.

H'-bomb', *n.* hydrogen bomb.

he, *pron.* 1. the male mentioned. 2. anyone.

head, *n.* 1. part of the body beyond the neck. 2. mind. 3. top or front part. 4. leader. 5. crisis. 6. poise. —*a.* 1. chief. 2. at the head. —*v.* 1. to lead. 2. set out; go. —**head off,** intercept. —**head over heels,** completely. —**not make head or tail of,** not to understand. —**over one's head,** beyond one's understanding. —**turn one's head,** make one vain.

head'ache, *n.* pain in the head.

head'ing, *n.* title; caption.

head'light, *n.* light at the front of a vehicle.

head'line, *n.* title of newspaper article. —*v.* feature.

head'long, *a. & adv.* with the head first. 2. rash(ly).

head'quar'ters, *n.pl.* center of operations; main office.

head'stone, *n.* grave marker.

head'strong, *a.* obstinate.

head'way, *n.* progress.

head'y, *a.* [-IER, -IEST] 1. intoxicating. 2. rash.

heal, *v.* cure or mend.

health, *n.* 1. soundness of body and mind. 2. physical condition. —**health'ful,** *a.* —**health'y** [-IER, -IEST] *a.*

heap, *n. & v.* pile; mass.

hear, *v.* [HEARD, HEARING] 1. receive (sounds) through the ear. 2. listen to. 3. be told. —**not hear of,** not permit.

hear'ing, *n.* 1. ability to hear. 2. chance to be heard

hark'en (härk'-) *v.* listen.

hear'say, *n.* gossip; rumor.

hearse (hürs) *n.* vehicle to carry a body to the grave.

heart, *n.* 1. organ that circulates the blood. 2. vital part. 3. love, sympathy, courage, etc. 4. figure shaped like ♥. —**by heart,** from memory. —**take to heart,** be troubled by.

heart'ache, *n.* sorrow.

heart'burn, *n.* burning sensation in the stomach.

heart'en, *v.* encourage.

heart'felt, *a.* sincere.

hearth (härth) *n.* 1. floor of a fireplace. 2. home.

heart'less, *a.* unkind.

heart'-rend'ing, *a.* agonizing.

heart'sick, *a.* very sad.

heart'y, *a.* [-IER, -IEST] 1. cordial. 2. vigorous. 3. strong and healthy. 4. nourishing. —**heart'i·ly,** *adv.*

heat, *n.* 1. hotness, or the perception of it. 2. strong feeling. 3. single race, etc. in a series. 4. sexual excitement of animals. —*v.* make or become hot. —**heat'ed·ly,** *adv.* —**heat'er,** *n.*

heath, *n.* tract of open wasteland.

hea·then (hē'thən) *a. & n.* (of) one not a Jew, Christian, or Moslem.

heath'er (heth'-) *n.* low plant with purple flowers.

heave, *v.* [alt. pp. HOVE] 1. lift, or lift and throw, with effort. 2. make (a sigh) with effort. 3. rise and fall in rhythm. 4. vomit. —*n.* act of heaving.

heav'en, *n.* 1. *Theol.* place where God and his angels are. 2. *pl.* sky. 3. state of bliss. —**heav'en·ly,** *a.*

heav'y, *a.* [-IER, -IEST] 1. weighing much. 2. very great, intense, etc. 3. sorrowful —*n.* [*pl.* -IES] stage villain. —**heav'i·ly,** *adv.* —**heav'i·ness,** *n.*

heav'y-hand'ed, *a.* awkward.

He'brew, *n.* language of ancient and modern Israel. —*a.* of the Jews.

heck′le, v. annoy with questions, taunts, etc. —**heck′-ler,** n.

hec′tic, a. feverish, frenzied, etc. —**hec′ti·cal·ly,** adv.

hedge, n. dense row of shrubs. —v. 1. put a hedge around. 2. avoid direct answers.

hedge′hog, n. porcupine.

he′don·ist (hē′-) n. pleasure-seeker. —**he′don·ism,** n. —**he′don·is′tic,** a.

heed, n. careful attention. —v. pay heed (to). —**heed′-ful,** a. —**heed′less,** a.

heel, n. 1. back part of the foot. 2. part of shoe, etc. at the heel. —v. 1. furnish with heels. 2. follow closely. 3. lean to one side, as a ship.

heif′er, n. young cow.

height (hīt) n. 1. highest point or degree. 2. distance from bottom to top. 3. altitude. 4. pl. high place.

height′en, v. make or become higher, greater, etc.

hei′nous (hā′-) a. outrageous.

heir (âr) n. one who inherits another's property, etc. —**heir′ess,** n.fem.

heir′loom, n. a possession handed down in a family.

held, pt. & pp. of **hold.**

hel′i·cop′ter, n. aircraft with a horizontal propellor above the fuselage.

he′li·um, n. very light, non-flammable gas, a chemical element.

hell, n. Theol. place of torment for sinners after death. —**hell′ish,** a.

he′ll, 1. he will. 2. he shall.

Hel·len′ic, a. Greek.

hel·lo′, int. exclamation of greeting.

helm, n. 1. tiller or wheel to steer a ship. 2. control.

hel′met, n. protective head covering of metal, etc.

helms′man, n. [pl. -MEN] man who steers a ship.

help, v. 1. give assistance (to); aid. 2. remedy. 3. avoid. 4. serve. —n. 1. aid; assistance. 2. remedy. 3. one that helps. 4. hired helper(s). —**help′er,** n. —**help′ful,** a.

help′ing, n. portion of food served to one person.

help′less, a. 1. unable to help oneself. 2. unprotected.

hem, v. [HEMMED, HEMMING] 1. fold the edge of and sew down. 2. surround or confine. 3. clear the throat audibly. —n. hemmed edge.

—**hem and haw,** hesitate in speaking.

hem′i·sphere, n. 1. half a sphere. 2. any of the halves (N or S, E or W) of the earth.

hem′lock, n. 1. evergreen tree. 2. poisonous weed.

hemo-, pref. blood.

he′mo·glo′bin, n. coloring matter of red blood cells.

he′mo·phil′i·a, n. prolonged bleeding due to failure of blood to clot.

hem′or·rhage (-ij) n. heavy bleeding. —v. bleed heavily.

hem′or·rhoids, n.pl. swollen veins near the anus.

hemp, n. tall plant with fibers used to make rope, etc.

hem′stitch, n. ornamental stitch, used esp. at a hem.

hen, n. female of the chicken or certain other birds.

hence, adv. 1. from this place or time. 2. therefore.

hence′forth′, adv. from now on: also **hence′for′ward.**

hench′man, n. [pl. -MEN] trusted helper.

hen′na, n. reddish-brown dye from a tropical shrub.

hep·a·ti′tis, n. inflammation of the liver.

her, pron. objective case of **she.** —a. of her.

her′ald, n. 1. messenger. 2. forerunner. —v. foretell.

her′ald·ry, n. 1. study of coats of arms, etc. 2. pomp. —**he·ral′dic,** a.

herb, n. nonwoody plant, now esp. one used as seasoning or in medicine.

her′bi·cide, n. chemical used to kill plants, esp. weeds.

her·biv′o·rous, a. plant-eating.

her′cu·le′an, a. [often H-] having or involving great strength, courage, etc.

herd, n. cattle, etc. feeding or living together. —v. form into a herd or group.

herds′man, n. [pl. -MEN] one who tends a herd.

here, adv. 1. in, at, or to this place. 2. at this point; now. —n. this place.

here′a·bout′, adv. near here: also **here′a·bouts′.**

here·af′ter, adv. from now on. —n. state after death.

here·by′, adv. by this means.

he·red′i·tar′y, a. of, or passed down by, heredity or inheritance.

he·red′i·ty, n. passing on of characteristics to offspring or descendants.

here·in′, adv. in this place,

matter, writing, etc.

her·e·sy (her'-) n. [pl. -SIES] unorthodox opinion or religious belief. —**her·e·tic,** n. —**he·ret·i·cal,** a.

here·to·fore', adv. until now.

her·it·a·ble (her'-) a. that can be inherited.

her·it·age, n. tradition, etc. handed down from the past.

her·met·ic (hēr-) a. airtight: also **her·met·i·cal.** —**her·met·i·cal·ly,** adv.

her·mit, n. one who lives alone in a secluded place.

her·ni·a, n. rupture, as of the abdominal wall.

he·ro, n. [pl. -ROES] 1. brave, noble man. 2. central male character in a story. —**he·ro'ic,** a. —**her·o·ine** (her'-ō-in) n.fem. —**her'o·ism,** n.

her·o·in (her'-) n. narcotic.

her·on, n. wading bird.

her·ring, n. food fish of the Atlantic.

her·ring·bone', n. pattern of parallel, slanting lines.

hers, pron. that or those belonging to her.

her·self', pron. intensive or reflexive form of **she.**

hertz, n. [pl. HERTZ] international unit of frequency.

hes·i·tate (hez'-) v. 1. feel unsure; waver. 2. pause. —**hes·i·tant,** a. —**hes·i·tan·cy,** n. —**hes·i·ta'tion,** n.

het·er·o·dox', a. unorthodox, as in religious beliefs. —**het·er·o·dox'y,** n.

het·er·o·ge·ne·ous, a. 1. dissimilar. 2. varied.

hew, v. [alt. pp. HEWN] chop, as with an ax.

hex, n. [Col.] something thought to bring bad luck. —v. cause bad luck to.

hex·a·gon, n. figure with 6 angles and 6 sides.

hey (hā) int. exclamation to get attention, etc.

hey·day, n. peak period.

hi, int. word of greeting.

hi·a·tus (hī·ā'-) n. gap.

hi·ber·nate, v. spend the winter in a sleeplike state. —**hi·ber·na'tion,** n.

hi·bis·cus, n. plant with large, colorful flowers.

hic·cup, **hic·cough** (-kəp) v. & n. (have) a muscle spasm that stops the breath.

hick·o·ry, n. [pl. -RIES] 1. hardwood tree. 2. its nut.

hide, v. [HID, HIDDEN or HID, HIDING] 1. put, or be, out of sight. 2. keep secret. —n. animal skin or pelt.

hid·e·ous, a. very ugly.

hie, v. [HIED, HIEING or HYING] hasten.

hi·er·arch'y (-ärk'-) n. [pl. -IES] (rule by) clergy or officials in graded ranks.

hi·er·o·glyph'ic (-glif'-) a. & n. (of) picture writing, as of the ancient Egyptians.

hi'-fi', a. of high fidelity.

high, a. 1. tall. 2. to, at, or from a height. 3. above others in rank, size, cost, etc. 4. raised in pitch; shrill. 5. elated. —adv. in or to a high level, etc. —n. 1. high level, degree, etc. 2. gear arrangement giving greatest speed. —**high'ly,** adv.

high'ball', n. liquor mixed with soda water, etc.

high'brow, **high'brow,** n. & a. [Sl.] intellectual.

high fidelity, accurate reproduction of sound.

high'-flown', a. too showy.

high'hand'ed, a. arrogant.

high light, brightest or most interesting part, scene, etc.

high'-mind'ed, a. having high ideals or principles.

high'ness, n. 1. height. 2. [H-] title of royalty.

high school, school from grades 8 (or 9) through 12.

high seas, ocean waters not belonging to any nation.

high'-strung', a. excitable.

high'-ten'sion, a. carrying a high voltage.

high'way, n. main road.

high'way·man, n. [pl. -MEN] highway robber.

hi'jack, v. [Col.] steal (goods in transit) by force.

hike, v. 1. take a long walk. 2. [Col.] raise. —n. a hiking.

hi·lar'i·ous, a. very gay or merry. —**hi·lar'i·ty,** n.

hill, n. mound of land. —**hill'y** [-IER, -IEST] a.

hill'ock, n. small hill.

hilt, n. handle of a sword, dagger, etc.

him, pron. objective case of **he.**

him·self', pron. intensive or reflexive form of **he.**

hind (hīnd) a. back; rear. —n. female of the red deer.

hin'der, v. keep back; stop or thwart. —**hin'drance,** n.

hind'most, a. farthest back.

hind'sight, n. recognition, after the event, of what one should have done.

Hin'du, n. native or language of India. —a. 1. of Hindus. 2. of Hinduism.

Hin'du·ism, n. main religion of India.

hinge, *n.* joint on which a door, etc. swings. —*v.* 1. attach by a hinge. 2. depend.

hint, *n.* slight indication. —*v.* give a hint.

hin'ter·land, *n.* remote area.

hip, *n.* part between the upper thigh and the waist.

hip'pie, *n.* [Sl.] young person alienated from conventional society.

hip'po·pot'a·mus, *n.* [*pl.* -MUSES, -MI (-mī')] large, thick-skinned animal of Africa.

hire, *v.* pay for the services or use of. —*n.* amount paid in hiring.

hire'ling, *n.* one who will do almost anything for pay.

hir'sute (hûr'-) *a.* hairy.

his, *pron.* & *a.* (that or those) of him.

hiss, *n.* a prolonged *s* sound. —*v.* 1. make this sound. 2. disapprove of by hissing.

his'to·ry, *n.* [*pl.* -RIES] study or record of past events. —**his·to'ri·an,** *n.* —**his·tor'i·cal, his·tor'ic,** *a.*

his·tri·on'ics, *n.pl.* dramatics. —**his·tri·on'ic,** *a.*

hit, *v.* [HIT, HITTING] 1. come against with force; bump. 2. give a blow (to); strike. 3. affect strongly. 4. come (on or upon). —*n.* 1. a blow. 2. collision. 3. successful song, play, etc. —**hit'ter,** *n.*

hitch, *v.* 1. move with jerks. 2. fasten with a hook, knot, etc. —*n.* 1. a tug; jerk. 2. hindrance. 3. kind of knot.

hitch'hike, *v.* travel by asking for rides from motorists.

hith'er, *adv.* to this place.

hith·er·to', *adv.* until now.

hive, *n.* 1. colony of bees or its shelter. 2. *pl.* skin allergy with raised, itching patches.

hoard, *n.* hidden supply. —*v.* accumulate and store away (money, etc.).

hoar'frost, *n.* frozen dew.

hoarse, *a.* sounding rough and husky.

hoar'y, *a.* [-IER, -IEST] 1. white. 2. white-haired and old. 3. very old.

hoax (hōks) *n.* a trick; practical joke. —*v.* to fool.

hob'ble, *v.* 1. to limp. 2. hamper by tying the legs. —*n.* a limp.

hob'by, *n.* [*pl.* -BIES] pastime activity.

hob'nail, *n.* broad-headed nail for shoe soles.

hob'nob, *v.* [-NOBBED, -NOBBING] be friendly (*with*).

ho'bo, *n.* [*pl.* -BOS, -BOES] a vagrant; tramp.

hock, *n.* hind-leg joint that bends backward.

hock'ey, *n.* team game played on ice skates.

hod, *n.* 1. trough for carrying bricks, etc. 2. coal scuttle.

hodge'podge, *n.* a jumble.

hoe, *n.* garden tool with a thin blade on a long handle. —*v.* [HOED, HOEING] cultivate with a hoe.

hog, *n.* 1. pig. 2. [Col.] greedy person. —*v.* [HOGGED, HOGGING] [Sl.] take all of.

hogs'head, *n.* large barrel.

hoi pol·loi (pa-loi') [Gr.] the common people.

hoist, *v.* raise; esp. with a crane, etc. —*n.* apparatus for lifting.

hold, *v.* [HELD, HOLDING] 1. keep in the hands. 2. keep in a certain position. 3. keep back. 4. occupy. 5. have (a meeting, etc.). 6. contain. 7. regard. 8. remain unyielding. —*n.* 1. grip. 2. strong influence. 3. ship's interior below deck. —**get hold of,** acquire. —**hold up,** 1. delay. 2. rob.

hold'ing, *n.* often *pl.* property owned.

hole, *n.* 1. hollow place. 2. burrow. 3. an opening, tear, etc. —**hole up,** hibernate, as in a hole.

hol'i·day (hol'ə-) *n.* 1. religious festival. 2. work-free day, usually set aside by law.

hol'i·ness, *n.* a being holy.

hol'ler, *v.* & *n.* [Col.] shout.

hol'low, *a.* 1. having a cavity within it. 2. concave; sunken. 3. insincere. 4. deep-toned and dull. —*n.* 1. cavity. 2. small valley. —*v.* make or become hollow.

hol'ly, *n.* evergreen shrub with red berries.

hol'ly·hock, *n.* tall plant with large, showy flowers.

hol·o·caust (hol'ə-kôst) *n.* great destruction, esp. of people or animals by fire.

hol'ster, *n.* leather pistol case.

ho'ly, *a.* [-LIER, -LIEST] 1. sacred. 2. sinless. 3. deserving reverence or worship.

Holy Communion, church rite in which bread and wine are received as (symbols of) the body and blood of Jesus.

Holy Ghost (or Spirit), 3d person of the Trinity.

hom·age (hom'ij, om'-) *n.*

anything done to show honor or respect.

home, *n.* 1. place where one lives. 2. household or life around it. —*a.* 1. domestic. 2. central. —*adv.* 1. at or to home. 2. to the target.

home′land, *n.* —**home′less,** *n.* —**home′mak′er,** *n.*

home′ly, *a.* [-LIER, -LIEST] 1. simple. 2. plain; ugly.

home run, *Baseball* hit by which the batter scores a run.

home′sick, *a.* longing for home.—**home′sick′ness,** *n.*

home′spun, *n.* cloth made of yarn spun at home. —*a.* plain or simple.

home′stead, *n.* 1. a home and its grounds. 2. public land granted as a farm.

home′ward, *adv. & a.* toward home: also **home′wards,** *adv.*

home′work, *n.* schoolwork done outside the classroom.

hom′i·cide (-sīd) *n.* 1. a killing of one person by another. 2. one who kills another. —**hom′i·cid′al,** *a.*

hom′i·let′ics, *n.* art of writing & preaching sermons.

hom′i·ly, *n.* [*pl.* -LIES] sermon.

hom′i·ny, *n.* coarsely ground dry corn.

homo-, *pref.* same; equal.

ho′mo·ge′ne·ous (-jē′ni-) *a.* 1. similar. 2. made up of similar parts.

ho·mog′e·nize (-moj′ə-nīz′) *v.* make uniform throughout.

hom′o·nym (-nim) *n.* word pronounced like another but having a different meaning and, usually, spelling.

Ho·mo sa′pi·ens (hō′mō sā′pi·enz) man; human being.

ho′mo·sex′u·al, *a.* of or having sexual desire for those of the same sex. —*n.* homosexual person.

hone, *n.* fine whetstone. —*v.* sharpen on a hone.

hon′est, *a.* 1. not cheating, stealing, or lying; upright. 2. sincere or genuine. 3. frank and open. —**hon′es·ty,** *n.*

hon′ey, *n.* sweet, syrupy substance made by bees (honeybees).

hon′ey·comb, *n.* structure of wax cells made by bees to hold their honey, etc.— *v.* fill with holes.

hon′ey·dew mel′on, muskmelon with a whitish rind.

hon′ey·moon, *n.* vacation for a newly married couple.

—*v.* have a honeymoon.

hon′ey·suck′le, *n.* vine with small, fragrant flowers.

honk, *n.* 1. call of a wild goose. 2. sound of an auto horn.—*v.* make this sound.

hon′or (on′ẽr) *n.* 1. high regard. 2. good reputation. 3. adherence to right principles. 4. glory or credit. 5. [H-] title of certain officials. 6. something showing respect. 7. source of respect or fame. —*v.* 1. treat with respect or high regard. 2. confer an honor on. 3. accept as valid.

hon′or·a·ble, *a.* deserving honor. —**hon′or·a·bly,** *adv.*

hon′o·rar′i·um, *n.* fee paid for professional services.

hon′or·ar′y, *a.* done, given, or held as an honor.

hon′our, *n.* honor: Br. sp.

hood, *n.* 1. covering for the head and neck. 2. cover over an automobile engine. —**hood′ed,** *a.*

-hood, *suf.* 1. state or quality. 2. whole group of.

hood′lum, *n.* [Col.] ruffian.

hood′wink, *v.* deceive.

hoof, *n.* [*pl.* HOOFS, rarely HOOVES] horny covering on the feet of cattle, horses, etc.

hook, *n.* 1. bent piece of metal used to catch or hold something. 2. fishhook. 3. sharp curve or curving motion. —*v.* catch, fasten, hit, etc. with a hook. —**hook up,** connect, as a radio.

hook′up, *n.* connection of parts, as in radio.

hoop, *n.* large, circular band.

hoo·ray′, *int. & n.* hurrah.

hoot, *n.* 1. cry an owl makes. 2. shout of scorn. —*v.* utter a hoot or hoots.

hop, *v.* [HOPPED, -PING] leap on one foot, or with all feet at once. —*n.* 1. a hopping. 2. [Col.] a dance. 3. *pl.* dried cones of a vine, used to flavor beer, etc.

hope, *n.* 1. trust that what is wanted will happen. 2. object of this. —*v.* want and expect. —**hope′ful,** *a.* —**hope′less,** *a.*

hop′per, *n.* trough from which material is conveyed.

horde, *n.* a crowd; pack.

ho·ri′zon (-rī′-) *n.* line where sky and earth seem to meet.

hor′i·zon′tal, *a.* 1. parallel to the horizon. 2. level.

hor′mone, *n.* substance that is formed by a gland and stimulates an organ.

horn, *n.* 1. bonelike growth

on the head of a cow, etc.
2. brass-wind instrument.
—**horned**, a.

hor'net, n. large wasp.

horn'pipe, n. sailor's dance.

horn'y, a. [-IER, -IEST] hard; callous.

hor'o·scope, n. chart of the zodiac used by astrologers.

hor'ri·ble, a. 1. causing horror. 2. [Col.] very bad, ugly, etc. —**hor'ri·bly**, adv.

hor'rid, a. horrible.

hor'ri·fy, v. [-FIED, -FYING] 1. make feel horror. 2. [Col.] shock greatly.

hor'ror, n. 1. strong fear or dislike. 2. cause of this.

hors d'oeu·vre (ôr' dûrv') [pl. D'OEUVRES] appetizer.

horse, n. 1. large animal domesticated for pulling loads, carrying a rider, etc. 2. supporting frame on legs.

horse'back, adv. & n. (on) the back of a horse.

horse'man, n. [pl. -MEN] skilled rider of horses. —**horse'man·ship**, n.

horse'play, n. rough play.

horse'pow'er, n. unit of power output, as of engines.

horse'rad·ish, n. plant with a pungent edible root.

horse'shoe', n. flat, U-shaped, metal plate nailed to a horse's hoof.

hor'ti·cul'ture, n. art of growing flowers, fruits, etc. —**hor'ti·cul'tur·al**, a.

ho·san'na, int. shout of praise to God.

hose, n. 1. [pl. HOSE] stocking. 2. flexible tube to convey liquids.

ho'sier·y (-zhēr-) n. stockings.

hos'pi·ta·ble, a. friendly to guests. —**hos'pi·tal'i·ty**, n.

hos'pi·tal, n. place of medical care for ill and hurt. —**hos'pi·tal·ize'**, v.

host, n. 1. man who entertains guests. 2. great number.

hos'tage (hos'tij) n. person held as a pledge.

hos'tel, n. lodging place.

hos'tess, n. 1. woman who acts as a host. 2. woman in charge of seating in a restaurant.

hos'tile, a. 1. of or like an enemy. 2. unfriendly.

hos·til'i·ty, n. [pl. -TIES] 1. enmity. 2. pl. warfare.

hot, a. [HOTTER, HOTTEST] 1. high in temperature; very warm. 2. spicy; peppery. 3. angry, violent, eager, etc. 4. close behind. 5. [Sl.]

fresh or new. —**hot'ly**, adv.

hot'bed, n. glass-covered bed of earth, for forcing plants.

hot'-blood'ed, a. excitable.

hot dog, [Col.] wiener.

ho·tel', n. place with rooms, food, etc. for travelers.

hot'head'ed, a. easily angered. —**hot'head**, n.

hot'house, n. greenhouse.

hot plate, small, portable stove.

hound, n. breed of hunting dog. —v. keep pursuing.

hour, n. 1. 1/24 of a day; 60 minutes. 2. a particular time. —**hour'ly**, a. & adv.

hour'glass, n. instrument for measuring time by the flow of sand in it.

house, n. 1. building to live in. 2. family. 3. building for specified use. 4. business firm. 5. legislative assembly. —v. (houz) cover, shelter, lodge, etc. —**keep house**, take care of a home.

house'bro'ken, a. trained to live in a house, as a dog.

house'hold, n. 1. all those living in one house. 2. home and its affairs.

house'keep'er, n. woman who manages a home.

house'work, n. work of cleaning, cooking, etc. in a house.

hous'ing (houz'-) n. 1. shelter or lodging; houses. 2. enclosing frame, box, etc.

hov'el, n. small, miserable dwelling.

hov'er, v. 1. flutter in the air near one place. 2. linger close by.

how, adv. 1. in what way. 2. in what condition. 3. why. 4. to what extent.

how·ev'er, adv. 1. by whatever means. 2. to whatever degree. —con. nevertheless.

how'itz·er, n. short cannon.

howl, v. 1. long, wailing cry of a wolf, dog, etc. 2. similar cry, as of pain. —v. 1. utter a howl. 2. laugh in scorn, mirth, etc.

how'so·ev'er, adv. however.

hoy'den, n. tomboy.

hub, n. 1. center of a wheel. 2. center of activity, etc.

hub'bub, n. tumult.

huck'le·ber'y, n. [pl. -RIES] edible dark-blue berry.

huck'ster, n. peddler.

hud'dle, v. 1. crowd close together. 2. draw (oneself) up tightly. —n. confused crowd or heap.

hue, n. color; tint. —**hue**

and cry, loud outcry.

huff, v. to blow; puff. —n. burst of anger. —**huff'y** [-IER, -IEST] a.

hug, v. [HUGGED, HUGGING] 1. embrace. 2. keep close to. —n. embrace.

huge, a. very large; immense.

hulk, n. 1. body of an old, dismantled ship. 2. big, clumsy person or thing. —**hulk'ing** a.

hull, n. 1. outer covering of a seed or fruit. 2. main body of a ship. —v. remove the hulls from.

hul'la·ba·loo', n. clamor.

hum, v. [HUMMED, HUMMING] 1. sing with closed lips. 2. make a low, steady murmur. —n. this sound.

hu'man, a. of or like a person or people. —n. a person: also **human being.** —**hu'man·ly,** adv.

hu·mane', a. kind, merciful, etc. —**hu·mane'ly,** adv.

hu·man'i·tar'i·an, n. one devoted to promoting the welfare of humanity. —a. helping humanity.

hu·man'i·ty, n. 1. a being human or humane. 2. the human race.

hum'ble, a. 1. not proud; modest. 2. lowly; unpretentious. —v. make humble. —**hum'bly,** adv.

hum'bug, n. fraud; sham.

hum'drum, n. a monotonous routine.

hu'mid, a. damp; moist. —**hu·mid'i·fy** [-FIED, -FYING] v. —**hu·mid'i·fi'er,** n.

hu·mid'i·ty, n. 1. dampness. 2. amount of moisture in the air.

hu·mil'i·ate, v. lower the pride or dignity of; mortify. —**hu·mil'i·a'tion,** n.

hu·mil'i·ty, n. humbleness.

hum'ming·bird', n. tiny bird able to hover.

hu'mor, n. 1. comical quality, talk, etc. 2. ability to see or express what is funny. 3. mood. 4. whim. —v. indulge. Br. sp. **humour.** —**hu'mor·ist,** n. —**hu'mor·ous,** a.

hump, n. rounded bulge. —v. to arch; hunch.

hump'back', n. (person having) a back with a hump.

hu'mus, n. dark soil made up of decayed leaves, etc.

hunch, v. arch into a hump. —n. 1. a hump. 2. [Col.] a feeling that something is going to happen.

hunch'back, n. humpback.

hun'dred, a. & n. ten times ten. —**hun'dredth,** a. & n.

hung, pt. & pp. of **hang.**

hun'ger, n. 1. need or craving for food. 2. strong desire. —v. feel hunger (for). —**hun'gry,** a. —**hun'gri·ly,** adv.

hunk, n. [Col.] large piece.

hunt, v. 1. search out (game) to catch or kill. 2. search; seek. 3. chase. —n. a chase or search. —**hunt'er,** n.

hur'dle, n. 1. frame for jumping over in a race. 2. obstacle. —v. 1. jump over. 2. overcome (an obstacle).

hurl, v. throw with force or violence. —**hurl'er,** n.

hurl'y-burl'y, n. turmoil.

hur·rah', int. & n. shout of joy, approval, etc.

hur·ray, int. & n. hurrah.

hur'ri·cane, n. violent storm from the tropics.

hur'ry, v. [-RIED, -RYING] move, act, etc. with haste; rush. —n. rush; haste. —**hur'ried·ly,** adv.

hurt, v. [HURT, HURTING] 1. cause pain or injury to. 2. damage. 3. offend. 4. have pain. —n. pain, injury, or harm. —**hurt'ful,** a.

hur'tle, v. move or throw swiftly and with violence.

hus'band (huz'-) n. married man. —v. manage thriftily.

hus'band·ry, n. 1. thrifty management. 2. farming.

hush, v. make or become silent. —n. silence; quiet.

husk, n. dry covering of some fruits and seeds. —v. remove the husk from.

husk'y, a. [-IER, -IEST] 1. hoarse. 2. big and strong. —n. [also H-] Eskimo dog.

hus'sy, n. [pl. -SIES] bold or shameless woman.

hus·tle (hus'l) v. 1. shove roughly. 2. move, work, etc. quickly or energetically. —n. a hustling.

hut, n. shedlike cabin.

hutch, n. 1. chest or cupboard. 2. pen or coop for small animals.

hy'a·cinth, n. plant with spikes of flowers.

hy'brid, n. offspring of two animals or plants of different species, etc.

hy·dran'ge·a (-drān'-) n. shrub with large clusters of flowers.

hy'drant, n. large pipe with a valve for drawing water from a water main.

hy·drau'lic (-drô'-) a. 1.

worked by force of a moving liquid. 2. of hydraulics.

hy·drau'lics, n. study and use of the mechanical properties of liquids.

hydro-, pref. water.

hy'dro·chlo'ric acid, acid formed of hydrogen & chlorine.

hy'dro·e·lec'tric, a. of the production of electricity by water power.

hy'dro·gen, n. colorless gas, the lightest chemical element.

hy'dro·gen·at·ed, a. treated with hydrogen.

hydrogen bomb, very destructive atomic bomb.

hydrogen peroxide, liquid bleach and disinfectant.

hy'dro·pho'bi·a, n. rabies.

hy'dro·pon'ics, n. science of growing plants in liquid mineral solutions.

hy'dro·ther'a·py, n. treatment of disease by external use of water.

hy·e'na, n. wolflike animal of Africa and Asia.

hy'giene (-jēn) n. set of principles for health.

hy'gi·en'ic, a. 1. of hygiene or health. 2. sanitary.

hy'men, n. membrane covering part of the opening of the vagina in a virgin.

hymn (him) n. song of praise, esp. a religious one.

hym'nal, n. book of hymns: also **hymn'book.**

hyper-, pref. over; excessive.

hy·per'bo·le (-ba-li) n. exaggeration for effect. **—hy'·per·bol'ic,** a.

hy'per·ten'sion, n. abnormally high blood pressure.

hy'phen, n. mark (-) used between parts or syllables of a word.

hy'phen·ate, v. join or write with a hyphen. **—hy'phen·a'tion,** n.

hyp·no'sis, n. sleeplike state in which one responds to the hypnotist's suggestions. **—hyp·not'ic,** a.

hyp'no·tize, v. induce hypnosis in. **—hyp'no·tism,** n. **—hyp'no·tist,** n.

hypo-, pref. 1. under. 2. less than; deficient in.

hy'po·chon'dri·ac' (-kon'-) n. one who suffers from abnormal anxiety over his health.

hy·poc'ri·sy, n. [pl. -SIES] condition of being, or action of, a hypocrite.

hyp'o·crite (-krit) n. one

who pretends to have a virtue, feeling, etc. he does not have. **—hyp·o·crit'i·cal,** a.

hy'po·der'mic, a. injected under the skin. **—n.** syringe and needle for giving hypodermic medical injections.

hy·pot'e·nuse, n. side of right-angled triangle opposite the right angle.

hy·poth'e·sis, n. tentative explanation.

hy'po·thet'i·cal, a. based on a hypothesis; supposed.

hys'ter·ec'to·my (his'-) n. surgical removal of the uterus.

hys·te'ri·a, n. outbreak of wild emotion. **—hys·ter'i·cal,** a.

hys·ter'ics, n.pl. hysteria.

I, pron. person speaking or writing.

i'bex, n. wild goat.

i'bis, n. large wading bird.

-ible, suf. 1. that can or should be. 2. tending to.

-ic, -ical, suf. 1. of or having to do with. 2. like. 3. produced by. 4. containing.

ICBM, intercontinental ballistic missile.

ice, n. 1. water frozen solid by cold. 2. frozen dessert of fruit juice, sugar, etc. **—v.** 1. change into ice. 2. cool with ice. 3. cover with icing. **—iced,** a.

ice'berg, n. great mass of ice afloat in the sea.

ice'box, n. refrigerator, esp. one in which ice is used.

ice cream, frozen cream dessert.

ich'thy·ol'o·gy (ik'thi-) n. study of fishes. **—ich'thy·ol'o·gist,** n.

i'ci·cle, n. hanging stick of ice.

ic'ing, n. sweet, soft coating for cakes; frosting.

i'con, n. sacred image or picture.

i·con'o·clast, n. one who attacks venerated institutions; stirs or ideas.

-ics, suf. art or science.

i'cy, a. [ICIER, ICIEST] 1. full of or covered with ice. 2. very cold. **—i'ci·ly,** adv. **—i'ci·ness,** n.

I'd, 1. I had. 2. I would.

i·de'a, n. 1. mental conception; thought or belief. 2. plan; scheme.

i·de'al, n. 1. conception of something in its perfect

form. 2. perfect model. —*a.* thought of as, or being, an ideal. —**i·de′al·ly,** *adv.*

i·de′al·ism, *n.* conception of, or striving for, an ideal. —**i·de′al·ist,** *n.* —**i·de′al·is′tic,** *a.*

i·de′al·ize, *v.* regard or show as perfect.

i·den′ti·cal, *a.* the same.

i·den′ti·fy, *v.* [-FIED, -FYING] 1. show to be a certain one. 2. associate closely (*with*). —**i·den′ti·fi·ca′tion,** *n.*

i·den′ti·ty, *n.* [pl. -TIES] 1. state or fact of being the same. 2. individuality.

i·de·ol′o·gy, *n.* [pl. -GIES] system of beliefs, as of a group. —**i·de·o·log′i·cal,** *a.*

id′i·om, *n.* 1. set phrase with a special meaning. 2. usual way of expression in words. —**id′i·o·mat′ic,** *a.*

id′i·o·syn′cra·sy, *n.* [pl. -SIES] personal oddity.

id′i·ot, *n.* person who is mentally very deficient. —**id′i·o·cy,** *n.* —**id′i·ot′ic,** *a.*

i′dle, *a.* 1. useless. 2. baseless. 3. not busy or working. 4. lazy. —*v.* 1. loaf. 2. be or make idle. —**i′dler,** *n.* —**i′dly,** *adv.*

i′dol, *n.* image or object worshiped or adored.

i·dol′a·try, *n.* worship of idols. —**i·dol′a·ter,** *n.* —**i·dol′a·trous,** *a.*

i′dol·ize, *v.* adore as an idol.

i′dyl, i·dyll (ī′d′l) *n.* short poem about pleasant rural life. —**i·dyl′lic** (-dil′-) *a.*

i.e., that is to say.

if, *con.* 1. in case that. 2. although. 3. whether. —**as if,** as it would be if.

ig′loo, *n.* [pl. -LOOS] Eskimo hut made of snow blocks.

ig′ne·ous, *a.* 1. of fire. 2. produced by great heat.

ig·nite′, *v.* 1. set fire to. 2. catch on fire.

ig·ni′tion, *n.* 1. an igniting. 2. electrical system for igniting the gases in an engine.

ig·no′ble, *a.* not noble; base.

ig′no·min′y, *n.* shame; disgrace. —**ig′no·min′i·ous,** *a.*

ig·no·ra′mus, *n.* [pl. -MUSES] ignorant person.

ig′no·rant, *a.* 1. showing lack of knowledge. 2. unaware. —**ig′no·rance,** *n.*

ig·nore′, *v.* pay no attention to.

i·gua′na (-gwä′-) *n.* large tropical lizard.

ilk, *n.* [Col.] kind; sort.

ill, *a.* [WORSE, WORST] 1. bad.

2. sick. —*n.* evil or disease. —*adv.* [WORSE, WORST] 1. badly. 2. scarcely. —**ill at ease,** uncomfortable.

I'll, 1. I shall. 2. I will.

ill′-bred′, *a.* rude; impolite.

il·le′gal, *a.* against the law. —**il·le′gal·ly,** *adv.*

il·leg′i·ble (-lej′-) *a.* hard or impossible to read.

il·le·git′i·mate (-mit) *a.* 1. born of unwed parents. 2. contrary to law, rules, etc. —**il·le·git′i·ma·cy,** *n.*

il·lib′er·al, *a.* 1. without culture. 2. narrow-minded.

il·lic′it (-lis′-) *a.* unlawful; improper.

il·lit′er·ate (-it) *a.* unable to read. —*n.* illiterate person. —**il·lit′er·a·cy,** *n.*

ill′ness, *n.* sickness; disease.

il·log′i·cal, *a.* not logical.

ill′-timed′, *a.* inappropriate.

il·lu′mi·nate, *v.* 1. light up. 2. explain. 3. decorate. —**il·lu′mi·na′tion,** *n.*

il·lu′mine, *v.* light up.

il·lu′sion, *n.* 1. false idea. 2. misleading appearance. —**il·lu′sive, il·lu′so·ry,** *a.*

il′lus·trate, *v.* 1. explain, as by examples. 2. furnish (books, etc.) with pictures. —**il′lus·tra′tion,** *n.* —**il·lus′tra·tive,** *a.* —**il·lus′tra·tor,** *n.*

il·lus′tri·ous, *a.* famous.

ill will, hate; dislike.

I'm, I am.

im′age (-ij) *n.* 1. a representation, as a statue. 2. reflection in a mirror, etc. 3. mental picture; idea. 4. copy. —*v.* reflect.

im′age·ry, *n.* 1. images. 2. descriptions.

i·mag′i·nar′y, *a.* existing only in the imagination.

i·mag·i·na′tion, *n.* 1. power to form mental pictures or 2. ideas. 2. thing imagined.

i·mag′i·na·tive, *a.*

i·mag′ine, *v.* 1. conceive in the mind. 2. suppose. —**i·mag′i·na·ble** (-na-b′l) *a.*

im′be·cile (-s′l) *a.* stupid. —*n.* person who is mentally deficient. —**im′be·cil′ic,** *a.* —**im′be·cil′i·ty,** *n.*

im·bed′, *v.* embed.

im·bibe′, *v.* 1. drink (in). 2. absorb into the mind.

im·bro′glio (-brōl′yō) *n.* [pl. -GLIOS] involved misunderstanding or disagreement.

im·bue′ (-bū′) *v.* 1. saturate. 2. dye. 3. fill, as the mind.

im′i·tate, *v.* 1. copy or mimic. 2. resemble. —**im′i·ta′tion,** *n.*

n. & a.

im·mac·u·late (-ū-lit) *a.* 1. perfectly clean. 2. without a flaw. 3. pure; sinless.

im·ma·te·ri·al, *a.* 1. unimportant. 2. spiritual.

im·ma·ture, *a.* not fully grown or developed. —**im'ma·tur'i·ty**, *n.*

im·meas·ur·a·ble, *a.* boundless; vast. —**im·meas'ur·a·bly**, *adv.*

im·me·di·ate (-it) *a.* 1. closest. 2. instant. 3. direct. —**im·me'di·ate·ly**, *adv.*

im·me·mo·ri·al, *a.* very old.

im·mense, *a.* vast; huge. —**im·men'si·ty**, *n.*

im·merse, *v.* 1. plunge into a liquid. 2. engross. —**im·mer'sion**, *n.*

im·mi·grant, *n.* one who immigrates. —**im·mi·grate**, *v.* enter a country, etc. in order to settle there. —**im'mi·gra'tion**, *n.*

im·mi·nent, *a.* likely to happen without delay. —**im'mi·nence**, *n.*

im·mo·bile, *a.* not moving or movable. —**im'mo·bil'i·ty**, *n.* —**im'mo·bi·lize**, *v.*

im·mod·er·ate (-it) *a.* without restraint; excessive.

im·mod·est, *a.* indecent. —**im·mod'es·ty**, *n.*

im·mor·al, *a.* not moral; esp., unchaste. —**im'mo·ral'i·ty**, *n.*

im·mor·tal, *a.* 1. living forever. 2. having lasting fame. —*n.* immortal being. —**im'mor·tal'i·ty**, *n.*

im·mov·a·ble, *a.* 1. firmly fixed. 2. unyielding.

im·mune (-mūn') *a.* exempt from or protected against something bad, as a disease, etc. —**im·mu'ni·ty**, *n.* —**im'mu·nize**, *v.*

im·mu·ta·ble, *a.* unchangeable. —**im·mu'ta·bly**, *adv.*

imp, *n.* 1. young demon. 2. mischievous child.

im·pact, *n.* (force of) a collision.

im·pair', *v.* make worse, less, etc. —**im·pair'ment**, *n.*

im·pale', *v.* pierce through with something pointed.

im·pal'pa·ble, *a.* that cannot be felt or easily perceived.

im·part', *v.* 1. give. 2. tell.

im·par'tial, *a.* fair; just. —**im·par'ti·al'i·ty**, *n.*

im·pass'a·ble, *a.* that cannot be traveled over.

im·passe (-pas) *n.* deadlock.

im·pas'sioned, *a.* passion-

ate; fiery.

im·pas'sive, *a.* calm.

im·pa'tient, *a.* annoyed because of delay, etc. —**im·pa'tience**, *n.*

im·peach', *v.* try (an official) on a charge of wrong-doing. —**im·peach'ment**, *n.*

im·pec'ca·ble, *a.* flawless.

im·pe·cu'ni·ous, *a.* having no money; poor.

im·pede', *v.* hinder.

im·ped'i·ment, *n.* thing that impedes; specif., a speech defect.

im·pel', *v.* [-PELLED, -PELLING] 1. drive forward. 2. force.

im·pend', *v.* be imminent. —**im·pend'ing**, *a.*

im·pen'e·tra·ble, *a.* that cannot be penetrated.

im·per'a·tive, *a.* 1. necessary; urgent. 2. of the mood of a verb expressing a command.

im'per·cep'ti·ble, *a.* not easily perceived; subtle.

im·per'fect, *a.* 1. not complete. 2. not perfect.

im'per·fec'tion, *n.* 1. a being imperfect. 2. fault.

im·pe'ri·al, *a.* of an empire, emperor, or empress.

im·pe'ri·al·ism, *n.* policy of forming and maintaining an empire, as by subjugating territories, etc. —**im·pe'ri·al·ist**, *a. & n.*

im·per'il, *v.* endanger.

im·pe'ri·ous, *a.* domineering.

im·per'ish·a·ble, *a.* indestructible.

im·per'son·al, *a.* 1. without reference to any one person. 2. not existing as a person.

im·per'son·ate, *v.* 1. assume the role of. 2. mimic. —**im·per'son·a'tion**, *n.*

im·per'ti·nent, *a.* 1. not relevant. 2. insolent. —**im·per'ti·nence**, *n.*

im·per'vi·ous, *a.* 1. incapable of being penetrated. 2. not affected by (with *to*).

im·pe·ti'go (-tī'-) *n.* skin disease with pustules.

im·pet'u·ous, *a.* impulsive; rash. —**im·pet'u·os'i·ty**, *n.*

im'pe·tus, *n.* 1. force of a moving body. 2. stimulus.

im·pinge' (-pinj') *v.* 1. strike, hit, etc. (*on*). 2. encroach (*on*).

im·pi·ous (-pi-) *a.* not pious. —**im·pi'e·ty** (-pī'-) *n.*

im·pla'ca·ble (-plā'kə-, -plak'ə-) *a.* not to be appeased.

im·plant', v. plant firmly.

im·plau'si·ble, a. not plausible.

im'ple·ment, n. tool or instrument. —v. put into effect.

im'pli·cate, v. show to be a party to a crime, connect.

im'pli·ca'tion, n. 1. an implying or implicating. 2. something implied.

im·plic'it (-plis'-) a. 1. implied. 2. absolute.

im·plore', v. beseech.

im·ply', v. [-PLIED, -PLYING] hint; suggest.

im·po·lite', a. discourteous.

im·port', v. 1. bring (goods) into a country. 2. signify. —n. (im'port) 1. thing imported. 2. meaning. 3. importance. —im·por·ta'tion, n.

im·por'tant, a. 1. having much significance. 2. having power or authority. —im·por'tance, n.

im·por·tune', v. urge repeatedly. —im·por'tu·nate (-chə-nit) a.

im·pose', v. put on (a burden, tax, etc.). —impose on, 1. take advantage of. 2. cheat. —im·po·si'tion, n.

im·pos'ing, a. impressive.

im·pos'si·ble, a. that cannot exist, be done, etc. —im·pos'i·bil'i·ty [pl. -TIES] n.

im·pos'tor, n. cheat pretending to be what he is not.

im'po·tent, a. lacking power; helpless. —im'po·tence, n.

im·pound', v. seize by law.

im·pov'er·ish, v. make poor.

im·prac'ti·ca·ble, a. that cannot be put into practice.

im·prac'ti·cal, a. not practical.

im'pre·cate, v. to curse. —im·pre·ca'tion, n.

im·preg'na·ble, a. that cannot be overcome by force.

im·preg'nate, v. 1. make pregnant. 2. saturate. —im'preg·na'tion, n.

im'pre·sa'ri·o (-sä'-) n. [pl. -os] manager, as of concerts.

im·press', v. 1. to stamp. 2. affect the mind or emotions of. 3. fix in the memory. —n. (im'pres) an imprint. —im·pres'sive, a.

im·pres'sion, n. 1. a mark. 2. effect produced on the mind. 3. vague notion.

im·pres'sion·a·ble, a. sensitive; easily influenced.

im·print', v. mark or fix as by pressing. —n. (im'print) 1. a mark; print. 2. characteristic effect.

im·pris'on, v. put in prison.

im·prob'a·ble, a. unlikely.

im·promp'tu, a. & adv. without preparation; offhand.

im·prop'er, a. not proper.

im·pro·pri'e·ty, n. [pl. -TIES] improper act.

im·prove', v. make or become better or more valuable. —im·prove'ment, n.

im·prov'i·dent, a. unthrifty.

im·pro·vise', v. 1. compose and perform without preparation. 2. make or do with whatever is at hand. —im'pro·vi·sa'tion, n.

im·pru'dent, a. rash; indiscreet. —im·pru'dence, n.

im'pu·dent, a. insolent. —im'pu·dence, n.

im·pugn' (-pūn') v. to challenge as false.

im'pulse, n. 1. driving force; impetus. 2. sudden inclination to act. —im·pul'sive, a.

im·pu'ni·ty, n. freedom from punishment or harm.

im·pure', a. 1. dirty. 2. immoral. 3. adulterated. —im·pu'ri·ty [pl. -TIES] n.

im·pute', v. attribute.

in, prep. 1. contained by. 2. wearing. 3. during. 4. at the end of. 5. with regard to. 6. because of. 7. into. —into or at the inside. —n. 1. pl. those in power. 2. [Col.] special access. —in that, because. —in with, associated with.

in-, pref. 1. in, into, or toward. 2. no, not, or lacking: for list below add not or lack of to meaning of base word.

in'a·bil'i·ty
in'ac·ces'si·ble
in·ac'cu·ra·cy
in·ac'cu·rate
in·ac'tive
in'a·de'qua·cy
in'a·de'quate
in'ad·mis'si·ble
in'ad·vis'a·ble
in·an'i·mate
in'ap·pro'pri·ate
in·apt'
in·ap'ti·tude
in'ar·tic'u·late
in'ar·tis'tic
in'at·ten'tion
in·au'di·ble
in'aus·pi'cious
in·ca'pa·ble
in'ca·pac'i·ty
in'co·her'ence
in'co·her'ent
in'com·pat'i·ble
in'com·pre·hen'si·ble
in'con·ceiv'a·ble

in'con·clu'sive
in'con·gru·ous
in'con·sid'er·a·ble
in'con·sid'er·ate
in'con·sist'en·cy
in'con·sist'ent
in·con'stant
in·con'ti·nence
in'con·tro·vert'i·ble
in'cor·rect'
in'cor·rupt'i·ble
in·cur'a·ble
in·de'cent
in·de·ci'sion
in·de·ci'sive
in·dec'o·rous
in·def'i·nite
in'di·gest'i·ble
in'di·rect'
in'dis·cern'i·ble
in'dis·creet'
in·dis·cre'tion
in'dis·pu'ta·ble
in·dis'tinct'
in'dis·tin'guish·a·ble
in·di·vis'i·ble
in·ed'i·ble
in'ef·fec'tive
in'ef·fec'tu·al
in·ef'fi·ca·cy
in'ef·fi'cient
in'e·las'tic
in·el'e·gant
in·el'i·gi·ble
in'e·qual'i·ty
in·eq'ui·ta·ble
in·eq'ui·ty
in·ex·act'
in'ex·cus'a·ble
in'ex·haust'i·ble
in'ex·pe'di·ent
in'ex·pen'sive
in'ex·pe'ri·enced
in·ex'pert
in'ex·tin'guish·a·ble
in·fer'tile
in·flex'i·ble
in·fre'quent
in·glo'ri·ous
in·grat'i·tude
in'har·mo'ni·ous
in·hos'pi·ta·ble
in·hu'mane'
in'ju·di'cious
in·of·fen'sive
in·op'er·a·tive
in·op'por·tune'
in·sen'si·tive
in·sep'a·ra·ble
in'sig·nif'i·cant
in'sin·cere'
in'sin·cer'i·ty
in·sol'u·ble
in'sta·bil'i·ty
in'suf·fi'cient
in'sur·mount'a·ble
in·tan'gi·ble
in·tol'er·a·ble
in·tol'er·ance
in·tol'er·ant

in·var'i·a·ble
in·vis'i·ble
in·vis'i·bly
in·vol'un·tar'y
in·vul'ner·a·ble

in·ad·vert'ent, *a.* not on purpose; accidental. —**in'-ad·vert'ence,** *n.*

in·al'ien·a·ble (-āl'yən-) *a.* that cannot be taken away.

in·ane', *a.* lacking sense; silly. —**in·an'i·ty,** *n.*

in·as·much' *as,* because.

in·au'gu·rate (-ô'gyoo-) *v.* 1. formally induct into office. 2. begin; open. —**in·au'gu·ral,** *a.* —**in·au'gu·ra'tion,** *n.*

in'born, *a.* present at birth; natural.

in·cal'cu·la·ble, *a.* too great to be calculated.

in'can·des'cent, *a.* 1. glowing with heat. 2. shining.

in·can·ta'tion, *n.* words chanted in magic spells.

in'ca·pac'i·tate (-pas'-) *v.* make unable or unfit.

in·car'cer·ate, *v.* imprison. —**in·car'cer·a'tion,** *n.*

in·car'nate (-nit) *a.* in human form; personified. —**in'car·na'tion,** *n.*

in·cen'di·ar'y, *a.* 1. causing fires. 2. stirring up strife. —*n.* one who willfully sets fire to property.

in'cense', *n.* 1. substance burned to produce a pleasant odor. 2. this odor. —*v.* (in·sens') enrage.

in·cen'tive, *n.* motive or stimulus.

in·cep'tion, *n.* a beginning.

in·ces'sant, *a.* constant.

in'cest, *n.* sexual intercourse between close relatives. —**in·ces'tu·ous,** *a.*

inch, *n.* measure of length, 1/12 foot. —*v.* move very slowly, by degrees.

in·cho'ate (-kō'it) *a.* just begun.

in'ci·dence, *n.* range of occurrence or effect.

in'ci·dent, *n.* event.

in'ci·den'tal, *a.* 1. happening along with something more important. 2. minor. —*n.* 1. something incidental. 2. *pl.* miscellaneous items. —**in'ci·den'tal·ly,** *adv.*

in·cin'er·ate, *v.* burn to ashes.

in·cin'er·a'tor, *n.* furnace for burning trash.

in·cip'i·ent, *a.* just beginning to exist or appear.

in·cise' (-sīz') *v.* cut into; engrave.

in·ci'sion (-sizh'ən) n. 1. a cutting into. 2. a cut; gash.

in·ci'sive (-sī'siv) a. piercing; acute.

in·ci'sor (-zēr) n. any of the front cutting teeth.

in·cite', v. urge to action. —**in·cite'ment**, n.

in·clem'ent, a. stormy.

in·cline' (in-klīn') v. 1. lean; bend; slope. 2. tend. 3. have a preference. 4. influence. —n. (in'klīn) a slope. —**in'cli·na'tion**, n.

in·close', v. enclose.

in·clude', v. have or take in as part of a whole; contain. —**in·clu'sion**, n.

in·clu'sive, a. 1. including everything. 2. including the limits mentioned.

in·cog'ni·to (in-kog'ni-tō, in'kəg-nē'tō) adv. & a. disguised under a false name.

in'come, n. money one gets as wages, salary, rent, etc.

in·com'pa·ra·ble, a. beyond comparison; matchless.

in·com'pe·tent, n. & a. (a person) without adequate skill or knowledge.

in·com·plete', a. lacking a part or parts; unfinished.

in'con·se·quen'tial, a. unimportant.

in·con·sol'a·ble, a. that cannot be comforted or cheered.

in·con·spic'u·ous, a. attracting little attention.

in·con·ven'ience, n. 1. lack of comfort, etc. 2. inconvenient thing. —v. cause bother, etc. to. —**in·con·ven'ient**, a.

in·cor'po·rate, v. 1. combine; include. 2. merge. 3. form (into) a corporation. —**in·cor'po·ra'tion**, n.

in·cor·ri·gi·ble, a. too bad to be reformed.

in·crease', v. make or become greater, larger, etc. —n. (in'krēs) 1. an increasing. 2. amount of this.

in·creas'ing·ly, adv. more and more.

in·cred'i·ble, a. too unusual to be believed.

in·cred'u·lous, a. showing doubt. —**in·cre·du'li·ty**, n.

in'cre·ment, n. 1. an increasing. 2. amount of this.

in·crim'i·nate, v. involve in, or make appear guilty of, a crime.

in·crust', v. cover with, or form into, a crust.

in'cu·ba'tor, n. 1. heated container for hatching eggs. 2. similar device in which

premature babies are kept.

in·cul'cate, v. fix in the mind, as by insistent urging.

in·cum'bent, a. resting (on or upon one) as a duty. —n. holder of an office, etc.

in·cur', v. [-CURRED, -CURRING] bring upon oneself.

in·cur'sion, n. raid.

in·debt'ed, a. 1. in debt. 2. owing gratitude.

in·debt'ed·ness, n. 1. a being indebted. 2. amount owed.

in·deed', adv. certainly. —int. exclamation of surprise, doubt, sarcasm, etc.

in·de·fat'i·ga·ble, a. not tiring; tireless.

in·de·fen'si·ble, a. that cannot be defended or justified.

in·del'i·ble, a. that cannot be erased, washed out, etc.

in·del'i·cate (-kit) a. lacking propriety; coarse.

in·dem'ni·fy, v. repay for or insure against loss. —**in·dem'ni·ty**, n.

in·dent', v. 1. to notch. 2. space in from the regular margin.

in'de·pend'ent, a. not ruled, controlled, supported, etc. by others. —**in'de·pend'ence**, n.

in·de·scrib'a·ble, a. beyond the power of description.

in·de·struct'i·ble, a. that cannot be destroyed.

in·de·ter'mi·nate (-nit) a. not definite; vague.

in'dex, n. [pl. -DEXES, -DICES] 1. forefinger: also **index finger**. 2. indication. 3. alphabetical list of names, etc. in a book showing pages where they can be found.

In'di·an, n. & a. 1. (native) of India. 2. (member) of any of the aboriginal races of the Western Hemisphere: also **American Indian**.

in'di·cate, v. 1. point out; show. 2. be a sign of. —**in'di·ca'tion**, n. —**in·dic'a·tive**, a. —**in'di·ca'tor**, n.

in·dict' (-dīt') v. charge with a crime. —**in·dict'ment**, n.

in·dif'fer·ent, a. 1. neutral. 2. unconcerned. 3. mediocre. —**in·dif'fer·ence**, n.

in·dig'e·nous (-dij'-) a. native.

in'di·gent, a. poor; needy. —**in'di·gence**, n.

in'di·ges'tion, n. difficulty in digesting food.

in·dig'nant, a. angry at unjust or mean action. —**in'dig·na'tion**, n.

in·dig'ni·ty, *n.* [*pl.* -TIES] an insult to one's pride.

in'di·go, *n.* 1. blue dye. 2. deep violet-blue.

in·dis·crim'i·nate (-nit) *a.* making no distinctions.

in·dis·pen'sa·ble, *a.* absolutely necessary.

in·dis·posed', *a.* 1. slightly ill. 2. unwilling.

in·dis·sol'u·ble, *a.* that cannot be dissolved or destroyed.

in·dite', *v.* write or compose.

in·di·vid'u·al, *n.* single person, thing, or being.—*a.* 1. single. 2. of, for, or typical of an individual.—**in·di·vid'u·al·ly,** *adv.*

in·di·vid·u·al'i·ty, *n.* distinct characteristics.

in·doc'tri·nate, *v.* teach a doctrine or belief to.—**in·doc'tri·na'tion,** *n.*

in'do·lent, *a.* idle; lazy.—**in'do·lence,** *n.*

in·dom'i·ta·ble, *a.* unyielding; unconquerable.

in'door, *a.* being, belonging, done, etc. in a building.

in'doors', *adv.* in or into a building.

in·du'bi·ta·ble, *a.* that cannot be doubted.

in·duce', *v.* 1. persuade. 2. bring on; cause.—**in·duce'ment,** *n.*

in·duct', *v.* 1. install in an office, a society, etc. 2. bring into the armed forces.—**in·duct·ee',** *n.*

in·duc'tion, *n.* 1. an inducting. 2. a coming to a general conclusion from particular facts.

in·dulge', *v.* 1. satisfy a desire. 2. gratify the wishes of.—**in·dul'gence,** *n.*—**in·dul'gent,** *a.*

in·dus'tri·al, *a.* having to do with industries or people working in industry.

in·dus'tri·al·ist, *n.* owner or manager of a large industry.

in·dus'tri·al·ize', *v.* build up industries in.

in·dus'tri·ous, *a.* working hard and steadily.

in'dus·try, *n.* [*pl.* -TRIES] 1. steady effort. 2. any branch of manufacture or trade.

in·e'bri·ate, *v.* make drunk.—*n.* (-it) drunkard.

in·ef'fa·ble, *a.* too sacred to be spoken.

in·ept', *a.* 1. unfit. 2. absurd. 3. awkward.

in·ert', *a.* 1. unable to move or act. 2. dull; slow.

in·er'tia (-shə) *n.* tendency

of matter to remain at rest, or to continue moving in a fixed direction.

in·es·cap'a·ble, *a.* that cannot be escaped.

in·es'ti·ma·ble, *a.* too great to be estimated.

in·ev'i·ta·ble, *a.* certain to happen.—**in·ev·i·ta·bil'i·ty,** *n.*

in·ex·cus'a·ble, *a.* unrelenting.—**in·ex'o·ra·bly,** *adv.*

in·ex·pli·ca·ble, *a.* that cannot be explained.

in·ex·tri·ca·ble, *a.* that cannot be disentangled.

in·fal'li·ble, *a.* never wrong.

in'fa·my (-fə-mi) *n.* 1. disgrace. 2. great wickedness.—**in'fa·mous,** *a.*

in'fant, *n.* baby.—*a.* 1. of infants. 2. in an early stage.—**in'fan·cy,** *n.*—**in'fan·tile,** *a.*

in'fan·try, *n.* soldiers trained to fight on foot.—**in'fan·try·man** [*pl.* -MEN] *n.*

in·fat'u·ate (-fach'oo) *v.* inspire with unreasoning passion.—**in·fat·u·a'tion,** *n.*

in·fect', *v.* make diseased.—**in·fec'tion,** *n.*

in·fec'tious, *a.* 1. caused by infection. 2. tending to spread to others.

in·fer' (-fûr') *v.* [-FERRED, -FERRING] conclude by reasoning.—**in'fer·ence,** *n.*

in·fe'ri·or, *a.* 1. lower in space, order, status, etc. 2. poor in quality.—**in·fe·ri·or'i·ty,** *n.*

in·fer'nal, *a.* of hell; hellish.

in·fest', *v.* overrun in large numbers.

in'fi·del, *n.* one who rejects (a) religion.

in·fi·del'i·ty, *n.* unfaithfulness.

in'field, *n. Baseball* area enclosed by base lines.—**in'field·er,** *n.*

in'fil·trate, *v.* 1. filter. 2. pass through.—**in'fil·tra'tion,** *n.*

in'fi·nite (-nit) *a.* 1. lacking limits; endless. 2. vast.

in·fin·i·tes'i·mal, *a.* too small to be measured.

in·fin'i·tive, *n.* form of a verb without reference to person, tense, etc.

in·fin'i·ty, *n.* unlimited space, time, or quantity.

in·firm', *a.* weak; feeble.—**in·firm'i·ty** [*pl.* -TIES] *n.*

in·fir'ma·ry, *n.* hospital.

in·flame', *v.* 1. excite. 2. make red, sore, and swollen.—**in·flam·ma'tion,** *n.*—

in·flam'ma·to·ry, a.

in·flam'ma·ble (-flam'-) a. easily set on fire.

in·flate', v. make swell out, as with gas.

in·fla'tion, n. 1. an inflating. 2. increase in the currency in circulation resulting in a fall in its value and a rise in prices. —in·fla'tion·ar·y, a.

in·flect', v. 1. vary the tone of (the voice). 2. change the form of (a word) to show tense, etc. —in·flec'tion, n.

in·flict', v. cause to suffer (a wound, punishment, etc.). —in·flic'tion, n.

in'flu·ence, n. 1. power to affect others. 2. one with such power. —v. have an effect on. —in·flu·en'tial, a.

in·flu·en'za, n. acute, contagious virus disease.

in'flux, n. a flowing in.

in·form', v. give information (to). —in·form'er, n.

in·for'mal, a. 1. not following fixed rules. 2. casual; relaxed. —in·for·mal'i·ty, n.

in·for·ma'tion, n. news or knowledge imparted. —in·form'a·tive, a.

in·frac'tion, n. violation of a law, etc.

in·fra·red', a. of those invisible rays having a penetrating, heating effect.

in·fringe', v. break (a law, etc.). —in·fringe on, encroach on (one's rights).

in·fu'ri·ate, v. enrage.

in·fuse', v. 1. instill. 2. inspire. 3. to steep. —in·fu'sion, n.

-ing, suf. used to form the present participle.

in·gen'ious (-jēn'-) a. clever; resourceful. —in·ge·nu'i·ty (-ja-nōō'-) n.

in·gen'u·ous (-jen'-) a. 1. frank. 2. naive.

in'got (iṅ'gat) n. mass of metal cast as a bar, etc.

in·grained', a. firmly fixed.

in'grate, n. ungrateful person.

in·gra'ti·ate, v. get (oneself) into another's favor.

in·gre'di·ent, n. component part of a mixture.

in'gress, n. entrance.

in·hab'it, v. live in.

in·hab'it·ant, n. person or animal inhabiting a place.

in·hale', v. breathe in. —in'ha·la'tion, n.

in·her'ent (-hēr'-, -her'-) a. inborn; natural; basic.

in·her'it, v. 1. receive as an

heir. 2. have by heredity. —in·her'it·ance, n.

in·hib'it, v. restrain; check. —in·hi·bi'tion, n.

in·hu'man, a. cruel, brutal, etc. —in·hu·man'i·ty, n.

in·im'i·cal, a. 1. hostile. 2. adverse; harmful.

in·im'i·ta·ble, a. that cannot be imitated.

in·iq'ui·ty (-ik'wa-) n. [pl. -TIES] sin or wicked act. —in·iq'ui·tous, a.

in·i'tial (ish'əl) a. first. —n. first letter of a name. —v. mark with one's initials. —in·i'tial·ly, adv.

in·i'ti·ate (i-nish'i-) v. 1. begin to use. 2. teach the fundamentals to. 3. admit as a new member. —in·i'ti·a'tion, n.

in·i'ti·a·tive, n. 1. first step. 2. ability to get things started.

in·ject', v. 1. force (a fluid) into tissue, etc. with a syringe, etc. 2. throw in; insert. —in·jec'tion, n.

in·junc'tion, n. order or command, esp. of a court.

in·jure', v. do harm to; hurt. —in·ju'ri·ous, a.

in'ju·ry, n. [pl. -RIES] harm or wrong.

in·jus'tice, n. 1. being unjust. 2. unjust act.

ink, n. colored liquid for writing, printing, etc. —v. mark or color with ink. —ink'y [-IER, -IEST] a.

ink'ling, n. hint or notion.

in'land, a. & adv. in or toward a country's interior.

in'-law, n. [Col.] a relative by marriage.

in·lay', v. [-LAID, -LAYING] decorate a surface with pieces of wood, etc. set in. —n. [pl. -LAYS] 1. inlaid decoration. 2. filling in a tooth.

in'let, n. narrow strip of water going into land.

in'mate, n. one kept in a prison, hospital, etc.

in'most, a. innermost.

inn, n. hotel or restaurant.

in'nate, a. inborn; natural.

in'ner, a. 1. farther in. 2. more secret.

in'ner·most, a. 1. farthest in. 2. most secret.

in'ning, n. Baseball round of play in which both teams have a turn at bat.

in'no·cent, a. 1. without sin. 2. not guilty. 3. harmless. 4. artless. —n. innocent person. —in'no·cence, n.

in·noc'u·ous, a. harmless.

in·no·va'tion, n. new method, device, etc. **—in'no·va'·tor,** n.

in·nu·en'do, n. [pl. -DOES] hint or sly remark.

in·nu'mer·a·ble, a. too numerous to be counted.

in·oc'u·late, v. inject a vaccine so as to immunize. **—in·oc'u·la'tion,** n.

in·or'di·nate (-nit) a. excessive.

in·or·gan'ic, a. not living; not animal or vegetable.

in'quest, n. judicial inquiry, as by a coroner.

in·quire', v. 1. ask; question. 2. investigate (into). **—in·quir'y** [pl. -IES] n.

in·qui·si'tion, n. 1. investigation. 2. strict suppression, as of heretics by a tribunal. **—in·quis'i·tor,** n.

in·quis'i·tive, a. asking many questions; prying.

in·roads, n.pl. injurious encroachments.

in·sane', a. 1. mentally ill; crazy. 2. of or for insane people. **—in·san'i·ty,** n.

in·sa'ti·a·ble (-sha-b'l) a. that cannot be satisfied.

in·scribe', v. mark or engrave (words, etc.) on. **—in·scrip'tion,** n.

in·scru'ta·ble, a. that cannot be understood.

in'sect, n. small animal with six legs, as a fly.

in·sec'ti·cide, n. substance used to kill insects.

in·se·cure', a. 1. not safe. 2. anxious. 3. not firm. **—in'se·cu'ri·ty,** n.

in·sem'i·nate, v. sow or impregnate.

in·sen'sate, a. not feeling.

in·sen'si·ble, a. 1. unconscious. 2. unaware.

in·sert', v. put into something else. **—n.** (in'sĕrt) thing inserted. **—in·ser'tion,** n.

in'side', n. inner side or part. **—a.** 1. internal. 2. secret. **—adv.** 1. within. 2. indoors. **—prep.** (in-sīd') in.

in·sid'i·ous, a. sly, treacherous, tricky, etc.

in'sight, n. understanding of a thing's true nature.

in·sig'ni·a, n.pl. badges, emblems, etc., as of rank or membership.

in·sin'u·ate, v. 1. hint; imply. 2. to get in artfully. **—in·sin'u·a'tion,** n.

in·sip'id, a. tasteless; dull.

in·sist', v. 1. demand strongly. 2. maintain a stand. **—in·sist'ence,** n. **—in·sist'ent,** a.

in·so·far', adv. to the degree that (with as).

in'so·lent, a. showing disrespect. **—in'so·lence,** n.

in·sol'vent, a. bankrupt.

in·som'ni·a, n. abnormal inability to sleep.

in·spect', v. 1. look at carefully. 2. examine officially. **—in·spec'tion,** n. **—in·spec'tor,** n.

in·spire', v. 1. stimulate, as to a creative effort. 2. arouse (a feeling). 3. inhale. **—in'spi·ra'tion,** n.

in·stall', v. 1. put formally in office. 2. establish in a place. 3. fix in place for use. **—in·stal·la'tion,** n.

in·stall'ment, in·stal'·ment, n. any of the several parts of a payment, magazine serial, etc.

in'stance, n. 1. example. 2. occasion. 3. instigation.

in'stant, a. 1. immediate. 2. quick to prepare. **—n.** moment. **—in'stant·ly,** adv.

in'stan·ta'ne·ous, a. done or happening in an instant.

in·stead', adv. in place of the other.

in'step, n. upper surface of the arch of the foot.

in'sti·gate, v. urge on to an action; incite. **—in'sti·ga'·tion,** n. **—in'sti·ga'tor,** n.

in·still', in·stil', v. put in gradually; implant.

in'stinct, n. 1. inborn tendency to do a certain thing. 2. knack. **—in·stinc'tive,** a.

in'sti·tute, v. establish. **—n.** organization for promoting art, science, etc.

in'sti·tu'tion, n. 1. establishment. 2. established law, custom, etc. 3. institute.

in·struct', v. 1. teach. 2. direct. **—in·struc'tion,** n. **—in·struc'tive,** a. **—in·struc'tor,** n.

in'stru·ment, n. 1. means; agent. 2. tool or device for doing exact work. 3. device producing musical sound.

in'stru·men'tal, a. 1. serving as a means. 2. of, for, or by musical instruments.

in·sub·or'di·nate (-nit) a. disobedient.

in·suf'fer·a·ble, a. intolerable.

in'su·lar, a. 1. of an island. 2. narrow in outlook.

in'su·late, v. 1. protect with a material to prevent the loss of electricity, heat, etc.

2. set apart. **—in·su·la′-tion,** n. **—in′su·la′tor,** n.

in·su·lin, n. pancreatic hormone used to treat diabetes.

in·sult′, n. act or remark meant to hurt one's feelings. —v. subject to an insult.

in·su′per·a·ble, a. that cannot be overcome.

in·sur′ance (-shoor′-) n. 1. an insuring. 2. contract whereby a company guarantees payment for a loss, death, etc. 3. amount for which a thing is insured.

in·sure′, v. 1. make sure. 2. protect. 3. get or give insurance on.

in·sur′gent, a. rising up in revolt; rebelling. —n. a rebel. **—in·sur′gence,** n.

in·sur·rec′tion, n. rebellion.

in·tact′, a. kept whole.

in·tagl′io (-tal′yō) n. [pl. -IOS] design carved below the surface.

in′take, n. 1. amount taken in. 2. place in a pipe, etc. where fluid is taken in.

in′te·ger (-jẽr) n. whole number.

in′te·gral, a. 1. essential to completeness. 2. entire.

in′te·grate, v. 1. form into a whole; unify. 2. desegregate. **—in′te·gra′tion,** n.

in·teg′ri·ty, n. 1. honesty, sincerity, etc. 2. wholeness.

in·teg′u·ment, n. skin, rind, shell, etc.

in′tel·lect, n. 1. ability to reason. 2. high intelligence.

in′tel·lec′tu·al, a. 1. of the intellect. 2. needing or showing high intelligence. —n. one with intellectual interests.

in·tel′li·gence, n. 1. ability to learn; or solve problems. 2. news; information. **—in·tel′li·gent,** a.

in·tel′li·gi·ble, a. that can be understood; clear.

in·tem′per·ate (-it) a. not moderate; excessive.

in·tend′, v. 1. to plan; purpose. 2. to mean.

in·tense′, a. 1. very strong, great, deep, etc. 2. very emotional. **—in·ten′si·fy** [-FIED, -FYING] v. **—in·ten′si·fi·ca′tion,** n. **—in·ten′si·ty,** n.

in·ten′sive, a. 1. thorough. 2. *Gram.* emphasizing.

in·tent′, a. firmly fixed in attention or purpose. —n. purpose; intention.

in·ten′tion, n. thing intended or planned; purpose. —

in·ten′tion·al, a.

in·ter′ (-tũr′) v. [-TERRED, -TERRING] bury.

inter-, *pref.* 1. between; among. 2. with each other.

in·ter·breed′ v. [-BRED, -BREEDING] to cross varieties of in breeding.

in·ter·cede′ (-sẽd′) v. 1. plead for another. 2. mediate. **—in·ter·ces′sion,** n.

in·ter·cept′, v. 1. seize or interrupt or intercept the way. **—in·ter·cep′tion,** n.

in·ter·change′, v. 1. exchange. 2. alternate. —n. (in′tẽr-chānj) 1. an interchanging. 2. traffic entrance or exit on a freeway. **—in·ter·change′a·ble,** a.

in′ter·course, n. 1. dealings between people, countries, etc. 2. sexual union.

in·ter·dict′, v. 1. prohibit. 2. restrain. **—in·ter·dic′tion,** n.

in′ter·est, n. 1. feeling of curiosity or concern. 2. thing causing this feeling. 3. share in something. 4. welfare; benefit. 5. group with a common concern. 6. (rate of) payment for the use of money. —v. have the interest or attention of.

in·ter·fere′, v. 1. come between; intervene. 2. meddle. **—interfere with,** hinder. **—in·ter·fer′ence,** n.

in′ter·im, n. time between; meantime. —a. temporary.

in·te′ri·or, a. 1. inner. 2. inland. 3. private. —n. 1. interior part. 2. domestic affairs of a country.

in·ter·ject′, v. throw in between; insert.

in·ter·jec′tion, n. 1. an interjecting. 2. thing interjected. 3. *Gram.* exclamation.

in·ter·lace′, v. join as by weaving together.

in·ter·lard′, v. intersperse.

in·ter·line′, v. write between the lines of.

in·ter·lock′, v. lock together.

in·ter·loc′u·to·ry, a. *Law* not final, as a decree.

in′ter·lop′er, n. intruder.

in′ter·lude, n. thing that fills time, as music between acts of a play.

in·ter·mar′ry, v. [-RIED, -RYING] marry, as persons of different races, religions, etc. **—in·ter·mar′riage,** n.

in·ter·me′di·ar·y, a. intermediate. —n. [pl. -IES] go-between.

in·ter·me′di·ate (-it) a. in

the middle; in between.

in·ter′ment, n. burial.

in·ter′mi·na·ble, a. lasting, or seeming to last, forever.

in·ter·mis′sion, n. interval, as between acts of a play.

in·ter·mit′tent, a. periodic; recurring at intervals.

in′tern, n. doctor in training at a hospital. —v. (in-tûrn′) confine within an area.

in·ter′nal, a. 1. inner. 2. within a country.

in·ter·na′tion·al, a. 1. among nations. 2. for all nations. —**in·ter·na′tion·al·ize**, v.

in·ter·ne′cine (-nē′sin) a. destructive to both sides.

in·ter·plan′e·tar·y, a. between planets.

in′ter·play, n. action or influence on each other.

in·ter′po·late, v. to insert (extra words, etc.).

in·ter·pose′, v. place or come between; interrupt.

in·ter′pret, v. explain or translate. —**in·ter′pre·ta′tion**, n. —**in·ter′pret·er**, n.

in·ter·ra′cial, a. among or for persons of different races.

in′ter·re·lat′ed, a. closely connected with one another.

in·ter′ro·gate (-ter′-) v. question formally. —**in·ter′ro·ga′tion**, n.

in·ter·rog′a·tive, n. & a. (word) asking a question.

in·ter·rupt′, v. 1. break in on (talk, etc.). 2. obstruct.

in′ter·scho·las′tic, a. between or among schools.

in·ter·sect′, v. 1. divide by passing across. 2. cross each other. —**in·ter·sec′tion**, n.

in·ter·sperse′, v. scatter among other things.

in′ter·state, a. between or among states of a country.

in·ter′stice (-stis) n. crevice.

in·ter·twine′, v. twist together.

in·ter·ur′ban, a. going between towns or cities.

in′ter·val, n. 1. space between things. 2. time between events. 3. difference in musical pitch. —**at intervals**, now and then.

in·ter·vene′, v. 1. come or be between. 2. come in so as to help settle something. —**in′ter·ven′tion**, n.

in′ter·view, n. meeting of people, as to confer, ask questions, etc. —v. have an interview with.

in·tes′tate, a. not having made a will.

in·tes′tine (-tin) n. usually pl. alimentary canal from the stomach to the anus. —**in·tes′ti·nal**, a.

in′ti·mate, v. hint. —a. (-mit) 1. most personal. 2. very familiar. —n. intimate friend. —**in′ti·ma·cy** [pl. -CIES] n. —**in′ti·ma′tion**, n.

in·tim′i·date, v. make afraid as with threats. —**in·tim′i·da′tion**, n.

in′to, prep. 1. toward and within. 2. to the form, state, etc., as divided into parts.

in·to·na′tion, n. manner of utterance with regard to rise and fall in pitch.

in·tone′, v. utter in a chant.

in·tox′i·cate, v. 1. make drunk. 2. excite greatly. —**in·tox′i·cant**, n. —**in·tox′i·ca′tion**, n.

intra-, pref. within; inside.

in·trac′ta·ble, a. unruly.

in·tra·mu′ral, a. among members of a school or college.

in·tran′si·gent (-jǝnt) a. refusing to compromise. —**in·tran′si·gence**, n.

in·tran′si·tive, a. not taking a direct object, as some verbs.

in′tra·ve′nous, a. into or within a vein.

in·trep′id, a. fearless.

in′tri·cate (-kit) a. hard to follow because complicated. —**in′tri·ca·cy** [pl. -CIES] n.

in·trigue′ (-trēg′) v. 1. plot secretly. 2. excite the curiosity of. —n. 1. secret plot. 2. secret love affair.

in·trin′sic, a. real; essential. —**in·trin′si·cal·ly**, adv.

in·tro·duce′, v. 1. insert. 2. bring into use. 3. make acquainted with. 4. give experience of. 5. begin. —**in′tro·duc′tion**, n. —**in′tro·duc′to·ry**, a.

in′tro·spec′tion, n. a looking into one's own thoughts, feelings, etc.

in′tro·vert, n. one more interested in his inner feelings than in external events.

in·trude′, v. force oneself upon others without welcome. —**in·trud′er**, n.

in·tru′sion, n. —**in·tru′sive**, a.

in·tu·i′tion (-ish′ǝn) n. immediate knowledge of something without conscious reasoning. —**in·tu′i·tive**, a.

in′un·date, v. flood. —**in′un·da′tion**, n.

in·ure′ (-yoor′) v. accustom to pain, trouble, etc.

in·vade', v. enter forcibly, as to conquer. —**in·vad'er**, n. —**in·va'sion**, n.

in'va·lid, n. one who is ill or disabled.

in·val'id, a. not valid, sound, etc. —**in·val'i·date**, v.

in·val'u·a·ble, a. priceless.

in·vec'tive, n. strong critical or abusive language.

in·veigh' (-vā') v. talk or write bitterly (against).

in·vei'gle (-vē'-, -vā'-) v. trick or lure into an action.

in·vent', v. 1. produce (a new device). 2. think up. —**in·ven'tor**, n.

in·ven'tion, n. 1. an inventing. 2. power of inventing. 3. something invented. —**in·ven'tive**, a.

in'ven·to·ry, n. [pl. -RIES] complete list or stock of goods.

in·verse' (or **in'vûrs**) a. inverted; directly opposite. —n. inverse thing.

in·vert', v. 1. turn upside down. 2. reverse. —**in·ver'sion**, n.

in·ver'te·brate, n. & a. (animal) having no backbone.

in·vest', v. 1. install in office. 2. furnish with authority. 3. put (money) into business, etc. for profit. —**in·vest'ment**, n. —**in·ves'tor**, n.

in·ves'ti·gate, v. search (into); examine. —**in·ves'ti·ga'tion**, n. —**in·ves'ti·ga'tor**, n.

in·vet'er·ate (-it) a. firmly fixed; habitual.

in·vid'i·ous, a. offensive, as an unfair comparison.

in·vig'or·ate, v. enliven.

in·vin'ci·ble, a. unconquerable. —**in·vin'ci·bil'i·ty**, n.

in·vi'o·la·ble, a. not to be profaned or injured.

in·vi'o·late, a. kept sacred or unbroken.

in·vi·ta'tion, n. 1. an inviting. 2. message or note used in inviting.

in·vite', v. 1. ask (a person) to come somewhere or do something. 2. request. 3. give occasion for. 4. tempt.

in·vo·ca'tion, n. prayer for blessing, help, etc.

in'voice, n. itemized list of goods shipped to a buyer, stating prices, etc.

in·voke', v. call on (God, etc.) for help, etc.

in·volve', v. 1. complicate. 2. draw into difficulty, etc. 3. include. 4. require. 5.

occupy the attention of. —**in·volve'ment**, n.

in'ward, a. 1. internal. 2. directed toward the inside. —adv. 1. toward the inside. 2. into the mind or soul. Also **in'wards**, adv. —**in'ward·ly**, adv.

i'o·dine, n. chemical element used in medicine, etc.

i'on, n. electrically charged atom or group of atoms. —**-ion**, suf. 1. act or state of. 2. result of.

i·o'ta (I-) n. a jot.

IOU, signed note acknowledging a debt.

ip'e·cac (-kak) n. emetic made from a plant root.

IQ, I.Q. n. number showing one's level of intelligence, based on a test.

i·ras'ci·ble (-ras'a-) a. easily angered.

i·rate', a. angry.

ire, n. anger.

i·ri·des'cent, a. showing a play of rainbowlike colors. —**ir'i·des'cence**, n.

i'ris, n. 1. colored part of the eye, around the pupil. 2. plant with sword-shaped leaves and showy flowers.

I'rish, a. & n. (of) the people or language of Ireland. —**I'rish·man** [pl. -MEN] n.

irk (ûrk) v. annoy; tire. —**irk'some**, a. annoying.

i'ron, n. 1. strong metal that is a chemical element. 2. device used for pressing cloth. 3. pl. iron shackles. —a. 1. of iron. 2. strong. —v. press with a hot iron. —**iron out**, smooth away.

i'ron·clad, a. 1. covered with iron. 2. difficult to change or break.

i'ro·ny, n. [pl. -NIES] 1. expression in which what is meant is the opposite of what is said. 2. event that is the opposite of what is expected. —**i·ron'ic**, **i·ron'i·cal**, a.

ir·ra'di·ate, v. 1. expose to X rays, ultraviolet rays, etc. 2. shine; radiate.

ir·ra'tion·al, a. lacking reason or good sense.

ir·rec'on·cil'a·ble, a. that cannot be reconciled or made to agree.

ir·re·fut'a·ble (-ref'yoo-, -ri·fū'-) a. that cannot be disproved.

ir·reg'u·lar, a. 1. not conforming to rule, standard, etc. 2. not straight or uniform. —**ir·reg'u·lar'i·ty**, n.

ir·rel'e·vant, *a.* not to the point. —ir·rel'e·vance, *n.*

ir·re·li'gious, *a.* not religious.

ir·rep'a·ra·ble, *a.* that cannot be repaired or remedied.

ir're·press'i·ble, *a.* that cannot be held back.

ir're·proach'a·ble, *a.* blameless; faultless.

ir're·sist'i·ble, *a.* that cannot be resisted.

ir·res'o·lute, *a.* not resolute; wavering.

ir're·spec'tive, *a.* regardless (of).

ir're·spon'si·ble, *a.* lacking a sense of responsibility.

ir're·triev'a·ble, *a.* that cannot be recovered.

ir·rev'er·ent, *a.* showing disrespect.

ir·rev'o·ca·ble, *a.* that cannot be undone or changed. —ir·rev'o·ca·bly, *adv.*

ir'ri·gate, *v.* 1. supply with water by means of ditches, etc. 2. wash out (a body cavity). —ir'ri·ga'tion, *n.*

ir'ri·ta·ble, *a.* easily irritated or angered. —ir'ri·ta·bil'i·ty, *n.*

ir'ri·tate, *v.* 1. to anger; annoy. 2. make sore. —ir'ri·tant, *a. & n.* —ir'ri·ta'tion, *n.*

is, pres. t. of **be**: used with *he, she,* or *it.*

-ise, -ize: Br. sp.

-ish, *suf.* 1. like; like that of. 2. somewhat.

i'sin·glass (ī'z'n-) *n.* 1. gelatin made from fish bladders. 2. mica.

Is'lam, *n.* Moslem religion.

is'land, *n.* land mass surrounded by water. —is'land·er, *n.*

isle (īl) *n.* small island.

-ism, *suf.* 1. theory or doctrine of. 2. act or result of. 3. condition or qualities of. 4. an instance of.

is'n't, *v.* is not.

i'so·late, *v.* place alone. —i'so·la'tion, *n.*

i·sos'ce·les (ī-sos'ə-lēz) *a.* designating a triangle with two equal sides.

i'so·tope, *n.* any of two or more forms of an element with different atomic weights.

is·sue (ish'ōō) *n.* 1. result. 2. offspring. 3. point under dispute. 4. an issuing or amount issued. —*v.* 1. emerge. 2. result. 3. put out; give out. 4. publish. —at issue, disputed. —take

issue, disagree. —is'su·ance, *n.*

-ist, *suf.* 1. one who practices. 2. adherent of.

isth·mus (is'məs) *n.* strip of land connecting two larger bodies of water.

it, *pron.* the animal or thing mentioned. *It* is also used as an indefinite subject or object.

I·tal'ian, *n. & a.* (native or language) of Italy.

i·tal'ic, *a. & n.* (of) type in which the letters slant upward to the right. —i·tal'i·cize, *v.*

itch, *n.* 1. tingling of the skin, with the desire to scratch. 2. restless desire. —*v.* have an itch. —itch'y [-IER, -IEST] *a.*

-ite, *suf.* 1. inhabitant of. 2. adherent of.

i'tem, *n.* 1. article; unit. 2. bit of news.

i'tem·ize, *v.* list the items of.

it'er·ate, *v.* repeat. —it'er·a'tion, *n.*

i·tin'er·ant, *a.* traveling. —*n.* traveler.

i·tin'er·ar'y, *n.* [pl. -IES] 1. route. 2. plan of a journey.

-itis, *suf.* inflammation of.

its, *a.* of it.

it's, 1. it is. 2. it has.

it·self', *pron.* intensive or reflexive form of **it**.

-ity, *suf.* state or quality.

I've, I have.

-ive, *suf.* 1. of, or having the nature of. 2. tending to.

i'vo·ry, *n.* [pl. -RIES] 1. hard, white substance in elephants' tusks, etc. 2. creamy white.

i'vy, *n.* [pl. IVIES] climbing evergreen vine.

-ize, *suf.* 1. make or become. 2. unite with. 3. engage in.

J

jab, *v. & n.* [JABBED, JAB-BING] punch or poke.

jab'ber, *v.* talk quickly or foolishly. —*n.* chatter.

ja·bot (zha-bō') *n.* [pl. -BOTS (-bōz')] front ruffle on a blouse.

jack, *n.* 1. device to lift something. 2. male of some animals. 3. fellow. 4. playing card with a page boy's picture. 5. *Naut.* small flag. 6. electric plug-in receptacle. 7. [Sl.] money. —*v.* raise as with a jack.

jack'al, *n.* wild dog of Asia, Africa, etc.

jack'ass, n. 1. male donkey. 2. fool.

jack'daw, n. European black bird.

jack'et, n. 1. short coat. 2. outer covering.

jack'knife, n. large pocketknife. —v. bend like a half-open jackknife.

jack'pot, n. cumulative stakes, as in a poker game.

jack rabbit, large hare of W. North America.

jade, n. 1. hard, green stone. 2. worn-out horse. 3. loose woman. —v. tire or satiate.

jag'ged, a. having sharp points.

jag'uar (-wär) n. animal like a large leopard.

jail, n. prison for short-term confinement. —v. put or keep in jail. —**jail'er, jail'or,** n.

ja·lop'y, n. [pl. -IES] [Sl.] old, worn-out automobile.

jal'ou·sie (-oo-sē) n. window or door made of slats fixed as in a Venetian blind.

jam, v. [JAMMED, JAMMING] 1. cram; stuff. 2. crush or crowd. 3. wedge tight. — n. 1. a jamming. 2. [Col.] difficult situation. 3. spread made by boiling fruit and sugar.

jamb (jam) n. side post of a doorway.

jam·bo·ree', n. [Col.] noisy revel.

jan'gle, v. & n. (make or cause to make) a harsh, inharmonious sound.

jan'ji·tor, n. one who takes care of a building.

Jan'u·ar'y, n. 1st month.

Jap·a·nese', n. [pl. -NESE] & a. (native or language of) Japan.

jar, v. [JARRED, JARRING] 1. make a harsh sound. 2. jolt. —n. 1. jolt. 2. wide-mouthed container.

jar'gon, n. special vocabulary of some work, class, etc.

jas'mine (-min) n. shrub with fragrant flowers.

jaun·dice (jôn'dis) n. disease that turns the skin, eyeballs, etc. yellow. —v. make bitter with envy.

jaunt, n. short pleasure trip.

jaun'ty, a. [-TIER, -TIEST] gay, easy, and carefree.

jave'lin (jav'-) n. light spear thrown in contests.

jaw, n. either of the two bony parts that hold the teeth. —v. [Sl.] to talk.

jay, n. 1. bird of the crow family. 2. bluejay.

jay'walk, v. cross a street heedlessly. —**jay'walk·er,** n.

jazz, n. popular American music with strong rhythms.

jeal'ous (jel'-) a. 1. resentfully suspicious or envious. 2. watchful in guarding. —**jeal'ous·y** [pl. -IES] n.

jeans, n.pl. trousers or overalls of twilled cotton cloth.

jeep, n. small, rugged, orig. military automobile.

jeer, v. & n. ridicule.

Je·ho'vah, n. God.

jell, v. [Col.] 1. become, or make into, jelly. 2. become definite.

jel'ly, n. [pl. -LIES] 1. soft, gelatinous food made from cooked fruit sirup. 2. gelatinous substance.

jel'ly·fish, n. jellylike sea animal with tentacles.

jeop'ard·ize (jep'-) v. to risk; endanger.

jeop'ard·y, n. risk; danger.

jerk, n. 1. sharp pull. 2. muscular twitch. 3. [Sl.] stupid person. —v. 1. move with a jerk. 2. twitch. —**jerk'y** [-IER, -IEST] a.

jer'kin, n. snug, usually sleeveless jacket.

jer'sey, n. 1. soft, knitted cloth. 2. [pl. -SEYS] upper garment of this.

jest, v. & n. 1. joke. 2. ridicule. —**jest'er,** n.

Je'sus, n. founder of the Christian religion.

jet, v. [JETTED, JETTING] shoot out in a stream. —n. 1. liquid or gas in such a stream. 2. spout that shoots a jet. 3. jet-propelled airplane. 4. black mineral. —a. 1. jet-propelled. 2. black.

jet'lin'er, n. commercial jet passenger plane.

jet propulsion, propulsion by gases from a rear vent. —**jet'-pro·pelled',** a.

jet'sam, n. cargo thrown overboard to lighten a ship.

jet'ti·son, v. 1. throw (goods) overboard to lighten a ship. 2. discard.

jet'ty, n. [pl. -TIES] 1. wall built into the water. 2. landing pier.

Jew, n. 1. descendant of people of ancient Israel. 2. believer in Judaism. —**Jew'ish,** a.

jew'el, n. 1. gem. 2. small gem used as a watch bearing. —**jew'el·er, jew'el·ler,** n. one

jew'el·ry, n. jewels or ornaments with jewels.

jib, n. triangular sail ahead of the foremast.

jibe (jīb) v. 1. shift a sail, the course, of a ship. 2. [Col.] be in accord. 3. to gibe. —n. gibe.

jif'fy, n. [Col.] an instant.

jig, n. 1. lively dance. 2. device to guide a tool. —v. [JIGGED, JIGGING] dance (a jig).

jig'ger, n. glass of 1½ ozs. for measuring liquor.

jig'gle, v. move in slight jerks. —n. a jiggling.

jig'saw, n. saw with a narrow blade set in a frame; also **jig saw**.

jigsaw puzzle, picture cut in pieces to be fitted together again.

jilt, v. reject (a lover).

jim'my, n. [pl. -MIES] short crowbar used by burglars. —v. [-MIED, -MYING] pry open.

jin'gle, v. make light, ringing sounds. —n. 1. jingling sound. 2. light verse.

jin·rik'i·sha (-rĭk'shō) n. two-wheeled oriental carriage pulled by one or two men.

jinx, n. [Sl.] person or thing supposed to cause bad luck. —v. [Sl.] cause bad luck to.

jit'ter·y, a. nervous or restless. —the jitters, nervous feeling.

jive, n. [Sl.] (jargon of) jazz.

job, n. 1. piece of work. 2. employment; work. —a. done by the job. —v. handle (goods) as a middleman.

job'ber, n. one who buys goods in quantity and sells them to dealers.

job lot, goods, often of various sorts, for sale as one quantity.

jock'ey, n. race-horse rider. —v. maneuver for advantage.

jo·cose', a. joking; playful.

joc'u·lar, a. joking; full of fun. —joc'u·lar'i·ty, n.

joc'und, a. genial; gay.

jodh'purs (jŏd'pẽrz) n.pl. riding breeches.

jog, v. [JOGGED, JOGGING] 1. nudge; shake. 2. move at a slow, steady, jolting pace. —n. 1. nudge. 2. jogging pace. 3. part that changes direction sharply.

join, v. 1. connect; unite. 2. become a part or member (of).

joint, n. 1. place where two things are joined. 2. one of the parts of a jointed whole. 3. [Sl.] saloon, etc. —a. 1. common to two or more. 2. sharing with another. —v. connect by a joint. —out of joint, 1. dislocated. 2. disordered. —joint'ly, adv.

joist, n. any of the parallel timbers holding up planks of a floor, etc.

joke, n. 1. anything said or done to arouse laughter. 2. thing not to be taken seriously. —v. make jokes.

jok'er, n. 1. one who jokes. 2. deceptive clause, as in a contract. 3. extra playing card used in some games.

jol'ly, a. [-LIER, -LIEST] merry; gay. —jol'li·ty, n.

jolt, v. & n. 1. jar; jerk. 2. shock or surprise.

jon'quil, n. narcissus with yellow or white flower.

josh, v. [Sl.] tease, fool, etc.

jos'tle, v. shove roughly.

jot, n. very small amount. —v. [JOTTED, JOTTING] write (down) briefly.

jounce, v. jolt or bounce.

jour'nal, n. 1. diary. 2. record of proceedings. 3. newspaper or magazine. 4. book for business records. 5. part of an axle, etc. that turns in a bearing.

jour'nal·ism, n. newspaper writing and editing. —jour'nal·ist, n.

jour'ney, n. a trip. —v. travel.

jour'ney·man, n. [pl. -MEN] worker skilled at his trade.

joust (just, joust) n. & v. fight with lances on horseback.

jo'vi·al, a. gay; jolly.

jowl, n. 1. cheek. 2. fleshy, hanging part under the jaw.

joy, n. gladness; delight.

joy'ful, a. —joy'ous, a.

ju'bi·lant, a. rejoicing. —ju'bi·la'tion, n.

ju'bi·lee, n. 1. a 50th or 25th anniversary. 2. time of rejoicing.

Ju'da·ism, n. Jewish religion.

judge (jŭj) v. 1. hear and decide cases in a law court. 2. determine the winner. 3. appraise or criticize. 4. think; suppose. —n. one who judges.

judg'ment, judge'ment, n. 1. a deciding. 2. legal decision. 3. opinion. 4. ability to make wise decisions.

ju·di·cial (jōō-dish'əl) a. 1. of judges, courts, etc. 2. careful in thought.

ju·di·ci·ar·y (-dish'i-) a. of judges or courts. —n. [pl. -IES] 1. part of government that administers justice. 2. judges collectively.

ju·di·cious (-dish'əs) a. showing good judgment. —**ju·di'cious·ly,** adv.

ju'do, n. kind of wrestling used for self-defense.

jug, n. container for liquids, with a small opening and a handle.

jug'gle, v. 1. do tricks with (balls, etc.). 2. handle in a tricky way. —**jug'gler,** n.

jug'u·lar, n. either of two large veins in the neck; in full, **jugular vein.**

juice, n. liquid from fruit or cooked meat. —**juic'y** [-IER, -IEST] a.

juke box, [Col.] coin-operated phonograph.

Ju·ly', n. 7th month.

jum'ble, v. & n. (mix in) a confused heap.

jum'bo, a. very large.

jump, v. 1. spring from the ground, etc. 2. leap or make leap over. 3. move or change suddenly. 4. rise or raise suddenly, as prices. —n. 1. a jumping. 2. distance jumped. 3. sudden move or change. —**jump at,** accept eagerly. —**jump'er,** n.

jumper, n. sleeveless dress worn over a blouse, etc.

jump'y a. [-IER, -IEST] 1. moving jerkily. 2. nervous.

junc'tion, n. 1. a joining. 2. place where things join.

junc'ture (-chər) n. 1. junction. 2. point of time.

June, n. 6th month.

jun'gle, n. dense forest in the tropics.

jun'ior, a. 1. the younger; written Jr. 2. of lower rank, etc. —n. high school or college student in the next-to-last year.

ju'ni·per, n. small evergreen with berrylike cones.

junk, n. 1. old metal, paper, etc. 2. Chinese ship with flat bottom. 3. [Col.] rubbish. —v. [Col.] to discard.

jun'ket, n. 1. pleasure trip. 2. milk thickened as curd.

ju'ris·dic'tion, n. (range of) authority, area of a court.

ju'ris·pru'dence, n. 1. science or philosophy of law. 2. a system of laws.

ju'rist, n. an expert in law.

ju'ror, n. member of a jury; also **ju'ry·man** [pl. -MEN] n.

ju'ry, n. [pl. -RIES] group of people chosen to give a decision, esp. in a law case.

just, a. 1. right or fair. 2. righteous. 3. well-founded. 4. correct; exact. —adv. 1. exactly. 2. only. 3. barely. 4. a very short time ago. 5. [Col.] really. —**just the same,** [Col.] nevertheless. —**just'ly,** adv.

jus'tice, n. 1. a being just. 2. reward or penalty as deserved. 3. the upholding of what is just. 4. a judge.

justice of the peace, local magistrate in minor cases.

jus'ti·fy, v. [-FIED, -FYING] 1. show to be just, right, etc. 2. free from guilt. —**jus'ti·fi'a·ble** a. —**jus'ti·fi·ca'tion,** n.

jut, v. [JUTTED, JUTTING] stick out.

jute, n. strong fiber used to make burlap, rope, etc.

ju've·nile (-və-n'l, -nīl) a. 1. child or young person. —a. 1. young; immature. 2. of or for juveniles.

K

kale, n. a cabbage with spreading, curled leaves.

ka·lei'do·scope (-lī'-) n. small tube containing bits of colored glass that change patterns as the tube is turned. —**ka·lei'do·scop'ic** (-skop'-) a.

kan·ga·roo', n. leaping animal of Australia.

ka'pok, n. silky fibers from tropical trees, used for stuffing pillows, etc.

kar'at, n. carat.

ka·ra'te, n. self-defense by blows with side of open hand.

ka'ty·did, n. insect resembling the grasshopper.

kay'ak (kī'-) n. Eskimo canoe.

keel, n. center piece along the bottom of a ship. —**keel over,** turn or fall over.

keen, a. 1. sharp. 2. piercing. 3. perceptive; eager. 4. eager. 5. intense. 6. [Sl.] excellent. —**keen'ly,** adv.

keep, v. [KEPT, KEEPING] 1. fulfill; observe. 2. protect; take care of. 3. preserve. 4. retain. 5. continue. 6. hold and not let go. 7. refrain. —n. food and shelter. —**keep to oneself,** 1. avoid others. 2. refrain from telling. —**keep'er,** n.

keep'ing, *n.* 1. care or protection. 2. conformity.

keep'sake, *n.* souvenir.

keg, *n.* small barrel.

kelp, *n.* brown seaweed.

ken, *n.* range of knowledge.

ken'nel, *n.* 1. doghouse. 2. *often pl.* place where dogs are bred or kept.

ker'chief, *n.* 1. cloth worn around the head or neck. 2. handkerchief.

ker'nel, *n.* 1. grain or seed. 2. soft, inner part of a nut or fruit pit.

ker'o·sene, ker'o·sine (-sēn) *n.* oil distilled from petroleum.

ketch, *n.* sailing vessel.

ketch'up, *n.* thick sauce of tomatoes, spices, etc.

ket'tle, *n.* 1. pot used in cooking. 2. teakettle.

ket'tle·drum, *n.* hemispheric copper drum with an adjustable parchment top.

key, *n.* 1. device for working a lock. 2. lever pressed in operating a piano, typewriter, etc. 3. thing that explains, as a code. 4. controlling factor. 5. mood or style. 6. low island. 7. *Mus.* scale based on a certain keynote. —*a.* controlling. —*v.* bring into harmony. —**key up,** excite. —**key'hole,** *n.*

key'board, *n.* row(s) of keys of a piano, typewriter, etc.

key'note, *n.* 1. *Mus.* lowest, basic note of a scale. 2. basic idea.

key'stone, *n.* top, supporting stone of an arch.

kha'ki (kak'-) *a. & n.* yellowish-brown (uniform).

kib'itz·er, *n.* [Col.] onlooker who gives unwanted advice.

kick, *v.* 1. strike (out) with the foot. 2. recoil, as a gun. 3. [Col.] complain. —*n.* 1. a kicking. 2. [Col.] thrill.

kick'back, *n.* [Sl.] forced or secret rebate.

kick'off, *n.* kick in football that begins play.

kid, *n.* 1. young goat. 2. leather from its skin: also **kid'skin.** 3. [Col.] child. —*v.* [KIDDED, KIDDING] [Col.] tease, fool, etc. —**kid'der,** *n.*

kid'nap, *v.* seize and hold a person, esp. for ransom. —**kid'nap·er,** *n.*

kid'ney, *n.* urine-forming gland.

kiel·ba·sa (kēl-bä′sə) *n.* smoked Polish sausage.

kill, *v.* 1. make die; slay. 2. destroy. 3. spend (time)

idly. —*n.* 1. a killing. 2. animal(s) killed. —**kill'er,** *n.*

kiln (kil, kiln) *n.* oven for baking bricks, etc.

ki·lo (kē′lō, kil′ō) *n.* [*pl.* -LOS] kilogram.

kilo-, *pref.* one thousand.

kil'o·cy·cle, *n.* 1,000 cycles (per second).

kil'o·gram, *n.* 1,000 grams.

kil'o·me'ter, *n.* 1,000 meters.

kil'o·watt, *n.* 1,000 watts.

kilt, *n.* skirt worn by men of the Scottish Highlands.

kil'ter, *n.* [Col.] working order.

ki·mo'no, *n.* [*pl.* -NOS] Japanese robe.

kin, *n.* relatives; family.

kind, *n.* sort; variety. —*a.* gentle, generous, etc. —**in kind,** in the same way. —**kind of,** [Col.] somewhat. —**kind'ly,** *a. & adv.* —**kind'ness,** *n.*

kin'der·gar'ten, *n.* class or school for children about five years old.

kind'heart'ed, *a.* kind.

kin'dle, *v.* 1. set on fire. 2. start burning. 3. excite.

kin'dling, *n.* bits of wood, etc. for starting a fire.

kin'dred, *n.* relatives; kin. —*a.* related or similar.

ki·net'ic, *a.* of motion.

king, *n.* 1. male ruler of a state. 2. playing card with a king's picture. 3. chess piece that has to be captured.

king'dom, *n.* country ruled by a king or queen.

king'fish·er, *n.* fish-eating diving bird.

kink, *n. & v.* curl or twist. —**kink'y** [-IER, -IEST] *a.*

kin'ship, *n.* 1. family relationship. 2. close connection.

kins'man, *n.* [*pl.* -MEN] male relative. —**kins'wom'an** [*pl.* -WOMEN] *n.fem.*

kip'per, *n.* salted and dried or smoked herring.

kis'met (kiz′-) *n.* fate.

kiss, *v.* caress with the lips in affection or greeting. —*n.* 1. act of kissing. 2. kind of candy.

kit, *n.* 1. set of tools, etc. 2. box or bag for it.

kitch'en, *n.* place for preparing and cooking food.

kitch·en·ette', kitch·en·et', *n.* small kitchen.

kite, *n.* 1. kind of hawk. 2. light frame covered with paper, tied to a string, and flown in the wind.

kith and kin, friends and relatives.

kit'ten, n. young cat: also **kit'ty** [pl. -TIES].

kit'ten·ish, a. coy.

klep'to·ma'ni·a, n. persistent impulse to steal. — **klep'to·ma'ni·ac,** n.

knack, n. special ability.

knap'sack, n. bag to carry supplies on the back.

knave, n. dishonest person; rogue. — **knav'ish,** a.

knav'er·y, n. dishonesty.

knead, v. press and squeeze.

knee, n. joint between thigh and lower leg.

knee'cap, n. movable bone at the front of the knee.

kneel, v. [KNELT or KNEELED, KNEELING] rest on the bended knee or knees.

knell, n. slow tolling of a bell, as at a funeral.

knew, pt. of **know.**

knick'ers, n.pl. breeches gathered below the knees: also **knick'er·bock'ers.**

knick'knack, n. small, showy article.

knife, n. [pl. KNIVES] sharp cutting blade set in a handle. — v. stab with a knife.

knight (nīt) n. 1. medieval, chivalrous soldier. 2. British man holding honorary rank. 3. chessman like a horse's head. — **knight'hood,** n.

knit, v. [KNITTED or KNIT, KNITTING] 1. make by looping yarn with needles. 2. draw or grow together.

knob, n. round handle, etc. — **knob'by** [-BIER, -BIEST] a.

knock, v. 1. hit; strike; rap. 2. make a pounding noise. 3. [Col.] find fault with. — n. 1. hit; blow. 2. pounding noise. — **knock off,** [Col.] 1. stop working. 2. deduct. — **knock out,** make unconscious. — **knock'er,** n. — **knock'out,** n.

knoll, n. little hill; mound.

knot, n. 1. lump in tangled thread, etc. 2. a tying together of string, rope, etc. 3. small group. 4. hard lump in wood where a branch has grown. 5. one nautical mile per hour. — v. [KNOTTED, KNOTTING] form a knot (in).

knot'ty, a. [-TIER, -TIEST] 1. full of knots. 2. puzzling.

know, v. [KNEW, KNOWN, KNOWING] 1. be informed (about). 2. be aware (of). 3. be acquainted with.

know'-how', n. [Col.] technical skill.

know'ing, a. 1. having knowledge. 2. shrewd; cunning.

knowl'edge, n. things known or learned.

knuck'le, n. joint of a finger. — **knuckle down,** work hard. — **knuckle under,** surrender.

kohl'ra·bi (kōl'rä'-) n. [pl. -BIES] kind of cabbage.

Ko·ran' (kō-) n. sacred book of Moslems.

ko'sher, a. fit to eat according to Jewish dietary laws.

kow·tow (kou'tou') v. show great deference (to).

ku·chen (kōō'khən) n. bread-like cake, with raisins, etc.

ku·dos (kū'dos) n. credit for achievement.

kum'quat (-kwät) n. small, oval, orangelike fruit.

L

lab, n. [Col.] laboratory.

la'bel, n. card, etc. marked and attached to an object to show its contents, etc. — v. 1. attach a label to. 2. classify as.

la'bi·al, a. of the lips.

la'bor, n. 1. work. 2. task. 3. all workers. 4. process of childbirth. — v. 1. work hard. 2. move with effort.

lab'o·ra·to·ry, n. [pl. -RIES] place for scientific work or research.

la'bored, a. with effort.

la'bor·er, n. a worker, esp. an unskilled worker.

la·bo'ri·ous, a. difficult.

labor union, association of workers to further their interests.

la'bour, n. & v. labor: Br. sp.

la·bur'num, n. shrub with drooping yellow flowers.

lab'y·rinth, n. maze.

lace (lās) n. 1. string used to fasten together parts of a shoe, etc. 2. openwork fabric woven in fancy designs. — v. 1. fasten with a lace. 2. intertwine. 3. whip.

lac'er·ate (las'-) v. tear jaggedly. — **lac'er·a'tion,** n.

lack, n. state of not having enough or any. — v. have little or nothing of.

lack'a·dai'si·cal (-dā'-) a. showing lack of interest.

lack'ey, n. [pl. -EYS] 1. menial male servant. 2. toady.

lack'lus'ter, a. dull.

la·con'ic (-kon'-) a. concise; brief.

lac·quer (lak'ēr) n. a varnish, often like enamel. —v. coat with lacquer.

la·crosse′, n. ball game using long-handled rackets.

lac′te·al, a. of or like milk.

lac′tic, a. 1. of milk. 2. of an acid in sour milk.

lac′tose, n. sugar found in milk.

la·cu′na (-kū′-) n. gap; space.

lac′y, a. [-IER, -IEST] of or like lace. —**lac′i·ness**, n.

lad, n. boy; youth.

lad′der, n. series of rungs framed by two sidepieces for climbing up or down.

lade, v. [alt. pp. LADEN] to load.

la′dle, n. long-handled, cup-like spoon for dipping. —v. dip out with a ladle.

la′dy, n. [pl. -DIES] 1. well-bred, polite woman. 2. any woman. —a. female. —**la′dy·like**, a.

la′dy·bug, n. small beetle with a spotted back.

la′dy·fin′ger, n. small, fin-ger-shaped spongecake.

lag, v. [LAGGED, LAGGING] fall behind. —n. 1. a falling be-hind. 2. amount of this.

la·ger (beer) (lä′gēr) n. a beer aged for several months.

lag′gard, a. backward; slow. —n. one who falls behind.

la·goon′, n. 1. shallow lake joined to a larger body of water. 2. water inside an atoll.

laid (lād) pt. & pp. of lay.

lain, pp. of lie (recline).

lair (lâr) n. animal's den.

lais·sez faire (les′ā fâr′) non-interference.

la′i·ty, n. all laymen, as a group.

lake, n. large inland body of water.

lam, n. [Sl.] headlong flight. —v. [LAMMED, LAMMING] [Sl.] flee.

la′ma (lä′-) n. Buddhist priest or monk in Tibet.

lamb (lam) n. 1. young sheep. 2. its flesh as food.

lam·baste′ (-bāst′) v. [Sl.] beat or scold soundly.

lam′bent, a. 1. flickering. 2. glowing softly. 3. light and graceful.

lame, a. 1. crippled. 2. stiff and painful. 3. poor; in-effectual. —v. make lame.

la·ment′, v. feel or show deep sorrow for. —n. 1. a lamenting. 2. elegy; dirge. —**lam′-en·ta·ble**, a. —**lam·en·ta′tion**, n.

lam′i·nate, v. form of into thin layers. —**lam′i·nat·ed**, a. —**lam′i·na′tion**, n.

lamp, n. 1. device for pro-ducing light. 2. such a de-vice set in a stand.

lamp′black, n. fine soot used as a black pigment.

lam·poon′, n. written satir-ical attack. —v. to attack in a lampoon.

lamp′post, n. post support-ing a street lamp.

lam′prey (-pri) n. eellike water animal.

lance, n. 1. long spear. 2. lancet. —v. cut open with a lancet.

lan′cet, n. surgical knife.

land, n. 1. solid part of earth's surface. 2. country or region. 3. ground; soil. —v. 1. put or go on shore or land. 2. arrive at a place, port, etc. 3. catch or get.

land′ed, a. 1. owning land. 2. consisting of land.

land′ing, n. 1. a coming to shore. 2. pier; dock. 3. platform at the end of stairs. 4. an alighting.

land′locked, a. 1. sur-rounded by land. 2. con-fined to fresh water.

land′lord, n. man who leases land, houses, rooms, etc. to others. —**land′la′dy**, n.fem.

land′lub′ber, n. one with little experience at sea.

land′mark, n. 1. identifying feature of a locality. 2. im-portant event.

land′scape, n. (picture of) natural scenery. —v. plant lawns, bushes, etc. on.

land′slide, n. 1. sliding of rocks or earth down a slope. 2. overwhelming victory.

lane, n. narrow path, road, etc.

lan′guage (-gwij) n. 1. speech or writing. 2. any means of communicating.

lan′guid (-gwid) a. 1. weak. 2. listless; sluggish.

lan′guish (-gwish) v. 1. be-come weak. 2. long; pine. —**lan′guish·ing**, a.

lan′guor (-gēr) n. lack of vigor. —**lan′guor·ous**, a.

lank, a. tall and lean.

lank′y, a. [-IER, -IEST] awk-wardly tall and lean.

lan′o·lin, n. fatty substance obtained from wool.

lan′tern, n. transparent case holding a light.

lan′yard (-yērd) n. Naut. short rope.

lap, n. 1. front part from the waist to the knees of a sitting person. 2. place in which one is cared for. 3. one circuit of a race track. 4. overlapping part. —v. [LAPPED, LAPPING] 1. fold or wrap. 2. lay or extend partly over. 3. dip up with the tongue. 4. splash lightly.

la·pel′, n. fold-back part at the upper front of a coat.

lap′i·dar·y, n. [pl. -IES] one who cuts & polishes gems.

lapse, n. 1. small error. 2. a falling into a lower condition. 3. passing, as of time. —v. 1. fall into a certain state. 2. deviate from virtue. 3. become void.

lar′board (-bērd) n. & a. left; port.

lar′ce·ny, n. theft. —**lar′ce·nous,** a.

larch, n. kind of pine tree.

lard, n. melted fat of hogs. —v. cover with lard.

lard′er, n. (place for keeping) food supplies.

large, a. of great size or amount. —adv. in a large way. —**at large,** 1. free; not jailed. 2. in general. —**large′ness,** n.

large′ly, adv. mainly.

lar·gess, lar·gesse (lär′jes) n. generous giving.

lar′go (lär′-) a. & adv. Mus. slow and stately.

lar′i·at (lar′-) n. a rope, esp. a lasso.

lark, n. 1. any of various songbirds. 2. gay time. —v. to play or frolic.

lark′spur, n. plant with spurred, esp. blue, flowers.

lar′va, n. [pl. -VAE (-vē)] insect in the earliest stage after hatching. —**lar′val,** a.

lar·yn·gi·tis (lar′in-jī′-) n. inflammation of the larynx.

lar′ynx (-inks) n. upper end of the trachea.

las·civ′i·ous (lə-siv′-) a. showing or exciting lust.

la·ser (lā′zēr) n. device that concentrates light rays in an intense beam.

lash, n. 1. striking part of a whip. 2. a stroke as with a whip. 3. eyelash. —v. 1. strike or drive as with a lash. 2. swing sharply. 3. tie with a rope, etc. ·

lass, n. young woman.

las′si·tude, n. weariness.

las′so (-ō) n. [pl. -SOS, -SOES] rope with a sliding noose, for catching cattle, etc. —v. catch with a lasso.

last, a. 1. after all others. 2. only remaining. 3. most recent. —adv. 1. after all others. 2. most recently. —n. 1. last one. 2. footlike form for making shoes. —v. go on; stay in use, etc. —**at last,** finally.

last′ly, adv. in conclusion.

latch, n. fastening for a door, window, etc.; esp., a bar that fits into a notch. —v. fasten with a latch.

late, a. 1. after the expected time. 2. near the end of a period. 3. recent. 4. recently dead. —adv. 1. after the expected time. 2. near the end of a period.

late′ly, adv. recently.

la′tent, a. undeveloped.

lat′er·al, a. sideways.

la′tex, n. milky fluid in certain plants and trees.

lath (lath) n. framework for plaster, as thin strip of wood.

lathe (lāth) n. machine for shaping wood, metal, etc., with a cutting tool.

lath′er (lath′-) n. 1. foam formed by soap and water. 2. foamy sweat. —v. cover with or form lather.

Lat′in, n. 1. language of ancient Rome. 2. speaker of a Latin language. —a. of or derived from Latin.

lat′i·tude, n. 1. unlimited freedom. 2. distance in degrees from the equator.

la·trine′ (-trēn′) n. toilet for the use of many people.

lat′ter, a. 1. nearer the end. 2. last mentioned of two.

lat′tice, n. structure of crossed strips of wood, etc.

laud (lôd) v. & n. praise. —**laud′a·to·ry,** a.

laud′a·ble, a. praiseworthy.

laugh, v. make vocal sounds showing mirth, scorn, etc. —n. act of laughing: also **laugh′ter.** —**laugh′a·ble,** a.

laugh′ing·stock′, n. object of ridicule.

launch (lônch) v. 1. send into space. 2. set afloat. 3. begin. —n. large motorboat.

laun′der, v. wash or wash and iron (clothes, etc.). —**laun′dress,** n.fem.

laun′dry, n. [pl. -DRIES] 1. place for laundering. 2. things to be (or are) laundered. —**laun′dry·man** [-MEN] n.

lau′rel, n. 1. evergreen with large, glossy leaves. 2. pl. fame; victory.

la·va (lä′və, lav′ə) n. rock from a volcano.

lav'a·to'ry, n. [pl. -RIES] 1. washbowl. 2. room with toilet and washbowl.

lav'en·der, a. pale purple.

lav'ish, a. very generous. —v. give or spend freely.

law, n. 1. any of the rules of conduct made by a government. 2. obedience to these. 3. profession of lawyers. 4. fundamental rule. 5. series of natural events always happening the same way. —**law'mak'er,** n.

law'-a·bid'ing, a. obeying the law.

law'ful, a. legal (sense 1).

law'less, a. disobeying the law.

lawn, n. grass cut short.

law'suit, n. case before a court for decision.

law'yer, n. person licensed to practice law.

lax, n. 1. not tight. 2. not strict. —**lax'i·ty,** n.

lax'a·tive, n. & a. (medicine) making the bowels move.

lay, v, [LAID, LAYING] 1. put down on something. 2. set in place. 3. put or place. 4. produce (an egg). 5. settle; allay. 6. bet. 7. devise. 8. present. —n. 1. position; arrangement. 2. short poem. —a. of or for laymen. —**lay aside, lay away,** or **lay by,** save for future use.

lay, pt. of **lie** (recline).

lay'er, n. single thickness.

lay·ette' (-et') n. complete outfit for a newborn baby.

lay'man, n. [pl. -MEN] one not belonging to the clergy or to a given profession.

lay'off', n. temporary unemployment.

lay'out, n. arrangement.

la'zy, a. [-ZIER, -ZIEST] 1. not willing to work. 2. sluggish. —**la'zi·ly,** adv. —**la'zi·ness,** n.

lead (lēd) v. [LED, LEADING] 1. direct or guide as by going before. 2. be at the head of. 3. go or pass. 4. bring as a result. 5. move first in a game, etc. —n. 1. guidance. 2. first place. 3. distance ahead. 4. clue. 5. leading role. —**lead'er,** n. —**lead'er·ship,** n.

lead (led) n. 1. heavy, soft metal, a chemical element. 2. graphite used in pencils.

lead'en, a. 1. of lead. 2. heavy. 3. gloomy.

lead'ing (lēd'-) a. chief.

leaf, n. [pl. LEAVES] 1. flat, thin, usually green part growing from a plant stem.

2. sheet of paper, etc. —v. turn the pages of.

leaf'let, n. 1. small leaf. 2. folded printed sheet.

leaf'y, a. [-IER, -IEST] having many leaves.

league (lēg) n. 1. association of nations, groups, etc. 2. unit of distance, about 3 miles. —v. join in a league.

leak, v. 1. pass or let pass out or in accidentally. 2. become known gradually. —n. accidental crack that allows leaking. —**leak'y,** a.

leak'age, n. 1. a leaking. 2. amount that leaks.

lean, v. 1. bend or slant. 2. rely (on). 3. tend. 4. rest against something. —a. 1. with little or no fat. 2. meager. —**lean'ness,** n.

leap, v. [alt. pt. & pp. LEAPT] jump (over). —n. a jump.

leap year, every fourth year, having 29 days in February.

learn, v. 1. get knowledge or skill by study. 2. hear (of). 3. memorize. —**learn'ing,** n.

learn'ed (-id) a. having or showing much learning.

lease, n. contract by which property is rented. —v. give or get by a lease.

leash, n. strap or chain for holding a dog, etc. in check.

least, a. smallest. —adv. in the smallest degree. —n. smallest in degree, etc. —**at least,** at any rate.

leath'er (leth'-) n. animal skin that has been tanned.

leave, v. [LEFT, LEAVING] 1. let remain. 2. have remaining after one. 3. bequeath. 4. go away (from). —n. 1. permission. 2. permitted absence from duty. —**leave out,** omit. —**take one's leave,** depart.

leav'en (lev'-) n. 1. yeast, etc. used to make dough rise. 2. permeating influence. —v. affect with leaven.

leaves, n. pl. of **leaf**.

lech'er, n. lewd man. —**lech'er·ous,** a.

lec'ture, n. 1. informative talk. 2. a scolding. —v. give a lecture (to). —**lec'tur·er,** n.

led, pt. & pp. of **lead** (guide).

ledge, n. 1. shelf. 2. projecting ridge of rocks.

ledg'er, n. book of final entry for transactions.

lee, n. & a. (on) the side away from the wind.

lee'ward, n., a., adv.

leech, n. bloodsucking worm

leek, n. onionlike vegetable.

leer, n. malicious or suggestive grin. —v. look with a leer.

leer'y, a. [Col.] wary.

lees, n.pl. dregs; sediment.

lee'way, n. [Col.] margin of time, money, etc.

left, a. of that side toward the west when one faces north. —n. 1. left side. 2. liberal or radical party, etc. —adv. toward the left.

left, pt. & pp. of **leave.**

left'-hand'ed, a. 1. using the left hand more easily. 2. for the left hand. 3. insincere. —adv. with the left hand.

left'ist, n. & a. liberal or radical.

leg, n. 1. limb used for standing and walking. 2. thing like a leg in shape or use.

leg'a·cy, n. [pl. -CIES] something handed down to one, esp. by a will.

le'gal, a. 1. of, based on, or permitted by law. 2. of lawyers. —le·gal'i·ty, n. —le'gal·ize, v. —le'gal·ly, adv.

leg'ate (-it) n. papal envoy.

le·ga'tion, n. envoy and his staff and headquarters.

leg'end (lej'-) n. 1. traditional tale. 2. inscription, title, etc. —leg'end·ar'y, a.

leg'er·de·main' (lej'-) n. sleight of hand.

leg'gings, n.pl. coverings for protecting the legs.

leg'i·ble (lej'-) a. that can be read. —leg'i·bly, adv.

le'gion (-jən) n. 1. large body of soldiers. 2. great number.

le'gion·naire' (-âr') n. member of a legion.

leg'is·late, v. 1. make laws. 2. bring (about) by laws. —leg'is·la'tion, n. —leg'is·la'tive, a. —leg'is·la'tor, n.

leg'is·la·ture, n. group of persons who make laws.

le·git'i·mate (-jit'ə·mit) a. 1. born of a married couple. 2. lawful. 3. reasonable. —le·gu'mi·nous, a.

leg·ume (leg'ūm) n. plant with pods, as the pea and bean. —le·gu'mi·nous, a.

le·i (lā, lā'ī) n. [pl. LEIS] garland or wreath of flowers.

lei'sure (lē'zhēr) a. & n. free (time) for rest, play, etc.

lei'sure·ly, a. slow. —adv. in an unhurried manner.

lem'on, n. small, sour, yellow citrus fruit.

lem'on·ade', n. drink of lemon juice, sugar, and water.

le'mur (lē'-) n. small mammal related to the monkey.

lend, v. [LENT, LENDING] 1. let another use (a thing) temporarily. 2. let out (money) at interest. 3. impart. —lend'er, n.

length, n. 1. distance from end to end. 2. extent in space or time. 3. long stretch. —at length, finally. —length'wise, a.

length'en, v. make or become longer.

length'y, a. [-IER, -IEST] long; esp. too long.

le'ni·ent, a. merciful; gentle. —le'ni·en·cy, n.

lens, n. 1. curved piece of glass, plastic, etc. for adjusting light rays passing through it: used in cameras, telescopes, etc. 2. similar part of the eye.

Lent, n. period of 40 weekdays before Easter.

lent, pt. and pp. of **lend.**

len'til, n. small, edible seed of a pealike plant.

Le'o, n. 5th sign of the zodiac; Lion.

le'o·nine, a. like a lion.

leop'ard (lep'-) n. large, black-spotted, wild cat of Asia and Africa.

lep'er, n. one having leprosy.

lep'ro·sy, n. disease with skin ulcers, scaling, etc.

le·sion (lē'zhən) n. injury of an organ or tissue.

less, a. not so much, so great, etc. —adv. to a smaller extent. —n. a smaller amount. —prep. minus.

-less, suf. 1. without. 2. not —ing or —ed.

les·see', n. one to whom property is leased.

less'en, v. make or become less.

less'er, a. smaller, less, etc.

les'son, n. 1. exercise for a student to learn. 2. something learned by experience.

les'sor, n. one giving a lease.

lest, con. for fear that.

let, v. 1. allow; permit. 2. leave. 3. rent. 4. cause to flow, as blood. —n. hindrance. —let down, 1. lower. 2. disappoint. —let up, 1. relax. 2. cease.

le'thal, a. fatal; deadly.

leth'ar·gy, n. lack of energy. —le·thar'gic (-thär'-) a.

let'ter, n. 1. a character of the alphabet. 2. message sent by mail. 3. literal meaning. 4. *pl.* literature. —*v.* mark with letters. —**let'tered,** *a.*

let'ter head, *n.* 1. name, etc. of a person or firm as a heading on letter paper. 2. sheet of this paper.

let'tuce, *n.* plant with crisp, green leaves used in salads.

leu ke'mi a (lōō-), *n.* disease characterized by an abnormal increase in the white blood corpuscles.

lev'ee, *n.* river embankment to prevent flooding.

lev'el, *n.* 1. instrument for determining the horizontal. 2. horizontal plane, line, etc. 3. height. 4. position, rank, etc. —*a.* 1. flat and even. 2. even in height (*with*). —*v.* 1. make or become level. 2. demolish. —**lev'el er,** *n.*

lev'el-head'ed, *a.* sensible.

lev'er (or lēv'ēr) *n.* bar turning on a fulcrum, used to lift or move weights.

lev'er age (-ij) *n.* action or power of a lever.

le vi'a than (-vī'-) *n.* 1. *Bible* sea monster. 2. huge thing.

lev'i ty *n.* improper gaiety; frivolity.

lev'y, *v.* [-IED, -YING] 1. impose (a tax, etc.). 2. enlist (troops). 3. wage (war). —*n.* [*pl.* -IES] a levying or something levied.

lewd (lōōd), *a.* indecent.

lex'i cog'ra phy, *n.* work of writing a dictionary. —**lex'i cog'ra pher,** *n.*

lex'i con, *n.* dictionary.

li'a bil'i ty, *n.* [*pl.* -TIES] 1. a being liable. 2. debt. 3. disadvantage.

li'a ble, *a.* 1. legally responsible. 2. subject to. 3. likely.

li ai son (lē-ā-zōn', -ə-zon') *n.* 1. communication between military units. 2. illicit love affair.

li'ar, *n.* one who tells lies.

li'bel, *n.* statement in writing that may unjustly hurt a reputation. —*v.* make a libel against. —**li'bel ous,** *a.*

lib'er al, *a.* 1. generous. 2. not strict. 3. tolerant. 4. favoring reform. —*n.* one who favors reform. —**lib'er al ism,** *n.* —**lib'er al'i ty,** *n.* —**lib'er al ize',** *v.*

liberal arts, literature, philosophy, history, etc.

lib'er ate, *v.* set free; release. —**lib'er a'tion,** *n.* —**lib'er a'tor,** *n.*

lib'er tine (-tēn) *n.* sexually promiscuous man.

lib'er ty, *n.* [*pl.* -TIES] 1. freedom from slavery, etc. 2. a particular right. 3. *pl.* excessive familiarity. —**at liberty,** 1. not confined. 2. permitted (*to*).

li bi'do (-bī'-, -bē'-) *n.* sexual urge. —**li bid'i nous,** *a.*

Li'bra (lī'-) *n.* 7th sign of the zodiac; Scales.

li'bra ry, *n.* [*pl.* -IES] collection of books or a place for it. —**li bra'ri an,** *n.*

li bret'to, *n.* [*pl.* -TOS, -TI (-ti)] text of an opera, etc. —**li bret'tist,** *n.*

lice, *n.* pl. of **louse.**

li'cense, *n.* 1. legal permit. 2. freedom from rules. 3. freedom that is abused. —*v.* permit formally. Br. sp. **li'cence.**

li cen'tious (-shəs) *a.* morally unrestrained.

li'chen (lī'kən) *n.* mosslike plant growing on rocks, trees, etc.

lick, *v.* 1. pass the tongue over. 2. [Col.] beat or conquer. —*n.* 1. a licking. 2. small quantity. —**lick up,** consume by licking.

lic'o rice (-ris) *n.* black flavoring from a plant root.

lid, *n.* 1. movable cover. 2. eyelid. —**lid'ded,** *a.*

lie, *v.* [LAY, LAIN, LYING] 1. be horizontal or rest horizontally. 2. be or exist. —*n.* position; lay.

lie, *v.* [LIED, LYING] make a false statement knowingly. —*n.* thing said in lying.

liege (lēj) *n.* feudal lord or vassal.

lien (lēn) *n.* legal claim on another's property until a debt is paid.

lieu (lōō) *n.* place. —**in lieu of,** instead of.

lieu ten'ant, *n.* 1. low-ranking commissioned officer. 2. deputy. —**lieu ten'an cy** [*pl.* -CIES] *n.*

life, *n.* [*pl.* LIVES] 1. active existence of plants and animals. 2. living things. 3. time of being alive. 4. way of living. 5. a biography. 6. liveliness. —**life'less,** *a.* —**life'like,** *a.*

life'boat, *n.* small rescue boat carried by a ship.

life'long, *a.* lasting for life.

life'-size', *a.* as big as the thing represented.

life'time, *a. & n.* (lasting for) the length of one's life.

lift, *v.* 1. bring higher; raise. 2. go up; rise. 3. [Sl.] steal. —*n.* 1. a lifting. 2. lifting force. 3. raising of one's spirits. 4. help; aid. 5. ride in the direction one is going. 6. [Br.] elevator.

lift′off′, *n.* vertical take-off of a spacecraft, etc.

lig′a·ment, *n.* connective tissue for bones or organs.

lig′a·ture, *n.* 1. a thing for tying, as surgical thread. 2. letters united, as *fl*.

light, *n.* 1. radiant energy by which one sees. 2. brightness. 3. lamp, lantern, etc. 4. daylight. 5. thing to ignite something. 6. aspect. 7. knowledge. —*a.* 1. bright. 2. pale; fair. 3. not heavy. 4. not important. 5. easy to bear or do. 6. happy. 7. dizzy. 8. moderate. —*adv.* 1. palely. 2. lightly. —*v.* [LIGHTED or LIT, LIGHTING] 1. ignite. 2. furnish with light. 3. brighten. 4. be lighted. 5. come to rest. 6. happen (on). —**in the light of,** considering.

light′en, *v.* make or become brighter, less heavy, etc.

light′heart′ed, *a.* gay.

light′house, *n.* tower with a light to guide ships.

light′ly, *adv.* 1. gently. 2. very little. 3. cheerfully. 4. carelessly.

light′ning, *n.* flash of light in the sky from a discharge of atmospheric electricity.

lightning bug, firefly.

lightning rod, metal rod to divert lightning.

light′-year′, *n.* distance that light travels in a year, about 6 trillion mi.

lik′a·ble, like′a·ble, *a.* pleasant, friendly, etc.

like, *a.* similar; equal. —*prep.* 1. similar(ly) to. 2. typical of. 3. in the mood for. 4. indicative of. —*con.* [Col.] as. 2. as if. —*v.* 1. be fond of; enjoy. 2. wish. —*n.* 1. an equal. 2. *pl.* preferences. [Col.] wildly. —**lik′ing,** *n.* —**like,** *suf.* like.

like′ly, *a.* 1. credible. 2. probable; expected. 3. suitable. —*adv.* probably. —**like′li·hood,** *n.*

lik′en, *v.* compare.

like′ness, *n.* 1. a being like. 2. picture; copy.

like′wise, *adv.* 1. in the same way. 2. also; too.

li′lac, *n.* shrub with tiny, pale-purple flower clusters.

lilt, *n.* light, swingy rhythm.

lil′y, *n.* [*pl.* -IES] plant with trumpet-shaped flowers.

lily of the valley, [*pl.* LILIES OF THE VALLEY] plant with a spike of bell-shaped flowers.

Li′ma bean (lī′-) large, flat, edible bean in pods.

limb, *n.* 1. arm, leg, or wing. 2. large tree branch.

lim′ber, *v. & a.* (make or become) flexible.

lim′bo, *n.* place of oblivion.

Lim′burg·er (cheese), white, strong-smelling cheese.

lime, *n.* 1. white substance obtained from limestone. 2. green, lemonlike fruit.

lime′light, *n.* prominent position before the public.

lim′er·ick, *n.* rhymed, funny poem of five lines.

lime′stone, *n.* rock used in building, making lime, etc.

lim′it, *n.* 1. point where something ends. 2. *pl.* bounds. —*v.* set a limit to. —**lim′i·ta′tion,** *n.*

lim′it·ed, *a.* confined.

lim′ou·sine (-ə-zēn) *n.* large, luxury automobile.

limp, *v. & n.* (walk with) lameness. —*a.* not firm.

lim′pet, *n.* shellfish that clings to rocks, etc.

lim′pid, *a.* transparent.

lin′den, *n.* tree with heart-shaped leaves.

line, *n.* 1. cord, rope, etc. 2. wire, pipe, etc. 3. long, thin mark. 4. boundary. 5. outline. 6. row or series. 7. conformity. 8. transportation system. 9. route; course. 10. stock of goods. 11. short letter. —*v.* 1. mark with lines. 2. form a line (with *up*). 3. put or serve as, a lining in.

lin·e·age (lin′i-ij) *n.* line of descent; ancestry.

lin′e·al, *a.* 1. directly descended. 2. linear.

lin′e·a·ment, *n.* distinctive facial feature.

lin′e·ar, *a.* 1. of a line or lines. 2. of length.

line′man, *n.* [*pl.* -MEN] man who puts up telephone or other electric lines.

lin′en, *n.* 1. cloth of flax. 2. things of linen or cotton.

lin′er (līn′-) *n.* ship or airplane of a line (sense 8).

line′-up′, line′up′, *n.* row of persons or things.

lin·ger (lin′gēr) *v.* 1. continue to stay. 2. loiter.

lin·ge·rie (län′zhə-rē) *n.*

women's underwear.

lin'go (ling'-) *n.* [*pl.* -GOES] unfamiliar jargon.

lin'guist, *n.* one adept in several languages.

lin·guis'tics, *n.pl.* science of (a) language.

lin'i·ment, *n.* medicated liquid for the skin.

lin'ing, *n.* material covering an inner surface.

link, *n.* 1. loop in a chain. 2. thing that connects. — *v.* join; connect.

li·no'le·um, *n.* hard, smooth floor covering.

lin'seed oil, yellow oil from seed of flax.

lint, *n.* bits of thread, fluff, etc. from cloth. —**lint'y** [-IER, -IEST] *a.*

lin'tel, *n.* horizontal piece over a door or window.

li'on, *n.* 1. large animal of the cat family, found in Africa & SW Asia. 2. very strong, brave person. 3. celebrity. —**li'on·ess,** *n.fem.*

lip, *n.* 1. upper or lower edge of the mouth. 2. thing like a lip, as a cup's rim.

lip'stick, *n.* small stick of rouge to color the lips.

liq'ue·fy' (-wə-) *v.* [-FIED, -FYING] change to a liquid.

li·queur' (-kūr') *n.* sweet alcoholic liquor.

liq'uid (-wid) *a.* 1. readily flowing. 2. readily changed into cash. —*n.* substance that flows easily.

liq'ui·date, *v.* 1. settle the accounts of (a business). 2. pay (a debt). 3. change into cash. —**liq'ui·da'tion,** *n.*

liq'uor (-ēr) *n.* alcoholic drink, as whisky.

lisle (līl) *n.* fabric woven of strong cotton thread.

lisp, *v.* substitute the sounds "th" and "*th*" for the sounds of "s" and "z." —*n.* act or sound of lisping.

list, *n.* series of names, words, etc. set forth in order. —*v.* put in a list.

list, *v.* tilt to one side, as a ship. —*n.* a listing.

lis'ten, *v.* 1. try to hear. 2. pay attention.

list'less, *a.* indifferent because ill, sad, etc.

lit, *pt.* & *pp.* of **light.**

lit'a·ny, *n.* [*pl.* -NIES] prayer with responses.

li'ter, li'tre (lē'-) *n.* metric unit of capacity (61.025 cu. in.).

lit'er·al, *a.* 1. precise; exact; strict. 2. prosaic. 3. re-stricted to fact. —**lit'er·al·ly,** *adv.*

lit'er·ar·y, *a.* having to do with literature.

lit'er·ate (-it) *a.* educated; esp., able to read and write. —**lit'er·a·cy,** *n.*

lit'er·a·ture (-chēr) *n.* 1. all the valuable writings of a specific time, nation, etc. 2. all writings on some subject.

lithe (līth) *a.* bending easily.

lith'o·graph (lith'-) *n.* print made from stone or metal treated with grease and water. —**li·thog'ra·phy,** *n.*

lit'i·gate, *v.* to contest in a lawsuit. —**lit'i·gant,** *n.* —**lit'i·ga'tion,** *n.*

lit'mus paper, treated paper that turns blue in bases and red in acids.

lit'ter, *n.* 1. portable couch. 2. stretcher. 3. young pigs born at one time by a dog, cat, etc. 4. things lying about in disorder. —*v.* make untidy.

lit'tle, *a.* 1. small in size or amount. 2. short; brief. 3. not important. —*adv.* 1. slightly. 2. not at all. —*n.* small amount or short time. —**little by little,** gradually.

lit'ur·gy, *n.* [*pl.* -GIES] ritual for public worship. —**li·tur'gi·cal,** *a.*

liv'a·ble, *a.* fit or pleasant to live in.

live, *v.* 1. have life. 2. stay alive; endure. 3. pass one's life in a certain way. 4. have a full life. 5. feed (on). 6. reside.

live, *a.* 1. having life. 2. energetic. 3. of interest now. 4. still burning. 5. unexploded. 6. carrying electrical current. 7. broad-cast while happening.

live'li·hood, *n.* means of supporting oneself.

live'long (liv'-) *a.* whole.

live'ly, *a.* [-LIER, -LIEST] 1. full of life. 2. exciting. 3. cheerful. 4. having much bounce. —**live'li·ness,** *n.*

liv'en (līv'-) *v.* cheer (*up*).

liv'er (līv'-) *n.* organ in vertebrates that makes bile.

liv'er·wurst, *n.* sausage made of ground liver.

liv'er·y, *n.* [*pl.* -IES] 1. uni-form as of a servant. 2. business of renting horses and carriages.

lives, *n.* pl. of **life.**

live'stock, *n.* animals kept or raised on a farm.

liv'id, *a.* 1. black-and-blue. 2. grayish-blue.

liv'ing, *a.* 1. having life. 2. in active use. 3. of persons alive. 4. true; lifelike. 5. of life. 6. enough to live on. —*n.* 1. a being alive. 2. livelihood. 3. way that one lives.

living room, room for lounging, entertaining, etc.

liz'ard, *n.* reptile with a long tail and four legs.

lla'ma (lä'-) *n.* S. American camellike animal.

lo, *int.* look! see!

load, *n.* 1. amount carried. 2. burden. —*v.* 1. put (a load) in or on. 2. burden. 3. put ammunition into.

load'stone, *n.* magnetic iron ore.

loaf, *n.* [*pl.* LOAVES] bread, etc. baked in one piece. —*v.* waste (time). —**loaf'er,** *n.*

loam, *n.* rich soil.

loan, *n.* 1. act of lending. 2. something lent, esp. money at interest. —*v.* lend.

loathe (lōth) *v.* abhor. **loath'some,** *a.*

lob'by, *n.* [*pl.* -BIES] 1. entrance hall. 2. group of lobbyists. —*v.* [-BIED, -BY-ING] act as a lobbyist.

lob'by·ist, *n.* one who tries to influence legislators.

lobe, *n.* rounded projection.

lob'ster, *n.* edible sea animal with large pincers.

lo'cal, *a.* of or for a particular place or area. —*n.* 1. bus, etc. making all stops. 2. branch, as of a labor union. —**lo'cal·ly,** *adv.*

lo·cale' (-kal') *n.* a place or setting for events, etc.

lo·cal'i·ty, *n.* [*pl.* -TIES] place or district.

lo'cal·ize, *v.* limit or trace to a certain place.

lo'cate, *v.* 1. establish in a certain place. 2. find or show the position of.

lo·ca'tion, *n.* 1. a locating. 2. position; place.

lock, *n.* 1. device for fastening a door, etc. as with a key. 2. part of a canal between gates. 3. curl of hair. —*v.* 1. fasten with a lock. 2. shut (*in* or *out*). 3. jam or link together.

lock'er, *n.* chest, closet, etc. that can be locked.

lock'et, *n.* little case worn on a necklace.

lock'jaw, *n.* tetanus.

lock'out, *n.* a locking out of

employees to force agreement to employer's terms.

lock'smith, *n.* one who makes or repairs locks and keys.

lock'up, *n.* jail.

lo·co·mo'tion, *n.* act or power of moving about.

lo·co·mo'tive, *n.* engine for a railroad train.

lo'cust, *n.* 1. grasshopper-like insect. 2. cicada. 3. tree with white flowers.

lo·cu'tion (-kū'-) *n.* phrase or phraseology.

lode, *n.* vein or stratum of metallic ore.

lode'stone, *n.* loadstone.

lodge, *n.* 1. a house for special use. 2. chapter of a society. —*v.* 1. to house or dwell for a time. 2. put in. 3. come to rest. —**lodg'er,** *n.*

lodg'ing, *n.* 1. place to live. 2. *pl.* rented rooms.

loft, *n.* 1. space below a roof. 2. upper story of a warehouse, etc. 3. gallery. —*v.* send (a ball) high into the air.

loft'y, *a.* [-IER, -IEST] 1. very high. 2. noble. 3. haughty. —**loft'i·ness,** *n.*

log, *n.* 1. section cut from a tree trunk. 2. daily record of a ship's progress. —*v.* [LOGGED, LOGGING] 1. cut down trees & remove the logs. 2. enter in a ship's log.

lo'gan·ber'ry, *n.* [*pl.* -RIES] purple-red berry.

loge (lōzh) *n.* theater box.

log'ger·head, *n.* stupid fellow. —**at loggerheads,** in disagreement.

log'ic (loj'-) *n.* 1. science of reasoning. 2. (correct) reasoning. —**lo·gi'cian** (lō-jish'ən) *n.*

log'i·cal, *a.* 1. using or used in logic. 2. expected as a result. —**log'i·cal·ly,** *adv.*

lo·gis'tics (-jis'-) *n.* military science of moving and supplying troops.

lo·gy (lō'gi) *a.* [-GIER, -GIEST] [Col.] dull or sluggish.

-logy, *suf.* science or study of.

loin, *n.* 1. lower back from ribs to hipbone. 2. *pl.* hips and lower abdomen.

loi'ter, *v.* 1. spend time idly. 2. move slowly.

loll, *v.* 1. lounge about. 2. droop or let hang loosely.

lol'li·pop, lol'ly·pop, *n.* piece of candy on a stick.

lone, *a.* by oneself or itself.

lone'ly, *a.* [-LIER, -LIEST] 1.

alone and unhappy. 2. unfrequented. —**lone′li·ness**, *n.*

lone′some, *a.* having or causing a lonely feeling.

long, *a.* 1. measuring much. 2. in length. 3. of great length. 4. tedious. 5. far-reaching. 6. well supplied. —*adv.* 1. for a long time. 2. for the time of. 3. at remote time. —*v.* to wish earnestly; yearn. —**as** (or **so**) **long as**, 1. while. 2. since. 3. provided that. —**before long**, soon.

lon·gev′i·ty (-jev′-) *n.* long life.

long′hand, *n.* ordinary handwriting.

long′ing, *n.* earnest desire.

lon′gi·tude (lon′jə-) *n.* distance, in degrees, east or west of a line through Greenwich, Eng. —**lon′gi·tu′di·nal** (-tōō′-) *a.* 1. of length. 2. of longitude.

long′-lived′ (-līvd′) *a.* having a long life span.

long′-range′, *a.* covering a long distance or time.

long′shore′man, *n.* [*pl.* -MEN] one whose work is loading and unloading ships.

long ton, 2,240 pounds.

long′ways′, *adv.* lengthwise.

look, *v.* 1. direct the eyes so as to see. 2. search. 3. seem. —*n.* 1. act of looking. 2. appearance. 3. *pl.* [Col.] personal appearance. —*int.* 1. see! 2. pay attention! —**look after**, care for. —**look into**, investigate. —**look up to**, admire.

looking glass, glass mirror.

look′out′, *n.* 1. careful watching. 2. guard; sentry.

loom (lōōm) *n.* machine for weaving. —*v.* come into sight suddenly.

loon, *n.* duck-like bird.

loop, *n.* figure of a line, etc. curving back to cross itself. —*v.* make a loop.

loop′hole′, *n.* means of evading something.

loose (lōōs) *a.* 1. free. 2. not firm or tight. 3. inexact. 4. sexually immoral. —*v.* 1. free. 2. make less tight, etc. 3. release. —**loose′ly**, *adv.* —**loos′en**, *v.*

loot, *n. & v.* plunder.

lop, *v.* [LOPPED, LOPPING] cut off.

lope (lōp) *v. & n.* (move with) a long swinging stride.

lop′sid′ed, *a.* heavier, lower, etc. on one side.

lo·qua′cious (-kwā′shəs) *a.* very talkative.

lord, *n.* 1. master. 2. [L-] God. 3. [L-] Jesus Christ. 4. Br. nobleman.

lore, *n.* knowledge.

lor·gnette′ (-nyet′) *n.* eyeglasses on a handle.

lor′ry, *n.* [*pl.* -RIES] [Br.] motor truck.

lose (lōōz) *v.* [LOST, LOSING] 1. become unable to find. 2. have taken from one by accident, death, etc. 3. fail to keep. 4. fail to win.

loss (lôs) *n.* 1. a losing, or damage, etc. from this. 2. person, thing, etc. lost.

lost, *v.* 1. ruined. 2. missing or mislaid. 3. wasted.

lot, *n.* 1. deciding of a matter by chance. 2. fate. 3. piece of land. 4. group. 5. *often pl.* [Col.] great amount. —*adv.* very much.

lo′tion, *n.* liquid for softening or healing the skin.

lot′ter·y, *n.* [*pl.* -IES] game in which numbered chances on prizes are sold.

lo′tus, *n.* tropical water lily.

loud, *a.* 1. strong in sound. 2. noisy. 3. [Col.] flashy. —*adv.* in a loud way. —**loud′-ly**, *adv.* —**loud′ness**, *n.*

loud′speak′er, *n.* device, as in a radio, for changing electric waves into sound and amplifying it.

lounge (lounj) *v.* 1. sit in a relaxed way. 2. to be idle. —*n.* 1. room furnished for lounging. 2. couch.

louse, *n.* [*pl.* LICE] small insect parasite. —**lous′y** (-zi) [-IER, -IEST] *a.*

lout, *n.* stupid fellow.

lou′ver (lōō′-) *n.* 1. an opening with boards slanted to let in air and keep out rain. 2. such a board.

love, *n.* 1. strong affection. 2. object of this. —*v.* feel love (for). —**in love**, feeling love. —**make love**, woo, embrace, etc. —**lov′a·ble**, **love′a·ble**, *a.* —**lov′er**, *n.* —**lov′ing·ly**, *adv.*

love′lorn, *a.* pining from love.

love′ly, *a.* [-LIER, -LIEST] 1. beautiful. 2. [Col.] very enjoyable. —**love′li·ness**, *n.*

low (lō) *a.* 1. not high. 2. below others in rank, size, cost, etc. 3. gloomy. 4. deep in pitch. 5. vulgar. 6. not loud. —*adv.* in or to a low level, etc. —*n.* 1. low level, degree, etc. 2. gear arrangement giving least speed. 3. moo. —v. moo. —**lay low**, kill. —**lie low**, stay hidden.

low'-brow', low'brow, n. & a. [Sl.] nonintellectual.

low'-down', n. [Sl.] pertinent facts (with *the*).

low'er, a. below in rank, etc. —v. 1. let or put down. 2. make or become less in amount, value, etc.

low'er, (lou'-) v. 1. to scowl. 2. appear threatening.

low'ly, a. 1. of low rank. 2. humble. —**low'li·ness,** n.

low'-mind'ed, a. having a coarse, vulgar mind.

loy'al, a. faithful to one's friends, country, etc. —**loy'al·ly,** adv. —**loy'al·ty** [pl. -TIES] n.

loz·enge (loz'inj) n. cough drop, candy, etc.

lu·au (loo-ou') n. Hawaiian feast.

lub'ber, n. clumsy person.

lu'bri·cant, a. that lubricates. —n. oil, grease, etc.

lu'bri·cate, v. apply oil or grease to reduce friction. —**lu'bri·ca'tion,** n.

lu'cid (-sid) a. 1. clear. 2. sane. 3. shining. —**lu·cid'i·ty,** n. —**lu'cid·ly,** adv.

luck, n. 1. chance; fortune. 2. good fortune. —**luck'less,** a.

luck'y, a. [-IER, -IEST] having, resulting in, or thought to bring good luck. —**luck'i·ly,** adv.

lu'cra·tive, a. profitable.

lu'cre (-kẽr) n. riches; money: chiefly derogatory.

lu'di·crous (-kras) a. so incongruous as to be funny.

luff, v. head a ship toward the wind.

lug, v. [LUGGED, LUGGING] carry with effort. —n. earlike handle or support.

lug'gage, n. suitcases, trunks, etc.

lu·gu'bri·ous, a. mawkishly mournful.

luke'warm', a. 1. slightly warm. 2. lacking enthusiasm.

lull, v. 1. soothe by gentle sound or motion. 2. calm. —n. short period of calm.

lull'a·by, n. [pl. -BIES] song for lulling a baby to sleep.

lum·ba'go, n. pain in the lower back.

lum'bar (-bẽr) a. of or near the loins.

lum'ber, n. wood sawed into beams, boards, etc. —v. move heavily.

lum'ber·jack, n. man who cuts timber for the sawmill.

lum'ber·man, n. 1. lumberjack. 2. lumber dealer.

lu'mi·nar·y, n. [pl. -IES] famous person.

lu'mi·nous, a. bright; shining. —**lu·mi·nos'i·ty,** n.

lump, n. 1. mass of something. 2. a swelling. —a. in a lump or lumps. —v. 1. group together. 2. [Col.] put up with anyhow. —**lump'y** [-IER, -IEST] a.

lu'nar, a. of the moon.

lu'na·tic, a. 1. insane. 2. utterly foolish. —n. insane person. —**lu'na·cy,** n.

lunch, n. midday meal. —v. eat lunch.

lunch'eon (-an) n. formal lunch.

lung, n. organ in the chest for breathing.

lunge (lunj) n. 1. sudden thrust. 2. forward plunge. —v. make a lunge.

lurch, v. 1. sway suddenly to one side. —n. 1. lurching movement. 2. danger; trouble.

lure, n. 1. thing that attracts. 2. fish bait. —v. attract; entice.

lu'rid, a. 1. shocking. 2. glowing strangely.

lurk, v. stay or be hidden, ready to attack.

lus·cious (lush'as) a. 1. delicious. 2. pleasing.

lush, a. of or having luxuriant growth.

lust, n. 1. strong sexual desire. 2. strong desire, as for power. —v. feel an intense desire. —**lust'ful,** a.

lus'ter, n. 1. gloss; brightness. 2. brilliant fame. —**lus'trous** (-tras) a.

lust'y, a. [-IER, -IEST] vigorous; robust. —**lust'i·ly,** adv.

lute, n. stringed, guitarlike instrument.

lux·u'ri·ant (lug-zhoor'-) a. 1. growing in abundance. 2. richly ornamented. —**lux·u'ri·ance,** n.

lux·u'ri·ate, v. 1. live in luxury. 2. revel (*in*).

lux·u'ri·ous, a. 1. giving a feeling of luxury. 2. fond of luxury.

lux'u·ry, n. [pl. -RIES] costly comfort(s) or pleasure(s).

-ly, suf. 1. like. 2. in a specified way, or at a specified time or place. 3. in sequence. 4. every.

lye (lī) n. strong alkaline substance.

ly'ing, ppr. of **lie.**

ly'ing-in', a. & n. (of or for) childbirth.

lymph (limf) n. clear, yellowish body fluid. —**lym·phat'ic,** a.

lynch, v. kill by mob action, without lawful trial.

lynx, n. N. American wildcat.

lyre (līr) n. ancient instrument like a small harp.

lyr'ic (lir'-) a. 1. suitable for singing. 2. expressing the poet's emotions. —n. 1. lyric poem. 2. pl. words of a song.

lyr'i·cal, a. 1. lyric. 2. very enthusiastic, etc. —**lyr'i·cal·ly,** adv.

M

ma, n. [Col.] mother.

ma'am, n. [Col.] madam.

ma·ca'bre (-kä'brə) a. grim and horrible.

mac·ad'am, n. 1. small broken stones, used to make some roads. 2. such a road. —**mac·ad'am·ize,** v.

mac·a·ro'ni, n. tubes of flour paste, cooked for food.

mac·a·roon', n. cooky made with almonds or coconut.

ma·caw', n. large parrot.

mace (mās) n. 1. heavy spiked club. 2. official's staff. 3. spice made from ground nutmeg shell.

mac'er·ate (mas'-) v. soften by soaking.

ma·che·te (mə-shet'i) n. large, heavy knife.

Mach'i·a·vel'li·an (mak'-) a. crafty.

mach'i·na'tion (mak'-) n. wily or evil scheme.

ma·chine' n. 1. device with moving parts, for doing work. 2. group in control of a political party. —a. of or done by machines. —v. to shape, etc. by machinery.
machine gun, automatic gun.

ma·chin'er·y, n. 1. machines. 2. working parts.

ma·chin'ist, n. one who makes or operates machines.

mack'er·el, n. edible fish of the N. Atlantic.

mack'i·naw (coat), short, heavy coat, often plaid.

mack'in·tosh, n. raincoat of rubberized cloth.

mac'ro·cosm, n. universe.

mad, a. [MADDER, MADDEST] 1. insane. 2. frantic. 3. foolish. 4. [Col.] angry. —**mad'ly,** adv.—**mad'ness,** n.

mad'am, n. polite title for a woman.

mad'ame (-əm) n. [pl. MESDAMES (mā-däm')] married woman: Fr. for *Mrs.*

mad'cap, n. reckless person.

mad'den, v. make mad. —**mad'den·ing,** a.

mad'der, n. 1. vine with berries. 2. red dye made from its root.

made, pt. & pp. of **make.**

ma'de·moi·selle' (-mə-zel') n. unmarried woman: Fr. for *Miss.*

mad'house, n. 1. insane asylum. 2. place of turmoil.

mad'man', n. [pl. -MEN] insane person.

Ma·don'na, n. Virgin Mary.

mad'ras, n. fine cotton cloth, usually striped.

mad'ri·gal, n. part song for small group.

mael'strom (māl'-) n. violent whirlpool.

maes'tro (mīs'-) n. [It.] master, as in music.

mag·a·zine' (-zēn') n. 1. periodical publication. 2. storage place, as for military supplies. 3. supply chamber, as in a rifle.

ma·gen'ta (-jen'-) n. purplish red.

mag'got, n. wormlike larva. —**mag'got·y,** a.

Ma·gi (mā'jī) n. pl. wise men in the Bible.

mag'ic, n. 1. use of charms, spells, etc. 2. sleight of hand. —a. of or as if by magic: also **mag'i·cal.** —**mag'i·cal·ly,** adv.

ma·gi'cian (-jish'ən) n. one who does magic.

mag·is·te'ri·al (maj'-) a. authoritative.

mag'is·trate (maj'-) n. official administering the law. —**mag·is·tra·cy,** n.

mag·nan'i·mous (mag-) a. generous in forgiving; noble. —**mag·na·nim'i·ty,** n.

mag'nate (-nāt) n. influential person in business.

mag·ne'sia (-shə) n. white powder (magnesium oxide) used as a laxative.

mag·ne'si·um (-shi-) n light, silvery metal, a chemical element.

mag'net, n. piece of iron, steel, etc. that attracts iron or steel.

mag'net·ism, n. 1. properties of magnets. 2. personal charm. —**mag·net'ic,** a.

mag'net·ize, v. 1. make a magnet of. 2. to charm.

mag·ne'to (-nē'-) n. [pl. -TOS] small electric generator.

mag·nif'i·cent, a. 1. grand and stately; splendid. 2. exalted. —**mag·nif'i·cence,** n.

mag'ni·fy, v. [-FIED, -FYING] 1. increase apparent size of, as with a lens. 2. exaggerate. —**mag'ni·fi·ca'tion,** n. —**mag'ni·fi'er,** n.

mag'ni·tude, n. greatness of size, extent, or importance.

mag·no'li·a, n. tree with large, fragrant flowers.

mag'pie, n. noisy bird of the crow family.

ma'ha·ra'jah, n. in India, a prince, formerly the ruler of a native state. —**ma·ha·ra'ni, ma'ha·ra'nee,** n.fem.

mah'-jongg', mah'jong' (-jŏn') n. Chinese game played with small tiles.

ma·hog'a·ny, n. reddish-brown wood of a tropical tree.

maid, n. 1. unmarried, esp. young, woman. 2. woman or girl servant.

maid'en, n. young unmarried woman. —a. 1. of or for a maiden. 2. unmarried. 3. first; earliest. —**maid'en·hood,** n. —**maid'en·ly,** a.

mail, n. 1. letters, etc. sent by postal service. 2. postal system. 3. metal mesh armor. —a. of mail. —v. send by mail. —**mail'box,** n. —**mail'man** [pl. -MEN] n.

maim, v. cripple; disable.

main, a. chief; leading; principal. —n. 1. chief pipe in a system. 2. [Poet.] ocean. —**in the main,** mostly. —**with might and main,** with all one's strength. —**main'ly,** adv.

main'land, n. main part of a continent.

main'spring, n. chief spring in a clock, etc.

main'stay, n. main support.

main·tain', v. 1. keep up. 2. keep in repair. 3. declare to be true. 4. support.

main'te·nance, n. 1. a maintaining. 2. means of support.

mal·tre' d'hô·tel (met'rə dō'tel') [Fr.] chief of waiters.

maize (māz) n. corn.

maj'es·ty, n. 1. grandeur; dignity. 2. [M-] title for a sovereign. —**ma·jes'tic,** a. —**ma·jes'ti·cal·ly,** adv.

ma'jor, a. 1. greater in size, rank, etc. 2. Mus. half tone higher than the minor. —n.

1. military officer above a captain. 2. main study. —v. specialize (in a subject).

ma'jor·do'mo, n. man in charge of a great house.

major general, officer above brigadier general.

ma·jor'i·ty, n. 1. more than half. 2. full legal age.

make, v. [MADE, MAKING] 1. bring into being; build, create, etc. 2. cause to be. 3. amount to; equal. 4. acquire; earn. 5. cause success of. 6. execute, do, etc. 7. force; compel. 8. [Col.] get a place on (a team). —n. 1. act of making. 2. style or build. —**make away with,** steal. —**make believe,** pretend. —**make out,** 1. see. 2. succeed. —**make over,** change. —**make up,** 1. put together. 2. invent. 3. compensate. 4. stop quarreling. —**mak'er,** n.

make'shift, a. & n. (as) a temporary substitute.

make'-up', n. 1. way a thing is put together. 2. cosmetics.

mal-, pref. bad or badly.

mal'ad·just'ed, a. badly adjusted, as to environment. —**mal'ad·just'ment,** n.

mal·a·droit', a. clumsy.

mal'a·dy, n. [pl. -DIES] illness.

mal'a·prop·ism, n. ridiculous misuse of words.

ma·lar'i·a, n. disease with chills and fever, carried by mosquitoes.

mal'con·tent', a. & n. dissatisfied (person).

male, a. 1. of the sex that fertilizes the ovum. 2. of, like, or for men or boys. —n. a male person, animal, or plant.

mal·e·dic'tion, n. a curse.

mal'e·fac'tor, n. evildoer. —**mal'e·fac'tion,** n.

ma·lev'o·lent, a. wishing harm to others. —**ma·lev'o·lence,** n.

mal·fea'sance (-fē'z'ns) n. wrongdoing in public office.

mal·for·ma'tion, n. faulty formation. —**mal·formed',** a.

mal·ice (-is) n. ill will; wish to harm. —**ma·li'cious** (-shəs) a.

ma·lign' (-līn') v. speak evil of. —a. evil; harmful.

ma·lig'nant, a. 1. evil. 2. very harmful. 3. likely to cause death. —**ma·lig'nan·cy,** n.

ma·lin'ger, v. feign illness

to escape duty. —**ma·lin′ger·er,** n.

mall, n. shaded public walk.

mal′lard, n. wild duck.

mal′le·a·ble, a. that can be hammered or pressed into shape. —**mal′le·a·bil′i·ty,** n.

mal′let, n. hammer with a wooden head.

mal′low, n. family of plants including the hollyhock.

mal·nu·tri′tion, n. faulty diet; lack of nourishment.

mal·o′dor·ous, a. having a bad smell; stinking.

mal·prac′tice, n. improper practice, as by a doctor.

malt, n. barley, etc. soaked and dried for use in brewing and distilling.

mal·treat′, v. to abuse.

ma′ma, mam′ma, n. mother: child's word.

mam′mal, n. any vertebrate the female of which suckles its offspring.

mam′mon, n. riches as an object of greed.

mam′moth, n. huge, extinct elephant. —a. huge.

man, n. 1. human being; person. 2. adult male person. 3. human race. —v. [MANNED, MANNING] furnish with men for work, etc. —**to a man,** with no exception.

man′a·cle, n. & v. handcuff.

man′age, v. 1. to control or guide. 2. have charge of. 3. succeed in doing. —**man′age·ment,** n. —**man′ag·er,** n.

man′a·ge′ri·al (-jēr′i-) a. of a manager.

man·a·tee′, n. large mammal living in tropical waters.

man·da·rin, n. 1. formerly, high Chinese official. 2. [M-] main Chinese dialect.

man′date, n. 1. an order; command. 2. will of voters as expressed in elections. 3. commission given to a nation to administer a region. 4. such a region. —**man′da·to′ry,** a.

man′di·ble, n. lower jaw.

man′do·lin, n. musical instrument with from 8 to 12 strings.

man′drake, n. root used in medicine.

mane, n. long hair on the neck of a horse, lion, etc.

ma·neu′ver (-nōō′-) n. 1. planned movement of troops, warships, etc. 2. scheme. —v. 1. perform maneuvers. 2. get. etc. by some scheme.

man′ga·nese, n. grayish metal in alloys, a chemical element.

mange (mānj) n. skin disease of animals. —**man′gy,** a.

man·ger (mān′jer) n. box from which livestock feed.

man′gle, v. 1. mutilate by hacking, etc. 2. botch. 3. press in a mangle. —n. machine with rollers for ironing.

man′go, n. [pl. -GOES, -GOS] yellow-red tropical fruit.

man′grove, n. tropical tree with branches that send down roots to form trunks.

man′han·dle, v. handle roughly.

man′hole, n. hole for entering a sewer, etc.

man′hood, n. 1. time of being a man. 2. manly qualities. 3. men collectively.

ma′ni·a, n. 1. wild insanity. 2. obsession. —**man′ic,** a.

ma′ni·ac, n. violently insane person.

man′i·cure, v. & n. (take) care of the fingernails. —**man′i·cur·ist,** n.

man′i·fest, a. obvious. —v. reveal; show. —n. list of a ship's cargo. —**man′i·fes·ta′tion,** n.

man′i·fes′to, n. [pl. -TOES] public declaration.

man′i·fold, a. of many parts, sorts, etc. —n. pipe with several outlets, as for carrying exhaust from an engine.

man′i·kin, n. mannequin.

ma·nip′u·late, v. 1. handle skillfully. 2. manage unfairly or dishonestly. —**ma·nip′u·la′tion,** n.

man′kind′, n. 1. human race. 2. all human males.

man′ly, a. [-LIER, -LIEST] of, like, or fit for a man. —**man′li·ness,** n.

man′na, n. thing provided as by a miracle.

man′ne·quin (-kin) n. 1. woman model (sense 5). 2. model of the human body.

man′ner, n. 1. way; style. 2. habit. 3. pl. (polite) ways of behaving. 4. kind; sort.

man′ner·ism, n. (affected) peculiarity of manner.

man′ner·ly, a. polite.

man′nish, a. masculine.

man′-of-war′, n. warship.

man′or, n. large estate.

man′pow′er, n. 1. human strength. 2. collective strength of a nation, etc.

man′sard (roof) (-särd) roof with two slopes on each side.

manse, n. residence of a

minister or clergyman.

man'sion, *n.* large, imposing house.

man'slaugh'ter, *n.* unintentional killing of a person.

man'tel, *n.* frame around or shelf above a fireplace.

man·til'la, *n.* woman's scarf for the hair and shoulders.

man'tis, *n.* large, predatory insect.

man'tle, *n.* 1. sleeveless cloak. 2. thing that covers. —*v.* to cover.

man'u·al, *a.* made or done by hand. —*n.* handbook.

man·u·fac'ture, *n.* making of goods by machinery. —*v.* make, esp. by machinery. —**man·u·fac'tur·er**, *n.*

ma·nure', *n.* animal waste as fertilizer.

man'u·script, *n.* written or typed book, article, etc.

man'y, *a.* [MORE, MOST] numerous. —*n. & pron.* large number (of persons or things).

map, *n.* drawing of the earth's surface or of the sky. —*v.* [MAPPED, MAPPING] 1. to make a map of. 2. plan.

ma'ple, *n.* 1. large shade tree. 2. its hard wood.

mar, *v.* [MARRED, MARRING] damage; spoil.

ma·ra'ca, (-rä'-) *n.* pebble-filled musical rattle.

mar·a·schi·no cherry (mar'ə-skē'nō) sirupy cherry.

mar'a·thon, *n.* 1. foot race of about 26 mi. 2. any endurance contest.

ma·raud'er (-rôd'-) *n.* raider. —**ma·raud'ing**, *a.*

mar'ble, *n.* hard limestone, white or colored. —*a.* of or like marble.

March, *n.* third month.

march, *v.* walk with regular steps. 2. advance steadily. —*n.* 1. a marching. 2. progress. 3. distance marched. 4. marching music.

Mar'di gras' (grä') last day before Lent begins.

mare (mâr) *n.* female horse, mule, donkey, etc.

mar·ga·rine (mär'jə-rin) *n.* a spread like butter, of vegetable oil and skim milk.

mar'gin, *n.* 1. edge, as the blank border of a page. 2. extra amount in reserve. —**mar'gin·al**, *a.*

mar'i·gold (mar'-) *n.* plant with yellow or orange flowers.

ma·ri·jua·na, ma·ri·hua·

na (mä'ri-hwä'nə) *n.* narcotic from the hemp plant.

ma·rim'ba, *n.* kind of xylophone.

ma·ri'na (-rē'-) *n.* small harbor with docks.

mar'i·nate (mar'-) *v.* soak in spiced vinegar, brine, etc.

ma·rine' (-rēn') *a.* of or in the sea, ships, etc. —*n.* member of the Marine Corps.

mar'i·ner (mar'-) *n.* sailor.

mar'i·o·nette', *n.* puppet.

mar'i·tal, *a.* of marriage.

mar'i·time, *a.* 1. on or near the sea. 2. of sailing.

mar'jo·ram (mär'-) *n.* plant used for flavoring.

mark, *n.* 1. spot, scratch, etc. 2. sign or label. 3. sign of quality. 4. grade. 5. impression. 6. target; goal. —*v.* 1. put a mark on. 2. show by a mark. 3. characterize. 4. listen to. 5. rate. —**mark'er**, *n.*

marked, *a.* 1. having a mark. 2. noticeable.

mar'ket, *n.* 1. place where goods are sold. 2. store selling food. 3. buying and selling. 4. demand for (goods, etc.). —*v.* buy or sell. —**mar'ket·a·ble**, *a.*

mark'ing, *n.* arrangement of marks, as on fur, etc.

marks'man, *n.* [*pl.* -MEN] one who shoots well. —**marks'man·ship**, *n.*

mark'up, *n.* price increase.

mar'lin, *n.* large, slender, deep-sea fish.

mar'ma·lade, *n.* preserve of oranges or other fruits.

mar'mo·set, *n.* small monkey.

mar'mot, *n.* thick-bodied rodent, as the woodchuck.

ma·roon', *n. & a.* dark brownish red. —*v.* put (a person) ashore in a lonely place.

mar·quee' (-kē') *n.* rooflike projection over an entrance.

mar'quis (-kwis) *n.* nobleman above an earl or count. —**mar'quise'** (-kēz') *n.fem.*

mar·qui·sette' (-kwi-) *n.* thin, netlike cloth.

mar'riage (mar'ij) *n.* 1. married life. 2. wedding. —**mar'riage·a·ble**, *a.*

mar'row, *n.* 1. soft core inside bones. 2. central part.

mar'ry, *v.* [-RIED, -RYING] 1. join as husband and wife. 2. take as spouse. 3. unite.

marsh, *n.* swamp. —**marsh'y** [-IER, -IEST] *a.*

mar'shal, *n.* 1. highest rank-

ing officer in some armies.
2. Federal officer like a
sheriff. 3. head of a police
or fire department. —v. arrange (troops, ideas, etc.).

marsh′mal′low, n. soft,
white, spongy candy.

mar·su′pi·al, n. animal with
a pouch for carrying its
young.

mart, n. market.

mar′ten, n. 1. weasellike
animal. 2. its fur; sable.

mar′tial (-shal) a. 1. of war.
2. military. 3. warlike.

martial law, military rule
over civilians.

mar′tin, n. kind of swallow.

mar·ti·net′, n. strict dis-
ciplinarian.

mar′tyr (-tēr) n. one who
suffers or dies for his beliefs. —v. treat as a martyr.
—**mar′tyr·dom,** n.

mar′vel, n. wonderful thing.
—v. be amazed. —**mar′vel-
ous, mar′vel·lous,** a.

Marx′ism, n. doctrine of
social**ism.** —**Marx′ist,**
Marx′i·an, a. & n.

mas·ca′ra (-kar′-) n. cosmetic to color eyelashes.

mas′cot, n. animal or thing
kept for good luck.

mas′cu·line, a. of or like
men. —**mas′cu·lin′i·ty,** n.

mash, n. 1. grain crushed in
water for brewing, etc. 2.
moist feed mixture for
horses, etc. —v. crush into a
soft mass.

mask, n. & v. cover to conceal or protect the face.

mas′och·ist (-ə-kist) n. one
who gets pleasure from being hurt. —**mas′och·ism,**
n. —**mas′och·is′tic,** a.

ma′son, n. construction
worker in brick, stone, etc.
—**ma′son·ry,** n. mason's work.

masque (mask) n. 1. mas-
querade (n. 1). 2. elaborate
verse play.

mas·quer·ade′ (-kēr-) n. 1.
party with masks and cos-
tumes. 2. disguise. —v.
be disguised.

mass, n. 1. quantity of matter. 2. large number. 3.
size. 4. [M-] R.C.Ch. service
of the Eucharist. —v. gather
into a mass.

mas′sa·cre (-kēr) n. indis-
criminate killing. —v. kill in
large numbers.

mas·sage′ (-säzh′) n. rubbing and kneading of part of
the body. —v. give a mas-
sage to.

mas·sour′ (-sūr′) n. man

whose work is massaging. —
mas·seuse′ (-sooz′) n.fem.

mas′sive, a. big and heavy.

mass production, production in large quantities.

mast, n. 1. tall, upright pole
on a ship, supporting sails.

mas′ter, n. 1. man who rules
others or is in control. 2.
expert. —a. 1. of a master.
2. chief; main. —v. 1. control. 2. become expert in.

mas′ter·ful, a. 1. domineering. 2. expert; skillful: also
mas′ter·ly.

Master of Arts (or **Scienec,**
etc.) advanced college degree.

mas′ter·piece, n. thing made
or done with expert skill.

mas′ter·y, n. 1. control. 2.
victory. 3. expert skill.

mas′ti·cate, v. chew up. —
mas·ti·ca′tion, n.

mas′tiff, n. big, strong dog.

mas′to·don, n. extinct animal like the elephant.

mas′toid, a. & n. (of) a bony
projection behind the ear.

mas′tur·bate, v. practice
genital self-excitation. —
mas·tur·ba′tion, n.

mat, n. 1. flat piece, as of
woven straw, for protecting
a floor, etc. 2. thick tangled
mass. 3. border around a
picture. —v. [MATTED, MAT-
TING] 1. cover with a mat.
2. weave or tangle together.

mat′a·dor, n. bullfighter.

match, n. 1. short sliver with
a tip that catches fire by
friction. 2. person or thing
like another. 3. contest. 4.
marriage. —v. 1. be equal
(to). 2. put in opposition.
3. get an equivalent to.

match′less, a. without equal.

match′mak′er, n. arranger
of marriages.

mate, n. 1. one of a pair.
2. husband or wife. 3. lower
officer on a ship. —v. join,
as in marriage.

ma·te′ri·al, n. 1. what a
thing is made of. 2. fabric.
—a. 1. physical. 2. essential.

ma·te′ri·al·ism, n. 1. concern with physical things
only. 2. belief that everything has a physical cause.
—**ma·te′ri·al·is′tic,** a.

ma·te′ri·al·ize, v. give or
take material form.

ma·te′ri·al·ly, adv. 1. phys-
ically. 2. considerably.

ma·te′ri·el′, n. military supplies.

ma·ter′nal (-tūr′-) a. of,
like, or from a mother.

ma·ter'ni·ty, n. motherhood. —a. for pregnant women.

math, n. [Col.] mathematics.

math·e·mat'ics, n. science dealing with quantities and forms, their relationships, etc. —**math·e·mat'i·cal,**a. —**math·e·ma·ti'cian,** n.

mat·i·nee', **mat·i·née'** (-nā') n. afternoon performance of a play, etc.

mat'ins, n.pl. morning prayer.

ma'tri·arch (-ärk) n. woman who rules her family or tribe. —**ma'tri·ar'chal,** a.

ma·tric'u·late, v. enroll, as in college. —**ma·tric'u·la'tion,** n.

mat'ri·mo·ny, n. marriage. —**mat'ri·mo'ni·al,** a.

ma'trix, n. [pl. -TRICES (-tra-sēz), -TRIXES] that within which a thing develops.

ma'tron, n. 1. wife or widow. 2. woman manager of domestic affairs, as of a prison. —**ma'tron·ly,** a.

mat'ter, n. 1. physical substance of a thing. 2. thing or affair. 3. occasion. 4. importance. 5. trouble. —v. be of importance. —**as a matter of fact,** really. —**no matter,** regardless of.

mat'ter-of-fact', a. sticking to facts; literal.

mat'ting, n. woven straw, etc. used as for mats.

mat'tock, n. kind of pickax.

mat'tress, n. casing filled with cotton, springs, etc., for use on a bed.

ma·ture' (-tyoor', -choor') a. 1. fully grown, developed, etc. 2. due for payment. —v. make or become mature. —**ma·tu'ri·ty,** n.

maud'lin (môd'-) a. foolishly sentimental.

maul, v. handle roughly.

mau·so·le'um, n. large, imposing tomb.

mauve (mōv) n. pale purple.

mav'er·ick, n. 1. lost, unbranded calf. 2. political independent.

maw, n. 1. bird's crop. 2. throat, gullet, jaws, etc.

mawk'ish, a. sentimental in a sickening way.

max·il'la, n. upper jawbone.

max'im, n. concise saying that is a rule of conduct.

max'i·mum, a. & n. greatest possible (quantity or degree).

May, n. fifth month.

may, v. [pt. MIGHT] be able, likely, permitted, etc. to.

may'be, adv. possibly.

may'hem, n. crime of maiming a person intentionally.

may·on·naise' (-nāz') n. creamy salad dressing.

may'or, n. head of a city. —**may'or·al·ty,** n.

maze, n. confusing network of paths.

M.C., Master of Ceremonies.

M.D., Doctor of Medicine.

me, pron. objective case of **I.**

mead (mēd) n. alcoholic liquor made from honey.

mead'ow (med'ō) n. level field of grass.

mea'ger, **mea'gre** (mē'gēr) a. 1. poor; scanty. 2. thin.

meal, n. 1. any of the times for eating. 2. food served then. 3. coarsely ground grain. —**meal'y,** a.

meal'y-mouthed, not sincere.

mean, v. [MEANT (ment), MEANING] 1. intend. 2. intend to express. 3. signify. 4. have a certain importance. —a. 1. low in quality or rank. 2. poor or shabby. 3. ignoble, petty, unkind, etc. 4. stingy. 5. halfway between extremes. —n. 1. middle point. 2. pl. that by which a thing is gotten or done. 3. pl. wealth. —**by all (or no) means,** certainly (not). —**by means of,** by using. —**mean'ly,** adv. —**mean'ness,** n.

me·an'der, v. 1. wind back & forth. 2. wander idly.

mean'ing, n. what is meant, indicated, etc. —**mean'ing·ful,** a. —**mean'ing·less,** a.

mean'time, adv. & n. (during) the intervening time: also **mean'while.**

mea'sles (mē'z'lz) n. contagious disease, usually of children.

meas'ure, v. 1. find out the extent, dimensions, etc. of. 2. mark off a certain amount. 3. be a thing for measuring. 4. be of specified dimensions. —n. 1. dimensions, capacity, etc. 2. unit of measuring. 3. system of measuring. 4. instrument for measuring. 5. definite quantity. 6. course of action. 7. a law. 8. notes and rests between two bars on a musical staff. —**meas'ur·a·ble,** a. —**meas'ure·less,** a. —**meas'ure·ment,** n.

meat, n. 1. flesh of animals used as food. 2. edible part.

3. essence. —**meat'y** [-IER, -IEST] *a.*

me·chan'ic (-kan'-) *n.* worker who repairs machines.

me·chan'i·cal, *a.* 1. of or run by machinery. 2. machinelike. —**me·chan'i·cal·ly,** *adv.*

me·chan'ics, *n.* 1. science of motion and the effect of forces on bodies. 2. knowledge of machinery. 3. technical aspect.

mech'a·nism (mek'-) *n.* 1. working parts of a machine. 2. system of interrelated parts.

mech'a·nize, *v.* 1. make mechanical. 2. equip with machinery, trucks, etc. —**mech'a·ni·za'tion,** *n.*

med'al, *n.* flat, inscribed piece of metal given as an honor or reward.

me·dal'lion (-yən) *n.* 1. large medal. 2. round, medallike design.

med'dle, *v.* interfere in another's affairs. —**med'dler,** *n.*

me'di·a, *n.* alt. pl. of **medium.**

me'di·an, *n. & a.* (number, point, etc.) in the middle.

me'di·ate, *v.* (try to) settle (differences) between two parties. —**me'di·a'tion,** *n.* —**me'di·a'tor,** *n.*

med'ic, *n.* [Col.] 1. doctor. 2. army medical corpsman.

med'i·cal, *a.* having to do with the practice or study of medicine.—**med'i·cal·ly,** *adv.*

med'i·cate, *v.* treat with medicine. —**med'i·ca'tion,** *n.*

me·dic'i·nal, *a.* that is or is used as a medicine.

med'i·cine (-s'n) *n.* 1. science of treating and preventing disease. 2. drug, etc. used in treating disease.

me'di·e'val, *a.* of or like the Middle Ages.

me'di·o'cre (-kēr) *a.* ordinary; average. —**me'di·oc'ri·ty** (-ok'-) [*pl.* -TIES] *n.*

med'i·tate, *v.* 1. think deeply. 2. plan. —**med'i·ta'tion,** *n.* —**med'i·ta'tive,** *a.*

me'di·um, *a.* intermediate in amount, degree, etc. —*n.* [*pl.* -DIUMS, -DIA] 1. medium thing or state. 2. thing through which a force acts. 3. means, agency, etc. 4. surrounding substance.

med'ley, *n.* 1. mixture of unlike things. 2. musical piece made up of several songs.

meek, *a.* 1. patient & mild. 2. easily imposed on.

meet, *v.* [MET, MEETING] 1. come upon. 2. be present at the arrival of. 3. be introduced (to). 4. come into contact (with). 5. come together. 6. satisfy. 7. pay. —*n.* a meeting. —*a.* suitable.

meet'ing, *n.* 1. a coming together. 2. a gathering of people. 3. junction.

meg'a·lo·ma'ni·a, *n.* delusion of grandeur or power.

meg'a·phone, *n.* funnel-shaped device to increase the volume of the voice.

meg'a·ton, *n.* explosive force of a million tons of TNT.

mel'an·chol'y (-kol'i) *n.* sadness and mental depression. —*a.* sad or saddening.

me·lee, mê·lée (mā'lā') *n.* brawling group fight.

mel'io·rate (mēl'yə-) *v.* make or become better.

mel·lif'lu·ous, *a.* smooth and sweet, as sounds: also **mel·lif'lu·ent.** —**mel·lif'lu·ence,** *n.*

mel'low, *a.* full, rich, gentle, etc.; not harsh. —*v.* make or become mellow.

me·lo'di·ous, *a.* 1. having melody. 2. pleasing to hear.

mel'o·dra'ma, *n.* sensational, extravagant drama. —**mel'o·dra·mat'ic,** *a.*

mel'o·dy, *n.* [*pl.* -DIES] a tune, song, etc. —**me·lod'ic** (-lod'-) *a.*

mel'on, *n.* large, juicy, many-seeded fruit.

melt, *v.* 1. change from solid to liquid, as by heat. 2. dissolve. 3. disappear or merge gradually. 4. soften.

mem'ber, *n.* 1. distinct part, as an arm. 2. person in an organization.

mem'ber·ship, *n.* 1. state of being a member. 2. all the members.

mem'brane, *n.* thin tissue lining an organ or part. —**mem'bra·nous,** *a.*

me·men'to, *n.* [*pl.* -TOS, -TOES] souvenir.

mem'o, *n.* [*pl.* -OS] [Col.] memorandum.

mem'oirs (-wärz) *n.pl.* account of one's past life.

mem'o·ra·ble, *a.* worth remembering.

mem'o·ran'dum, *n.* [*pl.* -DUMS, -DA] short note to remind one of something.

me·mo'ri·al, *n.* anything meant to help people remember a person or event.

mem'o·rize, *v.* commit to memory.

mem'o·ry, *n.* [*pl.* -RIES] 1. power or act of remembering. 2. something or everything remembered. 3. commemoration.

men, *n.* pl. of **man.**

men'ace (-is) *n.* a threat. —*v.* threaten.

me·nag'er·ie (-naj'-) *n.* collection of wild animals.

mend, *v.* 1. repair. 2. make or become better. —**mended place. —on the mend,** *improving.* —**mend'er,** *n.*

men·da'cious (-dā'shəs) *a.* lying. —**men·dac'i·ty,** *n.*

men'di·cant, *n.* beggar.

me'ni·al, *a.* servile. —*n.* servant.

men·in·gi'tis (-jī'-) *n.* inflammation of membranes of the brain and spinal cord.

men'o·pause, *n.* permanent cessation of menstruation.

men'stru·ate, *v.* have a flow of blood monthly from the uterus. —**men'stru·al,** *a.* —**men·stru·a'tion,** *n.*

men·su·ra'tion (-shə-) *n.* a measuring.

-ment, *suf.* 1. result of. 2. a means for. 3. act of. 4. state of being.

men'tal, *a.* 1. of or in the mind. 2. for the mentally ill. —**men'tal·ly,** *adv.*

men·tal'i·ty, *n.* mental power.

men'thol (-thôl) *n.* derivative of oil of peppermint. —**men'tho·lat'ed,** *a.*

men'tion, *n.* brief reference. —*v.* refer to briefly.

men'tor, *n.* wise adviser.

men'u (-ū) *n.* [*pl.* -US] list of foods at a meal.

me·ow', **me·ou'** (-ou') *v. & n.* (make) the sound of a cat.

mer'can·tile, *a.* of merchants or trade.

mer'ce·nar'y, *a.* thinking mainly of money. —*n.* [*pl.* -IES] soldier paid to serve in a foreign army.

mer'cer·ized, *a.* treated, as cotton, to strengthen it.

mer'chan·dise (-dīz) *v.* buy and sell. —*n.* (*or* -dis) things bought and sold.

mer'chant, *n.* 1. dealer in goods. 2. storekeeper.

merchant marine, ships of a nation used in trade.

mer·cu'ri·al (-kyoor'i-) *a.*

changeable, fickle, etc.

mer·cu'ry, *n.* 1. silvery liquid metal, a chemical element.

mer'cy, *n.* [*pl.* -CIES] 1. kindness; forbearance. 2. power to forgive. —**mer'ci·ful,** *a.* —**mer'ci·less,** *a.*

mere, *a.* [superl. MEREST] no more than; only.

mere'ly, *adv.* only; simply.

mer·e·tri'cious (-trish'əs) *a.* flashy; tawdry.

mer·gan'ser, *n.* large duck.

merge, *v.* unite or combine so as to lose identity.

merg'er, *n.* a merging, or thing formed by merging.

me·rid'i·an, *n.* 1. highest point. 2. circle through the earth's poles.

me·ringue' (-ranˈ) *n.* egg whites and sugar beaten stiff.

mer'it, *n.* 1. worth; value. 2. something deserving praise. —*v.* deserve.

mer·i·to'ri·ous, *a.* deserving reward, praise, etc.

mer'maid (mûr'-) *n.* imaginary creature like a woman with a fish's tail.

mer'ry, *a.* [-RIER, -RIEST] full of fun. —**make merry,** be gay. —**mer'ri·ly,** *adv.* —**mer'ri·ment,** *n.* —**mer'ry·mak·ing,** *n.*

mer'ry-go-round', *n.* revolving platform with seats, as in amusement parks.

me'sa (mā'-) *n.* high plateau with steep sides.

mesh, *n.* (cord or wire of) a net or network. —*v.* 1. entangle. 2. interlock.

mes'mer·ize, *v.* hypnotize. —**mes'mer·ism,** *n.* —**mes'mer·ist,** *n.*

mes·quite, **mes·quit** (mes-kēt') *n.* spiny shrub.

mess, *n.* 1. a jumble. 2. trouble. 3. untidy condition. 4. communal meal as in the army. —*v.* 1. make dirty, jumbled, etc. 2. meddle. —**mess'y,** *a.* [-IER, -IEST] *a.*

mes'sage, *n.* 1. a communication. 2. important idea.

mes'sen·ger, *n.* one who carries a message, etc.

Mes·si'ah, *n.* 1. *Judaism* expected deliverer of the Jews. 2. *Christianity* Jesus. —**Mes·si·an'ic,** *a.*

mes·ti'zo (-tē'-) *n.* [-ZOS, -ZOES] one of American Indian & Spanish parentage.

met, *pt. & pp.* of **meet.**

me·tab'o·lism, *n.* changing of food by organisms into

energy, new cells, etc. —**met'a·bol'ic,** a.

met'al, n. 1. shiny, usually solid, chemical element. 2. an alloy. —a. of metal. —**me·tal'lic,** a.

met·al·lur'gy, n. science of refining metals. —**met·al·lur'gi·cal,** a. —**met'al·lur'gist,** n.

met·a·mor·pho'sis, n. [pl. -SES (-sēz')] 1. change in form. 2. any change.

met'a·phor, n. word for one thing used for another.

met·a·phys'ics, n. philosophy that deals with first principles. —**met'a·phys'i·cal,** a.

mete (mēt) v. allot.

me'te·or, n. small, solid body entering the earth's atmosphere at high speed. —**me·te·or'ic,** a.

me'te·or·ite', n. part of a meteor fallen to earth.

me·te·or·ol'o·gy, n. science of weather, climate, etc. —**me'te·or·o·log'i·cal,** a. —**me'te·or·ol'o·gist,** n.

me'ter, n. 1. rhythmic pattern in verse. 2. metric unit of length (39.37 in.). 3. device to measure flow of fluid. —**met'ric, -ri·cal,** a.

meth'ane, n. colorless, odorless, inflammable gas.

meth'od, n. 1. way; process. 2. system. —**me·thod'i·cal,** a.

me·tic'u·lous, a. very careful about details; fussy.

mé·tier' (mā-tyā') n. one's trade, etc.

me'tre (-tēr) n. meter: Br. sp.

met'ri·ca'tion, n. a changing to the metric system.

metric system, decimal system of weights and measures.

met'ro·nome, n. device that beats time at a set rate.

me·trop'o·lis, n. main or important city. —**met'ro·pol'i·tan,** a.

met'tle, n. spirit; courage. —**on one's mettle,** ready to do one's best.

mew, v. & n. meow.

Mex'i·can, n. & a. (native) of Mexico.

mez'za·nine (-nēn) n. 1. low story built between two main stories. 2. first few rows of balcony seats.

mez'zo-so·pra'no (met'sō-) n. voice or singer between soprano and contralto.

mi·as'ma (mī-az'-) n. vapor from swamps, once believed poisonous.

mi'ca (mī'kə) n. mineral that forms into thin, heat-resistant layers.

mice, n. pl. of **mouse.**

micro-, pref. small.

mi'crobe, n. minute organism, esp. one causing disease.

mi'cro·cosm, n. universe on a small scale.

mi'cro·film, n. film on which documents, etc. are recorded in a reduced size.

mi·crom'e·ter, n. instrument for measuring very small distances, angles, etc.

mi'cron, n. one millionth of a meter.

mi'cro·or'gan·ism, n. microscopic organism.

mi'cro·phone, n. instrument for changing sound waves into electric impulses.

mi'cro·scope, n. device for magnifying minute objects.

mi'cro·scop'ic (-skop'-) a. so small as to be invisible except through a microscope.

mid, 'mid, prep. [Poet.] amid.

mid-, pref. middle of.

mid'day, n. & a. noon.

mid'dle, a. halfway between two points, etc. —n. middle point or part.

Middle Ages, period in Europe, c. 500-1450 A.D.

mid'dle·man, n. [pl. -MEN] 1. one who buys from a producer and sells at wholesale or retail. 2. go-between.

mid'dling, a. of middle size, quality, etc.

mid'dy, n. [pl. -DIES] loose blouse with a sailor collar.

midge, n. small gnat.

midg'et, n. very small person. —a. miniature.

mid'land, a. & n. (of) the middle region of a country.

mid'night, n. twelve o'clock at night.

mid'riff, n. part of body between abdomen and chest.

mid'ship·man, n. [pl. -MEN] naval officer trainee.

midst, n. the middle. —prep. [Poet.] in the midst of.

mid'sum'mer, n. period about June 21.

mid'way, a. & adv. in the middle; halfway. —n. location for side shows, etc. at a fair.

mid'wife, n. [pl. -WIVES] woman who helps others in childbirth.

mien (mēn) n. one's manner.

miff, v. [Col.] offend.

might (mīt) v. pt. of **may.** —n. strength; force.

might'y, a. [-IER, -IEST] powerful, great, etc. —adv. [Col.] very. —**might'i·ly,** adv.

mi'graine (-grān) n. periodic headache.

mi'grate, v. move from one place or region to another, as with the change in season. —**mi'grant,** a. & n. —**mi·gra'tion,** n. —**mi'gra·tor'y,** a.

mi·ka'do (mi-kä'-) n. [pl. -DOS] emperor of Japan.

mike, n. [Sl.] microphone.

mil, n. .001 of an inch.

mild, a. 1. gentle. 2. weak in taste. —**mild'ly,** adv.

mil'dew, n. whitish fungus on plants, damp cloth, etc.

mile, n. unit of measure, 5,280 ft. The **nautical** (or **air**) **mile** is 6,076.1 ft.

mile'age, n. 1. total miles traveled. 2. allowance per mile for traveling expenses.

mile'stone, n. significant event.

mi·lieu (mēl-yoo') n. surroundings; environment.

mil'i·tant, a. ready to fight. —**mil'i·tan·cy,** n.

mil'i·ta·rism, n. 1. warlike spirit. 2. maintenance of strong armed forces. —**mil'i·ta·rist,** n. —**mil'i·ta·ris'tic,** a.

mil'i·tar'y, a. of soldiers, war, etc. —n. the army.

mil'i·tate, v. work (for or against).

mi·li'tia (-lish'ə) n. citizens trained for emergency military service.

milk, n. 1. white liquid secreted by female mammals for suckling their young. 2. any liquid like this. —v. draw milk from (a mammal). —**milk'y** [-IER, -IEST] a. —**milk'i·ness,** n.

milk'man, n. [pl. -MEN] man who sells or delivers milk.

milk'sop, n. sissy.

milk'weed, n. plant with a milky juice.

mill, n. 1. place for grinding grain into flour. 2. machine for grinding. 3. factory. 4. 1/10 of a cent. —v. 1. grind by or in a mill. 2. move (around) confusedly, as a crowd. —**mill'er,** n.

mil·len'ni·um, n. [pl. -NI-UMS, -NIA (-ə)] 1. Theol. 1000-year period of Christ's future reign on earth. 2. period of peace and joy.

mil'let, n. cereal grass.

milli-, pref. 1/1000 part of.

mil'li·me'ter, n. one thousandth of a meter.

mil'li·ner, n. one who makes or sells women's hats.

mil'li·ner'y, n. 1. women's hats. 2. business of a milliner.

mil'lion (-yan) n. & a. a thousand thousands. —**mil'lionth,** a. & n.

mil'lion·aire' (-âr') n. one having at least a million dollars.

mill'stone, n. 1. flat, round stone used for grinding grain, etc. 2. heavy burden.

mill'wright, n. worker who installs or repairs heavy machinery.

mime, n. & v. clown or mimic.

mim'e·ograph', n. machine for making stenciled copies of typewritten matter. —v. make (such copies) of.

mim'ic, v. [-ICKED, -ICKING] 1. imitate, as in ridicule. 2. copy closely. —n. one who mimics. —**mim'ic·ry,** n.

mi·mo'sa, n. flowering tree or shrub of warm climates.

min·a·ret', n. mosque tower.

mince, v. 1. cut into small pieces. 2. lessen the force of (words). 3. act with affected daintiness. —**minc'ing,** a.

mince'meat, n. pie filling of raisins, spices, suet, etc.

mind, n. 1. center of thought, feeling, etc. 2. intellect. 3. sanity. 4. memory. 5. opinion, intention, etc. —v. 1. observe. 2. obey. 3. take care of. 4. be careful about. 5. object to. —**bear** (or **keep**) **in mind,** remember. —**have in mind,** intend. —**make up one's mind,** reach a decision. —**put in mind,** remind.

mind'ful, a. aware (of).

mine, pron. that or those belonging to me. —n. 1. large excavation from which to extract ores, coal, etc. 2. great source of supply. 3. explosive device hidden under land or water. —v. 1. dig (ores, etc.) from a mine. 2. hide mines in. —**min'er,** n.

min'er·al (min'-) n. ore, rock, etc. found naturally in the earth. —a. of or containing minerals.

min'er·al'o·gy, n. science of minerals. —**min'er·al'o·gist,** n.

mi'ne·stro'ne (-strō'ni) n. [It.] thick vegetable soup.

min'gle, v. 1. mix or become mixed. 2. join with others.

mini-, pref. miniature; very small; very short.

min'i·a·ture (-chēr) n. 1. very small copy or model. 2. tiny painting. —a. minute.

min'i·mize, v. reduce to or estimate at a minimum.

min'i·mum, n. 1. smallest quantity possible. 2. lowest degree reached. —a. lowest or least possible. —**min'i·mal,** a.

min'ing, n. work of removing ores, etc. from a mine.

min·ion (min'yən) n. faithful or servile follower.

min'is·ter, n. 1. head of a governmental department. 2. diplomatic official below an ambassador. 3. one who conducts religious services. —v. give help; serve. — **min'is·tra'tion,** n. — **min'is·te'ri·al,** a.

min'is·try, n. [pl. -TRIES] 1. office of a clergyman. 2. clergy. 3. government department headed by a minister. 4. a ministering.

mink, n. 1. weasellike mammal. 2. its valuable fur.

min'now (-ō) n. very small fresh-water fish.

mi'nor, a. 1. lesser in size, rank, etc. 2. Mus. half tone lower than the major. —n. 1. one under full legal age. 2. secondary field of study.

mi·nor'i·ty, n. 1. smaller part or number. 2. racial, religious, etc. group that differs from the larger group. 3. time of being a minor.

min'strel, n. 1. traveling singer of the Middle Ages. 2. entertainer in an old-style U.S. variety show.

mint, n. 1. place where the government makes coins. 2. large amount. 3. aromatic plant with leaves used for flavoring. —v. coin (money).

min'u·end, n. number from which another is to be subtracted.

min·u·et', n. slow, stately dance of 18th century.

mi'nus, prep. less. —a. 1. negative. 2. less than. —n. sign (−) showing subtraction or negative quantity.

min'ute, n. 1. sixtieth part of an hour. 2. moment. 3. pl. official record.

mi·nute', a. 1. very small. 2. exact. —**mi·nute'ly,** adv. **mi·nu'ti·ae** (-nū'shi-ē) n.pl. trifling details.

minx, n. bold or saucy girl.

mir'a·cle, n. 1. event that seems to contradict scientific laws. 2. remarkable thing. —**mi·rac'u·lous,** a.

mi·rage' (-räzh') n. optical illusion caused by reflection of light.

mire, n. deep mud or slush. —v. stick or cause to get stuck as in mire.

mir'ror, n. coated glass that reflects images.

mirth, n. gaiety with laughter. —**mirth'ful,** a.

mis-, pref. wrong(ly); bad(ly).

mis'ad·ven'ture, n. bad luck.

mis·an'thrope, n. one who hates all people: also **mis·an'thro·pist.** —**mis·an'throp'ic,** a. —**mis·an'thro·py,** n.

mis'ap·pre·hend', v. understand wrongly. —**mis'ap·pre·hen'sion,** n.

mis·ap·pro'pri·ate, v. use (funds, etc.) dishonestly. — **mis'ap·pro'pri·a'tion,** n.

mis·be·got'ten, a. illegitimate.

mis·be·have', v. behave badly. —**mis·be·hav'ior,** n.

mis·cal'cu·late, v. misjudge. —**mis·cal·cu·la'tion,** n.

mis·car'ry, v. 1. go wrong. 2. lose a fetus before full term. —**mis·car'riage,** n.

mis'ce·ge·na'tion (mis'i-jə-) n. interracial marriage.

mis·cel·la'ne·ous (-səl-) a. of various kinds; mixed.

mis'cel·la'ny, n. [pl. -NIES] collection of various kinds.

mis·chance', n. bad luck.

mis'chief, n. 1. harm or damage. 2. prank. 3. teasing. —**mis·chie'vous** (-chi-) a.

mis·ci·ble (mis'ə-) a. that can be mixed.

mis·con·ceive', v. misunderstand. —**mis·con·cep'tion,** n.

mis·con'duct, n. wrong conduct.

mis·con·strue', v. misinterpret.

mis'cre·ant, n. villain.

mis·deed', n. crime, sin, etc.

mis·de·mean'or, n. Law minor offense.

mi'ser, n. stingy hoarder of money. —**mi'ser·ly,** a.

mis'er·a·ble, a. 1. in misery. 2. causing misery. 3. bad, poor, etc. —**mis'er·a·bly,** adv.

mis'er·y, n. [pl. -IES] pain,

poverty, distress, etc.

mis·fire′, v. fail to go off.

mis·fit′, v. fit improperly. —n. 1. improper fit. 2. (misfit) maladjusted person.

mis·for′tune, n. 1. trouble. 2. mishap, calamity, etc.

mis·giv′ings, n.pl. feelings of fear, doubt, etc.

mis·guide′, v. mislead.

mis·han′dle, v. abuse.

mis′hap, n. misfortune.

mis·in·form′, v. give wrong information (to).

mis·in·ter′pret, v. interpret wrongly. —**mis·in′ter·pre·ta′tion**, n.

mis·judge′, v. judge wrongly.

mis·lay′, v. [-LAID, -LAYING] put in a place later forgotten.

mis·lead′, v. 1. lead astray. 2. deceive.

mis·man′age, v. manage badly.

mis·no′mer, n. name wrongly applied.

mi·sog′y·nist (-soj′-) n. one who hates women. —**mi·sog′y·ny**, n.

mis·place′, v. put in a wrong place.

mis·print′, n. printing error.

mis′pro·nounce′, v. pronounce wrongly.

mis·quote′, v. quote incorrectly.

mis′rep·re·sent′, v. give a false idea of.

mis·rule′, n. bad government.

miss, v. 1. fail to hit, meet, do, see, hear, etc. 2. avoid. 3. note or feel the loss of. —n. 1. failure to hit, etc. 2. [pl. MISSES] unmarried woman; also [M-] title used before her name.

mis′sal, n. R.C.Ch. prayer book for Mass for the year.

mis·shap′en, a. deformed.

mis′sile, n. object to be thrown or shot.

miss′ing, a. absent; lost.

mis′sion, n. 1. special task or duty. 2. group or station of missionaries. 3. diplomatic delegation.

mis′sion·ar′y, n. [pl. -IES] person sent by a church to make converts, esp. abroad.

mis′sive, n. letter or note.

mis·spell′, v. spell incorrectly.

mis·state′, v. state wrongly. —**mis·state′ment**, n.

mis·step′, n. 1. wrong step. 2. mistake in conduct.

mist, n. mass of water vapor; thin fog. —**mist′y** [-IER, -IEST] a.

mis·take′, v. [-TOOK, -TAKEN, -TAKING] understand or perceive wrongly. —n. error.

mis·tak′en, a. wrong or incorrect.

Mis′ter, n. title before a man's name: usually **Mr.**

mis′tle·toe, n. evergreen plant with white berries.

mis·treat′, v. treat badly. —**mis·treat′ment**, n.

mis′tress, n. 1. woman in charge or control. 2. woman kept as if she were a wife.

mis·tri′al, n. Law trial made void by an error, etc.

mis·trust′, n. lack of trust. —v. have no trust in; doubt.

mis′un·der·stand′, v. [-STOOD, -STANDING] understand incorrectly.

mis·use′ (-ūz′) 1. use improperly. 2. abuse. —n. (-ūs′) incorrect use.

mite, n. 1. tiny, parasitic arachnid. 2. tiny amount.

mi′ter, n. 1. tall cap of a bishop. 2. corner joint of two pieces cut at an angle.

mit′i·gate, v. make or become less severe. —**mit′i·ga′tion**, n.

mitt, n. 1. padded baseball glove. 2. [Sl.] hand.

mit′ten, n. glove without separate finger pieces.

mix, v. [alt. pt. & pp. MIXT] 1. stir or come together in a single mass. 2. make by mixing ingredients. 3. combine. —n. mixture, or its ingredients. —**mix up**, 1. confuse. 2. involve (in).

mixed, a. 1. blended. 2. of different kinds. 3. of both sexes.

mix′ture (-chēr) n. 1. a mixing. 2. thing mixed.

mne·mon′ic (ni-) a. of or helping the memory.

moan (mōn) n. low, mournful sound. —v. 1. utter (with) a moan. 2. complain.

moat, n. deep, usually water-filled ditch around a castle.

mob, n. crowd, esp. a disorderly one. —v. [MOBBED, MOBBING] crowd around and attack.

mo′bile (-b′l, -bēl) a. 1. readily movable. 2. expressive. —**mo·bil′i·ty**, n.

mo′bil·ize, v. make or become ready, as for war. —**mo′bil·i·za′tion**, n.

moc′ca·sin, n. heelless slipper of soft leather.

mo′cha (-kə) n. kind of coffee.

mock, v. 1. ridicule. 2. mimic & deride. —*a.* false.

mock'er·y, *n.* [*pl.* -**IES**] 1. a mocking. 2. poor imitation.

mock'ing·bird, *n.* small bird with imitative call.

mode, *n.* 1. way of acting or doing. 2. fashion.

mod'el, *n.* 1. small copy of something. 2. one to be imitated. 3. style. 4. one who poses for an artist. 5. one who displays clothes by wearing them. —*a.* serving as a model. —*v.* 1. plan or form. 2. work as a model.

mod'er·ate (-it) *v.* avoiding extremes. —*n.* moderate person. —*v.* (-āt) 1. make or become moderate. 2. preside over (a debate, etc.). — **mod'er·ate·ly,** *adv.* — **mod'er·a'tion,** *n.* — **mod'-er·a'tor,** *n.*

mod'ern, *a.* of recent times; up-to-date. —*n.* modern person. — **mod'ern·is'tic,** *a.* — **mod'ern·ize,** *v.*

mod'est, *a.* 1. not conceited. 2. decent. 3. moderate. — **mod'es·ty,** *n.*

mod'i·cum, *n.* small amount.

mod'i·fy, *v.* [-**FIED,** -**FYING**] change or limit slightly. — **mod'i·fi·ca'tion,** *n.* — **mod'i·fi·er,** *n.*

mod'ish (mōd'-) *a.* fashionable.

mod'u·late, *v.* adjust or vary, as the pitch of the voice. — **mod'u·la'tion,** *n.*

mod'ule, *n.* detachable section with a special function.

mo'gul, *n.* important person.

mo'hair, *n.* goat-hair fabric.

Mo·ham'med·an, *a.* & *n.* Moslem. — **Mo·ham'med-an·ism,** *n.*

moist, *a.* slightly wet.

mois'ten (-'n) *v.* make moist.

mois'ture (-chẽr) *n.* slight wetness.

mo'lar, *n.* back tooth.

mo·las'ses, *n.* dark sirup left after sugar is refined.

mold (mōld) *n.* 1. hollow form in which a thing is shaped. 2. thing shaped. 3. furry, fungous growth. —*v.* 1. make in a mold. 2. shape. 3. become moldy.

mold'er, *v.* crumble.

mold'ing, *n.* decorative strip of wood, etc.

mold'y, *a.* [-**IER,** -**IEST**] of or covered with mold (*n.* 3).

mole, *n.* 1. small, dark, congenital spot on the skin. 2. small, burrowing animal.

mol'e·cule, *n.* smallest particle of a substance that can exist alone. — **mo·lec'u·lar,** *a.*

mole'hill, *n.* small ridge made by a burrowing mole.

mo·lest', *v.* to trouble or harm. — **mo'les·ta'tion,** *n.*

moll, *n.* [Sl.] gangster's mistress.

mol'li·fy, *v.* [-**FIED,** -**FYING**] soothe; make calm.

mol'lusk, mol'lusc, *n.* invertebrate with a soft body enclosed in a shell.

mol'ly·cod'dle, *n.* sissy. —*v.* pamper.

molt (mōlt) *v.* shed hair, skin, etc. before getting a new growth.

mol'ten (mōl'-) *a.* melted by heat.

mom, *n.* [Col.] mother.

mo'ment, *n.* brief period of, or certain point in time.

mo'men·tar'i·ly, *adv.* 1. for a short time. 2. at any moment.

mo'men·tar'y, *a.* lasting for only a moment.

mo·men'tous, *a.* very important.

mo·men'tum, *n.* impetus of a moving object.

mon'arch (-ẽrk) *n.* hereditary ruler. — **mo·nar'chi·cal** (-när'ki-) *a.*

mon'arch·y, *n.* [*pl.* -**IES**] government by a monarch. — **mon'arch·ist,** *n.*

mon'as·ter'y, *n.* [*pl.* -**IES**] residence for monks.

mo·nas'tic, *a.* of or like monks or nuns. —*n.* monk. — **mo·nas'ti·cism,** *n.*

Mon'day, *n.* second day of the week.

mon'e·tar'y (mon'-) *a.* 1. of currency. 2. of money.

mon'ey, *n.* [*pl.* -**EYS,** -**IES**] 1. metal coins or paper notes used as the legal medium of exchange. 2. wealth. **make money,** become wealthy.

mon'eyed (-id) *a.* rich.

Mon·go'li·an, *n.* & *a.* (person) of the so-called yellow race.

mon'goose, *n.* [*pl.* -**GOOSES**] ferretlike animal of India.

mon'grel, *n.* & *a.* (animal or plant) of mixed breed.

mon'i·tor, *n.* 1. student who helps keep order, etc. 2. radio or TV receiver for checking on programs. —*v.* watch, or check on.

monk (munk) *n.* man who is a member of an ascetic religious order.

mon'key, *n.* [*pl.* -**KEYS**] small,

long-tailed primate. —v. [Col.] meddle; trifle.

monkey wrench, wrench with an adjustable jaw.

mono-, *pref.* one; alone.

mon'o·cle (mon'-) *n.* eyeglass for one eye.

mo·nog'a·my, *n.* practice of being married to only one person at a time. —**mo·nog'a·mous,** *a.*

mon'o·gram, *n.* initials of a name, made into a design.

mon'o·graph, *n.* book or article on a single subject.

mon'o·lith *n.* pillar, statue, etc. made of a single, large stone. —**mon'o·lith'ic,** *a.*

mon'o·logue, mon'o·log (-lôg) *n.* 1. long speech. 2. skit for one actor only.

mo·nop'o·ly, *n.* [*pl.* -LIES] 1. total control of a product or service. 2. company having this. —**mo·nop'o·lis'tic,** *a.* —**mo·nop'o·lize,** *v.*

mon'o·rail, *n.* railway with cars on a single rail.

mon'o·syl'la·ble, *n.* word of one syllable. —**mon'o·syl·lab'ic,** *a.*

mon'o·the·ism (-thē-) *n.* belief that there is only one God.—**mon'o·the·is'tic,** *a.*

mon'o·tone, *n.* sameness of tone, pitch, color, etc.

mo·not'o·ny, *n.* 1. lack of variety. 2. tiresome sameness. —**mo·not'o·nous,** *a.*

mon·ox'ide, *n.* oxide with one oxygen atom per molecule.

mon·sieur (mə·syûr') *n.* [*pl.* MESSIEURS (mes'ērz)] gentleman: Fr. for *Mr.*

Mon·si'gnor (-sēn'yēr) *n.* R.C.Ch.* title of high rank.

mon·soon' (-sōōn') *n.* wind bringing rainy season to S. Asia.

mon'ster, *n.* huge or abnormal plant or animal.

mon'strous, *a.* 1. horrible. 2. huge. 3. very abnormal. —**mon·stros'i·ty** [*pl.* -TIES] *n.*

mon·tage' (-täzh') *n.* superimposition of images, as in a movie.

month, *n.* any of the 12 divisions of the year.

month'ly, *a.* happening, appearing, etc. every month. —*n.* [*pl.* -LIES] monthly periodical. —*adv.* every month.

mon'u·ment, *n.* 1. memorial statue, building, etc. 2. famous work. —**mon'u·men'tal,** *a.*

moo, *v. & n.* (make) the vocal sound of a cow.

mood (mōōd) *n.* 1. state of mind. 2. verb form to express a fact, wish, or order.

mood'y, *a.* [-IER, -IEST] 1. changing in mood. 2. gloomy.

moon, *n.* body that revolves around a planet, spec. around the earth. —*v.* look dreamy or listless.—**moon'beam,** *n.*—**moon'light,** *n.*

moon'lit, *a.* lighted by the moon.

moon'shine, *n.* 1. moonlight. 2. [Col.] whisky made illegally.

moon'stone, *n.* milky-white gem.

Moor, *n.* N. Afr. Moslem. —**Moor'ish,** *a.*

moor (moor) *n.* [Br.] open wasteland. —*v.* to secure, as by cables, ropes, etc.

moor'ings, *n.pl.* cables, or place, for mooring a ship.

moose, *n.* [*pl.* MOOSE] largest animal of the deer family.

moot, *a.* debatable.

mop, *n.* rags, sponge, etc. on a stick, as for washing floors. —*v.* [MOPPED, MOPPING] clean up, as with a mop.

mope, *v.* be gloomy.

mo·raine' (-rān') *n.* heap of rocks, etc. left by a glacier.

mor'al, *a.* 1. of or dealing with right and wrong. 2. good; virtuous. 3. giving sympathy, but no active help. —*n.* 1. moral lesson. 2. *pl.* moral rules or standards. —**mor'al·ly,** *adv.*

mo·rale' (-ral') *n.* degree of courage, discipline, etc.

mo·ral'i·ty, *n.* 1. moral quality. 2. virtue.

mor'al·ize, *v.* discuss moral questions. —**mor'al·ist,** *n.*

mo·rass', *n.* bog; swamp.

mor'a·to'ri·um, *n.* authorized delay in paying debts.

mo'ray, *n.* voracious eel.

mor'bid, *a.* 1. diseased. 2. gloomy or unwholesome. —**mor·bid'i·ty,** *n.*

mor'dant, *a.* sarcastic.

more, *a. & n.* 1. greater (in) amount or degree. 2. (something) additional. —*adv.* 1. to a greater degree. 2. in addition. —**more or less,** somewhat.

more·o'ver, *adv.* besides.

mo·res (-rēz) *n.pl.* customs with the force of law.

morgue (môrg) *n.* place where bodies of accident victims, etc. are taken, as for autopsy.

mor'i·bund, *a.* dying.

morn, *n.* [Poet.] morning.

morn'ing, n. first part of the day, till noon.

morn'ing-glo'ry, n. [pl. -RIES] vine with trumpet-shaped flowers.

mo·roc'co, n. fine, soft leather made of goatskin.

mo'ron, n. person who is mentally somewhat deficient. —**mo·ron'ic,** a.

mo·rose' (-rōs') a. gloomy.

mor'phine (-fēn) n. opium drug used to relieve pain.

mor'row, n. [Poet.] 1. morning. 2. the following day.

Morse code, code of dots and dashes used in telegraphy.

mor'sel, n. bit, as of food.

mor'tal, a. 1. that must die. 2. causing death. 3. very great; extreme. —n. human being. —**mor'tal·ly,** adv.

mor·tal'i·ty, n. 1. a being mortal. 2. death rate.

mor'tar, n. 1. bowl for pulverizing things with a pestle. 2. small cannon. 3. cement mixture used between bricks, etc.

mort·gage (môr'gij) n. deed pledging property as security for a debt. —v. pledge by a mortgage.

mor·ti'cian (-tish'ən) n. undertaker.

mor'ti·fy, v. [-FIED, -FYING] 1. shame; humiliate. 2. control (desires) by fasting, etc. —**mor'ti·fi·ca'tion,** n.

mor'tise (-tis) n. hole cut for a tenon to fit in.

mor'tu·ar'y (-chōō-) n. [pl. -IES] place to keep dead bodies before burial.

mo·sa'ic (-zā'-) n. design made of colored stones inlaid in mortar.

Mos'lem, n. follower of the religion of Mohammed. —a. of Islam.

mosque (mosk) n. Moslem place of worship.

mos·qui'to (-kē'-) n. [pl. -TOES, -TOS] small biting insect that sucks blood.

moss, n. tiny green plant growing in clusters on rocks, etc. —**moss'y,** a.

most, a. 1. greatest in amount or number. 2. almost all. —n. the greatest amount or number. —adv. to the greatest degree.

most'ly, adv. mainly; chiefly.

mote, n. speck, as of dust.

mo·tel', n. roadside hotel for motorists.

moth, n. four-winged insect like a butterfly.

moth'er, n. 1. female parent.

2. woman head of a convent. —a. 1. of or like a mother. 2. native. —v. be a mother to. —**moth'er·hood,** n.

moth'er·ly, a.

moth·er·in·law', n. [pl. MOTHERS-IN-LAW] mother of one's husband or wife.

moth'er·of·pearl', n. hard, shiny lining of some shells.

mo·tif' (-tēf') n. main theme of an artistic work.

mo'tion, n. 1. a moving; change of position. 2. gesture. 3. proposal made at a meeting. —v. make, or direct by, gestures. —**mo'tion·less,** a.

motion picture, series of pictures flashed on a screen in rapid succession so that things in them seem to move.

mo'ti·vate, v. provide with motive. —**mo'ti·va'tion,** n.

mo'tive, n. reason for doing something. —a. of motion.

mot'ley, a. of many different elements; varied.

mo'tor, n. 1. machine using electricity to make something work. 2. engine, esp. a gasoline engine. —a. 1. of or run by a motor. 2. of or for motor vehicles. 3. producing motion. —v. travel by automobile. —**mo'tor·ist,** n.

mo'tor·boat, n. boat propelled by a motor.

mo'tor·car, n. automobile.

mo'tor·cy'cle, n. 2-wheeled, engine-powered vehicle.

mot'tle, v. to blotch.

mot'to, n. [pl. -TOES, -TOS] maxim or phrase, as used on seals, coins, etc., that shows one's ideals, etc.

mould (mōld) n. & v. mold. —**mould'y** [-IER, -IEST] a. mold.

moult (mōlt) v. molt.

mound, n. heap of earth, etc.

mount, v. 1. climb; go up. 2. get up on. 3. increase in amount. 4. fix on or in a mounting. —n. 1. act of mounting. 2. horse to ride. 3. mounting. 4. mountain.

moun'tain, n. very high rise of land on earth's surface.

moun·tain·eer', n. 1. mountain dweller. 2. mountain climber.

mountain lion, cougar.

moun'tain·ous, a. 1. full of mountains. 2. very big.

moun'te·bank, n. charlatan.

mount'ing, n. a backing, support, setting, etc.

mourn (môrn) v. feel or show grief or sorrow (for). —

mourn'er, *n.* —**mourn'-ful,** *a.*

mourn'ing, *n.* 1. grief at a death. 2. mourners' black clothes.

mouse, *n.* [*pl.* MICE] 1. small rodent. 2. timid person. —**mous'y** [-IER, -IEST] *a.*

mous·tache', *n.* mustache.

mouth, *n.* 1. opening in the face for food. 2. any opening. —*v.* (mou*th*) say affectedly. —**mouth'ful,** *n.*

mouth organ, harmonica.

mouth'piece, *n.* 1. part held in or near the mouth. 2. spokesman for others.

move, *v.* 1. change the place of. 2. set or keep in motion. 3. change one's residence. 4. be active or take action. 5. cause. 6. stir emotionally. 7. propose (a resolution). —*n.* 1. movement or action. 2. *Games* one's turn. —**mov'a·ble, move'a·ble,** *a.* & *n.* —**mov'er,** *n.*

move'ment, *n.* 1. a moving or way of moving. 2. action toward a goal. 3. moving parts of a clock, etc. 4. *Music* main division of a composition.

mov'ie, *n.* motion picture: also **moving picture.**

mow (mō) *v.* [alt. pp. MOWN] 1. cut down (grass). 2. kill; knock down. —**mow'er,** *n.*

mow (mou) *n.* heap of hay, esp. in a barn.

Mr. (mis'tĕr) [*pl.* MESSRS. (mes'ĕrz)] title used before a man's name.

Mrs. (mis'iz) title used before a married woman's name.

Ms. (miz) title used instead of *Miss* or *Mrs.*

much, *a.* [MORE, MOST] great in quantity, degree, etc. —*adv.* 1. greatly. 2. nearly. —*n.* 1. great amount. 2. something great.

mu'ci·lage (-lij) *n.* gluey or gummy adhesive. —**mu'ci·lag'i·nous** (-laj'-) *a.*

muck, *n.* 1. black earth. 2. dirt; filth.

muck'rake, *v.* expose corruption in politics & business. —**muck'rak'er,** *n.*

mu'cous (mū'-) *a.* 1. of or secreting mucus. 2. slimy.

mucous membrane, membrane lining body cavities.

mu'cus (mū'-) *n.* slimy secretion of mucous membranes.

mud, *n.* wet, soft earth.

mud'dle, *v.* 1. mix up; confuse. 2. act confusedly. —*n.* mess, confusion, etc.

mud'dy, *a.* [-DIER, -DIEST] 1. full of or covered with mud. 2. clouded or obscure. —*v.* [-DIED, -DYING] make or become muddy.

muff, *n.* cylindrical covering to warm the hands. —*v.* bungle; miss.

muf'fin, *n.* bread baked in a small cupcake mold.

muf'fle, *v.* 1. wrap up warmly. 2. deaden (sound).

muf'fler, *n.* 1. thick scarf. 2. device to deaden noise.

muf'ti, *n.* civilian clothes.

mug, *n.* 1. heavy drinking cup. 2. [Sl.] face.

mug'gy, *a.* [-GIER, -GIEST] hot and humid.

mu·lat'to, *n.* [*pl.* -TOES] one born of a Negro and a Caucasian.

mul'ber·ry, *n.* [*pl.* -RIES] a tree with berrylike fruit.

mulch, *v.* & *n.* (use) a cover of leaves, peat, etc. to keep plants from freezing.

mulct (mulkt) *v.* take from by fraud.

mule, *n.* 1. offspring of a male donkey and a female horse. 2. lounging slipper.

mul'ish (mūl'-) *a.* stubborn.

mull, *v.* 1. [Col.] ponder. 2. heat and flavor, as wine.

mul·lein, mul·len, *n.* tall plant with downy leaves.

mul'let, *n.* an edible fish.

mul·ti-, *pref.* of or having many or several.

mul'ti·far'i·ous (-fâr'-) *a.* of many kinds; varied.

mul'ti·ple, *a.* having many parts, etc. —*n.* product of two numbers, one specified.

mul'ti·pli·cand', *n.* the number to be multiplied by another.

mul'ti·plic'i·ty (-plis'-) *n.* great number.

mul'ti·ply, *v.* [-PLIED, -PLYING] 1. to increase in number, degree, etc. 2. find the product (of) by adding a certain number a certain number of times. —**mul'ti·pli·ca'tion,** *n.* —**mul'ti·pli·er,** *n.*

mul'ti·tude, *n.* large number.

mul'ti·tu'di·nous, *a.* many.

mum, *n.* [Col.] chrysanthemum.

mum, *a.* silent.

mum'ble, *v.* speak or say indistinctly. —*n.* mumbled utterance.

mum′mer, n. actor, esp. one with a mask or disguise.

mum′mer·y, n. [pl. -IES] foolish ritual; false show.

mum′my, n. [pl. -MIES] ancient embalmed body.

mumps, n. disease in which the salivary glands swell.

munch, v. chew noisily.

mun′dane, a. of the world.

mu·nic′i·pal (-nis′-) a. of a city or town.

mu·nic·i·pal′i·ty, n. [pl. -TIES] city or town having local self-government.

mu·nif′i·cent, a. very generous. —**mu·nif′i·cence,** n.

mu·ni′tions, n.pl. weapons and ammunition for war.

mu·ral (myoor′əl) a. of or on a wall. —n. picture painted on a wall.

mur′der, v. kill (a person) unlawfully and with malice. —n. act of murdering. —**mur′der·er,** n. —**mur′der·ess,** n.fem.

mur′der·ous, a. 1. of or like murder. 2. guilty of, or ready to, murder.

murk, n. darkness; gloom. —**murk′y** [-IER, -IEST] a.

mur′mur, n. 1. low, steady sound. 2. mumbled complaint. —v. 1. make a murmur. 2. say in a low voice.

mur′rain (-in) n. a plague, esp. of cattle.

mus′cle, n. 1. tissue forming the fleshy parts that move the body. 2. any single part of this tissue. 3. strength.

mus′cu·lar, a. 1. of or done by muscle. 2. strong.

muse, v. think deeply. —n. spirit inspiring an artist.

mu·se′um, n. place for showing artistic, historical, or scientific objects.

mush, n. 1. thick, soft mass. 2. boiled corn meal. 3. [Col.] maudlin sentimentality. —int. shout urging on sled dogs. —v. travel over snow. —**mush′y** [-IER, -IEST] a.

mush′room, n. fleshy, umbrella-shaped fungus, often edible. —v. grow rapidly.

mu′sic, n. 1. songs, symphonies, etc. 2. art of composing or performing these.

mu′si·cal, a. of, fond of, or set to music. —**mu′si·cal·ly,** adv.

mu·si′cian (-zish′ən) n. person skilled in music.

musk, n. strong-smelling animal secretion, used in perfumes. —**musk′y** [-IER, -IEST] a.

mus′ket, n. long gun.

musk′mel′on, n. cantaloupe.

musk′rat, n. water rodent.

mus′lin (muz′-) n. strong cotton cloth, as for sheets.

muss, v. [Col.] make messy. —n. mess. —**muss′y,** a.

mus′sel, n. bivalve mollusk.

must, v. 1. have to. 2. be likely or certain to. —n. thing that must be done.

mus·tache (mas-tash′, mus′tash) n. hair grown out on the upper lip of men.

mus′tang, n. small, wild horse.

mus′tard, n. yellow, spicy powder or paste.

mus′ter, v. 1. bring or come together, as troops. 2. summon. —n. a mustering.

mus′ty, a. [-TIER, -TIEST] stale and moldy.

mu′ta·ble, a. changeable.

mu·ta′tion (mū-) n. a change, esp. a sudden variation in a plant or animal.

mute, a. 1. silent. 2. not able to speak. —n. 1. a deafmute. 2. device to mute a musical instrument. —v. soften the sound of.

mu′ti·late, v. cut off or damage part of.

mu′ti·ny, n. [pl. -NIES] & v. [-NIED, -NYING] revolt, as against one's military superiors. —**mu·ti·neer′,** n. —**mu′ti·nous,** a.

mutt, n. [Sl.] mongrel dog.

mut′ter, v. 1. speak or say indistinctly. 2. grumble. —n. muttered utterance.

mut′ton, n. flesh of (grown) sheep used as food.

mu′tu·al (-chōō-) a. 1. of or for one another. 2. in common. —**mu′tu·al·ly,** adv.

muz′zle, n. 1. snout. 2. device for an animal's mouth to prevent biting. 3. front end of a gun barrel. —v. 1. put a muzzle on. 2. prevent from talking.

my, pronominal a. of me.

my′na, my′nah, n. Asian starling.

my·o′pi·a, n. nearsightedness. —**my·op′ic,** a.

myr′i·ad (mir′-) n. great number. —a. very many.

myrrh (mūr) n. resin used in incense, perfume, etc.

myr′tle (mūr′-) n. 1. evergreen shrub. 2. creeping evergreen plant.

my·self′, pron. intensive or reflexive form of I.

mys′ter·y (mis′-) n. [pl.

-IES] 1. unexplained or unknown thing. 2. obscurity or secrecy. —**mys·te'ri·ous,** *a.*

mys'tic, *a.* 1. of mysticism. 2. occult or mysterious. —*n.* believer in mysticism.

mys'ti·cal, *a.* 1. spiritually symbolic. 2. mystic.

mys'ti·cism, *n.* belief that God can be known directly.

mys'ti·fy, *v.* [-FIED, -FYING] perplex or puzzle. —**mys'ti·fi·ca'tion,** *n.*

myth (mith) *n.* 1. traditional story explaining some phenomenon. 2. fictitious person or thing. —**myth'i·cal,** *a.*

my·thol'o·gy (mi-) *n.* [*pl.* -GIES] 1. study of myths. 2. myths of a certain people. —**myth'o·log'i·cal,** *a.*

N

nab, *v.* [Col.] seize or arrest.

na'dir (nā'-) *n.* 1. lowest point. 2. the point directly beneath one.

nag, *v.* [NAGGED, NAGGING] scold or urge constantly — *n.* 1. [Col.] one who nags. 2. inferior horse.

nail, *n.* 1. horny layer at the ends of the fingers and toes. 2. narrow, pointed piece of metal driven into pieces of wood to hold them. —*v.* fasten as with nails.

na·ive, na·ïve (nä-ēv') *a.* innocent; simple.—**na·ive·te', na·ïve·te'** (-tā') *n.*

na'ked, *a.* 1. without clothing or covering. 2. plain.

name, *n.* 1. word or words for a person, thing, or place. 2. reputation. —*a.* well-known. —*v.* 1. give a name to. 2. mention or identify by name. 3. appoint.

name'less, *a.* 1. without a name. 2. obscure; vague.

name'ly, *adv.* that is to say.

name'sake, *n.* person named after another.

nap, *v.* [NAPPED, NAPPING] sleep briefly. —*n.* 1. short sleep. 2. fuzzy surface of fibers on cloth.

nape, *n.* back of the neck.

naph'tha (naf'-) *n.* oily liquid used as a solvent, etc.

nap'kin, *n.* small piece of paper or cloth to protect clothes while eating.

nar·cis'sus (när-) *n.* flowering bulbous plant.

nar·cot'ic, *n.* drug that causes deep sleep and les-

sens pain. —*a.* of or like a narcotic.

nar·rate (na-rāt', nar'āt) *v.* tell a story. —**nar'ra·tor,** *n.*

nar·ra'tion, *n.* 1. a narrating. 2. a narrative.

nar'ra·tive, *a.* in story form. —*n.* story; account.

nar'row, *a.* 1. not wide. 2. intolerant. 3. limited in size, degree, etc. —*v.* lessen in width, extent, etc.

nar'row-mind'ed, *a.* bigoted.

na'sal (-z'l) *a.* of or through the nose.

na·stur'tium (-shəm) *n.* yellowish-red flower.

nas'ty, *a.* [-TIER, -TIEST] 1. dirty. 2. obscene. 3. unpleasant; mean.—**nas'ti·ly,** *adv.*—**nas'ti·ness,** *n.*

na'tal, *a.* of one's birth.

na'tion, *n.* 1. a people with history, language, etc. in common. 2. people under one government.

na'tion·al, *a.* of a whole nation. —*n.* citizen.

na'tion·al·ism, *n.* 1. patriotism. 2. advocacy of national independence. —**na'tion·al·ist,** *a.* & *n.* —**na'tion·al·is'tic,** *a.*

na'tion·al'i·ty, *n.* [*pl.* -TIES] nation, esp. of one's birth or citizenship.

na'tion·al·ize, *v.* transfer control of to a government. —**na'tion·al·i·za'tion,** *n.*

na'tive, *a.* 1. belonging to a region or country by birth, source, etc. 2. being or of the place of one's birth. 3. inborn. —*n.* native person, animal, or plant.

na'tive-born', *a.* born in a specified place.

na·tiv'i·ty, *n.* birth.

nat'ty, *a.* [-TIER, -TIEST] neat and stylish.

nat'u·ral, *a.* 1. of or dealing with nature. 2. not artificial. 3. innate. 4. lifelike. 5. to be expected. 6. *Mus.* neither sharp nor flat. —**nat'u·ral·ly,** *adv.*

nat'u·ral·ist, *n.* one who studies plants and animals.

nat'u·ral·ize', *v.* confer citizenship upon (an alien). —**nat'u·ral·i·za'tion,** *n.*

na'ture, *n.* 1. basic quality of a thing. 2. inborn character. 3. kind; sort. 4. physical universe or [also N-] its forces. 5. natural scenery.

naught (nôt) *n.* 1. nothing. 2. zero.

naugh'ty, *a.* [-TIER, -TIEST]

1. mischievous. 2. not nice or proper. —**naugh'ti·ly**, *adv.* —**naugh'ti·ness**, *n.*

nau'se·a (*or* -sha) *n.* 1. feeling of wanting to vomit. 2. disgust. —**nau'se·ate**, *v.* —**nau'seous**, *a.*

nau'ti·cal, *a.* of sailors, ships, or navigation.

nau'ti·lus, *n.* tropical mollusk.

na'val, *a.* of or for a navy, its ships, etc.

nave, *n.* main, long part of some churches.

na'vel, *n.* small, abdominal scar where the umbilical cord was attached.

nav'i·ga·ble, *a.* 1. wide or deep enough for ship travel. 2. that can be steered.

nav'i·gate, *v.* 1. travel through or on (air, sea, etc.) in a ship or aircraft. 2. steer (a ship, etc.). —**nav'i·ga'tion**, *n.* —**nav'i·ga'tor**, *n.*

na'vy, *n.* [*pl.* -VIES] 1. entire fleet of warships, etc. of a nation. 2. very dark blue: also **navy blue**.

navy bean, small, white bean.

nay, *n.* 1. denial. 2. negative vote or voter.

Na·zi (nä'tsi) *n. & a.* (adherent) of the German fascist party (1933-45). —**Na'zism**, *n.*

neap tide, lowest high tide, occurring twice a month.

near, *adv.* at a short distance. —*a.* 1. close in distance, time, etc. 2. intimate. 3. stingy. —*v.* draw near to. —*prep.* close to. —**near'ness**, *n.*

near'-by', **near'by'**, *a. & adv.* near; close at hand.

near'ly, *adv.* almost.

near'sight'ed, *a.* seeing only near objects distinctly.

neat, *a.* 1. tidy; clean. 2. skillful. 3. trim in form. —**neat'ly**, *adv.* —**neat'ness**, *n.*

neb'u·la, *n.* [*pl.* -LÆ (-lē)] cloudlike patch seen in the night sky. —**neb'u·lar**, *a.*

neb'u·lous, *a.* vague.

nec'es·sar'i·ly, *adv.* 1. because of necessity. 2. as a necessary result.

nec'es·sar'y, *a.* 1. that must be had or done; essential. 2. inevitable. —*n.* [*pl.* -IES] necessary thing.

ne·ces'si·tate, *v.* make (something) necessary.

ne·ces'si·ty, *n.* [*pl.* -TIES] 1. great need. 2. something necessary. 3. poverty.

neck, *n.* 1. part that joins the head to the body. 2. narrow part, as of a bottle. —**neck and neck**, very close.

neck'er·chief, *n.* kerchief worn around the neck.

neck'lace (-lis) *n.* chain of gold, beads, etc. worn around the neck.

neck'tie, *n.* decorative neck band worn with a shirt.

nec'tar, *n.* 1. sweet liquid in flowers. 2. delicious drink.

nec·tar·ine' (-ēn') *n.* smooth-skinned peach.

nee, **née** (nā) *a.* born.

need, *n.* 1. lack of something required; also, the thing lacking. 2. poverty or distress. —*v.* 1. have need of. 2. be obliged. —**need'less**, *a.*

nee'dle, *n.* 1. very slender, pointed piece, as for sewing, knitting, playing phonograph records, etc. 2. anything needle-shaped. —*v.* [Col.] goad; tease.

needle point, embroidery of woolen threads on canvas.

need'y, *a.* [-IER, -IEST] very poor; destitute.

ne'er'-do-well', *a. & n.* shiftless & irresponsible (person).

ne·far'i·ous (-fâr'-) *a.* very wicked.

ne·gate', *v.* deny or nullify. —**ne·ga'tion**, *n.*

neg'a·tive, *a.* 1. saying "no." 2. not positive. 3. of the electricity made by friction on resin or wax. 4. being less than zero. —*n.* 1. a negative word, reply, etc. 2. photographic plate or film in which light and shadow are reversed.

neg·lect', *v.* 1. fail to do. 2. fail to care for properly. —*n.* a neglecting.

neg·li·gee' (-zhā') *n.* woman's dressing gown.

neg'li·gent, *a.* habitually careless. —**neg'li·gence**, *n.*

neg'li·gi·ble, *a.* trivial.

ne·go'ti·ate, *v.* 1. discuss so as to agree on. 2. arrange for (a loan, etc.). 3. transfer or sell. 4. [Col.] get across. —**ne·go'ti·a·ble**, *a.* —**ne·go'ti·a'tion**, *n.* —**ne·go'ti·a'tor**, *n.*

Ne'gro, *n.* [*pl.* -GROES] *& a.* (person) of the so-called black race. —**Ne'groid**, *a.*

neigh (nā) *v. & n.* (utter) the cry of a horse.

neigh'bor, *n.* 1. one that lives or is near another. 2. fellow man. —*a.* near-by. —*v.* live or be near.

neigh'bor·hood, n. one part of a city or the people in it. —**in the neighborhood of,** [Col.] near or nearly.

neigh'bor·ly, a. friendly.

nei'ther (nē'thēr or nī'-) a. & pron. not one or the other (of two). —con. correlative used with nor.

nem'e·sis, n. just punishment.

neo-, pref. new; recent.

ne·ol'o·gism (-jiz'm) n. new word.

ne'on, n. inert gas used in electric signs, a chemical element.

ne'o·phyte (-fīt) n. novice.

neph'ew, n. 1. son of one's brother or sister. 2. son of one's brother-in-law or sister-in-law.

nep'o·tism, n. giving of jobs, etc. to relatives.

nerve, n. 1. cordlike fiber carrying impulses to and from the brain. 2. courage. 3. pl. nervousness. 4. [Col.] impudence.

nerve'-rack'ing, nerve'-wrack'ing, a. very hard on one's patience.

nerv'ous, a. 1. of nerves. 2. easily upset; restless. 3. fearful. —**ner'vous·ness,** n.

nervous system, all the nerve cells and nervous tissues of an organism.

-ness, suf. quality; state.

nest, n. 1. place where a bird or other animal raises its young. 2. cozy place. 3. set of things in increasing sizes. —v. make a nest.

nest egg, money put aside.

nes'tle (nes''l) v. 1. settle down or hold close for comfort. 2. lie sheltered.

net, n. 1. openwork fabric as of string, for snaring fish, etc. 2. fine net to hold the hair. 3. netlike cloth. 4. net amount. —a. 1. of net. 2. left over after deductions, etc. —v. [NETTED, NETTING] 1. to snare. 2. to gain.

neth'er (neth'ēr) a. under.

net'ting, n. net fabric.

net'tle, n. weed with stinging hairs. —v. annoy.

net'work, n. 1. arrangement of wires or threads as in a net. 2. chain of radio or TV stations.

neu'ral (noo'-) a. of a nerve or nerves.

neu·ral'gia, n. pain along a nerve path.

neu·ri'tis, n. inflammation of nerves. —**neu·rit'ic,** a.

neuro-, pref. of nerves.

neu·rol'o·gy, n. branch of medicine dealing with the nervous system. —**neu·rol'o·gist,** n.

neu·ro'sis, n. [pl. -SES (-sēz)] mental disorder with abnormally intense anxieties, obsessions, etc. —**neu·rot'ic,** a. & n.

neu'ter, a. neither masculine nor feminine.

neu'tral, a. 1. supporting neither side in a war or quarrel. 2. not one or the other. 3. having no decided color. —n. 1. neutral nation, etc. 2. position of disengaged gears. —**neu·tral'i·ty,** n.

neu'tral·ize, v. counteract the effectiveness of.

neu'tron, n. uncharged particle of an atom.

nev'er, adv. 1. at no time. 2. in no way.

nev·er·the·less', adv. however.

new, a. 1. appearing, made, etc. for the first time. 2. unfamiliar. 3. fresh. 4. unused. 5. modern; recent. 6. more. 7. beginning again. —adv. 1. again. 2. recently.

new'born', a. 1. just born. 2. reborn.

new'fan'gled (-faŋ'g'ld) a. new and strange.

new'ly, adv. recently.

new'ly·wed, n. recently married person.

news (nōoz, nūz) n. 1. new information. 2. (reports of) recent events.

news'boy, n. boy who sells or delivers newspapers.

news'cast, n. radio or television news broadcast. —**news'cast'er,** n.

news'pa'per, n. daily or weekly news publication.

news'print, n. cheap paper used for newspapers, etc.

news'reel, n. motion picture of current news events.

news'stand, n. a stand for the sale of newspapers, etc.

news'y, a. [-IER, -IEST] [Col.] having much news.

newt, n. small salamander.

New Year's Day, January 1: also **New Year's.**

next, a. nearest; closest. —adv. in the nearest time, place, etc. —prep. beside.

next'-door', a. in or at the next house, building, etc.

nex'us, n. [pl. -USES, -US] connection or link.

ni'a·cin, n. nicotinic acid.

nib, *n.* 1. bird's beak. 2. (pen) point.

nib'ble, *v.* eat with quick, small bites. —*n.* small bite.

nice, *a.* 1. pleasant, kind, good, etc. 2. precise; accurate. 3. refined. —**nice'ly,** *adv.*

ni'ce·ty, *n.* [*pl.* -TIES] 1. accuracy. 2. refinement. 3. small detail; fine point. 4. something choice or dainty.

niche (nich) *n.* 1. recess in a wall for a statue, etc. 2. especially suitable position.

nick, *v.* make a small cut, chip, etc. in or on. —*n.* small cut, chip, etc. —**in the nick of time,** at the critical moment.

nick'el, *n.* 1. rust-resistant metal, a chemical element. 2. nickel and copper coin worth 5 cents.

nick'name, *n.* 1. substitute name, as "Slim." 2. familiar form of a proper name, as "Bob." —*v.* give a nickname to.

nic'o·tine (-tēn) *n.* poisonous liquid in tobacco leaves.

nic·o·tin'ic acid, member of the vitamin B complex.

niece (nēs) *n.* 1. daughter of one's brother or sister. 2. daughter of one's brother-in-law or sister-in-law.

nig'gard, *a. & n.* stingy (person). —**nig'gard·ly,** *a.*

nigh (nī) *adv., a., prep.* near.

night (nīt) *n.* period of darkness between sunset and sunrise. —**night'time,** *n.*

night'cap, *n.* 1. cap worn in bed. 2. alcoholic drink taken just before bedtime.

night club, place for eating, drinking, dancing, etc. at night.

night'gown, *n.* sleeping gown for women and children.

night'hawk, *n.* 1. night bird. 2. night owl.

night'in·gale, *n.* European thrush that sings at night.

night'ly, *a. & adv.* (done or happening) every night.

night'mare, *n.* frightening dream or experience.

night owl, one who stays up late.

night'shade, *n.* belladonna or related plant.

night'shirt, *n.* kind of nightgown for men.

nil, *n.* nothing.

nim'ble, *a.* quick in movement or thought. —**nim'bly,** *adv.*

nim'bus, *n.* 1. rain cloud. 2. halo.

nin'com·poop, *n.* fool.

nine, *a. & n.* one more than eight. —**ninth,** *a. & n.*

nine'teen', *a. & n.* nine more than ten. —**nine'teenth',** *a. & n.*

nine'ty, *a. & n.* [*pl.* -TIES] 9 times 10. —**nine'ti·eth,** *a. & n.*

nin'ny, *n.* [*pl.* -NIES] a fool.

nip, *v.* [NIPPED, NIPPING] 1. pinch or bite. 2. pinch off. 3. spoil, as by frost. —*n.* 1. stinging cold. 2. small drink of liquor. —**nip and tuck,** close as to outcome.

nip'per, *n.* 1. *pl.* pliers, pincers, etc. 2. claw of a crab or lobster.

nip'ple, *n.* 1. protuberance on a breast or udder. 2. thing shaped like this.

nip'py, *a.* [-PIER, -PIEST] sharp; biting.

nir·va'na (-vä'-) *n.* Buddhism perfect, passionless bliss.

nit, *n.* egg of a louse.

ni'ter, ni'tre, *n.* salt used in explosives, fertilizer, etc.

ni'trate, *n.* salt of nitric acid.

ni'tric acid, corrosive acid containing nitrogen.

ni'tro·gen (-jən) *n.* colorless, odorless gas, a chemical element. —**ni·trog'e·nous,** *a.*

ni'tro·glyc'er·in, ni'tro·glyc'er·ine (-glis'ēr-in) *n.* thick explosive oil, used in dynamite.

nit'wit, *n.* stupid person.

nix, *int.* no! stop!

no, *adv.* 1. not at all. 2. not so. —*a.* not a. —*n.* [*pl.* NOES] 1. refusal. 2. negative vote.

no·bil'i·ty, *n.* [*pl.* -TIES] 1. noble state or rank. 2. people of noble rank.

no'ble, *a.* 1. highly moral. 2. grand; splendid. 3. of high hereditary rank. —*n.* person of high rank. —**no'ble·man** (-MEN) *n.* —**no'bly,** *adv.*

no'bod·y, *pron.* no one. —*n.* [*pl.* -IES] unimportant person.

noc·tur'nal, *a.* 1. of the night. 2. done, happening, etc. at night.

noc'turne, *n.* romantic musical composition.

nod, *v.* [NODDED, NODDING] 1. bend the head quickly. 2. show (assent) thus. 3. let the head fall forward in dozing. —*n.* a nodding.

node, *n.* 1. knob; swelling.

2. point on a stem from which a leaf grows.

nod·ule (nŏj′ool) n. small knot or rounded lump.

nog′gin, n. small mug.

noise, n. sound, esp. a loud, unpleasant sound. —v. spread (a rumor). —**noise′-less**, a.

noi′some, a. 1. unhealthful. 2. foul-smelling.

nois′y, a. [-IER, -IEST] 1. making noise. 2. full of noise. —**nois′i·ly**, adv. —**nois′i·ness**, n.

no′mad, n. 1. member of a wandering tribe. 2. wanderer. —**no·mad′ic**, a.

no·men·cla·ture (klā′chĕr) n. system of names.

nom′i·nal, a. 1. in name only. 2. relatively small. —**nom′i·nal·ly**, adv.

nom′i·nate, v. 1. appoint; name. 2. name as a candidate. —**nom′i·na′tion**, n.

nom′i·na·tive, a. & n. Gram. (in) the case of the subject of a verb.

nom′i·nee′ (-nē′) n. person who is nominated.

non-, pref. not (as in the list below).

non′ab·sorb′ent
non′ac′tive
non′ag·gres′sion
non′al·co·hol′ic
non′be·liev′er
non′com·bus′ti·ble
non′com·mer′cial
non′com·mis′sioned
non′con·duc′tor
non′con·form′ist
non′con·ta′gious
non′es·sen′tial
non′ex·ist′ent
non′fac′tu·al
non′fa′tal
non′fic′tion
non′flow′er·ing
non′fly′ing
non′func′tion·al
non′in·ter·fer′ence
non′in·ter·ven′tion
non′in·tox′i·cat·ing
non′ir′ri·tat·ing
non′ma·lig′nant
non′me·tal′lic
non′mil′i·tar·y
non′of·fi′cial
non′pay′ment
non′per·ish·a·ble
non′poi′son·ous
non′po·lit′i·cal
non′po′rous
non′pro·duc′tive
non′pro·fes′sion·al
non′prof′it·a·ble
non′re·li′gious
non′res·i·den′tial

non′smok′er
non′sup·port′ing
non′sus·tain′ing
non′tax′a·ble
non′tech′ni·cal
non′tox′ic

non·age (nŏn′ij) n. state of being under legal age.

nonce, n. the present time.

non′cha·lant (-sha-lănt) a. casually indifferent. —**non′-cha·lance**, n.

non·com′bat·ant, n. 1. civilian in wartime. 2. soldier not in combat.

non·com·mit′tal, a. not taking a definite stand.

non·de·script, a. of no definite class or type.

none, pron. 1. no one. 2. not any. —adv. not at all. —**none the less**, nevertheless.

non·en′ti·ty, n. [pl. -TIES] unimportant person.

non·pa·reil′ (-pa-rel′) a. unequaled; peerless.

non·par′ti·san, a. not of any single party, faction, etc.

non·plus′, v. [-PLUSED or -PLUSSED, -PLUSING or -PLUS-SING] thoroughly bewilder.

non·prof′it, a. not for profit.

non·res′i·dent, n. & a. (person) not living in the locality of his work, etc.

non·sec·tar′i·an, a. not connected with any church.

non′sense, n. absurd or meaningless words or acts. —**non·sen′si·cal**, a.

non′stop′, a. & adv. without a stop.

non′sup·port′, n. failure to support a legal dependent.

non·un′ion, a. not belonging to, or done by, a labor union.

noo′dle, n. flat strip of dry dough.

nook (nook) n. 1. corner. 2. small secluded spot.

noon (noon) n. twelve o'clock in the daytime; midday: also **noon′day**, **noon′time**.

no one, no person: also **no′-one′**, pron.

noose, n. loop with a slipknot for tightening it.

nor, con. and not (either).

norm, n. standard or model.

nor′mal, a. 1. usual; natural. 2. average. —n. what is normal; usual state. —**nor′-mal·cy**, **nor·mal′i·ty**, n.

nor′mal·ly, adv. 1. in a normal way. 2. usually.

north, n. direction or region to the right of one facing the sunset. —*a. & adv.* in, toward, or from the north. —**north'er·ly,** *a. & adv.* —**north'ern,** *a.* —**north'ern·er,** *n.* —**north'ward,** *a. & (also* **north'wards)** *adv.*

north·east', *n.* direction or region between north and east. —*a. & adv.* in, toward, or from the northeast. —**north·east'er·ly,** *a. & adv.* —**north·east'ern,** *a.* —**north·east'ward,** *a. & (also* **north·east'wards)** *adv.*

northern lights, aurora borealis.

North Pole, northern end of the earth's axis.

north·west', *n.* direction or region between north and west. —*a. & adv.* in, toward, or from the northwest. —**north·west'er·ly,** *a. & adv.* —**north·west'ern,** *a.* —**north·west'ward,** *a. & (also* **north·west'wards)** *adv.*

nose, *n.* 1. part of the face with two openings for breathing and smelling. 2. sense of smell. 3. thing like a nose. —*v.* 1. find, as by smell. 2. push with the front forward. 3. meddle (in). —**nose out,** defeat narrowly.

nose'gay, *n.* bunch of flowers.

nos·tal'gia (-jə) *n.* a longing for something past or far away. —**nos·tal'gic,** *a.*

nos'tril, *n.* either of two outer openings of the nose.

nos'trum, *n.* quack medicine.

nos'y, nos'ey (nōz'-) *a.* [-IER, -IEST] [Col.] inquisitive.

not, *adv.* in no manner, degree, etc.

no'ta·ble, *a. & n.* remarkable or outstanding (person). —**no'ta·bly,** *adv.*

no'ta·rize, *v.* certify (a document) as a notary.

no'ta·ry, *n.* [*pl.* -RIES] one authorized to certify documents, etc.: in full, **notary public.**

no·ta'tion, *n.* 1. (use of) a system of symbols, as in music. 2. a note.

notch, *n.* 1. V-shaped cut. 2. [Col.] a step; degree. —*v.* cut notches in.

note, *n.* 1. brief writing, comment, letter, etc. 2. notice; heed. 3. written promise to pay. 4. musical tone or its symbol. 5. importance. —*v.* 1. to notice. 2. make a note of.

note'book, *n.* book for keeping memorandums, etc.

not'ed, *a.* renowned; famous.

note'wor'thy, *a.* outstanding.

noth'ing, *n.* 1. no thing. 2. unimportant person or thing. 3. zero. —*adv.* not at all. —**for nothing,** 1. free. 2. in vain. 3. without reason. —**noth'ing·ness,** *n.*

no'tice, *n.* 1. announcement or warning. 2. short review. 3. attention. —*v.* observe. —**take notice,** observe.

no'tice·a·ble, *a.* 1. easily seen. 2. significant. —**no'tice·a·bly,** *adv.*

no'ti·fy, *v.* [-FIED, -FYING] give notice to; inform. —**no'ti·fi·ca'tion,** *n.*

no'tion, *n.* 1. general idea. 2. belief; opinion. 3. whim. 4. *pl.* small wares.

no·to'ri·ous, *a.* widely known, esp. unfavorably. —**no·to·ri'e·ty,** *n.*

not'with·stand'ing, *prep. & adv.* in spite of this.

nought (nôt) *n.* naught.

noun, *n.* word that names a person, thing, etc.

nour'ish (nur'-) *v.* feed to promote health and growth. —**nour'ish·ment,** *n.*

nov'el, *a.* new & unusual. —*n.* long fictional narrative.

nov'el·ist, *n.* writer of novels.

nov'el·ty, *n.* [*pl.* -TIES] 1. newness. 2. novel thing. 3. small, cheap toy, etc.

No·vem'ber, *n.* 11th month.

nov'ice, *n.* 1. one in a religious order before taking final vows. 2. beginner.

no·vi'ti·ate, no·vi'ci·ate (nō-vish'i-it) *n.* period of being a novice.

now, *adv.* 1. at this moment; at present. 2. at that time; then. 3. with things as they are. —*con.* since. —*n.* the present time. —**now and then,** occasionally.

now'a·days, *adv.* in these days; at the present time.

no'where, *adv.* not in, at, or to any place.

nox'ious (nok'shəs) *a.* harmful to health or morals.

noz'zle, *n.* small spout at the end of a hose, etc.

nu·ance' (-äns') *n.* slight change in color, meaning, etc.

nub'by, *a.* [-BIER, -BIEST] rough and knotty, as cloth.

nu'cle·ar, *a.* of, like, or forming a nucleus or nuclei.

nuclear fission, splitting of nuclei of atoms, with the release of much energy, as in the atomic bomb.

nuclear fusion, fusion of nuclei of atoms, with the release of much energy, as in the hydrogen bomb.

nu'cle·us, n. [pl. -CLEI (-kli-ī), -CLEUSES] central part, spec. of an atom or of a living cell.

nude, a. & n. naked (figure).

nudge, v. push gently, as with the elbow to attract attention. —n. gentle push.

nud'ism, n. practice or cult of going nude. —nud'ist, a. & n.

nug'get, n. lump of gold ore.

nui'sance (nōō'-) n. annoying act, person, etc.

null (nul) a. without legal force: also **null and void.**

nul'li·fy, v. [-FIED, -FYING] 1. make null. 2. make useless. —nul'li·fi·ca'tion, n.

numb (num) a. not able to feel. —v. make numb.

num'ber, n. 1. symbol or word showing how many or what place in a series. 2. total. 3. also pl. many. 4. quantity. 5. single issue of a periodical. 6. one part of a program of entertainment. 7. form of a word showing it to be singular or plural. —v. 1. count. 2. give a number to. 3. include. 4. total or contain.

num'ber·less, a. countless.

nu'mer·al, n. figure, letter, or word expressing a number.

nu'mer·a'tor, n. part above the line in a fraction.

nu·mer'i·cal, a. 1. of or having to do with number(s). 2. (expressed) by numbers. —nu·mer'i·cal·ly, adv.

nu'mer·ous, a. 1. very many. 2. large in number.

nu'mis·mat'ics, n. study or collection of coins. —nu·mis'ma·tist, n.

num'skull, n. stupid person.

nun, n. woman living in a convent under vows.

nun'ci·o (-shi-ō) n. [pl. -OS] papal ambassador.

nun'ner·y, n. [pl. -IES] convent.

nup'tial (-shəl) a. of marriage or a wedding. —n. [in pl.] a wedding.

nurse, n. 1. one trained to care for the sick, help doctors, etc. 2. nursemaid. —v. 1. take care of (an invalid, etc.). 2. try to cure; treat. 3. suckle. 4. protect or conserve. 5. nourish.

nurse'maid, n. woman hired

to care for children.

nurs'er·y, n. [pl. -IES] 1. room set aside for children. 2. place where trees & plants are raised for sale.

nur'ture (-chēr) n. training; care. —v. 1. nourish. 2. train; rear.

nut, n. 1. dry fruit with a kernel inside a hard shell. 2. the kernel. 3. small metal block for screwing onto a bolt, etc. 4. [Sl.] odd or silly person.

nut'meat, n. kernel of a nut.

nut'meg, n. aromatic seed grated & used as a spice.

nu'tri·ent, a. & n. nutritious (substance).

nu'tri·ment, n. food.

nu·tri'tion (-trī'-) n. 1. process of taking in and assimilating food. 2. food. —nu·tri·tive (-tiv) a.

nu·tri'tious, a. nourishing.

nuts, a. [Sl.] crazy; silly.

nut'shell, n. shell of a nut.

nut'ty, a. [-TIER, -TIEST] 1. containing nuts. 2. tasting like nuts. 3. [Sl.] crazy, queer, enthusiastic, etc.

nuz'zle, v. 1. push against with the nose. 2. snuggle.

ny'lon, n. 1. synthetic material made into thread, etc. 2. pl. stockings of this.

nymph, n. minor Greek or Roman nature goddess.

nym'pho·ma'ni·a, n. uncontrollable sexual desire in a woman. —nym'pho·ma'ni·ac, a. & n.

O

O, int. 1. exclamation in direct address. 2. oh.

oaf (ōf) n. stupid, clumsy fellow. —oaf'ish, a.

oak (ōk) n. hardwood tree bearing acorns. —oak'en, a.

oak'um, n. hemp fiber used to calk seams in boats.

oar, n. pole with a broad blade at one end, for rowing. —oars'man [pl. -MEN] n.

oar'lock, n. device supporting an oar in rowing.

o·a'sis, n. [pl. -SES] fertile place with water in the desert.

oat, n. usually in pl. 1. a cereal grass. 2. its grain.

oath, n. 1. sworn declaration to tell the truth, etc. 2. word used in cursing.

oat'meal, n. ground or rolled oats, cooked as porridge.

ob'bli·ga'to (-gä'-) n. [pl. -TOS, -TI] elaborate musical accompaniment to a piece.

ob'du·rate (-rit) *a*. 1. stubborn; unyielding. 2. not repenting.　**—ob'du·ra·cy,** *n*.

o·be'di·ent, *a*. obeying or willing to obey.　**—o·be'di·ence,** *n*.　**—o·be'di·ent·ly,** *adv*.

o·bei'sance (-bā'-, -bē'-) *n*. 1. bow, curtsy, etc. 2. homsiged.

ob'e·lisk, *n*. slender, tapering, four-sided pillar.

o·bese', *a*. very fat.　**—o·bes'i·ty,** *n*.

o·bey', *v*. 1. carry out orders (of). 2. be guided by.

ob·fus'cate, *v*. obscure; confuse.　**—ob·fus·ca'tion,** *n*.

o·bit'u·ar·y, *n*. [*pl.* -IES] notice of death, often with a short biography.

ob'ject, *n*. 1. thing that can be seen or touched. 2. person or thing to which action, etc. is directed. 3. purpose; goal. 4. *Gram.* word receiving the action of the verb or governed by a preposition. —*v*. (ab-jekt') feel or express opposition or disapproval.　**—ob·jec'tion,** *n*.　**—ob·jec'tor,** *n*.

ob·jec'tion·a·ble, *a*. offensive; disagreeable.

ob·jec'tive, *n*. 1. real or actual; not subjective. 2. without bias. 3. *Gram.* of the case of an object of a preposition or verb. —*n*. goal.　**—ob·jec·tiv'i·ty,** *n*.　**—ob·jec'tive·ly,** *adv*.

ob'jur·gate, *v*. rebuke; upbraid.　**—ob·jur·ga'tion,** *n*.

ob'li·gate, *v*. bind by a promise, sense of duty, etc.　**—ob'li·ga'tion,** *n*.　**—ob·lig'a·to·ry,** *a*.

o·blige' (-blīj') *v*. 1. compel, as by law or duty. 2. make indebted; do a favor for.　**—o·blig'ing,** *a*. helpful.

ob·lique' (-lēk' *or* -līk') *a*. 1. slanting. 2. not direct.

ob·lit'er·ate, *v*. 1. blot out. 2. destroy.　**—ob·lit'er·a'tion,** *n*.

ob·liv'i·on, *n*. 1. state of being forgotten. 2. forgetful state.

ob·liv'i·ous, *a*. unmindful.

ob'long, *a*. rectangular and longer than broad. —*n*. oblong figure.

ob'lo·quy (-kwi) *n*. widespread censure or disgrace.

ob·nox'ious (-nok'shəs) *a*. offensive.

o'boe (-bō) *n*. double-reed wood-wind instrument.

ob·scene' (-sēn') *a*. offensive to decency.　**—ob·scen'i·ty** (-sen'-) *n*. [*pl.* -TIES] *n*.

ob·scure', *a*. 1. dim. 2. not clear or distinct. 3. not well-known. —*v*. make obscure.　**—ob·scu'ri·ty,** *n*.

ob'se·quies, *n.pl.* funeral rites.

ob·se'qui·ous (-kwi-) *a*. servile.

ob·serv'ance, *n*. 1. the observing of a law, etc. 2. customary act, rite, etc.

ob·serv'ant, *a*. 1. attentive. 2. perceptive; alert.

ob·serv'a·to·ry, *n*. [*pl.* -RIES] building for astronomical research.

ob·serve', *v*. 1. adhere to (a law, etc.). 2. celebrate (a holiday, etc.). 3. notice; watch. 4. remark.　**—ob·ser·va'tion,** *n*.　**—ob·serv'er,** *n*.

ob·ses'sion, *n*. idea, etc. that obsesses one.

ob'so·les'cent, *a*. becoming obsolete.　**—ob'so·les'cence,** *n*.

ob'so·lete, *a*. no longer used.

ob·stet'rics, *n*. branch of medicine dealing with childbirth.　**—ob·stet'ric, ob·stet'ri·cal,** *a*.　**—ob'ste·tri'cian,** *n*.

ob'sti·nate (-nit) *a*. 1. stubborn. 2. hard to treat or cure.　**—ob'sti·na·cy,** *n*.

ob·strep'er·ous, *a*. unruly.

ob·struct', *v*. 1. block. 2. hinder.　**—ob·struc'tion,** *n*.　**—ob·struc'tive,** *a*.

ob·tain', *v*. 1. get by trying. 2. prevail.

ob·trude', *v*. 1. push out. 2. force oneself upon others.

ob·tuse', *a*. 1. more than 90°: said of an angle. 2. blunt. 3. slow to understand.

ob·verse', *a*. facing the observer. —*n*. (ob'vûrs) front or main side of a coin, etc.

ob'vi·ate, *v*. prevent, as by proper measures.

ob'vi·ous, *a*. easy to understand.　**—ob'vi·ous·ly,** *adv*.

o·ca·ri'na (ok'ə-rē'-) *n*. small, oval musical toy.

oc·ca'sion, *n*. 1. happening. 2. special event. 3. opportunity. 4. cause. —*v*. cause.　**—on occasion,** sometimes.

oc·ca'sion·al, *a*. 1. for special times. 2. infrequent.　**—oc·ca'sion·al·ly,** *adv*.

Oc'ci·dent, *n*. Europe and the Western Hemisphere.　**—Oc'ci·den'tal,** *a*. & *n*.

oc·clude', v. close or shut. —**oc·clu'sion**, n.

oc·cult', a. 1. secret. 2. mysterious. 3. magical.

oc'cu·pan·cy, n. an occupying. —**oc'cu·pant**, n.

oc'cu·pa'tion, n. 1. an occupying. 2. work; vocation. —**oc'cu·pa'tion·al**, a.

oc'cu·py, v. [-PIED, -PYING] 1. take possession of. 2. dwell in. 3. employ.

oc·cur', v. [-CURRED, -CUR-RING] 1. exist. 2. come to mind. 3. happen. —**oc·cur'rence**, n.

o·cean (ō'shən) n. 1. body of salt water covering much of the earth. 2. one of its five main divisions. —**o·ce·an'ic**, a.

o'ce·lot (ō'sə–, os'ə–) n. large, spotted wild cat.

o·cher, o·chre (ō'kẽr) n. yellow or red clay pigment.

o'clock', by the clock.

oc'ta·gon, n. figure with eight sides and eight angles. —**oc·tag'o·nal**, a.

oc'tave, n. eight full steps of a musical scale.

oc·tet', oc·tette', n. group of eight, esp. of musical performers.

Oc·to'ber, n. tenth month.

oc'to·ge·nar'i·an (–jə–) n. & a. (person) between 80 and 90 years old.

oc'to·pus, n. mollusk with soft body and eight arms.

oc'u·lar (–yoo–) a. of, for, or by the eye.

oc'u·list, n. doctor who treats diseases of the eye.

odd, a. 1. having a remainder of one when divided by two. 2. left over, as from a pair. 3. with a few more. 4. occasional. 5. peculiar; queer. —**odd'ly**, adv.

odd'i·ty, n. 1. odd quality. 2. [pl. -TIES] odd person or thing.

odds, n.pl. 1. advantage; favoring difference. 2. betting ratio based on chances. —**at odds**, quarreling. —**odds and ends**, remnants.

ode, n. lofty poem in praise.

o'di·ous, a. disgusting.

o'di·um, n. 1. hatred. 2. disgrace.

o·dom'e·ter, n. device that measures distance traveled.

o'dor, n. smell; aroma. —**o'dor·ous**, a.

o'dor·if'er·ous, a. giving off an (esp. fragrant) odor.

o'dour, n. odor: Br. sp.

od·ys·sey (od'ə–si) n. long journey with adventures.

o'er (ōr) prep. & adv. [Poet.] over.

of, prep. 1. being or coming from. 2. belonging to. 3. having or containing. 4. concerning; about. 5. during.

off, adv. 1. farther away in space or time. 2. so as to be no longer on. 3. so as to be less. —prep. 1. not on. 2. dependent on. 3. away from. 4. below the standard of. —a. 1. not on. 2. on the way. 3. away from work. 4. below standard. 5. provided for. 6. wrong. —int. go away!

of'fal, n. refuse; garbage.

of·fend', v. 1. commit an offense. 2. make angry; displeased. —**of·fend'er**, n.

of·fense', n. 1. sin or crime. 2. an offending. 3. (ôf'ens) an attacking. —**take offense**, become offended.

of·fen'sive, a. 1. attacking. 2. disgusting. —n. position for attacking.

of'fer, v. 1. present or give. 2. suggest. —n. thing offered. —**of'fer·ing**, n.

of'fer·to·ry, n. [pl. -RIES] 1. offering of bread and wine at Mass. 2. collection of money at church service.

off'hand', adv. without preparation. —a. 1. said offhand. 2. rude; curt. Also **off'hand'ed**, a.

of'fice, n. 1. a favor. 2. post of authority. 3. place for doing business. 4. rite.

of'fice·hold'er, n. government official.

of'fi·cer, n. 1. one having a position of authority in business, the armed forces, etc. 2. policeman.

of·fi'cial (–fish'əl) a. 1. authorized. 2. formal. —n. one holding an office. —**of·fi'cial·ly**, adv.

of·fi'ci·ate, v. perform official duties or functions.

of·fi'cious (–fish'əs) a. meddlesome.

off'ing, n. distance: only in **in the offing**, at some future time.

off·set', v. [-SET, -SETTING] compensate for.

off'shoot', n. anything that comes from a main source.

off'shore', a. & adv. (moving) away from shore.

off'spring', n. child or children.

oft, adv. [Poet.] often.

of·ten (ôf'n) adv. many

times: also **of'ten·times**.

o·gle (ō'g'l) v. look at in a fond way. —n. ogling look.

o'gre (-gēr) n. 1. *Folklore* man-eating giant. 2. cruel man.

oh (ō) *int. & n.* [*pl.* OH'S, OHS] exclamation of surprise, fear, wonder, pain, etc.

ohm (ōm) n. unit of electrical resistance.

oil, n. 1. any greasy liquid. 2. petroleum. —v. lubricate with oil. —a. of, from, or like oil. —**oil'y**, a.

oil'cloth, n. cloth waterproofed with oil or paint.

oint'ment, n. oily cream for healing the skin.

O.K., OK, a., adv., int. all right. —n. approval. —v. [O.K.'D, OK'D; O.K.'ING, OK'ING] to approve. Also sp. **okay**.

o'kra, n. plant with green pods used in soups.

old, a. 1. having lived or existed for a long time. 2. of a certain age. 3. not new. 4. former. —n. time long past. —**old'ness**, n.

Old English, English before 1100 A.D.

old'-fash'ioned, a. of the past; out-of-date.

old maid, spinster.

Old Testament, Bible of Judaism, or the first part of the Christian Bible.

old'-tim'er, n. [Col.] longtime member, worker, etc.

o'le·an'der, n. flowering evergreen shrub.

o'le·o·mar'ga·rine (-ja-rin) n. margarine: also **o'le·o**.

ol·fac'to·ry, a. of the sense of smell.

ol'i·gar'chy (-gärk'-) n. [*pl.* -IES] 1. state rule by a few people. 2. these people.

ol'ive, n. 1. evergreen tree. 2. its small oval fruit. 3. yellowish green.

om'buds·man, n. [*pl.* -MEN] official who investigates complaints against government.

o·me'ga, n. last letter of the Greek alphabet.

om·e·let, om·e·lette (om'-lit) n. eggs beaten up and cooked as a pancake.

o'men, n. sign of something to come.

om'i·nous, a. threatening.

o·mis'sion (-mish'-) n. an omitting or thing omitted.

o·mit', v. [OMITTED, OMITTING] 1. leave out. 2. fail to do.

omni-, *pref.* all; everywhere.

om'ni·bus, a. providing for many things at once.

om·nip'o·tent, a. all-powerful. —**om·nip'o·tence**, n.

om·nis'cient (-nish'ənt) a. knowing all things. —**om·nis'cience**, n.

om·niv'o·rous, a. 1. eating all foods. 2. taking in everything.

on, *prep.* 1. held up by, covering, or attached to. 2. near to. 3. at the time of. 4. connected with. 5. in a state of. 6. by using. 7. concerning. —*adv.* 1. in a situation of touching, covering, or being held up by. 2. toward. 3. forward. 4. continuously. 5. into operation. —a. in action.

once, adv. 1. one time. 2. at any time. 3. formerly. —n. one time. —**at once**, 1. immediately. 2. simultaneously.

on'com'ing, a. approaching.

one, a. 1. being a single thing. 2. united. 3. a certain. 4. some. —n. 1. lowest number. 2. single person or thing. —*pron.* a person or thing.

one'ness, n. unity; identity.

one·self', *pron.* one's own self. —**be oneself**, function normally. —**by oneself**, alone.

one'-sid'ed, a. 1. unequal. 2. partial.

one'-way', a. in one direction only.

on·ion (un'yən) n. bulblike, sharp-tasting vegetable.

on'look'er, n. spectator.

on'ly, a. 1. alone of its or their kind. 2. best. —adv. 1. and no other. 2. merely. —con. [Col.] except that.

on'set', n. 1. attack. 2. start.

on'slaught (-slôt) n. violent attack.

on'to, *prep.* to and upon.

o'nus, n. responsibility.

on'ward, adv. forward: also **on'wards**. —a. advancing.

o'nyx (-iks) n. kind of agate.

ooze, v. flow out slowly. —n. 1. something that oozes. 2. soft mud or slime.

o'pal, n. iridescent gem.

o·paque' (-pāk') a. not transparent. —**o·pac'i·ty** (-pas'-) n.

o'pen, a. 1. not closed, covered, etc. 2. not enclosed. 3. unfolded. 4. free to be entered, used, etc. 5. not restricted. 6. available. 7. frank. —v. 1. cause to be or become open. 2. begin. 3. start operating. —**open to,** glad to consider.—**o'pen·er,** n.—**o'pen·ly,** adv.

o'pen·hand'ed, a. generous.

o'pen·ing, n. 1. open place. 2. beginning. 3. favorable chance. 4. unfilled job.

o'pen·mind'ed, a. impartial

o'pen·work', n. ornamental work with openings in it.

op·er·a, n. play set to music and sung with an orchestra. —**o'per·at'ic,** a.

op'er·a·ble, a. that can be treated by surgery.

op'er·ate, v. 1. be or keep in action. 2. have an effect. 3. perform an operation. 4. manage. —**op'er·a'tor,** n.

op'er·a'tion, n. 1. act or way of operating. 2. being in action. 3. one process in a series. 4. surgical treatment for an illness.

op'er·a·tive, a. 1. operating. 2. efficient.

op'er·et'ta, n. light opera.

oph'thal·mol'o·gy (of'-) n. branch of medicine dealing with diseases of the eye. —**oph'thal·mol'o·gist,** n.

o'pi·ate (-it) n. narcotic drug containing opium.

o·pin'ion (-yən) n. 1. what one thinks true. 2. estimation. 3. expert judgment.

o·pin'ion·at'ed, a. obstinate in holding an opinion.

o'pi·um, n. narcotic drug made from a certain poppy.

o·pos'sum, n. small, tree-dwelling mammal.

op·po'nent, n. person against one in a fight, etc.

op'por·tune', a. timely.

op'por·tun'ist, n. one willing to get ahead unethically. —**op'por·tun'ism,** n.

op'por·tu'ni·ty, n. [pl. -TIES] fit time to do something.

op·pose', v. 1. place opposite. 2. fight or resist. —**op·po·si'tion** (-zish'ən) n.

op'po·site, a. 1. entirely different. 2. opposed to. —n. anything opposed. —prep. across from.

op·press', v. 1. weigh down. 2. rule in a cruel way. —**op·pres'sion,** n. —**op·pres'sor,** n.

op·pres'sive, a. 1. burdensome. 2. cruel and unjust.

op·pro'bri·ous, a. 1. abusive. 2. disgraceful.

op·pro'bri·um, n. disgrace.

op'tic, a. of the eye.

op'ti·cal, a. 1. of vision. 2. aiding sight. 3. of optics.

op·ti'cian (-tish'ən) n. maker or seller of eyeglasses.

op'tics, n. science dealing with light and vision.

op'ti·mism, n. tendency to be cheerful about life. —**op'ti·mist,** n. —**op'ti·mis'tic,** a.

op'ti·mum, n. & a. (the) best.

op'tion, n. choice or right to choose. —**op'tion·al,** a.

op·tom'e·trist, n. one who tests eyes and fits eyeglasses. —**op·tom'e·try,** n.

op'u·lent, a. 1. wealthy. 2. abundant. —**op'u·lence,** n.

o'pus, n. [pl. OPERA, OPUSES] a work, esp. of music.

or, con. word introducing an alternative, synonym, etc.

-or, suf. person or thing that.

or'a·cle, n. ancient Gr. or Rom. priest who acted as prophet. —**o·rac'u·lar,** a.

o'ral, a. 1. spoken. 2. of the mouth. —**o'ral·ly,** adv.

or'ange, n. 1. sweet, reddish-yellow citrus fruit. 2. reddish yellow.

or'ange·ade', n. drink of orange juice, water, and sugar.

o·rang'u·tan, n. large ape.

o·ra'tion, n. formal, public speech. —**or'a·tor,** n.

or'a·to'ri·o, n. [pl. -OS] vocal and orchestral composition on a religious theme.

or'a·to·ry, n. skill in public speaking. —**or'a·tor'i·cal,** a.

orb, n. (heavenly) sphere.

or'bit, n. path of one heavenly body around another. —v. put or go in an orbit.

or'chard, n. grove of fruit trees.

or'ches·tra (-kis-) n. 1. group of musicians playing together. 2. main floor of a theater. —**or·ches'tral,** a.

or'ches·trate, v. arrange music for an orchestra. —**or'ches·tra'tion,** n.

or'chid (-kid) n. 1. plant having flowers with three petals, one of which is enlarged. 2. light bluish red.

or·dain', v. 1. to decree. 2. admit to the ministry.

or·deal', n. difficult or painful experience.

or'der, n. 1. peaceful, orderly, or proper state. 2. monastic or fraternal brotherhood. 3. general condition.

4. command. 5. (request for) items to be supplied. 6. class; kind. —v. 1. arrange. 2. command. 3. request (supplies). —in order that, so that.

or'der·ly, a. 1. neatly arranged. 2. well-behaved. —n. [pl. -LIES] 1. soldier acting as an officer's servant. 2. male hospital attendant. —or'der·li·ness, n.

or'di·nal number, number used to show order in a series, as first, second, etc.

or'di·nance, n. statute, esp. of a city government.

or'di·nar'y, a. 1. customary; usual. 2. common; average. —or·di·nar'i·ly, adv.

or·di·na'tion, n. an ordaining or being ordained.

ord'nance, n. Mil. heavy guns, ammunition, etc.

ore, n. rock or mineral containing metal.

or'gan, n. 1. keyboard musical instrument using pipes, reeds, or electronic tubes. 2. animal or plant part with a special function. 3. agency or medium. —or'gan·ist, n.

or'gan·dy, or'gan·die n. sheer, stiff cotton cloth.

or·gan'ic, a. 1. of a body organ. 2. systematically arranged. 3. of or from living matter. 4. of chemical compounds containing carbon.

or'gan·ism, n. living thing.

or'gan·i·za'tion, n. 1. act of organizing. 2. group organized for some purpose.

or'gan·ize, v. 1. arrange according to a system. 2. form into a group, union, etc. —or'gan·iz'er, n.

or'gasm, n. climax of a sexual act.

or'gy (-ji) n. [pl. -GIES] wild merrymaking.

o'ri·ent, n. [O-] Asia. —v. adjust (oneself) to a specific situation. —O'ri·en'tal, a. & n. —o'ri·en·ta'tion, n.

or'i·fice (-fis) n. mouth; opening.

or'i·gin, n. 1. beginning. 2. parentage. 3. source.

o·rig'i·nal, a. 1. first. 2. new; novel. 3. inventive. —n. an original work, form, etc. —o·rig'i·nal'i·ty, n. —o·rig'i·nal·ly, adv.

o·rig'i·nate, v. 1. create; invent. 2. begin; start. —o·rig'i·na'tion, n. —o·rig'i·na'tor, n.

o'ri·ole, n. bird with bright-orange and black plumage.

or'lon, synthetic fiber: trademark (O-).

or'na·ment (-mənt) n. decoration. —v. (-ment') decorate. —or'na·men'tal, a. —or'na·men·ta'tion, n.

or·nate', a. showy. —or·nate'ly, adv.

or'ner·y, a. [-IER, -IEST] [Col.] mean; obstinate.

or'ni·thol'o·gy, n. study of birds. —or'ni·thol'o·gist, n.

o'ro·tund, a. 1. full and deep in sound. 2. bombastic.

or'phan, n. child whose parents are dead. —v. cause to be an orphan. —or'phan·age, n.

or'tho·don'tics, or'tho·don'tia (-shə) n. dentistry of teeth straightening. —or'tho·don'tist, n.

or'tho·dox, a. 1. holding to the usual or fixed beliefs; conventional. 2. [O-] of a large eastern Christian church. —or'tho·dox'y, n.

or'tho·pe'dics, n. surgery dealing with bones. —or'tho·pe'dic, a. —or'tho·pe'dist, n.

-ory, suf. 1. of or like. 2. place or thing for.

os'cil·late, v. 1. swing to and fro. 2. fluctuate. —os'cil·la'tion, n.

os'cu·late, v. kiss.

os·mo'sis, n. diffusion of fluids through a porous membrane.

os'prey, n. [pl. -PREYS] large, fish-eating hawk.

os'si·fy, v. [-FIED, -FYING] change into bone.

os·ten'si·ble, a. seeming; apparent. —os·ten'si·bly, adv.

os'ten·ta'tion, n. showiness. —os'ten·ta'tious, a.

os'te·op'a·thy, n. a system of medical practice. —os'te·o·path', n.

os'tra·cize, v. banish; shut out. —os'tra·cism, n.

os'trich, n. large, nonflying bird.

oth'er, a. 1. being the one(s) remaining. 2. different. 3. additional. —pron. 1. the other one. 2. some other one. —adv. otherwise. —every other, every alternate.

oth'er·wise, adv. 1. differently. 2. in all other ways. 3. if not; else. —a. different.

oth'er·world'ly, a. apart from earthly interests.

ot'ter, n. weasellike animal.

ot'to·man, n. low, cushioned seat or footstool.

ouch, int. cry of pain.

ought, v. a helping verb showing: 1. duty. 2. desirability. 3. probability.

ounce, n. 1. unit of weight, $\frac{1}{16}$ pound. 2. fluid ounce, $\frac{1}{16}$ pint.

our, pronominal a. of us.

ours, pron. that or those belonging to us.

our·selves', pron. intensive or reflexive form of **we.**

-ous, suf. having; full of; characterized by.

oust, v. force out; expel.

oust'er, n. dispossession.

out, adv. 1. away from a place, etc. 2. outdoors. 3. into being or action. 4. thoroughly. 5. from a group. —a. 1. not used, working, etc. 2. having lost. —n. 1. [Sl.] excuse. 2. Baseball retirement of a batter or runner from play. —v. become known. —prep. out of. —**on the outs,** [Col.] quarreling. —**out of,** 1. from inside of. 2. beyond. 3. from (material). 4. because of. 5. no longer having. 6. so as to deprive.

out-, pref. 1. outside. 2. outward. 3. better or more than.

out'-and-out', a. thorough.

out'board, a. located on the outer surface of a boat.

out'break, n. a breaking out, as of disease or rioting.

out'build·ing, n. building apart from the main one.

out'burst, n. sudden show of feeling, energy, etc.

out'cast, a. & n. shunned (person).

out·class', v. surpass.

out'come, n. result.

out'crop, n. exposed rock layer.

out'cry, n. [pl. -CRIES] 1. a crying out. 2. strong protest.

out·dat'ed, a. out-of-date.

out·do', v. do better than.

out'door, a. in the open.

out'doors, adv. in or into the open; outside. —n. (out-dôrz') the outdoor world.

out'er, a. on or closer to the outside.

out'er·most, a. farthest out.

out'field, n. Baseball area beyond the base lines. —**out'field·er,** n.

out'fit, n. 1. equipment for some activity. 2. group;

esp., military unit. —v. [-FITTED, -FITTING] equip.

out'go, n. expenditure.

out'go'ing, a. 1. leaving. 2. sociable.

out·grow', v. grow too large for.

out'growth, n. 1. result. 2. an offshoot.

out·guess', v. outwit.

out'house, n. outdoor latrine.

out'ing, n. picnic, trip, etc.

out·land'ish, a. 1. strange. 2. fantastic.

out'law, n. notorious criminal. —v. declare illegal.

out'lay, n. money spent.

out'let, n. 1. passage or way out. 2. market for goods.

out'line, n. 1. bounding line. 2. sketch showing only outer lines. 3. general plan.

out·live', v. live longer than.

out'look, n. 1. viewpoint. 2. prospect.

out'ly·ing, a. remote.

out·mod'ed (-mōd'-) a. old-fashioned.

out·num'ber, v. be greater in number than.

out'-of-date', a. obsolete.

out'-of-doors', a. outdoor. —n. & adv. outdoors.

out·pa'tient, n. hospital patient not an inmate.

out'post, n. remote settlement or military post.

out'put, n. total quantity produced in a given period.

out'rage (-rāj) n. 1. shocking act or crime. 2. deep insult. —v. commit an outrage on. —**out·ra'geous,** a.

out'right, a. complete. —adv. entirely.

out'set, n. beginning.

out'side, n. 1. the exterior. 2. area beyond. —a. 1. outer. 2. from some other. 3. slight. —adv. on or to the outside. —prep. (out-sīd') on or to the outside of.

out·sid'er, n. one not of a certain group.

out'skirts, n.pl. outlying districts of a city, etc.

out·spo'ken, a. frank; bold.

out·stand'ing, a. 1. prominent. 2. unpaid.

out·stretched', a. extended.

out·strip', v. [-STRIPPED, -STRIPPING] excel.

out'ward, a. 1. outer. 2. visible. —adv. toward the outside. Also **out'wards,** adv. —**out'ward·ly,** adv.

out·wit', v. [-WITTED, -WITTING] to overcome by cleverness.

o'va, *n.* pl. of **ovum.**

o'val, *a. & n.* egg-shaped (thing).

o'va·ry, *n.* [*pl.* -RIES] 1. female gland where ova are formed. 2. part of a flower where the seeds form.

o·va'tion, *n.* loud and long applause for cheering.

ov'en, *n.* compartment for baking, drying, etc.

o'ver, *prep.* 1. above. 2. on; upon. 3. across. 4. during. 5. more than. 6. about. —*adv.* 1. above or across. 2. more. 3. down. 4. other side up. 5. again. —*a.* 1. finished. 2. on the other side.

over-, *pref.* excessive or excessively (as in the list below).

o'ver·a·bun'dance
o'ver·ac'tive
o'ver·anx'ious
o'ver·bur'den
o'ver·cau'tious
o'ver·con'fi·dent
o'ver·cook'
o'ver·crowd'
o'ver·dose'
o'ver·eat'
o'ver·em'pha·size
o'ver·es'ti·mate
o'ver·ex·ert'
o'ver·ex·pose'
o'ver·heat'
o'ver·in·dulge'
o'ver·load'
o'ver·pop'u·late
o'ver·pro·duc'tion
o'ver·ripe'
o'ver·stim'u·late
o'ver·stock'
o'ver·sup·ply'
o'ver·tire'

o'ver·all, *a.* 1. end to end. 2. total. —*n.* [in *pl.*] work trousers with attached bib.

o'ver·awe', *v.* subdue by inspiring awe.

o'ver·bear'ing, *a.* bossy.

o'ver·board', *adv.* from a ship into the water.

o'ver·cast, *a.* cloudy; dark.

o'ver·coat, *n.* coat worn over the usual clothing.

o'ver·come', *v.* get the better of; master.

o'ver·do', *v.* 1. do too much. 2. cook too long.

o'ver·drive, *n.* gear that reduces an engine's power without reducing its speed.

o'ver·due', *a.* past the time for payment, arrival, etc.

o'ver·flow', *v.* 1. flood; run over. 2. fill beyond capacity. —*n.* 1. an overflowing. 2. vent for overflowing liquids.

o'ver·grow', *v.* 1. grow over all of. 2. grow too much.

o'ver·hand, *a. & adv.* with the hand held higher than the elbow.

o'ver·haul', *v.* check thoroughly and make needed repairs.

o'ver·head, *a. & adv.* above the head. —*n.* continuing business costs, as of rent.

o'ver·hear', *v.* hear a speaker without his knowledge.

o'ver·joyed', *a.* delighted.

o'ver·land, *a. & adv.* by or across land.

o'ver·lap', *v.* lap over.

o'ver·look', *v.* 1. look down on. 2. fail to notice. 3. neglect. 4. excuse.

o'ver·ly, *adv.* too much.

o'ver·night', *adv.* during the night. —*a.* of or for a night.

o'ver·pass, *n.* bridge over a river, road, etc.

o'ver·pow'er, *v.* subdue.

o'ver·rate', *v.* estimate too highly.

o'ver·ride', *v.* overrule.

o'ver·rule', *v.* 1. set aside. 2. prevail over.

o'ver·run', *v.* 1. spread out over. 2. swarm over.

o'ver·seas', *a. & adv.* 1. across or beyond the sea. 2. foreign. Also **oversea.**

o'ver·see', *v.* supervise. —**o'ver·se'er,** *n.*

o'ver·shad'ow, *v.* be more important than.

o'ver·shoe', *n.* boot worn over the regular shoe to ward off dampness, etc.

o'ver·sight, *n.* 1. failure to see. 2. careless omission.

o'ver·sleep', *v.* sleep longer than intended.

o'vert (*or* ō-vûrt') *a.* 1. open; public. 2. done openly.

o'ver·take', *v.* 1. catch up with. 2. come upon suddenly.

o'ver·tax', *v.* 1. tax too much. 2. put a strain on.

o'ver·throw', *v. & n.* defeat.

o'ver·time, *n.* 1. time beyond a set limit. 2. pay for overtime work. —*a. & adv.* of or for overtime.

o'ver·tone, *n. Mus.* higher tone heard faintly when a main tone is played.

o'ver·ture (-chêr) *n.* 1. *Mus.* introduction. 2. proposal.

o'ver·turn', *v.* 1. turn over. 2. conquer.

o'ver·ween'ing, *a.* haughty.

o'ver·weight', *a.* above the normal or allowed weight.

o'ver·whelm', *v.* 1. cover over completely. 2. crush.

o'ver·work', v. work too hard.
—n. too much work.

o'ver·wrought' (-rôt') a. too nervous or excited.

o'void, a. egg-shaped.

o'vule, n. 1. immature ovum. 2. part of a plant that develops into a seed.

o'vum, n. [pl. -VA (-və)] female germ cell.

owe, v. 1. be in debt (to) for a certain sum. 2. feel obligated to give.

ow'ing (ō'-) a. due; unpaid. —**owing to**, resulting from.

owl, n. night bird of prey with large ears. —**owl'ish,** a.

own, a. belonging to oneself or itself. —n. what one owns. —v. 1. possess. 2. confess. —**own'er,** n. —**own'er·ship,** n.

ox, n. [pl. OXEN] 1. a cud-chewing animal, as a cow, bull, etc. 2. castrated bull.

ox'ford (-fērd) n. low shoe laced over the instep.

ox'ide, n. oxygen compound.

ox'i·dize, v. unite with oxygen. —**ox'i·da'tion,** n.

ox'y·gen, n. colorless gas, commonest chemical element.

oys'ter (ois'-) n. edible mollusk with hinged shell.

o'zone, n. form of oxygen with a strong odor.

P

pa, n. [Col.] father.

pace, n. 1. a step or stride. 2. rate of speed. 3. gait. —v. 1. walk back and forth across. 2. measure by paces. 3. set the pace for.

pace'mak'er, n. electronic device placed in the body to regulate heartbeat.

pach'y·derm (pak'-) n. large, thick-skinned animal.

pa·cif'ic, a. peaceful; calm.

pac'i·fism (pas'-) n. opposition to all war. —**pac'i·fist,** n.

pac'i·fy, v. [-FIED, -FYING] make calm. —**pac'i·fi·ca'tion,** n. —**pac'i·fi'er,** n.

pack, n. 1. bundle of things. 2. package of a set number. 3. group of animals, etc. —v. 1. put (things) in a box, bundle, etc. 2. crowd; cram. 3. fill tightly. 4. send (off). —**pack'age,** n. packed thing. —v. make a package of.

pack'et, n. small package.

pact, n. compact; agreement.

pad, n. 1. soft stuffing or cushion. 2. sole of an ani-

mal's foot. 3. water lily leaf. 4. paper sheets fastened at one edge. —v. [PADDED, PADDING] 1. stuff with material. 2. walk softly.

pad'dle, n. 1. oar for a canoe. 2. similar thing for games, etc. —v. 1. propel with a paddle. 2. spank.

pad'dock, n. small enclosure for horses.

pad'dy, n. [pl. -DIES] rice in a rice field.

pad'lock, n. a lock with a U-shaped arm. —v. fasten with a padlock.

pa'gan, n. & a. heathen. —**pa'gan·ism,** n.

page, n. 1. one side of a leaf of a book, etc. 2. the leaf. 3. boy attendant. —v. 1. number the pages of. 2. try to find (a person) by calling his name.

pag'eant (paj'ənt) n. elaborate show, parade, play, etc. —**pag'eant·ry,** n.

pa·go'da, n. towerlike temple of the Orient.

paid, pt. & pp. of **pay.**

pail, n. bucket. —**pail'ful,** n.

pain, n. 1. hurt felt in body or mind. 2. pl. great care. —v. cause pain to. —**pain'ful,** a. —**pain'less,** a.

pains'tak'ing, a. careful.

paint, n. pigment mixed with oil, water, etc. —v. 1. make pictures (of) with paint. 2. cover with paint. —**paint'er,** n. —**paint'ing,** n.

pair, n. two things, persons, etc. that match or make a unit. —v. form pairs (of).

pa·ja'mas, n.pl. jacket and trousers for sleeping.

pal, n. [Col.] close friend.

pal'ace, n. 1. monarch's residence. 2. magnificent building. —**pa·la'tial** (-shal) a.

pal'at·a·ble, a. pleasing to the taste.

pal'ate (-it) n. 1. roof of the mouth. 2. taste.

pale, a. 1. white; colorless. 2. not bright or intense. —n. 1. pointed fence stake. 2. bounds. —v. turn pale.

pa'le·on·tol'o·gy (pā'-) n. study of fossils. —**pa'le·on·tol'o·gist,** n.

pal'ette (-it) n. thin board on which artists mix paint

pal'frey (pôl'-) n. [pl. -FREYS] [Ar.] saddle horse.

pal·i·sade (pal-ə-sād') n. 1. fence of large pointed stakes for fortification. 2. pl. steep cliffs.

pall (pôl) v. [PALLED, PALL-ING] become boring. —n. dark covering as for a coffin.

pall'bear·er, n. bearer of a coffin at a funeral.

pal'let, n. straw bed.

pal'li·ate, v. 1. relieve; ease. 2. make seem less serious. —**pal·li·a'tion**, n. —**pal'li·a·tive**, a. & n.

pal'lid, a. pale. —**pal'lor**, n.

palm (päm) n. 1. tall tropical tree topped with a bunch of huge leaves. 2. its leaf: symbol of victory. 3. inside of the hand. —**palm off**, get rid of, sell, etc. by fraud.

pal·met'to, n. [pl. -TOS, -TOES] small palm tree.

palm'is·try, n. fortunetelling from the lines, etc. on a person's palm.

pal'o·mi'no (-mē'-) n. [pl. -NOS] pale-yellow horse with white mane and tail.

pal'pa·ble, a. 1. that can be touched, felt, etc. 2. obvious. —**pal'pa·bly**, adv.

pal'pi·tate, v. to throb. —**pal'pi·ta'tion**, n.

pal·sy (pôl'zi) n. paralysis in part of the body, often with tremors. —**pal'sied**, a.

pal·try (pôl'tri) a. [-TRIER, -TRIEST] trifling; petty.

pam'pas, n.pl. treeless plains of Argentina.

pam'per, v. be overindulgent with.

pam'phlet, n. thin, unbound booklet.

pan, n. broad, shallow container used in cooking, etc. —v.[PANNED, PANNING][Col.] criticize adversely. —**pan out**, [Col.] turn out (well).

pan-, pref. all; of all.

pan·a·ce'a, n. supposed remedy for all diseases.

pan'cake, n. thin cake of batter fried in a pan.

pan'cre·as, n. gland that secretes a digestive juice. —**pan'cre·at'ic**, a.

pan'da, n. white-and-black, bearlike animal of Asia.

pan·de·mo'ni·um, n. wild disorder or noise.

pan'der, v. 1. act as a pimp. 2. help others satisfy their desires. —n. pimp.

pane, n. sheet of glass.

pan·e·gyr'ic (-jir'-) n. speech or writing of praise.

pan'el, n. 1. flat section set off on a wall, door, etc. 2. group chosen for judging, discussing, etc. —v. provide with panels. —**pan'el·ing**, n.

pang, n. sudden, sharp pain.

pan'han'dle, v. [Sl.] beg on the streets.

pan'ic, n. sudden, wild fear. —v. [-ICKED, -ICKING] fill with panic. —**pan'ick·y**, a.

pan'o·ply, n. [pl. -PLIES] 1. suit of armor. 2. splendid display. —**pan'o·plied**, a.

pan·o·ra'ma (-ra'-) n. 1. unlimited view. 2. constantly changing scene.

pan'sy, n. [pl. -SIES] small plant with velvety petals.

pant, v. 1. breathe in pants. 2. long (for). 3. gasp out. —n. rapid, heavy breath.

pan·ta·loons', n.pl. trousers.

pan'ther, n. 1. cougar. 2. jaguar. 3. leopard.

pan'ties, n.pl. women's or children's short underpants.

pan'to·mime, n. & v. (make) use of gestures without words to present a play.

pan'try, n. [pl. -TRIES] a room for food, pots, etc.

pants, n.pl. trousers.

pap, n. soft food.

pa'pa, n. father: child's word.

pa'pa·cy, n. position, authority, etc. of the Pope.

pa'pal, a. of the Pope or the papacy.

pa·paw (pô'pô) n. tree with yellow fruit.

pa·pa'ya (-pä'-) n. tropical palmlike tree.

pa'per, n. 1. thin material in sheets, used to write or print on, wrap, etc. 2. sheet of this. 3. essay. 4. newspaper. 5. wallpaper. 6. pl. credentials. —a. of or like paper. —v. cover with wallpaper. —**pa'per·y**, a.

pa'per·back, n. book bound in paper.

pa'per·boy, n. boy who sells or delivers newspapers.

pa'pier-mâ·ché' (-pēr-mə-shā') n. wet paper pulp, molded into various objects.

pa·poose', n. North American Indian baby.

pap·ri'ka (-rē'-) n. ground, mild, red seasoning.

pa·py'rus, n. 1. paper made by ancient Egyptians from a water plant. 2. this plant.

par (pär) n. 1. equal rank. 2. average. 3. face value of stocks, etc. 4. expert score in golf.

par'a·ble (par'-) n. short, simple story with a moral.

par'a·chute (-shōōt) n. umbrellalike device used to slow down one dropping from an aircraft. —v. drop by para·chute. —par'a-chut·ist, n.

pa·rade', n. 1. showy display. 2. march or procession. —v. 1. march in a parade. 2. show off.

par'a·dise, n. 1. place or state of great happiness. 2. heaven.

par'a·dox, n. contradictory statement that is or seems false. —par'a·dox'i·cal, a.

par'af·fin, n. white, waxy substance used for making candles, sealing jars, etc.

par'a·gon, n. model of perfection or excellence.

par'a·graph, n. distinct section of a piece of writing, begun on a new line. —v. arrange in paragraphs.

par'a·keet, n. small parrot.

par'al·lel, a. 1. in the same direction and at a fixed distance apart. 2. similar. —n. 1. parallel line, surface, etc. 2. one like another. 3. circle parallel to the equator. —v. be parallel with.

par'al·lel'o·gram, n. 4-sided figure with opposite sides parallel and equal.

pa·ral'y·sis, n. 1. loss of power to move any part of the body. 2. a crippling.

par·a·lyt'ic (-lit'-) a. & n.

par'a·lyze (-līz) v. cause paralysis in.

par'a·mount, a. supreme.

par'a·mour (-moor) n. illicit lover or mistress.

par·a·noi'a, n. mental illness of feeling persecuted. —par'a·noid, a.

par'a·pet, n. wall for protection from enemy fire.

par·a·pher·na'li·a, n.pl. belongings or equipment.

par'a·phrase, n. a rewording. —v. reword.

par·a·ple'gi·a (-plē'ji-a) n. paralysis of the lower body. —par·a·ple'gic, a. & n.

par·a·pro·fes'sion·al, n. worker trained to assist a professional.

par'a·site, n. plant or animal that lives on or in another. —par'a·sit'ic, a.

par'a·sol (-sôl) n. light umbrella used as a sunshade.

par·a·troops, n.pl. unit of soldiers trained to parachute from airplanes behind enemy lines. —par'a·troop·er, n.

par'boil, v. boil until partly cooked.

par'cel (-s'l) n. 1. package. 2. piece (of land). —v. apportion (with out).

parcel post, postal branch which delivers parcels.

parch, v. 1. make hot and dry. 2. make thirsty.

parch'ment, n. skin of a sheep, etc. prepared as a surface for writing.

par'don, v. 1. to release from punishment. 2. excuse; forgive. —n. act of pardoning. —par'don·a·ble, a.

pare (pãr) v. 1. peel. 2. reduce gradually.

par·e·gor'ic, n. medicine with opium, for diarrhea, etc.

par'ent, n. 1. father or mother. 2. source. —pa·ren'tal, a. —par'ent·hood, n.

par'ent·age, n. descent from parents or ancestors.

pa·ren'the·sis, n. [pl. -SES (-sēz')] 1. word of explanation put into a sentence. 2. either of the marks ( ) used to set this off. —par'en·thet'i·cal, par'en·thet'ic, a.

par·fait' (pär-fā') n. icecream dessert in a tall glass.

pa·ri'ah (-ə) n. outcast.

par'ing, n. strip peeled off.

par'ish, n. 1. part of a diocese under a priest, etc. 2. church congregation.

pa·rish'ion·er, n. member of a parish.

par'i·ty, n. equality of value at a given ratio between moneys, commodities, etc.

park, n. public land for recreation or rest. —v. leave (a vehicle) temporarily.

par'ka, n. hooded coat.

parl'ance, n. mode of speech.

par'lay, v. bet winnings on another race, etc.

par'ley (-li) v. & n. talk to settle differences, etc.

par'lia·ment (-lə-) n. legislative body, spec. [P-] of Great Britain, Canada, etc. —par·lia·men'ta·ry, a.

par'lor, n. 1. living room. 2. business establishment, as a beauty parlor.

pa·ro'chi·al (-ki-əl) a. 1. of a parish. 2. limited; narrow.

par'o·dy, v. [-DIED, -DYING] & n. [-DIES] (write) a farcical imitation of a work.

pa·role', v. & n. release from prison on condition of future good behavior.

par'rot, n. brightly colored bird that can imitate speech. —v. repeat or copy without full understanding.

par'ry, v. [-RIED, -RYING] 1. ward off. 2. evade.

parse, v. analyze (a sentence) grammatically.

par'si·mo'ny, n. stinginess. —**par'si·mo'ni·ous,** a.

pars'ley, n. plant with leaves used to flavor some foods

pars'nip, n. sweet white root used as a vegetable.

par'son, n. minister or clergyman.

part, n. 1. portion, piece, element, etc. 2. duty. 3. role. 4. music for a certain voice or instrument in a composition. 5. usually pl. region. 6. dividing line formed in combing the hair. —v. 1. divide; separate. 2. go away from each other. —a. less than a whole. —**part with,** give up. —**take part,** participate.

par·take', v. [-TOOK, -TAKEN, -TAKING] have or take a share (of).

par'tial (-shəl) a. 1. favoring one over another. 2. not complete. —**partial to,** fond of. —**par'ti·al'i·ty,** n. —**par'tial·ly,** adv.

par·tic'i·pate (-tis'-) v. have or take a share with others (in). —**par·tic'i·pant,** n. —**par·tic'i·pa'tion,** n.

par'ti·ci·ple, n. verb form having the qualities of both a verb and adjective.

par'ti·cle, n. 1. tiny fragment. 2. preposition, article, or conjunction.

par·tic'u·lar, a. 1. of one; individual. 2. specific. 3. hard to please. —n. detail. —**par·tic'u·lar·ly,** adv.

part'ing, a. & n. 1. dividing. 2. departing.

par'ti·san (-z'n) n. 1. strong supporter; adherent. 2. guerrilla. —a. of a partisan.

par·ti'tion (-tish'ən) n. 1. division into parts. 2. thing that divides. —v. divide into parts.

part'ly, adv. not fully.

part'ner, n. one who undertakes something with another; associate; mate. —**part'ner·ship,** n.

part of speech, class of word, as noun, verb, etc.

par'tridge, n. game bird, as the pheasant, quail, etc.

part time, part of the usual time. —**part'-time',** a.

par·tu·ri'tion (-tish'-) n. childbirth.

par'ty, n. [pl. -TIES] 1. group working together for a political cause, etc. 2. social gathering. 3. one involved in a lawsuit, crime,

etc. 4. [Col.] person.

pas'chal (-k'l) a. of the Passover or Easter.

pass, v. 1. go by, beyond, etc. 2. go or change from one form, place, etc. to another. 3. cease; end. 4. approve or be approved. 5. cause or allow to go, move, qualify, etc. 6. spend time. 7. happen. 8. give as an opinion, judgment, etc. —n. 1. a passing. 2. free ticket. 3. brief military leave. 4. passage (n. 4). —**pass'a·ble,** a.

pas'sage, n. 1. a passing. 2. right to pass. 3. voyage. 4. road, opening, etc. 5. part of something written.

pas'sage·way', n. narrow way, as a hall, alley, etc.

pas'sen·ger, n. one traveling in a train, car, etc.

pass'er·by', n. [pl. PASSERSBY] one who passes by.

pass'ing, a. 1. that passes. 2. casual. —**in passing,** incidentally.

pas'sion, n. 1. strong emotion, as hate, love, etc. 2. object of strong desire. —**pas'sion·ate,** a.

pas'sive, a. 1. inactive, but acted upon. 2. yielding; submissive. —**pas·siv'i·ty,** n.

Pass'o·ver, n. Jewish holiday in the spring.

pass'port, n. government document identifying a citizen traveling abroad.

pass'word, n. secret word given to pass a guard.

past, a. 1. gone by. 2. of a former time. —n. 1. history. 2. time gone by. —prep. beyond in time, space, etc. —adv. to and beyond.

paste, n. 1. moist, smooth mixture. 2. adhesive mixture with flour, water, etc. —v. make adhere, as with paste. —**past'y,** a.

paste'board, n. stiff material of pasted layers of paper.

pas'tel', a. & n. soft and pale (shade).

pas'teur·ize (-tēr-, -chēr-) v. kill bacteria (in milk, etc.) by heating. —**pas'teur·i·za'tion,** n.

pas'time, n. way to spend spare time.

pas'tor, n. clergyman in charge of a congregation.

pas'to·ral, a. 1. of a pastor. 2. simple and rustic.

pas'try (pās'trĭ) n. [pl. -TRIES] fancy baked goods.

pas'ture (-chēr) n. ground

for grazing: also **pas'tur-age** (-ij). —v. let (cattle) graze.

pat, n. 1. gentle tap with something flat. 2. small lump, as of butter. —v. [PATTED, PATTING] give a gentle pat to. —a. suitable.

patch, n. 1. piece of material used to mend a hole, etc. 2. spot. —v. 1. put a patch on. 2. make crudely.

pate, n. top of the head.

pa·tel'la, n. [pl. -LAS, -LAE (-ē)] kneecap.

pat'ent, n. document granting exclusive rights over an invention. —a. 1. protected by patent. 2. (pā't'nt) obvious. —v. get a patent for.

patent leather, leather with a hard, glossy finish.

pa·ter'nal, a. 1. fatherly. 2. on the father's side. — **pa·ter'nal·ism,** n.

pa·ter'ni·ty, n. fatherhood.

path, n. 1. way worn by footsteps. 2. line of movement. 3. course of conduct.

pa·thet'ic, a. arousing pity. —**pa·thet'i·cal·ly,** adv.

pa·thol'o·gy, n. study of the nature and effect of disease. —**path'o·log'i·cal** (-loj'-) a. —**pa·thol'o·gist,** n.

pa'thos, n. the quality in a thing which arouses pity.

path'way, n. path.

pa'tient, a. 1. enduring pain, delay, etc. without complaint. 2. persevering. —n. one receiving medical care. —**pa'tience,** n. —**pa'tient·ly,** adv.

pat'i·na, n. green oxidized coating on bronze or copper.

pat'i·o, n. [pl. -os] 1. courtyard. 2. paved terrace near a house.

pa'tri·arch (-ärk) n. 1. father and head of a family or tribe. 2. dignified old man. —**pa'tri·ar'chal,** a.

pa·tri'cian (-shən) a. & n. aristocratic (person).

pat'ri·mo'ny, n. inheritance from one's father.

pa'tri·ot, n. one who shows love and loyalty for his country. —**pa'tri·ot'ic,** a. —**pa'tri·ot·ism,** n.

pa·trol', v. [-TROLLED, -TROLLING] make trips around in guarding. —n. a patrolling, or a group that patrols.

pa·trol'man, n. [pl. -MEN] policeman who patrols a certain area.

pa'tron, n. 1. a sponsor. 2. regular customer.

pa'tron·age (-ij) n. 1. help given by a patron. 2. customers, or their trade. 3. political favors.

pa'tron·ize, v. 1. sponsor. 2. be condescending to. 3. be a regular customer of.

pat'ter, v. 1. series of rapid taps. 2. glib talk. —v. make or utter (a) patter.

pat'tern, n. 1. one worthy of imitation. 2. plan used in making things. 3. design or decoration. 4. usual behavior, procedure, etc. —v. copy as from a pattern.

pat'ty, n. [pl. -TIES] flat cake of ground meat, etc.

pau'ci·ty (pô'-) n. 1. fewness. 2. scarcity.

paunch, n. fat belly.

pau'per, n. very poor person.

pause, v. & n. (make a) temporary stop.

pave, v. surface (a road, etc.) as with asphalt.

pave'ment, n. paved road, sidewalk, etc.

pa·vil'ion (-yən) n. 1. large tent. 2. building for exhibits, etc., as at a fair.

paw, n. foot of an animal with claws. —v. 1. touch, etc. with paws or feet. 2. handle roughly.

pawl, n. catch for teeth of a ratchet wheel.

pawn, v. give as security for a loan. —n. 1. chessman of lowest value. 2. person subject to another's will.

pawn'bro·ker, n. one whose business is lending money on things pawned with him.

pay, v. [PAID, PAYING] 1. give (money) to (one) for goods or services. 2. settle, as a debt. 3. give, as a compliment. 4. make, as a visit. 5. be profitable (to). —n. wages. —a. operated by coins. **pay out** [pt. PAYED OUT] let out, as a rope. —**pay·ee',** n. —**pay'er,** n. —**pay'ment,** n.

pay'a·ble, a. 1. that can be paid. 2. due to be paid.

pay'mas'ter, n. official in charge of paying employees.

pea, n. plant with pods having round, edible seeds.

peace, n. 1. freedom from war or strife. 2. agreement to end war. 3. law and order. 4. calm. —**peace'a·ble,** a.

peace'ful, a. 1. not fighting. 2. calm. 3. of a time of peace. —**peace'ful·ly,** adv.

peach, n. round, juicy, orange-yellow fruit.

pea′cock, *n.* male of a large bird (**pea′fowl**), with a long, showy tail.

peak, *n.* 1. pointed end or top. 2. mountain with pointed summit. 3. highest point.

peak′ed, *a.* thin and drawn.

peal, *n.* 1. loud ringing of bell(s). 2. loud, prolonged sound. —*v.* ring; resound.

pea′nut, *n.* 1. vine with underground pods and edible seeds. 2. the pod or a seed.

pear, *n.* soft, juicy fruit.

pearl (pûrl) *n.* 1. smooth, roundish stone formed in oysters, used as a gem. 2. mother-of-pearl. 3. bluish gray. —**pearl′y** [-IER, -IEST] *a.*

peas′ant (pez′-) *n.* farm worker of Europe, etc. —**peas′ant·ry,** *n.*

peat (pēt) *n.* decayed plant matter in bogs, dried for fuel.

peb′ble, *n.* small, smooth stone. —**peb′bly** [-BLIER, -BLIEST] *a.*

pe·can′, *n.* edible nut with a thin, smooth shell.

pec·ca·dil′lo, *n.* [*pl.* -LOES, -LOS] minor or petty sin.

pec′ca·ry, *n.* [*pl.* -RIES] wild piglike animal with tusks.

peck, *v.* strike as with a beak. —*n.* 1. stroke made as with a beak. 2. dry measure equal to 8 quarts.

pec′tin, *n.* substance in some fruits causing jelly to form.

pec′to·ral, *a.* of the chest.

pe·cul′iar (-kūl′yẽr) *a.* 1. of only one; exclusive. 2. special. 3. odd. —**pe·cu·li·ar′i·ty** [*pl.* -TIES] *n.*

pe·cu′ni·ar·y (-kū′-) *a.* of money.

ped′a·gogue, ped′a·gog (-gog) *n.* teacher. —**ped′a·go′gy** (-gō′ji) *n.* —**ped′a·gog′ic** (-goj′ik), **ped′a·gog′i·cal,** *a.*

ped′al, *n.* lever worked by the foot. —*v.* work by pedals. —*a.* of the foot.

ped′ant, *n.* one who stresses trivial points of learning. —**pe·dan′tic,** *a.* —**ped′ant·ry,** *n.*

ped′dle, *v.* go from place to place selling. —**ped′dler, ped′lar,** *n.*

ped′es·tal, *n.* base, as of a column, statue, etc.

pe·des′tri·an, *a.* 1. going on foot. 2. dull and ordinary. —*n.* one who goes on foot; walker.

pe′di·at′rics (pē′-) *n.* medical care and treatment of babies and children. —**pe′di·a·tri′cian** (-trish′ən) *n.*

ped′i·gree, *n.* ancestry; descent. —**ped′i·greed,** *a.*

peek, *v.* glance quickly and furtively. —*n.* glance.

peel, *v.* 1. cut away (the rind, etc.) of. 2. shed skin. —*n.* rind or skin of fruit. —**peel′ing,** *n.* rind peeled off.

peep, *v.* 1. make the chirping cry of a young bird. 2. look through a small opening. 3. appear partially. —*n.* 1. peeping sound. 2. furtive glimpse. —**peep′hole,** *n.*

peer, *n.* 1. an equal. 2. British noble. —*v.* look closely. —**peer′age** (-ij) *n.*

peer′less, *a.* without equal.

peeve, *v.* [Col.] make peevish. —*n.* [Col.] annoyance.

pee′vish, *a.* irritable.

peg, *n.* 1. short pin or bolt. 2. step or degree. —*v.* [PEGGED, PEGGING] fix or mark as with pegs.

pe′koe (-kō) *n.* a black tea.

pelf, *n.* mere wealth.

pel′i·can, *n.* water bird with a pouch in its lower bill.

pel·la′gra (-lā′grə *or* -lag′rə) *n.* disease caused by vitamin deficiency.

pel′let, *n.* little ball.

pell′-mell′, pell′mell′, *adv.* in reckless haste.

pel·lu′cid (-lōō′sid) *a.* clear.

pelt, *v.* 1. throw things at. 2. beat steadily. —*n.* skin of a fur-bearing animal.

pel′vis, *n.* cavity formed by bones of the hip and part of the backbone. —**pel′vic,** *a.*

pem′mi·can, pem′i·can, *n.* dried food concentrate.

pen, *n.* 1. enclosure for animals. 2. device for writing with ink. 3. [Sl.] penitentiary. —*v.* [PENNED (*for* 1 *also* PENT), PENNING] 1. enclose as in a pen. 2. write with a pen.

pe′nal, *a.* of or as punishment.

pe′nal·ize, *v.* punish.

pen′al·ty, *n.* [*pl.* -TIES] 1. punishment. 2. handicap.

pen′ance, *n.* voluntary suffering to show repentance.

pence, *n.* [Br.] *pl.* of penny.

pen′chant, *n.* strong liking.

pen′cil, *n.* device with a core of graphite, etc. for writing, etc. —*v.* write with a pencil.

pend, *v.* await decision.

pend′ant, *n.* hanging object used as an ornament.

pend′ent, *a.* suspended.

pend′ing, *a.* not decided. —

prep. 1. during. 2. until.

pen′du·lous (-joo-ləs) *a.* hanging freely.

pen′du·lum, *n.* weight hung so as to swing freely.

pen′e·trate, *v.* 1. enter by piercing. 2. affect throughout. 3. understand. —**pen′e·tra·ble**, *a.* —**pen′e·tra′tion**, *n.*

pen′guin (-gwin) *n.* flightless bird of the antarctic.

pen·i·cil′lin (-sil′-) *n.* antibiotic drug got from a mold.

pen·in′su·la, *n.* land area almost surrounded by water. —**pen·in′su·lar**, *a.*

pe′nis, *n.* male sex organ.

pen′i·tent, *a.* willing to atone. —*n.* penitent person. —**pen′i·tence**, *n.*

pen·i·ten′tia·ry (-shə-) *n.* [*pl.* -RIES] prison.

pen name, pseudonym.

pen′nant, *n.* 1. long, narrow flag. 2. championship.

pen′non, *n.* flag or pennant.

pen′ni·less, *a.* very poor.

pen′ny, *n.* 1. [*pl.* -NIES] cent. 2. [*pl.* PENCE] Br. coin, 1/12 shilling.

pe·nol′o·gy (pē-nol′-) *n.* study of prisons.

pen′sion, *n.* regular payment to a retired or disabled person. —*v.* pay a pension.

pen′sive (-siv) *a.* thoughtful; reflective.

pent, *a.* shut in; kept in.

pen′ta·gon, *n.* figure with five angles and five sides.

pen·tam′e·ter, *n.* line of verse of five metrical feet.

pent′house, *n.* apartment on the roof of a building.

pe·nu′ri·ous, *a.* stingy.

pen′u·ry (-yoo-) *n.* extreme poverty.

pe′on, *n.* Latin American worker. —**pe′on·age** (-ij) *n.*

pe′o·ny, *n.* [*pl.* -NIES] plant with large showy flowers.

peo′ple, *n.* [*pl.* -PLE] 1. human beings. 2. populace. 3. one's family. 4. [*pl.* -PLES] a nation, race, etc. —*v.* populate.

pep, *n.* [Sl.] energy. —*v.* [PEPPED, PEPPING] [Sl.] fill with pep (with *up*). —**pep′py**, *a.*

pep′per, *n.* 1. plant with a red or green, hot or sweet pod. 2. the pod. 3. spicy seasoning made from berries of a tropical plant. —*v.* 1. season with pepper (n. 3). 2. pelt with small objects.

pep′per·mint, *n.* mint plant yielding an oily flavoring.

pep′sin, *n.* stomach enzyme that helps digest proteins.

pep′tic, *a.* of digestion.

per, *prep.* 1. by means of. 2. for each.

per·am′bu·late, *v.* walk through or over.

per annum, by the year.

per·cale′ (-kāl′) *n.* cotton cloth used for sheets.

per cap′i·ta, for each person.

per·ceive′ (-sēv′) *v.* 1. grasp mentally. 2. become aware (of) through the senses.

per cent′, per cent.

per cent, out of every hundred. —*n.* [Col.] percentage.

per·cent′age, *n.* 1. rate per hundred. 2. portion.

per·cep′ti·ble, *a.* that can be perceived.

per·cep′tion, *n.* 1. ability to perceive. 2. knowledge got by perceiving.

per·cep′tive, *a.* able to perceive readily.

perch, *n.* 1. small food fish. 2. a pole or branch that birds roost on. —*v.* rest on a perch.

per·co·late, *v.* 1. filter. 2. make in a percolator.

per′co·la·tor, *n.* pot in which boiling water filters through ground coffee.

per·cus′sion (-kush′-) *n.* hitting of one thing against another.

per·di′tion (-dish′ən) *n.* 1. hell. 2. loss of one's soul.

per·emp′to·ry, *a.* 1. overbearing. 2. not to be refused.

per·en′ni·al, *a.* 1. lasting a year. 2. living more than two years. —*n.* plant living more than two years.

per′fect, *a.* 1. complete. 2. excellent. 3. completely accurate. —*v.* (pər-fekt′) make perfect. —**per·fect′i·ble**, *a.* —**per·fec′tion**, *n.*

per·fec′tion·ist, *n.*

per′fi·dy, *n.* [*pl.* -DIES] treachery. —**per·fid′i·ous**, *a.*

per′fo·rate, *v.* pierce with a hole or holes. —**per·fo·ra′tion**, *n.*

per·force′, *adv.* necessarily.

per·form′, *v.* 1. do; carry out. 2. act a role, play music, etc.

per·form′ance, *n.* 1. a doing or thing done. 2. display of one's skill or talent.

per·fume′ (-fūm′) *v.* scent with perfume. —*n.* (pûr′fūm) 1. fragrance. 2. liquid with a pleasing odor.

per·func′to·ry, *a.* done without care or interest.

per·haps', adv. possibly; probably.

per'i·gee (-jē) n. point nearest earth in a satellite's orbit.

per'il, v. & n. (put in) danger or risk. —**per'il·ous**, a.

per·im'e·ter, n. outer boundary of a figure or area.

pe'ri·od, n. 1. portion of time. 2. mark of punctuation (.).

pe'ri·od'ic, a. recurring at regular intervals.

pe'ri·od'i·cal, n. magazine published every week, month, etc. —a. periodic. —**pe'ri·od'i·cal·ly**, adv.

pe·riph'er·y, n. [pl. -IES] outer boundary or part. —**pe·riph'er·al**, a.

per'i·scope, n. tube with mirrors, etc., for seeing over or around an obstacle.

per'ish, v. be destroyed; die. **per·ish·a·ble**, n. & a. (food) liable to spoil.

per'i·to·ni'tis, n. inflammation of the membrane (**per'i·to·ne'um**) lining the abdominal cavity.

per'i·win'kle, n. myrtle (2).

per'jure, v. tell a lie while under oath.—**per'jur·er**, n. —**per'ju·ry** [pl. -RIES] n.

perk, v. 1. raise or liven (up). 2. make stylish or smart. —**perk'y** [-IER, -IEST] a.

per'ma·nent, a. lasting indefinitely. —**per'ma·nence**, n. —**per'ma·nent·ly**, adv.

per'me·ate, v. diffuse; penetrate (through or among). —**per'me·a·ble**, a.

per·mis'si·ble, a. allowable.

per·mis'sion, n. consent.

per·mis'sive, a. not restrictive.

per·mit', v. [-MITTED, -MITTING] allow. —n. (pûr'mit) document giving permission.

per'mu·ta'tion, n. a change, as in order.

per·ni'cious (-nish'əs) a. very harmful or damaging.

per'o·ra'tion, n. last part or summation of a speech.

per·ox'ide, n. see **hydrogen peroxide**.

per'pen·dic'u·lar, a. 1. at right angles to a given line or plane. 2. vertical. —n. perpendicular line.

per'pe·trate, v. do (something evil, wrong, etc.). —**per'pe·tra'tion**, n. —**per'pe·tra'tor**, n.

per·pet'u·al, a. 1. lasting forever. 2. constant.

per·pet'u·ate, v. cause to continue or be remembered. —**per·pet'u·a'tion**, n.

per·pe·tu'i·ty, n. existence forever.

per·plex', v. confuse or puzzle. —**per·plex'i·ty**, n.

per'qui·site (-zit) n. privilege or profit incidental to one's employment.

per se (sē) by (or in) itself.

per'se·cute', v. torment continuously for one's beliefs, etc. —**per'se·cu'tion**, n. —**per'se·cu'tor**, n.

per'se·vere' (-vēr') v. continue in spite of difficulty. —**per'se·ver'ance**, n.

per'si·flage (-fläzh) n. playful or joking talk.

per·sim'mon, n. orange-red, plumlike fruit.

per·sist', v. continue insistently or steadily. —**per·sist'ent**, a. —**per·sist'ence**, n.

per'son, n. 1. human being. 2. the body or self. 3. Gram. any of the three classes of pronouns indicating the identity of the subject, as I, you, he, etc.

per'son·age, n. (important) person.

per'son·al, a. 1. private; individual. 2. of the body. 3. of the character, conduct, etc. of a person. 4. indicating grammatical person. 5. other than real estate: said of property. —**per'son·al·ize'**, v. —**per'son·al·ly**, adv.

per'son·al'i·ty, n. [pl. -TIES] 1. distinctive or attractive character of a person. 2. notable person. 3. pl. offensive remarks about a person.

per·son'i·fy, v. [-FIED, -FYING]. 1. represent as a person. 2. typify. —**per·son'i·fi·ca'tion**, n.

per·son·nel', n. persons employed in any work, etc.

per·spec'tive, n. 1. appearance of objects from their relative distance and positions. 2. sense of proportion.

per'spi·ca'cious, a. having keen insight.

per·spire', v. to sweat. —**per'spi·ra'tion**, n.

per·suade', v. cause to do or believe by urging, etc. —**per·sua'sive**, a.

per·sua'sion, n. 1. a persuading. 2. belief.

pert, *a.* saucy; impudent.

per·tain′, *v.* 1. belong. 2. have reference.

per·ti·na′cious, *a.* persistent. —**per·ti·nac′i·ty,** *n.*

per′ti·nent, *a.* relevant; to the point. —**per′ti·nence,** *n.*

per·turb′, *v.* alarm; upset.

pe·ruse′ (-rōōz′) *v.* read. —**pe·rus′al,** *n.*

per·vade′, *v.* spread or be prevalent throughout. —**per·va′sive,** *a.*

per·verse′, *a.* 1. stubbornly contrary. 2. erring. 3. wicked. —**per·ver′si·ty,** *n.*

per·vert′, *v.* 1. lead astray; corrupt. —*n.* (pûr′vèrt) doer of abnormal sexual acts. —**per·ver′sion,** *n.*

pes′ky, *a.* [-KIER, -KIEST] [Col.] annoying.

pe·so (pā′sō) *n.* [*pl.* -SOS] monetary unit of Mexico, Cuba, etc.

pes′si·mism, *n.* tendency to expect the worst. —**pes′si·mist,** *n.* —**pes′si·mis′tic,** *a.*

pest, *n.* person or thing that causes trouble, etc.

pes′ter, *v.* annoy; vex.

pes′ti·cide, *n.* chemical for killing insects, weeds, etc.

pes′ti·lence, *n.* virulent or contagious disease. —**pes′ti·lent,** *a.*

pes′tle, *n.* tool used to pound or grind substances.

pet, *n.* 1. domesticated animal treated fondly. 2. favorite. 3. bad humor. —*a.* 1. favorite. 2. expressing fondness. —*v.* [PET-TED, PETTING] stroke gently.

pet′al, *n.* leaflike part of a blossom.

pet′cock, *n.* small valve for draining pipes, etc.

pe·tite′ (-tēt′) *a.* small and trim in figure.

pe·ti′tion, *n.* solemn, earnest request, esp. in writing. —*v.* address a petition to.

pet′rel, *n.* small sea bird.

pet′ri·fy, *v.* [-FIED, -FYING] 1. change into stony substance. 2. stun, as with fear.

pe·tro′le·um, *n.* oily liquid found in rock strata: it yields kerosene, gasoline, etc.

pet′ti·coat, *n.* skirt worn under an outer skirt.

pet′ty, *a.* [-TIER, -TIEST] 1. of little importance. 2. narrow-minded. 3. low in rank.

pet′u·lant (pech′-) *a.* impatient or irritable. —**pet′u·lance,** *n.*

pe·tu′ni·a, *n.* plant with funnel-shaped flowers.

pew (pū) *n.* row of fixed benches in a church.

pew′ter, *n.* alloy of tin with lead, brass, or copper.

pha′e·ton (fā′-) *n.* light, four-wheeled carriage.

pha′lanx, *n.* massed group of individuals.

phal′lus, *n.* image of the penis. —**phal′lic,** *a.*

phan′tom, *n.* 1. ghost; specter. 2. illusion. —*a.* unreal.

Phar·aoh (fâr′ō) *n.* title of ancient Egyptian rulers.

phar′i·see (fâr′-) *n.* self-righteous person.

phar′ma·ceu′ti·cal (fär′ma-sōō′-) *a.* 1. of pharmacy. 2. of or by drugs.

phar′ma·cist, *n.* one whose profession is pharmacy.

phar′ma·col′o·gy, *n.* study of drugs. —**phar′ma·col′o·gist,** *n.*

phar′ma·cy, *n.* [*pl.* -CIES] 1. science of preparing drugs and medicines. 2. drugstore.

phar′ynx (far′inks) *n.* cavity between mouth and larynx.

phase, *n.* 1. aspect; side. 2. one of a series of changes.

pheas′ant (fez′-) *n.* game bird with a long tail.

phe′no·bar′bi·tal′, *n.* white compound used as a sedative.

phe·nom′e·non, *n.* [*pl.* -NA] 1. observable fact or event. 2. anything very unusual. —**phe·nom′e·nal,** *a.*

phi′al (fī′-) *n.* vial.

phi·lan′der, *v.* make love insincerely. —**phi·lan′der·er,** *n.*

phi·lan′thro·py, *n.* 1. desire to help mankind. 2. [*pl.* -PIES] thing done to help mankind. —**phil′an·throp′ic,** *a.* —**phi·lan′thro·pist,** *n.*

phi·lat′e·ly, *n.* collection and study of postage stamps. —**phi·lat′e·list,** *n.*

phil′har·mon′ic, *a.* loving music.

Phi·lis′tine (-tin) *n.* one who is smugly conventional.

phil′o·den′dron, *n.* tropical American climbing plant.

phi·los′o·pher, *n.* one learned in philosophy.

phi·los′o·phize, *v.* to reason like a philosopher.

phi·los′o·phy, *n.* [*pl.* -PHIES] 1. study of ultimate reality, ethics, etc. 2. system of principles. 3. calmness. —**phil′o·soph′ic, phil′o·soph′i·cal,** *a.*

phle·bi′tis, *n.* inflammation of a vein.

phlegm (flem) *n.* mucus in the throat, as during a cold.

phleg·mat'ic, *a.* sluggish, unexcitable, etc.

phlox (floks) *n.* plant with clusters of flowers.

pho'bi·a, *n.* irrational, persistent fear of something.

phoe'be (fē'-) *n.* small bird.

phoe'nix, *n.* Egyptian myth. immortal bird.

phone, *n. & v.* [Col.] telephone.

pho·net'ics, *n.* science of speech sounds and the written representation of them. —**pho·net'ic,** *a.*

pho'no·graph, *n.* instrument that reproduces sound from grooved records.

pho'ny, *a.* [-NIER, -NIEST] & *n.* [*pl.* -NIES] [Sl.] fake.

phos'phate, *n.* 1. salt of phosphoric acid. 2. fertilizer containing phosphates.

phos'pho·res'cent, *a.* giving off light without heat. —**phos'pho·res'cence,** *n.*

phos'pho·rus, *n.* phosphorescent, waxy chemical element. —**phos·phor'ic, phos'pho·rous,** *a.*

pho'to, *n.* [*pl.* -TOS] [Col.] a photograph.

pho'to·e·lec'tric, *a.* of the electric effects produced by light on some substances.

pho'to·en·grav'ing, *n.* reproduction of photographs in relief on printing plates. —**pho'to·en·grav'er,** *n.*

pho·to·gen'ic (-jen'-) *a.* attractive to photograph.

pho'to·graph, *n.* picture made by photography. —*v.* take a photograph of. —**pho·tog'ra·pher,** *n.*

pho·tog'ra·phy, *n.* process of producing images on a surface sensitive to light. —**pho'to·graph'ic,** *a.*

pho'to·stat, *n.* 1. device for making photographic copies of printed matter, etc.: trademark (**P**-). 2. copy so made. —*v.* make a photostat of. —**pho'to·stat'ic,** *a.*

pho'to·syn'the·sis (-sin'-) *n.* formation of carbohydrates in plants by the action of sunlight.

phrase, *n.* 1. short, colorful expression. 2. group of words, not a sentence or clause, conveying a single idea. —*v.* express in words.

phra'se·ol'o·gy *n.* wording.

phy'lum (fī'-) *n.* [*pl.* -LA] basic division of plants or animals.

phys'ic (fiz'-) *n.* cathartic.

phys'i·cal, *a.* 1. of matter.

2. of physics. 3. of the body. —*n.* physical examination. —**phys'i·cal·ly,** *adv.*

physical therapy, treatment of disease by massage, exercise, etc.

phy·si'cian (-zish'ən) *n.* doctor of medicine.

phys'ics, *n.* science that deals with matter and energy. —**phys'i·cist,** *n.*

phys·i·og'no·my, *n.* [*pl.* -MIES] face.

phys·i·ol'o·gy, *n.* science of the functions of living organisms. —**phys'i·o·log'i·cal,** *a.* —**phys'i·ol'o·gist,** *n.*

phys'i·o·ther'a·py, *n.* physical therapy.

phy·sique' (-zēk') *n.* form or build of the body.

pi (pī) *n.* symbol (π) for the ratio of circumference to diameter, about 3.1416.

pi·a·nis'si·mo (pē'-) *a. & adv. Mus.* very soft.

pi·an'ist (or pē'ə-nist) *n.* piano player.

pi·an'o, *n.* [*pl.* -OS] keyboard instrument with hammers that strike steel wires: also **pi·an'o·for'te.** —*a. & adv.* (-än'-) *Mus.* soft.

pi·az'za, *n.* 1. in Italy, public square. 2. veranda.

pi·ca·yune', *a.* trivial.

pic'ca·lil'li, *n.* relish of vegetables, mustard, etc.

pic'co·lo, *n.* [*pl.* -LOS] small flute.

pick, *v.* 1. scratch or dig at with something pointed. 2. gather, pluck, etc. 3. choose; select. 4. provoke (a fight). —*n.* 1. choice. 2. the best. 3. pointed tool for breaking up soil, etc. 4. plectrum. —**pick on,** [Col.] criticize; tease. —**pick out,** choose. —**pick up,** 1. lift. 2. get, find, etc. 3. gain (speed). 4. improve. —**pick'er,** *n.*

pick'a·back, *adv.* on the back.

pick'ax, pick'axe, *n.* pick with one end of the head pointed, the other axlike.

pick'er·el, *n.* fish with a narrow, pointed snout.

pick'et, *n.* 1. pointed stake. 2. soldier(s) on guard duty 3. striking union member etc. stationed outside a factory, etc. —*v.* place or be a picket at.

pick'ings, *n.pl.* scraps.

pick'le, *n.* preserve in vinegar, brine, etc. —*n.* cucumber, etc. so preserved.

pick'pock'et, *n.* one who steals from pockets.

pick'up, *n.* 1. power of speeding up. 2. small truck.

pic'nic, *n.* outing with an outdoor meal. —*v.* [-NICKED, -NICKING] hold a picnic. —**pic'nick·er,** *n.*

pic·to'ri·al, *a.* of or expressed in pictures.

pic'ture, *n.* 1. likeness made by painting, photography, etc. 2. description. 3. motion picture. —*v.* 1. make a picture of. 2. describe. 3. imagine.

pic'tur·esque' ('-esk') *a.* 1. having natural beauty. 2. quaint. 3. vivid.

pid'dle, *v.* dawdle; trifle.

pidg'in English (pij'-) mixture of English & Chinese.

pie, *n.* fruit, meat, etc. baked on or in a crust.

pie'bald, *a.* covered with patches of two colors.

piece, *n.* 1. part broken off or separated. 2. part complete in itself. 3. single thing. —*v.* join (together) the pieces of.

piece'meal, *a.* & *adv.* (made or done) piece by piece.

piece'work, *n.* work which one is paid for by the piece.

pier (pēr) *n.* 1. landing place built over water. 2. heavy, supporting column.

pierce (pērs) *v.* 1. pass through as a needle does. 2. make a hole in. 3. sound sharply. —**pierc'ing,** *a.*

pi'e·ty, *n.* devotion to religious duties, etc.

pig, *n.* 1. fat farm animal; swine. 2. [Col.] greedy or filthy person. —**pig'gish,** *a.*

pi·geon (pij'ən) *n.* plump bird with a small head.

pi'geon·hole, *v.* & *n.* (put in) a compartment, as in a desk, for filing papers.

pi'geon-toed', *a.* having the toes or feet turned in.

pig'gy·back, *adv.* pickaback.

pig'head'ed, *a.* stubborn.

pig iron, molten iron.

pig'ment, *n.* coloring matter.

pig'men·ta'tion, *n.* coloration in plants or animals.

pig'my, *a.* & *n.* [*pl.* -MIES] pygmy.

pig'skin, *n.* leather made from the skin of a pig.

pig'tail, *n.* braid of hair hanging down the back.

pike, *n.* 1. slender, freshwater fish. 2. turnpike. 3. metal-tipped spear.

pi·las'ter, *n.* column projecting from a wall.

pile, *n.* 1. mass of things heaped together. 2. thick nap, as on a rug. 3. heavy, vertical beam. —*v.* 1. heap up. 2. accumulate. 3. crowd.

piles, *n.pl.* hemorrhoids.

pil'fer, *v.* steal; filch.

pil'grim, *n.* traveler to a holy place. —**pil'grim·age,** *n.*

pill, *n.* pellet of medicine to be swallowed whole.

pil'lage (-ij) *v.* & *n.* plunder.

pil'lar, *n.* upright support.

pil'lion (-yən) *n.* extra seat on a horse or motorcycle.

pil'lo·ry, *n.* [*pl.* -RIES] device with holes for head & hands, in which offenders were locked. —*v.* [-RIED, -RYING] expose to public scorn.

pil'low, *n.* bag of soft material, to support the head, as in sleeping. —*v.* rest as on a pillow.

pil'low·case', *n.* removable covering for a pillow: also **pil'low·slip'.**

pi'lot, *n.* 1. one whose job is steering ships in harbors, etc. 2. one who flies an airplane. 3. guide. —*v.* be pilot of, in, etc.

pi·men'to (-tō) *n.* [*pl.* -TOS] sweet, red pepper: also **pi·mien'to** (-myen'-).

pimp, *v.* & *n.* (act as) a prostitute's agent.

pim'ple, *n.* small, sore swelling of the skin. —**pim'ply** [-PLIER, -PLIEST] *a.*

pin, *n.* 1. pointed piece of wire to fasten things together. 2. thin rod to hold things with. 3. thing like a pin. 4. ornament with a pin to fasten it. 5. club at which a ball is bowled. —*v.* [PINNED, PINNING] fasten as with a pin.

pin'a·fore, *n.* apronlike garment for girls.

pin'cers, *n.pl.* 1. tool for gripping things. 2. claw of a crab, etc. Also **pinch'ers.**

pinch, *v.* 1. squeeze between two surfaces. 2. make look thin, gaunt, etc. 3. be stingy. —*n.* 1. a squeeze. 2. small amount. 3. emergency.

pinch'-hit', *v.* [-HIT, -HITTING] substitute (for one).

pin'cush'ion, *n.* small cushion to stick pins in.

pine, *n.* 1. evergreen tree with cones and needle-shaped leaves. 2. its wood. —*v.* 1. waste (away) through grief, etc. 2. yearn.

pine'ap'ple, n. large, juicy tropical fruit.

pin'feath'er, n. undeveloped feather.

ping, n. sound of a bullet striking something sharply.

ping'-pong', n. table tennis: trademark (**P-**).

pin'ion (-yən) n. 1. small cogwheel. 2. wing or wing feather. —v. bind the wings or arms of.

pink, n. 1. plant with paled-red flowers. 2. pale red. 3. finest condition. —v. cut a saw-toothed edge on (cloth).

pin'na·cle, n. 1. slender spire. 2. mountain peak. 3. highest point.

pi·noch·le (pē'nuk''l) n. card game using a double deck above the eight.

pin'point, v. show the precise location of.

pint, n. ½ quart.

pin'to, a. & n. piebald (horse).

pin'-up', a. that can be fastened to a wall. —n. [Sl.] pin-up picture, esp. of a girl.

pi'o·neer', n. early settler, first investigator, etc. —v. be a pioneer.

pi'ous, a. having, showing, or pretending religious devotion. —**pi'ous·ly,** adv.

pipe, n. 1. long tube for conveying water, gas, etc. 2. tube with a bowl at one end, for smoking tobacco. 3. tube for making musical sounds. —v. 1. utter in a shrill voice. 2. convey (water, etc.) by pipes. 3. play (a tune) on a pipe. —**pip'er,** n.

pip'ing, n. 1. music made by pipes. 2. shrill sound. 3. pipelike cloth trimming.

pip'pin, n. kind of apple.

pi·quant (pē'kənt) a. 1. agreeably pungent. 2. stimulating. —**pi'quan·cy,** n.

pique (pēk) n. resentment at being slighted. —v. 1. offend. 2. excite.

pi·qué' (-kā') n. cotton fabric with vertical cords.

pi'rate (-rit) n. 1. one who robs ships at sea. 2. one who uses a copyrighted or patented work without authorization. —v. be a pirate. —**pi'ra·cy,** n.

pir'ou·ette' (-ōō-et') n. a whirling on the toes. —v. [-ETTED, -ETTING] do a pirouette.

pis'ca·to'ri·al, a. of fishing.

pis·ta'chi·o (-tä'shi-) n.

[pl. -OS] greenish nut.

pis'til, n. seed-bearing organ of a flower.

pis'tol, n. small firearm held with one hand.

pis'ton, n. disk that moves back and forth in a hollow cylinder: it pushes against or is pushed by a fluid.

pit, n. 1. stone of a plum, peach, etc. 2. hole in the ground. 3. small hollow in a surface. 4. section for the orchestra in front of the stage. —v. [PITTED, PITTING] 1. remove the pit (stone) from. 2. mark with pits. 3. set in competition (*against*).

pitch, v. 1. set up (tents). 2. throw. 3. plunge forward. 4. set at some level, key, etc. 5. rise and fall, as a ship. —n. 1. throw. 2. point or degree. 3. degree of slope. 4. highness or lowness of a musical sound. 5. black, sticky substance from coal tar, etc. —**pitch in,** [Col.] begin working hard.

pitch'blende, n. dark, uranium-bearing mineral.

pitch'er, n. 1. container for holding and pouring liquids. 2. baseball player who pitches to the batters.

pitch'fork, n. large fork for lifting and tossing hay.

pit'e·ous, a. deserving pity. —**pit'e·ous·ly,** adv.

pit'fall, n. 1. covered pit as a trap. 2. hidden danger.

pith, n. 1. soft, spongy tissue in the center of plant stems. 2. essential part.

pith'y, a. [-IER, -IEST] full of meaning or force.

pit'i·a·ble, a. 1. deserving pity. 2. deserving contempt. —**pit'i·a·bly,** adv.

pit'i·ful, a. 1. arousing or deserving pity. 2. contemptible. —**pit'i·ful·ly,** adv.

pit'i·less, a. without pity.

pit'tance, n. small amount, esp. of money.

pit'ter-pat'ter, n. rapid series of tapping sounds.

pi·tu'i·tar'y, a. of a small endocrine gland attached to the brain.

pit'y, n. 1. sorrow for another's misfortune. 2. cause for sorrow or regret. —v. [-IED, -YING] feel pity (for).

piv'ot, n. 1. person or thing on which something turns or depends. 2. pivoting motion. —v. provide with or turn on a pivot. —**piv'ot·al,** a.

pix'y, pix'ie, n. [pl. -IES] fairy; sprite.

piz·za (pēt'sə) n. [It.] baked dish of thin dough, etc.

plac'ard (-ärd) v. & n. (put up) a sign in a public place.

pla'cate, v. appease.

place, n. 1. space. 2. region. 3. city or town. 4. residence. 5. particular building, site, part, position, etc. 6. job or its duties. —v. 1. put in a certain place. 2. identify by some relationship. —**in place of,** rather than. —**take place,** occur.

place'ment, n. a placing, esp. in a job.

pla·cen'ta, n. organ in the uterus to nourish the fetus.

plac'er (plas'-) n. gravel with gold, etc. in it.

plac'id (plas'-) a. calm.

plack'et, n. slit at the waist of a skirt or dress.

pla'gia·rize (-ja-) v. offer another's writings as one's own. —**pla'gia·rism,** n. —**pla'gia·rist,** n.

plague (plāg) n. 1. affliction. 2. deadly epidemic disease. —v. vex; trouble.

plaid (plad) n. & a. (cloth) with crisscross pattern.

plain, a. 1. clear. 2. outspoken. 3. obvious. 4. simple. 5. homely. 6. not fancy. 7. common. —n. extent of flat land. —adv. clearly. —**plain'ly,** adv. —**plain'ness,** n.

plaint, n. complaint.

plain'tiff, n. one who brings a suit into a court of law.

plain'tive, a. sad; mournful.

plait (plāt) v. & n. 1. braid. 2. pleat.

plan, n. 1. outline; map. 2. way of doing; scheme. —v. [PLANNED, PLANNING] 1. make a plan of or for. 2. intend. —**plan'ner,** n.

plane, a. flat. —n. 1. flat surface. 2. level or stage. 3. airplane. 4. carpenter's tool for leveling or smoothing. —v. smooth or level with a plane.

plan'et, n. any of nine heavenly bodies revolving around the sun. —**plan'e·tar'y,** a.

plan·e·tar'i·um, n. large domed room for projecting images of the heavens.

plank, n. 1. long, broad, thick board. 2. a principle in a political platform. —v. cover with planks.

plank'ton, n. tiny animals and plants floating in bodies of water.

plant, n. 1. living thing that cannot move, as a tree, flower, etc. 2. factory. —v. 1. put in the ground to grow. 2. set firmly in place.

plan'tain (-tin) n. 1. weed with broad leaves. 2. plant with bananalike fruit.

plan·ta'tion, n. estate with its workers living on it.

plaque (plak) n. flat, decorative piece of wood or metal.

plas'ma, n. fluid part of blood or lymph.

plas'ter, n. lime, sand, and water, mixed as a coating that hardens on walls. —v. cover as with plaster.

plaster of Paris, paste of gypsum and water that hardens quickly.

plas'tic, a. 1. that shapes or can be shaped. 2. of plastic. —n. substance that can be molded and hardened.

plastic surgery, surgical grafting of skin or bone.

plat, n. 1. map. 2. plot (n. 1).

plate, n. 1. shallow dish. 2. plated dinnerware. 3. cast of molded type. 4. engraved illustration. 5. denture. 6. metal in sheets for armor. —v. coat with metal.

pla·teau' (-tō') n. 1. tract of high, level land. 2. period of no progress.

plat'form, n. 1. raised horizontal surface. 2. political party's stated aims.

plat'i·num, n. silvery, precious metal, a chemical element.

plat'i·tude, n. trite remark.

pla·toon' (-tōōn') n. small group, as of soldiers.

plat'ter, n. large serving dish.

plat'y·pus, n. [pl. -PUSES, -PI (-pī)] duckbill.

plau'dits (plô'-) n. applause.

plau'si·ble, a. credible. —**plau'si·bil'i·ty,** n.

play, v. 1. have fun. 2. do in fun. 3. take part in a game or sport. 4. perform on a musical instrument. 5. trifle. 6. cause. 7. act in a certain way. 8. act the part of. —n. 1. recreation. 2. fun. 3. motion or freedom for motion. 4. move in a game. 5. drama. —**play up,** [Col.] emphasize.

play'boy, n. [Col.] rich man who dissipates much.

play'ful, a. full of fun; frisky. —**play'ful·ly,** adv.

—play′ful·ness, n.

play′ground, n. outdoor place for games and play.

playing cards, cards in four suits for playing games.

play′-off′, n. final match played to break a tie.

play on words, pun.

play′wright (-rīt) n. one who writes plays.

pla′za (plaz′ə or plä′zə) n. public square.

plea, n. 1. appeal; request. 2. statement in defense.

plead, v. 1. beg; entreat. 2. argue (a law case). 3. offer as an excuse.

pleas′ant, a. pleasing; agreeable. —pleas′ant·ly, adv.

pleas′ant·ry, n. [pl. -RIES] jocular remark.

please, v. 1. satisfy. 2. be the wish of. 3. be obliging enough to: used in polite requests. —pleased, a.

pleas′ing, a. giving pleasure. —pleas′ing·ly, adv.

pleas′ure, n. 1. delight or satisfaction. 2. one's wish. —pleas′ur·a·ble, a.

pleat, n. fold made by doubling cloth. —v. make pleats in.

ple·be′ian (-bē′ən) a. & n. common (person).

pleb′i·scite (-sīt) n. direct popular vote on an issue.

plec′trum, n. small device for plucking a banjo, etc.

pledge, n. 1. thing given as security for a contract, etc. 2. promise. —v. 1. give as security. 2. promise.

ple′na·ry, a. full or fully attended.

plen′i·po·ten′ti·a·ry (-shi-) a. having full authority. —n. [pl. -IES] ambassador.

plen′i·tude, n. fullness.

plen′ti·ful, a. abundant: also plen′te·ous.

plen′ty, n. 1. prosperity. 2. ample amount.

pleth′o·ra, n. overabundance.

pleu·ri·sy (ploor′ə-si) n. inflammation of membrane lining the chest cavity.

pli′a·ble, a. easily bent; flexible. —pli′a·bil′i·ty, n.

pli′ers, n.pl. small pincers.

plight (plīt) n. condition, esp. a bad or dangerous one. —v. 1. pledge. 2. betroth.

plod, v. [PLODDED, PLODDING] 1. trudge. 2. work steadily.

plop, n. sound of object falling into water. —v. [PLOPPED, PLOPPING] fall with a plop.

plot, n. 1. piece of ground. 2. diagram, plan, etc. 3. secret, esp. evil, scheme. —v. [PLOTTED, PLOTTING] 1. make a map, plan, etc. of. 2. scheme. —plot′ter, n.

plov′er (pluv′-) n. shore bird with long, pointed wings.

plow, plough (plou) n. 1. implement for cutting and turning up soil. 2. machine for removing snow. —v. 1. use a plow (on). 2. make one's way. —plow′man, plough′man [pl. -MEN] n.

plow′share, plough′share, n. blade of a plow.

pluck, v. 1. pull off or out. 2. pull at and release quickly. —n. 1. a pull. 2. courage.

pluck′y, a. 1. brave; spirited.

plug, n. 1. stopper. 2. device for making electrical contact. 3. worn-out horse. 4. [Sl.] insinuated advertisement. —v. [PLUGGED, PLUGGING] 1. stop up with a plug. 2. [Sl.] hit with a bullet. 3. [Sl.] advertise with a plug. 4. [Col.] work doggedly.

plum, n. 1. smooth-skinned, juicy fruit. 2. choice thing.

plum′age (ploom′-) n. a bird's feathers.

plumb (plum) n. weight on a line for checking a vertical wall or sounding a depth. —a. perpendicular. —adv. 1. straight down. 2. [Col.] entirely. —v. 1. test with a plumb. 2. solve.

plumb′er, n. one who fits and repairs water pipes, etc. —plumb′ing, n.

plume, n. feather or tuft of feathers. —v. 1. adorn with plumes. 2. preen.

plum′met, v. fall straight downward. —n. plumb.

plump, a. full and rounded. —v. drop heavily. —adv. suddenly; heavily.

plun′der, v. rob by force. —n. goods plundered.

plunge, v. 1. thrust suddenly (into). 2. dive or rush. —n. dive or fall.

plung′er, n. part that moves with a plunging motion.

plunk, v. 1. strum (a banjo, etc.). 2. put down heavily. —n. sound of plunking.

plu′ral, a. more than one. —n. Gram. word form designating more than one. —plu′ral·ize, v.

plu·ral′i·ty, n. 1. majority. 2. excess of winner's votes over his nearest rival's.

plus, prep. added to. —a. 1.

designating a sign (+) showing addition. 2. positive. 3. more than. —n. something added.

plush, n. fabric with a long pile. —a. [Sl.] luxurious.

plu′to·crat, n. wealthy person with great influence.

plu·to′ni·um, n. radioactive chemical element.

ply, n. [pl. PLIES] one layer in plywood, folded cloth, etc. —v. [PLIED, PLYING] 1. work at (a trade) or with (a tool). 2. keep supplying (with). 3. travel back and forth (between).

ply′wood, n. board made of glued layers of wood.

P.M., p.m., after noon.

pneu·mat′ic (noo-) a. 1. of or containing air or gases. 2. worked by compressed air.

pneu·mo′ni·a (noo-) n. acute disease of the lungs.

poach (pōch) v. 1. boil the contents of (an egg). 2. hunt or fish illegally. —**poach′er,** n.

pock′et, n. 1. little bag or pouch, esp. when sewed into clothing. 2. pouchlike cavity or hollow. —a. that can be carried in a pocket. —v. 1. put into a pocket. 2. hide; suppress. —**pock′et·ful,** n.

pock′et·book, n. purse.

pock′et·knife, n. [pl. -KNIVES] small knife with folding blades.

pock′mark, n. scar left by a pustule: also **pock.**

pod, n. shell of peas, beans, etc. containing the seeds.

po·di′a·trist (-dī′-), n. one who treats foot ailments. —**po·di′a·try,** n.

po′di·um, n. platform for an orchestra conductor.

po′em, n. piece of imaginative writing in rhythm, rhyme, etc.

po′et, n. writer of poems.

po′et·ry, n. 1. writing of poems. 2. poems. 3. rhythms, deep feelings, etc. of poems. —**po·et′ic, po·et′i·cal,** a.

poign·ant (poin′yant) a. 1. painful to the feelings. 2. keen. —**poign′an·cy,** n.

poin·set′ti·a (or -ta) n. plant with petallike red leaves.

point, n. 1. a dot. 2. specific place or time. 3. stage or degree reached. 4. item; detail. 5. special feature. 6. unit, as of a game score. 7. sharp end. 8. cape (land). 9. purpose; object. 10. mark showing direction on a compass. —v. 1. sharpen to a point. 2. call attention (to). 3. show. 4. aim. —**at the point of,** very close to. —**beside the point,** irrelevant. —**to the point,** pertinent.

point′-blank′, a. & adv. 1. (aimed) straight at a mark. 2. direct(ly).

point′er, n. 1. long, tapered rod for pointing. 2. indicator. 3. large hunting dog. 4. [Col.] hint; suggestion.

point′less a. without meaning. —**point′less·ly,** adv.

poise (poiz) n. 1. balance. 2. ease and dignity of manner. —v. balance.

poi′son, n. substance which can cause illness or death. —v. 1. harm or kill with poison. 2. put poison into. 3. corrupt. —**poi′son·ous,** a.

poke, v. 1. prod, as with a stick. 2. search (about or around). 3. move slowly (along). —n. jab; thrust.

poke fun (at), ridicule.

pok′er, n. 1. gambling game with cards. 2. iron bar for stirring a fire.

pok′y, pok′ey, a. [-IER, -IEST] slow; dull.

polar bear, large white bear of arctic regions.

pole, n. 1. long, slender piece of wood, metal, etc. 2. end of an axis, as of the earth. 3. either of two opposed forces, as the ends of a magnet. —v. propel (a boat) with a pole. —**po′lar,** a.

pole′cat, n. 1. weasellike animal of Europe. 2. skunk.

po·lem′ics, n. art or practice of disputation. —**po·lem′ic, a. & n.**

pole vault, a leap for height by vaulting with aid of a pole. —**pole′vault,** v.

po·lice′ n. 1. department of a city, etc. for keeping law and order. 2. [construed as pl.] members of such a department. —v. control, keep with police.

po·lice′man, n. [pl. -MEN] member of a police force.

pol′i·cy, n. [pl. -CIES] 1. governing principle, plan, etc. 2. insurance contract.

pol′i·o·my′e·li′tis, n. virus disease often resulting in paralysis: also **po′li·o.**

Pol′ish (pōl′-) n. & a. (language) of Poland.

pol′ish (pol′-) v. 1. smooth and brighten, as by rubbing.

2. refine (manners, etc.). — n. 1. surface gloss. 2. elegance. 3. substance used to polish.

po·lite′, a. 1. showing good manners. 2. refined. — **po·lite′ly**, adv.

pol′i·tic, a. wise or shrewd.

po·lit′i·cal, a. of government, politics, etc.

pol′i·ti′cian (-tish′ən) n. one active in politics.

pol′i·tics, n. 1. science of government. 2. political affairs.

pol′i·ty, n. [pl. -TIES] 1. system of government. 2. a state.

pol′ka (pōl′-) n. fast dance for couples.

pol′ka dot (pō′-) any of a pattern of dots on cloth.

poll (pōl) n. 1. a counting or listing as of voters. 2. number of votes recorded. 3. pl. voting place. 4. survey of opinion. —v. 1. take the votes or opinions of. 2. receive, as votes.

pol′len, n. powderlike sex cells on flower stamens.

pol′li·nate, v. put pollen on the pistil of. —**pol′li·na′tion**, n.

pol′li·wog, n. tadpole.

pol·lute′, v. make unclean or impure. —**pol·lu′tion**, n.

po′lo (-lō) n. team game played on horseback.

pol·troon′, n. coward.

poly–, pref. much; many.

po·lyg′a·my (-lig′ə-mi) n. a being married to more than one person at one time. —**po·lyg′a·mist**, n.

pol′y·gon, n. figure with more than four angles and sides.

pol′y·graph, n. device measuring bodily changes, used on one suspected of lying.

pol′yp (-ip) n. slender water animal with tentacles.

pol′y·syl′la·ble, n. word of more than three syllables. —**pol′y·syl·lab′ic**, a.

pol′y·the·ism (-thē′-) n. belief in more than one god. —**pol′y·the·is′tic**, a.

po·made′, n. perfumed ointment for the hair.

pome·gran′ate (pom′gran′-) n. round, red fruit with a hard rind and many seeds.

pom′mel (pum′-) n. rounded, upward-projecting front part of a saddle. —v. beat, as with the fists.

pomp, n. stately or ostentatious display.

pom′pa·dour (-dôr) n. hair style with the hair brushed up high from the forehead.

pom′pon, n. decorative tuft, as of silk.

pom′pous, a. pretentious. —**pom·pos′i·ty**, n.

pon′cho (-chō) n. [pl. -CHOS] cloak like a blanket.

pond, n. small lake.

pon′der, v. think deeply (about).

pon′der·ous, a. heavy; clumsy.

pone, n. corn meal bread.

pon·gee′ (-jē′) n. soft, silk cloth.

pon′iard (-yërd) n. dagger.

pon′tiff, n. 1. the Pope. 2. bishop. —**pon·tif′i·cal**, a.

pon·tif′i·cate, v. be dogmatic or pompous.

pon·toon′, n. one of the floats supporting a bridge or airplane on water.

po′ny, n. [pl. -NIES] small horse.

poo′dle, n. curly-haired dog.

pooh, int. exclamation of contempt, disbelief, etc.

pool, n. 1. small pond. 2. puddle. 3. tank for swimming. 4. billiards on a table with pockets. 5. common fund of money, etc. —v. put into a common fund.

poop, n. raised deck at the stern of a sailing ship.

poor, a. 1. having little money. 2. below average; inferior. 3. worthy of pity. —**poor′ly**, adv.

pop, n. 1. light, explosive sound. 2. flavored soda water. —v. [POPPED, POP-PING] 1. make, or burst with, a pop. 2. cause to pop. 3. move, go, etc. suddenly. 4. bulge. —adv. like a pop.

pop′corn, n. corn with kernels that pop when heated.

Pope, pope, n. head of the Roman Catholic Church.

pop′lar (-lēr) n. tall tree.

pop′lin, n. ribbed cloth.

pop′o′ver, n. hollow muffin.

pop′py, n. [pl. -PIES] plant with showy flowers.

pop′u·lace (-lis) n. the common people.

pop′u·lar, a. 1. of, by, or for people generally. 2. very well liked. —**pop′u·lar′i·ty**, n. —**pop′u·lar·ize′**, v.

pop′u·late, v. inhabit.

pop′u·la′tion, n. total number of inhabitants.

pop′u·lous, a. full of people.

por′ce·lain (-s′l-in) n. hard, fine, glazed earthenware.

porch, *n.* open or screen-enclosed room on the outside of a building.

por'cine, *a.* of or like pigs.

por'cu·pine, *n.* gnawing animal with long, sharp spines in its coat.

pore, *v.* study or ponder (*over*). —*n.* tiny opening, as in the skin, for absorbing or discharging fluids.

pork, *n.* flesh of a pig used as food.

por·nog'ra·phy, *n.* writings, pictures, etc. intended to arouse sexual desire. —**por'no·graph'ic,** *a.*

por'ous, *a.* full of pores or tiny holes. —**po·ros'i·ty,** *n.*

por'poise (-pəs) *n.* sea mammal with a blunt snout.

por'ridge, *n.* cereal or meal boiled in water or milk.

por'rin·ger (-jẽr) *n.* bowl for porridge, etc.

port, *n.* 1. harbor. 2. city with a harbor. 3. sweet, dark-red wine. 4. left side of a ship as one faces the bow. 5. porthole. 6. opening, as in a valve frame.

port'a·ble, *a.* that can be carried.

port'age, *n.* 1. carrying of boats and supplies overland between waterways. 2. route so used.

por'tal, *n.* doorway; gate.

por·tend', *v.* be an omen or warning of. —**por'tent,** *n.* —**por·ten'tous,** *a.*

por'ter, *n.* 1. doorman. 2. attendant who carries luggage, sweeps, etc.

por'ter·house (steak) beef steak.

port·fo'li·o, *n.* [*pl.* -os] brief case.

port'hole, *n.* window in a ship's side.

por'ti·co, *n.* [*pl.* -COES, -COS] porch consisting of a roof supported by columns.

por·tiere' (-tyâr') *n.* curtain hung in a doorway.

por'tion, *n.* part; share. —*v.* divide or give out in portions.

port'ly, *a.* stout and stately.

port·man'teau (-tō) *n.* kind of suitcase.

por'trait, *n.* painting, photograph, etc. of a person.

por·tray', *v.* 1. make a portrait of. 2. describe. 3. represent on the stage. —**por·tray'al,** *n.*

Por·tu·guese (-chə-gēz) *n.* [*pl.* -GUESE] *a.* (native or language) of Portugal.

pose (pōz) *v.* 1. present, as a question. 2. assume a bodily posture, a false role, etc. —*n.* assumed posture, etc.—**pos'er, po·seur'** (-zũr') *n.*

po·si'tion, *n.* 1. way of being placed. 2. opinion. 3. place; location. 4. status. 5. job. —*v.* to place.

pos'i·tive (poz'-) *a.* 1. explicit; definite. 2. sure or too sure. 3. affirmative. 4. real; absolute. 5. of the electricity made by friction on glass. 6. *Gram.* of an adjective, etc. in its uncompared degree. ·7. *Math.* greater than zero. —*n.* anything positive. —**pos'i·tive·ly,** *adv.*

pos·se (pos'i) *n.* body of men called to help a sheriff.

pos·sess', *v.* 1. own. 2. have as a quality, etc. 3. control. —**pos·ses'sor,** *n.*

pos·ses'sion, *n.* 1. a possessing. 2. thing possessed.

pos·ses'sive, *a.* 1. showing or desiring possession. 2. *Gram.* of a form, etc. indicating possession.

pos'si·ble, *a.* that can be, can happen, etc. —**pos'si·bil'i·ty** [*pl.* -TIES] *n.* —**pos'si·bly,** *adv.*

pos'sum, *n.* opossum. —**play possum,** feign sleep, ignorance, etc.

post, *n.* 1. piece of wood, etc. set upright as a support. 2. place where a soldier or soldiers are stationed. 3. job; position. 4. mail. —*v.* 1. put up (a notice, etc.). 2. assign to a post. 3. mail. 4. inform.

post-, *pref.* after; following.

post'age, *n.* amount charged for mailing a letter, etc.

post'al, *a.* of (the) mail.

post card, card, often a picture card, sent by mail.

post'date', *v.* 1. mark with a later date. 2. be later than.

post'er, *n.* large sign or notice posted publicly.

pos·te'ri·or, *a.* 1. at the back. 2. later. —*n.* buttocks.

pos·ter'i·ty, *n.* all future generations.

post'grad'u·ate, *a.* of study after graduation.

post'haste', *adv.* speedily.

post'hu·mous (pos'choo-məs) *a.* after one's death.

post'man, *n.* [*pl.* -MEN] mailman.

post'mark', *v. & n.* mark to show the date and place of mailing at the post office.

post'mas'ter, *n.* person in charge of a post office.

post'-mor'tem, *a.* after

death. —n. autopsy.

post office, place where mail is sorted, etc.

post'paid', a. with the sender paying the postage.

post·pone', v. put off; delay. —**post·pone'ment,** n.

post'script, n. note added at the end of a letter, etc.

pos'tu·late, v. assume to be true, real, etc. —n. (-lit) something postulated.

pos'ture (-chēr) n. way one holds the body. —v. pose.

post'war', a. after the war.

po'sy (-zi) n. [pl. -SIES] flower or bouquet.

pot, n. round container for cooking, etc. —v. [POTTED, POTTING] put into a pot. —**go to pot,** go to ruin.

po'ta·ble, a. drinkable.

pot'ash, n. white substance got from wood ashes.

po·tas'si·um, n. soft, white, metallic chemical element.

po·ta'to, n. [pl. -TOES] starchy tuber of a common plant, used as a vegetable.

po'tent, a. 1. powerful. 2. effective. —**po'ten·cy,** n.

po'ten·tate, n. person having great power; ruler, etc.

po·ten'tial (-shal) a. that can be; possible. —n. 1. something potential. 2. voltage at a given point in a circuit. —**po·ten'ti·al'i·ty** (-shi-al'-) [pl. -TIES] n. —**po·ten'tial·ly,** adv.

poth'er (poth'-) n. fuss.

po'tion, n. a drink, esp. of medicine or poison.

pot·pour'ri (pō'poo-rē') n. mixture.

pot'sherd, n. piece of broken pottery.

pot'ter, n. one who makes pots, dishes, etc. of clay.

pot'ter·y, n. earthenware.

pouch, n. 1. small sack or bag. 2. baglike part.

poul'tice (pōl'-) n. hot, soft mass applied to a sore part of the body.

poul'try, n. domestic fowls.

pounce, v. leap or swoop down, as if to seize. —n. a pouncing.

pound, n. 1. unit of weight, 16 ounces. 2. Br. monetary unit. 3. enclosure for stray animals. —v. 1. hit hard. 2. beat to pulp, powder, etc. 3. throb.

pour, v. 1. flow or make flow steadily. 2. rain heavily.

pout, v. 1. push out the lips, as in sullenness. 2. sulk. —n. a pouting.

pov'er·ty, n. 1. a being poor; need. 2. inadequacy.

pov'er·ty-strick'en, a. very poor.

pow'der, n. dry substance of fine particles. —v. 1. put powder on. 2. make into powder. —**pow'der·y,** a.

pow'er, n. 1. ability to do or act. 2. strength or energy. 3. authority. 4. powerful person, nation, etc. —**pow'er·less,** a.

pow'er·ful, a. strong; mighty. —**pow'er·ful·ly,** adv.

prac'ti·ca·ble, a. that can be done. —**prac'ti·ca·bil'i·ty,** n.

prac'ti·cal, a. 1. of or obtained through practice. 2. useful. 3. sensible. 4. virtual. —**prac'ti·cal'i·ty,** n. —**prac'ti·cal·ly,** adv.

prac'tice, v. 1. do repeatedly so as to gain skill. 2. make a habit of. 3. work at as a profession. —n. 1. a practicing. 2. acquired skill. 3. work or business of a professional person. Also, Br. sp., **prac'tise.**

prac'ticed, a. skilled.

prac·ti'tion·er, n. one who practices a profession, etc.

prag·mat'ic, a. 1. practical. 2. tested by results.

prai'rie (prâr'i) n. large area of grassy land.

prairie dog, small squirrel-like animal.

praise, v. 1. say good things about. 2. worship. —n. a praising. —**praise'wor·thy,** a.

prance, v. 1. move along on the hind legs, as a horse. 2. strut. —**pranc'er,** n.

prank, n. mischievous trick. —**prank'ster,** n.

prate, v. talk foolishly.

prat'tle, v. & n. chatter or babble.

prawn, n. shellfish like a shrimp but larger.

pray, v. 1. implore. 2. ask for by prayer. 3. say prayers.

prayer, n. 1. a praying. 2. words of worship or entreaty to God. 3. thing prayed for. —**pray'er·ful,** a.

pre-, pref. before.

preach, v. 1. give (a sermon). 2. urge as by preaching. —**preach'er,** n. —**preach'ment,** n.

pre·am'ble, n. introduction.

pre·ar·range', v. arrange beforehand.

pre·car'i·ous, a. not safe or sure; risky.

pre·cau'tion, *n.* care taken beforehand, as against danger. —**pre·cau'tion·ar'y,** *a.*

pre·cede' (-sēd') *v.* go or come before. —**pre·ced'ence** (or pres'ə-dəns) *n.*

prec'e·dent (pres'ə-) *n.* earlier case that sets an example.

pre'cept, *n.* rule of ethics.

pre·cep'tor, *n.* teacher.

pre'cinct (-sinkt) *n.* 1. subdivision of a city, ward, etc. 2. *pl.* grounds or environs.

pre'cious, *a.* 1. of great value. 2. beloved. 3. too refined. —**pre'cious·ly,** *adv.*

prec'i·pice (-pis) *n.* steep cliff.

pre·cip'i·tate, *v.* 1. bring on; hasten. 2. hurl down. 3. to separate out as a solid from solution. —*a.* (-tit) hasty; rash. —*n.* precipitated substance.

pre·cip'i·ta'tion, *n.* 1. a precipitating. 2. (amount of) rain, snow, etc.

pre·cip'i·tous, *a.* 1. steep. 2. hasty; rash.

pré·cis' (prā-sē') *n.* summary.

pre·cise', *a.* 1. exact; definite; accurate. 2. strict; scrupulous. —**pre·cise'ly,** *adv.* —**pre·ci'sion** (-sizh'ən) *n.*

pre·clude', *v.* make impossible, esp. in advance.

pre·co'cious (-kō'shəs) *a.* advanced beyond one's age. —**pre·coc'i·ty** (-kos'-) *n.*

pre·con·ceive', *v.* form an opinion of beforehand. —**pre·con·cep'tion,** *n.*

pre·cur'sor, *n.* forerunner.

pred'a·to'ry, *a.* 1. plundering. 2. preying on other animals.

pred·e·ces'sor, *n.* one preceding another, as in office.

pre·des'tine, *v.* destine or determine beforehand. —**pre·des'ti·na'tion,** *n.*

pre·de·ter'mine, *v.* set or decide beforehand.

pre·dic'a·ment, *n.* difficult situation.

pred'i·cate, *v.* base upon facts, conditions, etc. —*a. & n.* (-kit) *Gram.* (of) the word or words that make a statement about the subject.

pre·dict', *v.* tell about in advance. —**pre·dict'a·ble,** *a.* —**pre·dic'tion,** *n.*

pre·di·lec'tion, *n.* special liking; partiality.

pre'dis·pose', *v.* make likely to; get, etc.; incline. —**pre'dis·po·si'tion,** *n.*

pre·dom'i·nate, *v.* be greater in amount, power, etc.; prevail. —**pre·dom'i·nance,** *n.* —**pre·dom'i·nant,** *a.*

pre·em'i·nent, *a.* most outstanding. —**pre·em'i·nence,** *n.*

pre·empt', *v.* seize before anyone else can.

preen, *v.* 1. groom (its feathers): said of a bird. 2. groom (oneself).

pre·fab'ri·cat'ed, *a.* made in sections ready for quick assembly, as a house.

pref'ace (-is) *n.* introduction to a book, speech, etc. —*v.* give or be a preface to. —**pref'a·to·ry,** *a.*

pre'fect, *n.* administrator.

pre·fer', *v.* [-FERRED, -FER-RING] 1. like better. 2. bring (charges) before a court. —**pref'er·a·ble,** *a.*

pref'er·ence, *n.* 1. a preferring. 2. thing preferred. 3. advantage given to one over others. —**pref'er·en'tial,** *a.*

pre·fer'ment, *n.* promotion.

pre'fix, *n.* syllable(s) added to the beginning of a word to alter its meaning.

preg'nant, *a.* 1. bearing a fetus in the uterus. 2. filled (with). —**preg'nan·cy** [*pl.* -CIES], *n.*

pre·hen'sile, *a.* adapted for grasping, as the hand.

pre·his·tor'ic, *a.* of times before recorded history.

prej'u·dice (-dis) *n.* 1. preconceived idea. 2. hatred or intolerance of other races, etc. 3. disadvantage. —*v.* 1. harm. 2. fill with prejudice. —**prej·u·di'cial,** *a.*

prel'ate (-it) *n.* high-ranking clergyman.

pre·lim'i·nar'y, *a.* leading up to the main action. —*n.* [*pl.* -IES] preliminary step.

prel'ude, *n.* preliminary part, as of a musical piece.

pre·ma·ture', *a.* before the proper or usual time.

pre·med'i·tate, *v.* think out or plan beforehand. —**pre'med·i·ta'tion,** *n.*

pre'mi·er, *a.* foremost. —*n.* (pri-mîr') prime minister.

pre·mière' (-mîr') *n.* first performance of a play, etc.

prem'ise (prem'is) *n.* 1. basic assumption. 2. *pl.* piece of real estate.

pre'mi·um, *n.* 1. prize. 2. extra charge. 3. a payment. 4. high value.

pre'mo·ni'tion (prē'-) *n.* feeling of imminent evil.

pre·oc'cu·py, *v.* [-PIED, -PY-**

ING] engross; absorb. —**pre-oc'cu·pa'tion**, *n.*

pre·pare', *v.* 1. make or get ready. 2. equip. 3. put together. —**prep'a·ra'tion**, *n.* —**pre·par'a·to·ry**, *a.* —**pre·pared'·ness**, *n.*

pre·pay', *v.* pay in advance.

pre·pon'der·ate, *v.* predominate. —**pre·pon'der·ance**, *n.* —**pre·pon'der·ant**, *a.*

prep'o·si'tion (-zi'-) *n.* word that connects a noun or pronoun to another word. —**prep'o·si'tion·al**, *a.*

pre'pos·sess'ing, *a.* making a good impression.

pre·pos'ter·ous, *a.* absurd.

pre·req'ui·site (-rek'wə-zit) *n. & a.* (something) required beforehand.

pre·rog'a·tive, *n.* exclusive privilege.

pres'age, *n.* 1. warning. 2. foreboding. —*v.* (pri·sāj') 1. warn about. 2. predict.

pre'sci·ence (-shi-, presh'i-) *n.* foresight. —**pre'sci·ent**, *a.*

pre·scribe', *v.* 1. to order. 2. order to take a certain medicine or treatment.

pre·scrip'tion, *n.* 1. a prescribing, esp. by a doctor. 2 medicine prescribed.

pres'ence, *n.* 1. a being present. 2. one's appearance.

pres'ent, *a.* 1. being at a certain place. 2. of or at this time. —*n.* 1. present time. 2. gift. —*v.* (pri·zent') 1. introduce. 2. show. 3. offer for consideration. 4. give (to).

present'a·ble, *a.* 1. fit to present. 2. properly dressed.

pres'en·ta'tion, *n.* 1. a presenting. 2. thing presented.

pre·sen'ti·ment, *n.* premonition.

pres'ent·ly, *adv.* 1. soon. 2. now.

present'ment, *n.* presentation.

pre·serve', *v.* 1. keep from harm, spoiling, etc. 2. maintain. —*n.* [in *pl.*] fruit cooked with sugar. —**pre·ser·va'tion**, *a. & n.* —**pre·serv'a·tive**, *n.*

pre·side' (-zid') *v.* 1. act as chairman. 2. have control.

pres'i·dent, *n.* chief executive of a republic, company, etc. —**pres'i·den·cy**, *n.* -CIES.] —**pres'i·den'tial** (-shəl) *a.*

press, *v.* 1. push against; squeeze. 2. iron, as clothes. 3. force. 4. entreat. 5 urge

on. 6. keep moving. 7. crowd. —*n.* 1. pressure. 2. crowd. 3. machine for crushing, printing, etc. 4. newspapers. 5. journalists.

press'ing, *a.* urgent.

pres'sure (-shёr) *n.* 1. a pressing. 2. distress. 3. strong influence. 4. urgency. 5. force of weight. —*v.* [Col.] try to influence.

pres'ti·dig'i·ta'tion (-dij'-) *n.* sleight of hand.

pres·tige' (-tēzh') *n.* earned fame and respect.

pres'to, *adv. & a.* fast.

pre·sume', *v.* 1. dare. 2. suppose. 3. take liberties. —**pre·sump'tion**, *n.* —**pre·sump'tive**, *a.*

pre·sump'tu·ous (-chōō-əs) *a.* too bold or daring.

pre·sup·pose', *v.* assume beforehand.

pre·tend', *v.* 1. claim falsely. 2. make believe. 3. lay claim (with *to*).

pre·tense', *n.* 1. claim. 2. false claim or show. 3. a making believe.

pre·ten'sion, *n.* 1. claim. 2. pretext. 3. show; display.

pre·ten'tious (-shəs) *a.* showy; flashy.

pre'ter·nat'u·ral, *a.* supernatural.

pre'text, *n.* false reason used to hide the real one.

pret'ty, *a.* [-TIER, -TIEST] attractive and dainty. —*adv.* somewhat. —**pret'ti·ly**, *adv.* —**pret'ti·ness**, *n.*

pret'zel, *n.* hard, salted biscuit, twisted in a knot.

pre·vail', *v.* 1. win out or be successful. 2. become more common.

prev'a·lent, *a.* common; general. —**prev'a·lence**, *n.*

pre·var'i·cate, *v.* evade the truth; lie. —**pre·var'i·ca'tion**, *n.* —**pre·var'i·ca'tor**, *n.*

pre·vent', *v.* stop or keep from doing or happening. —**pre·vent'a·ble, pre·vent'i·ble**, *a.* —**pre·ven'tion**, *n.* —**pre·ven'tive, pre·ven'ta·tive**, *n. & a.* (something) that prevents. Also

pre'view, *n.* advance showing of (scenes from) a movie.

pre'vi·ous, *a.* coming before; prior. —**pre'vi·ous·ly**, *adv.*

prey (prā) *n.* 1. animal seized by another for food. 2. victim. —*v.* 1. hunt as prey. 2. plunder; rob. 3. harass.

price, *n.* 1. sum asked or paid for a thing. 2. value.

—*v.* get or put a price on.

price'less, *a.* beyond price.

prick, *v.* 1. pierce with a sharp point. 2. pain sharply. 3. raise (the ears). —*n.* 1. a pricking. 2. sharp pain.

prick'le, *n.* thorn or spiny point. —*v.* tingle. —**prick'ly** [-LIER, -LIEST] *a.*

pride, *n.* 1. overhigh opinion of oneself. 2. self-respect. 3. satisfaction in one's achievements. 4. person or thing one is proud of. **pride oneself on**, be proud of.

priest, *n.* one who conducts religious rites. —**priest'ess**, *n.fem.* —**priest'hood**, *n.* —**priest'ly**, *a.*

prig, *n.* smug, moralistic person. —**prig'gish**, *a.*

prim, *a.* [PRIMMER, PRIMMEST] stiffly proper. —**prim'ly**, *adv.*

pri'ma·cy, *n.* supremacy.

pri'ma don'na (prē'-) chief woman singer in an opera.

pri'ma·ry, *a.* 1. most important. 2. basic. 3. first in order. —*n.* [*pl.* -IES] preliminary election. —**pri·mar'i·ly**, *adv.*

pri'mate, *n.* 1. archbishop. 2. member of the highest order of mammals; man, ape, etc.

prime, *a.* first in rank, importance, or quality. —*n.* best period or part. —*v.* make ready. —**prim'er**, *n.*

prime minister, chief official in some countries.

prim'er, *n.* elementary textbook, esp. for reading.

pri·me'val (prī-) *a.* of the first age or ages.

prim'i·tive, *a.* 1. of earliest times. 2. crude; simple. —*n.* primitive person or thing.

primp, *v.* groom oneself fussily: also **prink**.

prim'rose, *n.* plant with tubelike flowers in clusters.

prince, *n.* 1. monarch's son. 2. ruler of a principality. —**prince'ly**, *a.* —**prin'cess**, *n.fem.*

prin'ci·pal, *a.* chief; main. —*n.* 1. principal person or thing. 2. head of a school. 3. sum owed, etc. aside from interest. —**prin'ci·pal·ly**, *adv.*

prin'ci·pal'i·ty, *n.* [*pl.* -TIES] land ruled by a prince.

prin'ci·ple, *n.* 1. basic truth, rule, action, etc. 2. rule of conduct. 3. integrity.

print, *n.* 1. cloth stamped

with a design. 2. impression made by inked type, plates, etc. 3. photograph. —*v.* 1. impress inked type, etc. on paper. 2. publish in print. 3. write in letters like printed ones. —**print'er**, *n.* —**print'ing**, *n. & a.*

pri'or, *a.* preceding in time, order, or importance. —*n.* head of a monastery or order. —**pri'or·ess**, *n.fem.* —**pri'o·ry** [*pl.* -RIES] *n.*

pri·or'i·ty, *n.* [*pl.* -TIES] 1. precedence. 2. prior right.

prism, *n.* clear glass, etc. of angular form, for dispersing light into its spectrum. —**pris·mat'ic**, *a.*

pris'on, *n.* place of confinement. —**pris'on·er**, *n.*

pris'tine (-tēn) *a.* fresh and untouched.

pri'vate, *a.* 1. of or for a particular person or group; not public. 2. secret. —*n.* *Mil.* lowest rank of enlisted man. —**pri'va·cy**, *n.* —**pri'vate·ly**, *adv.*

pri·va·teer', *n.* private ship commissioned to attack enemy ships.

pri·va'tion, *n.* lack of necessities.

priv'et, *n.* evergreen shrub.

priv'i·lege (-lij) *n.* special right, favor, etc. —*v.* grant a privilege to.

priv'y, *a.* private. —*n.* [*pl.* -IES] outhouse. —**privy to**, privately informed about.

prize, *v.* value highly. —*n.* 1. thing given to the winner of a contest, etc. 2. valued possession.

pro, *adv.* on the affirmative side. —*n.* 1. [*pl.* PROS] reason or vote for. 2. [Col.] professional.

pro-, *pref.* in favor of.

prob'a·ble, *a.* likely to occur or to be so. —**prob·a·bil'i·ty** [*pl.* -TIES] *n.* —**prob'a·bly**, *adv.*

pro'bate, *v.* establish the validity of (a will). —*a.* of suchaction.—*n.*a probating.

pro·ba'tion, *n.* 1. trial of ability, etc. 2. conditional suspension of a jail sentence. —**pro·ba'tion·a·ry**, *a.*

probe, *n.* 1. slender instrument for exploring a wound. 2. investigation. —*v.* 1. explore with a probe. 2. investigate. —**prob'er**, *n.*

pro'bi·ty (prō'bə-) *n.* honesty.

prob'lem, *n.* 1. question to be solved. 2. difficult matter, etc.

prob·lem·at'i·cal, *a.* not sure; uncertain.

pro·bos'cis (-bos'-) *n.* elephant's trunk, or similar snout.

pro·ce'dure (-jẽr) *n.* act or way of doing something.

pro·ceed', *v.* 1. go on after stopping. 2. carry on an action. 3. come forth.

pro·ceed'ing, *n.* 1. course of action. 2. *pl.* transactions. 3. *pl.* legal action.

pro'ceeds, *n.pl.* money from a business deal.

proc'ess, *n.* 1. series of changes in developing. 2. act or way of doing something. 3. court summons. 4. projecting part. —*v.* prepare by a special process.

pro·ces'sion, *n.* group moving forward, as in a parade.

pro·ces'sion·al, *n.* hymn or music for a procession.

pro·claim', *v.* announce officially. —**proc·la·ma'tion**, *n.*

pro·cliv'i·ty, *n.* [*pl.* -TIES] inclination; tendency.

pro·cras'ti·nate, *v.* put off; delay. —**pro·cras'ti·na'tion**, *n.* —**pro·cras'ti·na'tor**, *n.*

pro'cre·ate, *v.* produce (young). —**pro'cre·a'tion**, *n.*

pro·cure', *v.* get; obtain. —**pro·cur'a·ble**, *a.* —**pro·cure'ment**, *n.* —**pro·cur'er**, *n.*

prod, *n. & v.* [PRODDED, PRODDING] goad or jab.

prod'i·gal, *a.* very wasteful or generous. —*n.* spendthrift. —**prod'i·gal'i·ty**, *n.*

pro·di'gious (-dij'əs) *a.* 1. amazing. 2. enormous. —**pro·di'gious·ly**, *adv.*

prod'i·gy, *n.* [*pl.* -GIES] remarkable person or thing.

pro·duce', *v.* 1. show. 2. bring forth. 3. manufacture. 4. cause. 5. get (a play, etc.) ready for the public. —*n.* (prod'ōos) farm products. —**pro·duc'er**, *n.* —**pro·duc'tion**, *n.*

prod'uct, *n.* 1. thing produced. 2. result. 3. result of multiplying numbers.

pro·duc'tive, *a.* 1. producing much. 2. causing. —**pro'duc·tiv'i·ty**, *n.*

pro·fane', *a.* 1. not religious. 2. scornful of sacred things. —*v.* treat irreverently. —**pro·fane'ly**, *adv.*

pro·fan'i·ty, *n.* [*pl.* -TIES] swearing.

pro·fess', *v.* 1. declare openly.

2. claim to have or be. 3. declare one's belief in.

pro·fes'sion, *n.* 1. occupation requiring special study. 2. its members. 3. avowal.

pro·fes'sion·al, *n. & a.* (one) of a profession, or (one) paid to play in games, etc. —**pro·fes'sion·al·ly**, *adv.*

pro·fes'sor, *n.* college teacher. —**pro·fes·so'ri·al**, *a.*

prof'fer, *v. & n.* offer.

pro·fi'cient (-fish'ənt) *a.* skilled. —**pro·fi'cien·cy**, *n.*

pro'file, *n.* 1. side view of the face. 2. outline.

prof'it, *n.* 1. gain; benefit. 2. net income from business. —*v.* benefit. —**prof'it·a·ble**, *a.* —**prof'it·a·bly**, *adv.* —**prof'it·less**, *a.*

prof·it·eer' (-ẽr') *n.* one who makes excessive profits.

prof'li·gate (-git) *a.* 1. dissolute. 2. wasteful. —**prof'li·ga·cy**, *n.*

pro·found', *a.* 1. very deep. 2. complete. —**pro·fun'di·ty** [*pl.* -TIES] *n.*

pro·fuse' (-fūs') *a.* abundant. —**pro·fuse'ly**, *adv.* —**pro·fu'sion**, *n.*

pro·gen'i·tor (-jen'-) *n.* ancestor.

prog'e·ny (proj'-) *n.* offspring.

prog·no'sis, *n.* [*pl.* -SES (-sēz)] prediction.

prog·nos'ti·cate, *v.* predict. —**prog·nos'ti·ca'tion**, *n.*

pro'gram, pro'gramme, *n.* 1. list of things to be performed. 2. plan of procedure. —*v.* schedule in a program.

pro·gress' (prə-gres') *v.* advance, develop, or improve. —*n.* (prog'res) a progressing. —**pro·gres'sion**, *n.*

pro·gres'sive, *a.* 1. progressing. 2. favoring progress, reform, etc. —*n.* progressive person. —**pro·gres'sive·ly**, *adv.*

pro·hib'it, *v.* 1. forbid, as by law. 2. prevent. —**pro·hib'i·tive**, **pro·hib'i·to·ry**, *a.*

pro·hi·bi'tion, *n.* a forbidding, esp. of the making or selling of liquor. —**pro'hi·bi'tion·ist**, *n.*

proj'ect, *n.* 1. scheme. 2. undertaking. —*v.* (prə-jekt') 1. propose. 2. stick out. 3. cause (a light, etc.) to fall upon a surface. —**pro·jec'tion**, *n.* —**pro·jec'tor**, *n.*

pro·jec'tile (-t'l) *n.* object to be shot forth, as a bullet.

pro·le·tar'i·at, *n.* working

class. —**pro'le·tar'i·an,** a. & n.

pro·lif'ic, a. producing much.

pro·lix', a. wordy. —**pro·lix'i·ty,** n.

pro'logue (-lôg) n. introduction to a poem, play, etc.

pro·long', v. lengthen. —**pro'lon·ga'tion,** n.

prom, n. [Col.] formal dance at a college, etc.

prom·e·nade' (-nād', -näd') n. 1. walk for pleasure. 2. public place for walking. —v. take a promenade.

prom'i·nent, a. 1. projecting. 2. conspicuous. 3. famous. —**prom'i·nence,** n.

pro·mis'cu·ous, a. not discriminating. —**prom'is·cu'i·ty,** n.

prom·ise, n. 1. agreement to do or not do something. 2. sign as of future success. —v. 1. make a promise of or to. 2. cause to expect. —**prom'is·ing,** a.

prom'is·so·ry, a. containing or being a promise.

prom'on·to·ry, n. [pl. -RIES] peak of high land jutting out into the sea.

pro·mote', v. 1. raise in rank. 2. further the growth or sale of. —**pro·mo'tion,** n. —**pro·mot'er,** n.

prompt, a. ready; quick. —v. 1. help with a cue. 2. inspire or urge. —**prompt'er,** n. —**prompt'ly,** adv.

promp'ti·tude, n. quality of being prompt.

pro·mul'gate, v. proclaim; publish. —**pro'mul·ga'tion,** n.

prone, a. 1. lying face downward. 2. apt or likely.

prong, n. projecting point, as of a fork. —**pronged,** a.

pro'noun, n. word used in place of a noun. —**pro·nom'i·nal,** a.

pro·nounce', v. 1. declare officially. 2. utter the sounds of. —**pro·nounce'a·ble,** a. —**pro·nounce'ment,** n.

pro·nounced', a. definite.

pro·nun'ci·a'tion, n. act or way of pronouncing words.

proof, n. 1. convincing evidence. 2. a test. 3. strength of a liquor. —a. strong enough to resist.

-proof, suf. impervious to.

proof'read, v. to read in order to correct errors.

prop, n. a support or aid. —v. [PROPPED, PROPPING] to support or lean against.

prop·a·gan'da, n. 1. sys-

tematic spreading of ideas. 2. ideas so spread. —**prop'a·gan'dist,** a. & n. —**prop'a·gan'dize,** v.

prop'a·gate, v. 1. produce offspring. 2. raise; breed. 3. spread (ideas). —**prop'a·ga'tion,** n.

pro·pel', v. [-PELLED, -PELLING] drive forward.

pro·pel'ler, n. bladed end of a revolving shaft for propelling a ship or aircraft.

pro·pen'si·ty, n. [pl. -TIES] natural tendency.

prop'er, a. 1. suitable; fit. 2. correct. 3. belonging (to). 4. actual. —**prop'er·ly,** adv.

prop'er·ty, n. [pl. -TIES] 1. thing owned. 2. characteristic.

proph'e·cy (-si) n. [pl. -CIES] prediction.

proph'e·sy (-sī) v. [-SIED, -SYING] predict; foretell. —**pro·phet'ic,** a.

proph'et, n. 1. leader regarded as divinely inspired. 2. one who predicts.

pro'phy·lac'tic (-fə-) n. & a. (medicine, device, etc.) that prevents disease.

pro·pin'qui·ty, n. nearness.

pro·pi'ti·ate (-pish'i·āt) v. appease.

pro·pi'tious, a. favorable.

pro·po'nent, n. supporter.

pro·por'tion, n. 1. part in relation to the whole. 2. ratio. 3. symmetry. 4. pl. dimensions. —v. 1. make symmetrical. 2. make fit. —**pro·por'tion·al, pro·por'tion·ate** (-it) a.

pro·pose', v. 1. suggest for considering. 2. plan. 3. offer marriage. —**pro·pos'al,** n.

prop'o·si'tion, n. 1. a plan. 2. subject for debate.

pro·pound', v. suggest for consideration.

pro·pri'e·tar'y, a. held under a patent, etc.

pro·pri'e·tor, n. owner.

pro·pri'e·ty, n. [pl. -TIES] fitness; correctness.

pro·pul'sion, n. a propelling or a force that propels.

pro·rate', v. divide or assess proportionally.

pro·sa'ic, a. commonplace.

pro·scribe', v. forbid.

prose, n. nonpoetic language.

pros'e·cute, v. 1. engage in. 2. take legal action against. —**pros'e·cu'tion,** n. —**pros'e·cu'tor,** n.

pros'e·lyte (-līt) n. & v. convert. —**pros'e·lyt·ize',** v.

pros'pect, n. 1. outlook. 2.

likely customer, etc. —*v.* search (for). —**pros·pec'tor,** *n.*

pro·spec'tive, *a.* expected.

pro·spec'tus, *n.* report outlining a new work, etc.

pros'per, *v.* thrive.

pros·per'i·ty, *n.* wealth. —**pros'per·ous,** *a.* —**pros'per·ous·ly,** *adv.*

pros'tate, *a.* of a gland at the base of the bladder in males.

pros'ti·tute, *n.* woman who engages in sexual intercourse for pay. —*v.* sell (one's talents, etc.) for base purposes. —**pros'ti·tu'tion,** *n.*

pros'trate, *a.* 1. lying flat, esp. face downward. 2. overcome. —*v.* 1. lay flat. 2. overcome. —**pros·tra'tion,** *n.*

pro·tag'o·nist, *n.* main character or leading figure.

pro·tect', *v.* shield from harm. —**pro·tec'tion,** *n.* —**pro·tec'tive,** *a.* —**pro·tec'tor,** *n.*

pro·tec'tor·ate (-it) *n.* territory controlled and protected by a strong state.

pro'té·gé (-tə-zhā) *n.* one under another's patronage.

pro'tein (-tēn) *n.* nitrogenous substance essential to diet.

pro·test', *v.* 1. object. 2. assert. —*n.* (prō'test) objection. —**prot'es·ta'tion,** *n.*

Prot'es·tant, *n.* Christian not of the Roman Catholic or Orthodox Eastern Church. —**Prot'es·tant·ism,** *n.*

pro'to·col, *n.* code of etiquette among diplomats, etc.

pro'ton, *n.* positive particle in the nucleus of an atom.

pro'to·plasm, *n.* essential matter of all living cells. —**pro'to·plas'mic,** *a.*

pro'to·type, *n.* first thing of its kind.

pro'to·zo'an, *n.* [*pl.* -ZOA] one-celled animal.

pro·tract', *v.* draw out; prolong. —**pro·trac'tion,** *n.*

pro·trac'tor, *n.* device for drawing & measuring angles.

pro·trude', *v.* jut out. —**pro·tru'sion,** *n.*

pro·tu'ber·ance, *n.* bulge. —**pro·tu'ber·ant,** *a.*

proud, *a.* 1. haughty. 2. feeling or causing pride. 3. splendid. —**proud of,** highly pleased with. —**proud'ly,** *adv.*

prove, *v.* [alt. pp. PROVEN] 1. test by experiment. 2. establish as true.

prov'en·der, *n.* fodder.

prov'erb, *n.* wise saying. —**pro·ver'bi·al,** *a.*

pro·vide', *v.* 1. supply; furnish (with). 2. prepare (for or against). 3. stipulate. —**pro·vid'er,** *n.*

pro·vid'ed, pro·vid'ing, *con.* on condition (that).

prov'i·dence, *n.* 1. prudent foresight. 2. guidance of God or nature. 3. [P-] God. —**prov'i·dent,** *a.* —**prov'i·den'tial,** *a.*

prov'ince, *n.* 1. division of a country. 2. *pl.* parts of a country outside major cities. 3. sphere; field.

pro·vin'cial (-shəl) *a.* 1. of a province. 2. narrow-minded. —**pro·vin'cial·ism,** *n.*

pro·vi'sion, *n.* 1. a providing. 2. *pl.* stock of food. 3. stipulation. —*v.* supply with provisions.

pro·vi'sion·al, *a.* temporary.

pro·vi'so, *n.* [*pl.* -SOS, -SOES] stipulation.

prov'o·ca'tion, *n.* 1. a provoking. 2. thing that provokes. —**pro·voc'a·tive,** *a.*

pro·voke', *v.* 1. anger. 2. stir up or call forth.

prow (prou) *n.* forward part of a ship.

prow'ess, *n.* 1. bravery. 2. superior skill, etc.

prowl, *v.* stalk furtively.

prox·im'i·ty, *n.* nearness.

prox'y, *n.* [*pl.* -IES] authority to act for another.

prude, *n.* one overly modest. —**prud'er·y,** *n.* —**prud'ish,** *a.*

pru'dent, *a.* wisely careful. —**pru'dence,** *n.* —**pru·den'tial** (-shəl) *a.*

prune, *n.* dried plum. —*v.* trim twigs, etc. from.

pru'ri·ent, *a.* lustful.

pry, *n.* [*pl.* PRIES] lever. —*v.* [PRIED, PRYING] 1. raise with a lever. 2. look closely or inquisitively.

psalm (säm) *n.* sacred song or poem. —**psalm'ist,** *n.*

pseu·do (soō'dō) *a.* false.

pseu'do·nym (-nim) *n.* fictitious name assumed by an author, etc.

pshaw (shô) *int.* & *n.* exclamation of disgust, etc.

psy·che (sī'kē) *n.* 1. soul. 2. mind.

psy·chi·a·try (sī-kī'ə-tri) *n.* branch of medicine dealing with mental illness. —**psy·chi·at'ric,** *a.* —**psy·chi·a'trist,** *n.*

psy'chic (-kik) *a.* 1. of the mind. 2. supernatural. Also **psy'chi·cal.**

psycho-, *pref.* mind; mental processes: also **psych-.**

psy'cho·a·nal'y·sis, *n.* method of treating neuroses. —**psy'cho·an'a·lyst,** *n.* —**psy'cho·an'a·lyze,** *v.*

psy·chol'o·gy, *n.* science dealing with the mind and behavior. —**psy'cho·log'i·cal,** *a.* —**psy'cho·log'i·cal·ly,** *adv.* —**psy·chol'o·gist,** *n.*

psy'cho·path'ic, *a.* of mental disorder. —**psy'cho·path,** *n.*

psy·cho'sis, *n.* [*pl.* -SES (-sēz)] severe mental illness. —**psy·chot'ic,** *a. & n.*

psy'cho·so·mat'ic, *a.* of a physical disorder caused by emotional disturbance.

psy'cho·ther'a·py, *n.* treatment of mental illness. —**psy'cho·ther'a·pist,** *n.*

ptar'mi·gan (tär'mə·gən) *n.* northern grouse.

pto'maine (tō'-) *n.* a substance in decaying matter.

pub, *n.* [Br. Sl.] bar; tavern: in full, **public house.**

pu'ber·ty (pū'-) *n.* time of maturing sexually.

pub'lic, *a.* 1. of people as a whole. 2. for everyone. 3. known by all. —*n.* the people. —**in public,** in open view. —**pub'lic·ly,** *adv.*

pub'li·ca'tion, *n.* 1. printing and selling of books, etc. 2. thing published.

pub'li·cist, *n.* publicity agent.

pub·lic'i·ty, *n.* 1. public attention. 2. information meant to bring one this. —**pub'li·cize,** *v.*

pub'lish, *v.* 1. issue a (printed work) for sale. 2. announce. —**pub'lish·er,** *n.*

puck, *n.* hard rubber disk used in ice hockey.

puck'er, *n. & v.* wrinkle.

pud'ding, *n.* soft food of flour, milk, eggs, etc.

pud'dle, *n.* small pool of water.

pudg'y, *a.* [-IER, -IEST] short and fat.

pueb'lo, (pweb'-) *n.* [*pl.* -LOS] Southwestern Indian village.

pu'er·ile (pū'-) *a.* childish. —**pu'er·il'i·ty,** *n.*

puff, *n.* 1. brief burst of wind, etc. 2. draw at a cigarette. 3. light pastry shell. 4. soft pad. —*v.* 1. blow in puffs. 2. breathe rapidly.

3. smoke. 4. swell. —**puff'y** [-IER, -IEST] *a.*

puf'fin, *n.* northern seabird.

pug, *n.* small dog.

pu'gil·ism (pū'jəl-) *n.* sport of boxing. —**pu'gil·ist,** *n.* —**pu·gil·is'tic,** *a.*

pug·na'cious (-shəs) *a.* quarrelsome. —**pug·na'cious·ly,** *adv.* —**pug·nac'i·ty** (-nas'-) *n.*

puke (pūk) *v. & n.* vomit.

pul'chri·tude, *n.* beauty.

pull, *v.* 1. make move toward one. 2. pluck out. 3. rip. 4. strain. 5. [Col.] do. 6. move (*away, ahead,* etc.). —*n.* 1. act or effort of pulling. 2. handle, etc. 3. [Sl.] influence. —**pull through,** [Col.] get over (an illness).

pul'let, *n.* young hen.

pul'ley, *n.* [*pl.* -LEYS] wheel with a grooved rim in which a rope runs, to raise weights.

Pull'man (car), railroad car with berths for sleeping.

pul'mo·nar'y, *a.* of the lungs.

pulp, *n.* 1. soft, inside part, as of fruit. 2. moist wood fiber, ground to make paper. —**pulp'y** [-IER, -IEST] *a.*

pul'pit, *n.* clergyman's platform for preaching.

pul'sate, *v.* throb. —**pul·sa'tion,** *n.*

pulse, *n.* regular beat, as of blood in the arteries.

pul'ver·ize, *v.* grind into powder.

pu'ma (pū'-) *n.* cougar.

pum'ice, *n.* light, spongy rock, used for cleaning, etc.

pum'mel, *n. & v.* pommel.

pump, *n.* 1. machine that forces fluids in or out. 2. low-cut, strapless shoe. —*v.* 1. move or empty (fluids) with a pump. 2. move like a pump. 3. question persistently.

pumper'nick'el, *n.* coarse, dark rye bread.

pump'kin, *n.* large, round, orange-yellow gourd.

pun, *n.* humorous use of different words that sound alike. —*v.* [PUNNED, PUNNING] make puns. —**pun'ner,** *n.*

punch, *n.* 1. tool for piercing, etc. 2. fruit drink. 3. blow with the fist. —*v.* 1. pierce, etc. with a punch. 2. hit with the fist.

punc·til'i·ous, *a.* 1. careful in behavior. 2. precise.

punc'tu·al (-choo·əl) *a.* on time. —**punc'tu·al'i·ty,** *n.*

punc′tu·ate, v. use periods, commas, etc. in (writing). —**punc′tua′tion**, n.

punc′ture (-chēr) n. hole made by a sharp point. —v. pierce as with a point.

pun′dit, n. very learned man.

pun′gent (-jənt) a. 1. sharp in taste or smell. 2. keen and direct. —**pun′gen·cy**, n.

pun′ish, v. make suffer pain, loss, etc. as for a crime or offense. —**pun′ish·a·ble**, a. —**pun′ish·ment**, n.

pu′ni·tive, a. of or inflicting punishment.

punk, n. 1. substance that smolders, used to light fireworks. 2. [Sl.] insignificant young person. —a. [Sl.] poor in quality.

punt, v. 1. kick a dropped football before it touches the ground. 2. move (a boat) using a long pole. —n. 1. a punting. 2. square, flat-bottomed boat.

pu′ny, a. [-NIER, -NIEST] small or weak.

pup, n. young dog.

pu′pa (pū′-) n. [pl. -PAE (-pē), -PAS] insect just before the adult stage.

pu′pil, n. 1. person being taught. 2. contractile opening in iris of the eye.

pup′pet, n. doll moved by strings, etc. in a play.

pup′py, n. [pl. -PIES] young dog.

pur′chase (-chis) v. buy. —n. 1. thing bought. 2. act of buying. —**pur′chas·er**, n.

pure, a. 1. unmixed. 2. clean. 3. mere. 4. faultless. 5. chaste. 6. abstract. —**pure′ly**, adv. —**pu′ri·fy**, v. —**pu′ri·fi·ca′tion**, n. —**pu′ri·ty**, n.

pu·rée′ (-rā′) n. 1. mashed, strained food. 2. thick soup.

pur′ga·tive (-ga-) a. purging. —n. a cathartic.

pur′ga·to′ry, n. R.C.Ch. state or place for expiating sins after death.

purge, v. 1. cleanse; make pure. 2. move (the bowels). 3. get rid of. —n. 1. a purging. 2. cathartic.

pu′ri·tan, n. one very strict in morals and religion. —**pu′ri·tan′i·cal**, a.

pur′lieu (-lōō) n. outlying part; suburb.

pur·loin′, v. steal.

pur′ple, n. & a. bluish red. —**pur′plish**, a.

pur·port′, v. seem or claim to mean or be. —n. (pûr′pôrt) meaning.

pur′pose, n. 1. intention; aim. 2. determination. —on purpose, intentionally. —**pur′pose·ful**, a. —**pur′pose·less**, a. —**pur′pose·ly**, adv.

purr, v. & n. (make) the sound of a cat at ease.

purse, n. 1. small bag for money. 2. woman's hand bag. 3. prize money. —v. to pucker.

purs′er, n. ship's officer in charge of accounts, etc.

pur·su′ant to, following. —according to.

pur·sue′, v. 1. try to overtake; chase. 2. go on with. 3. seek. —**pur·su′ance**, n.

pur·suit′, n. 1. a pursuing. 2. occupation.

pur′vey′ (-vā′) v. supply, as food. —**pur·vey′or**, n.

pus, n. yellowish matter forming in infections.

push, v. 1. move by pressing against. 2. urge on. —n. 1. a pushing. 2. an advance.

pu′sil·lan′i·mous, a. cowardly; timid.

puss, n. cat: also **puss′y**.

pussy willow, willow with soft, silvery catkins.

pus′tule (-chool) n. inflamed, pus-filled pimple.

put, v. [PUT, PUTTING] 1. make be in some place, state, relation, etc. 2. impose or assign. 3. express. 4. go (in, out, etc.). —a. [Col.] fixed. —**put down**, repress. —**put off**, postpone. —**put on**, pretend. —**put out**, 1. extinguish. 2. inconvenience. —**put up**, 1. preserve, as fruits. 2. give lodgings to. 3. provide (money); tolerate. —**put up with**, tolerate.

pu′tre·fy, v. [-FIED, -FYING] rot. —**pu′tre·fac′tion**, n.

pu′trid, a. rotten; stinking.

putt, v. & n. Golf (make) a stroke to get the ball into the hole.

put′ter, v. busy oneself futilely. —n. club for putting.

put′ty, n. pliable substance to fill cracks, etc. —v. [-TIED, -TYING] fill with putty.

puz′zle, v. perplex. —n. 1. thing that puzzles. 2. problem to test cleverness.

pyg′my, n. [pl. -MIES] dwarf.

py·ja′mas, n.pl. pajamas: Br. sp.

py′lon, n. towerlike shaft.

py·lo′rus, n. [pl. -RI] opening from the stomach into intestines. —**py·lor′ic**, a.

py·or·rhe·a, py·or·rhoe·a, (pī'ə-rē'ə) *n.* infection of the gums & tooth sockets.

pyr'a·mid (pîr'-) *n.* 1. solid figure or structure with triangular sides meeting at a point. —*v.* build up. —**py·ram'i·dal,** *a.*

pyre (pîr') *n.* pile of wood for burning a dead body.

py·ro·ma'ni·a, *n.* compulsion to start fires. —**py·ro·ma'ni·ac,** *n.*

py'ro·tech'nics (-tek'-) *n.pl.* display of fireworks.

py'thon, *n.* large snake that crushes its prey to death.

Q

quack, *v.* utter the cry of a duck. —*n.* 1. this cry. 2. one who practices medicine fraudulently. —**quack'er·y** [*pl.* -IES] *n.*

quad·ran'gle, *n.* 1. plane figure with 4 angles & 4 sides. 2. four-sided area surrounded by buildings.

quad'rant, *n.* quarter section of a circle.

quad'ri·lat'er·al, *a.* & *n.* four-sided (figure).

qua·drille', *n.* square dance for four couples.

quad'ru·ped, *n.* four-footed animal.

quad'ru·ple, *a.* & *adv.* four times as much. —*v.* make or become quadruple.

quad'ru·plet, *n.* any of four children born at one birth.

quaff, *v.* drink deeply. —*n.* a quaffing.

quag'mire, *n.* a bog.

quail, *v.* draw back in fear. —*n.* game bird.

quaint, *a.* pleasingly odd or old-fashioned. —**quaint'ly,** *adv.* —**quaint'ness,** *n.*

quake, *v.* shake. —*n.* 1. a quaking. 2. earthquake.

qual'i·fy, *v.* [-FIED, -FYING] 1. make or be fit for a job, etc. 2. modify; restrict. 3. moderate. —**qual'i·fi·ca'tion,** *n.*

qual'i·ty, *n.* [*pl.* -TIES] 1. characteristic. 2. kind. 3. degree (of excellence). —**qual'i·ta'tive,** *a.*

qualm, *n.* scruple; misgiving.

quan'da·ry, *n.* [*pl.* -RIES] state of perplexity; dilemma.

quan'ti·ty, *n.* [*pl.* -TIES] 1. amount. 2. large amount. 3. number or symbol expressing measure. —**quan'ti·ta'tive,** *a.*

quar'an·tine (-tēn) *n.* isola-tion to keep contagious disease from spreading. —*v.* place under quarantine.

quar'rel, *v.* & *n.* (have) an argument or disagreement. —**quar'rel·some,** *a.*

quar'ry, *n.* [*pl.* -RIES] 1. animal, etc. being hunted down. 2. place where stone is excavated. —*v.* [-RIED, -RYING] excavate from a quarry.

quart, *n.* ¼ gallon.

quar'ter, *n.* 1. any of four equal parts; ¼. 2. 25-cent coin. 3. district. 4. *pl.* lodgings. 5. mercy. —*v.* 1. divide into quarters. 2. provide lodgings for. —**at close quarters,** at close range.

quar'ter·back, *n.* Football back who calls signals.

quar'ter·ly, *a.* occurring regularly four times a year. —*adv.* once every quarter of the year. —*n.* [*pl.* -LIES] publication issued quarterly.

quar'ter·mas'ter, *n.* army officer in charge of supplies.

quar·tet', quar·tette' *n.* musical composition for four performers.

quar'to, *n.* book-page size about 9x12 in.

quartz, *n.* bright mineral.

quash, *v.* 1. annul. 2. suppress.

qua'si, *a.* & *adv.* seeming(ly).

quat'rain (kwät'-) *n.* stanza of four lines.

qua'ver, *v.* 1. tremble. 2. be tremulous: said of the voice. —*n.* tremulous tone.

quay (kē) *n.* wharf.

quea'sy (kwē'-) *a.* [-SIER, -SIEST] feeling nausea.

queen, *n.* 1. wife of a king. 2. woman monarch. 3. female in an insect colony. 4. playing card with a queen's picture. 5. most powerful chess piece.

queer, *a.* 1. odd. 2. [Col.] eccentric. —*v.* [Sl.] spoil the success of. —**queer'ly,** *adv.*

quell, *v.* subdue or quiet.

quench, *v.* 1. extinguish. 2. satisfy. —**quench'less.** *a.*

quer'u·lous (kwer'-) *a.* 1. fretful. 2. complaining.

que'ry (kwēr'-) *n.* [*pl.* -RIES] & *v.* [-RIED, -RYING] question.

quest, *n.* a seeking.

ques'tion, *n.* 1. inquiry. 2. thing asked. 3. doubt. 4. problem. 5. point being debated. —*v.* 1. inquire. 2. doubt. 3. challenge. —**out of the question,** impossible. —**ques′tion·er,** n.

ques′tion·a·ble, a. 1. doubtful. 2. not well thought of.

question mark, mark of punctuation (?).

ques′tion·naire′ (-nâr′) n. list of questions for gathering information.

queue (kū) n. 1. pigtail. 2. line of persons.

quib′ble, v. evade a point by carping.

quick, a. 1. swift. 2. prompt. —adv. rapidly. —n. 1. the living. 2. one's deepest feelings. —**quick′ly,** adv.

quick′en, v. 1. enliven. 2. hasten.

quick′sand, n. wet, deep sand that engulfs heavy things.

quick′sil·ver, n. mercury.

quick′-wit′ted, a. alert.

qui·es′cent (kwī-) a. quiet, inactive.

qui′et, a. 1. still. 2. silent. 3. gentle. —n. 1. stillness. 2. silence. —v. make or become quiet. —**qui′et·ly,** adv. —**qui′et·ness,** n.

quill, n. 1. large feather. 2. pen made from this. 3. spine of a porcupine.

quilt, n. & v. (make) a bed-cover stitched in layers.

quince, n. hard yellowish fruit.

qui′nine (-nīn) n. alkaloid used in treating malaria.

quin′sy (-zi) n. sore throat.

quin·tes′sence, n. 1. pure essence. 2. perfect example.

quin·tet′, quin·tette′, n. musical composition for five performers.

quin′tu·plet, n. any of five children born at one birth.

quip, v. [QUIPPED, QUIPPING] & n. (make) a witty remark.

quire, n. set of 24 or 25 sheets of the same paper.

quirk, n. peculiarity.

quis′ling, n. traitor.

quit, v. [QUIT, QUITTED, QUITTING] 1. give up. 2. leave. 3. stop. —a. free.

quit′claim, n. deed resigning a claim, as to property.

quite, adv. 1. completely. 2. really. 3. [Col.] somewhat. —**quite a few,** [Col.] many.

quits, a. on even terms.

quit′tance, n. 1. discharge of a debt. 2. recompense.

quit′ter, n. [Col.] one who gives up easily.

quiv′er, v. tremble. —n. 1. tremor. 2. case for arrows.

quix·ot′ic, a. idealistic but impractical.

quiz, n. [pl. QUIZZES] test of knowledge. —v. [QUIZZED, QUIZZING] give a quiz to.

quiz′zi·cal, a. 1. comical. 2. perplexed. —**quiz′zi·cal·ly,** adv.

quoit (kwoit, koit) n. 1. ring thrown to encircle an upright peg. 2. pl. game so played.

quon′dam, a. former.

Quon′set hut (kwon′-) metal shelter with a curved roof.

quo′rum, n. minimum number needed to transact business at an assembly.

quo′ta, n. [pl. -TAS] share assigned to each one.

quo·ta′tion, n. 1. a quoting. 2. words quoted. 3. current price of a stock or bond.

quotation marks, marks ("…") around quoted words.

quote, v. 1. repeat (the words of). 2. state (the price of). —n. [Col.] 1. quotation. 2. quotation mark. —**quot′a·ble,** a.

quoth (kwōth) v. [Ar.] said.

quo′tient (-shant) n. number got by dividing one number into another.

R

rab′bi (-bī) n. [pl. -BIS, -BIES] ordained teacher of the Jewish law. —**rab·bin′-i·cal,** a.

rab′bit, n. burrowing rodent with soft fur and long ears.

rab′ble, n. a mob.

rab′id, a. 1. fanatical. 2. of or having rabies.

ra′bies, n. disease of dogs, etc., transmitted by biting.

rac·coon′, n. small, furry mammal with black-ringed tail.

race, n. 1. a competition, esp. of speed. 2. swift current. 3. division of mankind, esp. based on skin color. 4. any group or class. —v. 1. be in a race. 2. move swiftly. —**rac′er,** n. —**ra′cial,** a.

rac′ial, a. see **race.**

rac′ism, n. racial discrimination or persecution. —**rac′ist,** a. & n.

rack, n. 1. framework for holding things. 2. ancient torture device. 3. great torment. 4. toothed bar meshing with a gearwheel. —v. to torture. —**rack one's brains,** think hard.

rack′et, n. 1. noisy confusion. 2. dishonest scheme. 3. netted frame used as a bat in tennis: also sp. **rac'-quet.** —**rack'et·eer'**, n.

rac'on·teur' (-tūr') n. one clever at telling stories.

rac·y (rās'ē) a. [-IER, -IEST] 1. lively. 2. risqué.

ra'dar, n. device for locating objects by their reflection of radio waves.

ra'di·al, a. of or like a ray or rays.

ra'di·ant, a. 1. beaming. 2. shining bright. 3. issuing in rays. —**ra'di·ance**, n.

ra'di·ate', v. 1. send out rays, as of heat or light. 2. branch out as from a center. —**ra'di·a'tion**, n.

ra'di·a'tor, n. device for radiating heat.

rad'i·cal, a. 1. basic. 2. favoring extreme change. —n. 1. one with radical views. 2. Chem. group of atoms acting as one. —**rad'i·cal·ism**, n. —**rad'i·cal·ly**, adv.

ra'di·o, n. [pl. -OS] 1. way of sending sounds through space by electromagnetic waves. 2. set for receiving radio waves. 3. broadcasting by radio. —a. of radio. —v. [-OED, -OING] send by radio.

ra'di·o·ac'tive, a. emitting radiant energy by the disintegration of atomic nuclei. —**ra'di·o·ac·tiv'i·ty**, n.

ra'di·ol'o·gy, n. medical use of radiant energy. —**ra'di·ol'o·gist**, n.

rad'ish, n. edible pungent root of a certain plant.

ra'di·um, n. radioactive metallic chemical element.

ra'di·us, n. [pl. -DII (-dī-ī), -DIUSES] straight line from the center to the outside of a circle or sphere.

raf·fi'a, n. fiber from leaves of a palm, used in weaving.

raf'fle, n. lottery. —v. offer as a prize in a raffle.

raft, n. floating platform of logs fastened together.

raft'er, n. beam in a roof.

rag, n. 1. piece of torn or waste cloth. 2. pl. tattered clothes. —**rag'ged**, a.

rag'a·muf'fin, n. dirty, ragged child.

rage, n. 1. furious anger. 2. craze; fad. —v. 1. show violent anger. 2. be unchecked.

rag'lan, a. designating a sleeve that continues in one piece to the collar.

ra·gout (ra-gōō') n. stew.

rag'time, n. early jazz.

rag'weed, n. common weed

whose pollen causes hay fever.

raid, n. sudden attack or invasion. —v. make a raid on.

rail, n. 1. bar put between posts as a guard or support. 2. either of the bars of a railroad track. 3. railroad. 4. small wading bird. —v. speak bitterly.

rail'ing, n. fence made of rails and posts.

rail'ler·y, n. playful teasing.

rail'road, n. 1. road with steel rails for trains. 2. system of such roads. —v. [Col.] rush through unfairly.

rail'way, n. 1. [Br.] railroad. 2. track with rails for cars.

rai'ment (rā'-) n. [Ar.] attire.

rain, n. water falling in drops from the clouds. —v. fall as or like rain. —**rain'drop**, n. —**rain'fall**, n. —**rain'storm**, n. —**rain'y** [-IER, -IEST] a.

rain'bow, n. arc of colors formed by sunshine on rain.

rain'coat, n. waterproof coat.

raise, v. 1. lift up. 2. increase in amount, degree, etc. 3. build or put up. 4. bring up. 5. collect. 6. make grow. —n. a pay increase.

rai'sin, n. sweet dried grape.

rake, n. 1. long-handled tool with teeth at one end. 2. debauched man. —v. 1. gather (leaves, etc.) with a rake. 2. search carefully. 3. sweep with gunfire.

rak'ish (rāk'-) a. jaunty.

ral'ly, v. [-LIED, -LYING] 1. regroup to set in order. 2. gather for a common aim. 3. revive. —n. 1. a rallying. 2. mass meeting.

ram, n. 1. male sheep. 2. device for battering down walls, etc. —v. [RAMMED, RAMMING] 1. strike against with force. 2. force into place.

ram'ble, v. 1. stroll; roam. 2. talk or write aimlessly. 3. spread, as vines. —n.a stroll. —**ram'bler**, n.

ram·bunc'tious (-shəs) a. [Col.] disorderly; unruly.

ram'i·fy, v. [-FIED, -FYING] spread out into branches. —**ram'i·fi·ca'tion**, n.

ramp, n. sloping passage joining different levels.

ram·page', v. rush wildly about. —n. (ram'pāj) wild, angry action: usually in **on** the (or a) **rampage**.

ramp'ant, a. 1. raging; wild. 2. rearing up.

ram'part, n. fortified embankment.

ram'rod, n. rod for ramming down a charge in a gun.

ram'shack·le, a. rickety.

ran, pt. of **run.**

ranch, n. large farm for raising livestock. —**ranch'-er, ranch'man** [pl. -MEN] n.

ran'cid, a. stale, as oil or fat; spoiled.

ran'cor, n. bitter hate or ill will. —**ran'cor·ous,** a.

ran'dom, a. haphazard. —**at random,** haphazardly.

rang, pt. of **ring.**

range, v. 1. set in rows. 2. roam about. 3. extend. —n. 1. row or line, esp. of mountains. 2. effective distance. 3. extent. 4. open land. 5. place for shooting practice. 6. cooking stove.

rang'er, n. 1. trooper who patrols a region. 2. warden who patrols forests.

rang'y, a. [-IER, -IEST] long-limbed and thin.

rank, n. 1. row; line. 2. class or grade. 3. pl. enlisted soldiers. —v. 1. place in, or hold, a certain rank. 2. outrank. —a. 1. growing wildly. 2. bad in taste or smell. 3. utter. —**rank and file,** 1. enlisted men. 2. common people.

ran'kle, v. cause mental pain, resentment, etc.

ran'sack, v. 1. search thoroughly. 2. plunder; loot.

ran'som, n. 1. the freeing of a captive by paying money. 2. price asked. —v. buy a captive's freedom.

rant, v. talk wildly; rave.

rap, v. [RAPPED, RAPPING] strike or knock sharply. —n. quick, sharp knock.

ra·pa'cious (-shas) a. greedy; voracious. —**ra·pac'i·ty,** n.

rape, n. crime of sexually attacking a woman. —v. commit rape on. —**rap'ist,** n.

rap'id, a. swift. —**ra·pid'i·ty,** n. —**rap'id·ly,** adv.

rap'ids, n.pl. part of a river with very swift current.

ra'pi·er, n. light, sharp sword.

rap'ine (rap'in) n. plunder.

rap·port', n. sympathetic relationship; harmony.

rapt, a. engrossed (in).

rap'ture, n. ecstasy.

rare, a. 1. scarce; uncommon. 2. very good. 3. not dense. 4. partly raw.

rare'ness, n. —**rar'i·ty** [-TIES] n.

rare'bit, n. Welsh rabbit.

rar'e·fy, v. [-FIED, -FYING] make or become less dense.

rare'ly, adv. seldom.

ras'cal, n. 1. rogue. 2. mischievous child. —**ras·cal'i·ty,** n.

rash, a. too hasty; reckless. —n. red spots on the skin. —**rash'ly,** adv.

rasp, v. 1. scrape harshly. 2. irritate. —n. 1. rough file. 2. grating sound.

rasp'ber'ry, n. [pl. -RIES] 1. shrub with red or black berries. 2. the berry.

rat, n. long-tailed rodent, larger than a mouse. —v. [RATTED, RATTING] [Sl.] inform on others.

ratch'et, n. wheel or bar with slanted teeth that catch on a pawl.

rate, n. 1. relative amount or degree. 2. price per unit. 3. rank. —v. 1. appraise. 2. rank. 3. [Col.] deserve.

rath'er, adv. 1. preferably. 2. with more reason. 3. more truly. 4. on the contrary. 5. somewhat.

rat'i·fy, v. [-FIED, -FYING] approve formally. —**rat'i·fi·ca'tion,** n.

rat'ing (rāt'-) n. 1. rank. 2. appraisal.

ra'tio (-shō) n. [pl. -TIOS] relation of one thing to another in size, etc.

ra'tion (rā'- or ra'-) n. fixed share, as of food. —v. give in rations. —**ra'tion·ing,** n.

ra'tion·al (ra'-) a. 1. able to reason. 2. reasonable. —**ra'tion·al'i·ty,** n. —**ra'tion·al·ly,** adv.

ra'tion·al·ize, v. give plausible explanations for. —**ra'tion·al·i·za'tion,** n.

rat·tan', n. palm stems used in wickerwork, etc.

rat'tle, v. 1. make or cause to make a series of sharp, short sounds. 2. chatter. 3. [Col.] upset. —n. 1. a rattling. 2. baby's toy that rattles.

rat'tle·snake, n. snake with a tail that rattles: also **rat'tler.**

rau'cous (rô'-) a. hoarse.

rav'age (-ij) v. & n. ruin.

rave, v. 1. talk wildly. 2. praise greatly. —n. [Sl.] enthusiastic praise.

rav'el, v. untwist; fray.

ra'ven, n. large black crow. —a. black and shiny.

rav'e·nous, *a.* greedily hungry. —**rav'e·nous·ly**, *adv.*

ra·vine' (-vēn') *n.* long, deep hollow in the earth.

rav'ish, *v.* 1. fill with great joy. 2. rape.

rav'ish·ing, *a.* delightful.

raw, *a.* 1. uncooked. 2. unprocessed. 3. inexperienced. 4. sore and inflamed. 5. cold and damp. 6. [Sl.] unfair. —**raw'ness**, *n.*

raw'hide', *n.* untanned cattle hide.

ray, *n.* 1. thin beam of light. 2. stream of radiant energy. 3. tiny amount. 4. broad, flat fish.

ray'on, *n.* fabric made from cellulose.

raze, *v.* demolish.

ra'zor, *n.* sharp-edged instrument for shaving.

razz, *v.* [Sl.] make fun of.

re (rē) *prep.* regarding.

re-, *pref.* 1. back. 2. again: for list below add *again* to meaning of base word.

re·ad·just'
re·af·firm'
re·ap·pear'
re·ap·point'
re·arm'
re·as·sem'ble
re·as·sign'
re·a·wak'en
re·born'
re·broad'cast
re·build'
re·cap'ture
re·con·sid'er
re·con·struct'
re·dis·cov'er
re·do'
re·dou'ble
re·ech'o
re·ed·u·cate
re'·e·lect'
re'·en·act'
re'·en·list'
re·en'ter
re'·ex·am'ine
re·fill'
re·fu'el
re·heat'
re·in·vest'
re·learn'
re·live'
re·load'
re·lo'cate
re·make'
re·mar'ry
re·o'pen
re·or'der
re·phrase'
re·play'
re·print'
re·read'
re·tell'
re·u·nite'

reach, *v.* 1. extend the hand, etc. 2. touch. 3. get to. 4. influence. 5. get in touch with. 6. try to get. —*n.* act or extent of reaching.

re·act', *v.* 1. respond to stimulus. 2. return to an earlier state. 3. act with another substance in a chemical change. —**re·ac'tion**, *n.*

re·ac'tion·ar'y, *n.* [*pl.* -IES] & *a.* ultraconservative.

re·ac'tor, *n.* device for producing atomic energy.

read, *v.* [READ (red), READ-ING] 1. understand or utter (written or printed matter). 2. study. 3. register, as a gauge. —**read'er**, *n.*

read'ing, *n.* 1. act of one that reads. 2. thing to be read. 3. interpretation.

read'y (red'i) *a.* [-IER, -IEST] 1. prepared to act. 2. willing. 3. available. —*v.* [-IED, -YING] prepare. —**read'i·ly**, *adv.* —**read'i·ness**, *n.*

read'y-made', *a.* ready for use or sale at once.

re'al, *a.* 1. actual; true. 2. genuine. [Col.] very. —*adv.* **re'al·ly**, *adv.*

real estate, land, including buildings, etc. on it.

re'al·ism, *n.* awareness of things as they really are. —**re'al·ist**, *n.* —**re'al·is'tic**, *a.* —**re'al·is'ti·cal·ly**, *adv.*

re·al'i·ty, *n.* [*pl.* -TIES] 1. state of being real. 2. real thing; fact.

re'al·ize, *v.* 1. understand fully. 2. make real. 3. gain. —**re'al·i·za'tion**, *n.*

realm (relm) *n.* 1. kingdom. 2. region; sphere.

re'al·tor, *n.* certified real-estate broker.

re'al·ty, *n.* real estate.

ream, *n.* quantity of 480 to 516 sheets of paper. —*v.* enlarge (a hole). —**ream'er**, *n.*

reap, *v.* cut and gather (grain, etc.). —**reap'er**, *n.*

rear, *n.* back part or place. —*a.* of or at the rear. —*v.* 1. bring up; raise. 2. rise on the hind legs.

rear admiral, naval officer above a captain.

re·ar·range', *v.* arrange in a different way. —**re'ar·range'ment**, *n.*

rea'son, *n.* 1. explanation. 2. cause. 3. power to think. 4. good sense. —*v.* think or argue with logic. —**rea'son·ing**, *n.*

rea'son·a·ble, *a.* 1. fair. 2.

sensible. 3. not expensive.
—**rea'son·a·bly,** adv.

re'as·sure', v. restore to confidence.—**re'as·sur'ance,** n.

re'bate, v. & n. return (of) part of a payment.

reb'el, n. one who openly resists authority. —a. rebellious. —v. (ri-bel') [-ELLED, -ELLING] resist authority. —**re·bel'lion,** n. —**re·bel'lious,** a.

re'bound', v. & n. recoil.

re·buff', v. & n. snub.

re·buke', v. scold sharply. —n. sharp scolding.

re'bus, n. puzzle in which pictures stand for words.

re·but', v. [-BUTTED, -BUTTING] contradict formally. —**re·but'tal,** n.

re·cal'ci·trant, a. refusing to obey. —**re·cal'ci·trance,** n.

re·call', v. 1. call back. 2. remember. 3. revoke. —n. (rē'kôl) a recalling.

re·cant', v. renounce (one's beliefs).

re'ca·pit'u·late, v. summarize. —**re'ca·pit'u·la'tion,** n.

re·cede', v. move or slope backward.

re·ceipt' (-sēt') n. 1. a receiving. 2. written acknowledgment of sum received. 3. pl. amount received.

re·ceive', v. 1. get; be given. 2. greet (guests).

re·ceiv'er, n. 1. one who receives. 2. one holding in trust property in bankruptcy, etc. 3. apparatus that converts electrical signals into sound or light, as in radio & TV.

re'cent, a. of a short time ago. —**re'cent·ly,** adv.

re·cep'ta·cle, n. container.

re·cep'tion, n. 1. a receiving or being received. 2. social function. 3. the receiving of signals on radio or TV.

re·cep'tion·ist, n. employee who receives callers, etc.

re·cep'tive, a. ready to receive suggestions, etc.

re·cess', n. 1. hollow in a wall. 2. break from work. —v. 1. take a recess. 2. set back.

re·ces'sion, n. temporary falling off of business.

rec'i·pe, n. directions for preparing dish or drink.

re·cip'i·ent, n. one that receives.

re·cip'ro·cal, a. 1. done, etc. in return. 2. mutual. —**re·**

cip'ro·cal·ly, adv. —**rec'i·proc'i·ty,** n.

re·cit'al (-sīt'-) n. 1. account told. 2. musical program.

re·cite', v. 1. repeat something memorized. 2. narrate. —**rec'i·ta'tion,** n.

reck'less, a. heedless; rash. —**reck'less·ly,** adv. —**reck'less·ness,** n.

reck'on, v. 1. count. 2. estimate. 3. [Col.] suppose. —**reckon with,** deal with.

reck'on·ing, n. 1. a figuring out. 2. settlement of accounts.

re·claim', v. restore for use. —**rec'la·ma'tion,** n.

re·cline', v. lie down or lean back.

rec'og·nize, v. 1. identify as known before. 2. perceive. 3. acknowledge; notice formally. —**rec'og·ni'tion,** n. —**rec'og·niz'a·ble,** a.

re·coil', v. 1. pull back. —n. (rē'koil) a recoiling.

rec'ol·lect', v. remember. —**rec'ol·lec'tion,** n.

rec'om·mend', v. 1. suggest as fit or worthy. 2. advise. —**rec'om·men·da'tion,** n.

rec'om·pense, v. pay or pay back. —n. compensation.

rec'on·cile (-sīl) v. 1. make friendly again. 2. settle (a quarrel). 3. make agree or fit. 4. make acquiescent (to). —**rec'on·cil'a·ble,** a. —**rec'on·cil'i·a'tion** (-sil'-) n.

rec'on·dite', a. abstruse.

re'con·di'tion, v. put back in good condition.

re·con'nais·sance (-ə-səns) n. a spying on an area.

rec'on·noi'ter, v. examine or spy on an area.

rec'ord', v. 1. keep a written account of. 2. show on a dial, etc. 3. put sound on a grooved disk, etc. —n. (rek'ērd) 1. official account. 2. known facts. 3. disk with recorded sound. 4. the best yet done. —a. (rek'ērd) best.

re·cord'er, n. 1. person or machine that records. 2. early form of flute.

re·cord'ing, n. phonograph record.

re·count', v. narrate.

re'-count', v. count again. —n. (rē'kount) second count.

re·coup' (-kōōp') v. make up for, as a loss.

re'course, n. 1. a turning for aid. 2. source of aid.

re·cov'er, v. 1. get back; regain. 2. become normal. 3. keep from a fall. 4. reclaim. —**re·cov'er·y** [pl. -IES] n.

rec're·ant, a. cowardly. —n. coward.

rec·re·a'tion, n. refreshing play. —**rec're·a'tion·al,** a.

re·crim'i·nate, v. accuse one's accuser. —**re·crim'i·na'tion.**

re·cruit' (-krōōt') n. new member, soldier, etc. —v. enlist (recruits).

rec'tan·gle, n. four-sided figure with four right angles. —**rec·tan'gu·lar,** a.

rec'ti·fy, v. [-FIED, -FYING] to correct. —**rec'ti·fi·ca'tion.** —**rec'ti·fi·er,** n.

rec'ti·tude, n. honesty.

rec'tor, n. head of some schools or parishes.

rec'to·ry, n. [pl. -RIES] rector's residence.

rec'tum, n. lowest part of the intestine. —**rec'tal,** a.

re·cum'bent, a. lying down.

re·cu'per·ate, v. recover health, losses, etc. —**re·cu'per·a'tion,** n.

re·cur', v. [-CURRED, -CURRING] 1. occur again. 2. return in talk, etc. —**re·cur'rence,** n. —**re·cur'rent,** a.

red, n. 1. color of blood. 2. [R-] communist. —a. [REDDER, REDDEST] of the color red. —**red'dish,** a. —**red'ness,** n.

red'cap, n. porter in a railroad or bus station.

red'den, v. make or become red.

re·deem', v. 1. buy back. 2. pay off. 3. turn in for a prize. 4. free, as from sin. 5. atone for. —**re·deem'a·ble,** a. —**re·deem'er,** n. —**re·demp'tion,** n.

red'-hand'ed, a. while committing a crime.

red'head, n. person with red hair. —**red'head·ed,** a.

red'-hot', a. 1. glowing hot. 2. very excited. 3. very new.

red'-let'ter, a. memorable.

red'o·lent, a. 1. fragrant. 2. smelling (of). 3. suggesting. —**red'o·lence,** n.

re·doubt' (-dout') n. stronghold.

re·doubt'a·ble, a. 1. formidable. 2. deserving respect.

re·dound', v. have a result.

re·dress', v. correct and make up for. —n. (rē'dres) a redressing.

red snapper, ocean food fish.

red tape, rules and details that waste time and effort.

re·duce', v. 1. lessen; decrease. 2. change the form of. 3. lower. 4. lose weight. —**re·duc'tion,** n.

re·dun'dant, a. 1. excess; superfluous. 2. wordy. —**re·dun'dan·cy** [pl. -CIES] n.

red'wood, n. 1. giant evergreen. 2. its reddish wood.

reed, n. 1. a hollow-stemmed grass. 2. musical pipe made of this. 3. vibrating strip in some musical instruments. —**reed'y** [-IER, -IEST] a.

reef, n. ridge of land near the surface of water. —v. take in part of a sail.

reek, v. & n. (emit) a strong, offensive smell.

reel, n. 1. spool or frame on which thread, film, etc. is wound. 2. amount wound on it. 3. lively dance. —v. 1. to wind (in or out) on a reel. 2. tell fluently (with off). 3. stagger.

re·fec'to·ry, n. [pl. -RIES] dining hall.

re·fer', v. [-FERRED, -FERRING] 1. go to, or direct someone to, for aid, information, etc. 2. allude (to).

ref·er·ee', n. 1. one chosen to decide something. —v. judge in sports. —v. act as referee in.

ref'er·ence, n. 1. a referring. 2. relation or connection. 3. mention of a source of information. 4. recommendation, or person giving it. —**make reference to,** mention.

ref'er·en'dum, n. submission of a law to direct popular vote.

re·fine', v. free from impurities, coarseness, etc. —**re·fine'ment,** n.

re·fined', a. 1. purified. 2. cultivated or elegant.

re·fin'er·y, n. [pl. -IES] plant for purifying materials.

re·flect', v. 1. throw back, as an image or sound. 2. result in (credit, etc.). —**reflect on** (or **upon**), 1. ponder. 2. cast blame. —**re·flec'tion,** n. —**re·flec'tive,** a. —**re·flec'tor,** n.

re·flex', a. & n. (designating or of) an involuntary reaction to a stimulus.

re·flex'ive, a. 1. designating a verb whose subject and object are the same. 2. designating a pronoun used as object of such a verb.

re·form', v. 1. improve. 2. behave or make behave better. —n. improvement. —**re·form'er**, n.

ref·or·ma'tion, n. 1. a reforming. 2. [R-] 16th-century movement establishing the Protestant churches.

re·form'a·to·ry, n. [pl. -RIES] institution for reforming young lawbreakers.

re·fract', v. bend (a light ray, etc.) —**re·frac'tion**, n.

re·frac'to·ry, a. obstinate.

re·frain', v. hold back. —n. repeated verse of a song.

re·fresh', v. make fresh or stronger; renew or revive. —**re·fresh'ment**, n. 1. a refreshing. 2. pl. food or drink.

re·frig'er·ate (-frij'-) v. make cold, as for preserving. —**re·frig·er·a'tion**, n. —**re·frig'er·ant**, a. & n.

re·frig'er·a'tor, n. box or room for refrigerating.

ref·uge (-ūj) n. protection from danger or pursuit.

ref·u·gee' (-jē') n. one who flees to seek refuge.

re·fund', v. give back (money, etc.) —n. (rē'fund) amount refunded.

re·fur'bish, v. renovate.

re·fuse' (-fūz') v. 1. reject. 2. decline (to do, etc.). —n. (ref'ūs) rubbish. —**re·fus'al**, n.

re·fute', v. prove wrong. —**ref'u·ta'tion**, n.

re·gain', v. get back; recover.

re'gal, a. royal.

re·gale', v. entertain, as with a feast.

re·ga'li·a, n.pl. insignia or decorations, as of a rank.

re·gard', n. 1. concern. 2. affection and respect. 3. reference. 4. pl. good wishes. —v. 1. gaze upon. 2. think of; consider. 3. concern. —**as regards**, concerning. —**re·gard'ful**, a. —**re·gard'less**, a. & adv.

re·gard'ing, prep. about.

re·gat'ta, n. boat race.

re·gen'er·ate, v. 1. give new life to; renew. 2. improve. —a. (-it) renewed or improved. —**re·gen·er·a'tion**, n.

re·gent (-jənt) n. interim ruler in place of a monarch. —**re'gen·cy** [pl. -CIES] n.

re·gime (rā-zhēm') n. political or ruling system.

reg'i·men (rej'-) n. system of diet, exercise, etc.

reg'i·ment, n. section of an army division. —v. control

and discipline strictly. —**reg·i·men'tal**, a. —**reg·i·men·ta'tion**, n.

re'gion, n. area, division, or part. —**re'gion·al**, a.

reg'is·ter, n. 1. list of names, etc. 2. recording device, as for cash transactions. 3. device for adjusting passage of air. 4. musical range. —v. 1. enter in a list. 2. show. 3. [Col.] make an impression. —**reg'is·tra'tion**, n.

reg'is·trar' (-trär') n. keeper of records, as in a college.

re·gress', v. go backward. —**re·gres'sion**, n.

re·gret', v. [-GRETTED, -GRET-TING] be sorry for (a mistake, etc.). —n. a being sorry. —**re·gret'ful**, a. —**re·gret'ta·ble**, a.

reg'u·lar, a. 1. according to rule; orderly. 2. usual. 3. unchanging. —**reg·u·lar'i·ty**, n. —**reg'u·lar·ly**, adv.

reg'u·late, v. 1. control. 2. adjust to a standard, etc. —**reg'u·la'tor**, n.

reg·u·la'tion, n. 1. a regulating. 2. rule. —a. usual.

re·gur'gi·tate (-jə-) v. bring up from the stomach. —**re·gur'gi·ta'tion**, n.

re·ha·bil'i·tate, v. restore to earlier state. —**re·ha·bil'i·ta'tion**, n.

re·hash', v. repeat. —n. (rē'hash) a rehashing.

re·hearse' (-hûrs') v. 1. recite. 2. practice for a performance. —**re·hears'al**, n.

reign (rān) n. (period of) a sovereign's rule. —v. rule as sovereign.

re'im·burse', v. pay back. —**re'im·burse'ment**, n.

rein (rān) n. strap hooked to a bit for controlling a horse. —**give (free) rein to**, free from restraint.

re'in·car·na'tion, n. rebirth (of the soul). —**re'in·car'nate**, v.

rein'deer (rān'-) n. [pl. -DEER] large northern deer.

re'in·force', v. strengthen. —**re'in·force'ment**, n.

re'in·state', v. restore. —**re'in·state'ment**, n.

re·it'er·ate', v. repeat. —**re·it'er·a'tion**, n.

re·ject', v. 1. refuse to accept. 2. discard. —n. (rē'jekt) thing rejected. —**re·jec'tion**, n.

re·joice', v. be or make happy. —**re·joic'ing**, n.

re·join', v. 1. join again. 2. answer. —**re·join'der**, n.

re·ju've·nate, v. make young

again. —re·ju've·na'tion, n.

re·lapse', v. & n. fall back into a past state.

re·late', v. 1. narrate. 2. connect, as in meaning. 3. have reference (to).

re·lat'ed, a. of the same family or kind.

re·la'tion, n. 1. a relating or being related. 2. kinship. 3. a relative. 4. pl. dealings, as between people. —re·la'tion·ship, n.

rel'a·tive, a. 1. related. 2. relevant. 3. comparative. —n. related person.

rel'a·tiv'i·ty, n. 1. a being relative. 2. modern theory of the universe.

re·lax', v. 1. loosen up. 2. rest, as from work. —re'lax·a'tion, n.

re'lay, n. fresh group of workers, runners, etc. —v. (ri-lā') get and pass on.

re·lease', v. 1. set free. 2. allow to be issued. —n. 1. a releasing. 2. device to release a catch.

rel'e·gate, v. 1. exile. 2. put into a lower position. 3. assign. —rel'e·ga'tion, n.

re·lent', v. become less stern. —re·lent'less, a.

rel'e·vant, a. pertinent. —rel'e·vance, rel'e·van·cy, n.

re·li'a·ble, a. that can be relied on. —re·li'a·bil'i·ty, n. —re·li'a·bly, adv.

re·li'ance, n. trust or confidence. —re·li'ant, a.

rel'ic, n. 1. something from the past. 2. sacred object.

re·lief', n. 1. a relieving. 2. thing that relieves. 3. public aid, as to the poor. 4. projection, as sculpture, from a flat surface.

re·lieve', v. 1. to ease; comfort. 2. give aid to. 3. free by replacing. 4. bring a pleasant change to.

re·li'gion, n. 1. belief in God or gods. 2. system of worship. —re·li'gious, a.

re·lin'quish, v. let go.

rel'ish, n. 1. pleasing flavor. 2. enjoyment. 3. pickles, etc. served with a meal. —v. enjoy.

re·luc'tant, a. unwilling. —re·luc'tance, n. —re·luc'tant·ly, adv.

re·ly', v. [-LIED, -LYING] trust; depend (on or upon).

re·main', v. 1. be left when part is gone. 2. stay. 3. continue. —re·main'der, n.

re·mains', n.pl. 1. part left. 2. dead body.

re·mand', v. send back.

re·mark', v. & n. (make) a brief comment or observation.

re·mark'a·ble, a. unusual. —re·mark'a·bly, adv.

re·me'di·al, a. corrective.

rem'e·dy, n. [pl. -DIES] thing that corrects, etc. —v. again. 2. bear in mind. —re·mem'brance, n.

re·mem'ber, v. 1. think of again. 2. bear in mind. —re·mem'brance, n.

re·mind', v. cause to remember. —re·mind'er, n.

rem'i·nis'cence, n. 1. memory. 2. pl. account of remembered events. —rem'i·nisce', v. —rem'i·nis'cent, a.

re·miss', a. careless.

re·mit', v. [-MITTED, -MITTING] 1. forgive. 2. refrain from exacting. 3. slacken. 4. send money. —re·mis'sion, n. —re·mit'tance, n.

rem'nant, n. part left over.

re·mod'el, v. rebuild.

re·mon'strate, v. say in protest. —re·mon'strance, n.

re·morse', n. deep sense of guilt. —re·morse'ful, a. —re·morse'less, a.

re·mote', a. 1. distant. 2. slight. —re·mote'ly, adv.

re·move', v. 1. take away. 2. dismiss. 3. get rid of. —re·mov'al, n.

re·mu'ner·ate, v. pay for; reward. —re·mu'ner·a'tion, n. —re·mu'ner·a·tive, a.

ren·ais·sance' (-ə-säns') n. rebirth; revival: also re·nas'cence, n. —re·nas'cent, a.

re'nal, a. of the kidneys.

rend, v. [RENT, RENDING] tear; split apart.

ren'der, v. 1. submit. 2. give in return. 3. cause to be. 4. perform. 5. translate. 6. melt (fat). —ren·di'tion, n.

ren·dez·vous (rän'də-vōō) n. appointed meeting (place). —v. meet as agreed.

ren'e·gade, n. traitor.

re·nege (ri-nig') v. 1. [Col.] go back on a promise.

re·new', v. 1. make new again. 2. begin again. 3. replenish (a supply).

re·nounce', v. 1. give up (a claim, etc.). 2. disown. —re·nounce'ment, n.

ren'o·vate, v. make like new; restore. —ren'o·va'tion, n. —ren'o·va'tor, n.

re·nown', n. fame. —re·nowned', a.

rent, n. 1. payment for the use of property. 2. a rip. —v. get or give rent for.

rent'al, n. 1. rate of rent. 2. thing for rent. —a. of or for rent.

re·nun'ci·a'tion, n. a renouncing, as of a right.

re·pair', v. 1. fix; mend. 2. make amends for. 3. go (to). —n. a repairing or being repaired.

rep'a·ra'tion, n. 1. a making of amends. 2. compensation, as for war damage.

rep·ar·tee', n. quick, witty reply or conversation.

re·past', n. a meal.

re·pay', v. [-PAID, -PAYING] pay back. —re·pay'ment, n.

re·peal', v. revoke; annul (a law). —n. revocation.

re·peat', v. say or do again. —n. 1. a repeating. 2. thing repeated. —re·peat'ed·ly, adv. —re·peat'er, n.

re·pel', v. [-PELLED, -PELLING] 1. force back. 2. disgust. —re·pel'lent, a. & n.

re·pent', v. feel sorry for (a sin, etc.). —re·pent'ance, n. —re·pent'ant, a.

re'per·cus'sion (-kush'ən) n. 1. echo. 2. reaction, often an indirect one.

rep'er·toire (-twär) n. stock of plays, songs, etc. one is prepared to perform: also rep'er·to'ry [pl. -RIES].

rep'e·ti'tion, n. 1. a repeating. 2. thing repeated. rep'e·ti'tious, a.

re·pine', v. feel or express discontent (at).

re·place', v. 1. put back. 2. take the place of. 3. put another in place of. —re·place'ment, n.

re·plen'ish, v. fill again. —re·plen'ish·ment, n.

re·plete', a. filled —re·ple'tion, n.

rep'li·ca, n. exact copy.

re·ply', v. [-PLIED, -PLYING] & n. [pl. -PLIES] answer.

re·port', v. 1. give an account of. 2. tell as news; announce. 3. denounce (an offender, etc.) to one in authority. 4. present oneself. —n. 1. statement or account. 2. rumor. 3. explosive noise. —re·port'ed·ly, adv.

re·port'er, n. one who gathers and reports news.

re·pose', v. & n. rest.

re·pos'i·to'ry, n. [pl. -RIES] place where things may be put for safekeeping.

rep're·hend', v. scold or blame. —rep're·hen'si·ble, a.

rep're·sent', v. 1. portray or describe. 2. symbolize. 3. act in place of. 4. be an example of. —rep're·sen·ta'tion, n.

rep're·sent'a·tive, a. 1. representing. 2. typical. —n. 1. typical example. 2. one chosen to act for others. 3. [R-] Congressional or State legislator.

re·press', v. 1. hold back. 2. subdue. 3. force (painful ideas, etc.) into the unconscious. —re·pres'sion, n. —re·pres'sive, a.

re·prieve', n. & v. delay (in) the execution of (one sentenced to die).

rep'ri·mand, n. & v. rebuke.

re·pri'sal, n. injury done for injury received.

re·proach', v. blame; rebuke. —n. 1. disgrace. 2. a scolding or blaming. —re·proach'ful, a.

rep'ro·bate, a. & n. depraved (person).

re·pro·duce', v. produce copies, offspring, etc. —re'pro·duc'tion, n. —re'pro·duc'tive, a.

re·proof', n. a reproving; rebuke: also re·prov'al.

re·prove', v. find fault with.

rep'tile, n. cold-blooded, creeping vertebrate, as a snake, lizard, etc. —rep·til'i·an, a.

re·pub'lic, n. government by elected representatives. —re·pub'li·can, a. & n.

re·pu'di·ate, v. disown; cast off. —re·pu'di·a'tion, n.

re·pug'nant, a. 1. opposed. 2. distasteful; offensive. —re·pug'nance, n.

re·pulse', v. 1. repel. 2. rebuff. —re·pul'sion, n.

re·pul'sive, a. disgusting.

rep'u·ta·ble, a. having a good reputation.

rep'u·ta'tion, n. 1. others' opinion of one. 2. good character. 3. fame.

re·pute', v. consider to be. —n. reputation. —re·put'ed, a. —re·put'ed·ly, adv.

re·quest', n. 1. an asking for. 2. thing asked for. —v. ask for.

Re'qui·em, re'qui·em, n. R. C. Ch. Mass for the dead.

re·quire', v. 1. demand. 2.

re·quire′ment, n.

req·ui·site (rek′wə-zit) n. & a. (something) necessary.

req·ui·si′tion, n. written order.—v. demand or take.

re·quite′, v. repay for.—**re·quit′al,** n.

re·route′, v. send by a different route.

re·scind′ (-sind′) v. cancel; repeal.

res′cue, v. free or save.—n. a rescuing.—**res′cu·er,** n.

re·search′ (or rē′sûrch) n. careful study in a subject.

re·sem′ble, v. be like.—**re·sem′blance,** n.

re·sent′, v. feel anger at.—**re·sent′ful,** a.—**re·sent′ment,** n.

res·er·va′tion, n. 1. a reserving, as of a hotel room. 2. public land set aside as for Indians.

re·serve′, v. keep back; set aside.—n. 1. thing reserved. 2. limitation. 3. reticence. 4. pl. troops subject to call.—**re·served′,** a.

res′er·voir (-vwär) n. 1. place for storing water. 2. large supply.

re·side′, v. 1. live (in or at). 2. be present (in).

res′i·dence, n. 1. a residing. 2. home.—**res′i·dent,** a. & n.—**res′i·den′tial** (-shal) a.

res′i·due, n. part that is left.—**re·sid′u·al,** a.

re·sign′, v. 1. give up, as a claim, position, etc. 2. be submissive.—**res′ig·na′tion,** n.—**re·signed′,** a.

re·sil′ient, a. 1. bouncing back; elastic.—**re·sil′ience, re·sil′i·en·cy,** n.

res′in, n. 1. substance from trees used in varnish, etc. 2. rosin.—**res′in·ous,** a.

re·sist′, v. 1. withstand. 2. fight against.

re·sist′ance, n. 1. power to resist. 2. opposition to another force.—**re·sist′ant,** a.

res′o·lute, a. firm; determined.—**res′o·lute·ly,** adv.

res′o·lu′tion, n. 1. a resolving. 2. formal statement. 3. determination.

re·solve′, v. 1. decide. 2. solve. 3. change.—n. fixed purpose.—**re·solved′,** a.

res′o·nant, a. 1. resounding. 2. intensifying sound.—**res′o·nance,** n.

re·sort′, v. 1. go often. 2. turn for help (to.)—n. 1. place for help or a vacation, etc. 2. source of help.

re·sound′ (-zound′) v. make

an echoing sound.

re·source′ (or rē′sôrs) n. 1. emergency supply. 2. pl. wealth. 3. resourcefulness.

re·source′ful, a. able to handle problems, etc.

re·spect′, v. 1. think highly of. 2. show concern for. 3. concern.—n. 1. honor. 2. concern. 3. pl. regards. 4. reference.—**re·spect′ful,** a.

re·spect′ful·ly, adv.

re·spect′a·ble, a. 1. of good reputation. 2. good enough.—**re·spect′a·bil′i·ty,** n.

re·spect′ing, prep. concerning.

re·spec′tive, a. of or for each separately.—**re·spec′tive·ly,** adv.

res′pi·ra′tion, n. act or process of breathing.—**res′pi·ra·to′ry,** a.

res′pi·ra′tor, n. device to aid breathing artificially.

res′pite, n. 1. a delay. 2. period of relief or rest.

re·splend′ent, a. dazzling.

re·spond′, v. 1. to answer. 2. react.

re·sponse′, n. 1. a reply. 2. reaction.—**re·spon′sive,** a.

re·spon′si·ble, a. 1. obliged to do or answer for. 2. involving duties. 3. dependable.—**re·spon′si·bil′i·ty** [pl. -TIES] n.

rest, n. 1. ease or inactivity. 2. peace. 3. support. 4. pause. 5. remainder.—v. 1. get, or be at, ease. 2. become still. 3. lie or lay. 4. depend.—**rest′ful,** a.

res′tau·rant (-tə-) n. place for buying and eating meals.

res′ti·tu′tion, n. 1. a giving back. 2. reimbursement.

rest′ive, a. restless.

rest′less, a. 1. uneasy. 2. disturbed. 3. active.

re·store′, v. 1. give back. 2. return to a former position, condition, etc.—**res′to·ra′tion,** n.—**re·stor′a·tive,** a. & n.

re·strain′, v. hold back from action; suppress.

re·straint′, n. 1. a restraining. 2. thing that restrains. 3. self-control.

re·strict′, v. limit; confine.—**re·stric′tion,** n.—**re·stric′tive,** a.

rest′-room, n. public room with toilets and washbowls: also rest room.

re·sult′, v. 1. happen as an effect. 2. end (in).—n. 1. what is caused; outcome. 2. mathematical answer.

re·sume′, v. 1. take again. 2. continue after interruption. —**re·sump′tion**, n.

ré·su·mé (rā-zoo-mā′, rez′-yoo-) n. summary.

re·sur′gent, a. rising again. —**re·sur′gence**, n.

res·ur·rect′, v. bring back to life, use, etc. —**res′ur·rec′tion**, n.

re·sus′ci·tate (-sus′ə-) v. revive, as one almost dead. —**re·sus′ci·ta′tion**, n.

re′tail, n. sale of goods in small amounts to consumers. —a. of such sale. —v. sell at retail. —**re′tail·er**, n.

re·tain′, v. 1. keep in possession, use, etc. 2. keep in mind. 3. hire (a lawyer).

re·tain′er, n. 1. one that retains. 2. servant to a rich person or family. 3. fee paid to hire a lawyer.

re·take′, v. take again. —n. (rē′tāk) scene photographed again.

re·tal′i·ate, v. return injury for injury. —**re·tal′i·a′tion**, n. —**re·tal′i·a·to′ry**, a.

re·tard′, v. slow down; delay. —**re′tar·da′tion**, n.

retch, v. strain to vomit.

re·ten′tion, n. 1. a retaining. 2. ability to retain. —**re·ten′tive**, a.

ret′i·cent, a. disinclined to speak. —**ret′i·cence**, n.

ret′i·na, n. part at the back of the eyeball, on which images are formed.

ret′i·nue (-′n-ōō) n. attendants on a person of rank.

re·tire′, v. 1. withdraw or retreat. 2. withdraw from one's career, etc. 3. go to bed. —**re·tire′ment**, n.

re·tir′ing, a. shy; modest.

re·tort′, v. reply sharply or cleverly. —n. 1. sharp or clever reply. 2. container for distilling, etc.

re·touch′, v. touch up.

re·trace′, v. go back over.

re·tract′, v. 1. draw back or in. 2. withdraw, as a charge. —**re·trac′tion**, n.

re·treat′, n. 1. withdrawal, esp. under attack. 2. quiet place. 3. period of contemplation. —v. withdraw.

re·trench′, v. economize.

ret′ri·bu′tion, n. deserved punishment.

re·trieve′ (-trēv′) v. 1. get back or bring back. 2. make good (a loss or error).

ret′ro·ac′tive, a. effective as of a prior date.

ret′ro·grade, a. 1. moving backward. 2. getting worse.

ret′ro·gress, v. move backward, esp. into a worse state. —**ret′ro·gres′sion**, n.

ret′ro·spect, n. contemplation of the past. —**ret′ro·spec′tive**, a.

re·turn′, v. 1. go or come back. 2. bring or send back. 3. repay, as a visit. —n. 1. a returning. 2. something returned. 3. recurrence. 4. requital. 5. often in pl. yield or profit. 6. official report. —a. of or for a return. —in return, as a reward.

re·un′ion, n. a coming together again.

re·vamp′, v. renovate; redo.

re·veal′, v. 1. make known, as a secret. 2. show.

re·veil·le (rev′ə-li) n. Mil. morning signal to waken.

rev·el, v. 1. make merry. 2. take pleasure (in). —n. merrymaking. —**rev′el·ry** [pl. -RIES] n.

rev′e·la′tion, n. 1. a revealing. 2. striking disclosure.

re·venge′, n. harm in return. —v. avenge. —**re·venge′ful**, a.

rev′e·nue, n. government's income from taxes, etc.

re·ver′ber·ate, v. re-echo. —**re·ver′ber·a′tion**, n.

re·vere′, v. show deep respect or love for. —**rev′er·ence**, n. —**rev′er·ent**, a.

rev′er·end, a. respected: [R-] clergyman's title.

rev′er·ie, n. daydreaming.

re·vers′ (-vēr′) n. [pl. -VERS] lapel.

re·verse′, a. opposite. —n. 1. the opposite. 2. the back of a coin, etc. 3. change for the worse. 4. gear for reversing. —v. 1. turn about or inside out. 2. revoke. 3. go or make go in the opposite direction. —**re·ver′sal**, n. —**re·vers′i·ble**, a.

re·vert′, v. go back to a former state, owner, etc — **re·ver′sion**, n.

re·view′, n. 1. general survey. 2. re-examination. 3. a criticism of a book, play, etc. 4. formal inspection. —v. 1. survey. 2. study again. 3. inspect formally. 4. write a review of (a book, etc.). —**re·view′er**, n.

re·vile′, v. use abusive language (to or about).

re·vise′, v. change, esp. after reading. —**re·vi′sion**, n.

re·viv′al, n. 1. a reviving.

2. meeting to stir up religious feeling.—**re·viv'al·ist,** *n.*

re·vive', *v.* return to life, health, use, etc.

re·voke', *v.* put an end to; cancel.—**rev'o·ca·ble,** *a.*—**rev·o·ca'tion,** *n.*

re·volt', *v.* 1. to rebel. 2. disgust or be disgusted.—*n.* a rebellion.—**re·volt'ing,** *a.*

rev·o·lu'tion, *n.* 1. movement in an orbit. 2. complete cycle. 3. complete change. 4. overthrow of a government, etc.—**rev·o·lu'tion·ar·y,** *a.* & *n.* [*pl.* -IES].—**rev·o·lu'tion·ist,** *n.*

rev·o·lu'tion·ize, *v.* make a drastic change in.

re·volve', *v.* 1. rotate. 2. move in an orbit. 3. think about.

re·volv'er, *n.* pistol with a revolving cylinder for bullets.

re·vue', *n.* musical show.

re·vul'sion, *n.* disgust.

re·ward', *n.* thing given in return for something done.—*v.* give a reward to or for.

re·word', *v.* put into other words.

rhap'so·dy (rap'-) *n.* [*pl.* -DIES] 1. ecstatic speech or writing. 2. musical piece of free form.—**rhap·sod'i·cal,** **rhap·sod'ic,** *a.*

rhe·a (rē'a) *n.* large, ostrich-like bird.

rhe'o·stat, *n.* device for regulating electric current.

rhe'sus (monkey), small, brownish monkey of India.

rhet'o·ric, *n.* effective or showy use of words.—**rhe·tor'i·cal,** *a.*—**rhet·o·ri'cian** (-rish'an) *n.*

rhetorical question, question with an obvious answer.

rheumatic fever, disease with fever, aching joints, etc.

rheu'ma·tism, *n.* painful condition of the joints, etc.—**rheu·mat'ic,** *a.* & *n.*—**rheu'ma·toid,** *a.*

rhine'stone (rīn'-) *n.* artificial gem of glass, etc.

rhi'no, *n.* [*pl.* -NOS] [Col.] rhinoceros.

rhi·noc'er·os (-nos'-) *n.* large mammal with one or two horns on the snout.

rho·do·den'dron (rō'-) *n.* shrub with showy flowers.

rhom'bus, *n.* [*pl.* -BUSES -BI] equilateral parallelogram with oblique angles.

rhu'barb (rōō'-) *n.* 1. plant with edible leafstalks. 2. [Sl.] heated argument.

rhyme (rīm) *n.* 1. likeness of end sounds in words. 2. verse using this.—*v.* make (a) rhyme.

rhythm (rith'm) *n.* pattern of regular beat, accent, etc.—**rhyth'mi·cal,** **rhyth'mic,** *a.*—**rhyth'mi·cal·ly,** *adv.*

rib, *n.* 1. any of the curved bones around the chest. 2. anything riblike.—*v.* [RIBBED, RIBBING] 1. form with ribs. 2. [Sl.] tease.—**rib'bing,** *n.*

rib'ald, *a.* coarsely joking.—**rib'ald·ry,** *n.*

rib'bon, *n.* 1. narrow strip, as of silk, etc. 2. *pl.* shreds.

ri'bo·fla'vin (rī'-) *n.* a vitamin in milk, eggs, etc.

rice, *n.* a food grain grown in warm climates.

rich, *a.* 1. wealthy. 2. well supplied. 3. costly. 4. full of fats or sugar. 5. full and deep. 6. producing much.—**the rich,** wealthy people.—**rich'ly,** *adv.*—**rich'ness,** *n.*

rich'es, *n.pl.* wealth.

rick, *n.* stack of hay, etc.

rick'ets, *n.* disease causing a softening of the bones.

rick'et·y, *a.* weak; shaky.

ric'o·chet' (-shā') *n.* & *v.* [-CHETED (-shād'), -CHETING (-shā'in)] rebound at an angle.

rid, *v.* [RID or RIDDED, RIDDING] free or relieve of.—**get rid of,** dispose of.—**rid'dance,** *n.*

rid'dle, *n.* puzzling question, thing, etc.—*v.* perforate.

ride, *v.* [RODE, RIDDEN, RIDING] 1. sit on and make go. 2. move along, as in a car. 3. be carried along on or by. 4. dominate. 5. [Col.] tease.—*n.* a riding.

rid'er, *n.* 1. one who rides. 2. addition to a document.

ridge, *n.* 1. crest. 2. narrow, raised strip.—*v.* form into ridges.

rid'i·cule, *n.* remarks meant to make fun of another.—*v.* make fun of.

ri·dic'u·lous, *a.* foolish; absurd.—**ri·dic'u·lous·ly,** *adv.*

rife, *a.* 1. widespread. 2. abounding.

riff'raff, *n.* people thought of as low, common, etc.

ri'fle, *n.* gun with spiral grooves in the barrel.—*v.* rob.—**ri'fle·man** [*pl.* -MEN] *n.*

rift, *n.* & *v.* crack; split.

rig, *v.* [RIGGED, RIGGING] 1. equip. 2. arrange dishonestly. —*n.* 1. equipment. 2. arrangement of sails.

rig′ging, *n.* ropes, etc. to work the sails of a ship.

right, *a.* 1. straight. 2. just and good. 3. correct. 4. suitable. 5. normal. 6. of that side toward the east when one faces north. —*n.* 1. what is right. 2. right side. 3. power or privilege. 4. conservative party, etc. — *adv.* 1. directly. 2. properly. 3. completely. 4. toward the right. —*v.* set right. —**right away,** at once. —**right′ful,** *a.* —**right′ly,** *adv.*

right angle, 90-degree angle.

right·eous (rī′chəs) *a.* 1. virtuous. 2. morally right. —**right′eous·ly,** *adv.* — **right′eous·ness,** *n.*

right′-hand′ed, *a.* 1. using the right hand more easily. 2. for the right hand.

right′ist, *n. & a.* conservative or reactionary.

right of way, legal right to proceed, pass over, etc.

rig′id (rij′-) *a.* 1. stiff and firm. 2. severe; strict. —**ri·gid′i·ty,** *n.* —**rig′id·ly,** *adv.*

rig′ma·role, *n.* nonsense.

rig′or, *n.* strictness; hardship. —**rig′or·ous,** *a.*

rig′or mor′tis, stiffening of muscles after death.

rile, *v.* [Col.] to anger.

rill, *n.* little brook.

rim, *n.* edge, esp. of something round. —*v.* [RIMMED, RIMMING] form a rim around.

rime, *n. & v.* rhyme.

rime, *n.* white frost.

rind, *n.* firm outer layer.

ring, *v.* [RANG, RUNG] 1. make, or cause to make, the sound of a bell. 2. resound. 3. encircle. —*n.* 1. sound of a bell. 2. band for the finger. 3. hollow circle. 4. group with selfish aims. 5. enclosed area. — **ring′er,** *n.*

ring′lead′er, *n.* leader of a group, as of lawbreakers.

ring′let, *n.* long curl.

ring′worm, *n.* skin disease.

rink, *n.* smooth area for skating.

rinse, *v.* 1. wash lightly. 2. wash soap from. —*n.* rinsing or liquid for this.

ri′ot, *n. & v.* (take part in) mob violence. —**ri′ot·er,** *n.* —**ri′ot·ous,** *a.*

rip, *v.* [RIPPED, RIPPING] 1. tear apart roughly. 2. be-

come torn. —*n.* torn place.

ripe, *a.* 1. ready to be harvested, eaten, etc. 2. ready. —**rip′en,** *v.* —**ripe′ness,** *n.*

rip′-off′, *n.* [Sl.] a stealing, cheating, etc.

rip′ple, *v.* form small surface waves. —*n.* small wave.

rise, *v.* [ROSE, RISEN, RISING] 1. stand up. 2. come or go up. 3. increase. 4. begin. 5. revolt. —*n.* 1. ascent. 2. upward slope. 3. increase. 4. origin.

ris′er, *n.* vertical piece between steps.

ris·i·bil′i·ty (riz′-) *n.* laughter.

risk, *n.* chance of harm, loss, etc. —*v.* 1. put in danger. 2. take the chance of. — **risk′y** [-IER, -IEST] *a.*

ris·qué (-kā′) *a.* almost indecent.

rite, *n.* ceremonial act.

rit′u·al (rich′ōō-) *a.* of a rite. —*n.* system of rites.

ri′val, *n.* competitor. —*a.* competing. —*v.* compete with. —**ri′val·ry** [*pl.* -RIES] *n.*

riv′en, *a.* split.

riv′er, *n.* large stream. — **riv′er·side,** *n. & a.*

river basin, area drained by a river and its tributaries.

riv′et, *n.* metal bolt used to fasten by hammering the ends into heads. —*v.* fasten firmly. —**riv′et·er,** *n.*

riv′u·let, *n.* little stream.

roach (rōch) *n.* cockroach.

road, *n.* 1. way made for traveling. 2. *pl.* place for anchoring ships near shore. —**road′side,** *n. & a.*

roam, *v.* wander about; rove.

roan, *a.* reddish-brown, etc. thickly sprinkled with white. —*n.* roan horse.

roar, *v. & n.* 1. (make) a loud, deep, rumbling sound. 2. (burst out in) loud laughter.

roast, *v.* cook (meat, etc.) in an oven or over an open fire. —*n.* roasted meat. — *a.* roasted. —**roast′er,** *n.*

rob, *v.* [ROBBED, ROBBING] take property from unlawfully by force. —**rob′ber,** *n.* —**rob′ber·y** [*pl.* -IES] *n.*

robe, *n.* 1. long, loose, outer garment. 2. covering. —*v.* dress in a robe.

rob′in, *n.* red-breasted N. American thrush.

ro′bot, *n.* automatic manlike device.

ro·bust′, *a.* strong and

healthy. —**ro·bust'ness**, *n.*

rock, *n.* **1.** mass or pieces of stone. **2.** popular music based on jazz, folk music, etc. —*v.* move back and forth. **—on the rocks**, [Col.] ruined; bankrupt. —**rock'i·ness**, *n.* —**rock'y** [-IER, -IEST] *a.*

rock bottom, lowest level.

rock'er, *n.* chair mounted on curved pieces for rocking: also **rocking chair.**

rock'et, *n.* projectile propelled by the thrust of escaping gases.

ro·co·co (rə-kō'kō) *a.* full of elaborate decoration.

rod, *n.* **1.** straight stick or bar. **2.** linear measure, 5½ yds. **3.** [Sl.] pistol.

rode, pt. of **ride.**

ro'dent, *n.* gnawing mammal, as a rat, rabbit, etc.

ro·de·o (*or* rō-dā'ō) *n.* [*pl.* -DEOS] public exhibition of the skills of cowboys.

roe (rō) *n.* **1.** fish eggs. **2.** [*pl.* ROE, ROES] small deer.

rogue (rōg) *n.* **1.** scoundrel. **2.** mischievous person. — **ro'guish** (-gish) *a.*

roil, *v.* **1.** make muddy or cloudy. **2.** displease; vex.

roist'er, *v.* revel; carouse. —**roist'er·er,** *n.*

role, **rôle** (rōl) *n.* **1.** part played by an actor. **2.** function assumed by one.

roll, *v.* **1.** move by turning. **2.** move on wheels. **3.** wind into a ball or cylinder. **4.** flatten with a roller. **5.** rock. **6.** trill. —*n.* **1.** a rolling **2.** scroll. **3.** list of names. **4.** small cake of bread. **5.** a swaying motion. **6.** loud, echoing sound. —**roll'er,** *n.*

roller skate, skate with 4 small wheels instead of a runner. —**roll'er-skate',** *v.*

rol'lick·ing, a lively & gay.

roll'ing pin, cylinder used to roll out dough.

ro'ly-po'ly, *a.* pudgy.

Ro'man, *n.* **1.** of Rome. **2.** [r-] type with non-slanting letters. —*n.* native of Rome.

Roman Catholic, **1.** of the Christian church headed by the Pope. **2.** member of this church.

ro·mance', *a.* [R-] of any language derived from Latin. —*n.* **1.** tale of love, adventure, etc. **2.** exciting quality. **3.** love affair. —*v.* [Col.] make love to.

Roman numerals, Roman letters used as numerals:

I=1, V=5, X=10, L=50, C=100, D=500, M=1,000.

ro·man'tic, *a.* **1.** of romance. **2.** visionary. **3.** full of feelings of romance. —*n.* romantic person. —**ro·man'ti·cal·ly,** *adv.* —**ro·man'ti·cism,** *n.*

romp, *v.* play boisterously. —*n.* a romping.

romp'ers, *n.pl.* loose, one-piece outer garment for a small child.

rood (rood) *n.* crucifix.

roof, *n.* [*pl.* ROOFS] outside top covering of a building. —*v.* cover as with a roof.

rook (rook) *n.* **1.** European crow. **2.** *Chess* castle. —*v.* cheat.

rook'ie, *n.* [Sl.] beginner.

room, *n.* **1.** enough space. **2.** space set off by walls. **3.** *pl.* quarters. —*v.* to lodge. —**room'er,** *n.* —**room'ful,** *n.* —**room'mate,** *n.* —**room'y** [-IER, -IEST] *a.*

roost, *n.* perch for birds. —*v.* perch on a roost.

roost'er, *n.* male chicken.

root, *n.* **1.** underground part of a plant. **2.** embedded part, as of a tooth. **3.** cause. **4.** quantity multiplied by itself. —*v.* **1.** take root. **2.** place firmly. **3.** [Sl.] support a team, etc. — **take root,** **1.** grow by putting out roots. **2.** become fixed.

root beer, carbonated drink made of root extracts.

rope, *n.* strong cord of twisted strands. —*v.* **1.** mark off with a rope. **2.** catch with a lasso.

ro'sa·ry, *n.* [*pl.* -RIES] string of beads used when praying.

rose, *n.* **1.** sweet-smelling flower that has a prickly stem. **2.** pinkish red. —**rose'bud,** *n.* —**rose'bush,** *n.* —**rose'col'ored,** *a.*

ro'se·ate, *a.* rose-colored.

ro·sette', *n.* roselike ornament.

rose'wood, *n.* reddish wood.

ros'in (roz'-) *n.* hard resin.

ros'ter (ros'-) *n.* list; roll.

ros'trum, *n.* speakers' platform.

ros'y, *a.* [-IER, -IEST] **1.** rose red or pink. **2.** bright or promising. —**ros'i·ly,** *adv.* —**ros'i·ness,** *n.*

rot, *v.* [ROTTED, ROTTING] decay; spoil. —*n.* **1.** a rotting. **2.** plant disease.

ro'ta·ry, *a.* **1.** rotating. **2.** having rotating parts.

ro'tate, v. 1. turn around, as a wheel. 2. alternate. —**ro·ta'tion**, n.

rote, n. fixed routine. —**by rote**, by memory alone.

ro·tis'ser·ie, n. electric grill with a turning spit.

rot'ten, a. 1. decayed. 2. corrupt. —**rot'ten·ness**, n.

ro·tund', a. round; plump. —**ro·tun'di·ty**, n.

ro·tun'da, n. round building with a dome.

rou·é (rōō-ā') n. rake (n. 2).

rouge (rōōzh) n. 1. cosmetic to redden cheeks and lips. 2. red polish for jewelry. —v. put rouge on.

rough, a. 1. not smooth; uneven. 2. disorderly. 3. harsh. 4. not perfected. 5. [Col.] difficult. —adv. in a rough way. —n. rough part. —v. 1. treat roughly (with up). 2. shape roughly. —**rough it**, live without comforts. —**rough'en**,v.—**rough'ly**, adv. —**rough'ness**, n.

rough'age (-ij) n. coarse food.

rough'hew', v. hew or form roughly; also roughhew.

rou·lette' (rōō-let') n. gambling game played with a ball in a whirling bowl.

round, a. 1. that forms a circle or curve. 2. complete. 3. that is a whole number. 4. vigorous. —n. 1. thigh of beef. 2. course or series. 3. pl. regular circuit. 4. single gun shot. 5. outburst. 6. period of action or time. 7. simple song for 3 or 4 voices. —v. 1. make round. 2. finish. 3. turn. 4. pass around. —adv. 1. in a circle. 2. through a cycle. 3. from one to another. 4. in the opposite direction. —prep. 1. so as to encircle. 2. near. 3. in a circuit through. —**round'ly**, adv. —**round'ness**, n.

round'a·bout', a. indirect.

round'house,n. round building for repairing and storing locomotives.

round'-shoul'dered, a. having the shoulders stooped.

round trip, trip to a place and back.

round'up', n. a bringing together, esp. of cattle.

rouse, v. 1. excite. 2. wake.

roust'a·bout', n. unskilled, transient worker.

rout, n. 1. confused flight. 2. crushing defeat. —v. 1. make flee. 2. defeat. 3. force out. 4. gouge out.

route (rōōt, rout) n. course

traveled, as to make deliveries. —v. send by a certain route.

rou·tine', n. regular procedure. —a. regular; customary. —**rou·tine'ly**, adv.

rove, v. roam. —**rov'er**, n.

row (rō) n. 1. line of people, seats, etc. 2. a trip by rowboat. —v. move (in) a boat with oars.

row (rou) n. & v. [Col.] quarrel; brawl.

row'boat, n. boat to row.

row'dy, a. [-DIER, -DIEST] rough, disorderly, etc. —n. [pl. -DIES] rowdy person.

row'el (rou'-) n. small wheel with points, as on a spur.

roy'al, a. of a monarch, kingdom, etc. —**roy'al·ist**, a. & n. —**roy'al·ly**, adv.

roy'al·ty, n. [pl. -TIES] 1. royal rank, person, or persons. 2. set payment for use of copyright or patent.

R.S.V.P., please reply.

rub, v. [RUBBED, RUBBING] 1. move over a surface with pressure and friction. 2. spread on, erase, injure, etc. by rubbing. —n. 1. a rubbing. 2. difficulty; trouble. —**rub down**, to massage.

rub'ber, n. 1. elastic substance. 2. pl. overshoes. —**rub'ber·ize**,v.—**rub'ber·y**, a.

rub'bish, n. 1. worthless material; trash. 2. nonsense.

rub'ble, n. broken stones, bricks, etc.

rub'down, n. a massage.

ru·bel'la, n. contagious disease with red skin spots.

ru·bi·cund, a. reddish.

ru'ble, n. monetary unit of U.S.S.R.

ru'by, n. [pl. -BIES] deepred precious stone.

ruck'sack, n. knapsack.

rud'der, n. steering piece at ship's stern or aircraft's tail.

rud'dy, a. [-DIER, -DIEST] 1. healthily red. 2. reddish. —**rud'di·ness**, n.

rude, a. 1. coarse; crude. 2. impolite. —**rude'ly**, adv. —**rude'ness**, n.

ru'di·ment, n. 1. first principle of a subject. 2. trace. —**ru'di·men'ta·ry**, a.

rue, v. regret. —**rue'ful**, a.

ruff, n. 1. high, frilled collar. 2. raised ring of feathers or fur about a bird's or beast's neck.

ruf'fi·an, n. brutal, lawless person.

ruf'fle, v. 1. to ripple. 2.

make ruffles in or on. 3. make (feathers, etc.) stand up. 4. disturb. —*n.* narrow, pleated cloth trimming.

rug, *n.* floor covering of thick fabric in one piece.

rug'ged, *a.* 1. uneven; rough. 2. harsh; severe. 3. strong.

ru'in, *n.* 1. anything destroyed, etc. 2. *pl.* remains of this. 3. downfall; destruction. —*v.* bring or come to ruin. —**ru'in·a'tion,** *n.* —**ru'in·ous,** *a.*

rule, *n.* 1. a set guide for conduct, etc. 2. custom; usage. 3. government. 4. ruler (sense 2). —*v.* 1. to guide. 2. govern. 3. decide officially. 4. mark lines (on). —**as a rule,** usually. —**rul'ing,** *a. & n.*

rul'er, *n.* 1. one who governs. 2. straight-edged strip for drawing lines, measuring, etc.

rum, *n.* alcoholic liquor made from molasses, etc.

rum'ba, *n.* Cuban dance.

rum'ble, *v. & n.* (make) a deep, rolling sound.

ru'mi·nant, *a.* cud-chewing. —*n.* cud-chewing mammal.

ru'mi·nate, *v.* 1. chew the cud. 2. meditate. —**ru'mi·na'tion,** *n.*

rum'mage, *v.* search thoroughly.

rummage sale, sale of miscellaneous articles.

rum'my, *n.* card game.

ru'mor, *n.* unconfirmed report or story. —*v.* spread as a rumor.

rump, *n.* 1. animal's hind part. 2. buttocks.

rum'ple, *n. & v.* wrinkle.

rum'pus, *n.* [Col.] uproar.

run, *v.* [RAN, RUN, RUNNING] 1. go by moving the legs fast. 2. make a quick trip. 3. compete (in). 4. ravel. 5. spread over. 6. continue. 7. operate. 8. follow (a course). 9. undergo. 10. cause to run. —*n.* 1. act or period of running. 2. trip. 3. brook. 4. a kind. 5. enclosed area. 6. freedom. 7. a ravel. 8. Baseball point scored by a circuit of the bases. —**run across,** happen on. —**run down,** 1. stop. 2. knock down, capture, or kill. 3. disparage. —**run out of,** use up. —**run over,** 1. ride over. 2. overflow.

run'a·round, *n.* [Sl.] series of evasions.

run'a·way, *n.* person or ani-

mal that runs away. —*a.* 1. running away. 2. out of control.

run'-down, *a.* 1. not wound, as a watch. 2. in poor condition. —*n.* quick summary.

rung, pp. of **ring.** —*n.* rod-like step of a ladder, etc.

run'ner, *n.* 1. one that runs. 2. long, narrow rug. 3. ravel. 4. either of the pieces on which a sled slides.

run'ner-up', *n.* the second to finish in a contest.

run'ning, *a.* 1. that runs. 2. measured straight. 3. continuous. 4. successive. —*n.* act of one that runs.

running mate, lesser candidate, as for vice-president.

runt, *n.* stunted animal or plant.

run'way, *n.* a landing strip.

rup'ture (-chēr) *n.* 1. a breaking apart. 2. hernia. —*v.* 1. burst. 2. induce a hernia.

ru'ral, *a.* of or living in the country.

ruse (rōōz) *n.* artful trick.

rush, *v.* 1. move, push, attack, etc. swiftly. 2. hurry. —*n.* 1. a rushing. 2. busyness. 3. grassy marsh plant. —**rush up,** [Col.] get together. —**rush'er,** *n.*

rus'set, *n.* yellowish (or reddish) brown.

Rus'sian, *n. & a.* (native or language) of Russia.

rust, *n.* 1. reddish-brown coating formed on iron, etc. 2. plant disease. —*v.* 1. form rust on. 2. deteriorate, as through disuse. —**rust'y** [-IER, -IEST] *a.*

rus'tic, *a.* 1. rural. 2. plain or rough. —*n.* country person. —**rus'ti·cal·ly,** *adv.* —**rus·tic'i·ty** (-tis'-) *n.*

rus·tle (rus'l) *v.* 1. steal cattle. 2. make soft, rubbing sounds. —*n.* these sounds. —**rustle up,** [Col.] get together. —**rus'tler,** *n.*

rut, *n.* 1. groove as made by wheels. 2. fixed routine. 3. heat (*n.* 4). —*v.* [RUTTED, RUTTING] make ruts in.

ru'ta·ba'ga, *n.* yellow turnip.

ruth'less, *a.* without pity. —**ruth'less·ly,** *adv.*

-ry, *suf.* same as **-ery.**

rye (rī) *n.* 1. cereal grass. 2. its grain, used for flour.

S

Sab'bath, *n.* day of rest and worship: Saturday for Jews, Sunday for many Christians.

sa'ber, sa'bre, *n.* cavalry sword.

sa'ble, n. weasellike animal with dark fur.

sab'o·tage (-täzh) n. destruction of factories, etc. as by enemy agents or strikers. —v. destroy by sabotage.

sab'o·teur' (-tûr') n. one who commits sabotage.

sac, n. pouchlike part.

sac'cha·rin (sak'ə-) n. sugar substitute.

sac'cha·rine (-rin) a. very sweet. —n. saccharin.

sac'er·do'tal (sas'-) a. of priests.

sa·chet (sa-shā') n. small bag of perfumed powder.

sack, n. 1. bag. 2. large, coarse bag. 3. plunder. 4. [Sl.] bed. —v. 1. put in sacks. 2. plunder.

sack'cloth, n. coarse cloth worn to show sorrow.

sac'ra·ment, n. sacred Christian rite, as Communion. —**sac'ra·men'tal,** a.

sa'cred, a. 1. consecrated to a god or God. 2. venerated. 3. inviolate. —**sa'cred·ly,** adv. —**sa'cred·ness,** n.

sac'ri·fice, v. 1. offer (something) to a deity. 2. give up something for another. 3. take a loss in selling. —n. a sacrificing. —**sac'ri·fi'cial** (-fish'əl) a.

sac'ri·lege (-lij) n. desecration of sacred things. —**sac'ri·le'gious** (-lē'jəs) a.

sac'ro·sanct' (-saŋkt') a. very holy.

sad, a. [SADDER, SADDEST] showing or causing sorrow; unhappy. —**sad'den,** v. —**sad'ly,** adv. —**sad'ness,** n.

sad'dle, n. seat for a rider on a horse, etc. —v. 1. put a saddle on. 2. burden.

sad'ist, n. one who gets pleasure from hurting others. —**sad'ism,** n. —**sa·dis'tic,** a.

sa·fa'ri (-fä'-) n. hunting trip, esp. in Africa.

safe, a. 1. free from danger. 2. unharmed. 3. trustworthy. 4. cautious. —n. metal box with a lock. —**safe'ly,** adv. —**safe'ty,** n.

safe'guard, n. protection; precaution. —v. protect.

safe'keep'ing, n. protection.

saf'flow·er, n. plant whose seeds yield an edible oil.

saf'fron, n. orange-yellow dye and seasoning.

sag, v. [SAGGED, SAGGING] 1. sink in the middle. 2. hang unevenly. 3. lose strength. —n. place that sags.

sa'ga (sä'-) n. long story of heroic deeds.

sa·ga'cious (-gā'shəs) a. very wise or shrewd. —**sa·gac'i·ty** (-gas'-) n.

sage, a. very wise. —n. 1. very wise man. 2. green leaves used as seasoning. 3. sagebrush.

sage'brush, n. shrub of the western plains of the U.S.

Sag'it·ta'ri·us (saj'-) n. 9th sign of the zodiac; Archer.

sa·hib (sä'ib) n. title for a European once used in India.

said, pt. & pp. of **say.** —a. aforesaid.

sail, n. 1. canvas sheet to catch the wind and move a vessel. 2. boat trip. —v. 1. move by means of sails. 2. travel on water. 3. glide. —**set sail,** begin a trip by water. —**sail'boat,** n.

sail'fish, n. ocean fish with a tall dorsal fin.

sail'or, n. 1. enlisted man in the navy. 2. one who sails.

saint, n. holy person. —**saint'ly** [-LIER, -LIEST] a. —**saint'li·ness,** n.

saith (seth) [Ar.] says.

sake, n. 1. motive; cause. 2. behalf.

sa'ke (sä'-) n. Japanese alcoholic drink.

sa·laam' (-läm') n. Oriental greeting of bowing low.

sal'a·ble, sale'a·ble, a. that can be sold.

sa·la'cious (-lā'shəs) a. obscene.

sal'ad, n. vegetables, fruit, etc., with salad dressing.

sal'a·man'der, n. lizardlike amphibian.

sa·la'mi (-lä'-) n. spiced, salted sausage.

sal'a·ry, n. [pl. -RIES] fixed payment at regular intervals for work. —**sal'a·ried,** a.

sale, n. 1. a selling. 2. special selling of goods at reduced prices.

sales'man, n. [pl. -MEN] man employed to sell goods. —**sales'wom'an** [pl. -WOMEN] n.fem. —**sales'man·ship,** n. —**sales'per·son,** n.

sa'li·ent (-lē-) a. 1. prominent; conspicuous. 2. jutting. —n. salient part. —**sa'li·ence,** n.

sa'line (-līn) a. salty.

sa·li'va, n. watery fluid secreted by glands in the mouth. —**sal'i·var'y,** a.

sal'low, a. sickly yellow.

sal'ly, n. [pl. -LIES] 1. sudden rush forward. 2. quip. 3.

short trip. —v. [-LIED, -LY- ING] start out briskly.

salm'on (sam'-) n. large, edible ocean fish.

sa·lon' (-lon') n. 1. parlor. 2. gathering of notables.

sa·loon', n. 1. public place where liquor is sold and drunk. 2. large public room.

salt, n. 1. white substance found in the earth, sea water, etc., used to flavor food. 2. compound formed from an acid. 3 [Col.] sailor. —a. containing salt. —v. add salt to. —**salt'y** [-IER, -IEST] a.

salt water, sea water. —**salt'-wa'ter**, a.

sa·lu'bri·ous, a. healthful.

sal'u·tar'y, a. 1. healthful. 2. beneficial.

sal'u·ta'tion, n. act or form of greeting.

sa·lute', n. formal gesture, act, etc. expressing respect. —v. greet with a salute.

sal'vage (-vij) n. 1. rescue of a ship, etc. from shipwreck. 2. reclaimed property or goods. —v. 1. save from shipwreck, etc. 2. utilize (damaged goods, etc.).

sal·va'tion, n. 1. a saving or being saved. 2. one that saves. 3. saving of the soul.

salve (sav) n. soothing ointment. —v. soothe.

sal'ver, n. tray.

sal'vo, n. discharge of a number of guns together.

same, a. 1. being the very one. 2. alike. 3. unchanged. 4. before-mentioned. —pron. the same person or thing. —adv. in like manner. —all (or just) the same, nevertheless. —**same'ness**, n.

sam'o·var (-vär) n. metal urn to heat water for tea.

sam'pan, n. small Oriental boat, rowed with a scull.

sam'ple, n. 1. part typical of a whole. 2. example. —v. take a sample of.

sam'pler, n. cloth embroidered with designs, etc.

san·a·to'ri·um, n. sanitarium.

sanc'ti·fy, v. to make holy or free from sin. —**sanc'ti·fi·ca'tion**, n.

sanc·ti·mo'ni·ous, a. pretending to be pious. —**sanc'ti·mo'ny**, n.

sanc'tion, n. 1. authorization. 2. approval. 3. pl. punitive measures against a nation. —v. 1. authorize. 2. approve.

sanc'ti·ty, n. 1. holiness. 2. sacredness.

sanc'tu·ar'y, n. [pl. -IES] 1. holy place, as a church. 2. place of refuge.

sanc'tum, n. 1. sacred place. 2. one's own private room.

sand, n. 1. loose grains of disintegrated rock. 2. pl. area of sand. —v. to sandpaper. —**sand'er**, n.

san'dal, n. shoe with sole tied to the foot by straps.

san'dal·wood, n. tree with sweet-smelling wood.

sand'blast, v. clean with a blast of air and sand.

sand'box, n. box with sand, as for children to play in.

sand'man, n. supposed bringer of sleep to children.

sand'pa'per, n. paper coated with sand. —v. smooth with sandpaper.

sand'pip'er (-pip'-) n. shore bird with a long bill.

sand'stone, n. kind of rock much used in building.

sand'storm, n. windstorm with clouds of blown sand.

sand'wich, n. slices of bread with meat, etc. between them. —v. squeeze between.

sand'y, a. [-IER, -IEST] 1. of or like sand. 2. dull yellow.

sane, a. 1. mentally healthy. 2. sensible. —**sane'ly**, adv.

sang, pt. of **sing**.

san'guin·ar'y (-gwi-) a. 1. of or with bloodshed. 2. bloodthirsty.

san'guine, a. 1. blood-red. 2. cheerful.

san·i·tar'i·um, n. institution for invalids, etc.

san'i·tar'y, a. 1. of health. 2. clean and healthful.

san·i·ta'tion, n. 1. hygienic conditions. 2. sewage disposal.

san'i·ty, n. soundness of mind or judgment.

sank, pt. of **sink**.

sap, n. 1. juice of a plant. 2. vigor. 3. [SL.] a fool. —v. 1. undermine. 2. weaken. —**sap'py** [-PIER, -PIEST] a.

sa'pi·ent (sā'-) a. wise. —**sa'pi·ence**, n.

sap'ling, n. young tree.

sap'phire (saf'īr) n. deep-blue precious stone.

sap'suck·er, n. small woodpecker.

sar'casm, n. taunting, ironical remark. —**sar·cas'tic**, a.

sar·coph'a·gus, n. [pl. -GI (-jī'), -GUSES] stone coffin.

sar·dine', n. small herring preserved in oil.

sar·don·ic, a. bitterly sarcastic.

sa·ri (sä′rē) n. scarflike garment of Hindu women.

sa·rong′, n. skirtlike garment of East Indies.

sar′sa·pa·ril′la (or sas′pə-) n. root-flavored drink.

sar·to′ri·al, a. 1. of tailors. 2. of men's dress.

sash, n. 1. band worn over the shoulder or around the waist. 2. sliding frame for glass in a window.

sas′sa·fras, n. tree whose root bark is used for flavoring.

sass′y, a. [-IER, -IEST] [Col.] impudent.

sat, pt. & pp. of **sit.**

Sa′tan, n. the Devil. —

sa·tan′ic, a.

satch′el, n. small traveling bag.

sate, v. 1. satisfy fully. 2. satiate.

sa·teen′, n. satinlike cotton.

sat′el·lite, n. 1. small planet revolving around a larger one. 2. man-made object orbiting in space. 3. small state dependent on a larger one.

sa·ti·ate (-shi-) v. give too much to, causing disgust. —**sa·ti′e·ty,** n.

sat′in, n. smooth & glossy silk, nylon, or rayon cloth.

sat′ire, n. 1. use of ridicule, irony, etc. to attack vice or folly. 2. literary work in which this is done.—**sa·tir′i·cal** (-tir′-), **sa·tir′ic,** a. —**sat′i·rist,** n.

sat′i·rize, v. attack with satire.

sat′is·fy, v. [-FIED, -FYING] 1. fulfill the needs and desires of. 2. convince. 3. pay in full. —**sat′is·fac′tion,** n. —**sat′is·fac′to·ry,** a.

sat′u·rate (sach′oo-) v. 1. soak thoroughly. 2. fill completely. —**sat′u·ra′tion,** n.

Sat′ur·day, n. seventh day of the week.

sat′ur·nine, a. gloomy.

sat′yr, n. Gr. myth. woodland god with goat's legs.

sauce, n. 1. tasty, liquid or soft dressing for food. 2. mashed, stewed fruit.

sauce′pan, n. metal cooking pot with a long handle.

sau′cer, n. shallow dish, esp. one for holding a cup.

sau′cy, a. [-CIER, -CIEST] 1. impudent. 2. lively and bold. —**sau′ci·ly,** adv. —**sau′ci·ness,** n.

sauer·kraut (sour′krout) n. chopped, fermented cabbage.

sau′na, n. Finnish bath with exposure to hot, dry air.

saun′ter (sôn′-) v. & n. stroll.

sau′sage (sô′sij) n. chopped, seasoned pork, etc., often stuffed into a casing.

sau·té (sō-tā′) v. fry quickly in a little fat.

sav′age, a. 1. fierce; untamed. 2. primitive; barbarous. —n. uncivilized or brutal person. —**sav′age·ly,** adv. —**sav′age·ry,** n.

sa·vant (sə-vänt′) n. scholar.

save, v. 1. rescue; keep safe. 2. keep or store up for future use. 3. avoid waste (of). —prep. & con. except; but.

sav′ing, a. that saves. —n. 1. reduction in time, cost, etc. 2. pl. money saved.

sav′ior, sav′iour (-yēr) n. 1. one who saves or rescues. 2. [S-] Jesus Christ.

sa·voir-faire (sav′wär-fâr′) n. social poise; tact.

sa′vor, v. & n. (have) a special taste, smell, or quality.

sa′vor·y, a. [-IER, -IEST] tasting or smelling good.

saw, pt. of **see.** —n. 1. thin, metal blade with sharp teeth, for cutting. 2. proverb. —v. cut with a saw. —**saw′yer,** n.

saw′dust, n. fine bits of wood formed in sawing wood.

saw′horse, n. rack to hold wood while sawing it: also **saw′buck.**

sax′o·phone, n. single-reed, metal wind instrument.

say, v. [SAID, SAYING] 1. speak. 2. state. 3. suppose. —n. 1. chance to speak. 2. power to decide. —**that is to say,** in other words.

say′ing, n. proverb.

scab, n. 1. crust over a healing sore. 2. strikebreaker. —v. [SCABBED, SCABBING] 1. form a scab. 2. be a scab.

scab′bard, n. sheath for a sword, dagger, etc.

sca′bies (-bēz) n. itch caused by mites.

scaf′fold, n. 1. framework to hold workmen, painters, etc. 2. platform on which criminals are executed.

scald (skôld) v. 1. burn with hot liquid or steam. 2. heat almost to a boil. —n. burn caused by scalding.

scale, n. 1. series of gradations or degrees. 2. ratio of distances on a map, etc. 3. any of the thin, hard plates on fish, etc. 4. flake. 5. either pan of a balance. 6. *often pl.* weighing machine. 7. *Mus.* series of consecutive tones. —*v.* 1. climb up. 2. set according to a scale. 3. scrape scales from. 4. flake off in scales. —**scal'y** [-IER, -IEST] *a.* —**scal'i·ness**, *n.*

scal'lion (-yən) *n.* green onion.

scal'lop, *n.* 1. edible mollusk. 2. any of the curves forming a fancy edge. —*n.* 1. edge in scallops. 2. bake with a milk sauce, etc.

scalp, *n.* skin on top of the head. —*v.* 1. cut the scalp from. 2. sell (tickets, etc.) above current prices.

scal'pel, *n.* sharp knife used in surgery, etc.

scamp, *n.* rascal.

scam'per, *v.* run quickly. —*n.* quick dash.

scan, *v.* [SCANNED, SCANNING] 1. look at quickly. 2. examine. 3. show meter in verse.

scan'dal, *n.* 1. disgrace or thing that disgraces. 2. gossip. —**scan'dal·ous**, *a.*

scan'dal·ize, *v.* outrage one's feeling of decency.

scant, *a.* not enough. —**scant'y** [-IER, -IEST] *a.* —**scant'i·ly**, *adv.* —**scant'i·ness**, *n.*

scape'goat, *n.* one who is blamed for others' mistakes.

scape'grace, *n.* rogue.

scap'u·la, *n.* shoulder bone.

scar, *n.* mark left after a wound has healed. —*v.* [SCARRED, SCARRING] mark with or form a scar.

scar'ab (skar'-) *n.* beetle.

scarce, *a.* 1. not common. 2. hard to get. —*adv.* scarcely. —**scarce'ness**, *n.* —**scar'ci·ty** [*pl.* -TIES] *n.*

scarce'ly, *adv.* hardly.

scare, *v.* frighten. —*n.* sudden fear. —**scar'y** [-IER, -IEST] [Col.] *a.*

scare'crow, *n.* figure set up to scare birds away.

scarf, *n.* [*pl.* SCARFS, SCARVES] long or broad cloth piece for the neck, etc.

scar'let, *n.* bright red.

scarlet fever, contagious disease with fever and a rash.

scat, *v.* [Col.] go away!

scath'ing (skāth'-) *a.* harsh; bitter. —**scath'ing·ly**, *adv.*

scat'ter, *v.* 1. throw about. 2. move in several directions.

scav'eng·er (-inj-) *n.* 1. one who collects refuse. 2. animal that eats decaying matter. —**scav'enge**, *v.*

sce·nar'i·o' (si-) *n.* [*pl.* -OS] 1. movie script. 2. outline for proposed action.

scene, *n.* 1. place; setting. 2. view. 3. division of a play. 4. show of emotion.

scen'er·y, *n.* [*pl.* -IES] 1. painted backdrops for a stage play. 2. outdoor views.

sce'nic (sē'-) *a.* 1. of scenery. 2. picturesque.

scent (sent) *v.* 1. to suspect. 2. to perfume. —*n.* 1. odor. 2. perfume. 3. sense of smell.

scep'ter, scep'tre (sep'-) *n.* a staff as symbol of a ruler's power.

scep'tic (skep'-) *n.* skeptic.

sched·ule (skej'ool) *n.* 1. timetable. 2. timed plan. 3. list of details. —*v.* place in a schedule.

scheme, *n.* 1. plan; system. 2. plot; intrigue. 3. diagram. —*v.* plot. —**schem'er**, *n.* —**sche·mat'ic**, *a.*

schism (siz'm) *n.* split, esp. in a church, over doctrine. —**schis·mat'ic**, *a.*

schist (shist) *n.* rock in layers.

schiz'o·phre'ni·a (skiz'-) *n.* severe mental illness. —**schiz'o·phren'ic**, *a. & n.*

schnau'zer (shnou'-) *n.* small terrier.

schol'ar (skol-) *n.* 1. learned person. 2. student. —**schol·ar·ly**, *a.*

schol'ar·ship, *n.* 1. knowledge; learning. 2. money given to help a student.

scho·las'tic, *a.* of schools, students, teachers, etc.

school, *n.* 1. place for teaching and learning. 2. its students and teachers. 3. education. 4. group with the same beliefs. 5. group of fish. —*v.* train; teach. —*a.* of, in, or for school. —**school'mate**, *n.* —**school'teach'er**, *n.*

school board, group in charge of local public schools.

schoon'er, *n.* ship with two or more masts.

schwa (shwä) *n.* vowel sound in an unaccented syllable symbol ə.

sci·at'i·ca (sī-) *n.* neuritis in the hip and thigh.

sci'ence, *n.* systematized knowledge or a branch of it. —**sci·en·tif'ic**, *a.* —**sci'en·tif'i·cal·ly**, *adv.*

sci'en·tist, *n.* expert in science.

scim'i·tar, scim'i·ter (sim'-) *n.* curved sword.

scin·til'la (sin-) n. tiny bit.

scin'til·late, v. 1. sparkle. 2. be clever and witty. —**scin'til·la'tion,** n.

sci'on (sī'-) n. 1. bud or shoot. 2. descendant.

scis'sors (siz'-) n.pl. cutting tool with two pivoted blades.

scle·ro'sis (skli-) n. a hardening of body tissues.

scoff, n. scornful remark. —v. mock or jeer (at).

scold, v. find fault with angrily. —n. one who scolds.

sconce (skons) n. wall bracket for candles.

scone, n. small tea cake.

scoop, n. 1. small, shovellike utensil. 2. bucket of a dredge, etc. 3. a scooping. —v. 1. take up with a scoop. 2. hollow out.

scoot, v. [Col.] scurry off.

scoot'er, n. 1. child's two-wheeled vehicle. 2. small motorcycle.

scope, n. 1. range of understanding, action, etc. 2. chance.

-scope, suf. for seeing.

scorch, v. 1. burn slightly. 2. parch. —n. surface burn.

score, n. 1. points made in a game, etc. 2. grade on a test. 3. piece of music showing all parts. 4. scratch or mark. 5. twenty. 6. pl. very many. 7. debt. —v. 1. make a score or scores. 2. evaluate. 3. achieve. 4. keep score. 5. upbraid. —**scor'er,** n.

scorn, n. contempt; disdain. —v. 1. treat with scorn. 2. refuse. —**scorn'ful,** a. —**scorn'ful·ly,** adv.

Scor'pi·o, n. 8th sign of the zodiac; Scorpion.

scor'pi·on, n. arachnid with a poisonous sting.

Scotch (skoch) n. whisky made in Scotland. —a. Scottish. —n. [s] put an end to.

scot'-free', a. unpunished.

Scot'tish, a. & n. (of) the people or language of Scotland.

scoun'drel, n. villain.

scour, v. 1. to clean by rubbing with abrasives. 2. go through thoroughly, as in search.

scourge (skûrj) n. & v. 1. whip. 2. torment; plague.

scout, n. & v. (one sent ahead) to spy, search, etc.

scow, n. flat-bottomed boat.

scowl, n. & v. 1. (have) an angry frown.

scrag'gly, a. [-GLIER, -GLIEST] rough; jagged.

scram'ble, v. 1. climb or crawl with the hands and feet. 2. struggle for something. 3. mix together, as eggs while cooking. —n. a scrambling.

scrap, n. 1. fragment. 2. discarded material. 3. pl. bits of food. —a. discarded. —v. 1. discard. 2. [Sl.] fight. [SCRAPPED, SCRAPPING] 1.

scrap'py [-PIER, -PIEST] a.

scrap'book, n. book in which to paste pictures, etc.

scrape, v. 1. rub smooth or rub away. 2. scratch. 3. gather bit by bit. —n. 1. scraped place. 2. harsh sound. 3. predicament. —**scrap'er,** n.

scratch, v. 1. cut the surface. 2. scrape or dig with one's nails. 3. scrape noisily. 4. cross out. —n. mark from scratching. —a. for hasty notes, etc. —**from scratch,** from nothing. —**scratch'y** [-IER, -IEST] a.

scrawl, v. write carelessly. —n. poor handwriting.

scraw'ny, a. [-NIER, -NIEST] lean; thin.

scream, v. & n. (make) a loud, shrill cry or noise.

screech, v. & n. (give) a harsh, high shriek.

screen, n. 1. thing used to shield, conceal, etc. 2. wire mesh in a frame. 3. surface for showing movies, etc. —v. 1. conceal or shelter. 2. sift or sift out.

screen'play, n. script for a motion picture.

screw, n. 1. naillike fastener with a spiral groove. 2. propeller. —v. 1. to turn; twist. 2. fasten, as with a screw.

screw'driv'er, n. tool for turning screws; also **screw driver.**

scrib'ble, v. 1. write carelessly. 2. draw marks. —n. scribbled writing.

scribe, n. writer; author.

scrim'mage (-mij) n. 1. confused struggle. 2. play in football that follows the pass from center.

scrimp, v. spend or use as little as possible.

scrip, n. certificate redeemable for stocks, money, etc.

script, n. 1. handwriting. 2. working copy of a play.

Scrip'ture (-chēr) n. often pl. the Bible. —**Scrip'tur·al,** a.

scrof'u·la, n. tuberculosis

of the lymphatic glands.

scroll, *n.* 1. roll of paper, etc. with writing on it. 2. coiled or spiral design.

scro'tum, *n.* skin pouch containing the testicles.

scrounge, *v.* [Sl.] hunt around for and take; pilfer.

scrub, *v.* [SCRUBBED, SCRUBBING] rub hard, as in washing. —*n.* 1. a scrubbing. 2. growth of stunted trees or bushes. —*a.* 1. inferior. 2. undersized. —**scrub'by** [-BIER, -BIEST] *a.*

scruff, *n.* nape of the neck.

scru'ple, *n.* a doubt as to what is right, proper, etc. —*v.* hesitate from doubt.

scru'pu·lous, *a.* 1. showing scruples. 2. precise.

scru'ti·nize, *v.* examine closely. —**scru'ti·ny**, *n.*

scud, *v.* [SCUDDED, SCUDDING] move swiftly.

scuff, *v.* 1. scrape with the feet. 2. wear a rough place on. —*n.* worn spot.

scuf'fle, *n.* rough, confused fight. —*v.* be in a scuffle.

scull, *n.* 1. large oar at the stern of a boat. 2. light rowboat for racing. —*v.* propel with a scull.

scul'ler·y, *n.* [*pl.* -IES] room for rough kitchen work.

sculp'ture, *v.* carve wood, stone, etc. into statues, etc. —*n.* art of sculpturing or work sculptured. —**sculp'tor**, *n.* —**sculp'tur·al**, *a.*

scum, *n.* 1. surface impurities on a liquid. 2. vile people. —**scum'my** [-MIER, -MIEST] *a.*

scup'per, *n.* side opening for water to run off a deck.

scurf, *n.* scales shed by skin.

scur'ril·ous, *a.* vulgarly abusive. —**scur·ril'i·ty** [*pl.* -TIES] *n.*

scur'ry, *v. & n.* [-RIED, -RYING] scamper.

scur'vy, *a.* [-VIER, -VIEST] low; mean. —*n.* disease due to vitamin C deficiency.

scut'tle, *n.* bucket for coal. —*v.* [-TLED, -TLING] 1. scamper. 2. cut holes in a ship to sink it.

scythe (sīth) *n.* long-bladed tool to cut grass, etc.

sea, *n.* 1. the ocean. 2. a smaller body of salt water. 3. large body of fresh water. 4. heavy wave.

sea'board, *n.* land along the sea: also **sea'coast.**

sea'far·ing (-fâr'-) *a. & n.* (of) sea travel or a sailor's work. —**sea'far·er**, *n.*

sea food, ocean fish or shellfish used as food.

sea gull, a gull (bird).

sea horse, small fish with a head like that of a horse.

seal, *n.* 1. sea mammal with flippers. 2. official design stamped on a letter, etc. 3. thing that seals. —*v.* 1. certify as with a seal. 2. close tight. 3. settle finally.

sea lion, N. Pacific seal.

seam, *n.* 1. line where two pieces are sewed or welded together. 2. layer of ore or coal. —*v.* join with a seam.

sea'man, *n.* [*pl.* -MEN] 1. sailor. 2. navy enlisted man.

seam'stress, *n.* woman whose work is sewing.

seam'y, *a.* [-IER, -IEST] showing seams. —**the seamy side**, unpleasant side.

sé·ance (sā'äns) *n.* spiritualists' meeting.

sea'plane, *n.* airplane which can land on water.

sea'port, *n.* port for ocean ships.

sear, *a.* withered. —*v.* 1. wither. 2. burn the surface of.

search, *v.* look through or examine to find something. —*n.* a searching.

search'light, *n.* 1. strong light. 2. device to project it.

sea shell, mollusk shell.

sea'shore, *n.* land along the sea.

sea'sick·ness, *n.* nausea caused by a ship's rolling. —**sea'sick**, *a.*

sea'son, *n.* 1. any of the four divisions of the year. 2. special time. —*v.* 1. to flavor. 2. age. 3. accustom. —**sea'son·al**, *a.*

sea'son·a·ble, *a.* timely.

sea'son·ing, *n.* flavoring for food.

seat, *n.* 1. place to sit. 2. thing or part one sits on. 3. right to sit as a member. 4. chief location. —*v.* 1. set on a seat. 2. have seats for.

sea'way, *n.* inland waterway for ocean-going ships.

sea'weed, *n.* any sea plant(s).

se·cede' (-sēd') *v.* withdraw formally from a group, etc. —**se·ces'sion**, *n.*

se·clude', *v.* isolate. —**se·clu'sion**, *n.*

sec'ond, *a.* 1. next after the first. 2. another, like the first. —*n.* 1. one that is second. 2. thing not of first quality. 3. assistant.

4. 1/60 of a minute. —v. support (a suggestion, motion, etc.). —adv. in the second place, etc. —sec'ond·ly, adv.

sec'ond·ar·y, a. 1. second in order. 2. less important. 3. derivative.

sec'ond-guess', v. [Col.] use hindsight in judging.

sec'ond-hand', a. 1. not from the original source. 2. used before.

second nature, deeply fixed, acquired habit.

sec'ond-rate', a. inferior.

se'cret, a. 1. kept from being known by others. 2. hidden. —n. secret fact, etc. —se'cre·cy, n. —se'cret·ly, adv.

sec're·tar'i·at, n. staff headed by a secretary.

sec're·tar'y, n. [pl. -IES] 1. one who keeps records, writes letters, etc. for a person or group. 2. head of a department of government. 3. tall desk. —sec're·tar'i·al, a.

se·crete', v. 1. hide. 2. make (a body substance), as a gland. —se·cre'tion, n.

se·cre'tive (or sē'krə-) a. not frank or open. —se·cre'tive·ly, adv.

sect, n. group having the same beliefs, esp. in religion.

sec·tar'i·an, a. 1. of or like a sect. 2. narrow-minded.

sec'tion, n. distinct part. —v. divide into sections. —sec'tion·al, a.

sec'tor, n. 1. part of a circle like a pie slice. 2. district for military operations.

sec'u·lar, a. not connected with church or religion.

se·cure', a. 1. free from danger, care, etc. 2. firm; stable. 3. sure. —v. 1. make secure. 2. get. —se·cure'ly, adv.

se·cu'ri·ty, n. [pl. -TIES] 1. secure state or feeling. 2. protection. 3. thing given as a pledge of repayment, etc. 4. pl. stocks, bonds, etc.

se·dan', n. closed automobile with front and rear seats.

se·date', a. quiet and dignified. —se·date'ly, adv.

sed'a·tive, a. making one calmer. —n. sedative medicine. —se·da'tion, n.

sed'en·tar'y, a. characterized by much sitting.

sedge, n. coarse, grasslike plant of marshes.

sed'i·ment, n. matter that settles from a liquid.

se·di'tion (-di'-) n. stirring up of rebellion. —se·di'tious, a.

se·duce', v. 1. lead astray. 2. induce to give up one's chastity. —se·duc'er, n. —se·duc'tion, n. —se·duc'tive, a.

sed'u·lous, a. diligent.

see, v. [SAW, SEEN, SEEING] 1. look at. 2. understand. 3. find out. 4. make sure. 5. escort. 6. meet; visit with. 7. consult. 8. have the power of sight. —n. office or district of a bishop. —see to, attend to.

seed, n. [pl. SEEDS, SEED] 1. the part of a plant from which a new one will grow. 2. source. 3. sperm. —v. 1. plant with seed. 2. take the seeds from. —seed'less, a.

seed'ling, n. young plant grown from a seed.

seed'y, a. [-IER, -IEST] 1. full of seeds. 2. shabby; untidy.

see'ing, con. considering.

seek, v. [SOUGHT, SEEKING] 1. search for. 2. try (to get).

seem, v. look, feel, etc. (to be).

seem'ing, a. not actual. —seem'ing·ly, adv.

seep, v. leak through; ooze. —seep'age, n.

seer, n. prophet.

seer'suck·er, n. crinkled fabric.

see'saw, n. balanced plank ridden at the ends for swinging up and down. —v. move up and down or back and forth.

seethe (sēth) v. boil.

seg'ment, n. section. —v. divide into segments.

seg're·gate, v. set apart. —seg're·ga'tion, n.

seine (sān) n. fishing net.

seis'mic (sīz'-) a. of an earthquake.

seis'mo·graph, n. instrument to record earthquakes.

seize, v. 1. take suddenly or by force. 2. attack. 3. capture. —sei'zure, n.

sel'dom, adv. rarely.

se·lect', a. 1. chosen with care. —v. choose; pick out. —se·lec'tion, n. —se·lec'tive, a.

selective service, compulsory military training.

se·lect'man, n. [pl. -MEN] New England town official.

self, n. [pl. SELVES] one's own person, welfare, etc.

self-, pref. of, by, in, to, or with oneself or itself: see the list following.

self'-ad·dressed'

self'-ap·point'ed

self'-de·fense'

self'-de·ni'al

self'-dis'ci·pline

self'-ed'u·cat'ed

self'-es·teem'

self'-ex·plan'a·to'ry

self'-ex·pres'sion

self'-gov'ern·ment

self'-in·dul'gence

self'-pit'y

self'-pres·er·va'tion

self'-re·li'ance

self'-re·spect'

self'-sat'is·fied

self'-sup·port'ing

self'-taught'

self'-as·sur'ance, *n.* self-confidence.

self'-cen'tered, *a.* selfish.

self'-con'fi·dent, *a.* sure of oneself. —**self'-con'fi·dence,** *n.*

self'-con'scious, *a.* ill at ease. —**self'-con'scious·ly,** *adv.*

self'-con·tained', *a.* 1. self-controlled. 2. reserved. 3. self-sufficient.

self'-con·trol', *n.* control of one's emotions, actions, etc. —**self'-con·trolled',** *a.*

self'-de·ter'mi·na'tion, *n.* 1. free will. 2. right to choose one's government.

self'-ev'i·dent, *a.* evident without proof.

self'-im·por'tance, *n.* pompous conceit. —**self'-im·por'tant,** *a.*

self'-in'ter·est, *n.* (selfish) interest in one's own welfare.

self'ish, *a.* caring too much about oneself. —**self'ish·ly,** *adv.* —**self'ish·ness,** *n.*

self'less, *a.* unselfish.

self'-made', *a.* successful through one's own efforts.

self'-pos·ses'sion, *n.* full control over one's actions, etc. —**self'-pos·sessed',** *a.*

self'-re·straint', *n.* self-control. —**self'-re·strained',** *a.*

self'-right'eous, *a.* feeling more righteous than others.

self'same, *a.* identical.

self'-serv'ice, *n.* practice of serving oneself in a store, cafeteria, etc.

self'-styled', *a.* so called by oneself.

self'-suf·fi'cient, *a.* independent. —**self'-suf·fi'cien·cy,** *n.*

self'-willed', *a.* stubborn.

sell, *v.* [SOLD, SELLING] 1. exchange for money. 2. offer for sale. 3. be sold (*for*).

sel'vage, sel'vedge (-vij) *n.* edge woven to prevent raveling.

se·man'tics, *n.* study of words. —**se·man'tic,** *a.*

sem'a·phore (-fôr) *n.* flags or lights for signaling.

sem'blance, *n.* outward show.

se'men, *n.* reproductive fluid of the male.

se·mes'ter, *n.* either of the terms in a school year.

sem'i (-ī) *n.* [Col.] tractor with trailer attached.

semi-, *pref.* 1. half. 2. partly. 3. twice in some period (**sem'i·an'nu·al, sem'i·month'ly, sem'i·week'ly**).

sem'i·cir'cle, *n.* half circle.

sem'i·co'lon, *n.* mark of punctuation (;).

sem'i·fi'nal, *n. & a.* (contest) just before the finals.

sem'i·nar, *n.* supervised course of research.

sem'i·nar'y, *n.* [*pl.* -IES] 1. school for women. 2. school to train ministers, etc.

sem'i·pre'cious, *a.* less valuable than precious gems.

sen'ate, *n.* 1. lawmaking assembly. 2. [S] upper branch of Congress or of a State legislature. —**sen'a·tor,** *n.* —**sen'a·to'ri·al,** *a.*

send, *v.* [SENT, SENDING] 1. cause to go or be carried. 2. impel; drive. —**send for,** summon. —**send'er,** *n.*

se'nile (-nīl) *a.* 1. of old age. 2. weak in mind and body. —**se·nil'i·ty,** *n.*

sen'ior, *a.* 1. the older: written *Sr.* 2. of higher rank, etc. —*n.* high school or college student in the last year.

sen·ior'i·ty, *n.* status gained by length of service.

se·ñor' (-nyôr') *n.* [Sp.] Mr.

se·ño'ra, *n.* [Sp.] Mrs.

se·ño·ri'ta (-rē'-) *n.* [Sp.] Miss.

sen·sa'tion, *n.* 1. sense impression or the power to receive it. 2. exciting thing.

sen·sa'tion·al, *a.* shocking. —**sen·sa'tion·al·ism,** *n.*

sense, *n.* 1. power to see, hear, taste, feel, etc. 2. sound judgment. 3. meaning. —*v.* perceive. —**in a sense,** to some extent. —**make sense,** be intelligible.

sense'less, *a.* 1. unconscious. 2. foolish or stupid.

sen'si·bil'i·ty, *n.* [*pl.* -TIES] 1. power of feeling. 2. *pl.* delicate feelings.

sen'si·ble, *a.* 1. reasonable; wise. 2. aware. 3. noticeable. —**sen'si·bly,** *adv.*

sen'si·tive, *a.* 1. quick to feel, notice, etc. 2. susceptible to stimuli. 3. tender or sore. 4. touchy. —**sen'si·tiv'i·ty**, *n.*

sen'si·tize', *v.* make sensitive.

sen'so·ry, *a.* of the senses.

sen'su·al (-shoo-) *a.* of or enjoying the pleasures of the body.—**sen'su·al·ly**,*adv.* —**sen'su·al'i·ty**, *n.*

sen'su·ous, *a.* having to do with the senses.

sent, pt. & pp. of **send**.

sen'tence, *n.* 1. group of words stating something. 2. court decision. 3. punishment. —*v.* pronounce punishment on.

sen·ten'tious, *a.* 1. pithy. 2. pompously boring.

sen'tient (-shənt) *a.* conscious.

sen'ti·ment, *n.* 1. a feeling. 2. opinion. 3. tender feelings. 4. maudlin emotion.

sen'ti·men'tal, *a.* —**sen'ti·men'tal·ist**, *n.* —**sen'ti·men'tal·i·ty**, *n.* —**sen'ti·men'tal·ly**, *adv.*

sen'ti·nel, *n.* guard; sentry.

sen'try, *n.* [*pl.*- TRIES] guard posted to protect a group.

se'pal, *n.* leaf at the base of a flower.

sep'a·rate, *v.* 1. divide; set apart. 2. keep apart. 3. go apart. —*a.* (-rit) set apart; distinct. —**sep'a·ra·ble**, *a.* —**sep'a·rate·ly**, *adv.* —**sep'a·ra'tion**, *n.* —**sep'a·ra'tor**, *n.*

se'pi·a, *n.& a.* reddish brown.

sep'sis, *n.* blood infection. —**sep'tic**, *a.*

Sep·tem'ber, *n.* ninth month.

septic tank, tank into which house waste drains.

sep'ul·cher (-kēr) *n.* tomb: also, Br. sp., **sepulchre.** —**se·pul'chral**, *a.*

se'quel (-kwəl) *n.* 1. result. 2. book that continues an earlier book.

se'quence, *n.* 1. succession or the order of this. 2. series. 3. scene; episode.

se·ques'ter, *v.* hide; isolate. —**se'ques·tra'tion**, *n.*

se'quin, *n.* small, shiny disk for decorating cloth.

se·quoi'a (-kwoi'-) *n.* giant evergreen tree.

ser'aph (ser'-) *n.* [*pl.* -APHS, -APHIM] angel of the highest rank. —**se·raph'ic**, *a.*

sere, *a.* [Poet.] withered.

ser·e·nade', *n.& n.* (perform) music sung or played at night, esp. by a lover.

se·rene', *a.* undisturbed; calm. —**se·rene'ly**, *adv.* —**se·ren'i·ty**, *n.*

serf, *n.* feudal farmer, almost a slave.—**serf'dom**, *n.*

serge (sūrj) *n.* twilled, worsted fabric.

ser'geant (sär'jənt) *n.* 1. low-ranking police officer. 2. noncommissioned officer above a corporal.

ser'geant-at-arms', *n.* [*pl.* SERGEANTS-AT-ARMS] one who keeps order, as in a court.

se'ri·al, *a.* of, in, or published in a series. —*n.* serial story. —**se'ri·al·i·za'tion**, *n.*—**se'ri·al·ize'**, *v.*

se'ries, *n.* [*pl.* SERIES] number of similar things coming one after another.

se'ri·ous, *a.* 1. earnest. 2. important. 3. dangerous.

ser'mon, *n.* 1. religious speech by a clergyman. 2. serious talk on duty, etc.

ser'pent, *n.* snake.

ser'pen·tine (-tēn) *a.* winding.

ser'rate, *a.* edged like a saw.

ser'ried, *a.* placed close together.

se'rum (sēr'-) *n.* 1. yellowish fluid in blood. 2. antitoxin from the blood of an immune animal. —**se'rous**, *a.*

serv'ant, *n.* one hired to work in another's home.

serve, *v.* 1. be a servant to. 2. aid. 3. do official service. 4. spend a prison term. 5. offer (food, etc.) to. 6. be used by. 7. deliver. 8. hit a ball to start play. —*n.* serving (v. 8). —**serv'er**, *n.*

serv'ice, *n.* 1. a serving. 2. governmental work. 3. armed forces. 4. religious ceremony. 5. set of silverware, etc. 6. aid. —*v.* 1. supply. 2. repair. —**of service**, helpful. —**serv'ice·a·ble**, *a.*

serv'ice·man, *n.* [*pl.* -MEN] member of the armed forces.

ser'vile (-v'l) *a.* humbly submissive. —**ser·vil'i·ty**, *n.*

ser'vi·tude, *n.* slavery.

ses'a·me, *n.* edible seeds.

ses'sion, *n.* meeting of a court, legislature, class, etc.

set, *v.* [SET, SETTING] 1. put; place. 2. put in the proper condition, position, etc. 3. make or become firm or fixed. 4. establish; fix. 5. sit on eggs, as a hen. 6.

start.   7. mount (gems) 8. furnish (an example). 9. sink below the horizon. 10. fit (words) to music. —*a.* 1. fixed. 2. obstinate. 3. ready. —*n.* 1. way in which a thing is set. 2. scenery for a play. 3. group of like persons or things. 4. assembled parts, as of a radio. —**set about** (or **in, to**), begin. —**set forth**, state. —**set off,** 1. show off by contrast. 2. explode. —**set on** (or **upon**), attack. —**set up,** 1. erect. 2. establish.

set'back, *n.* relapse.

set-tee', *n.* small sofa.

set'ter, *n.* long-haired hunting dog.

set'ting, *n.* 1. that in which a thing is set. 2. time, place, etc., as of a story. 3. surroundings.

set'tle, *v.* 1. put in order. 2. set in place firmly or comfortably. 3. go to live in. 4. deposit sediment, etc. 5. calm. 6. decide. 7. pay, as a debt. 8. come to rest. 9. sink. —**set'tler**, *n.*

set'tle·ment, *n.* 1. a settling. 2. a colonizing of new land. 3. colony. 4. village. 5. an agreement. 6. payment.

sev'en, *a. & n.* one more than six. —**sev'enth**, *a. & n.*

sev'en·teen', *a. & n.* seven more than ten. —**sev'en·teenth'**, *a. & n.*

sev'en·ty, *a. & n. [pl. -TIES]** seven times ten. —**sev'en·ti·eth**, *a. & n.*

sev'er, *v.* cut off; separate. —**sev'er·ance**, *n.*

sev'er·al, *a.* 1. more than two but not many. 2. separate. —*n.* several persons or things. —**sev'er·al·ly**, *adv.*

se·vere', *a.* 1. harsh; strict. 2. grave. 3. very plain. 4. intense. —**se·vere'ly**, *adv.* —**se·ver'i·ty**, *n.*

sew (sō), *v.* [alt. pp. SEWN] fasten, make, etc. by means of needle and thread. —**sew'er**, *n.* —**sew'ing**, *n.*

sew'age (sōo'-) *n.* waste matter carried off by sewers.

sew'er, *n.* underground drain for water & waste matter.

sex, *n.* 1. either of the two divisions of organisms, male or female. 2. character of being male or female. —**sex'u·al**, *a.* —**sex'u·al·ly**, *adv.* —**sex'y** [-IER, -IEST] *a.*

sex'ism, *n.* unfair treatment of one sex by the other, esp. of women by men.

sex'tant, *n.* ship's instrument for navigation.

sex'ton, *n.* official who maintains church property.

shab'by, *a.* [-BIER, -BIEST] 1. worn out. 2. clothed poorly. 3. mean. —**shab'bi·ly**, *adv.* —**shab'bi·ness**, *n.*

shack, *n.* shanty.

shack'le, *n.* metal fastening for a prisoner's wrist or ankle. —*v.* 1. put shackles on. 2. restrain.

shad, *n.* salt-water fish.

shade, *n.* 1. partial darkness caused by cutting off light rays. 2. device to cut off light. 3. degree of darkness of a color. 4. small difference. —*v.* 1. screen from light. 2. change slightly. —**shad'y** [-IER, -IEST] *a.*

shad'ow, *n.* 1. shade cast by a body blocking light rays. 2. sadness. 3. small amount. —*v.* follow in secret. —**shad'ow·y**, *a.*

shaft, *n.* 1. arrow or spear, or its stem. 2. long, slender part or thing. 3. bar transmitting motion to a mechanical part. 4. vertical opening.

shag, *n.* long nap on cloth.

shag'gy, *a.* [-GIER, -GIEST] 1. having long, coarse hair. 2. unkempt.

shah, *n.* ruler of Iran.

shake, *v.* [SHOOK, SHAKEN, SHAKING] 1. move quickly up & down, back & forth, etc. 2. tremble. 3. weaken, disturb, upset, etc. 4. clasp (another's hand), as in greeting. —*n.* a shaking. —**shake off**, get rid of. —**shake up,** 1. mix by shaking. 2. jar. 3. reorganize. —**shak'y** [-IER, -IEST] *a.*

shale, *n.* rock of hard clay.

shall, *v.* [pt. SHOULD] a helping verb showing: 1. futurity or expectation. 2. determination or obligation.

shal·lot', *n.* onionlike plant.

shal'low, *a.* not deep. —*n.* shoal.

shalt, *v.* [Ar.] form of **shall** used with *thou.*

sham, *n. & a.* (something) false or fake. —*v.* [SHAMMED, SHAMMING] pretend.

sham'ble, *v.* walk clumsily. —*n.* [in *pl.*] scene of great destruction.

shame, *n.* 1. guilt, embarrassment, etc. felt for a wrong act. 2. dishonor. 3. a misfortune. —*v.* 1. make ashamed. 2. dishonor. 3.

force by a sense of shame. —**shame′ful,** *a.*

shame′faced, *a.* 1. bashful. 2. ashamed.

shame′less, *a.* showing no shame or modesty.

sham·poo′, *v.* wash (the hair, etc.). —*n.* a shampooing, or soap, etc. for this.

sham′rock, *n.* cloverlike plant with three leaflets.

shang′hai (-hī) *v.* [-HAIED, -HAIING] to kidnap for service aboard ship.

shank, *n.* the leg, esp. between the knee and ankle.

shan′t, shall not.

shan′tung′, *n.* silk fabric.

shan′ty, *n.* [*pl.* -TIES] small, shabby dwelling.

shape, *n.* 1. outer form. 2. definite form. 3. [Col.] condition. —*v.* form or adapt.

shape′ly, *a.* [-LIER, -LIEST] well-shaped.

share, *n.* part each gets or has. —*v.* 1. give in shares. 2. have a share (of).

share′crop, *v.* [-CROPPED, -CROPPING] work (land) for a share of the crop. —**share′crop′per,** *n.*

shark, *n.* a large, fierce fish.

shark′skin, *n.* smooth, silky cloth.

sharp, *a.* 1. having a fine point or cutting edge. 2. abrupt. 3. distinct. 4. clever or shrewd. 5. vigilant. 6. harsh or intense. 7. *Mus.* above the true pitch. —*n. Mus.* a note one half step above another: symbol (♯). —*adv.* 1. in a sharp way. 2. precisely. —**sharp′en,** *v.* —**sharp′en·er,** *n.* —**sharp′ly,** *adv.* —**sharp′ness,** *n.*

sharp′shoot′er, *n.* good marksman.

shat′ter, *v.* 1. break into pieces. 2. damage badly.

shave, *v.* [*alt. pp.* SHAVEN] 1. cut into slices from. 2. cut the hair or beard (of) to the skin. —*n.* act of shaving. —**close shave,** [Col.] narrow escape. —**shav′er,** *n.*

shav′ing, *n.* 1. act of one who shaves. 2. thin piece shaved off.

shawl, *n.* cloth covering for the head and shoulders.

she, *pron.* the female mentioned.

sheaf, *n.* [*pl.* SHEAVES] bundle of stalks, papers, etc.

shear, *v.* [*alt. pp.* SHORN] 1. cut or cut off as with shears. 2. clip hair from. —*n.* [in *pl.*] large scissors.

sheath [shēth] *n.* 1. case for a knife blade, etc. 2. any covering like this.

sheathe (shēth) *v.* put into or cover with a sheath.

shed, *n.* small shelter or storage place. —*v.* [SHED, SHEDDING] 1. make flow. 2. radiate. 3. throw or cast off.

sheen, *n.* luster; gloss.

sheep, *n.* [*pl.* SHEEP] cud-chewing animal with heavy wool. —**sheep′skin,** *n.*

sheep′ish, *a.* bashful or embarrassed.

sheer, *v.* to swerve. —*a.* 1. very thin. 2. absolute. 3. very steep. —*adv.* completely.

sheet, *n.* 1. large cloth of cotton, etc. used on beds. 2. piece of paper. 3. broad, thin piece of glass, etc. 4. rope to control a sail.

sheet′ing, *n.* cloth material for sheets.

sheik, sheikh (shēk) *n.* Arab chief.

shek′el, *n.* ancient Hebrew coin.

shelf, *n.* [*pl.* SHELVES] 1. thin, flat board for holding things. 2. ledge or reef.

shell, *n.* 1. hard outer covering, as of an egg. 2. narrow rowboat for racing. 3. missile from a large gun. 4. cartridge. —*v.* 1. remove the shell from. 2. bombard.

she′ll, 1. she will. 2. she shall.

shel·lac′, shel·lack′, *n.* thin varnish of resin and alcohol. —*v.* [SHELLACKED, SHELLACKING] 1. put shellac on. 2. [Sl.] to beat.

shell′fish, *n.* aquatic animal with a shell.

shel′ter, *n.* something that covers or protects. —*v.* give shelter to.

shelve, *v.* 1. put on a shelf. 2. lay aside.

shelv′ing, *n.* 1. material for shelves. 2. shelves.

shep′herd, *n.* 1. one who herds sheep. 2. religious leader. —*v.* be a shepherd. —**shep′herd·ess,** *n. fem.*

sher′bet, *n.* frozen dessert of fruit juice, milk, etc.

sher′iff, *n.* chief law officer of a county.

sher′ry, *n.* a strong wine.

shib′bo·leth, *n.* password.

shield, *n.* 1. armor carried on the arm. 2. thing that protects. —*v.* protect.

shift, *v.* 1. move or change from one person, place, di-

rection, etc. to another. 2. get along. —*n.* 1. a shifting. 2. time at work. 3. trick.

shift′less, *a.* lazy.

shift′y, *a.* [-IER, -IEST] tricky; evasive.

shil′ling, *n.* Br. coin, 1/20 of a pound.

shil′ly-shal′ly, *v.* [-LIED, -LY-ING] hesitate.

shim′mer, *v. & n.* (shine with) a wavering light.

shim′my, *n. & v.* [-MIED, -MYING] shake or wobble.

shin, *n.* front of the leg between knee and ankle. —*v.* [SHINNED, SHINNING] climb, as a rope, with hands and legs.

shine, *v.* [SHONE, SHINING] 1. be or make be bright. 2. excel. 3. [pt. & pp. SHINED] make shiny by polishing. —*n.* 1. brightness. 2. polish.

shin′gle, *n.* 1. piece of wood, slate, etc. for roofing. 2. [Col.] small signboard. —*v.* put shingles on (a roof).

shin′gles, *n.* virus skin disease along a nerve.

shin′y, *a.* [-IER, -IEST] bright; shining.

ship, *n.* 1. large water craft. 2. aircraft. —*v.* [SHIPPED, SHIPPING] 1. put or go in a ship. 2. transport. —**on shipboard**, on a ship. —**ship′load**, *n.* —**ship′ment**, *n.* —**ship′per**, *n.*

-ship, *suf.* 1. state of. 2. rank or office. 3. skill as.

ship′shape, *a.* neat; trim.

ship′wreck, *v. & n.* (cause) loss or ruin of a ship.

ship′yard, *n.* place where ships are built or repaired.

shire, *n.* [Br.] county.

shirk, *v.* neglect (a duty). —**shirk′er**, *n.*

shirr, *v.* 1. pull stitches tight in rows. 2. bake (eggs) with crumbs.

shirt, *n.* 1. upper garment for men. 2. undershirt.

shiv′er, *v.* 1. shake or tremble. 2. shatter. —*n.* 1. a trembling. 2. sliver.

shoal, *n.* 1. school of fish. 2. shallow place in water.

shock, *n.* 1. sudden blow or jar. 2. sudden emotional upset. 3. effect of electric current on the body. 4. bundle of grain. 5. thick mass of hair. —*v.* 1. astonish; horrify. 2. give an electric shock to.

shod′dy, *a.* [-DIER, -DIEST] inferior. —**shod′di·ness**, *n.*

shoe, *n.* 1. outer covering for the foot. 2. horseshoe.

3. part of a brake that presses on the wheel. —*v.* [SHOD, SHOEING] put shoes on.

shoe′horn, *n.* device to help slip a shoe on the foot.

shoe′lace, *n.* lace (*n.* 1): also **shoe′string**

shoe tree, form put in a shoe to hold its shape.

shone, *pt. & pp.* of **shine**.

shook, *pt.* of **shake**.

shoot, *v.* [SHOT, SHOOTING] 1. send out, or move, with force, speed, etc. 2. send a bullet, etc. from. 3. wound or kill with a bullet, etc. 4. to photograph. 5. score (a point, etc.) in sports. 6. grow rapidly. 7. variegate. —*n.* new growth; sprout. —**shoot′er**, *n.*

shop, *n.* 1. place where things are sold. 2. manufacturing place. —*v.* [SHOPPED, SHOPPING] look at or buy goods in shops. —**shop′per**, *n.*

shop′lift′er, *n.* one who steals from store counters.

shore, *n.* 1. land next to water. 2. prop; support. —*v.* prop (up).

short, *a.* 1. not measuring much. 2. not tall. 3. brief. 4. brusque. 5. less than enough. —*n.* 1. short movie. 2. *pl.* short pants. 3. short circuit. —*adv.* abruptly or briefly. —*v.* short-circuit. —**in short**, briefly. —**short′en**, *v.* —**short′ness**, *n.*

short′age, *n.* 1. lack; deficiency. 2. deficit.

short′cake, *n.* light biscuit or sweet cake.

short-change′, *v.* [Col.] give less change than is due.

short circuit, side circuit of low resistance that deflects electric current. —**short′-cir′cuit**, *v.*

short′com′ing, *n.* defect.

short cut, 1. shorter route. 2. way of saving time, etc.

short′en·ing, *n.* fat used to make baked goods flaky.

short′hand, *n.* system of symbols for writing fast.

short′-hand′ed, *a.* short of workers or helpers.

short′-lived′ (-līvd′) *a.* lasting only a short time.

short′ly, *adv.* 1. briefly. 2. soon. 3. curtly.

short′sight′ed, *a.* lacking in foresight.

short′-tem′pered, *a.* easily angered.

short wave, radio wave 60 meters or less in length. —

short'-wave', a.

short'-wind'ed (-win'did) a. easily put out of breath.

shot, pt. & pp. of **shoot**. —n. 1. act of shooting. 2. range; scope. 3. attempt. 4. throw, etc., as of a ball. 5. projectile(s) for a gun. 6. marksman. 7. photograph. 8. [Sl.] dose or drink. —**shot'gun**, n.

should (shood) pt. of **shall**. *Should* is used to express obligation, probability, etc.

shoul'der, n. 1. part of the body to which an arm or foreleg is connected. 2. edge of a road. —v. 1. push with the shoulder. 2. assume the burden of.

shout, v. & n. (utter) a loud, sudden cry or call.

shove, v. 1. push along a surface. 2. push roughly. —n. a push.

shov'el, n. tool with a broad scoop and a handle. —v. move or dig with a shovel. —**shov'el·ful** [pl. -FULS] n.

show, v. [pp. SHOWN or SHOWED] 1. bring into sight; reveal. 2. appear. 3. be noticeable. 4. guide. 5. point out. 6. prove; explain. —n. 1. a display, performance, etc. 2. pompous display. 3. pretense. —**show off**, make a display of. —**show'case**, n. —**show'room**, n.

show'down, n. [Col.] disclosure of facts to force a settlement.

show'er (shou'-) n. 1. brief fall of rain. 2. any sudden fall or flow. 3. party with gifts for a bride, etc. 4. bath of fine water spray. —v. 1. to spray with water. 2. give, or fall, abundantly.

show'man, n. [pl. -MEN] one who produces shows skillfully. —**show'man·ship**, n.

show'y, a. [-IER, -IEST] 1. of striking appearance. 2. gaudy; flashy. —**show'i·ly**, adv. —**show'i·ness**, n.

shrap'nel, n. fragments of an exploded artillery shell.

shred, n. 1. torn strip. 2. fragment. —v. [SHREDDED or SHRED, SHREDDING] cut or tear into shreds.

shrew, n. 1. small, mouselike mammal. 2. nagging woman. —**shrew'ish**, a.

shrewd, a. clever or sharp in practical affairs. —**shrewd'ly**, adv. —**shrewd'ness**, n.

shriek (shrēk) v. & n. (utter) a loud, piercing cry.

shrill, a. high-pitched and piercing in sound. —**shrill'ness**, n. —**shril'ly**, adv.

shrimp, n. 1. small, longtailed, edible shellfish. 2. [Col.] small person.

shrine, n. saint's tomb or other sacred place.

shrink, v. [SHRANK or SHRUNK, SHRUNK or SHRUNKEN, SHRINKING] 1. lessen in size; contract. 2. draw back. —**shrink'age**, n.

shriv'el, v. dry up; wither.

shroud, n. cloth used to wrap a corpse. 2. cover; veil. 3. pl. ropes supporting ship's masts. —v. hide; cover.

shrub, n. bush. —**shrub'ber·y**, n.

shrug, v. & n. [SHRUGGED, SHRUGGING] (draw up the shoulders in) a gesture of doubt, indifference, etc.

shuck, v. & n. husk; shell.

shud'der, v. shake, as in horror. —n. a shuddering.

shuf'fle, v. 1. walk with feet dragging. 2. mix or jumble together. —n. a shuffling.

shuf'fle·board, n. game in which disks are pushed toward numbered squares.

shun, v. [SHUNNED, SHUNNING] keep away from.

shunt, v. 1. move to one side. 2. switch or shift.

shush, int. be quiet! —v. say "shush" to.

shut, v. [SHUT, SHUTTING] 1. close (a door, etc.). 2. prevent entrance to or from. —a. closed. —**shut off**, prevent passage of or on. —**shut up**, 1. enclose. 2. [Col.] stop talking.

shut'ter, n. 1. movable window cover. 2. light-controlling device on a camera lens.

shut'tle, n. device to carry thread back and forth in weaving. —v. move rapidly to and fro.

shut'tle·cock, n. feathered cork ball in badminton.

shy, a. [SHIER or SHYER, SHIEST or SHYEST] 1. timid. 2. bashful. 3. distrustful. 4. [Sl.] lacking. —v. [SHIED, SHYING] 1. be startled. 2. hesitate. 3. fling sideways. —**shy'ly**, adv. —**shy'ness**, n.

shy'ster (shī'-) n. [Sl.] dishonest lawyer.

Si·a·mese' twins, pair of twins born joined.

sib'i·lant, a. & n. hissing (sound). —**sib'i·lance**, n.

sib'ling, n. a brother or sister.

sib'yl, n. prophetess of ancient Greece or Rome.

sick, *a.* 1. having disease; ill. 2. nauseated. 3. of or for sick people. 4. disgusted. —*n.* sick people. —**sick'ness,** *n.*

sick, sic, *v.* to urge (a dog) to attack.

sick'en, *v.* make or become sick. —**sick'en·ing,** *a.*

sick'le, *n.* curved blade with a short handle, for cutting tall grass.

sick'ly, *a.* [-LIER, -LIEST] 1. in poor health. 2. faint or weak.

side, *n.* 1. right or left half. 2. a bounding line. 3. a surface. 4. aspect. 5. relative position. 6. party; faction. —*a.* 1. of, at, or to a side. 2. secondary. —**side with,** support. —**take sides,** support one faction.

side'board, *n.* dining-room cabinet for linen, etc.

side'burns, *n.pl.* hair on the cheeks, beside the ears.

side'long, *adv. & a.* toward or to the side.

si·de're·al, *a.* of or measured by the stars.

side'-step', *v.* avoid as by stepping aside.

side'track', *v.* turn aside from a course, subject, etc.

side'walk, *n.* path for pedestrians alongside a street.

side'ways, *a. & adv.* 1. to or from one side. 2. side first. Also **side'wise.**

sid'ing, *n.* 1. outside boards, etc. on a building. 2. short railroad track off the main track.

si'dle, *v.* move sideways cautiously.

siege (sēj) *n.* 1. encircling of a place to effect its capture. 2. persistent attack.

si·es'ta, *n.* brief rest or nap, esp. in the afternoon.

sieve (siv) *n.* strainer with many small holes.

sift, *v.* 1. pass through a sieve, as to separate. 2. examine with care, as evidence.

sigh, *v.* 1. let out a deep breath, as in sorrow. 2. long (*for*). —*n.* a sighing.

sight, *n.* 1. something seen. 2. act or power of seeing. 3. range of vision. 4. aiming device. —*v.* 1. to see. 2. aim (a gun, etc.). —**at** (or **on**) **sight,** as soon as seen. —**sight'less,** *a.*

sight'ly, *a.* [-LIER, -LIEST] pleasing to look at.

sign, *n.* 1. mark or symbol. 2. meaningful gesture. 3. signboard, road marker, etc. 4. trace; vestige. —*v.* write

one's name (on). —**sign off,** stop broadcasting. —**sign'er,** *n.*

sig'nal, *n.* 1. gesture, device, etc. to warn, order, etc. 2. radio wave. —*a.* notable. —*v.* make signals (to).

sig'nal·ize, *v.* 1. make noteworthy. 2. point out.

sig'na·to'ry, *n.* [*pl.* -RIES] nation signing a pact, etc.

sig'na·ture, *n.* one's name written by oneself.

sign'board, *n.* board bearing advertising.

sig'net, *n.* small official seal.

sig·nif'i·cance, *n.* 1. meaning. 2. importance. —**sig-nif'i·cant,** *a.*

sig'ni·fy, *v.* [-FIED, -FYING] 1. to mean. 2. make known, as by a sign. —**sig'ni·fi·ca'-tion,** *n.*

si'lence, *n.* absence of sound. —*v.* 1. make silent. 2. repress. —*int.* be silent.

si'lent, *a.* 1. not speaking. 2. still; quiet. 3. inactive. —**si'lent·ly,** *adv.*

sil·hou·ette' (-ōō et') *v. & n.* (make) a dark shape against a light background.

sil'i·ca, *n.* glassy mineral found as sand, etc.

sil'i·con, *n.* chemical element forming silica, etc.

silk, *n.* thread or fabric of soft fiber made by silkworms. —**silk'en,** **silk'y** [-IER, -IEST] *a.*

silk'worm, *n.* moth caterpillar that spins silk fiber.

sill, *n.* bottom of a door frame or window frame.

sil'ly, *a.* [-LIER, -LIEST] foolish; absurd. —**sil'li·ness,** *n.*

si'lo, *n.* [*pl.* -LOS] tower for storing green fodder.

silt, *n.* fine particles of soil floating in or left by water. —*v.* fill with silt.

sil'ver, *n.* 1. white, precious metal, a chemical element. 2. silver coins. 3. silverware. 4. grayish white. —*a.* of silver. —*v.* cover as with silver. —**sil'ver·y,** *a.*

sil'ver·smith, *n.* one who makes things of silver.

sil'ver·ware, *n.* tableware of or plated with silver.

sim'i·an, *n.* ape or monkey.

sim'i·lar, *a.* nearly alike. —**sim'i·lar'i·ty** [-TIES] *n.* —**sim'i·lar·ly,** *adv.*

sim'i·le (-lē) *n.* a likening of dissimilar things.

si·mil'i·tude, *n.* likeness.

sim'mer, *v. & n.* (keep at or near) a gentle boiling.

sim'o·ny (sīm'-) n. buying or selling of sacred things.

sim'per, v. smile in a silly way. —n. silly smile.

sim'ple, a. 1. having only one or a few parts. 2. easy to do or understand. 3. plain. 4. natural. 5. common. 6. foolish. —**sim·plic'i·ty** [pl. -TIES] n.

sim'ple-mind'ed, a. 1. foolish. 2. feeble-minded.

sim'ple·ton, n. fool.

sim'pli·fy, v. [-FIED, -FYING] make easier. —**sim'pli·fi·ca'tion,** n.

sim'ply, adv. 1. in a simple way. 2. merely. 3. completely.

sim'u·late, v. pretend. —**sim'u·la'tion,** n.

si'mul·ta'ne·ous, a. done, etc. at the same time. —**si'mul·ta'ne·ous·ly,** adv.

sin, n. breaking of religious or moral law. —v. [SINNED, SINNING] commit a sin. —**sin'ful,** a. —**sin'ner,** n.

since, adv. & prep. 1. from then until now. 2. at some time between then and now. —con. 1. after the time that. 2. because.

sin·cere', a. 1. without deceit. 2. genuine. —**sin·cere'ly,** adv. —**sin·cer'i·ty,** n.

si'ne·cure (sī'-) n. well-paid job with little work.

sin'ew (-ū) n. 1. tendon. 2. strength. —**sin'ew·y,** a.

sing, v. [SANG, SUNG, SINGING] 1. make musical sounds with the voice, etc. 2. perform by singing. 3. hum, buzz, etc. 4. tell in song. —n. [Col.] group singing. —**sing'er,** n.

singe (sinj) v. [SINGED, SINGEING] burn superficially. —n. a singeing.

sin'gle, a. 1. one only. 2. of or for one person or family. 3. unmarried. —v. select from others. —n. 1. single thing. 2. pl. tennis game with only two players. —**sin'gle·ness,** n.

single file, column of persons one behind the other.

sin'gle-hand'ed, a. without help.

sin'gly, adv. 1. alone. 2. one by one.

sing'song, a. & n. (having) a monotonous cadence.

sin'gu·lar, a. 1. unique. 2. separate. 3. exceptional. 4. unusual. —n. Gram. word form designating only one.

—sin'gu·lar'i·ty, n. —**sin'gu·lar·ly,** adv.

sin'is·ter, a. 1. threatening. 2. wicked or evil.

sink, v. [SANK or SUNK, SUNK, SINKING] 1. go or put beneath the surface of water, etc. 2. go down slowly. 3. become lower. 4. pass gradually (into sleep, etc.). 5. invest. 6. defeat. —n. basin with a drain pipe.

sink'er, n. lead weight used on a fishing line.

sin'u·ous, a. crooked.

si'nus, n. [pl. -NUSES] any air cavity in the skull opening into the nasal cavities.

si'nus·i'tis, n. inflammation of the sinuses.

-sion, suf. act, state, or result of.

sip, v. [SIPPED, SIPPING] drink a little at a time. —n. small amount sipped.

si'phon, n. tube for carrying liquid from one container to another below it. —v. drain through a siphon.

sir, n. 1. polite title for a man. 2. [S-] title for a knight or baronet.

sire, n. male parent. —v. be the male parent of.

si'ren, n. 1. warning device with a wailing sound. 2. seductive woman.

sir'loin, n. choice cut of beef from the loin.

sir'up, n. sweet, thick liquid. —**sir'up·y,** a.

si'sal, n. strong rope fiber.

sis'sy, n. [pl. -SIES] [Col.] unmanly boy or man. —**sis'si·fied,** a.

sis'ter, n. 1. female related to one by having the same parents. 2. female fellow member. 3. nun. —**sis'ter·hood,** n. —**sis'ter·ly,** a.

sis'ter-in-law', n. [pl. SISTERS-IN-LAW] 1. sister of one's spouse. 2. brother's wife.

sit, v. [SAT, SITTING] 1. rest on one's buttocks or haunches. 2. perch. 3. be in session. 4. pose, as for a portrait. 5. be located. 6. baby-sit. —**sit down,** take a seat. —**sit in,** take part. —**sit'ter,** n.

site, n. location; scene.

sit'u·ate (sich'ōō-) v. put or place; locate.

sit'u·a'tion, n. 1. location. 2. condition. 3. job.

six, a. & n. one more than five. —**sixth,** a. & n.

six'teen', a. & n. six more

than ten. —**six′teenth′**, *a.* & *n.*

six′ty, *a.* & *n.* [*pl.* -TIES] six times ten. —**six′ti·eth**, *a.* & *n.*

siz′a·ble, size′a·ble, *a.* fairly large.

size, *n.* 1. dimensions. 2. any of a series of measures, often numbered. 3. pasty glaze: also **siz′ing**. —*v.* 1. arrange by size (*n.* 2). 2. apply size (*n.* 3).

siz′zle, *v.* to hiss when hot. —*n.* such a sound.

skate, *n.* 1. metal runner fastened to a shoe, for gliding on ice: also **ice skate**. 2. roller skate. —*v.* move along on skates.

skein (skān) *n.* coil of yarn or thread.

skel′e·ton, *n.* framework, as of the bones of a body. —**skel′e·tal**, *a.*

skep′tic, *n.* one who questions matters generally accepted. —**skep′ti·cal**, *a.* —**skep′ti·cism**, *n.*

sketch, *n.* 1. rough drawing or design. 2. outline. —*v.* make a sketch (of). —**sketch′y** [-IER, -IEST]

skew′er, *n.* long pin to hold meat together as it cooks.

ski (skē) *n.* [*pl.* SKIS] long, flat runner fastened to the shoe for snow travel. —*v.* travel on skis. —**ski′er**, *n.*

skid, *n.* 1. plank, log, etc. on which to support or slide something heavy. 2. act of skidding. —*v.* [SKIDDED, SKIDDING] slide sideways.

skiff, *n.* small sailboat.

skill, *n.* 1. great ability. 2. art or craft involving use of the hands or body. —**skilled**, *a.* —**skil′ful, skil′ful**, *a.*

skil′let, *n.* frying pan.

skim, *v.* [SKIMMED, SKIMMING] 1. take floating matter from a liquid. 2. read quickly. 3. glide lightly.

skim milk, milk with the cream removed.

skimp, *v.* [Col.] scrimp.

skimp′y, *a.* [-IER, -IEST] [Col.] barely enough; scanty.

skin, *n.* 1. tissue covering the body. 2. pelt. 3. covering like skin, as fruit rind. —*v.* [SKINNED, SKINNING] remove the skin from.

skin′flint, *n.* miser.

skin′ny, *a.* [-NIER, -NIEST] very thin. —**skin′ni·ness**, *n.*

skip, *v.* [SKIPPED, SKIPPING] 1. move by hopping on alternate feet. 2. leap lightly

(over). 3. bounce. 4. omit. —*n.* act of skipping.

skip′per, *n.* ship's captain.

skir′mish, *v.* & *n.* (take part in) a small, brief battle.

skirt, *n.* 1. part of a dress. coat, etc. below the waist. 2. woman's garment that hangs from the waist. —*v.* go along the edge of.

skit, *n.* short, funny play.

skit′tish, *a.* 1. lively; playful. 2. very nervous.

skul·dug′ger·y, *n.* [Col.] mean trickery.

skulk, *v.* move or lurk in a stealthy way.

skull, *n.* bony framework of the head.

skunk, *n.* small mammal that ejects a smelly liquid.

sky, *n.* [*pl.* SKIES] often *pl.* upper atmosphere or space around the earth.

sky′lark, *n.* Old World lark.

sky′light, *n.* window in a roof or ceiling.

sky′line, *n.* outline of a city, etc. seen against the sky.

sky′rock′et, *n.* firework rocket. —*v.* [Col.] rise fast.

sky′scrap′er, *n.* very tall building.

sky′ward, *a.* & *adv.* toward the sky: also **sky′wards**, *adv.*

slab, *n.* flat, thick piece.

slack, *a.* 1. loose. 2. not busy. 3. slow; sluggish. —*n.* slack part or time. —*v.* slack off (or up), slacken.

slack′en, *v.* 1. slow down. 2. loosen.

slack′er, *n.* one who shirks.

slacks, *n.pl.* trousers.

slag, *n.* smelting refuse.

slain, pp. of **slay**.

slake, *v.* 1. satisfy (thirst). 2. mix (lime) with water.

slam, *v.* [SLAMMED, SLAMMING] shut, hit, etc. with force. —*n.* heavy impact.

slan′der, *n.* spoken falsehood harmful to another. —*v.* speak slander against. —**slan′der·ous**, *a.*

slang, *n.* vigorous, short-lived, informal language.

slant, *v.* & *n.* 1. incline; slope. 2. (show) a special attitude.

slap, *n.* a blow with something flat. —*v.* [SLAPPED, SLAPPING] strike with a slap

slap′stick, *n.* crude comedy

slash, *v.* 1. cut at with a knife. 2. cut slits in. 3. reduce. —*n.* a slashing; cut.

slat, *n.* narrow strip.

slate, *n.* 1. bluish-gray rock in thin layers. 2. tile, etc. of

slate. 3. list of candidates.
—v. designate.

slat′tern, n. untidy woman.
—slat′tern·ly, a. & adv.

slaugh′ter (slô′-) v. 1. kill
(animals) for food. 2. kill
(people) brutally. —n. a
slaughtering.

slaugh′ter·house, n. place
for butchering animals.

slave, n. human being owned
by another. —v. to toil.
—slav′ish, a.

slav′er (slav′-) v. drool.

slav′er·y, n. 1. condition of
slaves. 2. ownership of
slaves. 3. drudgery.

Slav′ic, a. of the Russians,
Poles, Slovaks, etc.

slay, v. [SLEW, SLAIN, SLAY-
ING] kill by violent means.
—slay′er, n.

slea′zy (slē′-) a. [-ZIER,
-ZIEST] flimsy; thin.

sled, n. vehicle with runners,
for snow. —v. [SLEDDED,
SLEDDING] ride a sled.

sledge, n. 1. long, heavy
hammer. 2. heavy sled.

sleek, a. 1. glossy. 2. well-
groomed. —v. make sleek.

sleep, n. natural regular rest,
as at night. —v. [SLEPT,
SLEEPING] to be in a state of
sleep. —sleep′less, a.

sleep′er, n. 1. one who sleeps.
2. railway car with berths.

sleep′y, a. [-IER, -IEST] 1.
drowsy. 2. dull; quiet.

sleet, n. partly frozen rain.
—v. to shower as sleet.

sleeve, n. part of a garment
covering the arm.

sleigh (slā) n. vehicle on runners for travel on snow.

sleight of hand (slīt) 1. skill
in doing tricks with the
hands. 2. such tricks.

slen′der, a. 1. long and thin.
2. small in size or force.

slept, pt. & pp. of sleep.

sleuth (slōōth) n. [Col.] de-
tective.

slew, pt. of slay. —n. [Col.]
large number or amount.

slice, n. 1. thin, broad piece
cut off. 2. share. —v. cut
into slices or as a slice.
—slic′er, n.

slick, v. make smooth. —a.
1. smooth. 2. slippery. 3.
clever. —n. smooth area, as
of oil on water.

slide, v. [SLID, SLID or SLID-
DEN, SLIDING] 1. move along
a smooth surface. 2. glide.
3. slip. —n. 1. a sliding. 2.
inclined surface to slide on.
3. picture for projection on
a screen.

slide fastener, fastener with
interlocking tabs worked by
a sliding part.

slide rule, rapid computer
that looks like a ruler.

slight, a. 1. slender. 2. unimportant. 3. small or weak.
—v. & n. neglect or snub.
—slight′ly, adv.

slim, a. [SLIMMER, SLIMMEST]
1. long and thin. 2. small. —
v. [SLIMMED, SLIMMING] make
or become slim.

slime, n. soft, wet, sticky
matter. —slim′y [-IER,
-IEST] a.

sling, n. 1. device for hurling
stones. 2. band or looped
cloth for raising or supporting. —v. [SLUNG, SLINGING]
hurl as with a sling.

sling′shot, n. Y-shaped piece
with elastic band for shooting stones, etc.

slink, v. [SLUNK, SLINKING]
move in a sneaking way.

slip, v. [SLIPPED, SLIPPING]
1. go quietly. 2. put or pass
smoothly or quickly. 3. slide
accidentally. 4. escape from.
5. become worse. 6. err. —
n. 1. dock for ships. 2. woman's undergarment. 3. a falling down. 4. error. 5. plant
stem or root, for planting,
etc. 6. small piece of paper.

slip′knot, n. knot that can
slip along a rope.

slip′per, n. light, low shoe.

slip′per·y, a. [-IER, -IEST]
1. that can cause slipping.
2. tending to slip. 3. tricky.

slip′shod, a. careless.

slit, v. [SLIT, SLITTING] cut or
split open. —n. straight,
narrow opening.

slith′er (slith′-) v. slide or
glide along.

sliv′er, n. thin, pointed piece
cut or split off.

slob′ber, v. & n. drool.

sloe, n. dark-blue fruit.

slog, v. [SLOGGED, SLOGGING]
plod.

slo′gan, n. motto or phrase,
as for advertising purposes.

sloop, n. boat with one mast.

slop, n. 1. spilled liquid. 2.
slush. 3. watery food. 4.
often pl. liquid waste. —v.
[SLOPPED, SLOPPING] splash.

slope, n. 1. rising or falling
surface, line, etc. 2. amount
of this. —v. have a slope.

slop′py, a. [-PIER, -PIEST] 1.
slushy. 2. [Col.] careless.

slot, n. narrow opening.

sloth (slôth) n. 1. laziness.
2. S. American animal living
in trees. —sloth′ful, a.

slouch, *n.* 1. lazy person. 2. drooping posture. —*v.* have a drooping posture.

slough (sluf) *v.* to shed; discard. —*n.* (slou) swamp.

slov'en (sluv'-) *n.* slovenly person.

slov'en·ly, *a.* careless or untidy.

slow, *a.* 1. taking longer than usual. 2. low in speed. 3. behind the right time. 4. stupid. 5. sluggish. —*v.* make or become slow. —*adv.* in a slow way. —**slow'ly,** *adv.* —**slow'ness,** *n.*

sludge, *n.* 1. mud or mire. 2. slimy waste.

slug, *n.* 1. small mollusk. 2. bullet. 3. false coin. —*v.* [SLUGGED, SLUGGING] [Col.] hit hard. —**slug'ger,** *n.*

slug'gard, *n.* lazy person.

slug'gish, *a.* slow-moving.

sluice (sloos) *n.* water channel or gate to control it.

slum, *n.* populous area with very poor living conditions.

slum'ber, *v. & n.* sleep.

slump, *v.* 1. fall suddenly. 2. slouch. —*n.* sudden fall.

slur, *v.* [SLURRED, SLURRING] 1. pass over quickly. 2. pronounce indistinctly. 3. insult. —*n.* a slurring. 2. insult.

slush, *n.* partly melted snow. —**slush'y,** *a.*

slut, *n.* immoral woman.

sly, *a.* [SLIER or SLYER, SLIEST or SLYEST] 1. cunning; crafty. 2. playfully mischievous. —**on the sly,** secretly. —**sly'ly,** *adv.*

smack, *n.* 1. slight taste. 2. sharp noise made by parting the lips suddenly. 3. sharp slap. 4. loud kiss. 5. fishing boat. —*v.* 1. have a taste. 2. make a smack with one's lips. 3. slap loudly. —*adv.* directly.

small, *a.* 1. little in size, extent, etc. 2. trivial. 3. mean; petty. —*n.* small part. —**small'ish,** *a.*

small'pox, *n.* contagious disease with fever and sores.

smart, *v.* 1. cause or feel stinging pain. 2. suffer. —*a.* 1. that smarts. 2. brisk; lively. 3. bright; clever. 4. neat. 5. stylish. —**smart'ly,** *adv.*

smash, *v.* 1. break violently. 2. crash. 3. destroy. —*n.* 1. a smashing. 2. wreck; collision.

smat'ter·ing, *n.* a little knowledge.

smear, *v.* 1. make greasy,

dirty, etc. 2. spread. 3. slander. —*n.* a smearing.

smell, *v.* [SMELLED or SMELT, SMELLING] 1. catch the odor of. 2. sniff. 3. have an odor. —*n.* 1. power to smell. 2. thing smelled; odor.

smell'y, *a.* [-IER, -IEST] having a bad smell.

smelt, *n.* 1. small, silvery food fish. —*v.* melt (ore or metal) so as to remove the impurities. —**smelt'er,** *n.*

smile, *v.* 1. show pleasure, amusement, etc. by curving the mouth upward. 2. show with a smile. —*n.* act of smiling.

smirch, *v. & n.* smear.

smirk, *v. & n.* smug smile.

smite, *v.* [SMOTE, SMITTEN, SMITING] 1. hit or strike hard. 2. affect strongly.

smith, *n.* one who makes or repairs metal objects.

smith'y, *n.* [*pl.* -IES] blacksmith's shop.

smock, *n.* loose, protective outer garment.

smog, *n.* fog and smoke.

smoke, *n.* vapor, as from something burning. —*v.* 1. give off smoke. 2. use cigarettes, a pipe, etc. 3. cure (meats, etc.) with smoke. —**smoke'less,** *a.* —**smok'er,** *n.* —**smok'y** [-IER, -IEST] *a.*

smoke'stack, *n.* tall chimney.

smol'der, *v.* 1. burn without flame. 2. exist suppressed. Also sp. **smoulder**

smooth, *a.* 1. having no roughness or bumps; even. 2. with no trouble. 3. ingratiating. —*v.* make smooth. —*adv.* in a smooth way. —**smooth'ness,** *n.*

smor'gas·bord (-gas-) *n.* variety of tasty foods served buffet style.

smoth'er (smuth'-) *v.* 1. suffocate. 2. cover thickly.

smudge, *n.* 1. dirty spot. 2. fire with dense smoke. —*v.* to smear. —**smudg'y,** *a.*

smug, *a.* [SMUGGER, SMUGGEST] too self-satisfied. —**smug'ly,** *adv.*

smug'gle, *v.* 1. bring in or take out secretly or illegally. —**smug'gler,** *n.*

smut, *n.* 1. dirt. 2. obscene matter. 3. plant disease. —**smut'ty** [-TIER, -TIEST] *a.*

snack, *n.* light meal.

snag, *n.* 1. sharp projection. 2. tear made by this. 3. hidden difficulty. —*v.*

[SNAGGED, SNAGGING] 1. tear on a snag. 2. hinder.

snail, *n.* mollusk with a spiral shell.

snake, *n.* long, legless reptile. —*v.* twist like a snake. —**snak'y** [-IER, -IEST] *a.*

snap, *v.* [SNAPPED, SNAPPING] 1. bite or grasp suddenly. 2. shout (at). 3. break suddenly. 4. make a cracking sound. 5. move quickly. 6. take a snapshot of. —*n.* 1. sharp sound. 2. fastening that clicks shut. 3. [Sl.] easy job. —*a.* quick. —**snap'per,** *n.* —**snap'pish,** *a.*

snap'drag'on, *n.* plant with red or yellow flowers.

snap'py, *a.* [-PIER, -PIEST] [Col.] lively; brisk.

snap'shot, *n.* picture taken with a hand camera.

snare, *n.* 1. trap for small animals. 2. dangerous lure. 3. string across the bottom of a drum. —*v.* to trap.

snarl, *v.* 1. growl, baring the teeth. 2. speak sharply. 3. tangle. —*n.* 1. a snarling. 2. tangle; disorder.

snatch, *v.* seize; grab. —*n.* 1. brief time. 2. fragment.

sneak, *v.* move, do, etc. secretly. —*n.* one who sneaks. —**sneak'y** [-IER, -IEST] *a.*

sneak'ers, *n.pl.* [Col.] canvas shoes with rubber soles.

sneer, *v.* show scorn. —*n.* sneering look or remark.

sneeze, *v.* expel breath from the nose and mouth in a sudden, uncontrolled way. —*n.* act of sneezing.

snick'er, *v. & n.* (give) a silly, partly stifled laugh.

snide, *a.* slyly malicious.

sniff, *v.* inhale forcibly through the nose, as in smelling. —*n.* act of sniffing.

snif'fle, *v. & n.* sniff to check mucus flow.

snip, *v.* [SNIPPED, SNIPPING] cut in a quick stroke. —*n.* small piece cut off.

snipe, *n.* wading bird. —*v.* shoot at from a hidden place. —**snip'er,** *n.*

sniv'el, *v.* 1. cry and sniffle. 2. whine.

snob, *n.* one who disdains his supposed inferiors. —**snob'bish,** *a.* —**snob'ber·y,** *n.*

snood, *n.* kind of hair net.

snoop, *v.* [Col.] pry in a sneaky way. —*n.* [Col.] one who snoops.

snoot'y, *a.* [-IER, -IEST] [Col.] snobbish.

snooze, *v. & n.* (take) a nap.

snore, *v.* breathe noisily while asleep. —*n.* a snoring.

snort, *v.* force breath audibly from the nose. —*n.* a snorting.

snout, *n.* projecting nose and jaws of an animal.

snow, *n.* flakes of frozen water vapor from the sky. —*v.* fall as snow. —**snow'drift,** *n.* —**snow'fall,** *n.* —**snow'flake,** *n.* —**snow'storm,** *n.* —**snow'y** [-IER, -IEST] *a.*

snow'ball, *n.* ball of packed snow. —*v.* increase rapidly.

snow'bound, *a.* confined by snow.

snow'mo·bile, *n.* motor vehicle for snow travel, with runners and tractor treads.

snow'plow, *n.* machine for removing snow.

snow'shoe, *n.* racketlike footgear for walking on snow.

snub, *v.* [SNUBBED, SNUBBING] 1. treat with scorn. 2. stop abruptly. —*n.* a slight. —*a.* short and turned up, as a nose.

snuff, *v.* put out (a candle, etc.). —*n.* powdered tobacco. —**up to snuff,** [Col.] up to the usual standard.

snug, *a.* [SNUGGER, SNUGGEST] 1. cosy. 2. compact. 3. tight in fit.

snug'gle, *v.* cuddle; nestle.

so, *adv.* 1. in such a way. 2. to such a degree. 3. very. 4. therefore. 5. more or less. 6. also. 7. then. 8. [Col.] very much. —*con.* 1. in order (that). 2. [Col.] with the result (that). —*int.* word showing surprise. —**and so on** (or forth), and the rest.

soak, *v.* 1. make wet. 2. stay in liquid. —**soak up,** absorb.

soap, *n.* substance that makes suds in water for washing. —*v.* rub with soap. —**soap'y** [-IER, -IEST] *a.*

soar, *v.* fly high in the air.

sob, *v.* [SOBBED, SOBBING] weep aloud with short gasps. —*n.* act of sobbing.

so'ber, *a.* 1. not drunk. 2. serious; sedate. 3. plain. —*v.* make or become sober. —**so·bri'e·ty,** *n.*

so'-called', *a.* called thus, but usually inaccurately.

soc'cer, *n.* kind of football.

so'cia·ble (-sha-) *a.* friendly; genial. —**so·cia·bil'i·ty,** *n.* —**so'cia·bly,** *adv.*

so'cial, *a.* 1. of society. 2.

living in groups. 3. sociable. 4. of social work. —n. a party. —**so'cial·ly,** adv.

so'cial·ism, n. public ownership of the means of production. —**so'cial·ist,** n. & a. —**so'cial·is'tic,** a.

so'cial·ize, v. 1. put under public ownership. 2. [Col.] take part in social affairs.

social security, federal insurance for old age, unemployment, etc.

social work, work of clinics, agencies, etc. to improve living conditions.

so·ci'e·ty, n. [pl. -TIES] 1. community of people. 2. all people. 3. companionship. 4. organized group. 5. the fashionable class.

so'ci·ol'o·gy (-si-) n. study of the organization, problems, etc. of society. —**so'·ci·o·log'i·cal,** a. —**so'ci·ol'o·gist,** n.

sock, n. 1. short stocking. 2. [Sl.] a blow. —v. [Sl.] hit with force.

sock'et, n. hollow part into which something fits.

sod, n. earth surface with grass. —v. [SODDED, SODDING] cover with sod.

so'da, n. 1. substance containing sodium. 2. soda water. 3. beverage of soda water and ice cream.

soda cracker, crisp cracker.

soda water, carbonated water.

sod'den, a. soaked or soggy.

so'di·um, n. silver-white metallic chemical element.

sodium bi·car'bon·ate (-it) baking soda.

sodium chloride, common salt.

sod'om·y, n. abnormal sexual intercourse.

so'fa, n. couch with back and arms.

soft, a. 1. not hard; easy to crush, cut, etc. 2. not harsh; mild, gentle, etc. 3. without minerals that hinder lathering. 4. weak. 5. nonalcoholic. —adv. gently. —**soft'ly,** adv. —**soft'ness,** n.

sof'ten, v. make or become soft. —**soft'en·er,** n.

sog'gy, a. [-GIER, -GIEST] very wet and heavy; soaked.

soil, n. earth or ground, esp. surface. —v. make or become dirty.

soi·ree, soi·rée (swä-rā') n. an evening social.

so'journ, n. & v. visit, as in a foreign land.

sol'ace (-is) n. relief or comfort. —v. comfort.

so'lar, a. of or having to do with the sun.

so·lar'i·um, n. glassed-in room for sunning.

solar system, the sun and all its planets.

sold, pt. & pp. of **sell.**

sol·der (sod'er) n. metal alloy for joining metal parts. —v. join with solder.

sol'dier, n. member of an army, esp. an enlisted man. —v. be a soldier.

sole, n. 1. bottom of the foot, or of a shoe. 2. sea flatfish. —v. put a sole on (a shoe). —a. one and only.

sole'ly, adv. 1. alone. 2. only.

sol'emn, a. 1. formal. 2. serious. —**sol'emn·ly,** adv.

so·lem'ni·ty, n. [pl. -TIES] 1. solemn ritual. 2. seriousness.

sol'em·nize, v. celebrate or perform formally.

so·lic'it (-lis'-) v. ask for with force. —**so·lic'i·ta'tion,** n.

so·lic'i·tor, n. 1. one who solicits trade, etc. 2. [Br.] lawyer not a barrister. 3. lawyer for a city, etc.

so·lic'i·tous, a. 1. showing concern. 2. anxious. —**so·lic'i·tude,** n.

sol'id, a. 1. firm or hard. 2. not hollow. 3. three-dimensional. 4. of one piece, solid etc. —n. 1. firm or hard substance. 2. three-dimensional object. —**so·lid'i·fy** [-FIED, -FYING] v. —**so·lid'i·ty,** n.

sol'i·dar'i·ty, n. firm unity.

so·lil'o·quy (-kwi) n. [pl. -QUIES] a talking to oneself. —**so·lil'o·quize,** v.

sol'i·taire (-tār) n. 1. gem set by itself. 2. card game for one person.

sol'i·tar·y, a. 1. alone; lonely. 2. single.

sol'i·tude, n. loneliness.

so'lo, n. & a. (piece of music) for one performer. —**so'lo·ist,** n.

sol'stice (-stis) n. longest day (June 21 or 22) or shortest day (Dec. 21 or 22).

sol'u·ble, a. 1. that can be dissolved. 2. solvable. —**sol'u·bil'i·ty,** n.

so·lu'tion, n. 1. solving of a problem. 2. explanation or answer. 3. liquid with something dissolved in it.

solve, v. find the answer to. —**solv'a·ble,** a.

sol'vent, a. 1. able to pay

one's debts. 2. able to dissolve a substance. —n. substance used to dissolve another. —**sol'ven·cy**, n.

som'ber, **som'bre**, a. 1. dark and gloomy. 2. sad.

som·bre'ro (-brâr'ō) n. [pl. -ROS] broad-brimmed hat.

some, a. 1. certain but unspecified. 2. of indefinite quantity. 3. about. —pron. indefinite quantity.

-some, suf. tending to (be).

some'bod·y, n. [pl. -IES] important person. —pron. person not named or known.

some'day, adv. sometime.

some'how, adv. in some way.

some'one, pron. somebody.

som·er·sault (sum'ēr-sôlt) v. & n. (perform) a turning of the body, heels over head.

some'thing, n. thing not named or known.

some'time, adv. at some unspecified time. —a. former.

some'times, adv. at times.

some'what, n. some part, amount, etc. —adv. a little.

some'where, adv. in, to, or at some unnamed place.

som·nam'bu·lism, n. act of walking while asleep.

som'no·lent, a. sleepy. —**som'no·lence**, n.

son, n. male in relation to his parents.

so·na'ta (-nä'-) n. piece of music for one or two instruments.

song, n. 1. music or poem to be sung. 2. singing sound.

song'ster, n. singer. —**song'stress**, n.fem.

son'ic (son'-) a. of or having to do with sound.

son'-in-law, n. [pl. SONS-IN-LAW] husband of one's daughter.

son'net, n. 14-line poem.

so·no'rous, a. resonant. —**so·nor'i·ty**, n.

soon, adv. 1. in a short time. 2. early. 3. readily.

soot (soot) n. black particles in smoke. —**soot'y** [-IER, -IEST] a.

soothe (sooth) v. 1. make calm, as by kindness. 2. ease, as pain. —**sooth'ing·ly**, adv.

sooth'say'er (sooth'-) n. one who pretends to prophesy.

sop, n. bribe. —v. [SOPPED, SOPPING] soak (up).

so·phis'ti·cat'ed, a. worldly-wise. —**so·phis'ti·cate** (-kit) n. —**so·phis'ti·ca'tion**, n.

soph'o·more, n. second-year student in high school or college.

so·po·rif'ic, n. & a. (drug) causing sleep.

so·pra'no, n. [pl. -NOS] highest female voice.

sor'cer·y, n. witchcraft. —**sor'cer·er**, n. —**sor'cer·ess**, n.fem.

sor'did, a. 1. dirty; filthy. 2. mean; selfish.

sore, a. 1. painful. 2. sad. 3. [Col.] angry. —n. injured body tissue. —**sore'ness**, n.

sore'ly, adv. greatly.

sor'ghum (-gam) n. grass grown for grain, sirup, etc.

so·ror'i·ty, n. [pl. -TIES] social club for women.

sor'rel, n. 1. reddish brown. 2. horse of this color.

sor'row, n. & n. (feel) sadness. —**sor'row·ful**, a.

sor'ry, a. [-RIER, -RIEST] 1. full of sorrow, regret, etc. 2. pitiful; wretched.

sort, n. kind; class. —v. arrange according to kind. —**of sorts** or **of a sort**, of an inferior kind. —**out of sorts**, [Col.] ill-humored. —**sort of**, [Col.] somewhat.

sor'tie (-ti) n. raid by besieged troops.

SOS, signal of distress.

so'-so', a. & adv. fair or fairly well: also so so.

sot, n. habitual drunkard.

souf·flé (soo-flā') n. food made puffy by being baked with beaten egg whites.

sought, pt. & pp. of seek.

soul, n. 1. spiritual part of a person. 2. vital part. 3. person. —**soul'ful**, a.

sound, n. 1. that which is heard. 2. strait or inlet of the sea. —v. 1. (cause) to make a sound. 2. seem. 3. measure the depth of water. 4. seek the opinion of (with out). —a. 1. free from defect; healthy, secure, wise, etc. 2. deep or thorough. —**sound'ly**, adv. —**sound'ness**, n.

sound'proof, v. & a. (make) impervious to sound.

soup, n. liquid food with meat, vegetables, etc. in it.

sour, a. 1. having an acid taste. 2. fermented. 3. unpleasant. —v. make or become sour. —**sour'ness**, n.

source, n. 1. starting point. 2. place of origin.

souse, n. 1. pickled food. 2. brine. —v. 1. to pickle. 2. soak in liquid.

south, n. direction or region to the left of one facing the sunset. —a. & adv. in, toward, or from the south.—**south′-er·ly**, *a. & adv.*—**south′-ern**, *a.*—**south′ern·er**, *n.*—**south′ward**, *a. &* (also **south′wards**) *adv.*

south′east′, *n.* direction or region between south and east.—*a. & adv.* in, toward, or from the southeast.—**south′east′er·ly**, *a. & adv.*—**south′east′ern**, *a.*—**south′east′ward**, *a. &* (also **south′east′wards**) *adv.*

South Pole, southern end of the earth's axis.

south′west′, *n.* direction or region between south and west.—*a. & adv.* in, toward, or from the southwest.—**south′west′er·ly**, *a. & adv.*—**south′west′ern**, *a.*—**south′west′ward**, *a. &* (also **south′west′wards**) *adv.*

sou·ve·nir (sōō-və-nēr′) *n.* thing kept as a reminder.

sov·er·eign (sov′rən) *a.* 1. chief; supreme. 2. independent.—*n.* 1. monarch. 2. former Br. gold coin.—**sov′er·eign·ty** [*pl.* -TIES] *n.*

sow (sou) *n.* adult female pig.

sow (sō) *v.* [SOWN (sōn) or SOWED, SOWING] scatter, or plant with, seed for growing.

soy, *n.* sauce from soybeans.

soy′bean, *n.* seed of a plant of the pea family.

spa (spä) *n.* (resort having a) mineral spring.

space, *n.* 1. limitless expanse containing all things. 2. distance or area. 3. interval of time.—*v.* divide by spaces.

space′craft, *n.* [*pl.* -CRAFT] vehicle for outer-space travel, exploration, etc.

space′ship, *n.* rocket-propelled vehicle for travel in outer space.

spa′cious (-shəs) *a.* having much space; vast.

spade, *n.* 1. flat-bladed digging tool. 2. playing card marked with a ♠.—*v.* dig with a spade.

spa·ghet′ti (-ghe′-) *n.* (cooked) strings of dried flour paste.

span, *n.* 1. nine inches. 2. extent. 3. period of time.—*v.* extend over.

span′gle, *n.* shiny decoration, as a sequin.—*v.* decorate with spangles.

span′iel (-yal) *n.* dog with large drooping ears.

Span′ish, *a. & n.* (of) the people or language of Spain.

spank, *v. & n.* slap on the buttocks.

spar, *n.* pole supporting a

ship's sail.—*v.* [SPARRED, SPARRING] box cautiously.

spare, *v.* 1. save or free from something. 2. avoid using. 3. give up, as time or money.—*a.* 1. extra. 2. lean; meager.—*n.* extra thing.

spare′rib, *n.* thin end of pork rib.

spar′ing, *a.* frugal.

spark, *n.* 1. small glowing piece from a fire. 2. particle. 3. flash from an electrical discharge across a gap.—*v.* 1. make sparks. 2. excite.

spar′kle, *v.* 1. give off sparks. 2. glitter. 3. effervesce.—*n.* glitter.—**spar′kler**, *n.*

spark plug, piece in an engine cylinder, that ignites the fuel mixture.

spar′row, *n.* small songbird.

sparse (spärs) *a.* thinly spread.—**sparse′ly**, *adv.*—**spar′si·ty**, **sparse′ness**, *n.*

Spar′tan, *a.* brave; hardy.

spasm, *n.* 1. involuntary muscular contraction. 2. short, sudden burst of activity.—**spas·mod′ic**, *a.*

spas′tic, *n. & a.* (one) having muscular spasms.

spat, *pt. & pp.* of **spit**.—*n.* 1. [Col.] brief quarrel. 2. cloth ankle covering.

spa′tial (-shəl) *a.* of, or existing in, space.

spat′ter, *v.* 1. spurt out in drops. 2. splash.—*n.* mark made by spattering.

spat′u·la (spach′oo-) *n.* tool with a broad, flexible blade.

spawn (spôn) *n.* 1. eggs of fishes, etc. 2. offspring.—*v.* produce (spawn).

speak, *v.* [SPOKE, SPOKEN, SPEAKING] 1. utter words. 2. tell; express. 3. make a speech. 4. use (a language) in speaking.—**speak for**, ask for.—**speak′er**, *n.*

spear, *n.* long, slender sharp-pointed weapon.—*v.* pierce or stab as with a spear.

spear′head, *n.* leading person or group, as in an attack.

spear′mint, *n.* fragrant mint.

spe′cial, *a.* 1. distinctive. 2. unusual. 3. main: chief. 4. for a certain use.—*n.* special thing.—**spe′cial·ly**, *adv.*

spe′cial·ize, *v.* concentrate on a certain type of study, work, etc.—**spe′cial·ist**, *n.*—**spe′cial·i·za′tion**, *n.*

spe′cial·ty, *n.* [*pl.* -TIES] 1. special feature, interest, etc. 2. special article.

spe·cie (spē′shi) *n.* metal money.

spe′cies, *n.* [*pl.* -CIES] distinct kind of plant or animal.

spe·cif′ic, *a.* definite; explicit. —**spe·cif′i·cal·ly**, *adv.*

spec′i·fi·ca′tion (spes′-) *n.* 1. a specifying. 2. *usually pl.* detailed description.

spec′i·fy, *v.* [-FIED, -FYING] state explicitly.

spec′i·men, *n.* sample.

spe′cious (-shǝs) *a.* plausible but not genuine.

speck, *n.* small spot or bit. —*v.* mark with specks.

speck′le, *n. & v.* speck.

spec′ta·cle, *n.* 1. unusual sight. 2. public show. 3. *pl.* eyeglasses.

spec·tac′u·lar, *a.* showy; striking.

spec·ta′tor, *n.* one who watches.

spec′ter, *n.* ghost: also, Br. sp., **spec′tre**. —**spec′tral**, *a.*

spec′tro·scope, *n.* instrument that forms spectra for study.

spec′trum, *n.* [*pl.* -TRA, -TRUMS] row of colors formed by diffraction.

spec′u·late, *v.* 1. ponder. 2. take risky chances in business. —**spec′u·la′tion**, *n.* —**spec′u·la′tor**, *n.*

speech, *n.* 1. act or way of speaking. 2. power to speak. 3. something said. 4. public talk. —**speech′less**, *a.*

speed, *n.* 1. rapid motion. 2. rate of movement. —*v.* [SPED, SPEEDING] 1. move fast. 2. aid. —**speed′y** [-IER, -IEST] *a.*

speed·om′e·ter, *n.* device to indicate speed.

spell, *n.* 1. supposedly magic words. 2. fascination; charm. 3. period of work, duty, etc. —*v.* 1. give in order the letters of (a word). 2. mean. 3. [Col.] relieve (another).

spell′bound, *a.* fascinated.

spell′ing, *n.* 1. a forming words from letters. 2. way a word is spelled.

spend, *v.* [SPENT, SPENDING] 1. use up. 2. pay out (money). 3. pass (time).

spend′thrift, *n.* one who wastes money. —*a.* wasteful.

sperm, *n.* 1. semen. 2. any of the germ cells in it.

spew, *v.* throw up; vomit.

sphere, *n.* 1. globe; ball. 2. place or range of action. —**spher′i·cal** (sfer′-) *a.*

sphe′roid, *n.* almost spherical body.

spice, *n.* 1. any aromatic seasoning. 2. stimulating qual-

ity. —*v.* add spice to.

spic′y [-IER, -IEST] *a.*

spick′-and-span′, *a.* fresh or tidy.

spi′der, *n.* arachnid that spins webs.

spig′ot, *n.* faucet or tap.

spike, *n.* 1. sharp-pointed projection. 2. long, heavy nail. 3. ear of grain. 4. long flower cluster. —*v.* 1. fasten or pierce as with a spike. 2. thwart.

spill, *v.* [SPILLED *or* SPILT, SPILLING] 1. let run over. 2. overflow. 3. shed (blood). 4. [Col.] make fall. —*n.* [Col.] a fall.

spill′way, *n.* channel for excess water.

spin, *v.* [SPUN, SPINNING] 1. twist fibers into thread. 2. make a web, cocoon, etc. 3. tell (a story). 4. whirl. 5. move fast. —*n.* 1. a whirling movement. 2. fast ride.

spin′ach, *n.* plant with dark-green, edible leaves.

spi′nal, *a.* of the spine. **spinal column**, long row of connected bones in the back. **spinal cord**, cord of nerve tissue in the spinal column.

spin′dle, *n.* 1. rod used in spinning thread. 2. rod that acts as an axis.

spin′dling, *a.* long and thin: also **spin′dly** [-DLIER, -DLIEST].

spine, *n.* 1. thorn, quill, etc. 2. spinal column. —**spin′y** [-IER, -IEST] *a.*

spine′less, *a.* 1. having no spine. 2. weak or cowardly.

spin′et, *n.* small upright piano.

spin′ster, *n.* unmarried, older woman.

spi′ral, *a.* circling around a center. —*n.* spiral curve or coil. —*v.* move in a spiral.

spire, *n.* tapering, pointed part, as of a steeple.

spir′it, *n.* 1. soul. 2. ghost, angel, etc. 3. *often pl.* mood. 4. courage. 5. loyalty. 6. essential quality. 7. *often pl.* alcoholic liquor. —*v.* carry away secretly.

spir′it·ed, *a.* lively.

spir′it·u·al, *a.* 1. of the soul. 2. religious; sacred. —*n.* Negro religious song. —**spir′it·u·al′i·ty**, *n.*

spir′it·u·al·ism, *n.* seeming communication with the dead. —**spir′it·u·al·ist**, *n.*

spit, *n.* 1. thin rod to roast meat on. 2. shoreline narrowed to a point. 3. saliva.

—*v.* [SPITTED, SPITTING] 1. fix as on a spit. 2. [pt. & pp. SPAT or SPIT] to eject (saliva, etc.) from the mouth.

spite, *n.* malice. —*v.* annoy; hurt. —**in spite of,** regardless of. —**spite'ful,** *a.*

spit'tle, *n.* spit; saliva.

spit·toon', *n.* container to spit into.

splash, *v.* 1. dash liquid, etc. (on). —*n.* 1. a splashing. 2. spot made by splashing.

splat'ter, *n.* & *v.* splash.

splay, *v.* & *a.* spread out.

spleen, *n.* 1. large abdominal organ. 2. malice; spite. —**sple·net'ic,** *a.*

splen'did, *a.* magnificent; grand. —**splen'dor,** *n.*

splice, *n.* & *v.* (make) a joint with ends overlapped.

splint, *n.* stiff strip to hold a broken bone in place.

splin'ter, *n.* thin, sharp piece. —*v.* split in splinters.

split, *v.* [SPLIT, SPLITTING] separate into parts. —*n.* break; crack. —*a.* divided.

splotch, *n.* & *v.* spot; stain. —**splotch'y** [-IER, -IEST] *a.*

splurge, *v.* & *n.* [Col.] (make) a showy display, etc.

splut'ter, *v.* 1. make spitting sounds. 2. speak confusedly. —*n.* a spluttering.

spoil, *v.* [SPOILED or SPOILT, SPOILING] to damage, ruin, decay, etc. —*n.* [in pl.] plunder. —**spoil'age** (-ij) *n.*

spoke, *pt.* of **speak.** —*n.* rod from hub to rim.

spo'ken, *pp.* of **speak.** —*a.* oral; voiced.

spokes'man, *n.* [pl. -MEN] one who speaks for another.

sponge, *n.* 1. absorbent substance made from a sea animal, plastic, etc. 2. the sea animal. —*v.* 1. clean, etc. with a sponge. 2. [Col.] live off others. —**spon'gy** [-GIER, -GIEST] *a.*

spon'sor, *n.* 1. promoter; supporter. 2. advertiser who pays for a radio or TV program. —*v.* be sponsor for.

spon·ta'ne·ous, *a.* 1. without effort. 2. within or by itself. —**spon·ta·ne'i·ty,** *n.*

spook, *n.* [Col.] ghost. —**spook'y** [-IER, -IEST] *a.*

spool, *n.* cylinder upon which thread, etc. is wound.

spoon, *n.* small bowl with a handle, used in eating. —**spoon'ful** [pl. -FULS] *n.*

spoor (spoor) *n.* wild animal's trail or track.

spo·rad'ic, *a.* not regular.

—**spo·rad'i·cal·ly,** *adv.*

spore, *n.* tiny reproductive cell of mosses, ferns, etc.

sport, *n.* 1. athletic game. 2. fun. 3. abnormal plant or animal. —*v.* 1. [Col.] display. 2. play. —*a.* for play.

sport'ing, *a.* 1. of sports. 2. fair. 3. risky.

sports, *a.* sport.

sports'man, *n.* [pl. -MEN] 1. participant in sports. 2. one who plays fair. —**sports'man·like,** *a.*

spot, *n.* 1. stain; mark. 2. place. —*v.* [SPOTTED, SPOTTING] 1. mark with spots. 2. [Col.] see. —*a.* made at random. —**spot'less,** *a.*

spot'light, *n.* 1. strong beam of light, or lamp that throws it. 2. public notice.

spot'ty, *a.* [-TIER, -TIEST] 1. spotted. 2. not uniform.

spouse, *n.* husband or wife.

spout, *n.* 1. pipe, etc. by which a liquid pours. 2. stream of liquid. —*v.* 1. shoot out with force. 2. talk loudly on and on.

sprain, *v.* twist a muscle or ligament in a joint. —*n.* injury caused by this.

sprang, *pt.* of **spring.**

sprat, *n.* small herring.

sprawl, *v.* sit or spread out in a relaxed or awkward way. —*n.* sprawling position.

spray, *n.* 1. mist or stream of tiny liquid drops. 2. branch with leaves, flowers, etc. 3. spray gun. —*v.* apply, or emit in, a spray.

spray gun, device that sprays a liquid, as paint.

spread, *v.* [SPREAD, SPREADING] 1. open out. 2. extend in time or space. 3. make known. 4. cover. 5. go or make go. —*n.* 1. act or extent of spreading. 2. cloth cover. 3. butter, jam, etc.

spree, *n.* 1. lively time. 2. drinking bout.

sprig, *n.* little twig.

spright'ly, *a.* [-LIER, -LIEST] gay; lively. —*adv.* briskly.

spring, *v.* [SPRANG or SPRUNG, SPRUNG, SPRINGING] 1. leap. 2. grow; develop. 3. snap back or shut. 4. make or become bent, split, etc. 5. make known. —*n.* 1. a leap. 2. resilience. 3. resilient coil of wire, etc. 4. flow of water from the ground. 5. source. 6. season after winter. —*a.* of, for, or in the spring (*n.* 6). —**spring'y** [-IER, -IEST] *a.*

spring'board, *n.* springy

board, as to dive from.

sprin'kle, v. 1. scatter drops of or on. 2. rain lightly. —n. a sprinkling.

sprint, v. & n. race at full speed for a short distance.

sprite, n. elf, fairy, etc.

sprock'et, n. any tooth in a series on a wheel made to fit the links of a chain.

sprout, v. begin to grow. —n. new growth; shoot.

spruce, n. evergreen tree. —v. & a. (make) neat or trim.

spry, a. [SPRIER or SPRYER, SPRIEST or SPRYEST] lively.

spume, n. foam; froth.

spun, pt. and pp. of **spin.**

spunk, n. [Col.] courage. —**spunk'y** [-IER, -IEST] a.

spur, n. 1. pointed device on a shoe to prick a horse. 2. stimulus. 3. projecting part. —v. [SPURRED, SPURRING] 1. prick with spurs. 2. urge on.

spu'ri·ous (spyoor'-) a. false; not genuine.

spurn, v. reject in scorn.

spurt, v. 1. shoot forth; squirt. 2. make a sudden effort. —n. a spurting.

sput'nik, n. Russian man-made satellite.

sput'ter, v. 1. speak in a fast, confused way. 2. spit out bits. 3. make hissing sounds. —n. a sputtering.

spu'tum, n. saliva.

spy, v. [SPIED, SPYING] 1. watch closely and secretly. 2. see. —n. [pl. SPIES] one who spies, esp. to get another country's secrets.

squab (skwäb) n. young pigeon.

squab'ble, v. & n. quarrel over a small matter.

squad, n. small group.

squad'ron, n. unit of warships, aircraft, etc.

squal'id, a. 1. foul; unclean. 2. wretched. —**squal'or,** n.

squall, n. 1. brief, violent windstorm. 2. harsh, loud cry. —v. cry loudly.

squan'der, v. spend or use wastefully.

square, n. 1. rectangle with all sides equal. 2. area with streets on four sides. 3. tool for making right angles. 4. product of a number multiplied by itself. —v. 1. make square. 2. make straight, even, etc. 3. settle; adjust. 4. multiply by itself. —a. 1. shaped like a square. 2. forming a right angle. 3. straight, level, or even. 4. just; fair. 5. [Col.] filling, as a meal. —adv.

in a square way. —**square'-ly,** adv. —**square'ness,** n.

squash, v. 1. press into a soft, flat mass. 2. suppress. —n. 1. a squashing. 2. game played in a walled court with rackets. 3. fleshy vegetable growing on a vine.

squat, v. [SQUATTED or SQUAT, SQUATTING] 1. crouch. 2. settle on land without title to it. —a. short and heavy: also **squat'ty.** —n. position of squatting. —**squat'ter,** n.

squaw, n. American Indian woman or wife.

squawk, v. 1. utter a loud, harsh cry. 2. [Sl.] complain. —n. a squawking. —**squawk'er,** n.

squeak, v. make a sharp, high-pitched sound. —n. such a sound. —**squeak'y,** a.

squeal, v. & n. (utter) a long, shrill cry.

squeam'ish, a. 1. easily nauseated. 2. easily shocked.

squee'gee (-jē) n. rubber-edged tool to wash windows.

squeeze, v. 1. press hard. 2. extract by pressure. 3. force by pressing. —n. a squeezing. —**squeez'er,** n.

squelch, n. [Col.] crushing retort. —v. suppress or silence completely.

squid, n. long, slender sea mollusk with ten arms.

squint, v. 1. peer with eyes partly closed. 2. be cross-eyed. —n. a squinting.

squire, n. 1. English country gentleman. 2. man escorting a woman. —v. escort.

squirm, v. twist and turn.

squir'rel, n. tree-dwelling rodent with a bushy tail.

squirt, v. & n. (shoot out in) a jet; spurt.

stab, v. [STABBED, STABBING] pierce or wound as with a knife. —n. 1. a thrust, as with a knife. 2. [Col.] a try.

sta'bi·lize, v. 1. make stable, or firm. 2. keep from changing. —**sta'bi·li·za'tion,** n. —**sta'bi·liz'er,** n.

sta'ble, a. not apt to change; firm. —n. building for horses or cattle. —v. keep in a stable. —**sta·bil'i·ty,** n.

stac·ca·to (sta-kä'tō) a. & adv. Mus. with abrupt tones.

stack, n. 1. orderly pile. 2. smokestack. 3. set of bookshelves. —v. pile in a stack.

sta'di·um, n. place for outdoor games, surrounded by tiers of seats.

staff, n. [pl. STAVES; for 2 &

3 STAFFS] 1. stick or rod used for support, etc. 2. group of people assisting a leader. 3. the five lines and between which music is written. —v. provide with workers.

stag, n. full-grown male deer. —a. for men only.

stage, n. 1. platform, esp. one on which plays are presented. 2. the theater. 3. part of a journey. 4. period in growth or development. —v. 1. present as on a stage. 2. carry out.

stage′coach, n. horse-drawn public coach for long trips.

stag′ger, v. 1. (cause to) totter, reel, etc. 2. shock. 3. arrange alternately. —n. a staggering.

stag′nant, a. 1. not flowing, therefore foul. 2. sluggish. **stag′nate,** v. become stagnant. —**stag·na′tion,** n.

staid (stād) a. sober; sedate.

stain, v. 1. discolor; spot. 2. dishonor. 3. color (wood, etc.) with a dye. —n. 1. a spot; mark. 2. dishonor. 3. dye for wood, etc. —**stain′less,** a.

stair, n. 1. one of a series of steps between levels. 2. usually pl. flight of stairs: also **stair′case, stair′way.**

stake, n. 1. pointed stick to be driven in the ground. 2. often pl. money risked as a wager. —v. 1. mark the boundaries of. 2. wager. — **at stake,** being risked.

sta·lac′tite, n. stick of lime hanging from a cave roof.

sta·lag′mite, n. stick of lime built up on a cave floor.

stale, a. 1. no longer fresh. 2. trite. 3. out of condition.

stale′mate, n. deadlock.

stalk, v. 1. stride haughtily. 2. track secretly. —n. 1. a stalking. 2. plant stem.

stall, n. 1. section for one animal in a stable. 2. market booth. —v. 1. put in a stall. 2. stop. 3. delay by evading.

stal′lion (-yən) n. uncastrated male horse.

stal′wart, a. strong or brave. —n. stalwart person.

sta′men, n. pollen-bearing part of a flower.

stam′i·na, n. endurance.

stam′mer, v. & n. pause or halt in speaking.

stamp, v. 1. put the foot down hard. 2. pound with the foot. 3. cut out with a die. 4. impress a design on.

5. put a stamp on. —n. 1. a stamping. 2. gummed piece of paper, as for postage. 3. stamped mark. 4. stamping device.

stam·pede′, n. sudden, headlong rush, as of a herd. —v. move in a stampede.

stance, n. way one stands.

stanch, v. check the flow of blood from a wound. —a. staunch.

stan′chion (-shən) n. upright support.

stand, v. [STOOD, STANDING] 1. be or get in an upright position. 2. place or be placed. 3. hold a certain opinion. 4. halt. 5. endure or resist. —n. 1. a halt. 2. a position. 3. platform, rack, counter, etc. 4. a growth (of trees). —**stand by,** be ready to help. —**stand for,** 1. represent. 2. [Col.] tolerate. —**stand out,** to project, be prominent, etc.

stand′ard, n. 1. flag, banner, etc. 2. thing set up as a rule or model. 3. upright support. —a. that is a standard or rule. 2. proper.

stand′ard·ize, v. make standard or uniform.

stand′-in′, n. a substitute.

stand′ing, n. 1. status or rank. 2. duration. —a. 1. upright. 2. continuing.

stand′off, n. tie in a contest.

stand′off·ish, a. aloof.

stand′point, n. viewpoint.

stand′still, n. a stop or halt.

stan′za, n. group of lines making a section of a poem.

sta′ple, n. 1. main product, part, etc. 2. fiber. 3. U-shaped piece of metal used to fasten. —v. fasten with a staple. —a. regular or principal. —**sta′pler,** n.

star, n. 1. heavenly body seen as a point of light at night. 2. flat figure with five or more points. 3. asterisk. 4. one who excels, as in acting. —v. [STARRED, STARRING] 1. mark with stars. 2. present in, or play, a leading role. —**star′ry** [-RIER, -RIEST] a.

star′board (-bērd) n. right side of a ship, etc. as one faces the bow.

starch, n. 1. white food substance in potatoes, etc. 2. powdered form of this. —v. stiffen (laundry) with starch. —**starch′y** [-IER, -IEST] a.

stare, v. gaze steadily. — n. long, steady look.

star'fish, n. small, star-shaped sea animal.

stark, a. 1. bleak. 2. complete; utter. 3. rigid. —adv. entirely. **—stark'ly,** adv.

star'ling, n. bird with shiny, black feathers.

start, v. 1. begin to go, do, etc. 2. set in motion. 3. jump or jerk. —n. 1. a starting. 2. jump or jerk. 3. place or time of beginning. 4. lead; advantage. —**start in,** begin to do. —**start out,** begin a trip, etc. **—start'er,** n.

star'tle, v. 1. frighten suddenly. 2. surprise.

starve, v. 1. suffer or die from lack of food. 2. cause to starve. **—star·va'tion,** n.

state, n. 1. the way a person or thing is. 2. formal style. 3. nation. 4. [often S-] a unit of a federal government. —v. express in words.

stat'ed, a. fixed; set.

state'ly, a. [-LIER, -LIEST] grand or dignified.

state'ment, n. 1. a stating. 2. something stated. 3. report, as of money owed.

state'room, n. private room in a ship or railroad car.

states'man, n. [pl. -MEN] man skillful in government.

stat'ic, a. 1. at rest. 2. of electricity caused by friction. —n. electrical disturbances in radio reception.

sta'tion, n. 1. assigned place. 2. stopping place. 3. place for radio or TV transmission. 4. social rank. —v. assign to a station.

sta'tion·ar·y (-er'-) a. not moving or changing.

sta'tion·er·y (-er'-) n. writing materials.

sta·tis'tics, n.pl. 1. analysis of numerical data. 2. the data. **—sta·tis'ti·cal,** a. **—stat'is·ti'cian** (-tish'ən) n.

stat'u·ar'y, n. statues.

stat'ue (stach'ōō) n. likeness done in stone, metal, etc.

stat'u·esque' (-esk') a. stately; imposing.

stat'u·ette', n. small statue.

stat'ure (stach'-) n. 1. person's height. 2. development.

sta'tus, n. 1. rank. 2. condition.

status quo (kwō) [L.] existing state of affairs.

stat'ute (stach'-) n. a law.

stat'u·to·ry, a. authorized, or punishable, by statute.

staunch (stônch) a. firm, loyal, etc. —v. stanch.

stave, n. 1. any of the wood side strips of a barrel. 2. staff. 3. stanza. —v. [STAVED or STOVE, STAVING] smash. **—stave off,** hold off.

stay, v. 1. remain. 2. dwell. 3. stop or delay. 4. support. —n. 1. a staying. 2. prop. 3. guy rope. 4. stiffening strip.

stead (sted) n. place for a substitute.

stead'fast, a. constant; firm.

stead'y, a. [-IER, -IEST] 1. firm. 2. regular. 3. calm. 4. reliable. —v. [-IED, -YING] make or become steady.

steak, n. slice of meat or fish.

steal, v. [STOLE, STOLEN, STEALING] 1. take dishonestly and secretly. 2. move stealthily.

stealth (stelth) n. secret action. **—stealth'i·ly,** adv. **—stealth'y** [-IER, -IEST] a.

steam, n. water changed to a vapor by boiling: source of heat and power. —a. using steam. —v. 1. expose to steam. 2. give off steam. —**steam'boat, steam'ship,** n. **—steam'y,** a.

steam'er, n. thing run by steam.

steed, n. [Poet.] riding horse.

steel, n. hard alloy of iron with carbon. —a. of steel. —v. make strong. **—steel'y,** a.

steel wool, steel shavings used for cleaning, etc.

steel'yard, n. weighing scale.

steep, a. having a sharp rise or slope. —v. soak.

stee'ple, n. high tower.

stee'ple·chase, n. horse race over a course with obstacles.

steer, v. guide; direct. —n. male of beef cattle; ox.

steer'age, n. part of a ship for passengers poorer section.

stein (stīn) n. beer mug.

stel'lar, a. 1. of or like a star. 2. most important.

stem, n. 1. stalk of a plant, flower, etc. 2. stemlike part. 3. prow of a ship. 4. root of a word. —v. [STEMMED, STEMMING] 1. remove the stem of. 2. advance against. 3. stop. 4. derive.

stench, n. offensive smell.

sten'cil, n. sheet cut with letters, etc. to print when inked over. —v. mark with a stencil.

ste·nog'ra·phy, n. transcription of dictation in shorthand. **—ste·nog'ra·pher,** n. **—sten'o·graph'ic,** a.

sten·to·ri·an, a. very loud.

step, n. 1. one foot movement, as in walking. 2. footstep. 3. way of stepping. 4. stair tread. 5. degree; rank. 6. act in a series. —v. 1. move with a step. 2. press the foot down. —**in** (or **out of**) **step**, (not) in rhythm with others. —**step up**, 1. advance. 2. increase in rate.

step'broth'er, n. stepparent's son.

step'child, n. spouse's child (**stepdaughter** or **stepson**) by a former marriage.

step'lad'der, n. four-legged ladder with flat steps.

step'par'ent, n. spouse (**stepfather** or **stepmother**) of one's remarried parent.

steppe, n. great plain.

step'sis'ter, n. stepparent's daughter.

ster'e·o·phon'ic, a. of sound reproduced to show directions it came from.

ster'e·o·scope', n. device for giving three-dimensional effect to pictures.

ster'e·o·type', v. & n. (express in) a set, trite form.

ster·ile (ster'l) a. 1. unable to reproduce itself. 2. free of germs. —**ste·ril'i·ty**, n.

ster'i·lize, v. make sterile. —**ster'i·li·za'tion**, n.

ster'ling (stûr'-) a. 1. (made) of silver at least 92.5% pure. 2. of British money. 3. excellent.

stern, a. severe; unyielding. —n. rear end of a ship, etc.

ster'num, n. front chest bone to which ribs are joined.

steth'o·scope, n. instrument for hearing chest sounds.

ste've·dore, n. one hired to load and unload ships.

stew, v. cook by boiling slowly. —n. meat with vegetables, cooked in this way.

stew'ard, n. 1. one put in charge of funds, supplies, etc. 2. servant on a ship, etc. —**stew'ard·ess**, n.fem.

stick, n. 1. small branch broken or cut off. 2. long, thin piece, as of wood. —v. [STUCK, STICKING] 1. pierce. 2. attach or be attached as by pinning or gluing. 3. extend. 4. become fixed, jammed, etc. 5. persevere. 6. hesitate. 7. [Col.] puzzle.

stick'er, n. gummed label.

stick'ler, n. one who is stubbornly fussy.

stick'y, a. [-IER, -IEST] adhesive. —**stick'i·ness**, n.

stiff, a. 1. hard to bend or move. 2. thick; dense. 3. strong, as a wind. 4. difficult. 5. tense. —**stiff'en**, v. —**stiff'ly**, adv.

sti'fle, v. 1. suffocate. 2. suppress; restrain.

stig'ma, n. [pl. -MAS, -MATA] 1. sign of disgrace. 2. upper tip of a pistil.

stig'ma·tize, v. mark as disgraceful.

stile, n. step(s) for climbing over a fence or wall.

sti·let'to (-tō) n. [pl. -TOS, -TOES] small, thin dagger.

still, a. 1. quiet. 2. motionless. 3. calm. —n. device to distill liquor. —adv. 1. until then or now. 2. even; yet. 3. nevertheless. —con. nevertheless. —v. make or become still. —**still'ness**, n.

still'born, a. dead at birth.

stilt, n. supporting pole, esp. one of a pair for walking high off the ground.

stilt'ed, a. pompous.

stim'u·lant, n. thing that stimulates, as a drug.

stim'u·late, v. make (more) active. —**stim'u·la'tion**, n.

stim'u·lus, n. [pl. -LI (-lī)] anything causing activity.

sting, v. [STUNG, STINGING] 1. hurt with a sting. 2. cause or feel sharp pain. —n. a stinging, or pain from it.

stin'gy, a. [-GIER, -GIEST] miserly; grudging.

stink, v. [STANK or STUNK, STUNK, STINKING] & n. (have) a strong, unpleasant smell.

stint, v. restrict to a small amount. —n. 1. limit. 2. assigned task.

sti'pend, n. regular payment.

stip'ple, v. paint or draw in small dots.

stip'u·late, v. specify as an essential condition.

stir, v. [STIRRED, STIRRING] 1. move, esp. slightly. 2. move around as with a spoon. 3. excite. —n. 1. a stirring. 2. commotion.

stir'rup, n. ring hung from a saddle as a footrest.

stitch, n. 1. single movement or loop made by a needle in sewing, knitting, etc. 2. sudden pain. —v. sew.

stock, n. 1. tree trunk. 2. ancestry. 3. biological breed. 4. rifle part holding the barrel. 5. pl. frame with holes for feet and hands, once used for punishment. 6. broth from meat or fish. 7. livestock. 8. goods on hand.

9. shares in a business. —*v.* supply or keep in stock. —*a.* 1. kept in stock. 2. common. —**in stock,** available.

stock·ade′, *n.* defensive wall of tall stakes.

stock′bro′ker, *n.* broker for stocks and bonds.

stock exchange (or **mar′ket),** place of sale for stocks and bonds.

stock′ing, *n.* knitted covering for the leg and foot.

stock′pile, *v. & n.* (accumulate) a reserve supply.

stock′-still′, *a.* motionless.

stock′y, *a.* [-IER, -IEST] short and heavy.

stock′yard, *n.* place to pen livestock till slaughtered.

stodg′y, *a.* [-IER, -IEST] dull; uninteresting.

sto′ic, *a. & n.* stoical (person).

sto′i·cal, *a.* indifferent to joy, grief, pain, etc. —**sto′i·cism,** *n.*

stoke, *v.* stir up and feed fuel to (a fire). —**stok′er,** *n.*

stole, *pt. of* **steal.**

stol′en, *pp. of* **steal.**

stol′id, *a.* unexcitable.

stom′ach, *n.* 1. digestive organ into which food passes. 2. abdomen. 3. appetite. —*v.* tolerate.

stone, *n.* 1. solid nonmetallic mineral matter. 2. piece of this. 3. seed of certain fruits. 4. abnormal stony mass in the kidney, etc. 5. [*pl.* STONE] [Br.] 14 pounds. —*v.* throw stones at.

ston′y, *a.* [-IER, -IEST] 1. full of stones. 2. unfeeling.

stood, *pt. & pp. of* **stand.**

stooge, *n.* [Col.] lackey.

stool, *n.* 1. single seat with no back or arms. 2. feces.

stoop, *v.* 1. bend the body forward. 2. lower one's dignity. —*n.* 1. position of stooping. 2. small porch.

stop, *v.* [STOPPED, STOPPING] 1. close by filling, shutting off, etc. 2. cease; end; halt. 3. block; obstruct. 4. stay. —*n.* 1. a stopping. 2. place stopped at. 3. obstruction, plug, etc. —**stop off,** stop for a while. —**stop′page,** *n.*

stop′gap, *n.* temporary substitute.

stop′per, *n.* something inserted to close an opening.

stor′age (-ij) *n.* 1. a storing. 2. place for, or cost of, storing goods.

store, *n.* 1. supply; stock. 2. establishment where goods are sold. —*v.* put aside for future use. —**in store,** set aside for the future.

store′house, *n.* warehouse.

store′keep′er, *n.* person in charge of a store.

store′room, *n.* room where things are stored.

stork, *n.* large, long-legged wading bird.

storm, *n.* 1. strong wind with rain, snow, etc. 2. any strong disturbance. 3. strong attack. —*v.* 1. blow violently, rain, etc. 2. rage. 3. rush or attack violently. —**storm′y** [-IER, -IEST] *a.*

sto′ry, *n.* [*pl.* -RIES] 1. telling of an event. 2. fictitious narrative. 3. one level of a building. 4. [Col.] falsehood. —**sto′ried,** *a.*

stout, *a.* 1. brave. 2. firm; strong. 3. fat. —*n.* strong, dark beer. —**stout′ly,** *adv.*

stove, *n.* apparatus for heating, cooking, etc.

stow (stō) *v.* 1. pack or store away. —**stow away,** hide aboard a ship, etc. for a free ride. —**stow′a·way,** *n.*

strad′dle, *v.* 1. sit or stand astride. 2. take both sides of (an issue). —*n.* a straddling.

strafe, *v.* attack with machine guns from aircraft.

strag′gle, *v.* 1. wander from the group. 2. spread out unevenly. —**strag′gler,** *n.*

straight, *a.* 1. not crooked, bent, etc. 2. direct. 3. in order. 4. honest. 5. undiluted. —*adv.* 1. in a straight line. 2. directly. —**straight away** (or **off),** without delay. —**straight′en,** *v.*

straight′for′ward, *a.* 1. direct. 2. honest.

straight′way, *adv.* at once.

strain, *v.* 1. stretch tight or hard. 2. strive hard. 3. sprain. 4. filter. —*n.* 1. a straining or being strained. 2. excessive demand on one's emotions, etc. 3. ancestry. 4. inherited tendency. 5. trace; streak. 6. tune. —**strain′er,** *n.*

strait, *n.* often in *pl.* 1. narrow waterway. 2. distress.

strait′en, *v.* impoverish.

strait jacket, coatlike device for restraining a person.

strait′-laced′, *a.* strict.

strand, *v. n.* 1. any of the threads, wires, etc. that form a string, cable, etc. 2. string, as of pearls. 3. shore. —*v.* put into a helpless position.

strange, *a.* 1. unfamiliar. 2. unusual. 3. peculiar; odd. —**strange'ly,** *adv.*

stran'ger, *n.* 1. newcomer. 2. person not known to one.

stran'gle, *v.* 1. choke to death. 2. stifle. —**stran'gler,** *n.*

strap, *n.* narrow strip of leather, etc., as for binding things. —*v.* [STRAPPED, STRAPPING] fasten with a strap.

strap'ping, *a.* [Col.] robust.

strat'a·gem (-jəm) *n.* tricky ruse or move to gain an end.

strat'e·gy, *n.* [*pl.* -GIES] 1. science of military operations. 2. artful managing. —**stra·te'gic,** *a.* —**strate'gi·cal·ly,** *adv.* —**strat'e·gist,** *n.*

strat'i·fy, *v.* form in layers. —**strat'i·fi·ca'tion,** *n.*

strat'o·sphere, *n.* upper atmosphere.

stra'tum, *n.* [*pl.* -TA, -TUMS] any of a series of layers.

stra'tus (strā'-) *n.* [*pl.* -TI] long, low cloud layer.

straw, *n.* 1. grain stalk or stalks after threshing. 2. tube for sucking a drink.

straw'ber'ry, *n.* [*pl.* -RIES] small, red, juicy fruit of a vinelike plant.

straw vote, unofficial poll of public opinion.

stray, *v.* 1. wander; roam. 2. deviate. —*a.* 1. lost. 2. occasional. —*n.* stray one.

streak, *n.* 1. long, thin mark. 2. layer. 3. tendency in behavior. 4. [Col.] spell, as of luck. —*v.* 1. mark with streaks. 2. go fast.

stream, *n.* 1. small river. 2. steady flow, as of air. —*v.* 1. flow in a stream. 2. move swiftly.

stream'er, *n.* 1. long, narrow flag or strip.

stream'line, *v. & a.* (make) streamlined.

stream'lined, *a.* 1. shaped to move easily in air, etc. 2. made more efficient.

street, *n.* road in a city.

street'car, *n.* passenger car on rails along streets.

strength, *n.* 1. force; power. 2. durability. 3. intensity. —**strength'en,** *v.*

stren'u·ous, *a.* needing or showing much energy.

strep'to·coc'cus, *n.* [*pl.* -COCCI (-kok'sī)] kind of spherical bacteria.

strep'to·my'cin (-mī'sin) *n.* antibiotic drug.

stress, *n.* 1. strain; pressure. 2. importance; emphasis. 3. special force on a syllable, etc. —*v.* 1. strain. 2. accent; emphasize.

stretch, *v.* 1. reach out. 2. draw out to full extent. 3. strain. 4. exaggerate. —*n.* 1. a stretching. 2. ability to be stretched. 3. extent.

stretch'er, *n.* 1. one that stretches. 2. canvas-covered frame to carry the sick.

strew, *v.* [*alt. pp.* STREWN] 1. scatter. 2. cover by scattering.

stri'at·ed, *a.* striped.

strick'en, *a.* struck, wounded, afflicted, etc.

strict, *a.* 1. exact or absolute. 2. rigidly enforced or enforcing. —**strict'ly,** *adv.* —**strict'ness,** *n.*

stric'ture (-chēr) *n.* strong criticism.

stride, *v.* [STRODE, STRIDDEN, STRIDING] walk with long steps. —*n.* long step.

stri'dent, *a.* shrill; grating. —**strife,** *n.* a quarrel(ing).

strike, *v.* [STRUCK, STRUCK or STRICKEN, STRIKING] 1. hit. 2. sound by hitting some part. 3. ignite (a match). 4. make by stamping. 5. attack. 6. reach or find. 7. occur to. 8. assume (a pose). 9. take down or apart. 10. stop working until demands are met. —*n.* 1. a striking. 2. *Baseball* a pitched ball struck at but missed, etc. 3. *Bowling* a knocking down of all the pins at once. —**strike out,** 1. erase. 2. *Baseball* put or go out on three strikes. —**strike up,** begin. —**strik'er,** *n.*

strik'ing, *a.* very attractive, impressive, etc.

string, *n.* 1. thick thread, etc. used as for tying. 2. numbers of things on a string or in a row. 3. thin cord bowed, etc. to make music, as on a violin. —*v.* [STRUNG, STRINGING] 1. provide with strings. 2. put on a string. 3. extend. —**string'y,** *a.*

string bean, thick bean pod, eaten as a vegetable.

strin'gent (-jənt) *a.* strict.

strip, *v.* [STRIPPED, STRIPPING] 1. take off clothing, covering, etc. (of). 2. make bare. 3. break the teeth of (a gear, etc.). —*n.* long, narrow piece.

stripe, *n.* 1. narrow band of different color or material.

2. kind; sort. —v. mark with stripes.

strip'ling, n. a youth.

strive, v. [STROVE, STRIVEN or STRIVED, STRIVING] 1. try very hard. 2. struggle.

strode, pt. of **stride**.

stroke, n. 1. sudden blow, attack, action, etc. 2. a single movement of the arm, a tool, etc. 3. striking sound. —v. draw one's hand, etc. gently over.

stroll, n. leisurely walk. —v. 1. take a stroll. 2. wander.

strong, a. 1. powerful. 2. healthy. 3. durable. 4. intense. —**strong'ly**, adv.

strong'hold, n. fortress.

stron'ti·um (-shi-əm) n. chemical element with radioactive isotope.

struck, pt. & pp. of **strike**.

struc'ture (-chēr) n. 1. thing built. 2. plan, design, etc. —**struc'tur·al**, a.

strug'gle, v. 1. fight. 2. strive. —n. a struggling.

strum, v. [STRUMMED, STRUMMING] pluck, as a guitar.

strum'pet, n. prostitute.

strung, pt. & pp. of **string**.

strut, v. [STRUTTED, STRUTTING] walk arrogantly. —n. 1. strutting walk. 2. rod used as a support.

strych·nine (strik'nīn) n. poisonous drug used as a stimulant.

stub, n. short, leftover or blunt part. —v. [STUBBED, STUBBING] bump (one's toe).

stub'ble, n. 1. short grain stumps. 2. short growth.

stub'born, a. obstinate. —**stub'born·ness**, n.

stub'by, a. [-BIER, -BIEST] short and thick.

stuc'co, n. [-COED, -COING & n. (cover with) rough plaster.

stuck, pt. & pp. of **stick**.

stud, n. 1. decorative nail. 2. removable button. 3. upright support in a wall. 4. breeding stallion. —v. [STUDDED, STUDDING] be set thickly on.

stu'dent, n. one who studies.

stud'ied, a. done on purpose.

stu'di·o, n. [pl. -OS] 1. artist's work area. 2. place for producing movies, or radio or TV programs.

stu'di·ous, a. 1. fond of study. 2. attentive.

stud'y, v. [-IED, -YING] 1. learn by reading, thinking, etc. 2. investigate. —n. [pl. -IES] 1. act of studying.

2. pl. education. 3. deep thought. 4. place to study.

stuff, n. 1. material; substance. 2. (worthless) objects. —v. 1. fill. 2. cram. —**stuff'ing**, n.

stuff'y, a. [-IER, -IEST] 1. poorly ventilated. 2. stopped up. 3. [Col.] dull.

stul'ti·fy, v. [-FIED, -FYING] make seem foolish, useless.

stum'ble, v. 1. walk unsteadily; trip. 2. speak confusedly. 3. come by chance. —n. a stumbling.

stump, n. part left after cutting off the rest. —v. 1. make a speaking tour. 2. walk heavily. 3. [Col.] perplex.

stun, v. [STUNNED, STUNNING] 1. make unconscious, as by a blow. 2. shock deeply.

stung, pt. & pp. of **sting**.

stun'ning, a. [Col.] very attractive.

stunt, v. keep from growing. —n. daring show of skill.

stu'pe·fy, v. [-FIED, -FYING] stun. —**stu'pe·fac'tion**, n.

stu·pen'dous, a. overwhelming.

stu'pid, a. 1. not intelligent. 2. foolish. 3. dull. —**stu·pid'i·ty** [pl. -TIES] n.

stu'por, n. dazed condition.

stur'dy, a. [-DIER, -DIEST] 1. firm. 2. strong.

stur'geon (-jən) n. food fish.

stut'ter, n. & v. stammer.

sty, n. [pl. STIES] pigpen.

sty, stye (stī) n. [pl. STIES] swelling on the rim of the eyelid.

style, n. 1. way of making, writing, etc. 2. fine style. 3. fashion. —v. 1. name. 2. design the style of.

styl'ish, a. fashionable.

sty'lus, n. 1. pointed writing tool. 2. phonograph needle.

sty'mie (-mi) v. [-MIED, -MIEING] obstruct; block.

styp'tic (stip'-) a. that halts bleeding; astringent.

suave (swäv) a. smoothly polite. —**suav'i·ty**, n.

sub-, pref. 1. under. 2. somewhat. 3. being a division.

sub·al'tern (-ôl'-) n. Br. army officer below a captain.

sub·con'scious, a. & n. (of) one's feelings, wishes, etc. of which one is unaware.

sub·di·vide', v. 1. divide again. 2. divide land into small sections for sale. —**sub'di·vi'sion**, n.

sub·due', v. 1. get control over. 2. make less intense.

sub'ject, a. 1. that is a subject. 2. liable. 3. contingent upon. —n. 1. one controlled by another. 2. topic of discussion or study. 3. *Gram.* word or words about which something is said. —v. (sab-jekt′) 1. bring under control. 2. make undergo. —sub·jec′tion, n.

sub·jec′tive, a. of one's feelings rather than from facts. —sub·jec·tiv′i·ty, n.

sub′ju·gate, v. conquer.

sub′lease, n. lease granted by a lessee. —v. (sub-lēs′) grant or hold a sublease of.

sub·let′, v. 1. sublease. 2. let out work one has contracted to do.

sub′li·mate, v. 1. to sublime. 2. refine instinctive conduct. —sub′li·ma′tion, n.

sub·lime′, a. noble; lofty. —v. purify (a solid) by heating and then condensing. —sub·lim′i·ty, n.

sub′ma·rine (-rēn) n. warship operating under water.

sub·merge′, v. put or go under water. —sub·mer′gence, sub·mer′sion, n.

sub·mis′sion, n. 1. a submitting. 2. obedience. —sub·mis′sive, a.

sub·mit′, v. [-MITTED, -MITTING] 1. present for consideration, etc. 2. surrender.

sub·nor′mal, a. below normal, as in intelligence.

sub·or′di·nate (-nit) a. lower in rank; secondary. —n. subordinate person. —v. (-nāt) make subordinate.

sub·orn′, v. induce to commit perjury.

sub·poe′na, sub·pe′na (sa-pē′-) n. legal paper ordering one to appear in court. —v. order with a subpoena.

sub·scribe′, v. 1. promise to contribute. —subscribe to, 1. agree to take and pay for, as a magazine. 2. approve of. —sub·scrip′tion, n.

sub′se·quent, a. following.

sub·ser′vi·ent, a. servile.

sub·side′, v. 1. sink lower. 2. become quieter.

sub·sid′i·ar′y (-er′ē) a. helping in a lesser way. —n. [pl. -IES] company controlled by another.

sub′si·dize′, v. support with a subsidy.

sub′si·dy, n. [pl. -DIES] (government) grant of money.

sub·sist′, v. live; exist.

sub·sist′ence, n. 1. a subsisting. 2. livelihood.

sub′stance, n. 1. essence. 2. physical matter. 3. central meaning. 4. wealth.

sub·stan′tial (-shal) a. 1. material. 2. strong. 3. large. 4. wealthy. 5. in essentials.

sub·stan′ti·ate (-shi-) v. prove to be true or real.

sub′sti·tute′, n. one that takes the place of another. —v. use as or be a substitute. —sub′sti·tu′tion, n.

sub′ter·fuge, n. scheme used to evade something.

sub′ter·ra′ne·an, a. 1. underground. 2. secret.

sub′tle (sut′'l) a. 1. keen; acute. 2. crafty. 3. delicate. —sub′tle·ty [pl. -TIES] n. —sub′tly, adv.

sub·tract′, v. take away, as one number from another. —sub·trac′tion, n.

sub′urb, n. district, town, etc. on the outskirts of a city. —sub·ur′ban, a.

sub·vert′, v. overthrow (something established). —sub·ver′sion, n. —sub·ver′sive, a. & n.

sub′way, n. underground electric railroad in a city.

suc·ceed′, v. 1. come next after. 2. have success.

suc·cess′, n. 1. favorable result. 2. the gaining of wealth, fame, etc. 3. successful one. —suc·cess′ful, a. —suc·cess′ful·ly, adv.

suc·ces′sion, n. 1. a coming after another. 2. series.

suc·ces′sive, a.

suc·ces′sor, n. one who succeeds another, as in office.

suc·cinct′ (sǝksint′) a. terse.

suc′cor, n. & v. help.

suc′co·tash, n. beans and corn kernels cooked together.

suc′cu·lent, a. juicy.

suc·cumb′ (-kum′) v. 1. give in; yield. 2. die.

such, a. 1. of this or that kind. 2. some. 3. so much. —pron. such a one. —such as, for example.

suck, v. 1. draw into the mouth. 2. suck liquid from. 3. dissolve in the mouth. —n. act of sucking.

suck′er, n. 1. one that sucks or clings. 2. sprout. 3. [Col.] lollipop. 4. [Sl.] dupe.

suck′le, v. give or get milk from the breast.

su′crose, n. sugar found in sugar cane, sugar beets, etc.

suc′tion, n. creation of a vacuum with its sucking action. —a. worked by suction.

sud′den, a. 1. unexpected.

2. hasty. —**sud'den·ly**, adv.

suds, n.pl. foam on soapy water. —**suds'y**, a.

sue, v. 1. begin a lawsuit against. 2. petition.

suede (swād) n. 1. leather with one side buffed into a nap. 2. cloth like this.

su'et, n. hard animal fat.

suf'fer, v. 1. undergo or endure (pain, loss, etc.). 2. tolerate. —**suf'fer·ance**, n.

suf·fice' (-fīs') v. be enough.

suf·fi'cient, a. enough. —**suf·fi'cien·cy**, n. —**suf·fi'cient·ly**, adv.

suf'fix, n. syllable(s) added at the end of a word to alter its meaning, etc.

suf'fo·cate, v. 1. kill by cutting off air. 2. die from lack of air. 3. stifle. —**suf'fo·ca'tion**, n.

suf'frage (-rij) n. right to vote.

suf·fuse' (-fūz') v. overspread, as with color.

sug'ar, n. sweet carbohydrate found in sugar cane, etc.

sugar cane, tall tropical grass grown for its sugar.

sug·gest', v. 1. bring to mind. 2. propose as a possibility. 3. imply. —**sug·ges'tion**, n.

sug·ges'tive, a. suggesting ideas, esp. indecent ideas.

su'i·cide, n. 1. act of killing oneself intentionally. 2. one who commits suicide. —**su'i·cid'al**, a.

suit, n. 1. coat and trousers (or skirt). 2. any of the four sets of playing cards. 3. lawsuit. 4. a suing, pleading, etc. —v. 1. be suitable for. 2. make suitable. 3. please. —**follow suit**, follow the example set.

suit'a·ble, a. appropriate; fitting. —**suit'a·bly**, adv.

suit'case, n. traveling bag.

suite (swēt) n. 1. group of connected rooms. 2. set of matched furniture.

suit'or, n. man who courts a woman.

sul'fa, a. of a family of drugs used in combating certain bacterial infections.

sul'fate, n. salt of sulfuric acid.

sul'fide, n. compound of sulfur.

sul'fur, n. yellow solid substance, a chemical element. —**sul·fu'ric** (-fyoor'ik), a. —**sul·fu'rous**, a.

sulfuric acid, acid formed of hydrogen, sulfur, and oxygen.

sulk, v. be sulky. —n. often pl. sulky mood.

sulk'y, a. [-IER, -IEST] sullen; glum. —n. [pl. -IES] light, two-wheeled carriage. —**sulk'i·ly**, adv.

sul'len, a. 1. showing illhumor by morose withdrawal. 2. gloomy. —**sul'len·ly**, adv.

sul'ly, v. [-LIED, -LYING] soil, stain, defile, etc.

sul'phur, n. sulfur.

sul'tan, n. Moslem ruler.

sul'try, a. [-TRIER, -TRIEST] 1. hot and humid. 2. inflamed, as with passion.

sum, n. 1. amount of money. 2. summary. 3. total. —v. [SUMMED, SUMMING] summarize.

su·mac, su·mach (shoo'mak, soo'-) n. plant with lance-shaped leaves and red fruit.

sum'ma·rize, v. make or be a summary of.

sum'ma·ry, n. [pl. -RIES] brief report; digest. —a. 1. concise. 2. prompt. —**sum·ma'ri·ly**, adv.

sum·ma'tion, n. summarizing of arguments, as in a trial.

sum'mer, n. warmest season of the year. —a. of or for summer. —v. pass the summer. —**sum'mer·y**, a.

sum'mit, n. highest point.

sum'mon, v. 1. call together. 2. send for. 3. rouse.

sum'mons, n. official order to appear in court.

sump'tu·ous (-choo-əs) a. costly; lavish.

sun, n. 1. incandescent body about which the planets revolve. 2. heat or light of the sun. —v. [SUNNED, SUNNING] expose to sunlight.

sun'burn, n. inflammation of the skin from exposure to the sun. —v. [alt. pt. & pp. SUNBURNT] give or get sunburn.

sun'dae (-di) n. ice cream covered with sirup, nuts, etc.

Sun'day, n. first day of the week.

sun'der, v. break apart.

sun'di'al, n. instrument that shows time by the shadow cast by the sun.

sun'down, n. sunset.

sun'dry, a. various.

sun'fish, n. 1. small freshwater fish. 2. large sea fish.

sun'flow'er, n. tall plant with big, daisylike flowers.

sung, pp. of **sing**.

sunk, pp. & alt. pt. of **sink.**

sunk′en, a. 1. sunk in liquid. 2. depressed; hollow.

sun′ny, a. 1. full of sunshine. 2. cheerful.

sun′rise, n. daily rising of the sun in the east.

sun′set, n. daily setting of the sun in the west.

sun′shine, n. 1. shining of the sun. 2. light from the sun. —**sun′shin·y,** a.

sun′stroke, n. illness from overexposure to the sun.

sup, v. [SUPPED, SUPPING] have supper.

super-, pref. 1. over; above. 2. very; very much. 3. greater than others. 4. extra.

su·per·an′nu·at·ed, a. 1. retired on a pension. 2. too old to work or use.

su·perb′, a. excellent.

su′per·charge, v. increase an engine's power.

su·per·cil′i·ous (-sil′-) a. disdainful; haughty.

su·per·fi′cial (-fish′əl) a. 1. of or on the surface. 2. shallow; hasty. —**su′per·fi′cial·ly,** adv.

su·per·flu′ous, a. unnecessary. —**su′per·flu′i·ty,** n.

su′per·hu′man, a. 1. divine. 2. greater than normal.

su′per·im·pose′, v. put on top of something else.

su′per·in·tend′, v. direct or manage. —**su′per·in·tend′ent,** n.

su·pe′ri·or, a. 1. higher in rank, etc. 2. above average. 3. haughty. —n. one that is superior. —**superior to,** unaffected by. —**su·pe′ri·or′i·ty,** n.

su·per′la·tive, a. of the highest degree; supreme. —n. 1. highest degree. 2. third degree in the comparison of adjectives and adverbs.

su′per·man′, n. [pl. -MEN] seemingly superhuman man.

su′per·mar′ket, n. large, self-service food store.

su′per·nat′u·ral, a. beyond known laws of nature. —**the supernatural** supernatural things.

su′per·nu′mer·ar′y, a. & n. [pl. -IES] extra (person or thing).

su·per·scribe′, v. write on the top or outside.

su·per·sede′, v. replace, succeed, or supplant.

su′per·son′ic, a. 1. of sounds too high to hear. 2. (traveling) faster than sound.

su′per·star′, n. famous athlete, entertainer, etc.

su′per·sti′tion, n. belief or practice based on fear or ignorance. —**su′per·sti′tious,** a.

su′per·struc′ture, n. 1. part above a ship's deck. 2. upper part of a building.

su′per·vene′, v. come unexpectedly.

su′per·vise′, v. oversee or direct. —**su′per·vi′sion,** n. —**su′per·vi′sor,** n. —**su′per·vi′so·ry,** a.

su·pine′, a. 1. lying on the back. 2. lazy.

sup′per, n. evening meal.

sup·plant′, v. take the place of, esp. by force.

sup′ple, a. flexible.

sup′ple·ment, n. something added. —v. add to. —**sup′ple·men′ta·ry,** a.

sup′pli·cate, v. implore. —**sup′pli·cant, sup′pli·cant,** n. & a. —**sup′pli·ca′tion,** n.

sup·ply′, v. [-PLIED, -PLYING] 1. furnish; provide. 2. make up for. —n. [pl. -PLIES] 1. amount available. 2. pl. materials. —**sup·pli′er,** n.

sup·port′, v. 1. hold up. 2. help. 3. provide for. 4. help prove. —n. 1. a supporting. 2. that which supports.

sup·pose′, v. 1. take as true; assume. 2. guess; think. 3. expect. —**sup·posed′,** a. —**sup′po·si′tion,** n.

sup·pos′i·to′ry, n. [pl. -RIES] medicated substance put in the rectum or vagina.

sup·press′, v. 1. put down by force. 2. keep back; conceal. —**sup·pres′sion,** n.

sup′pu·rate (-yoo-) v. become filled with pus.

su·prem′a·cy, n. supreme power or authority.

su·preme′, a. highest in rank, power, or degree.

sur′charge, n. 1. extra charge. 2. overload. —v. put a surcharge in or on.

sure, a. 1. reliable; certain. 2. without doubt. 3. bound to happen or do. —adv. [Col.] surely. —**for sure,** certainly.

sure′ly, adv. 1. with confidence. 2. without doubt.

sure′ty, n. [pl. -TIES] 1. security. 2. guarantor of another's debts.

surf, n. ocean waves breaking on a shore or reef.

sur′face, n. 1. outside of a thing. 2. any face of a solid.

3. outward look. —*a.* superficial. —*v.* 1. give a surface to. 2. rise to the surface.

surf'board, *n.* long board used in riding the surf.

surf'eit (-fit) *n.* 1. excess, as of food. 2. sickness caused by this. —*v.* overindulge.

surf'ing, *n.* sport of riding the surf on a surfboard.

surge, *v. & n.* (move in) a large wave or sudden rush.

sur'geon (-jən) *n.* doctor who practices surgery.

sur'ger·y, *n.* 1. treatment of disease or injury by operations. 2. a room for this. —**sur'gi·cal,** *a.*

sur'ly, *a.* [-LIER, -LIEST] bad-tempered; uncivil.

sur·mise' (-mīz') *n. & v.* guess.

sur·mount', *v.* 1. overcome. 2. climb over. 3. top. —**sur·mount'a·ble,** *a.*

sur'name, *n.* family name.

sur·pass', *v.* 1. excel. 2. go beyond the limit of.

sur'plice (-plis) *n.* clergyman's loose, white tunic.

sur'plus, *n. & a.* (quantity) over what is needed or used.

sur·prise', *v.* 1. come upon unexpectedly. 2. astonish. —*n.* 1. a surprising or being surprised. 2. thing that surprises. —**sur·pris'ing,** *a.*

sur·re'al·ism, *n.* art specifying the unconscious. —**sur·re'al·ist,** *a. & n.*

sur·ren'der, *v.* 1. give oneself up. 2. give up; abandon. —*n.* act of surrendering.

sur·rep·ti'tious (-tish'əs) *a.* secret; stealthy.

sur'rey, *n.* [*pl.* -REYS] light, four-wheeled carriage.

sur·round', *v.* 1. encircle on all sides.

sur·round'ings, *n.pl.* things, conditions, etc. around a person or thing.

sur·veil'lance (-vāl'-) *n.* watch kept over a person.

sur·vey', *v.* 1. examine in detail. 2. determine the form, boundaries, etc. of a piece of land. —*n.* (sūr'vā) 1. general or comprehensive study. 2. act of surveying an area. —**sur·vey'or,** *n.*

sur·vive', *v.* 1. outlive 2. continue to live. —**sur·viv'al,** *n.* —**sur·vi'vor,** *n.*

sus·cep'ti·ble (sə-sep'-) *a.* easily affected; sensitive.

sus·pect', *v.* 1. believe to be guilty on little evidence. 2. distrust. 3. surmise. —*n.* (sus'pekt) one suspected.

sus·pend', *v.* 1. exclude, stop, etc. for a time. 2. hold back (judgment, etc.). 3. hang. —**sus·pen'sion,** *n.*

sus·pend'ers, *n.pl.* shoulder straps to hold up trousers.

sus·pense', *n.* tense uncertainty.

sus·pi'cion, *n.* 1. a suspecting or being suspected. 2. feeling of one who suspects. 3. trace. —**sus·pi'cious,** *a.*

sus·tain', *v.* 1. maintain; prolong. 2. provide for. 3. support. 4. suffer. 5. uphold as valid. 6. confirm.

sus'te·nance, *n.* 1. means of livelihood. 2. food.

su'ture (-chēr) *n.* stitching up of a wound, or stitch so used.

swab (swäb) *n.* 1. a mop. 2. piece of cotton, etc. used to medicate or clean the throat, etc. —*v.* [SWABBED, SWABBING] clean with a swab.

swad'dle, *v.* wrap (a baby) in narrow bands of cloth.

swag'ger, *v.* 1. walk with a bold stride. 2. brag loudly. —*n.* swaggering walk.

swal'low, *v.* 1. pass (food, etc.) from the mouth into the stomach. 2. take in; absorb. 3. tolerate. 4. suppress. —*n.* 1. act of swallowing. 2. amount swallowed. 3. small, swift-flying bird.

swam, pt. of **swim.**

swamp, *n.* piece of wet, spongy ground. —*v.* 1. flood with water. 2. overwhelm. —**swamp'y,** *a.*

swan, *n.* large water bird with a long graceful neck.

swank, *a.* [Sl.] ostentatiously stylish: also **swank'y.**

swap (swäp) *n. & v.* [SWAPPED, SWAPPING] [Col.] trade.

swarm, *n.* 1. colony of bees. 2. large, moving mass of insects, etc. —*v.* move in a swarm.

swarth'y, *a.* [-IER, -IEST] dark-skinned.

swash'buck·ler (swäsh'-) *n.* swaggering fighting man.

swas'ti·ka (swäs'-) *n.* cross with bent arms: Nazi emblem.

swat, *v.* [SWATTED, SWATTING] & *n.* [Col.] (hit with) a quick, sharp blow. —**swat'ter,** *n.*

swatch, *n.* sample bit of cloth.

swath (swäth) *n.* a strip cut by a scythe, mower, etc.

swathe (swāth) *v.* 1. wrap up in a bandage. 2. envelop.

sway, *v.* 1. swing from side to side or to and fro. 2.

incline. 3. influence. —n. 1. a swaying. 2. influence.

swear, v. [SWORE, SWORN, SWEARING] 1. make a solemn declaration or promise. 2. curse. 3. make take an oath.

sweat, n. 1. salty liquid given off through the skin. 2. moisture collected on a surface. —v. [SWEAT or SWEATED, SWEATING] 1. give forth sweat. 2. work so hard as to cause sweating. —**sweat'y,** a.

sweat'er, n. knitted garment for the upper body.

sweep, v. [SWEPT, SWEEPING] 1. clean, or clear away, with a broom. 2. carry away or pass over swiftly. 3. reach in a long line. —n. 1. a sweeping. 2. range or extent. —**sweep'ing,** a.

sweep'ings, n.pl. things swept up.

sweep'stakes, n. [pl. -STAKES] lottery on a horse race.

sweet, a. 1. tasting of sugar. 2. pleasant. 3. fresh. —n. a candy. —**sweet'en,** v. —**sweet'ly,** adv.

sweet'bread, n. calf's pancreas or thymus, used as food.

sweet'bri·er, sweet'bri·ar, n. kind of rose.

sweet'heart, n. loved one.

sweet pea, climbing plant with fragrant flowers.

sweet potato, thick, yellow root of a tropical vine.

swell, v. [alt. pp. SWOLLEN] 1. bulge. 2. increase in size, force, etc. 3. fill, as with pride. —n. 1. a swelling. 2. large wave. 3. [Sl.] excellent.

swell'ing, n. 1. swollen part. 2. increase.

swel'ter, v. feel oppressed with great heat.

swel'ter·ing, a. very hot.

swept, pt. & pp. of **sweep.**

swerve, v. & n. (make) a quick turn aside.

swift, a. 1. moving fast. 2. prompt. —n. swallowlike bird. —**swift'ly,** adv.

swig, v. [SWIGGED, SWIGGING] [Col.] drink in large gulps. —n. large gulp.

swill, v. drink greedily. —n. garbage fed to pigs.

swim, v. [SWAM, SWUM, SWIMMING] 1. move in water by moving the limbs, fins, etc. 2. float on a liquid. 3. overflow. 4. be dizzy. —n. a swimming. —**swim'mer,** n.

swin'dle, v. defraud; cheat. —n. a swindling.

swine, n. [pl. SWINE] pig or hog. —**swin'ish,** a.

swing, v. [SWUNG, SWINGING] 1. sway back and forth. 2. turn, as on a hinge. 3. manage to get, win, etc. —n. 1. a swinging. 2. sweeping blow. 3. musical rhythm. 4. seat hanging from ropes.

swipe, n. [Col.] hard, sweeping blow. —v. 1. [Col.] hit with a swipe. 2. [Sl.] steal.

swirl, v. & n. whirl; twist.

swish, v. (move with) a hissing or rustling sound.

Swiss, a. of Switzerland.

switch, n. 1. thin stick used for whipping. 2. control device for an electric circuit. 3. movable section of railroad track. 4. shift; change. —v. 1. to whip. 2. jerk. 3. turn a light, etc. on or off. 4. move a train to another track. 5. shift.

switch'board, n. control panel for electric switches.

swiv'el, n. fastening with free-turning parts. —v. turn as on a swivel.

swol'len, alt. pp. of **swell.** —a. bulging.

swoon, v. & n. faint.

swoop, v. sweep down or pounce upon. —n. a swooping.

sword (sôrd) n. weapon with a handle and a long blade.

sword'fish, n. large ocean fish with a swordlike jaw.

sworn, a. bound by an oath.

swum, pp. of **swim.**

syc'a·more (sik'-) n. shade tree with shedding bark.

syc'o·phant, n. flatterer.

syl·lab'i·fy (sil-) v. [-FIED, -FYING] divide into syllables: also **syl·lab'i·cate.** —**syl·lab'i·fi·ca'tion,** n.

syl'la·ble, n. 1. single vocal sound. 2. written form of this. —**syl·lab'ic,** a.

syl'la·bus, n. [pl. -BUSES, -BI (-bī)] summary or outline.

syl'lo·gism (-jizm) n. two premises and a conclusion.

sylph (silf) n. slender, graceful woman.

syl'van, a. of, living in, or covered with trees.

sym'bol, n. object, mark, etc. that represents another object, an idea, etc. —**sym·bol'ic, sym·bol'i·cal,** a. —**sym'bol·ize,** v.

sym'bol·ism, n. 1. use of symbols. 2. set of symbols.

sym'me·try, n. balance of opposite parts in position or size. —**sym·met'ri·cal,** a.

sym·pa·thet·ic, a. of, in, or feeling sympathy. —**sym'-pa·thet'i·cal·ly**, adv.

sym·pa·thize, v. feel or show sympathy.

sym·pa·thy, n. [pl. -THIES] 1. sameness of feeling. 2. agreement. 3. compassion.

sym·pho·ny, n. [pl. -NIES] full orchestra or composition for it. —**sym·phon'ic**, a.

sym·po·si·um, n. [pl. -UMS, -A (-ə)] meeting for discussion.

symp'tom, n. indication or sign, of disease. —**symp'-to·mat'ic**, a.

syn'a·gogue (-gôg) n. building where Jews worship.

syn'chro·nize (sĭn'krə-) v. 1. move or occur at the same time or rate. 2. make agree in time or rate.

syn'co·pate, v. Mus. shift the beat to unaccented notes. —**syn'co·pa'tion**, n.

syn'di·cate (-kĭt) n. 1. business association of bankers, corporations, etc. 2. organization selling news stories, etc. —v. (-kāt) publish through a syndicate.

syn'od, n. council of churches or church officials.

syn'o·nym, n. word meaning the same as another. —**syn·on'y·mous**, a.

syn·op'sis, n. [pl. -SES (-sēz)] summary.

syn'tax, n. way words are arranged in a sentence. —**syn·tac'ti·cal**, a.

syn·the·sis, n. [pl. -SES (-sēz)] combining of parts into a whole. —**syn'the·size**, v.

syn·thet'ic, a. 1. of or using synthesis. 2. artificial; not natural. —n. synthetic thing. —**syn·thet'i·cal·ly**, adv.

syph'i·lis, n. infectious venereal disease. —**syph·i·lit'ic**, a. & n.

syr'inge (sə-rĭnj') n. ball with a tube, for ejecting fluids.

syr'up, n. sirup.

sys'tem, n. 1. whole formed of related things. 2. set of organized facts, rules, etc. 3. orderly way of doing things. —**sys'tem·a·tize'**, v.

sys·tem·at'ic, a. orderly; methodical. —**sys·tem·at'i·cal·ly**, adv.

T

tab, n. small flap or tag. —**keep tab** (or **tabs**) **on**, [Col.] keep informed about.

tab'by, n. [pl. -BIES] pet cat.

tab'er·na·cle, n. large place of worship.

ta'ble, n. 1. flat surface set on legs. 2. table set with food. 3. orderly list or arrangement. —v. postpone.

tab'leau (-lō) n. [pl. -LEAUX (-lōz), -LEAUS] scene by persons posing in costume.

ta'ble·land, n. plateau.

ta'ble·spoon, n. spoon holding ½ fluid ounce. —**ta'ble·spoon'ful** [pl. -FULS] n.

tab'let, n. 1. flat, inscribed piece of stone, metal, etc. 2. writing pad. 3. flat, hard cake of medicine.

table tennis, game like tennis, played on a table.

ta'ble·ware, n. dishes, forks, etc. used for eating.

ta·boo', ta·bu', n. sacred or social prohibition. —v. prohibit.

tab'u·lar, a. of or arranged in a table or list.

tab'u·late, v. put in tabular form. —**tab·u·la'tion**, n.

tac'it (tas'-) a. not expressed openly, but implied.

tac·i·turn (tas'-) a. usually silent. —**tac·i·tur'ni·ty**, n.

tack, n. 1. short, flat-headed nail. 2. course of action. 3. ship's direction relative to position of sails. —v. 1. fasten with tacks. 2. add. 3. change course.

tack'le, n. 1. equipment. 2. set of ropes & pulleys. 3. a tackling. —v. 1. undertake. 2. Football bring down (the ball carrier).

tact, n. skill in dealing with people. —**tact'ful**, a.

tac'tic, n. skillful method.

tac'tics, n. science of battle maneuvers. —**tac'ti·cal**, a. —**tac·ti'cian** (-tĭsh'ən) n.

tad'pole, n. frog or toad in an early stage.

taf'fe·ta, n. stiff silk cloth.

taf'fy, n. a chewy candy.

tag, n. 1. hanging end. 2. card, etc. attached as a label. 3. children's chasing game. —v. 1. provide with a tag. 2. touch as in game of tag. 3. [Col.] follow closely.

tail, n. 1. appendage at rear end of an animal's body. 2. hind or end part. —v. [Col.] follow closely. —a. at or from the rear. —**tail'less**, a.

tail'light, n. red light at the back of a vehicle.

tai'lor, n. one who makes or repairs clothes. —v. 1. make by a tailor's work. 2. form, alter, etc. to suit.

tail'spin, n. sharp downward plunge of a plane with tail spinning in circles.

taint, v. 1. spoil; rot. 2. make corrupt or depraved. —n. trace of contamination.

take, v. [TOOK, TAKEN, TAKING] 1. grasp. 2. capture, seize, win, etc. 3. obtain, select, assume, etc. 4. use, consume, etc. 5. buy; rent. 6. travel by. 7. deal with. 8. occupy. 9. derive from. 10. write down. 11. photograph. 12. require. 13. engage in. 14. understand. 15. have or feel. 16. carry, lead, etc. 17. remove. 18. subtract. —n. amount taken. —**take after,** act or look like. —**take in,** 1. admit; receive. 2. make smaller. 3. understand. 4. trick. —**take over,** begin managing. —**take up,** 1. make tighter or shorter. 2. absorb. 3. engage in.

take'-off', n. 1. a leaving the ground, as in flight. 2. [Col.] mocking imitation.

tal'cum (powder), powder for the body and face made from a soft mineral (**talc**).

tale, n. 1. story. 2. lie. 3. gossip.

tal'ent, n. special, natural ability. —**tal'ent-ed,** a.

tal'is-man, n. [pl. -MANS] anything supposed to have magic power.

talk, v. 1. say words; speak. 2. gossip. 3. confer. 4. discuss. —n. 1. a talking. 2. conversation. 3. speech. 4. conference. 5. gossip. —**talk back,** answer impertinently. —**talk'er,** n.

talk'a·tive, a. talking a great deal: also **talk'y.**

tall, a. high, as in stature.

tal'low, n. hard animal fat used in candles and soap.

tal'ly, n. [pl. -LIES] record, account, etc. —v. 1. record; score. 2. add. 3. agree.

tal'ly·ho', int. fox hunter's cry. —n. [pl. -HOS] coach drawn by four horses.

tal'on, n. claw of a bird of prey.

tam, n. tam-o'-shanter.

ta·ma'le (-mä'li) n. [Mex. Sp.] peppery chopped meat rolled in corn meal.

tam'a·rack, n. swamp larch.

tam·bou·rine' (-bə-rēn') n. small, shallow drum with metal disks around it.

tame, a. 1. trained from a wild state. 2. gentle. 3. not lively; dull. —v. make tame.

—**tame'ly,** adv. —**tam'er,** n.

am'-o'-shan'ter, n. flat, round Scottish cap.

tamp, v. pack down by tamping. —**tamp'er,** n.

tam'per, v. interfere (with).

tan, n. yellowish brown. —a. [TANNER, TANNEST] yellowish-brown. —v. [TANNED, TANNING] 1. make (hide) into leather by soaking in tannic acid. 2. brown by sun's rays.

tan'bark, n. tree bark containing tannic acid.

tan'dem, adv. one behind another.

tang, n. strong taste or odor. —**tang'y** [-IER, -IEST] a.

tan'gent (-jənt) a. touching a curve at one point. —n. a tangent curve, line, etc. —**go off at (or on) a tangent,** change suddenly to another line of action. —**tan·gen'tial** (-jen'shəl) a.

tan·ge·rine' (-jə-rēn') n. small, loose-skinned orange.

tan'gi·ble (-jə-) a. 1. real or solid. 2. definite.

tan'gle, v. 1. make or become knotted, confused, etc. 2. catch, as in a snare. —n. tangled mass or condition.

tan'go, n. [pl. -GOS] South American dance. —v. dance the tango.

tank, n. 1. large container for liquid or gas. 2. armored vehicle carrying guns.

tank'ard, n. large drinking cup with a hinged lid.

tank'er, n. ship for transporting liquids, esp. oil.

tan'ner·y, n. [pl. -IES] place where leather is made by tanning hides. —**tan'ner,** n.

tan'nic acid, acid used in tanning, dyeing, etc.: also **tan'nin,** n.

tan'ta·lize, v. show but withhold something; tease.

tan'ta·mount, a. equal.

tan'trum, n. fit of rage.

tap, v. [TAPPED, TAPPING] 1. hit lightly. 2. make a hole in. 3. draw off, as liquids. 4. connect into. —n. 1. light blow. 2. pl. signal for lights to be out. 3. faucet or spigot. 4. plug or cork. 5. place for connection.

tape, n. narrow strip of cloth, paper, etc. —v. 1. bind with a tape. 2. record on tape.

tape measure, tape with marks for measuring.

ta'per, v. decrease or lessen gradually in thickness, loudness, etc. —n. 1. a tapering.

2. slender candle.

tape recorder, recording device using magnetic tape.

tap·es·try, n. [pl. -TRIES] cloth with woven designs.

tape·worm, n. tapelike worm found in the intestines.

tap·i·o·ca, n. starchy substance from cassava roots.

ta·pir, n. hoglike animal.

tap·root, n. main root.

tar, n. 1. black liquid distilled from wood or coal. 2. [Col.] sailor. —v. [TARRED, TARRING] cover with tar. —**tar′ry,** a.

ta·ran·tu·la (-choo-) n. large, hairy spider.

tar′dy, a. [-DIER, -DIEST] 1. slow. 2. late.

tare, n. 1. weed. 2. container's weight.

tar′get, n. thing aimed at, shot at, or attacked.

tar′iff (tar′-) n. 1. tax on exports or imports. 2. list of prices, charges, etc.

tar′nish, v. stain; discolor. —n. dullness; stain.

ta′ro (tä′-) n. tropical plant with edible root.

tar·pau·lin (-pô′-) n. waterproofed canvas.

tar′pon, n. large ocean fish.

tar′ry (tar′-) v. [-RIED, -RYING] 1. linger. 2. delay.

tart, a. 1. sour; acid. 2. sharp in meaning. —n. pastry filled with jam, etc. —**tart′ly,** a. —**tart′ness,** n.

tar′tan, n. plaid cloth.

tar′tar, n. hard deposit forming on the teeth.

task, n. work that must be done. —v. burden; strain. —**take to task,** scold.

task′mas′ter, n. one who assigns severe tasks.

tas′sel, n. 1. bunch of threads hanging from a knob. 2. tuft of corn silk.

taste, v. 1. notice or test the flavor of in one's mouth. 2. eat or drink sparingly. 3. have a certain flavor. —n. 1. sense for telling flavor. 2. flavor. 3. small amount. 4. sense of the beautiful, proper, etc. 5. liking. —**taste′ful,** a. —**taste′less,** a.

tast′y, a. [-IER, -IEST] that tastes good.

:at, v. [TATTED, TATTING] make lace with a hand shuttle.

:at′ter, n. 1. rag; shred. 2. pl. ragged clothes. —**tat′tered,** a.

:at′tle, v. 1. tell secrets. 2. gossip. —n. gossip.

tat·too′, v. [-TOOED, -TOOING] make designs on the skin. —n. [pl. -TOOS] 1. tattooed design. 2. steady beating, as on a drum.

taught (tôt) pt. & pp. of **teach.**

taunt (tônt) v. mock; tease. —n. scornful remark.

taupe (tōp) n. dark, brownish gray.

Tau·rus (tôr′-) n. 2nd sign of the zodiac; Bull.

taut (tôt) a. 1. tightly stretched. 2. tense.

tav′ern, n. saloon or inn.

taw′dry, a. [-DRIER, -DRIEST] gaudy and cheap.

taw′ny, a. [-NIER, -NIEST] dark yellow or tan.

tax, n. 1. compulsory payment to a government. 2. burden; strain. —v. 1. levy, or make pay, a tax. 2. burden. 3. accuse; charge. —**tax′a·ble,** a. —**tax·a′tion,** n. —**tax′pay′er,** n.

tax′i, n. [pl. -IS] taxicab. —v. [-IED, -IING or -YING] 1. go in a taxicab. 2. move along the ground or water, as an airplane.

tax′i·cab, n. automobile for passengers who pay.

tax′i·der′my, n. art of stuffing animal skins. —**tax′i·der′mist,** n.

TB, T.B., tuberculosis.

tea, n. 1. leaves of an Asiatic shrub. 2. drink made from these. 3. afternoon party with tea. —**tea′cup,** n.

teach, v. [TAUGHT, TEACHING] give lessons (in). —**teach′er,** n.

teak, n. East Indian tree.

tea′ket·tle, n. kettle with a spout, used to heat water.

teal (tēl) n. wild duck.

team, n. 1. two or more animals harnessed together. 2. group working or playing together. —v. join in a team. —**team′work,** n.

team′ster, n. truck driver.

tea′pot, n. pot with spout and handle for brewing tea.

tear (târ) v. [TORE, TORN, TEARING] 1. pull apart, up, etc. by force. 2. make by tearing. 3. move fast. —n. 1. a tearing. 2. torn place. —**tear down,** wreck.

tear (tēr) n. drop of liquid from the eye. —**in tears,** weeping. —**tear′ful,** a.

tear gas, gas that blinds the eyes with tears.

tease, v. 1. annoy by poking fun at, etc. 2. fluff up, as hair. —n. one who teases.

tea'spoon, n. small spoon. —**tea'spoon·ful** [pl. -FULS] n.

teat (tēt) n. nipple on a breast or udder.

tech'ni·cal (tek'-) a. 1. dealing with industrial arts or skills. 2. of a specific art, science, etc. 3. of technique. —**tech'ni·cal·ly,** adv.

tech'ni·cal'i·ty, n. [pl. -TIES] 1. technical detail. 2. minute formal point.

tech·ni'cian (-nish'ən) n. one skilled in a technique.

tech·nique (-nēk') n. method of procedure, as in art.

tech·nol'o·gy, n. study of applied arts and sciences. —**tech'no·log'i·cal,** a.

te'di·ous, a. tiring; boring.

te'di·um, n. a being tedious.

tee, n. Golf 1. small peg to rest the ball on. 2. starting place for each hole. —v. [TEED, TEEING] hit a ball from a tee (with off).

teem, v. abound; swarm.

teens, n.pl. years of one's age from 13 to 19. —**teen'-age,** a. —**teen'ag·er,** n.

tee'pee, n. tepee.

tee'ter, v. & n. seesaw.

tee'ter-tot'ter, n. & v. seesaw.

teeth, n. pl. of tooth.

teethe (tēth) v. have teeth cutting through the gum.

tee·to'tal·er, n. one who never drinks liquor.

tel'e·cast, v. [-CAST or -CASTED, -CASTING] & n. broadcast over television.

tel'e·gram, n. message sent by telegraph.

tel'e·graph, n. device or system for sending messages through by electric signals through a wire. —v. send a message by telegraph. —**te·leg'ra·pher,** n. —**tel'e·graph'ic,** a. —**te·leg'ra·phy,** n.

te·lep'a·thy, n. supposed communication between minds without help of speech, sight, etc. —**tel'e·path'ic,** a.

tel'e·phone, n. device or system for talking over distances through wires. —v. talk (to) by telephone.

tel'e·scope, n. device with lenses that magnify distant objects. —v. slide one into another. —**tel'e·scop'ic** (-skop'-) a.

tel'e·vise, v. transmit by television.

tel'e·vi'sion, n. 1. way of sending pictures through space by radio waves to a re-

ceiving set. 2. such a set.

tell, v. [TOLD, TELLING] 1. report; narrate. 2. put into words. 3. show. 4. inform. 5. recognize. 6. order. —**tell off,** [Col.] criticize sharply.

tell'er, n. 1. one who tells. 2. cashier at a bank.

tell'tale, a. revealing what is meant to be secret.

te·mer'i·ty (-mer'-) n. rashness; boldness.

tem'per, v. 1. make less intense. 2. make hard, as steel. —n. 1. state of mind. 2. self-control. 3. rage.

tem'per·a·ment, n. (moody or excitable) disposition. —**tem'per·a·men'tal,** a.

tem'per·ance, n. 1. self-restraint; moderation. 2. abstinence from liquor.

tem'per·ate (-it) a. 1. moderate; self-restrained. 2. not very hot or very cold.

tem'per·a·ture (-chēr) n. 1. degree of hotness or coldness. 2. fever.

tem'pered, a. having a certain kind of temper.

tem'pest, n. wild storm. —**tem·pes'tu·ous** (-choo-) a.

tem'ple, n. 1. a building for worship service or for some special purpose. 2. area near eye and ear.

tem'po, n. [pl. -POS, -PI (-pi)] rate of speed, esp. for playing music.

tem'po·ral, a. 1. worldly. 2. of time.

tem'po·rar'y, a. lasting only a while. —**tem'po·rar'i·ly,** adv.

tempt, v. 1. entice, esp. to an immoral act. 2. provoke. 3. incline strongly. —**temp·ta'tion,** n.

ten, a. & n. one more than nine. —**tenth,** a. & n.

ten'a·ble, a. that can be defended or believed.

te·na'cious (-shəs) a. 1. holding firmly. 2. retentive. 3. stubborn. —**te·nac'i·ty** (-nas'-) n.

ten'ant, n. occupant (who pays rent). —**ten'an·cy,** n.

tend, v. 1. take care of. 2. be apt; incline. 3. lead.

tend'en·cy, n. [pl. -CIES] a being likely to move or act in a certain way.

ten'der, a. 1. soft or delicate. 2. sensitive. 3. loving. 4. young. —n. 1. thing offered, as in payment. 2. car with locomotive's coal. 3. one who tends. —v. give to one to take. —**ten'der·ly,** adv.

ten'der·foot, n. [pl. -FOOTS, -FEET] newcomer, esp. one not used to hardships.

ten'der·ize, v. make tender.

ten'der·loin, n. tenderest part of a loin of meat.

ten'don, n. cord of tissue binding a muscle to a bone.

ten'dril, n. threadlike, clinging part of a climbing plant.

ten'e·ment, n. apartment house, esp. an old one.

ten'et, n. opinion or belief.

ten'nis, n. game played by hitting a ball over a net with a racket.

ten'on, n. projecting part to fit in a mortise.

ten'or, n. 1. highest singing voice. 2. general course. 3. meaning.

ten'pins, n. bowling.

tense, a. 1. taut. 2. anxious. —v. make or become tense. —n. verb form showing time.

ten'sile (-s'l) a. of or under tension.

ten'sion, n. 1. a stretching. 2. stress from this. 3. nervous strain. 4. voltage.

tent, n. canvas shelter.

ten'ta·cle, n. slender growth on an animal's head, for feeling, grasping, etc.

ten'ta·tive, a. not final.

ten'u·ous, a. 1. thin; fine. 2. not dense. 3. flimsy.

ten'ure, n. right or duration of holding a position, etc.

te'pee, n. cone-shaped tent.

tep'id, a. lukewarm.

term, n. 1. fixed time period. 2. pl. conditions of a contract, etc. 3. pl. personal relationship. 4. word or phrase. 5. either part of a fraction, etc. —v. name.

ter'ma·gant (-gənt) n. nagging woman.

ter'mi·nal, a. of or at the end. —n. 1. end (part). 2. main station, as for buses.

ter'mi·nate, v. 1. stop; end. 2. form the end of. —**ter'mi·na'tion**, n.

ter'mi·nol'o·gy, n. [pl. -GIES] special words or phrases.

ter'mi·nus, n. [pl. -NUSES, -NI (-nī)] an end limit, etc.

ter'mite, n. antlike insect that eats wood.

tern, n. gull-like sea bird.

ter'race (-ris) n. 1. patio. 2. flat mound with sloping side. 3. row of houses on this. —v. make a terrace of.

ter'ra cot'ta, brown-red earthenware or its color.

terra fir'ma, solid ground.

ter·rain', n. area of land.

ter'ra·my'cin (-mī'sin) n. antibiotic drug.

ter'ra·pin, n. fresh-water turtle.

ter·res'tri·al, a. 1. worldly. 2. of the earth. 3. of, or living on, land.

ter'ri·ble, a. 1. causing terror. 2. extreme. 3. [Col.] very bad. —**ter'ri·bly**, adv.

ter'ri·er, n. breed of small, lively dog.

ter·rif'ic, a. 1. terrifying. 2. [Col.] very great, etc.

ter'ri·fy, v. [-FIED, -FYING] fill with terror.

ter'ri·to'ry, n. [pl. -RIES] 1. land ruled by a nation. 2. national region not yet a State. 3. region. —**ter'ri·to'ri·al**, a.

ter'ror, n. great fear, or cause of this.

ter'ror·ism, n. use of force and threats to intimidate. —**ter'ror·ist**, n. & a.

ter'ror·ize, v. 1. terrify. 2. coerce by terrorism.

ter'ry (cloth), cloth having a pile of uncut loops.

terse, a. concise; to the point. —**terse'ly**, adv.

ter'ti·ar·y (-shi-) a. third.

test, n. examination or trial to determine a thing's value, one's knowledge, etc. —v. subject to a test.

tes'ta·ment, n. 1. [T-] either part of the Bible. 2. legal will.

tes'ti·cle, n. male sex gland.

tes'ti·fy, v. [-FIED, -FYING] 1. give evidence in court. 2. indicate.

tes'ti·mo'ni·al, n. 1. statement of recommendation. 2. thing given as a tribute.

tes'ti·mo'ny, n. [pl. -NIES] 1. statement of one who testifies in court. 2. indication.

test tube, tubelike glass container.

tes'ty, a. [-TIER, -TIEST] irritable; touchy.

tet'a·nus, n. acute infectious disease.

tête-à-tête (tāt'ə-tāt') a. & n. (of) a private talk between two people.

teth'er (teth'-) n. rope or chain tied to an animal to confine it. —v. tie with this.

text, n. 1. an author's words. 2. main part of a printed page. 3. textbook. 4. Biblical passage. 5. topic. —**tex'tu·al** (-chōō-) a.

text'book, n. book used in teaching a subject.

tex'tile, n. woven fabric —a.

1. of weaving. 2. woven.

tex'ture (-chër) *n.* 1. look and feel of a fabric. 2. structure. —**tex'tur**al, *a.*

than, *con.* compared to.

thank, *v.* give thanks to.

thank'ful, *a.* showing thanks. —**thank'ful**ly,*adv.*

thank'less, *a.* ungrateful or unappreciated.

thanks, *n.pl.* expression of gratitude. —*int.* I thank you. —**thanks to,** 1. thanks be given to. 2. because of.

thanks'giv'ing, *n.* 1. thanks to God. 2. [T-] U.S. holiday: 4th Thursday in Nov.

that, *pron.* [*pl.* THOSE] 1. the one mentioned. 2. the farther one or other one. 3. who, whom, or which. 4. when. —*a.* being that one. —*con.* That is used to introduce certain dependent clauses. —*adv.* to that extent. —**in that,** because.

thatch, *v.* & *n.* (cover with) a roof of straw, etc.

thaw, *v.* melt or become so warm that ice melts. —*n.* period of thawing weather.

the, *a. definite article* that or this one in particular or of a certain kind. —*adv.* that much or by that much.

the'a·ter, the'a·tre, *n.* 1. place where plays, movies, etc. are shown. 2. scene of events. 3. dramatic art. —**the·at'ri·cal,** *a.*

thee (*thē*) *pron.* objective case of **thou.**

theft, *n.* act of stealing.

their, *a.* of them.

theirs, *pron.* that or those belonging to them.

the'ism (*thē'-*) *n.* belief in god(s). —**the'ist,** *n.* & *a.*

them, *pron.* objective case of **they.**

theme, *n.* 1. topic. 2. short essay. 3. main melody.

them·selves', *pron.* intensive or reflexive form of **they.**

then, *adv.* 1. at that time. 2. next. 3. in that case. 4. besides. —*n.* that time.

thence, *adv.* from that place.

thence'forth', *adv.* from that time on: also **thence'·for'ward.**

the·oc'ra·cy (*thē-*) *n.* [*pl.* -CIES] (a) government by a church.

the·ol'o·gy (*thē-*) *n.* study of God and of religious beliefs. —**the·o·lo'gi·an,** *n.* —**the·o·log'i·cal,** *a.*

the'o·rem, *n. Math.* statement (to be) proved.

the'o·ret'i·cal, *a.* based on theory, not on practice.

the'o·ry, *n.* [*pl.* -RIES] 1. explanation based on scientific study and reasoning. 2. principles of an art or science. 3. guess, conjecture, etc. —**the'o·rize,** *v.*

ther'a·peu'tic (-pū'-) *a.* serving to cure or heal.

ther'a·py, *n.* [*pl.* -PIES] method of treating disease. —**ther'a·pist,** *n.*

there, *adv.* 1. at, in, or to that place. 2. at that point. 3. in that respect. —*n.* that place.

there'a·bouts', *adv.* near that place, time, amount, etc.: also **there'a·bout.**

there·af'ter, *adv.* after that.

there·by', *adv.* by that.

there'fore, *adv.* & *con.* for this or that reason.

there·in', *adv.* in that place, matter, writing, etc.

there·of', *adv.* 1. of that. 2. from that as a cause.

there·on', *adv.* 1. on that. 2. thereupon.

there·to', *adv.* to that place, thing, etc.

there'to·fore', *adv.* up to that time.

there·up·on', *adv.* 1. just after that. 2. because of that.

there·with', *adv.* 1. with that or this. 2. just after that.

ther'mal, *a.* of heat.

ther·mom'e·ter, *n.* device for measuring temperature.

ther'mo·nu'cle·ar, *a.* of or using the heat energy released in nuclear fission.

ther'mos (bottle) container for keeping liquids at the same temperature.

ther'mo·stat, *n.* device for regulating temperature.

the·sau'rus (-sô'-) *n.* book containing lists of synonyms or related words.

these, *pron.* & *a.* pl. of **this.**

the'sis, *n.* [*pl.* -SES (-sēz)] 1. statement to be defended. 2. essay written to obtain an academic degree.

Thes'pi·an, *n.* actor.

they, *pron.* 1. the ones mentioned. 2. people.

they're (*thâr*) they are.

thi'a·mine (-min) *n.* vitamin B₁, found in liver, etc.

thick, *a.* 1. great in extent from side to side. 2. as measured from side to side. 3. dense. 4. not clear. —*n.* the most active part. —**thick'en,** *v.* —**thick'ly,** *adv.*

thick'et *a.* thick growth of shrubs or small trees.

thick'set', *a.* thick in body.

thick'-skinned', *a.* unfeeling.

thief, *n.* [pl. THIEVES] one who steals.

thieve, *v.* steal. —**thiev'er·y** [pl. -IES] *n.* —**thiev'ish**, *a.*

thigh, *n.* the leg between the knee and the hip.

thim'ble, *n.* protective cap worn on the finger in sewing.

thin, *a.* [THINNER, THINNEST] 1. small in extent from side to side. 2. lean; slender. 3. sparse. 4. watery. 5. weak. 6. transparent; flimsy. —*v.* [THINNED, THINNING] make or become thin. —**thin'ness**, *n.*

thine, *pron.* [Ar.] yours. —*a.* [Ar.] your.

thing, *n.* 1. real object or substance. 2. a happening, act, event, etc. 3. matter or affair. 4. *pl.* belongings.

think, *v.* [THOUGHT, THINKING] 1. form in or use the mind. 2. consider. 3. believe. —**think of**, 1. remember. 2. have an opinion of. 3. invent. 4. consider.

thin'-skinned', *a.* sensitive.

third, *a.* preceded by two others. —*n.* 1. third one. 2. one of three equal parts.

thirst, *n.* 1. need or craving for water. 2. strong desire. —*v.* feel thirst. —**thirst'y**, *a.*

thir'teen', *a. & n.* three more than ten. —**thir'teenth'**, *a. & n.*

thir'ty, *a. & n.* [pl. -TIES] three times ten. —**thir'ti·eth**, *a. & n.*

this, *a. & pron.* [pl. THESE] (being) the one mentioned or nearer. —*adv.* to this extent.

this'tle, *n.* prickly plant.

thith'er (thith'-) *adv.* there.

tho, tho' (thō) *con. & adv.* though.

thong, *n.* strip of leather used as a lace, strap, etc.

tho'rax, *n.* 1. chest (sense 3). 2. middle segment of an insect.

thorn, *n.* short, sharp point on a plant stem. —**thorn'y**, *a.*

thor'ough (thŭr'ō) *a.* 1. complete. 2. very exact.

thor'ough·bred, *n. & a.* (an animal) of pure breed.

thor'ough·fare, *n.* main highway.

thor'ough·go'ing, *a.* very thorough.

those, *a. & pron.* pl. of **that**.

thou, *pron.* [Ar.] you (sing. subject of *v.*).

though, *con.* 1. although.

2. yet. 3. even if. —*adv.* however.

thought, *n.* 1. act or way of thinking. 2. idea, plan, etc.

thought, *pt. & pp.* of **think**.

thought'ful, *a.* 1. full of thought. 2. considerate.

thought'less, *a.* 1. careless. 2. inconsiderate.

thou'sand, *a. & n.* ten hundred. —**thou'sandth**, *a. & n.*

thrash, *v.* 1. thresh. 2. beat. 3. toss about violently.

thread, *n.* 1. fine cord of spun cotton, silk, etc. 2. spiral ridge of a screw, etc. —*v.* 1. put a thread through a needle. 2. make one's way.

thread'bare, *a.* shabby.

threat, *n.* 1. warning of plan to harm. 2. sign of danger.

threat'en, *v.* make or be a threat.

three, *a. & n.* one more than two.

three'score', *a.* sixty.

thresh, *v.* beat out (grain) from its husk.

thresh'old, *n.* 1. sill of a door. 2. beginning point.

threw, *pt.* of **throw**.

thrice, *adv.* three times.

thrift, *n.* careful managing of money, etc. —**thrift'i·ly**, *adv.* —**thrift'less**, *a.* —**thrift'y** [-IER, -IEST] *a.*

thrill, *v. & n.* 1. (feel or make feel) great excitement.

thrive, *v.* [THROVE or THRIVED, THRIVED or THRIVEN, THRIVING] 1. be successful. 2. grow luxuriantly.

throat, *n.* 1. front of the neck. 2. upper passage from mouth to stomach or lungs.

throb, *v.* [THROBBED, THROBBING] beat or vibrate strongly. —*n.* a throbbing.

throe (thrō) *n.* pang of pain.

throm·bo'sis, *n.* a clotting in the circulatory system.

throne, *n.* 1. official chair, as of a king. 2. his power.

throng, *n. & v.* crowd.

throt'tle, *n.* valve to control fuel mixture. —*v.* choke.

through, *prep.* 1. from end to end of. 2. by way of. 3. to places in. 4. throughout. 5. by means of. 6. because of. —*adv.* 1. in and out of. 2. all the way. 3. entirely. —*a.* 1. open; free. 2. to the end without stops. 3. finished.

through·out', *adv. & prep.* in every part (of).

throw, *v.* [THREW, THROWN, THROWING] 1. send through the air from the hand. 2. make fall. 3. put suddenly.

4. move, as a switch. 5. direct, cast, etc. —n. 1. a throwing. 2. distance thrown. —**throw off,** get rid of, expel, etc. —**throw together,** assemble hastily. —**throw up,** 1. give up. 2. vomit.

throw′back, n. (a) return to an earlier type.

thru, prep., adv., a. through.

thrush, n. any of a large group of songbirds.

thrust, v. [THRUST, THRUSTING] push with sudden force. —n. 1. sudden push. 2. stab. 3. forward force.

thud, v. & n. [THUDDED, THUDDING] (hit with) a dull sound.

thug, n. rough criminal.

thumb, n. short, thick finger nearest the wrist.

thumb′nail, n. nail of the thumb. —a. brief.

thump, n. 1. a blow with a heavy, blunt thing. 2. its dull sound. —v. hit or pound with a thump.

thun′der, n. loud noise after lightning. —v. 1. cause thunder. 2. shout loudly. —**thun′der·ous,** a.

thun′der·bolt, n. flash of lightning and its thunder.

thun′der·struck, a. amazed.

Thurs′day, n. fifth day of the week.

thus, adv. 1. in this way. 2. to this or that degree. 3. therefore.

thwack, v. & n. whack.

thwart, v. block; hinder.

thy, a. [Ar.] your.

thyme (tīm) n. plant of the mint family.

thy′mus (thī′-) n. small gland in the throat.

thy′roid, a. & n. (of) a gland secreting a growth hormone.

thy·self′, pron. [Ar.] yourself.

ti·ar′a (-âr′-) n. woman's crownlike headdress.

tib′i·a, n. thicker bone of the lower leg.

tic, n. muscle spasm.

tick, n. 1. light clicking sound. 2. blood-sucking insect. —v. make a ticking sound.

tick′er, n. 1. one that ticks. 2. telegraphic device recording stock prices on paper tape.

tick′et, n. 1. printed card entitling one to a theater seat, etc. 2. tag, label, etc. 3. list of a party's candidates. —v. put a ticket on.

tick′ing, n. cloth holding a

pillow's contents.

tick′le, v. 1. stroke lightly and make twitch or laugh. 2. feel tickled. 3. amuse; delight. —n. a tickling.

tick′lish, a. 1. sensitive to tickling. 2. touchy.

tid′al, a. of, having, or caused by a tide.

tidal wave, destructive wave sent inshore as by an earthquake.

tid′bit, n. choice morsel.

tide, n. 1. rise and fall of the ocean twice a day. 2. trend. —v. help (over) a difficulty.

ti′dings, n.pl. news.

ti′dy, a. [-DIER, -DIEST] 1. neat; orderly. 2. [Col.] quite large. —v. [-DIED, -DYING] make tidy.

tie, v. [TIED, TYING] 1. fasten with string, rope, etc. 2. make (a knot). 3. bind in any way. 4. to equal, as in a score. —n. 1. thing that ties or joins. 2. necktie. 3. contest with equal scores.

tier (têr) n. any of a series of rows, one above another.

tie′-up′, n. 1. temporary stoppage, as of traffic. 2. [Col.] connection.

tiff, n. slight quarrel.

ti′ger, n. large, striped jungle cat. —**ti′gress,** n.fem.

tight, a. 1. made to keep water, air, etc. out or in. 2. fitting closely or too closely. 3. taut. 4. difficult. 5. [Col.] stingy. —adv. closely. —**tight′en,** v. —**tight′ly,** adv.

tight′rope, n. taut rope on which acrobats perform.

tights, n.pl. tight garment from the waist to the feet.

tight′wad, n. [Sl.] miser.

til′de, n. diacritical mark (~).

tile, n. thin piece of baked clay, stone, plastic, etc. for roofing, flooring, etc. —v. cover with tiles.

till, prep. & con. until. —v. cultivate land for crops. —n. drawer for money.

till′er, n. bar or handle to turn a boat's rudder.

tilt, v. & n. 1. slope; tip. 2. joust. —**at full tilt,** at full speed.

tim′ber, n. 1. wood for building houses, etc. 2. wooden beam. 3. trees.

tim·bre (tim′bĕr, tam′-) n. the distinctive sound of a voice or musical instrument.

time, n. 1. period; duration. 2. the right instant, hour, etc. 3. the passing hours, days, etc.; or, system of measuring them. 4. an occasion. 5. set period of work, or pay for this. 6. tempo or rhythm. —*v.* 1. choose a right time for. 2. measure the speed of. —*a.* 1. of time. 2. set to work at a given time. —**at times,** sometimes. —**in time,** 1. eventually. 2. before it is too late. —**on time,** 1. not late. 2. by installment payments. —**times,** multiplied by. —**tim′er,** *n.*

time′keep′er, *n.* one who records time played, as in games, or hours worked.

time′less, *a.* eternal.

time′ly, *a.* [-LIER, -LIEST] at the right time.

time′piece, *n.* clock; watch.

time′ta′ble, *n.* schedule of arrivals and departures.

tim′id, *a.* shy; easily frightened. —**ti·mid′i·ty,** *n.*

tim′or·ous, *a.* timid.

tim′o·thy, *n.* a tall grass used for fodder.

tim′pa·ni, *n.pl.* kettledrums.

tin, *n.* soft, silvery metal, a chemical element. —**tin′ny** [-NIER, -NIEST] *a.*

tinc′ture (-chēr) *n.* solution of medicine in alcohol. —*v.* tinge.

tin′der, *n.* any dry, easily ignited material.

tine, *n.* prong, as of a fork.

tin foil, thin sheet of tin.

tinge (tinj) *n.* 1. tint. 2. slight trace. —*v.* give a tinge to.

tin′gle, *n.* sting slightly; prickle. —*n.* a tingling.

tink′er, *n.* mender of pots and pans. —*v.* 1. mend clumsily. 2. to putter.

tin′kle, *n.* ring of a small bell. —*v.* make a tinkle.

tin′sel, *n.* 1. thin strips of metal foil, for decorating. 2. showy, cheap thing.

tin′smith, *n.* one who works with tin: also **tin′ner.**

tint, *n.* 1. light color. 2. a shading of a color. —*v.* give a tint to.

ti′ny, *a.* [-NIER, -NIEST] very small.

-tion, *suf.* 1. act of. 2. condition of being. 3. thing that is.

tip, *n.* 1. a point or end. 2. thing fitted to an end. 3. light blow; tap. 4. secret information. 5. warning. 6. gratuity. 7. slant. —*v.* [TIPPED, TIPPING] 1. make or put a tip on. 2. give a tip. 3. overturn. 4. slant.

tip′-off′, *n.* a tip (n. 4 & 5).

tip′pet, *n.* long scarf.

tip′ple, *v.* drink liquor.

tip′sy, *a.* [-SIER, -SIEST] 1. unsteady. 2. drunk.

tip′toe, *n.* tip of the toes. —*v.* [-TOED, -TOEING] walk stealthily on one's toes.

tip′top, *a., adv. & n.* (at) the highest point.

ti′rade, *n.* long, angry speech.

tire, *v.* 1. make or become weary, bored, etc. —*n.* hoop or rubber tube around a wheel. —**tire′less,** *a.*

tired, *a.* weary; exhausted.

tire′some, *a.* tiring.

tis·sue (tish′ōō) *n.* 1. tissue paper. 2. cellular material of organisms. 3. thin cloth.

tissue paper, thin, soft paper.

ti′tan, *n.* giant. —**ti·tan′ic,** *a.*

tit for tat, this for that.

tithe (tīth) *v. & n.* (pay) a tenth part of one's income.

ti′tian (tish′ən) *n. & a.* reddish yellow.

tit′il·late, *v.* excite pleasurably. —**tit′il·la′tion,** *n.*

ti′tle, *n.* 1. name of a book, picture, etc. 2. word showing rank or occupation. 3. legal right. 4. championship. —*v.* name.

tit′mouse, *n.* [*pl.* -MICE] small, dull-colored bird.

tit′ter, *v. & n.* giggle.

tit′tle, *n.* small bit; jot.

tit′u·lar, *a.* 1. in name only. 2. of or having a title.

to, *prep.* 1. toward. 2. as far as. 3. on, onto, or against. 4. until. 5. causing. 6. with. 7. in each. *To* may indicate an infinitive or a receiver of action. —*adv.* 1. forward. 2. shut.

toad, *n.* froglike land animal.

toad′stool, *n.* poisonous mushroom.

toad′y, *n.* [*pl.* -IES] servile flatterer. —*v.* [-IED, -YING] be a toady (to).

toast, *v.* 1. brown by heating, as bread. 2. warm. 3. drink in honor of. —*n.* 1. toasted bread. 2. a toasting.

toast′mas′ter, *n.* one who presides at a banquet.

to·bac′co, *n.* [*pl.* -COS] plant with leaves dried for smoking, chewing, etc.

to·bog′gan, *v. & n.* (coast on) a flat, runnerless sled.

toc′sin, *n.* alarm bell.

to·day′, to-day′, *adv.* 1. during this day. 2. nowadays. —*n.* this day or time.

tod'dle, v. walk unsteadily, as a child. —**tod'dler,** n.

tod'dy, n. [pl. -DIES] whisky, etc. mixed with hot water, sugar, etc.

to-do (tə-dōō') n. [Col.] a fuss.

toe, n. any of five end parts of the foot. —v. [TOED, TOE-ING] touch with the toes. —**on one's toes,** alert. —**toe'nail,** n.

tof'fee, tof'fy, n. taffy.

to'ga, n. loose garment worn in ancient Rome.

to-geth'er, adv. 1. in one group or place. 2. at the same time. 3. so as to meet, agree, etc.

togs, n.pl. [Col.] clothes.

toil, v. 1. work hard. 2. go with effort. —n. hard work.

toi'let, n. 1. fixture to receive body waste. 2. bathroom. 3. one's grooming: also **toi·lette'.**

toi'let·ry, n. [pl. -RIES] soap, cosmetics, etc.

toilet water, cologne.

toils, n.pl. snare or net.

to'ken, n. 1. sign or symbol. 2. keepsake. 3. metal disk, as for fare. —a. pretended.

told, pt. & pp. of **tell.**

tol'er·a·ble, a. 1. endurable. 2. fairly good. —**tol'er·a·bly,** adv.

tol'er·ance, n. 1. a tolerating, as of another's ways. 2. power to resist a drug's effect. 3. deviation allowed. —**tol'er·ant,** a.

tol'er·ate, v. 1. put up with; endure. 2. permit.

toll (tōl) n. 1. charge on a turnpike, for a long-distance phone call, etc. 2. the number lost, etc. —v. ring with slow, regular strokes, as a bell.

tom'a·hawk, n. light ax used by Am. Indians.

to·ma'to, n. [pl. -TOES] red, round, juicy vegetable.

tomb (tōōm) n. vault or grave for the dead.

tom'boy, n. girl who behaves like an active boy.

tomb'stone, n. stone marking a tomb or grave.

tom'cat, n. male cat.

tome (tōm) n. large book.

tom'fool'er·y, n. [pl. -IES] foolish behavior; silliness.

to·mor'row, to-mor'row, adv. & n. (on) the day after today.

tom'-tom', n. primitive drum.

ton, n. 2,000 pounds.

tone, n. 1. vocal or musical sound, spec. as to pitch. 2. style, character, feeling, etc. 3. shade or tint. 4. healthy condition, as of muscles. —**tone down,** give a less intense tone to. —**ton'al,** a.

tongs, n.pl. device for seizing, lifting, etc., made of two long, hinged arms.

tongue, n. 1. movable muscle in the mouth, used in eating and speaking. 2. act or manner of speaking. 3. language. 4. tonguelike part.

ton'ic, n. medicine, etc. that invigorates.

to·night', to-night', adv. & n. (on) this night.

ton'nage (-ij) n. 1. amount in tons of shipping, etc. 2. carrying capacity of a ship.

ton'sil, n. either of two oval masses of tissue at the back of the mouth.

ton'sil·lec'to·my, n. [pl. -MIES] surgical removal of the tonsils.

ton'sil·li'tis, n. inflammation of the tonsils.

ton'sure, n. shaven crown of a priest's or monk's head.

too, adv. 1. also. 2. more than enough. 3. very.

took, pt. of **take.**

tool, n. 1. instrument, implement, etc. used for some work. 2. stooge. —v. shape or work with a tool.

tooth, n. [pl. TEETH] 1. any of a set of bony structures in the jaws, used for biting and chewing. 2. toothlike part, as of a saw, gear, etc. —**tooth and nail,** with all one's strength. —**tooth'-ache,** n. —**tooth'brush,** n.

tooth'pick, n. pointed stick for picking food from between the teeth.

tooth'some, a. tasty.

top, n. 1. highest point or surface. 2. uppermost part or covering. 3. highest degree or rank. 4. toy that spins round. —a. of, at, or being the top. —v. [TOPPED, TOPPING] 1. provide with a top. 2. be at the top of. 3. surpass; exceed. —**on top of,** 1. resting upon. 2. besides. —**top off,** complete.

to'paz, n. yellow gem.

top'coat, n. light overcoat.

top hat, man's tall, black hat.

top'-heav'y, a. too heavy at the top and, thus, unstable.

top'ic, *n.* subject of an essay, speech, etc.

top'i·cal, *a.* of current or local interest.

top'mast, *n.* second mast above the deck of a ship.

top'most, *a.* uppermost.

top'-notch', *a.* [Col.] first-rate.

to·pog'ra·phy, *n.* 1. surface features of a region. 2. science of showing these, as on maps. —**top'o·graph'i·cal, top'o·graph'ic,** *a.*

top'ple, *v.* (make) fall over.

top'sail, *n.* sail next above the lowest sail on a mast.

top'soil, *n.* upper layer of soil, usually richer.

top'sy-tur'vy, *adv. & a.* 1. upside down. 2. in disorder.

to'rah (tō'rə) *n.* Jewish scriptures; spec. [T-] first 5 books of the Bible.

torch, *n.* 1. portable flaming light. 2. device that makes a very hot flame, as in welding. —**torch'light,** *n.*

tore, *pt.* of **tear** (pull apart).

tor'e·a·dor', *n.* bullfighter.

tor'ment, *n.* great pain. —*v.* (tôr·ment') make suffer. —**tor·men'tor,** *n.*

torn, *pp.* of **tear** (pull apart).

tor·na'do, *n.* [*pl.* -DOES] violent wind with a whirling, funnel-shaped cloud.

tor·pe'do, *n.* [*pl.* -DOES] large, cigar-shaped, underwater projectile. —*v.* [-DOED, -DOING] destroy or ruin.

tor'pid, *a.* dull; sluggish. —**tor'por,** *n.*

torque (tôrk) *n.* force that gives a twisting motion.

tor'rent, *n.* swift, violent stream. —**tor·ren'tial** (-shəl) *a.*

tor'rid, *a.* very hot.

tor'sion, *n.* a twisting or being twisted.

tor'so, *n.* [*pl.* -SOS] human body minus head and limbs.

tor·til'la (-tē'yä) *n.* flat, unleavened corn cake.

tor'toise (-təs) *n.* turtle, esp. one living on land.

tor'tu·ous (-chōō-) *a.* full of twists and turns.

tor'ture (-chēr) *n.* 1. inflicting of great pain. 2. great pain. —*v.* 1. subject to torture. 2. twist.

To'ry, *n.* [*pl.* -RIES] 1. Br. loyalist in Am. Revolution. 2. [often t-] a conservative.

toss, *v.* [TOSSED, TOSSING] 1. throw lightly from the hand. 2. fling or be flung about. 3. jerk upward. —*n.* a tossing.

toss'up, *n.* 1. flipping of a coin to decide. 2. even chance.

tot, *n.* young child.

to'tal, *n.* the whole amount; sum. —*a.* 1. entire; whole. 2. complete. —*v.* add (up to). —**to·tal'i·ty,** *n.* —**to'tal·ly,** *adv.*

to·tal'i·tar'i·an, *a.* of a dictatorship.

tote, *v.* [Col.] carry; haul.

to'tem pole, pole with the animal symbol of an Am. Indian tribe.

tot'ter, *v.* 1. rock as if about to fall. 2. stagger.

tou'can (tōō'-) *n.* tropical bird with a large beak.

touch, *v.* 1. put the hand, etc. on so as to feel. 2. bring or come into contact. 3. tap lightly. 4. handle; use. 5. concern. 6. arouse pity, etc. —*n.* 1. a touching. 2. way things feel. 3. sense of this. 4 small bit. —**in touch,** in contact. —**touch on,** mention. —**touch up,** improve by additions.

touch'down', *n.* goal scored in football, for 6 points.

touch'stone, *n.* criterion.

touch'y, *a.* [-IER, -IEST] 1. irritable. 2. difficult.

tough, *a.* 1. hard to chew, cut, break, etc. 2. strong or rough. 3. very difficult. —*n.* ruffian. —**tough'en,** *v.*

tou·pee (tōō-pā') *n.* small wig for a bald spot.

tour, *n.* long trip, as to see sights, put on plays, etc. —*v.* go on a tour (through). —**tour'ist,** *n. & a.*

tour'na·ment, *n.* 1. series of contests for a championship. 2. knights' jousting contest.

tour'ney, *n.* [*pl.* -NEYS] tournament.

tour'ni·quet (-ket) *n.* device for compressing a blood vessel to stop bleeding.

tou·sle (tou'z'l) *v.* muss.

tout (tout) *v.* 1. [Col.] praise highly. 2. [Sl.] sell tips on (race horses). —*n.* one who touts.

tow, *v.* pull by a rope or chain. —*n.* a towing.

toward (tôrd) *prep.* 1. in the direction of. 2. concerning. 3. near. 4. for. Also **towards.**

tow'el, *n.* piece of cloth or paper to wipe things dry.

tow'er, *n.* high structure, often part of another building. —*v.* rise high.

tow′head, (tō′-) *n.* person with light yellow hair.

town, *n.* 1. small city. 2. business center. —**towns′-peo′ple, towns′folk**, *n.pl.*

town′ship, *n.* 1. part of a county. 2. U.S. land unit 6 miles square.

tox′ic, *a.* 1. of or caused by a toxin. 2. poisonous.

tox′in, *n.* poison, esp. from bacteria, viruses, etc.

toy, *n.* thing to play with.— *a.* small. —*v.* play (with).

trace, *n.* 1. mark or track left. 2. small bit. 3. harness strap connecting to vehicle. —*v.* 1. follow (the trail or course of). 2. draw, outline, etc. —**trac′er**, *n.*

trac′er·y, *n.* [pl. -IES] design of interlacing lines.

tra·che·a (trā′kē-ə) *n.* air passage from the larynx to the bronchial tubes.

track, *n.* 1. footprint, wheel rut, etc. 2. path, trail, or course. 3. running sports, etc. 4. pair of rails a train runs on. —*v.* 1. follow the track of. 2. leave footprints on. —**keep (or lose) track of**, keep (or fail to keep) informed about.

tract, *n.* 1. large stretch of land. 2. system of bodily organs. 3. booklet.

trac′ta·ble, *a.* manageable.

trac′tion, *n.* 1. power to grip a surface. 2. a pulling.

trac′tor, *n.* 1. motor vehicle to pull farm machines, etc. 2. truck to haul a trailer.

trade, *n.* 1. skilled work. 2. buying and selling. 3. an exchange. —*v.* 1. buy and sell. 2. exchange.

trade′-in, *n.* thing used as part payment.

trade′mark, trade′-mark, *n.* special mark or name (**trade name**) put on a product.

trades′man, *n.* [pl. -MEN] storekeeper.

trade union, labor union.

trade wind, wind that blows toward the equator.

tra·di′tion, *n.* 1. custom, etc. handed down from the past. 2. such handing down. —**tra·di′tion·al**, *a.*

tra·duce′ *v.* to slander.

traf′fic, *n.* 1. vehicles moving along streets, etc. 2. amount of business done. 3. trade (*n.* 2). —*v.* [-FICKED, -FICKING] do business, esp. illicitly.

tra·ge′di·an, *n.* actor of

tragedy. —**tra·ge′di·enne′**, *n.fem.*

trag′e·dy, *n.* [pl. -DIES] 1. serious play with a sad ending. 2. tragic event.

trag′ic, *a.* 1. of or like tragedy. 2. very sad. —**trag′i·cal·ly**, *adv.*

trail, *v.* 1. drag or lag behind. 2. follow or drift behind. 3. dwindle. —*n.* 1. thing trailing behind. 2. beaten path.

trail′er, *n.* wagon or van pulled by a car or truck, sometimes used as a home.

train, *n.* 1. thing that drags behind. 2. procession. 3. connected series. 4. locomotive with cars. —*v.* 1. guide the development of. 2. instruct or prepare. 3. aim. —**train·ee′**, *n.*

trait, *n.* characteristic.

trai′tor, *n.* disloyal person. —**trai′tor·ous**, *a.*

tra·jec′to·ry, *n.* [pl. -RIES] curved path of a missile.

tram′mel, *n. & v.* (thing) to hinder or restrain.

tramp, *v.* 1. walk, or step, heavily. 2. roam about. —*n.* 1. vagrant. 2. a tramping.

tram′ple, *v.* step hard on or crush underfoot.

trance, *n.* state of shock, hypnosis, or deep thought.

tran′quil, *a.* calm; quiet. —**tran·quil′i·ty, tran·quil′i·ty**, *n.*

tran′quil·ize, tran′-quil·lize, *v.* make tranquil. —**tran′quil·iz·er, tran′-quil·liz·er**, *n.*

trans-, *pref.* over, across, beyond.

trans·act′, *v.* do; complete. —**trans·ac′tion**, *n.*

trans·cend′ (-send′) *v.* exceed. —**trans·cend′ent**, *a.*

tran·scen·den′tal, *a.* 1. transcendent. 2. supernatural.

tran·scribe′, *v.* 1. write or type out. 2. record for rebroadcast. —**tran·scrip′-tion**, *n.*

tran′script, *n.* written or typewritten copy.

tran′sept, *n.* shorter part of a cross-shaped church.

trans·fer′, *v.* [-FERRED, -FER-RING] move or change from one person, place, etc. to another. —*n.* a transferring. —**trans·fer′a·ble**, *a.* —**trans·fer′ence**, *n.*

trans·fig′ure, *v.* 1. transform. 2. make seem glorious. —**trans·fig′u·ra′tion**, *n.*

trans·fix', v. pierce through.

trans·form', v. change the form or condition of. —**trans'for·ma'tion**, n.

trans·form'er, n. device that changes voltage.

trans·fuse', v. 1. imbue; fill. 2. transfer blood to another. —**trans·fu'sion**, n.

trans·gress', v. 1. break a law; do wrong. 2. go beyond. —**trans·gres'sion**, n. —**trans·gres'sor**, n.

tran'sient (-shant) a. temporary. —n. one who stays only a short time.

tran·sis'tor, n. device used like an electron tube.

tran'sit, n. 1. passage across. 2. a conveying.

tran·si'tion, n. a passing from one condition, place, etc. to another.

tran'si·tive, a. taking a direct object, as some verbs.

tran'si·to'ry, a. temporary.

trans·late', v. put into another language, form, etc. —**trans·la'tion**, n. —**trans·la'tor**, n.

trans·lu'cent, a. letting a little light pass through.

trans·mis'sion, n. 1. a transmitting. 2. car part sending power to wheels.

trans·mit', v. [-MITTED, -MITTING] 1. transfer. 2. pass or convey. 3. send out radio or TV signals. —**trans·mit'ter**, n.

tran'som, n. small window above a door or window.

trans·par'ent, a. that can be seen through; clear.

trans·pire', v. 1. become known. 2. happen.

trans·plant', v. 1. dig up and plant in another place.

trans·port', v. 1. carry from one place to another. 2. carry away with emotion. —n. (trans'pôrt) thing for transporting. —**trans'por·ta'tion**, n.

trans·pose', v. 1. to interchange. 2. Mus. change the key of.

trans·verse', a. situated, placed, etc. across.

trap, n. 1. device for catching animals. 2. tricky ruse. 3. bend in a drainpipe. —v. [TRAPPED, TRAPPING] 1. catch in a trap. 2. set traps for animals. —**trap'per**, n.

trap door, door in a roof or floor.

tra·peze', n. swinglike bar for acrobats.

trap'e·zoid, n. figure with

two of four sides parallel.

trap'pings, n.pl. adornments.

trash, n. rubbish. —**trash'y** [-IER, -IEST] a.

trau'ma (trô'-) n. emotional shock with lasting psychic effects. —**trau·mat'ic**, a.

trav·ail' (or trə-vāl') n. 1. labor. 2. agony.

trav'el, v. 1. make a journey (through). 2. move or pass. —n. 1. a traveling. 2. pl. journeys. —**trav'el·er**, n.

trav'e·logue, trav'e·log (-lôg) n. illustrated lecture or movie of travels.

trav·erse' (or trə-vûrs') v. to cross. —a. of drapes drawn by pulling cords.

trav·es·ty, n. [pl. -TIES] farcical imitation. —v. [-TIED, -TYING] make a travesty of.

trawl (trôl) v. & n. (fish with) a large dragnet. —**trawl'er**, n.

tray, n. flat, low-sided server to carry things.

treach'er·ous (trech'-) a. 1. disloyal. 2. not safe or reliable. —**treach'er·y**, n.

tread (tred) v. [TROD, TRODDEN or TROD, TREADING] 1. walk on, along, over, etc. 2. trample. —n. 1. way or sound of treading. 2. part for treading or moving on.

trea'dle (tred'-) n. foot pedal to operate a wheel, etc.

tread'mill, n. device worked by treading an endless belt.

trea'son (trē'z'n) n. betrayal of one's country. —**trea'son·a·ble, trea'son·ous**, a.

treas'ure, n. 1. accumulated money, jewels, etc. 2. valued person or thing. —v. 1. save up. 2. cherish.

treas'ur·y, n. [pl. -IES] 1. place where money is kept. 2. funds of a state, corporation, etc. —**treas'ur·er**, n.

treat, v. 1. deal with or act toward. 2. pay for the food, etc. of. 3. subject to a process, medical care, etc. —n. 1. food, etc. paid for by another. 2. thing giving pleasure. —**treat'ment**, n.

trea·tise (trē'tis) n. a formal writing on a subject.

trea'ty, n. [pl. -TIES] agreement between nations.

tre'ble (treb'-) a. 1. triple. 2. of or for the treble. —n. 1. Mus. highest part. 2. high-pitched voice or sound. —v. to triple.

tree, n. large, woody plant with one main trunk and

many branches. —v. [TREED, TREEING] chase up a tree.

tre'foil, n. 1. plant with three-part leaves. 2. design like a leaf.

trek, v. [TREKKED, TREKKING] & n. (make) a slow, hard journey.

trel'lis, n. lattice on which vines, etc. are grown.

trem'ble, v. 1. shake from cold, fear, etc. 2. quiver or vibrate. —n. act or fit of trembling.

tre·men'dous, a. [Col.] 1. very large. 2. wonderful.

trem'or, n. a trembling, shaking, etc.

trem'u·lous, a. trembling.

trench, n. ditch, esp. one dug for cover in battle.

trench'ant, a. incisive.

trend, n. & v. (have) a general direction or tendency.

trep'i·da'tion, n. fear.

tres'pass, v. 1. enter another's property unlawfully. 2. sin. —n. a trespassing. —**tres'pass·er,** n.

tress, n. lock of hair.

tres'tle, n. 1. framework support, as for a bridge. 2. sawhorse.

trey (trā) n. playing card with three spots.

tri-, pref. three.

tri'ad, n. group of three.

tri'al, n. 1. hearing and deciding of a case in a law court. 2. attempt. 3. test. 4. pain, trouble, etc.

tri'an·gle, n. three-sided figure with three angles. — **tri·an'gu·lar,** a.

tribe, n. 1. group of people living together under a chief. 2. group or class. —**trib'al,** a. —**tribes'man,** n.

trib·u·la'tion, n. great misery or distress.

tri·bu'nal, n. law court.

trib'une, n. public defender.

trib'u·tar'y, n. [pl. -IES] river that flows into a larger one.

trib'ute, n. 1. forced payment, as by a weak nation to a stronger. 2. gift, speech, etc. showing respect.

trick, n. 1. something done to fool, cheat, etc. 2. prank. 3. clever act or skillful way. 4. turn at work. 5. personal habit. 6. cards played in one round. —v. fool or cheat. —**trick'er·y,** n.

trick'le, v. 1. flow in drops or a thin stream. 2. move slowly. —n. slow flow.

trick'y, a. [-IER, -IEST] 1.

deceitful. 2. difficult.

tri'col'or, n. flag having three colors.

tri'cy·cle (-si-k'l) n. three-wheeled vehicle.

tri'dent, n. three-pronged spear.

tried, pt. & pp. of **try.** —a. tested or trustworthy.

tri'fle, n. 1. thing of little value. 2. small amount. —v. 1. act jokingly. 2. play.

tri'fling, a. unimportant.

trig'ger, n. lever pressed in firing a gun.

trig·o·nom'e·try, n. mathematics dealing with relations between sides and angles of triangles. —**trig·o·no·met'ric,** a.

trill, n. (sing or play with) a rapid alternation of two close notes.

tril'lion, n. thousand billions. —**tril'lionth,** a. & n.

tril'o·gy (-ji) n. [pl. -GIES] set of three plays, etc.

trim, v. [TRIMMED, TRIMMING] 1. clip, lop, etc. 2. decorate. 3. put (sails) in order. —n. 1. good condition. 2. decoration. —a. [TRIMMER, TRIMMEST] 1. orderly; neat. 2. in good condition. — **trim'mer,** n.

trim'ming, n. 1. decoration. 2. pl. parts trimmed off.

Trin'i·ty, n. Father, Son, and Holy Ghost as one God.

trin'ket, n. small ornament.

tri'o (trē'ō) n. [pl. -OS] musical composition for three performers.

trip, v. [TRIPPED, TRIPPING] 1. move with light, rapid steps. 2. stumble or make stumble. 3. err or cause to err. —n. a journey.

tri·par'tite (trī-) a. 1. having three parts. 2. between three parties, as a treaty.

tripe, n. stomach of a cow, etc. used as food.

tri'ple, a. 1. of or for three. 2. three times as much or as many. —n. Baseball hit putting the batter on third. —v. make or become triple. — **tri'ply,** adv.

tri'plet, n. any of three children born at one birth.

trip'li·cate (-kit) a. triple. —n. one of three exact copies.

tri'pod, n. three-legged stool, support, etc.

trite, a. worn-out; stale.

tri'umph, n. victory; success. —v. gain victory or success. —**tri·um'phal,** a. —**tri·um'phant,** a.

tri·um'vi·rate (-rit) n. government by three men.

triv'et, n. three-legged stand for holding pots.

triv'i·a, n.pl. trifles.

triv'i·al, a. unimportant. —**triv·i·al'i·ty** [pl. -TIES] n.

tro'che (-ki) n. small medicinal lozenge.

trog·lo·dyte (trog'lə-dīt) n. 1. cave dweller. 2. hermit.

troll (trōl) v. 1. fish with a moving line. 2. sing loudly. —n. Folklore cave-dwelling giant.

trol'ley, n. [pl. -LEYS] 1. overhead device that sends electric current to a streetcar. 2. electric streetcar. also **trolley car.**

trol'lop, n. 1. slattern. 2. prostitute.

trom'bone, n. brass-wind instrument with a sliding tube.

troop, n. 1. group of persons. 2. pl. soldiers. 3. cavalry unit. —v. move in a group.

troop'er, n. 1. cavalryman. 2. mounted policeman.

tro'phy, n. [pl. -PHIES] souvenir of victory, etc.

trop'ic, n. 1. either of two parallels of latitude (**Tropic of Cancer** and **Tropic of Capricorn**) N. & S. of the equator. 2. [also T-] pl. hot region between these latitudes. —**trop'i·cal,** a.

trot, v. [TROTTED, TROTTING] go at a trot. —n. 1. running gait of a horse. 2. slow, jogging run. —**trot'ter,** n.

troth, n. [Ar.] 1. promise, esp. to marry. 2. truth.

trou·ba·dour (trōō'bə-dôr) n. medieval lyric poet.

trou'ble, n. 1. worry, distress, bother, etc. 2. disturbance. 3. difficulty. —v. be or give trouble to. —**trou'ble·some,** a.

trough (trôf) n. 1. long, narrow, open container, as for feeding animals. 2. long, narrow hollow.

trounce, v. beat; flog.

troupe (trōōp) n. troop of actors, etc. —**troup'er,** n.

trou'sers, n.pl. man's two-legged outer garment.

trous·seau (trōō'sō) n. [pl. -SEAUS, -SEAUX (-sōz)] bride's outfit of clothes, linen, etc.

trout, n. fresh-water food fish of the salmon family.

trow'el (trou'-) n. 1. flat tool for smoothing. 2. scooplike tool for digging.

troy (weight), system of weights for gold, silver, etc.

in which 12 ozs. = 1 lb.

tru'ant, n. 1. pupil who stays away from school without leave. 2. one who shirks his duties. —**tru'an·cy,** n.

truce, n. cessation of fighting by mutual agreement.

truck, n. 1. large motor vehicle for carrying loads. 2. wheeled frame. 3. vegetables raised for market. 4. [Col.] dealings. —v. carry on a truck. —**truck'er,** n.

truck'le, v. be servile.

truc'u·lent, a. fierce. —**truc'u·lence,** n.

trudge, v. walk wearily.

true, a. 1. loyal. 2. not false. 3. accurate. 4. lawful. 5. real; genuine. —adv. exactly. —n. that which is true. —**tru'ly,** adv.

tru'ism, n. an obvious truth.

trump, n. (playing card of) a suit ranked highest. —v. take with a trump. —**trump up,** devise deceitfully.

trump'er·y, n. [pl. -IES] showy but worthless thing.

trum'pet, n. brass-wind instrument with a flared end. —v. proclaim loudly.

trun'cate, v. cut off a part. —**trun·ca'tion,** n.

trun'dle, v. roll along.

trundle bed, low bed on small wheels.

trunk, n. 1. main stem of a tree. 2. body, not including the head and limbs. 3. long snout of an elephant. 4. large box for clothes, etc. 5. main line. 6. pl. very short pants worn for sports.

truss, v. tie, fasten, or tighten. —n. supporting framework or device.

trust, n. 1. belief in the honesty, reliability, etc. of another. 2. one trusted. 3. responsibility. 4. custody. 5. credit (n. 4). 6. property managed for another. 7. monopolistic group of corporations. —v. 1. have trust in. 2. put in the care of. 3. believe. 4. hope. 5. let buy on credit. —**trust'ful,** a. —**trust'wor·thy,** a.

trus·tee', n. 1. one put in charge of another's property. 2. member of a controlling board. —**trus·tee'ship,** n.

trust'y, a. [-IER, -IEST] dependable. —n. [pl. -IES] a convict with privileges.

truth, n. 1. a being true, honest, etc. 2. that which is true. 3. established fact. —**truth'ful,** a.

try, v. [TRIED, TRYING] 1. conduct the trial of. 2. test. 3. afflict. 4. attempt. —n. [pl. TRIES] attempt; effort.

try'ing, a. hard to bear.

try'out, n. test of fitness.

tryst (trist) n. appointment to meet made by lovers.

T'-shirt, n. short-sleeved, pull-over undershirt.

T square, T-shaped ruler.

tub, n. 1. large, open container. 2. bathtub.

tu'ba, n. large, deep-toned brass-wind instrument.

tube, n. 1. slender pipe for fluids. 2. tubelike, sealed container. 3. electron tube. —tu'bu·lar, a.

tu'ber, n. thickened part of an underground stem. —tu'ber·ous, a.

tu'ber·cle, n. 1. small, round projection. 2. hard growth.

tu·ber·cu·lo'sis, n. wasting disease, esp. of the lungs. —tu·ber'cu·lous, tu·ber'cu·lar, a.

tube'rose, n. flower with a bulblike root.

tuck, v. 1. gather up in folds. 2. push the edges of something under. 3. cover snugly. 4. press into a small space. —n. sewed fold.

tuck'er, v. [Col.] tire (out).

-tude, suf. like -ness.

Tues'day, n. third day of the week.

tuft, n. bunch of hairs, grass, etc. growing or tied together. —v. form in tufts.

tug, v. [TUGGED, TUGGING] pull; drag. —n. 1. hard pull. 2. tugboat.

tug'boat, n. small boat for towing or pushing ships.

tug of war, contest with two teams pulling at a rope.

tu·i'tion (-i'-) n. charge for instruction.

tu'lip, n. bulb plant with cup-shaped flower.

tulle (tool) n. fine netting for veils, etc., made of silk, etc.

tum'ble, v. 1. fall or move suddenly or clumsily. 2. toss about. 3. do acrobatics. —n. 1. a fall. 2. disorder.

tum'ble-down, a. dilapidated.

tum'bler, n. 1. drinking glass. 2. acrobat. 3. part of a lock moved by a key.

tu'mid, a. 1. swollen; bulging. 2. inflated; pompous.

tum'my, n. [pl. -MIES] stomach: child's word.

tu'mor, n. abnormal growth in or on the body.

tu'mult, n. 1. uproar. 2. confusion. —tu·mul'tu·ous (-chōō-əs) a.

tun, n. large cask.

tu'na (fish), large ocean fish with oily flesh.

tun'dra, n. large arctic plain without trees.

tune, n. 1. melody. 2 Mus. right pitch. 3. agreement. —v. put in tune (n. 2).

tune in (on), set a radio for a station. —tun'er, n.

tune'ful, a. full of melody.

tung'sten, n. hard metal in alloys, a chemical element.

tu'nic, n. 1. loose gown worn in ancient Greece and Rome. 2. long, belted blouse.

tun'nel, n. underground passageway. —v. make a tunnel.

tun'ny, n. [pl. -NIES] tuna.

tur'ban, n. Moslem headdress, a scarf wound round the head.

tur'bid, a. 1. muddy or cloudy. 2. confused.

tur'bine (-bin or -bīn) n. engine driven by the pressure of air, steam, or water on the vanes of a wheel.

tur'bo·jet, n. airplane engine with a jet-driven turbine to work the air compressor.

tur'bo·prop, n. airplane engine with a jet-driven turbine to drive the propeller.

tur'bu·lent, a. 1. disorderly. 2. agitated. —tur'bu·lence, n.

tu·reen', n. large, deep dish with a lid, for soup, etc.

turf, n. top layer of earth with grass. —the turf, (track for) horse racing.

tur'gid (-jid) a. 1. swollen. 2. pompous. —tur·gid'i·ty, n.

Turk, n. native of Turkey.

tur'key, n. 1. large bird with a spreading tail. 2. its flesh, used as food.

Turk'ish, n. & a. (language) of Turkey.

tur'moil, n. noisy, excited condition.

turn, v. 1. revolve or rotate. 2. change in position or direction. 3. make or perform. 4. reverse. 5. change in feelings, etc. 6. change in form, etc. 7. drive, set, etc. 8. upset. 9. depend. 10. reach or pass. —n. 1. a turning around. 2. change in position or direction. 3. short walk, ride, etc. 4. bend; twist. 5. chance; try. 6. deed. 7. turning point.

8. style; form. 9. [Col.] shock. **—in** (or **out of**) **turn**, in (or not in) proper order. **—turn down**, reject. **—turn in**, 1. hand in. 2. [Col.] go to bed. **—turn off**, shut off. **—turn on**, make go on. **—turn out**, 1. shut off. 2. come. 3. make. 4. result. **—turn to**, rely on.

turn'a·bout, n. reversal.

turn'buck'le, n. metal loop used as a coupling.

turn'coat, n. traitor.

tur'nip, n. plant with an edible, round root.

turn'key, n. [pl. -KEYS] jailer.

turn'out, **turn'-out**, n. gathering of people.

turn'o'ver, n. 1. small pie with crust folded over. 2. rate of replacement of workers, goods, etc.

turn'pike, n. highway, esp. one on which a toll is paid.

turn'stile, n. gate admitting only one at a time.

turn'ta'ble, n. round, revolving platform.

tur'pen·tine, n. oil from trees, used in paints, etc.

tur'pi·tude, n. vileness.

tur'quoise (-koiz, -kwoiz) n. greenish-blue gem.

tur'ret, n. 1. small tower on a building. 2. armored dome, as on a tank. 3. lathe part holding cutting tools.

tur'tle, n. hard-shelled land and water reptile.

tur'tle·dove, n. wild dove.

turtle neck, high, snug, turned-down collar.

tusk, n. long, projecting tooth, as of an elephant.

tus'sle, n. & v. struggle.

tu'te·lage (-lij) n. 1. instruction. 2. protection.

tu'tor, n. private teacher. — v. teach. **—tu·to'ri·al**, a.

tut·ti-frut'ti (tōō'ti-frōō'ti) n. & a. (ice cream, etc.) made with mixed fruits.

tux·e'do, n. [pl. -DOS] man's semiformal suit.

TV, television.

twad'dle, n. nonsense.

twain, n. & a. [Poet.] two.

twang, n. 1. sharp, vibrating sound. 2. nasal sound. —v. make, or utter with, a twang. 'twas, it was.

tweak, v. & n. (give) a sudden, twisting pinch.

tweed, n. 1. rough wool fabric. 2. pl. clothes of tweed.

tweet, v. & n. chirp.

tweez'ers, n.pl. small pincers for plucking hairs.

twelve, a. & n. two more

than ten. **—twelfth**, a. & n.

twen'ty, a. & n. [pl. -TIES] two times ten. **—twen'ti·eth**, a. & n.

twice, adv. 1. two times. 2. two times as much.

twid'dle, v. twirl idly.

twig, n. small branch.

twi'light, n. dim light after sunset.

twill, n. cloth woven with parallel diagonal lines.

twin, n. 1. either of two born at the same time. 2. either of two very much alike. —a. being a twin or twins.

twine, n. strong cord made of twisted strands. —v. 1. interweave. 2. wind around.

twinge (twinj) v. & n. (have) a sudden pain or a qualm.

twin'kle, v. 1. sparkle. 2. light up. —n. a twinkling.

twirl, v. & n. spin; twist.

twist, v. 1. wind together or around something. 2. force out of shape. 3. pervert meaning of. 4. sprain. 5. rotate. 6. curve. —n. 1. something twisted. 2. a twisting.

twit, v. [TWITTED, TWITTING] & n. taunt; tease.

twitch, v. pull or move with a sudden jerk. —n. sudden, spasmodic motion.

twit'ter, v. 1. chirp rapidly. 2. tremble excitedly. —n. a twittering.

two, a. & n. one more than one. **—in two**, in two parts.

two'-faced', a. deceitful.

two'fold, a. 1. having two parts. 2. having twice as much or as many. —adv. twice as much or as many.

two'some, n. couple.

two'-way', a. allowing passage in two directions.

-ty, suf. quality or condition of.

ty·coon' (tī-) n. [Col.] powerful industrialist.

ty'ing, ppr. of tie.

tyke (tīk) n. [Col.] small child.

tym·pan'ic membrane (tim-) eardrum.

tym'pa·num, n. 1. cavity beyond eardrum. 2. drum.

type, n. 1. kind or sort. 2. model; example. 3. metal piece or pieces for printing. 4. printed letters, etc. —v. 1. classify. 2. typewrite.

type'write, v. write with a typewriter.

type'writ'er, n. keyboard machine for making printed letters on paper.

ty'phoid, n. infectious disease with intestinal disorders: also **typhoid fever.**

ty·phoon' (tī-) n. cyclonic storm, esp. in the W Pacific.

ty'phus, n. infectious disease with fever, skin rash, etc.: also **typhus fever.**

typ'i·cal (tip'-) a. 1. being a true example of its kind. 2. characteristic. —**typ'i·cal·ly,** adv.

typ'i·fy, v. [-FIED, -FYING] be typical of; exemplify.

typ'ist, n. one who operates a typewriter.

ty·pog'ra·phy, n. 1. setting of, and printing with, type. 2. style, design, etc. of matter printed from type. —**ty·pog'ra·pher,** n. —**ty'po·graph'i·cal,** a.

tyr·an'ny (tir'-) n. 1. government of a tyrant. 2. cruel and unjust use of power. —**ty·ran'ni·cal,** a. —**tyr'an·nize,** v.

ty'rant (tī'-) n. 1. absolute ruler. 2. cruel, unjust ruler.

ty'ro, n. [pl. -ROS] novice.

U

u·biq'ui·tous (ū-bik'wə-) a. everywhere at the same time. —**u·biq'ui·ty,** n.

ud'der, n. large, milk-secreting gland of cows, etc.

ugh, int. exclamation of disgust, horror, etc.

ug'ly, a. [-LIER, -LIEST] 1. unpleasant to see. 2. bad. 3. dangerous. —**ug'li·ness,** n.

u'ku·le'le (-lā'li) n. small guitar.

ul'cer, n. open sore, as on the skin. —**ul'cer·ate,** v. —**ul'cer·ous,** a.

ul·te'ri·or, a. beyond what is expressed.

ul'ti·mate (-mit) a. 1. farthest. 2. final. 3. basic. —n. final point or result. —**ul'ti·mate·ly,** adv.

ul·ti·ma'tum, n. final offer or demand.

ul'tra-, pref. 1. beyond. 2. extremely.

ul'tra·vi'o·let, a. of the invisible rays just beyond the violet end of the spectrum.

um'ber, n. reddish brown.

um·bil'i·cal cord, cord connecting a fetus with the placenta.

um'brage (-brij) n. resentment and displeasure.

um·brel'la, n. cloth screen on a folding frame, carried for protection against rain.

um'pire, n. 1. one who judges

a dispute. 2. an official in certain sports. —v. act as umpire.

UN, U.N., United Nations.

un-, pref. 1. not. 2. reversing action. See list below.

un·a'ble
un·a·fraid'
un·aid'ed
un·au'thor·ized
un'a·void'a·ble
un·bear'a·ble
un·be·liev'a·ble
un·bi'ased
un·bro'ken
un·but'ton
un·changed'
un·com'fort·a·ble
un·con·trol'la·ble
un·de·served'
un·de·sir'a·ble
un'de·vel'oped
un'dis·cov'ered
un·earned'
un·em·ployed'
un'em·ploy'ment
un·e'ven
un'ex·plained'
un'ex·plored'
un·fair'
un·fas'ten
un·fa'vor·a·ble
un·fit'
un'fore·seen'
un·for'tu·nate
un·friend'ly
un·gra'cious
un·harmed'
un·heed'ed
un·hurt'
un·im·por'tant
un'in·hab'it·ed
un·in'jured
un'in·ter·est·ing
un'in·vit'ed
un·just'
un·kind'
un·lace'
un·like'ly
un·man'ly
un·mar'ried
un·named'
un·nec'es·sar'y
un·no'ticed
un·of·fi'cial
un·o'pened
un·or'gan·ized
un·paid'
un·pop'u·lar
un'pre·pared'
un'pro·tect'ed
un·qual'i·fied
un·re·li'a·ble
un·ripe'
un'sat·is·fac'to·ry
un·self'ish
un·sight'ly
un·skilled'
un·sound'
un·spoiled'

un·suit'a·ble
un·ti'dy
un·tir'ing
un·tried'
un·trou'bled
un·true'
un·war'y
un·war'rant·ed
un·whole'some
un·will'ing
un·wise'
un·wor'thy
un·wrap'
un·yield'ing

un'ac·count'a·ble, *a.* 1. inexplicable. 2. not responsible.

un'ac·cus'tomed, *a.* 1. not accustomed (*to*). 2. unusual.

u·nan'i·mous, *a.* without dissent. —**u'na·nim'i·ty,** *n.* —**u·nan'i·mous·ly,** *adv.*

un'ap·proach'a·ble, *a.* 1. aloof. 2. without equal.

un·armed', *a.* having no weapon.

un'as·sum'ing, *a.* modest.

un·at·tached', *a.* 1. not attached. 2. not engaged or married.

un·a·ware', *a.* not aware. —*adv.* unawares.

un·a·wares', *adv.* 1. unintentionally. 2. by surprise.

un·bal'anced, *a.* 1. not in balance. 2. mentally ill.

un·be·com'ing, *a.* 1. not suited. 2. not proper.

un·be·lief', *n.* lack of belief, esp. in religion. —**un·be·liev'er,** *n.*

un·bend', *v.* [-BENT or -BENDED, -BENDING] 1. relax. 2. straighten.

un·bend'ing, *a.* 1. rigid; stiff. 2. firm; unyielding.

un·born', *a.* 1. not born. 2. not yet born; future.

un·bos'om, *v.* tell (secrets).

un·bri'dled, *a.* 1. with no bridle on. 2. uncontrolled.

un·called'-for', *a.* unnecessary and out of place.

un·can'ny, *a.* 1. weird. 2. unusually good, acute, etc.

un·cer'tain, *a.* 1. not sure or certain. 2. vague. 3. not steady or constant. —**un·cer'tain·ty** [*pl.* -TIES] *n.*

un'cle, *n.* 1. brother of one's father or mother. 2. husband of one's aunt.

un·com'mon, *a.* 1. not usual. 2. extraordinary.

un'com·pro·mis'ing, *a.* unyielding; firm.

un·con·cern', *n.* lack of interest or worry; indifference. —**un·con·cerned',** *a.*

un·con'scion·a·ble (-shən-)

a. 1. unscrupulous. 2. unreasonable.

un·con'scious, *a.* 1. not conscious. 2. not aware (*of*). 3. unintentional.

un·count'ed, *a.* 1. not counted. 2. innumerable.

un·couth', *a.* rude; crude.

un·cov'er, *v.* 1. disclose. 2. remove the cover from.

unc'tion, *n.* 1. an anointing. 2. anything soothing.

unc'tu·ous (-chōō-) *a.* 1. oily. 2. insincerely earnest.

un·de·cid'ed, *a.* not (having) decided.

un·de·ni'a·ble, *a.* that cannot be denied.

un'der, *prep.* 1. lower than; below; beneath. 2. covered by. 3. less than. 4. below and across. 5. subject to. 6. undergoing. —*adv.* 1. in or to a lower position. 2. so as to be covered. —*a.* lower.

under-, *pref.* 1. below. 2. less than usual or proper.

un'der·brush, *n.* small trees, bushes, etc. in a forest.

un'der·clothes, *n.pl.* clothes worn next to the skin: also **un'der·cloth'ing.**

un'der·cov'er, *a.* secret.

un'der·dog, *n.* one that is expected to lose.

un'der·es'ti·mate', *v.* make too low an estimate.

un'der·foot', *adv. & a.* 1. under the feet. 2. in the way.

un'der·ge' *v.* experience; endure.

un'der·grad'u·ate, *n.* college student who does not yet have a degree.

un'der·ground', *a. & adv.* 1. beneath the earth's surface. 2. (in) secret. —*n.* secret revolutionary movement.

un'der·growth, *n.* undgrowth brush.

un'der·hand, *a.* 1. with the hand held below the elbow. 2. secret; sly: also **un'der·hand'ed.** —*adv.* in an underhand way.

un·der·lie', *v.* 1. lie beneath. 2. support.

un'der·line', *v.* 1. draw a line under. 2. stress.

un'der·ling, *n.* subordinate

un'der·ly'ing, *a.* basic.

un'der·mine', *v.* 1. dig beneath. 2. weaken gradually.

un'der·neath', *adv. & prep.* 1. under; below.

un'der·pass, *n.* road under a railway or highway.

un'der·priv'i·leged, *a.* poor; needy.

un·der·rate', v. rate too low.

un·der·score', v. underline.

un·der·stand', v. [-STOOD, -STANDING] 1. get the meaning (of). 2. take as a fact. 3. know the nature, etc. of. 4. sympathize with.

un·der·stand'a·ble, a.

un·der·stand'ing, n. 1. comprehension. 2. intelligence. 3. mutual agreement.

un·der·state', v. say with little or no emphasis.

un·der·stud'y, v. & n. [pl. -IES] (be ready to) substitute for an actor.

un·der·take', v. 1. begin (a task, etc.). 2. promise. —**un·der·tak'ing**, n.

un·der·tak'er, n. person who manages funerals.

un·der·tone', n. subdued tone.

un·der·tow', n. strong flow of water back under breaking waves.

un·der·wear', n. underclothes.

un·der·weight', a. weighing too little.

un·der·world', n. 1. criminal world. 2. Hades.

un·der·write', v. 1. agree to finance. 2. write insurance for. —**un·der·writ'er**, n.

un·do', v. [-DID, -DONE, -DOING] 1. open, untie, etc. 2. cancel or destroy.

un·doubt'ed, a. certain.

un·dress', v. take the clothes off.

un·due', a. more than is proper. —**un·du'ly**, adv.

un·du·late, v. 1. move in waves. 2. have or give a wavy form. —**un·du·la'tion**, n.

un·dy'ing, a. eternal.

un·earth', v. 1. dig up from the earth. 2. find.

un·earth'ly, a. 1. supernatural. 2. weird.

un·eas'y, a. [-IER, -IEST] uncomfortable. —**un·eas'i·ness**, n.

un·e'qual, a. not equal in size, value, etc. —**unequal to**, not able to do, etc.

un·e'qualed, a. without equal.

un·e·quiv'o·cal, a. straightforward; clear.

un·ex·pect'ed, a. not expected; sudden. —**un·ex·pect'ed·ly**, adv.

un·fail'ing, a. always dependable.

un·faith'ful, a. 1. not faithful. 2. adulterous.

un·fa·mil'iar, a. 1. not well-known. 2. ignorant about.

un·feel'ing, a. 1. insensible. 2. hardhearted; cruel.

un·feigned' (-fānd') a. real; genuine.

un·fin'ished, a. 1. incomplete. 2. not painted, etc.

un·flinch'ing, a. steadfast.

un·fold', v. 1. spread out. 2. make or become known.

un·found'ed, a. not based on fact or reason.

un·furl', v. unfold.

un·gain'ly, a. awkward.

un·gov'ern·a·ble, a. unruly.

un·guent (-gwənt) n. salve.

un'gu·late (-lit) a. having hoofs. —n. ungulate mammal.

un·hand', v. let go of.

un·hap'py, a. [-PIER, -PIEST] 1. unlucky. 2. sad; wretched.

un·health'y, a. [-IER, -IEST] 1. not well. 2. harmful to health.

un·heard', a. not heard or listened to.

un·heard'-of', a. never known or done before.

un·hinge', v. remove from the hinges.

un·ho'ly [-LIER, -LIEST] a. 1. not sacred. 2. wicked; sinful.

un·horse', v. make fall from a horse.

uni-, pref. having only one.

u'ni·corn, n. mythical horse with a horn in its forehead.

u'ni·form, a. 1. never changing. 2. all alike. —n. special clothes for some group. —v. dress in a uniform. —**u'ni·form'i·ty**, n.

u'ni·fy, v. make into one. —**u'ni·fi·ca'tion**, n.

u'ni·lat'er·al, a. 1. of one side only. 2. involving only one of several parties.

un'im·peach'a·ble, a. without fault.

un·ion, n. 1. a uniting. 2. group of nations or states united. 3. marriage. 4. labor union.

un'ion·ize, v. organize into a labor union.

u·nique' (-nēk') a. 1. one and only. 2. without equal. 3. unusual.

u'ni·son, n. 1. Mus. sameness of pitch. 2. agreement.

u'nit, n. 1. single part of a whole. 2. special part. 3. a standard measure. 4. one.

u·nite', v. 1. put together as one; combine. 2. join together (in).

u'ni·ty, n. 1. a being united. 2. harmony; agreement.

u'ni·ver'sal, a. 1. of or for all. 2. present everywhere.

—u'ni·ver·sal'i·ty, n.

u'ni·ver'sal·ly, adv. 1. in every case. 2. everywhere.

u'ni·verse, n. space and all things in it. 2. the world.

u'ni·ver'si·ty, n. [pl. -TIES] school made up of colleges and, often, graduate schools.

un·kempt', a. untidy; messy.

un·known', a. 1. not known; strange. 2. not identified.

un·law'ful, a. against the law. —un·law'ful·ly, adv.

un·learned', a. not educated.

un·less', con. except if.

un·let'tered, a. 1. ignorant. 2. illiterate.

un·like', a. not alike. —prep. not like.

un·lim'it·ed, a. without limits or bounds.

un·load', v. 1. remove (a load). 2. take a load from. 3. get rid of.

un·lock', v. open by undoing a lock.

un·luck'y, a. [-IER, -IEST] having or bringing bad luck.

un·mask', v. 1. remove a mask (from). 2. expose.

un·mis·tak'a·ble, a. that cannot be mistaken; clear. —un'mis·tak'a·bly, adv.

un·mit'i·gat'ed, a. 1. not lessened. 2. absolute.

un·nat'u·ral, a. 1. abnormal. 2. artificial.

un·nerve', v. make lose nerve, courage, etc.

un·num'bered, a. 1. countless. 2. not numbered.

un·pack', v. take things out of a trunk, box, etc.

un·par'al·leled, a. that has no equal or counterpart.

un·pleas'ant, a. offensive; disagreeable.

un·prec'e·dent'ed, a. having no precedent; unique.

un·prin'ci·pled, a. without good principles.

un·print'a·ble, a. not fit to be printed.

un·ques'tion·a·ble, a. certain. —un·ques'tion·a·bly, adv.

un·quote', int. that ends the quotation.

un·rav'el, v. 1. undo the threads of. 2. make clear.

un·re'al, a. fantastic.

un·rea'son·a·ble, a. 1. not reasonable. 2. excessive.

un·re·lent'ing, a. 1. refusing to relent. 2. cruel.

un·rest', n. restlessness.

un·ri'valed, un·ri'valled,a. having no rival or equal.

un·roll', v. open (something rolled up).

un·ruf'fled, a. calm; smooth.

un·ru'ly, a. [-IER, -IEST] not obedient or orderly.

un·sa'vor·y, a. 1. tasting or smelling bad. 2. disgusting.

un·scathed' (-skāthd') a. uninjured.

un·screw', v. detach or loosen by removing screws.

un·scru'pu·lous, a. without scruples; dishonest.

un·seal', v. to open.

un·seat', v. 1. throw from a seat. 2. remove from office.

un·seem'ly, a. improper.

un·set'tle, v. disturb, displace, or disorder.

un·speak'a·ble, a. inexpressibly bad, evil, etc.

un·sta'ble, a. 1. not fixed, firm, etc. 2. changeable.

un·stead'y, a. unstable.

un·strung', a. nervous; upset.

un'sub·stan'tial (-shəl) a. not solid, firm, real, etc.

un·sung', a. not honored.

un·tan'gle, v. free from tangles; straighten out.

un·taught', a. 1. uneducated. 2. got without teaching.

un·think'a·ble, a. that cannot be considered.

un·think'ing, a. thoughtless.

un·tie', v. unfasten (something tied or knotted).

un·til', prep. 1. up to the time of. 2. before. —con. 1. to the time or place that. 2. before.

un·time'ly, a. 1. premature. 2. at the wrong time. —adv. too soon. —un·time'li·ness, n.

un·to, prep. [Poet.] to.

un·told', a. 1. not told or revealed. 2. very great.

un·to·ward' (-tôrd') a. 1. unfortunate. 2. hard to control.

un·truth', n. lie; falsehood. —un·truth'ful, a.

un·used', a. 1. not in use. 2. unaccustomed. 3. never used before.

un·u'su·al, a. not usual; rare. —un·u'su·al·ly, adv.

un·ut'ter·a·ble, a. that cannot be spoken or described —un·ut'ter·a·bly, adv.

un·var'nished, a. 1. not varnished. 2. plain; simple.

un·veil', v. remove a veil from; disclose.

un·wield'y, a. [-IER, -IEST] 1. hard to handle because of size, etc. 2. clumsy. —un·wield'i·ness, n.

un·wit'ting, a. 1. not knowing. 2. not intentional. —

un·wit'ting·ly, adv.
un·wont'ed, a. 1. not accustomed (to). 2. rare.
un·writ'ten, a. 1. not in writing. 2. observed through custom, as some laws.
up, adv. 1. to, in, or on a higher place, level, etc. 2. to a later time. 3. upright. 4. into action, discussion, etc. 5. aside; away. 6. so as to be even. 7. completely. 8. apiece. —prep. up along, on, in, etc. —a. 1. put, brought, going, or gone up. 2. at an end. —v. [UPPED, UPPING] [Col.] increase. — **ups and downs,** changes in fortune. —**up to,** [Col.] 1. doing or scheming. 2. capable of. 3. to be decided or done by.
up·braid', v. scold.
up'bring·ing, n. training received as a child.
up·end', v. set on end.
up'grade', n. upward slope. —v. raise in grade or rank.
up·heav'al, n. 1. a heaving up. 2. quick, violent change.
up'hill', a. & adv. 1. upward. 2. with difficulty.
up·hold', v. 1. support. 2. confirm; sustain.
up·hol'ster, v. fit out (furniture) with coverings, etc. —**up·hol'ster·y,** n.
up'keep', n. 1. maintenance. 2. cost of maintenance.
up·lift', v. 1. lift up. 2. raise to a better level. —n. (up' lift) a lifting up.
up·on', prep. & adv. on, or up and on.
up'per, a. higher in place, rank, etc. —n. part of a shoe above the sole.
up'per·most, a. highest in place, power, etc. —adv. in the highest place; first.
up'right', a. 1. standing up; erect. 2. honest; just. —adv. in an upright position. —n. upright pole, beam, etc.
up'ris·ing, n. a revolt.
up'roar', n. loud, confused noise or condition.
up·roar'i·ous, a. 1. making an uproar. 2. boisterous.
up·root', v. 1. pull up by the roots. 2. remove entirely.
up·set', v. [-SET, -SETTING] 1. overturn. 2. disturb or distress. 3. defeat unexpectedly. —n. (up'set) an upsetting. —a. 1. overturned. 2. disturbed.
up'shot', n. result; outcome.
up'side down, 1. with the top part underneath. 2. in

disorder. —**up'side-down',** a.
up'stairs', adv. & a. to or on an upper floor. —n. upper floor or floors.
up·stand'ing, a. honorable.
up'start', n. presumptuous newcomer.
up'stream', adv. & a. against the current of a stream.
up'tight', up'-tight', a. [Sl.] very tense, nervous, etc.
up'-to-date', a. 1. having the latest facts, ideas, etc. 2. of the newest or latest kind.
up'turn, n. upward trend.
up'ward, adv. & a. toward a higher place, position, etc.: also **up'wards,** adv. —**up·ward(s) of,** more than.
u·ra'ni·um, n. radioactive metallic chemical element.
ur'ban, a. of or in a city.
ur·bane', a. suave; refined. —**ur·ban'i·ty,** n.
ur'chin, n. small mischievous child, esp. a boy.
-ure, suf. 1. act, result, or means of. 2. state of being.
u·re'mi·a, n. toxic condition caused by kidney failure. —**u·re'mic,** a.
u·re'ter, n. tube from a kidney to the bladder.
u·re'thra, n. duct for discharge of urine from bladder.
urge, v. 1. insist on. 2. force onward. 3. plead with. 4. incite. —n. impulse.
ur'gent, a. 1. needing quick action. 2. insistent. —**ur'gen·cy,** n.
u'ri·nal, n. fixture in which to urinate.
u'ri·nar·y, a. of the organs that secrete or discharge urine.
u'ri·nate, v. discharge urine from the body.
u'rine, n. waste fluid from the kidneys, which passes through the bladder.
urn, n. 1. footed vase. 2. container with a faucet.
us, pron. the objective case of we.
us'a·ble, use'a·ble, a. that can be used.
us'age, n. 1. treatment. 2. custom; habit.
use (ūz) v. 1. put into action. 2. treat. 3. consume. —n. (ūs) 1. a using or being used. 2. power or right to use. 3. need to use. 4. utility or function. —**used to,** 1. did once. 2. familiar with. —**us'er,** n.
used, a. not new; secondhand.

use'ful, *a.* that can be used; helpful. —**use'ful·ness**, *n.*

use'less, *a.* worthless.

ush'er, *v.* show the way to or bring in. —*n.* one who ushers.

u'su·al, *a.* in common use; ordinary. —**u'su·al·ly**, *adv.*

u·surp', *v.* take by force and without right. —**u·sur·pa'tion**, *n.* —**u·surp'er**, *n.*

u'su·ry (ū'zhoo-) *n.* lending of money at an excessive interest rate. —**u'su·rer**, *n.* —**u·su'ri·ous**, *a.*

u·ten'sil, *n.* container or tool for a special purpose.

u'ter·us, *n.* hollow female organ in which a fetus grows. —**u·til'i·tar'i·an** (-târ'-) *a.* useful or practical.

u·til'i·ty, *n.* [*pl.* -**TIES**] 1. usefulness. 2. water, gas, etc. for public use. 3. company providing this.

u'ti·lize, *v.* put to use. —**u'ti·li·za'tion**, *n.*

ut'most, *a.* 1. most distant. 2. greatest or highest. —*n.* the most possible.

U·to'pi·a, u·to'pi·a, *n.* any imaginary place where all things are perfect. —**U·to'pi·an, u·to'pi·an**, *a. & n.*

ut'ter, *a.* complete; absolute. —*v.* express with the voice. —**ut'ter·ly**, *adv.*

ut'ter·ance, *n.* 1. an uttering. 2. something said.

ut'ter·most, *a. & n.* utmost.

u'vu·la (yōō'vyoo-) *n.* [-**LAS**, -**LAE** (-lē)] small part hanging down above the back of the tongue.

V

va'cant, *a.* 1. empty; unoccupied. 2. free from work. 3. stupid. —**va'can·cy** [*pl.* -**CIES**] *n.*

va'cate, *v.* 1. make a place empty. 2. annul.

va·ca'tion, *n. & n.* rest from work, study, etc. —**va·ca'tion·ist, va·ca'tion·er**, *n.*

vac'cine (-sēn) *n.* preparation injected for immunity to a disease. —**vac'ci·nate**, *v.* —**vac·ci·na'tion**, *n.*

vac'il·late (vas'-) *v.* 1. waver. 2. show indecision. —**vac'il·la'tion**, *n.*

vac'u·ous, *a.* 1. empty. 2. stupid; senseless. —**va·cu'i·ty** [*pl.* -**TIES**] *n.*

vac'u·um, *n.* 1. completely empty space. 2. space with most of the air or gas taken out. —*a.* of, having, or working by a vacuum. —*v.* [Col.] use a vacuum cleaner.

vacuum cleaner, machine that cleans by means of suction.

vacuum tube, electron tube.

vag'a·bond, *a. & n.* vagrant.

va·ga·ry (-gâr'-) *n.* [*pl.* -**IES**] odd action or idea.

va·gi'na (-jī'-) *n.* canal leading to the uterus. —**vag'i·nal**, *a.*

va'grant *n.* homeless wanderer; tramp. —*a.* 1. nomadic. 2. wayward. —**va'gran·cy**, *n.*

vague (vāg) *a.* indefinite; unclear. —**vague'ly**, *adv.* —**vague'ness**, *n.*

vain, *a.* 1. conceited. 2. futile. 3. worthless. —**in vain**, 1. without success. 2. profanely.

vain'glo'ry, *n.* boastful pride. —**vain'glo'ri·ous**, *a.*

val'ance (val'ans) *n.* short drapery forming a border.

vale, *n.* [Poet.] valley.

val'e·dic'to·ry, *n.* farewell speech, as at graduation. —**val'e·dic·to'ri·an**, *n.*

va'lence, *n.* Chem. combining capacity of an element.

val'en·tine, *n.* sweetheart or card for St. Valentine's Day.

val'et (val'it, -ā) *n.* male servant to another man.

val'iant (-yənt) *a.* brave.

val'id, *a.* 1. true or sound. 2. having legal force. —**val'i·date**, *v.* —**va·lid'i·ty**, *n.*

va·lise' (-lēs') *n.* suitcase.

val'ley, *n.* [*pl.* -**LEYS**] 1. low land between hills. 2. land drained by a river system.

val'or, *n.* courage; bravery. —**val'or·ous**, *a.*

val'u·a·ble, *a.* 1. having value. 2. worth much money. —*n.* valuable thing.

val'u·a'tion, *n.* 1. the fixing of a thing's value. 2. value set on a thing.

val'ue, *n.* 1. importance, desirability, utility, etc. 2. worth in money. 3. buying power. 4. *pl.* standards. —*v.* 1. set the value of. 2. think highly of. —**val'ue·less**, *a.*

valve, *n.* 1. device in a pipe, etc. to control the flow of a gas or liquid. 2. body membrane like this.

vamp, *n.* part of a shoe over the instep.

vam'pire, *n.* 1. one who preys on others. 2. bat that lives on other animals' blood: also **vampire bat**.

van, *n.* 1. vanguard. 2. large closed truck.

van'dal, *n.* one who destroys things on purpose.

Van·dyke' (beard) (-dīk') short, pointed beard.

vane, *n.* 1. device that swings to show wind direction. 2. blade of a windmill, etc.

van'guard, *n.* 1. front part of an army. 2. leading group or position in a movement.

va·nil'la, *n.* flavoring made from the pods of an orchid.

van'ish, *v.* disappear.

van'i·ty, *n.* [pl. -TIES] 1. a being vain, or conceited. 2. futility.

van'quish, *v.* conquer.

van'tage, *n.* advantage.

vap'id, *a.* tasteless; dull.

va'por, *n.* 1. thick mist, as fog or steam. 2. gas formed by heating a liquid or solid. —**va'por·ous,** *a.*

va'por·ize, *v.* change into vapor. —**va·por·i·za'tion,** *n.* —**va'por·iz'er,** *n.*

var'i·a·ble (vâr'-) *a.* that varies or can be varied. —*n.* variable thing.

var'i·ance, *n.* a varying. — **at variance,** disagreeing.

var'i·ant, *a.* slightly different. —*n.* variant form.

var'i·a'tion, *n.* 1. change in form, etc. 2. amount of change.

var'i·col'ored, *a.* of several or many colors.

var'i·cose, *a.* swollen, as veins.

var'ied, *a.* 1. of different kinds. 2. changed.

var'i·e·gat'ed, *a.* 1. marked with different colors. 2. varied.

va·ri'e·ty, *n.* [pl. -TIES] 1. change. 2. kind; sort. 3. number of different kinds.

var'i·ous, *a.* 1. of several kinds. 2. several or many.

var'mint, *n.* [Dial.] vermin; vile creature.

var'nish, *n.* resinous liquid forming a hard, glossy surface. —*v.* cover with this.

var'si·ty, *n.* [pl. -TIES] school's team in contests.

var'y, *v.* [-IED, -YING] 1. make or become different; change. 2. differ.

vas'cu·lar (-kyoo-) *a.* of vessels carrying blood, etc.

vase, *n.* open container for flowers, etc.

vas'sal, *n.* 1. feudal tenant. 2. subject, servant, etc.

vast, *a.* very great in size, degree, etc. —**vast'ly,** *adv.* —**vast'ness,** *n.*

vat, *n.* large tank or cask.

vaude'ville (vōd'vil) *n.* stage show with song and dance acts, skits, etc.

vault, *n.* 1. arched roof or ceiling. 2. arched room. 3. burial chamber. 4. room for keeping money, etc. as in a bank. —*v.* 1. provide with a vault. 2. leap over, balancing on a pole or the hands.

vaunt, *n. & v.* boast.

veal, *n.* meat from a calf.

veer, *v. & n.* shift; turn.

veg'e·ta·ble (vej'-) *n.* 1. plant eaten raw or cooked. 2. any plant.

veg'e·tar'i·an, *n.* one who eats no meat. —*a.* 1. of vegetarians. 2. of vegetables only.

veg'e·tate, *v.* live or grow like a plant.

veg'e·ta'tion, *n.* plant life.

ve'he·ment, *a.* 1. showing strong feeling. 2. violent. —**ve'he·mence,** *n.*

ve'hi·cle (-ə-k'l) *n.* means of conveying, esp. a device on wheels. —**ve·hic'u·lar,** *a.*

veil (vāl) *n.* 1. piece of thin fabric worn by women over the face or head. 2. thing that conceals. —*v.* 1. cover with a veil. 2. conceal.

vein (vān) *n.* 1. blood vessel going to the heart. 2. line in a leaf or an insect's wing. 3. fissure of mineral in rock. 4. colored streak. 5. trace or quality. —*v.* mark as with veins.

veld, veldt (velt, felt) *n.* S. African grassy land.

vel'lum, *n.* fine parchment.

ve·loc'i·pede (-los'-) *n.* tricycle.

ve·loc'i·ty, *n.* speed.

vel'vet, *n.* fabric of silk, rayon, etc. with a soft, thick pile. —**vel'vet·y,** *a.*

vel·vet·een', *n.* cotton cloth with a nap like velvet.

ve'nal, *a.* open to bribery. —**ve·nal'i·ty,** *n.*

vend, *v.* sell. —**ven'dor,** *n.*

vend'er, *n.*

ve·neer', *n.* thin, covering layer, as of fine wood. —*v.* cover with a veneer.

ven'er·a·ble, *a.* worthy of respect because of age, etc. —**ven'er·a·bil'i·ty,** *n.*

ven'er·ate, *v.* show deep respect for. —**ven'er·a'tion,** *n.*

ve·ne're·al, *a.* of or passed on by sexual intercourse.

venge'ance, *n.* revenge. —**with a vengeance,** 1. with great force. 2. very much.

venge'ful, a. seeking revenge.

ve'ni·al, a. pardonable.

ven'i·son, n. flesh of deer.

ven'om, n. 1. poison of some snakes, spiders, etc. 2. malice. —**ven'om·ous,** a.

vent, n. 1. outlet. 2. opening to let gas, etc. out. —v. let out.

ven'ti·late, v. circulate fresh air in. —**ven'ti·la'tion,** n. —**ven'ti·la'tor,** n.

ven'tral, a. of, near, or on the belly.

ven'tri·cle, n. either lower chamber of the heart.

ven·tril'o·quism, n. art of making one's voice seem to come from another point. —**ven·tril'o·quist,** n.

ven'ture (-chēr) n. risky undertaking. —v. 1. place in danger. 2. dare to do, say, etc.

ven'ture·some, a. 1. daring; bold. 2. risky.

ven'tur·ous, a. venturesome.

ve·ra'cious (-shəs) a. truthful or true. —**ve·rac'i·ty** (-ras'-) n.

ve·ran'da, ve·ran'dah, n. open, roofed porch.

verb, n. word expressing action or being.

ver'bal, a. 1. of or in words. 2. in speech. 3. like or derived from a verb. —n. verbal derivative, as a gerund. —**ver'bal·ly,** adv.

ver·ba'tim, adv. & a. word for word.

ver'bi·age (-ij) n. wordiness.

ver·bose', a. wordy. —**ver·bos'i·ty** (-bos'-) n.

ver'dant, a. covered with green vegetation.

ver'dict, n. decision, as of a jury in a law case.

ver'di·gris (-grēs, -gris) n. greenish coating on brass, copper, or bronze.

ver'dure (-jēr) n. 1. green vegetation. 2. color of this.

verge, v. & n. (be on) the edge or border.

ver'i·fy (ver'-) v. [-FIED, -FYING] 1. prove to be true. 2. test the accuracy of. —**ver'i·fi·ca'tion,** n.

ver'i·ly, adv. [Ar.] really.

ver'i·ta·ble, a. true; real.

ver'i·ty (-ti) n. [pl. -TIES] (a) truth.

ver·mil'ion (vēr-mil'yən) n. bright yellowish red.

ver'min, n. [pl. -MIN] small, destructive animal, as a fly or rat.

ver·mouth' (-mōōth') n. a white wine.

ver·nac'u·lar, a. & n. (of) the everyday speech of a country or place.

ver'nal, a. 1. of or in the spring. 2. springlike.

ver'sa·tile (-til) a. able to do many things well. —**ver'sa·til'i·ty,** n.

verse, n. 1. poetry. 2. stanza. 3. short division of a Bible chapter.

versed, a. skilled.

ver'si·fy, v. [-FIED, -FYING] 1. write poetry. 2. tell in verse. —**ver'si·fi·ca'tion,** n. —**ver'si·fi'er,** n.

ver'sion, n. 1. translation. 2. account; report.

ver'sus, prep. against.

ver'te·bra, n. [pl. -BRAE (-brē), -BRAS] any single bone of the spinal column.

ver'te·brate, n. & a. (animal) having a spinal column.

ver'tex, n. [pl. -TEXES, -TICES (-tə-sēz)] highest or farthest point.

ver'ti·cal, n. & a. (line, plane, etc.) that is straight up and down.

ver·ti'go, n. dizzy feeling.

verve, n. vigor; enthusiasm.

ver'y, a. 1. complete; absolute. 2. same. 3. actual. —adv. 1. extremely. 2. truly.

ves'per, n. 1. evening. 2. pl. [also V-] evening church service.

ves'sel, n. 1. container. 2. ship or boat. 3. tube of the body, as a vein.

vest, n. 1. man's sleeveless garment. 2. undershirt. —v. 1. clothe. 2. give power over or right to.

ves'ti·bule (-būl) n. 1. small entrance hall. 2. enclosed passage.

ves'tige (-tij) n. a trace or mark, esp. of something gone. —**ves·tig'i·al,** a.

vest'ment, n. garment, esp. one for a clergyman.

ves'try, n. [pl. -TRIES] 1. church meeting room. 2. lay church group with certain powers.

vet, n. [Col.] 1. veterinarian. 2. veteran.

vetch, n. plant grown for fodder.

vet'er·an, a. experienced. —n. 1. former member of the armed forces. 2. long-time employee, etc.

vet'er·i·nar'i·an, n. doctor for animals.

vet'er·i·nar·y, a. of the medical care of animals. —n. veterinarian.

ve′to, *n.* [*pl.* -TOES] 1. power, or right, to prohibit or reject. 2. use of this. —*v.* [-TOED, -TOING] use a veto on.

vex, *v.* annoy; disturb. —**vex-a′tion**, *n.* —**vex-a′tious**, *a.*

vi-a (vī′ə, vē′ə) *prep.* by way of.

vi′a-ble, *a.* able to exist.

vi′a-duct, *n.* bridge held up by a series of towers.

vi′al, *n.* small bottle.

vi′and, *n.* 1. article of food. 2. *pl.* fine food.

vi′brant, *a.* 1. quivering. 2. resonant. 3. energetic.

vi′brate, *v.* 1. move rapidly back and forth; quiver. 2. thrill. —**vi-bra′tion**, *n.* —**vi′bra-tor**, *n.*

vic′ar, *n.* 1. Church of England priest. 2. R.C.Ch. deputy of a bishop, etc.

vic′ar-age (-ij) *n.* vicar's residence.

vi-car′i-ous, *a.* 1. felt by imagined participation. 2. taking another's place. —**vi-car′i-ous-ly**, *adv.*

vice, *n.* 1. bad or evil conduct. 2. bad or evil habit.

vice-, *pref.* substitute or subordinate.

vice′-pres′i-dent, *n.* officer next in rank to a president.

vice′roy, *n.* deputy ruler for a sovereign.

vi-ce ver′sa (vī′si or vīs′) the other way around.

vi-cin′i-ty, *n.* [*pl.* -TIES] 1. nearness. 2. near-by area.

vi-cious (vish′əs) *a.* 1. evil. 2. unruly. 3. malicious. —**vi′cious-ly**, *adv.* —**vi′cious-ness**, *n.*

vi-cis′si-tude, *n.* any of one's ups and downs; change.

vic′tim, *n.* 1. one killed, hurt, etc. 2. one cheated, tricked, etc. —**vic′tim-ize**, *v.*

vic′tor, *n.* winner.

vic-to′ri-ous, *a.* having won a victory; conquering.

vic′to-ry, *n.* [*pl.* -RIES] success in war or any struggle.

vict′uals (vit′'lz) *n.pl.* [Dial. or Col.] food.

vid′e-o, *a.* & *n.* (of) television.

vie, *v.* [VIED, VYING] to compete in a contest.

view (vū) *n.* 1. a looking. 2. range of vision. 3. idea or thought. 4. scene. 5. opinion. 6. aim; goal. —*v.* 1. look at or see. 2. consider. —**in view of**, because of.

view′point, *n.* 1. place of observation. 2. attitude.

vig′il, *n.* 1. watchful staying awake. 2. watch kept. 3. eve of a religious festival.

vig′i-lant (vij′-) *a.* watchful. —**vig′i-lance**, *n.*

vig′i-lan′te, *n.* one of a group illegally organized to punish crime.

vi-gnette (vin-yet′) *n.* 1. short literary sketch. 2. picture that shades off at the edges.

vig′or, *n.* active force; strength and energy. —**vig′or-ous**, *a.* —**vig′or-ous-ly**, *adv.*

vik′ing (vik′-) *n.* early Scandinavian pirate.

vile, *a.* 1. evil; wicked. 2. disgusting. 3. lowly or bad.

vil′i-fy, *v.* [-FIED, -FYING] defame or slander.

vil′la, *n.* showy country house.

vil′lage, *n.* small town.

vil′lain (-lən) *n.* evil or wicked person. —**vil′lain-ous**, *a.* —**vil′lain-y**, *n.*

vim, *n.* energy; vigor.

vin′di-cate, *v.* 1. clear from criticism, blame, etc. 2. justify. —**vin′di-ca′tion**, *n.*

vin-dic′tive, *a.* 1. revengeful in spirit. 2. done in revenge.

vine, *n.* plant with a stem that grows along the ground or climbs a support.

vin′e-gar, *n.* sour liquid made by fermenting cider, wine, etc. —**vin′e-gar-y**, *a.*

vine′yard (vin′-) *n.* land where grapevines are grown.

vin′tage (-tij) *n.* wine of a certain region and year.

vi-nyl (vī′nil) *a.* of a group of chemical compounds used in making plastics.

vi′o-la, *n.* instrument like, but larger than, the violin. —**vi′o-list**, *n.*

vi′o-late, *v.* 1. break (a law, etc.) 2. rape. 3. desecrate. 4. disturb. —**vi′o-la′tion**, *n.* —**vi′o-la′tor**, *n.*

vi′o-lent, *a.* 1. showing or acting with wild force or feeling. 2. intense. —**vi′o-lence**, *n.*

vi′o-let, *n.* delicate spring flower, usually bluish-purple.

vi′o-lin′, *n.* four-stringed instrument played with a bow. —**vi′o-lin′ist**, *n.*

vi′o-lon-cel′lo, *n.* [*pl.* -LOS] cello.

vi′per, *n.* 1. venomous snake. 2. treacherous person.

vi·ra·go, n. [pl. -GOES, -GOS] shrewish woman.

vir'gin, n. woman who has not had sexual intercourse. —a. chaste, pure, untouched, etc. —**vir·gin'i·ty,** n.

vir'ile, a. 1. masculine. 2. strong, vigorous, etc. —**vi·ril'i·ty,** n.

vir'tu·al (-choo-) a. being so in effect if not in fact. —**vir'tu·al·ly,** adv.

vir'tue, n. 1. moral excellence. 2. good quality, esp. a moral one. 3. chastity. —**by** (or **in**) **virtue of,** because of. —**vir'tu·ous,** a. —**vir'tu·ous·ly,** adv.

vir·tu·o'so, n. [pl. -SOS] musician, etc. having great skill. —**vir·tu·os'i·ty,** n.

vir'u·lent, a. 1. deadly. 2. full of hate. —**vir'u·lence,** n.

vi'rus, n. infective agent that causes disease.

vi·sa (vē'zə) n. endorsement on a passport, granting entry into a country.

vis·age (viz'ij) n. the face.

vis·cer·a (vis'ēr-ə) n.pl. internal organs of the body. —**vis'cer·al,** a.

vis·cid (vis'id) a. viscous.

vis'count (vī'-) n. nobleman above a baron.

vis'cous (-kəs) a. thick, sirupy, and sticky. —**vis·cos'i·ty,** n.

vise (vīs) n. device with adjustable jaws for holding an object firmly.

vis·i·bil'i·ty (viz'-) n. distance within which things can be seen.

vis'i·ble, a. that can be seen; evident. —**vis'i·bly,** adv.

vi'sion, n. 1. power of seeing. 2. something seen in a dream, trance, etc. 3. mental image. 4. foresight.

vi'sion·ar'y, a. & n. [pl. -IES] idealistic and impractical person.

vis'it, v. 1. go or come to see. 2. stay with as a guest. 3. afflict. —n. a visiting. —**vis'i·tor,** n.

vis·it·a'tion, n. 1. visit to inspect. 2. punishment sent by God.

vi'sor (-zēr) n. 1. movable part of a helmet, covering the face. 2. brim on a cap for shading the eyes.

vis'ta, n. view; scene.

vis'u·al (vizh'oo-) a. 1. of or used in seeing. 2. visible.

vis'u·al·ize', v. form a mental image of.

vi'tal, a. 1. of life. 2. essential to life. 3. very important. 4. full of life. —**vi'tal·ly,** adv.

vi·tal'i·ty, n. 1. energy; vigor. 2. power to survive.

vi'tal·ize, v. give life or vigor to.

vi'ta·min, n. any of certain substances vital to good health. Vitamins A and D are found in fish-liver oil, eggs, etc.; Vitamin C, in citrus fruits.

vi'ti·ate (vish'i-) v. make bad; spoil. —**vi'ti·a'tion,** n.

vit're·ous, a. of or like glass.

vit'ri·fy, v. [-FIED, -FYING] change into glass by heating.

vit'ri·ol, n. 1. sulfuric acid. 2. metal sulfate. 3. caustic remarks. —**vit'ri·ol'ic,** a.

vi·tu'per·ate', v. berate.

vi·va'cious (-shus) a. spirited; lively. —**vi·vac'i·ty,** n.

viv'id, a. 1. full of life. 2. bright; intense. 3. strong; active. —**viv'id·ly,** adv.

viv'i·fy, v. [-FIED, -FYING] give life to.

vi·vip'a·rous (vī-) a. bearing living young.

viv'i·sec'tion, n. surgery on living animals for medical research.

vix'en, n. 1. female fox. 2. shrewish woman.

vo·cab'u·lar'y, n. [pl. -IES] all the words used by a person, group, etc. or listed in a dictionary, etc.

vo'cal, a. 1. of or by the voice. 2. speaking freely. —**vo'cal·ly,** adv.

vocal cords, membranes in the larynx that vibrate to make voice sounds.

vo'cal·ist, n. singer.

vo'cal·ize, v. speak or sing.

vo·ca'tion, n. one's profession, trade, or career. —**vo·ca'tion·al,** a.

vo·cif'er·ous (-sif'-) a. loud; clamorous. —**vo·cif'er·ate',** v.

vod'ka, n. Russian alcoholic liquor made from grain.

vogue (vōg) n. 1. current fashion. 2. popularity.

voice, n. 1. sound made through the mouth. 2. ability to make such sound. 3. sound like this. 4. right to express one's opinion, etc. 5. expression. —v. utter or express.

void, a. 1. empty; vacant. 2. lacking. 3. of no legal force. —n. empty space. —v. 1. to empty. 2. cancel.

voile (voil) n. thin fabric.

vol'a·tile (-t'l) a. 1. quickly evaporating. 2. changeable.

—**vol·a·til·i·ty**, n.

vol·ca·no, n. [pl. -NOES, -NOS] mountain formed by erupting molten rock. —**vol·can·ic**, a.

vo·li·tion, n. will (n. 3).

vol·ley, n. [pl. -LEYS] & v. 1. discharge (of) a number of weapons together. 2. return (of) a tennis ball before it hits the ground.

vol·ley·ball, n. game between teams hitting a large ball back and forth over a net.

volt (vōlt), n. unit of electromotive force.

volt·age (-ij) n. electromotive force, shown in volts.

vol·u·ble, a. talkative.

vol·ume, n. 1. a book. 2. cubic measure. 3. amount. 4. loudness of sound.

vo·lu·mi·nous, a. 1. filling volumes. 2. large; full.

vol·un·tar·y, a. 1. by choice; of one's own free will. 2. controlled by the will. —**vol·un·tar·i·ly**, adv.

vol·un·teer, v. offer, give, etc. of one's own free will. —n. one who volunteers.

vo·lup·tu·ous, a. sensual.

vom·it, v. & n. (have) matter from the stomach ejected through the mouth.

voo·doo, n. primitive religion of the West Indies.

vo·ra·cious (-shəs) a. 1. greedy. 2. very eager.

vor·tex, n. [pl. -TEXES, -TICES (-tə-sēz)] 1. whirlpool. 2. whirlwind.

vo·ta·ry, n. [pl. -RIES] worshiper; devotee.

vote, n. 1. a decision or choice shown on a ballot, etc. 2. all the votes. 3. the right to vote. —v. 1. cast a vote. 2. decide by vote. —**vot·er**, n.

vo·tive, a. given or done to fulfill a vow or promise.

vouch, v. give or be a guarantee (for).

vouch·er, n. a paper serving as proof of payment, etc.

vouch·safe', v. be kind enough to grant.

vow, v. & n. (make) a solemn promise or statement.

vow·el, n. speech sound of the letters a, e, i, o, u.

voy·age, n. & v. journey by ship.

vul·can·ize, v. treat rubber to make it stronger and more elastic.

vul·gar, a. 1. popular. 2. lacking culture; crude. —**vul·gar·ly**, adv.

vul·gar·ism, n. coarse word or phrase, thought improper.

vul·gar·i·ty, n. 1. vulgar state or quality. 2. [pl. -TIES] vulgar act, etc.

vul·ner·a·ble, a. 1. that can be hurt, attacked, etc. 2. easily hurt; sensitive. —**vul·ner·a·bil'i·ty**, n.

vul·ture (-chēr), n. 1. large bird of prey. 2. greedy, ruthless person.

vul·va, n. external female sex organs.

W

wab·ble, n. & v. wobble.

wad, n. 1. small, soft mass. 2. small lump. —v. [WADDED, WADDING] 1. roll into a wad. 2. stuff as with padding.

wad·dle, v. & n. walk with short steps, swaying from side to side.

wade, v. 1. walk through water, mud, etc. 2. proceed with difficulty. 3. cross by wading.

wa·fer, n. 1. thin, crisp cracker. 2. disklike thing.

waf·fle, n. crisp cake baked between two flat, studded plates (**waffle iron**).

waft, v. carry or move lightly over water or through the air. —n. 1. odor, sound, etc. carried through the air. 2. wafting motion.

wag, v. [WAGGED, WAGGING] move rapidly back and forth or up and down. —n. 1. a wagging. 2. a wit; comic.

wage, v. take part in. —n. usually pl. money paid for work done.

wa·ger, n. & v. bet.

wag·gle, v. wag abruptly.

wag·on, n. four-wheeled vehicle, esp. for hauling.

waif, n. homeless child.

wail, v. & n. 1. (make a) loud, sad cry. 2. lament.

wain·scot, n. wall paneling of wood. —v. panel with wood

waist, n. 1. body part between the ribs and the hips. 2. waistline.

waist·coat (or wes'kət) n. [Br.] man's vest.

waist·line, n. middle or narrow part of the waist.

wait, v. 1. remain until something occurs. 2. remain undone. 3. serve food at. 4. await. —n. act or time of waiting. —**wait on** (or **upon**), 1. be a servant to. 2. serve.

wait'er, *n.* man who serves food at table. **--wait'ress,** *n.fem.*

waive, *v.* 1. give up, as a right. 2. postpone.

waiv'er, *n.* *Law* waiving of a right, claim, etc.

wake, *v.* [alt. pt. WOKE] 1. come or bring out of a sleep. 2. become alert (*to*). 3. stir up. --*n.* 1. all-night vigil over a corpse. 2. track or trail left behind.

wake'ful, *a.* 1. watchful. 2. unable to sleep.

wak'en, *v.* to wake.

wale, *n.* 1. welt. 2. ridge, as on corduroy.

walk, *v.* 1. go on foot at moderate speed. 2. walk along, over, with, etc. --*n.* 1. way of walking. 2. stroll; hike. 3. path for walking. **walk of life,** way of living.

walk'ie-talk'ie, *n.* portable radio for sending and receiving.

wall, *n.* upright structure that encloses, divides, etc. --*v.* divide, or close up, with a wall.

wal'la-by, *n.* [pl. -BIES or -BY] small kangaroo.

wal'let, *n.* flat case for carrying money, cards, etc.

wall'flow-er, *n.* [Col.] shy or unpopular person.

wal'lop, *v.* [Col.] 1. hit hard. 2. defeat completely. --*n.* [Col.] hard blow.

wal'low, *v.* 1. roll around in mud or filth, as pigs do. 2. live selfishly.

wall'pa-per, *n.* & *v.* (apply) paper for covering walls or ceilings.

wal'nut, *n.* tree bearing an edible nut in a hard shell.

wal'rus, *n.* large seallike animal with two tusks.

waltz, *n.* ballroom dance in ¾ time. --*v.* dance a waltz.

wam'pum (wäm'-) *n.* beads used as money by N. Am. Indians.

wan (wän) *a.* sickly pale.

wand, *n.* slender rod, as one of supposed magic power.

wan'der, *v.* 1. roam idly about. 2. go astray; stray. **--wan'der-er,** *n.*

wan'der-lust, *n.* strong urge to wander or travel.

wane, *v.* 1. get smaller, weaker, etc. 2. approach the end. --*n.* a waning.

wan'gle, *v.* [Col.] get by sly or tricky means.

want, *v.* 1. wish for; desire. 2. need. 3. lack. --*n.* 1. lack;

need. 2. poverty. 3. desire. **want'ing,** *a.* 1. lacking. 2. inadequate. --*prep.* minus.

wan'ton, *a.* 1. senseless and cruel. 2. irresponsible. 3. immoral. --*n.* wanton person.

wap'i-ti (wäp'-) *n.* N. Am. elk.

war, *n.* 1. armed conflict, as between nations. 2. any fight. --*v.* [WARRED, WARRING] carry on war. **--war'like,** *a.*

war'ble, *v.* sing with trills, runs, etc. --*n.* a warbling. **--war'bler,** *n.*

ward, *n.* 1. one under the care of a guardian. 2. division of a hospital. 3. voting district of a city. **--ward off,** turn aside.

ward'en, *n.* 1. one who takes care of something. 2. head official of a prison.

ward'er, *n.* watchman; guard.

ward'robe, *n.* 1. closet for clothes. 2. all one's clothes.

ware, *n.* 1. usually in *pl.* thing for sale. 2. pottery.

ware'house, *n.* building where goods are stored.

war'fare, *n.* war or any conflict.

war'head, *n.* front part of a bomb, etc., with the explosive.

warm, *a.* 1. moderately hot. 2. enthusiastic. 3. kind and loving. --*v.* make or become warm. **--warm'ly,** *adv.*

warm'heart'ed, *a.* kind; loving.

war'mon-ger (-mun'-) *n.* one who tries to cause war.

warmth, *n.* 1. a being warm. 2. strong feeling.

warn, *v.* 1. tell of danger; advise to be careful. 2. inform; let know. **--warn'ing,** *n.* & *a.*

warp, *v.* 1. bend or twist out of shape. 2. distort. --*n.* 1. a warping or twist. 2. long threads in a loom.

war'rant, *n.* 1. justification. 2. legal writ authorizing an arrest, search, etc. --*v.* 1. authorize. 2. justify. **warrant officer,** officer just above enlisted man.

war'ran-ty, *n.* [pl. -TIES] guarantee (*n.* 1).

war'ren, *n.* area in which rabbits are raised.

war'ri-or, *n.* soldier.

war'ship, *n.* ship for combat use.

wart, *n.* small, hard growth on the skin. **--wart'y,** *a.*

war·y (wâr′i) a. [-IER, -IEST] on guard; cautious. —**wary of,** careful of. —**war′i·ly,** adv.

was, pt. of **be:** used with he, she, or it.

wash, v. 1. clean with water. 2. wash clothes. 3. flow over or against. 4. remove by washing. 5. coat thinly. —n. 1. a washing. 2. clothes (to be) washed. 3. rush of water. 4. eddy from propeller, oars, etc. —a. that can be washed. —**wash′a·ble,** a.

wash′board, n. ridged board to scrub clothes on.

wash′bowl, n. bowl for washing the hands and face: also **wash′ba′sin.**

wash′cloth, n. small cloth to wash the face or body.

wash′er, n. 1. machine for washing. 2. flat ring used to make a bolt, nut, etc. fit tight. 3. one who washes.

wash′room, n. rest-room.

wash′stand, n. plumbing fixture with a washbowl.

was′n't, was not.

wasp, n. flying insect: some have a sharp sting.

wasp′ish, a. bad-tempered.

was·sail (wäs′'l) n. [Ar.] toast (drink).

waste, v. 1. use up needlessly. 2. fail to take advantage of. 3. wear away. 4. lose strength or weaken. 5. destroy. —a. 1. barren or wild, as land. 2. left over. —n. 1. a wasting. 2. wasted matter; refuse, etc. 3. waste land. —**go to waste,** be wasted. —**lay waste,** devastate. —**waste′ful,** a.

waste′bas′ket, n. container for discarded paper, etc.

wast′rel (wāst′-) n. profligate person.

watch, n. 1. act of guarding or observing. 2. guard(s), or period of guard duty. 3. small clock for wrist or pocket. 4. Naut. period of duty, or crew on duty. —v. 1. keep vigil. 2. observe. 3. guard or tend. 4. be alert (for). —**watch out,** be alert or careful. —**watch′ful,** a.

watch′dog, n. dog kept to guard property.

watch′man, n. [pl. -MEN] person hired to guard.

watch′word, n. slogan.

wa′ter, n. 1. colorless liquid of rivers, lakes, etc. 2. water solution. 3. body

secretion, as urine. —v. 1. supply with water. 2. dilute with water. 3. fill with tears. 4. secrete saliva —a. of, for, in, or by water.

water buffalo, oxlike work animal of Asia & Africa.

water color, 1. paint made by mixing pigment and water. 2. a picture painted with water colors. —**wa′ter·col′or,** a.

wa′ter·course, n. river, brook, canal, etc.

water cress, water plant with leaves used in salads.

wa′ter·fall, n. steep fall of water, as from a cliff.

wa′ter·fowl, n. swimming bird.

wa′ter·front, n. land or docks at the edge of a river, harbor, etc.

water lily, water plant with large, showy flowers.

wa′ter·logged, a. soaked or filled with water.

wa′ter·mark, n. 1. mark showing how high water has risen. 2. design pressed into paper. —v. mark (paper) with a watermark.

wa′ter·mel′on, n. large melon with juicy, red pulp.

water moccasin, large, poisonous snake of southern U.S.

wa′ter·proof′, v. & a. (make) impervious to water.

wa′ter·shed, n. 1. area a river system drains. 2. ridge between two such areas.

wa′ter·ski′, v. be towed over water on a kind of ski.

wa′ter·spout, n. whirling water funnel rising from sea.

wa′ter·tight, a. so tight no water can get through.

wa′ter·way, n. navigable river, lake, canal, etc.

wa′ter·works, n.pl. system of reservoirs, pumps, etc. supplying water to a city.

wa′ter·y, a. 1. of, like, or full of water. 2. diluted.

watt (wät) n. unit of electric power. —**watt′age,** n.

wat′tle (wät′-) n. 1. sticks woven with twigs. 2. flap of skin hanging at the throat of a chicken, etc.

wave, v. 1. move to and fro. 2. wave the hand, etc., or signal thus. 3. arrange in curves. —n. 1. curving swell moving along on the ocean, etc. 2. wavelike vibration. 3. curve(s), as in the hair. 4. a waving, as of the hand.

—**wav′y** [-IER, -IEST] a.

wa′ver, v. 1. flutter, falter, flicker, etc. 2. show indecision. —n. a wavering.

wax, n. 1. plastic substance secreted by bees. 2. substance like this, as paraffin. —v. 1. put polish or wax on. 2. get larger, stronger, etc. 3. become. —**wax′y** [-IER, -IEST], **wax′en**, a.

way, n. 1. road or route. 2. movement forward. 3. method, manner, etc. 4. distance. 5. direction. 6. particular. 7. wish; will. 8. pl. framework on which a ship is built. —adv. [Col.] far. —**by the way**, incidentally. —**by the way of**, 1. passing through. 2. as a means of. —**give way**, 1. yield. 2. break down. —**under way**, moving ahead.

way′far′er (-fâr′-) n. traveler, esp. on foot. —**way′far′ing**, a. & n.

way′lay′ v. [-LAID, -LAYING] ambush.

way′side, a. & n. (at or along) the edge of a road.

way′ward (-wērd) a. 1. willful; disobedient. 2. irregular. —**way′ward·ness**, n.

we, pron. persons speaking or writing.

weak, a. lacking strength, power, etc.; not strong, effective, etc. —**weak′en**, v.

weak′-kneed′, a. timid; cowardly.

weak′ling, n. weak person.

weak′ly, a. [-LIER, -LIEST] sickly. —adv. in a weak way.

weak′ness, n. 1. a being weak. 2. fault. 3. special liking.

weal (wēl) n. 1. skin welt. 2. [Ar.] welfare.

wealth, n. 1. riches. 2. large amount. —**wealth′y** [-IER, -IEST] a.

wean, v. 1. stop suckling. 2. withdraw from a certain habit, etc.

weap′on (wep′-) n. 1. thing used for fighting. 2. means of attack or defense.

wear, v. [WORE, WORN, WEARING] 1. have on the body as clothes. 2. make or become damaged by use. 3. endure in use. 4. tire or exhaust. —n. 1. clothing. 2. impairment.

wea′ry, a. [-RIER, -RIEST] 1. tired. 2. bored. —v. [-RIED, -RYING] make or become weary. —**wea′ri·ness**, n. —**wea′ri·some**, a.

wea′sel (wē′z'l) n. small, flesh-eating mammal.

weath′er (weth′-) n. conditions outside as to temperature, humidity, etc. —v. 1. pass through safely. 2. be exposed to sun, rain, etc.

weath′er-beat′en, a. roughened, etc. by the weather.

weath′er man, n. [pl. -MEN] [Col.] weather forecaster.

weather vane, vane (sense 1).

weave, v. [WOVE, WOVEN, WEAVING] 1. make cloth by interlacing threads, as on a loom. 2. twist or move from side to side or in and out. —n. pattern of weaving.

web, n. 1. network, esp. one spun by a spider. 2. skin joining the toes of a duck, frog, etc.

web′bing, n. strong fabric woven into strips.

web′foot, n. [pl. -FEET] foot with a web (sense 2). —**web′-foot′ed**, a.

wed, v. [WEDDED, WEDDED or WED, WEDDING] 1. marry. 2. unite.

wed′ding, n. ceremony of marrying.

wedge, n. piece of wood, etc. tapering to a thin edge. —v. 1. fix in place with a wedge. 2. pack tightly.

wed′lock, n. matrimony.

Wednes′day (wenz′-) n. fourth day of the week.

wee, a. very small; tiny.

weed, n. unwanted plant, as in a lawn. —v. 1. remove weeds. 2. take (out) as useless, etc.

weeds, n.pl. black clothes for mourning.

week, n. 1. period of 7 days, esp. Sunday through Saturday. 2. the hours or days one works each week.

week′day, n. any day of the week except Sunday and, often, Saturday.

week′end′, week′-end′, n. Saturday and Sunday. —v. spend the weekend.

week′ly, a. 1. lasting a week. 2. done, etc. once a week. —adv. once a week. —n. [pl. -LIES] periodical coming out weekly.

weep, v. [WEPT, WEEPING] 1. shed tears. 2. mourn (for).

wee′vil, n. beetle larva that destroys cotton, grain, etc.

weft, n. woof in weaving.

weigh (wā) v. 1. determine the heaviness of, as on a scale. 2. have a certain weight. 3. consider well. 4. burden (with down). 5. hoist (an anchor).

weight, n. 1. (amount of) heaviness. 2. unit of heaviness. 3. solid mass. 4. burden. 5. importance or influence. —v. to burden. —**weight′y** [-IER, -IEST] a.

weird (wērd) a. 1. mysterious. 2. [Col.] queer.

wel′come a. 1. gladly received. 2. freely permitted. 3. under no obligation. —n. a welcoming. —v. greet with pleasure.

weld, v. unite by melting together. —n. welded joint.

wel′fare′ n. health, happiness, and comfort.

well, n. 1. natural spring. 2. hole dug in the earth to get water, oil, etc. 3. hollow shaft. 4. source. —v. gush or flow. —adv. [BETTER, BEST] 1. in a pleasing, good, or right way. 2. prosperously. 3. much. 4. thoroughly. —a. in good health. —int. exclamation of surprise. —**as well (as),** 1. in addition (to). 2. equally (with).

well′-be′ing, n. welfare.

well′-bred′, a. showing good manners; courteous.

well′-dis·posed′, a. friendly or receptive.

well′-done′, a. 1. done with skill. 2. thoroughly cooked.

well′-found′ed, a. based on facts or good judgment.

well′-known′, a. famous or familiar.

well′-man′nered, a. polite.

well′-mean′ing, a. with good intentions. —**well′-meant′,** a.

well′-nigh′, adv. almost.

well′-off′, a. 1. fortunate. 2. prosperous.

well′-read′, a. having read much.

well′spring, n. 1. spring. 2. continual source.

well′-to-do′, a. wealthy.

well′-worn′, a. much worn or used.

Welsh, a. & n. (of) the people or language of Wales.

Welsh rabbit (or **rarebit**), melted cheese on toast.

welt, n. 1. leather strip in the seam between shoe sole and upper. 2. ridge raised on the skin by a blow.

wel′ter, v. wallow. —n. confusion.

wen, n. skin cyst.

wench, n. young woman: derogatory or humorous.

wend, v. [Poet.] go; travel.

went, pt. of **go.**

wept, pt. & pp. of **weep.**

were, pt. of **be,** used with *you, we,* and *they.*

weren′t, were not.

were′wolf (wer′-) n. [pl. -WOLVES] Folklore person changed into a wolf.

west, n. 1. direction in which sunset occurs. 2. region in this direction. 3. [W-] Europe and N. & S. America. —a. & adv. in, toward, or from the west. —**west′er·ly,** a. & adv. —**west′ern,** a. —**west′ern·er,** n. —**west′ward,** a. & (also **west′wards**) adv.

wet, a. [WETTER, WETTEST] 1. covered or soaked with water. 2. rainy. 3. not dry yet. —n. water, rain, etc. —v. [WET or WETTED, WETTING] make or become wet.

we′ve, we have.

whack, v. & n. [Col.] hit or slap with a sharp sound.

whale, n. huge, fishlike sea mammal. —v. 1. hunt for whales. 2. [Col.] beat.

whale′bone, n. horny substance from a whale's jaw.

whal′er, n. man or ship engaged in hunting whales.

wharf, n. [pl. WHARVES, WHARFS] platform at which ships dock to load, etc.

what, pron. 1. which thing, event, etc.? 2. that which. —a. 1. which or which kind of. 2. as much or as many as. 3. how great! —adv. 1. how. 2. partly. —int. exclamation of surprise, etc. —**what for?** why? —**what if,** suppose.

what·ev′er, pron. 1. anything that. 2. no matter what. 3. what. —a. 1. of any kind. 2. no matter what.

what′so·ev′er, pron. & a. whatever.

wheat, n. cereal grass with seed ground for flour, etc.

whee′dle, v. coax.

wheel, n. round disk turning on an axle. —v. 1. move on wheels. 2. turn, revolve, etc.

wheel′bar′row, n. single-wheeled cart with handles.

wheel′base, n. distance from front to rear axle.

wheeze, v. & n. (make) a whistling, breathy sound.

whelk, n. large sea snail with a spiral shell.

whelp, n. puppy or cub. —v. give birth to whelps.

when, adv. at what time? —con. 1. at what time. 2. at which time. 3. at the time that. **4.** if. —*pron.* what or which time.

whence, *adv.* from where.

when·ev'er, *adv.* [Col.] when. —*con.* at whatever time.

where, *adv.* **1.** in or to what place? **2.** in what way? **3.** from what source? —*con.* **1.** at what place. **2.** at which place. **3.** to the place that. —*pron.* **1.** what place? **2.** the place at which.

where'a·bouts, *adv.* at what place? —*n.* location.

where·as', *con.* **1.** because. **2.** while on the contrary.

where·by', *adv.* by which.

where'fore, *adv.* why? —*con.* therefore. —*n.* the reason.

where·in', *adv.* **1.** in what way? **2.** in which.

where·of', *adv.* of what, which, or whom.

where·up·on', *con.* at or after which. —*adv.* on what?

wher·ev'er, *adv.* [Col.] where? —*con.* in or to whatever place.

where·with', *adv.* with which.

where·with·al', *n.* necessary means, esp. money.

whet, *v.* [WHETTED, WHETTING] **1.** sharpen, as by grinding. **2.** stimulate.

wheth'er, *con.* **1.** if it is true or likely that. **2.** in either case that.

whet'stone, *n.* abrasive stone for sharpening knives.

whey (hwā) *n.* watery part of curdled milk.

which, *pron.* **1.** what one or ones of several. **2.** the one or ones that. **3.** that. —*a.* **1.** what one or ones. **2.** whatever.

which·ev'er, *pron. & a.* any one that; no matter which.

whiff, *n.* **1.** light puff of air. **2.** slight odor.

while, *n.* period of time. —*con.* **1.** during the time that. **2.** although. —*v.* spend (time).

whim, *n.* sudden notion.

whim'per, *v. & n.* (make) a low, broken cry.

whim'sy (-zi) *n.* [pl. -SIES] **1.** whim. **2.** fanciful humor. —**whim'si·cal,** *a.*

whine, *v. & n.* (make) a long, high cry, as in complaining.

whin'ny, *v.* [-NIED, -NYING] *& n.* [pl. -NIES] (make) a low, neighing sound.

whip, *v.* [WHIPPED, WHIPPING] **1.** move suddenly. **2.** strike, as with a strap. **3.** beat (cream, etc.) into a froth. **4.** [Col.] defeat. —*n.* **1.** rod with a lash at one end. **2.** dessert of whipped cream, fruit, etc.

whip'lash, *n.* severe jolting of the neck back and forth.

whip'pet, *n.* small, swift dog.

whip'poor·will, *n.* N. Am. bird active at night.

whir, *v.* [WHIRRED, WHIRRING] fly or revolve with a buzzing sound. —*n.* this sound.

whirl, *v.* **1.** move or spin rapidly. **2.** seem to spin. —*n.* **1.** a whirling. **2.** confused condition.

whirl'pool, *n.* water in violent, whirling motion.

whirl'wind, *n.* air whirling violently and moving forward.

whisk, *v.* move, pull, etc. with a quick, sweeping motion. —*n.* this motion.

whisk broom, small broom.

whisk'er, *n.* **1.** *pl.* long hair on a man's face. **2.** long hair, as on a cat's upper lip.

whis'ky, *n.* [pl. -KIES] strong liquor made from grain: also sp. **whis'key** [pl. -KEYS].

whis'per, *v.* **1.** say very softly. **2.** tell as a secret. —*n.* a whispering.

whist, *n.* card game like bridge.

whis'tle, *v.* **1.** make, or move with, a high, shrill sound. **2.** blow a whistle. —*n.* **1.** device for making whistling sounds. **2.** a whistling.

whit, *n.* least bit; jot.

white, *a.* **1.** of the color of snow. **2.** pale. **3.** pure; innocent. **4.** having light skin. —*n.* **1.** color of pure snow. **2.** a white thing, as egg albumen. —**white'ness,** *n.*

white ant, termite.

white'cap, *n.* wave with its crest broken into foam.

white'-col'lar, *a.* of clerical or professional workers.

white elephant, useless thing expensive to maintain.

white'fish, *n.* white lake fish of the salmon family.

whit'en, *v.* make or become white.

white'wash, *n.* mixture of lime, water, etc. as for whitening walls. —*v.* **1.** cover with whitewash. **2.** conceal the faults of.

whith'er (hwith'-) *adv* where.

whit'ing (hwīt') *n.* sea fish of the cod family.

whit'ish, *a.* somewhat white.

whit′tle, *v.* 1. cut shavings from wood with a knife. 2. reduce gradually.

whiz, whizz, *v. & n.* [WHIZZED, WHIZZING] (make) the hissing sound of a thing rushing through air.

who, *pron.* 1. what person? 2. which person. 3. that.

whoa (hwō) *int.* stop!: command to a horse.

who·ev′er, *pron.* 1. any person that. 2. no matter who.

whole, *a.* 1. not broken, damaged, etc. 2. complete. 3. not divided up. 4. healthy. —*n.* 1. entire amount. 2. thing complete in itself. —**on the whole,** in general. —**whole′ness,** *n.*

whole·heart′ed, *a.* sincere.

whole·sale, *n.* sale of goods in large amounts, as to retailers. —*a.* 1. of such sale. 2. extensive. —*v.* sell at wholesale. —**whole′sal·er,** *n.*

whole′some, *a.* 1. healthful. 2. improving one's morals. 3. healthy. —**whole′some·ness,** *n.*

whol′ly, *adv.* completely.

whom, *pron.* obj. case of who.

whoop, *v. & n.* (utter) a loud shout, cry, etc.

whooping cough, infectious disease, esp. of children.

whop′per, *n.* 1. [Col.] any large thing. 2. big lie.

whore (hôr) *n.* prostitute.

whorl (hwûrl, hwôrl) *n.* design of circular ridges.

whose, *pronominal a.* of who or of which.

who·so·ev′er, *pron.* whoever.

why, *adv.* 1. for what reason. 2. because of which. 3. reason for which. —*n.* [pl. WHYS] the reason. —*int.* exclamation of surprise, etc.

wick, *n.* piece of cord, etc. for burning, as in a candle.

wick′ed, *a.* 1. evil. 2. unpleasant. 3. naughty.

wick′er, *n.* 1. long, thin twigs or strips. 2. wickerwork. —*a.* made of wicker.

wick′er·work, *n.* baskets, etc. made of wicker.

wick′et, *n.* 1. small door, gate, or window. 2. wire arch used in croquet.

wide, *a.* 1. great in width, amount, degree, etc. 2. of a specified width. 3. far from the goal. —*adv.* 1. over or to a large extent. 2. so as to be wide. —**wide′ly,** *adv.* —**wid′en,** *v.*

wide′spread′, *a.* occurring over a wide area.

wid′ow, *n.* woman whose husband has died. —*v.* make a widow of. —**wid′ow·hood,** *n.*

wid′ow·er, *n.* man whose wife has died.

width, *n.* 1. distance side to side. 2. a piece so wide.

wield, *v.* 1. handle with skill. 2. use (power, etc.).

wie′ner (wē′-) *n.* frankfurter.

wife, *n.* [pl. WIVES] married woman. —**wife′ly,** *a.*

wig, *n.* false covering of hair for the head.

wig·gle, *v. & n.* twist and turn from side to side. —**wig′gly** [-GLIER, -GLIEST] *a.*

wig′wag, *v.* [-WAGGED, -WAGGING] 1. wag. 2. send messages by visible code.

wig′wam, *n.* cone-shaped tent of N. Am. Indians.

wild, *a.* 1. in its natural state. 2. not civilized. 3. unruly. 4. stormy. 5. enthusiastic. 6. reckless. 7. missing the target. —*adv.* in a wild way. —*n.* [in pl.] wilderness.

wild′cat, *n.* fierce animal of the cat family. —*a.* unsound or risky.

wil′der·ness, *n.* wild region.

wile, *v. & n.* trick; lure.

will, *n.* 1. wish; desire. 2. strong purpose. 3. power of choice. 4. attitude. 5. legal document disposing of one's property after death. —*v.* 1. decide. 2. control by the will. 3. bequeath. —**at will,** when one wishes.

will, *v.* [pt. WOULD] helping verb showing: 1. futurity. 2. determination or obligation. 3. ability or capacity.

will′ful, *a.* 1. done deliberately. 2. stubborn. Also sp. **wil′ful.** —**will′ful·ly,** *adv.* —**will′ful·ness,** *n.*

will′ing, *a.* 1. consenting. 2. doing or done gladly. —**will′ing·ly,** *adv.* —**will′ing·ness,** *n.*

will′-o′-the-wisp′, *n.* anything elusive.

wil′low, *n.* tree with narrow leaves.

wil′low·y, *a.* slender.

will power, self-control.

wil′ly-nil′ly, *a. & adv.* (happening) whether one wishes it or not.

wilt, *v.* 1. make or become limp. 2. make or become weak.

wi′ly, *a.* [-LIER, -LIEST] crafty; sly. —**wi′li·ness,** *n.*

win, *v.* [WON, WINNING] 1. gain a victory. 2. get by

work, effort, etc. 3. persuade. —n. [Col.] victory.

wince, v. draw back; flinch.

winch, n. machine for hoisting by a chain wound on a drum.

wind (wīnd) v. [WOUND, WINDING] 1. turn, coil, or twine around. 2. cover, or tighten, by winding. 3. move or go indirectly. —n. a turn. —**wind up**, finish.

wind (wind) n. 1. air in motion. 2. gales. 3. breath. 4. smell. —v. put out of breath.

wind'break, n. fence, trees, etc. protecting a place from the wind.

wind'ed, a. out of breath.

wind'fall, n. unexpected gain, as of money.

wind instrument, Mus. instrument played by blowing air, esp. breath, through it.

wind'lass (-ləs) n. winch.

wind'mill, n. machine operated by the wind's rotation of a wheel of vanes.

win'dow, n. 1. opening for light and air in a building, car, etc. 2. glass in a frame set in this.

win'dow-pane, n. pane of glass in a window.

wind'pipe, n. trachea.

wind'shield, n. in cars, etc., glass shield in the front.

wind'up (wīnd'-) n. end.

wind'ward, a., adv. & n. (in or toward) the direction from which the wind blows.

wind'y, a. [-IER, -IEST] 1. with much wind. 2. talky.

wine, n. fermented juice of grapes or of other fruits. —v. entertain with wine.

wing, n. 1. organ used by a bird, insect, etc. in flying. 2. thing like a wing in use or position. 3. political faction. —v. 1. to fly. 2. send swiftly. 3. wound in the wing or arm. —**on the wing**, in flight. —**take wing**, fly away. —**winged**, a. —**wing'less**, a.

wink, v. 1. close and open the eyelids quickly. 2. do this with one eye, as a signal. 3. twinkle. —n. 1. a winking. 2. an instant.

win'ner, n. one that wins.

win'ning, a. 1. victorious. 2. charming. —n. 1. a victory. 2. pl. something won.

win'now (-ō) v. 1. blow the chaff from grain. 2. sort out.

win'some (-səm) a. charming.

win'ter, n. coldest season of the year. —a. of or for winter. —v. spend the winter.

win'ter-green, n. oil from the leaves of an evergreen plant, used for flavoring.

win'try (-tri) a. [-TRIER, -TRIEST] of or like winter.

wipe, v. 1. clean or dry by rubbing. 2. rub (a cloth, etc.) over something. —n. a wiping. —**wipe out**, 1. remove. 2. kill. —**wip'er**, n.

wire, n. 1. metal drawn into a long thread. 2. telegraph. 3. [Col.] telegram. —a. made of wire. —v. 1. furnish or fasten with wire(s). 2. [Col.] telegraph.

wire'less, a. 1. operating by electric waves, not with conducting wire. —n. 1. wireless telegraph or telephone. 2. [Chiefly Br.] radio.

wir'ing, n. system of wires, as for carrying electricity.

wir'y, a. [-IER, -IEST] 1. like wire; stiff. 2. lean and strong. —**wir'i-ness**, n.

wis'dom, n. 1. a being wise; good judgment. 2. knowledge.

wisdom tooth, back tooth on each side of each jaw.

wise, a. 1. having good judgment. 2. informed or learned. —**wise'ly**, adv.

-wise, suf. 1. in a certain direction, position, or manner. 2. with regard to.

wise'crack, v. & n. [Sl.] (make) a flippant remark.

wish, v. 1. to want; desire. 2. express a desire concerning. 3. request. —n. 1. a wishing. 2. something wished for. 3. request.

wish'ful, a. showing a wish.

wish'y-wash'y, a. weak.

wisp, n. slight thing or bit. —**wisp'y** [-IER, -IEST] a.

wis-te'ri-a, n. twining shrub with clusters of flowers.

wist'ful, a. yearning. —**wist'ful-ly**, adv.

wit, n. 1. (one with) the ability to make clever remarks. 2. pl. powers of thinking. —**to wit**, namely.

witch, n. woman supposed to have evil, magic power.

witch'craft, n. power or practices of witches.

witch hazel, lotion made from a plant extract.

with, prep. 1. against. 2. near to; in the care or company of. 3. into. 4. as a member of. 5. concerning. 6. compared to. 7. as well as. 8. in the opinion of. 9. as a result of. 10. by means of. 11. having or showing. 12. to; onto. 13. from. 14. after.

with·draw', v. [-DREW, -DRAWN, -DRAWING] 1. take back. 2. move back. 3. leave. —**with·draw'al**, n.

with·drawn', a. shy, reserved, etc.

with·er (with'-) v. wilt.

with·ers (with'-) n.pl. highest part of a horse's back.

with·hold', v. [-HELD, -HOLD-ING] 1. keep back; restrain. 2. refrain from granting.

with·in', adv. in or to the inside. —prep. 1. inside. 2. not beyond.

with·out', adv. on the outside. —prep. 1. outside. 2. lacking. 3. avoiding.

with·stand', v. [-STOOD, -STANDING] resist; endure.

wit'less, a. stupid.

wit'ness, n. 1. one who saw and can testify to a thing. 2. testimony. 3. attesting signer. —v. 1. see. 2. act as a witness of. 3. be proof of.

wit'ti·cism, n. witty remark.

wit'ty, a. [-TIER, -TIEST] cleverly amusing.

wives, n. pl. of **wife**.

wiz'ard, n. magician.

wiz'ard·ry, n. magic.

wiz'ened, a. dried up and wrinkled.

wob'ble, v. move unsteadily from side to side. —n. a wobbling. —**wob'bly**, a.

woe, n. grief or trouble. —**woe'ful**, a. —**woe'ful·ly**, adv.

woe'be·gone', a. showing woe.

woke, pt. of **wake**.

wolf, n. [pl. WOLVES] 1. wild, doglike animal. 2. cruel or greedy person. —v. eat greedily. —**wolf'ish**, a.

wol'ver·ine' (-ēn') n. strong animal like a small bear.

wom'an, n. [pl. WOMEN] adult female person. —**wom'an·hood'**, n. —**wom'an·ly**, a.

womb (wōōm) n. uterus.

won, pt. of **win**.

won'der, n. 1. amazing thing; marvel. 2. feeling caused by this. —v. 1. feel wonder. 2. be curious about.

won'der·ful, a. 1. causing wonder. 2. [Col.] excellent.

won'drous, a. & adv. [Poet.] amazing(ly).

wont (wunt) a. accustomed. —n. habit. —**wont'ed**, a.

won't, will not.

woo, v. seek to win, esp. as one's spouse.

wood, n. 1. hard substance under a tree's bark. 2. lumber. 3. often pl. forest. —a. 1. of wood. 2. of the woods. —**wood'ed**, a.

wood alcohol, poisonous alcohol used as fuel, etc.

wood'bine, n. climbing plant.

wood'chuck', n. N. Am. burrowing animal.

wood'cut', n. print made from a wood engraving.

wood'en, a. 1. made of wood. 2. lifeless, dull, etc.

wood'land, n. & a. forest.

wood'peck·er, n. bird that pecks holes in bark.

wood winds, wind instruments as the clarinet, oboe, flute. —**wood'-wind'**, a.

wood'work, n. wooden doors, frames, moldings, etc.

wood'y, a. [-IER, -IEST] 1. tree-covered. 2. of or like wood.

woof, n. threads woven across the warp in a loom.

wool, n. 1. soft curly hair of sheep, goats, etc. 2. yarn or cloth made of this.

wool'en, **wool'len**, a. of wool. —n. [in pl.] woolen goods.

wool'gath·er·ing, n. daydreaming.

wool'ly, a. [-LIER, -LIEST] of, like, or covered with wool. Also sp. **wooly**.

word, n. 1. a sound or sounds as a speech unit. 2. letter or letters standing for this. 3. brief remark. 4. news. 5. promise. 6. pl. quarrel. —v. put into words.

word'ing, n. choice and arrangement of words.

word'y, a. [-IER, -IEST] using too many words. —**word'i·ness**, n.

wore, pt. of **wear**.

work, n. 1. effort of doing or making; labor. 2. occupation, trade, etc. 3. task; duty. 4. thing made, done, etc. 5. pl. factory. 6. pl. moving parts of a machine 7. workmanship. —v. [alt. pt. & pp. WROUGHT] 1. do work; toil. 2. function. 3. cause to work. 4. be employed. 5. bring about. 6. come or bring to some condition. 7. solve (a problem). —**at work**, working. —**work out**, develop or result. —**work up**, 1. advance. 2.

develop. 3. excite. —**work'-a·ble,** *a.* —**work'er,** *n.* —**work'man,** *n.*

work'a·day, *a.* ordinary.

work'house, *n.* jail where prisoners are put to work.

work'ing·man, *n.* [pl. **-MEN**] worker, esp. in industry.

work'man·like, *a.* done well.

work'man·ship, *n.* worker's skill or product.

work'out, *n.* [Col.] strenuous exercise, practice, etc.

work'shop, *n.* room or building where work is done.

world, *n.* 1. the earth. 2. the universe. 3. all people. 4. any sphere or domain. 5. everyday life. 6. *often pl.* great deal.

worm, *n.* 1. long, slender creeping animal. 2. thing like a worm. 3. *pl.* disease caused by worms. —*v.* 1. move like a worm. 2. get in a sneaky way. —**worm'y,** *a.*

worm'wood, *n.* bitter herb.

worn, *pp.* of **wear.**

worn'-out', *a.* 1. no longer usable. 2. very tired.

wor'ry, *v.* [-RIED, -RYING] 1. make, or be, troubled or uneasy. 2. annoy. 3. shake with the teeth. —*n.* [*pl.* -RIES] 1. troubled feeling. 2. cause of this. —**wor'ri·er,** *n.* —**wor'ri·some,** *a.*

worse, *a.* 1. more evil, bad, etc. 2. more ill. —*adv.* in a worse way. —*n.* that which is worse.

wors'en, *v.* make or become worse.

wor'ship, *n.* 1. prayer, service, etc. in reverence to a deity. 2. intense love or admiration. —*v.* 1. show reverence for. 2. take part in worship service.

worst, *a.* most evil, bad, etc. —*adv.* in the worst way. —*n.* that which is worst.

wor'sted (woos'tid) *n.* wool fabric with a smooth surface.

worth, *n.* 1. value or merit. 2. equivalent in money. —*a.* 1. deserving. 2. equal in value to. —**worth'less,** *a.*

worth'-while', *a.* worth the time or effort spent.

wor'thy, *a.* [-THIER, -THIEST] 1. having worth or value. 2. deserving. —*n.* worthy person. —**wor'thi·ness,** *n.*

would (wood) *pt.* of **will.** *Would* is used to express futurity, a wish, a request, etc.

would'-be', *a.* wishing, pretending, or meant to be.

wound (woond) *n.* 1. injury

to the body tissue. 2. scar. 3. injury to the feelings, etc. —*v.* injure; hurt.

wound (wound) *pt.* & *pp.* of **wind** (turn).

wove, *pt.* of **weave.**

wo'ven, *pp.* of **weave.**

wow, *int.* expression of surprise, pleasure, etc.

wrack (rak) *n.* destruction.

wraith (rāth) *n.* ghost.

wran'gle (ran'-) *v.* & *n.* quarrel; dispute.

wrap, *v.* [WRAPPED or WRAPT, WRAPPING] 1. wind or fold (a covering) around. 2. enclose in paper, etc. —*n.* outer garment. —**wrap'per,** *n.*

wrath, *n.* great anger; rage. —**wrath'ful,** *a.*

wreak (rēk) *v.* 1. inflict (vengeance, etc.). 2. give vent to (anger, etc.).

wreath (rēth) *n.* [pl. WREATHS (rēthz)] twisted ring of leaves, etc.

wreathe (rēth) *v.* 1. encircle. 2. decorate with wreaths.

wreck, *n.* 1. remains of a thing destroyed. 2. rundown person. 3. a wrecking. —*v.* 1. destroy or ruin. 2. tear down. —**wreck'age** (-ij) *n.* —**wreck'er,** *n.*

wren, *n.* small songbird.

wrench, *n.* 1. sudden, sharp twist. 2. injury caused by a twist. 3. tool for turning nuts, bolts, etc. —*v.* 1. twist or jerk sharply. 2. injure with a twist.

wrest, *v.* take by force.

wres'tle, *v.* 1. struggle with (an opponent) trying to throw him. 2. contend (*with*). —*n.* struggle. —**wres'tler,** *n.* —**wres'tling,** *n.*

wretch, *n.* 1. very unhappy person. 2. person despised. —**wretch'ed,** *a.* 1. very unhappy. 2. distressing. 3. unsatisfactory.

wrig'gle, *v.* twist and turn, or move along thus. —*n.* a wriggling. —**wrig'gler,** *n.*

wring, *v.* [WRUNG, WRINGING] 1. squeeze and twist. 2. force out by this means. 3. get by force. —**wring'er,** *n.*

wrin'kle, *n.* small crease or fold. —*v.* make wrinkles in.

wrist, *n.* joint between the hand and forearm.

writ, *n.* formal court order.

write, *v.* [WROTE, WRITTEN, WRITING] 1. form (words, letters, etc.). 2. produce (writing or music). 3. write a letter. —**write off,** cancel, as a debt. —**writ'er,** n.

writhe (rīth) v. twist and turn, as in pain.

wrong, a. 1. not right or just. 2. not true or correct. 3. not suitable. 4. mistaken. 5. out of order. 6. not meant to be seen. —adv. incorrectly. —n. something wrong. —v. treat unjustly.

wrong'do'ing, n. unlawful or bad behavior. —**wrong'-do'er,** n.

wrong'ful, a. unjust, unlawful, etc. —**wrong'ful·ly,** adv.

wrought (rôt) a. 1. made. 2. shaped by hammering.

wrought iron, tough, malleable iron used for fences, etc. —**wrought'-i'ron,** a.

wrought'-up', a. excited.

wrung, pt. & pp. of wring.

wry, a. [WRIER, WRIEST] twisted or distorted. —**wry'ly,** adv. —**wry'ness,** n.

X, Y, Z

Xmas, n. Christmas.

X ray, 1. ray that can penetrate solid matter. 2. photograph made with X rays. —**X'-ray',** a. of or by X rays. —v. examine, treat, or photograph with X rays.

xy'lem (zī'-) n. woody plant tissue.

xy'lo·phone (zī'-) n. musical instrument of a row of wooden bars struck with hammers.

-y, suf. 1. full of or like. 2. rather. 3. apt to. 4. state of being. 5. act of.

yacht (yät) n. small ship. —v. sail in a yacht. —**yachts'-man** [pl. -MEN] n.

yak, n. wild ox of Asia.

yam, n. 1. starchy, edible root of a tropical plant. 2. [Dial.] sweet potato.

yank, v. & n. [Col.] jerk.

Yan'kee, n. U.S. citizen, esp. a Northerner.

yap, v. & n. [YAPPED, YAP-PING] (make) a sharp, shrill bark.

yard, n. 1. measure of length, three feet. 2. ground around a building. 3. enclosed place. 4. slender spar.

yard'age, n. distance or length in yards.

yard'stick, n. 1. measuring stick one yard long. 2. standard for judging.

yarn, n. 1. spun strand of wool, cotton, etc. 2. [Col.] tale or story.

yaw, v. & n. turn from the course, as of a ship.

yawl, n. kind of sailboat.

yawn, v. open the mouth widely, as when one is sleepy. —n. a yawning.

yaws, n.pl. tropical, infectious skin disease.

ye (yē) pron. [Ar.] you. —a. [Ar.] (thə) the.

yea (yā) adv. 1. yes. 2. truly. —n. vote of "yes."

year, n. 1. period of 365 days (366 in leap year) or 12 months. 2. pl. age.

year'book, n. book with data of the preceding year.

year'ling, n. animal in its second year.

year'ly, a. 1. every year. 2. of a year. —adv. every year.

yearn (yûrn) v. feel longing. —**yearn'ing,** n. & a.

yeast (yēst) n. 1. frothy substance causing fermentation. 2. yeast mixed with flour or meal: also **yeast cake.**

yell, v. & n. scream; shout.

yel'low, a. 1. of the color of ripe lemons. 2. [Col.] cowardly. —n. yellow color. —v. make or become yellow. —**yel'low·ish,** a.

yellow fever, tropical disease carried by a mosquito.

yellow jacket, bright-yellow wasp or hornet.

yelp, v. & n. (utter) a short, sharp cry or bark.

yen, n. [Col.] deep longing.

yeo'man (yō'-) n. [pl. -MEN] 1. U.S. Navy clerk. 2. [Br.] small-farm owner.

yes, adv. 1. it is so. 2. not only that, but more. —n. [pl. YESES] 1. consent. 2. affirmative vote.

yes'ter·day, n. 1. day before today. 2. recent time. —adv. on the day before today.

yet, adv. 1. up to now. 2. now. 3. still. 4. nevertheless. —con. nevertheless.

yew, n. evergreen tree.

Yid'dish, n. German dialect using the Hebrew alphabet.

yield (yēld) v. 1. produce; give. 2. surrender. 3. concede; grant. 4. give way to force. —n. amount produced.

yo'del, v. sing with abrupt, alternating changes to the falsetto. —n. a yodeling.

yo'gurt, yo'ghurt (-goort) n. thick, semisolid food made from fermented milk.

yoke, n. 1. frame for harnessing together a pair of oxen, etc. 2. thing that binds or unites. 3. servitude. 4. part of a garment at the shoulders. —v. 1. harness to.

2. join together.

yo'kel, *n.* simple rustic.

yolk (yōk) *n.* yellow part of an egg.

yon, *a. & adv.* [Ar.] yonder.

yon'der, *a. & adv.* over there.

yore, *adv.* [Obs.] long ago.

you, *pron. sing. & pl.* 1. the person(s) spoken to. 2. person(s) generally.

young, *a.* 1. in an early stage of life or growth. 2. fresh. —*n.* young offspring. —**young'ish,** *a.*

young'ster, *n.* child.

your, *pronominal a.* of you.

you're, you are.

yours, *pron.* that or those belonging to you.

your·self', *pron.* [*pl.* -SELVES] intensive or reflexive form of **you.**

youth, *n.* 1. state or quality of being young. 2. adolescence. 3. young people. 4. young man. —**youth'ful,** *a.*

you've, you have.

yowl, *v. & n.* howl; wail.

yuc'ca, *n.* lilylike plant.

yule, *n.* Christmas.

yule'tide, *n.* Christmas time.

za'ny, *a.* [-NIER, -NIEST] of or like a foolish or comical person. —*n.* [*pl.* -NIES] such a person. —**za'ni·ness,** *n.*

zeal, *n.* eager endeavor or devotion.

zeal'ot (zel'-) *n.* one showing zeal, esp. fanatic zeal.

zeal'ous (zel'-) *a.* full of zeal. —**zeal'ous·ly,** *adv.*

ze'bra, *n.* striped African animal related to the horse.

ze·bu (zē'bū) *n.* oxlike animal with a hump.

ze'nith, *n.* 1. point in the sky directly overhead. 2. highest point.

zeph·yr (zef'ēr) *n.* breeze.

zep'pe·lin, *n.* dirigible.

ze'ro, *n.* [*pl.* -ROS, -ROES] 1. the symbol 0. 2. point marked 0 in a scale. 3.

nothing. —*a.* of or at zero.

zest, *n.* 1. stimulating quality. 2. keen enjoyment. —**zest'ful,** *a.*

zig'zag, *n.* line with sharp turns back and forth. —*a. & adv.* in a zigzag. —*v.* [-ZAGGED, -ZAGGING] to move or form in a zigzag.

zinc, *n.* bluish-white metal, a chemical element.

zing, *n.* [Sl.] shrill, whizzing sound.

zin'ni·a, *n.* daisylike flower thick with petals.

zip, *v.* [ZIPPED, ZIPPING] 1. make a short, sharp hissing sound. 2. [Col.] move fast. 3. fasten with a zipper. —*n.* 1. a zipping sound. 2. [Col.] vim. —**zip'py** [-PIER, -PIEST] *a.*

zip'per, *n.* slide fastener.

zir'con, *n.* transparent gem.

zith'er, *n.* stringed instrument, played by plucking.

zo'di·ac, *n.* imaginary belt along the sun's apparent path divided into 12 parts named for constellations.

zom'bi, *n.* [*pl.* -BIS] animated corpse in folklore.

zone, *n.* 1. any of the five areas into which the earth is divided according to climate. 2. area set apart in some way. —*v.* mark off into zones. —**zoned,** *a.*

zoo, *n.* place with wild animals on exhibition.

zoological garden, zoo.

zo·ol'o·gy, *n.* science of animal life. —**zo'o·log'i·cal,** *a.* —**zo·ol'o·gist,** *n.*

zoom, *v.* 1. make a loud, buzzing sound. 2. speed upward or forward. —*n.* a zooming.

zuc·chi·ni (zōō-kē'ni) *n.* cucumberlike squash.

zwie·back (tswē'bäk, swī'bak) *n.* dried, toasted slices of a kind of bread.

PUNCTUATION

The **Period** (.) is used: 1) to end a sentence; 2) after most abbreviations; 3) before a decimal; 4) as one of a series (usually three spaced periods) to indicate an omission, an interruption, or a break in continuity.

The **Comma** (,) is used: 1) between short independent clauses in parallel construction and between clauses joined by the conjunctions *and, but, yet, nor*, etc.; 2) after a fairly long dependent clause that precedes an independent one; 3) before and after a dependent clause that comes in the middle of a sentence; 4) to set off a nonrestrictive word, phrase, or clause; 5) to set off transitional words and phrases; 6) to separate words, phrases, or clauses in series; 7) to set off the one spoken to in direct address; 8) to set off a direct quotation; 9) to set off titles, addresses, names of places, dates, etc.; 10) after the salutation of an informal letter; 11) after the complimentary close of letters.

The **Semicolon** (;) is used: 1) in compound sentences between independent clauses that are not joined by connectives, or when such clauses are joined by conjunctive adverbs; 2) to separate phrases or clauses that are broken by internal punctuation.

The **Colon** (:) is used: 1) to introduce a long series; 2) before a lengthy quotation; 3) between chapter and verse, volume and page, hour and minute, etc.; 4) after the salutation of a business letter.

The **Question Mark** (?) is used: 1) after a direct question; 2) to show uncertainty or doubt.

The **Exclamation Mark** (!) is used after a word, phrase, or sentence to indicate strong emotion, surprise, etc.

The **Hyphen** (-) is used: 1) to separate the parts of a compound word or numeral; 2) to indicate syllabication.

The **Dash** (—) is used: 1) to show a break in continuity; 2) between numbers, dates, times, places, etc. that mark limits.

Quotation Marks (" ") are used: 1) to enclose a direct quotation; 2) to enclose the titles of articles, short stories, short poems, etc., or divisions or chapters of books, periodicals, long poems, etc.

Italic Type is used: 1) to set off the titles of books, periodicals, newspapers, etc.; 2) to indicate foreign words or phrases.

The **Apostrophe** (') is used: 1) to indicate an omitted letter or letters in a word or contraction; 2) with an added *s* to form the possessive case of all nouns that do not end in an *s* or *z* sound; 3) with an added *s* to form the possessive of monosyllabic, singular nouns that end in an *s* or *z* sound; 4) without an added *s* to form the possessive of all nouns that end in an *s* or *z* sound except monosyllabic, singular forms and forms ending in *-ce*; 5) to form the plurals of letters, numbers, etc.

Parentheses, ( ), are used: 1) to enclose nonessential material in a sentence; 2) to enclose letters or numbers of reference as in an outline form.

Brackets, [ ], are used to indicate insertions, comments, corrections, etc. made by a person other than the original author of the material.

A **Capital Letter** is used: 1) to begin a sentence, or a quotation or direct question within a sentence; 2) to begin every word in all proper nouns; 3) to begin every word, except conjunctions, articles, and short prepositions that are not the first word, in the names of books, magazines, works of music or art, businesses, agencies, religions, holidays, etc.; 4) to begin every word in the names of days, months, eras, etc.; 5) in many abbreviations; 6) to begin nouns and pronouns referring to the Deity; 7) to begin all salutations and all complimentary closes of letters.

ABBREVIATIONS

A., a. acre(s).
A.B. Bachelor of Arts.
abbr. abbreviation.
A.C. alternating current.
A/C, a/c, account.
acc., acct. account.
A.D. in the year of our Lord.
ad lib. at pleasure.
Adm. Admiral.
aet., aetat. aged.
A.M. Master of Arts.
A.M., a.m. before noon.
Amer. America(n).
amp. ampere.
anon. anonymous.
app. appendix.
apt(s). apartment(s).
ar., arr. arrive(s).
assn. association.
asst. assistant.
Atl. Atlantic.
att(y). attorney.
Aus. Australia(n).
av. average; avoirdupois.
Av(e). Avenue.
b. born.
B.A. Bachelor of Arts.
bal. balance.
bbl. barrel(s).
B.C. before Christ.
bd. board; bond.
Bib. Bible; Biblical.
B/L, bill of lading.
bldg. building.
Blvd. Boulevard.
bro(s). brother(s).
B.S. Bachelor of Science.
B/S, bill of sale.
bu. bushel(s).
bul., bull. bulletin.
C. centigrade.
c(a). circa (about).
Can. Canada.
canc. cancel(lation).
cap. capital(ized).
c.c. carbon copy; cubic centimeters.
cent. a hundred; century.
cert. certificate.
cf. compare.
Ch. Church; China.
chap. chapter; chaplain.
chem. chemistry; chemist.
chg(d). charge(d).
cm. centimeter(s).
Co. Company; County.
c/o, care of.
C.O.D. collect on delivery.
Col. Colonel; Colo(u)mbia.
com. commerce; commander.
Cong. Congress(ional).
cont. continued; contents.
Corp. Corporation; Corporal.
cr. credit(or).
ct(s). centime(s); cent(s).
cwt. a hundredweight.
d. died; daughter; penny.
D.A. District Attorney.
D.C. direct current.

D.D. Doctor of Divinity.
D.D.S. Doctor of Dental Surgery.
dept. department; deputy.
dict. dictionary.
diff. difference.
dir. director.
dist. distributor; district.
div. division.
doc. document.
dol(s). dollar(s).
d(o)z. dozen(s).
Dr. Doctor; debtor.
dup. duplicate.
E. east(ern); English.
ea. each.
econ. economics.
ed. editor; edition.
e.g. for example.
elem. elementary.
enc(l). enclosure.
ency. encyclopedia.
Eng. England; English.
eng. engineer; engraver.
env. envelope.
eq. equal; equivalent.
equiv. equivalent.
esp., espec. especially.
est. estimated; established.
et al. and (the) others.
etc., &c. and so forth.
et seq. and the following.
Eur. Europe(an).
ex. example; exception.
exec. executive; executor.
ex lib. from the books (of).
ext. extension; extra.
fac. facsimile.
fcp. foolscap.
ff. following; folios.
fig. figurative(ly); figure.
fl. he flourished.
f.o.b. free on board.
Fr. Father; French.
freq. frequent(ly).
ft. foot; feet.
fwd. forward.
gal(s). gallon(s).
G.B. Great Britain.
Ger. German(y).
G.M. general manager.
gm. gram(s).
Gov. Governor.
govt. government.
Gr. Greek; Greece.
gr. grain(s); gram(s); gross.
grad. graduate(d).
gram. grammar.
Gr.Br. or Brit. Great Britain.
hdqrs. headquarters.
her. heraldry.
hist. history.
H.J. here lies (buried).
hosp. hospital.
H.P., h.p. horsepower.
H.R. House of Representatives.
hr. hour.
H.S. high school.

303

ABBREVIATIONS

ht. height.
hyp. hypothesis.
I. Island(s).
ib., ibid. in the same place.
i.e. that is.
id. the same.
illus. illustrated.
in. inch(es).
inc. incorporated; inclosure.
incl. inclusive.
incog. incognito.
inf. infantry; infinitive.
ins. insurance.
insp. inspected.
Inst. Institute.
inst. instant (the present month).
instr. instrument; instructor.
int. interest; international.
inv. invoice.
IOU. I owe you.
I.Q. intelligence quotient.
Ir. Ireland; Irish.
is. island; isle.
It. Italian; Italy.
ital. italics.
Jap. Japan(ese).
jct. junction.
J.P. Justice of the Peace.
jr. junior.
juv. juvenile.
K., k. King; kilogram.
kc. kilocycle(s).
kg. kilogram(s).
kilo. kilometer(s).
km. kilometer(s); kingdom.
kw. kilowatt(s).
L., lb. a pound (weight).
L., l. a pound (sterling).
lab. laboratory.
lang. language.
lat. latitude.
Lat. Latin.
lb(s). pound(s).
l.c. in the place cited; lower case.
leg. legal; legislature.
Legis. Legislature.
lib. book; library.
lin. lineal; linear.
liq. liquid; liquor.
lit. literature; liter; literal(ly).
loc. cit. in the place cited.
log. logarithm.
lon., long. longitude.
loq. he or she speaks.
l.s.d. pounds, shillings, pence.
Ltd., ltd. limited.
lv. leave(s).
M. a thousand; Monsieur.
m. male; married; meridian; noon; mile(s).
M.A. Master of Arts.
mach. machinery.
Mad. Madam.
mag. magazine.
Maj. Major.
mas., masc. masculine.

math. mathematics.
max. maximum.
M.C. Master of Ceremonies; Member of Congress.
M.D. Doctor of Medicine.
mdse. merchandise.
mech. mechanics.
med. medicine; medieval.
Medit. Mediterranean.
mem. memorandum.
Messrs. Messieurs.
met. metropolitan.
Mex. Mexican; Mexico.
mfg. manufacturing.
mfr. manufacture(r).
mgr. manager; monsignor.
mi. mile(s); mill(s).
mid. middle.
mil. military.
min. minimum; minute(s).
misc. miscellaneous.
Mile(s). Mademoiselle(s).
MM. Messieurs.
mm. millimeter(s).
Mme(s). Madame(s).
m.o. money order.
mo. month.
mod. modern; moderate.
Mons. Monsieur.
mph., miles per hour.
MS. manuscript.
M.S. Master of Science.
mt. mount(ain).
mtg. mortgage.
mun. municipal.
mus. museum; music.
N, north(ern).
n. born; noun.
N. Am(er). North America(n).
nat. national; native.
naut. nautical.
nav. naval; navigation.
n.b. note well.
n.d. no date.
neg. negative(ly).
neut. neuter.
No. north(ern).
no(s). number(s).
non seq. it doesn't follow.
nt. wt. net weight.
ob. he (she) died.
obs. obsolete.
op. cit. in the work cited.
opp. opposed; opposite.
orch. orchestra.
oz. ounce.
p. page; participle.
Pac. Pacific.
par. paragraph; parallel.
pass. passenger; passive.
pat(d). patent(ed).
pc. piece.
p.c. per cent.
p.d. per diem; police department.
pd. paid.
per. period; person.
perf. perfect; perforated.
pers. person(al).

ABBREVIATIONS

pert. pertaining.
Ph.D. Doctor of Philosophy.
phr. phrase.
phys. physician; physics.
pkg(s). package(s).
pl. place; plural.
P.M., p.m. after noon.
p.o. post office.
poet. poetic(al).
polit. political; politics.
pop. population; popularly.
pos. positive.
poss. possession; possessive.
pr. pair(s); price.
pref. preferred; prefix.
prelim. preliminary.
prep. preparatory;
    preposition.
pres. present; presidency.
prim. primary.
prin. principal; printing.
priv. private.
prob. problem; probably.
proc. proceeding.
prof. professor.
pron. pronunciation;
    pronoun.
prop. properly; proposition.
prop(r). proprietor.
P.S. postscript.
pt. part; payment; point.
pub. public; publisher.
punc. punctuation.
Q.E.D. that which was to
    be demonstrated.
qt. quantity; quart(s).
qu. quart; question.
ques. question.
quot. quotation.
q.v. which see.
Rd. road.
rec. receipt; record(ed).
recd. received.
ref. referee; reference;
    reformed; reformation.
reg. region; register(ed);
    regular; regulation;
    regiment.
rel. relative(ly); religion.
rep. report; representative;
    republic(an).
res. reserve; residence.
resp. respective(ly).
ret. retired; returned.
Rev. Reverend.
rev. revenue; revise(d);
    revolution.
R.F.D. Rural Free Delivery.
rhet. rhetoric(al).
R.I.P. may he (she, they)
    rest in peace.
R.N. registered nurse;
    Royal Navy.
Rom. Roman; Romance.
R.O.T.C. Reserve Officers'
    Training Corps.
r.p.m. revolutions per
    minute.
R.R. railroad.

R.S.V.P. please reply.
rt(s). right(s).
Ry. railway.
S, south(ern).
s. singular; son.
S.A. South America.
sc. science; scilicet (that
    is to say; namely).
Scot. Scotland; Scottish.
Sc.D. Doctor of Science.
sec. second(s); secretary;
    section(s).
Sen. Senate; Senator.
sep. separate.
seq(q). the following.
sgt. sergeant.
Shak. Shakespeare.
shpt. shipment.
soc. society.
sol. solution; soluble.
SOS, distress signal.
sov. sovereign.
Sp. Spain; Spanish.
sp. spelling; species;
    specimen.
spec. special; specifically.
sq. square.
Sr. Senior; Señor; Sir.
S.R.O. standing room only.
St. Street; Saint; Strait.
stat. statute(s); statue.
sub. substitute; suburb.
subj. subject(ive);
    subjunctive.
suff. suffix.
sup. supplement(ary);
    supra (above).
supt. superintendent.
syn. synonym(y).
synop. synopsis.
t. temperature; time; ton.
t.b. tuberculosis.
tbs. tablespoon(s).
tel. telephone; telegram.
temp. temperature.
terr. territory; terrace.
term. terminal; terminus.
tr. transitive; translation;
    transpose; trustee.
trans. transaction(s); trans-
    lated; transportation.
treas. treasurer; treasury.
U. University; Union.
ult. ultimate(ly).
v, volt(s); velocity.
v. verb; verse; version;
    versus; vide (see); volume.
vet. veteran; veterinary.
viz. videlicet (namely).
vol(s). volume(s); volun-
    teer(s).
V.P. Vice President.
vs. versus.
W, west(ern).
w, watt(s).
wk(s). week(s); work(s).
wt. weight.
yd(s). yard(s).
yr(s). year(s).
z. zone.

305

WEIGHTS AND MEASURES

Linear

12 inches	=	1 foot
3 feet	=	1 yard
5½ yards	=	1 rod
40 rods	=	1 furlong
8 furlongs	=	1 mile

Liquid

4 gills	=	1 pint
2 pints	=	1 quart
4 quarts	=	1 gallon
31½ gals.	=	1 barrel
2 barrels	=	1 hogshead

Metric Equivalents

1 inch	=	2.5400 centimeters
1 foot	=	0.3048 meter
1 yard	=	0.9144 meter
1 mile	=	1.6093 kilometers
1 centimeter	=	0.3937 inch
1 decimeter	=	3.9370 inches
1 meter	=	39.3701 inches
1 kilometer	=	0.6213 mile
1 quart (dry)	=	1.1012 liters
1 quart (liq.)	=	0.9463 liter
1 gallon	=	3.7853 liters
1 liter	=	0.9081 dry quart
1 liter	=	1.0567 liquid quarts

Square

144	sq. inches	= 1 sq. foot
9	sq. feet	= 1 sq. yard
30¼	sq. yards	= 1 sq. rod
160	sq. rods	= 1 acre
640	acres	= 1 sq. mile

Circular

60 sec.	=	1 min.
60 min.	=	1 degree
90 deg.	=	1 quadrant
180 deg.	=	1 semicircle
360 deg.	=	1 circle

Metric Equivalents

1 sq. inch	=	6.452 sq. centimeters
1 sq. foot	=	929.030 sq. centimeters
1 sq. mile	=	2.590 sq. kilometers
1 sq. centimeter	=	0.155 sq. inch
1 sq. meter	=	1.196 sq. yards
1 sq. kilometer	=	0.386 sq. mile

Cubic

1,728 cu. inches	=	1 cu. foot
27 cu. feet	=	1 cu. yard
128 cu. feet	=	1 cord (wood)

Dry

2 pints	=	1 quart
8 quarts	=	1 peck
4 pecks	=	1 bushel

Metric Equivalents

1 cu. inch	=	16.3872 cu. centimeters
		0.0164 liter
1 cu. foot	=	0.0283 cu. meter
		28.3170 liters
1 cu. meter	=	35.3145 cu. feet
1 ounce (avdp.)	=	28.3495 grams
1 pound	=	0.4536 kilogram
1 gram	=	0.0353 ounce
1 kilogram	=	2.2046 lbs.
1 ton (2000 lbs.)	=	907.1848 kilograms

Longitude and Time

1 second of longitude	=	1/15 sec. of time
1 minute " "	=	4 sec. of time
1 degree " "	=	4 min. of time
15 degrees " "	=	1 hour
360 degrees " "	=	24 hours

PERPETUAL CALENDAR

To find the day of the week for any date the first step is to find the Dominical letter in the column under the desired Century and in line horizontally with the last two figures of the desired year. The second step is to find the vertical column in which that Dominical letter appears in line horizontally with the desired month. (Two letters are given for leap years; the first, for January and February, the second for other months.) The last step is to find the day of the week in that same vertical column which appears in line horizontally with the desired date. Ex.: July 4, 1965, will fall on Sunday. Bold face type in the calendar illustrates these three steps.

CENTURY					YEAR			
Gregorian Calendar Oct. 15, 1582 to 2400					(Last two figures of desired year)			
1500	1600 2000	1700 2100	1800 2200	1900 2300				
Dominical Letter								
—	BA	C	E	G	00			
F	G	B	D	F	01	29	57	85
E	F	A	C	E	02	30	58	86
D	E	G	B	D	03	31	59	87
CB	DC	FE	AG	CB	04	32	60	88
A	B	D	F	A	05	33	61	89
G	A	C	E	G	06	34	62	90
F	G	B	D	F	07	35	63	91
ED	FE	AG	CB	ED	08	36	64	92
C	D	F	A	**C**	09	37	**65**	93
B	C	E	G	B	10	38	66	94
A	B	D	F	A	11	39	67	95
GF	AG	CB	ED	GF	12	40	68	96
E	F	A	C	E	13	41	69	97
D	E	G	B	D	14	42	70	98
C	D	F	A	C	15	43	71	99
—	CB	ED	GF	BA	16	44	72	
—	A	C	E	G	17	45	73	
—	G	B	D	F	18	46	74	
—	F	A	C	E	19	47	75	
—	ED	GF	BA	DC	20	48	76	
—	C	E	G	B	21	49	77	
—	B	D	F	A	22	50	78	
—	A	C	E	G	23	51	79	
—	GF	BA	DC	FE	24	52	80	
—	E	G	B	D	25	53	81	
C	D	F	A	C	26	54	82	
B	C	E	G	B	27	55	83	
AG	BA	DC	FE	AG	28	56	84	

MONTH	DOMINICAL LETTER						
Jan., Oct.	A	B	C	D	E	F	G
Feb., Mar., Nov.	D	E	F	G	A	B	C
Apr., July	G	A	B	**C**	D	E	F
May	B	C	D	E	F	G	A
June	E	F	G	A	B	C	D
Aug.	C	D	E	F	G	A	B
Sept., Dec.	F	G	A	B	C	D	E

DAY					DOMINICAL LETTER				
1	8	15	22	29	Sun.	Sat.	Fri.	Th.	Wed. Tu. Mon.
2	9	16	23	30	Mon.	Sun.	Sat.	Fri.	Th. Wed. Tu.
3	10	17	24	31	Tu.	Mon.	Sun.	Sat.	Fri. Th. Wed.
4	11	18	25		Wed.	Tu.	Mon.	**Sun.**	Sat. Fri. Th.
5	12	19	26		Th.	Wed.	Tu.	Mon.	Sun. Sat. Fri.
6	13	20	27		Fri.	Th.	Wed.	Tu.	Mon. Sun. Sat.
7	14	21	28		Sat.	Fri.	Th.	Wed.	Tu. Mon. Sun.

Reprinted by permission of the Smithsonian Institution.

THE UNITED STATES

STATE	DATE ADMITTED	POP. 1970	CAPITAL
Alabama (Ala.)	1819	3,444,165	Montgomery
Alaska (Alas.)	1959	302,173	Juneau
Arizona (Ariz.)	1912	1,772,482	Phoenix
Arkansas (Ark.)	1836	1,923,295	Little Rock
California (Cal.)	1850	19,953,134	Sacramento
Colorado (Colo.)	1876	2,207,259	Denver
*Connecticut (Conn.)	1788	3,032,217	Hartford
*Delaware (Del.)	1787	548,104	Dover
Dist. of Columbia (D.C.)	—	756,510	‡
Florida (Fla.)	1845	6,789,443	Tallahassee
*Georgia (Ga.)	1788	4,589,575	Atlanta
Hawaii	1959	768,561	Honolulu
Idaho (I.)	1890	712,567	Boise
Illinois (Ill.)	1818	11,113,976	Springfield
Indiana (Ind.)	1816	5,193,669	Indianapolis
Iowa (Ia.)	1846	2,825,041	Des Moines
Kansas (Kans.)	1861	2,249,071	Topeka
Kentucky (Ky.)	1792	3,219,311	Frankfort
Louisiana (La.)	1812	3,643,180	Baton Rouge
Maine (Me.)	1820	992,048	Augusta
*Maryland (Md.)	1788	3,922,399	Annapolis
*Massachusetts (Mass.)	1788	5,689,170	Boston
Michigan (Mich.)	1837	8,875,083	Lansing
Minnesota (Minn.)	1858	3,805,069	St. Paul
Mississippi (Miss.)	1817	2,216,912	Jackson
Missouri (Mo.)	1821	4,677,399	Jefferson City
Montana (Mont.)	1889	694,409	Helena
Nebraska (Nebr.)	1867	1,483,791	Lincoln
Nevada (Nev.)	1864	488,738	Carson City
*New Hampshire (N.H.)	1788	737,681	Concord
*New Jersey (N.J.)	1787	7,168,164	Trenton
New Mexico (N.Mex.)	1912	1,016,000	Santa Fe
*New York (N.Y.)	1788	18,190,740	Albany
*North Carolina (N.C.)	1789	5,082,059	Raleigh
North Dakota (N.Dak.)	1889	617,761	Bismarck
Ohio (O.)	1803	10,652,017	Columbus
Oklahoma (Okla.)	1907	2,559,253	Oklahoma City
Oregon (Oreg.)	1859	2,091,385	Salem
*Pennsylvania (Pa.)	1787	11,793,909	Harrisburg
*Rhode Island (R.I.)	1790	949,723	Providence
*South Carolina (S.C.)	1788	2,590,516	Columbia
South Dakota (S.Dak.)	1889	665,507	Pierre
Tennessee (Tenn.)	1796	3,924,164	Nashville
Texas (Tex.)	1845	11,196,730	Austin
Utah (Ut.)	1896	1,059,273	Salt Lake City
Vermont (Vt.)	1791	444,330	Montpelier
*Virginia (Va.)	1788	4,648,494	Richmond
Washington (Wash.)	1889	3,409,169	Olympia
West Virginia (W.Va.)	1863	1,744,237	Charleston
Wisconsin (Wis.)	1848	4,417,933	Madison
Wyoming (Wyo.)	1890	332,416	Cheyenne

*The 13 Original States.
‡Governed by Congress.

THE LARGEST CITIES IN
THE UNITED STATES
Census of 1970

New York, N.Y.	7,867,760	Shreveport, La. 182,064
Chicago, Ill.	3,366,957	Warren, Mich. 179,260
Los Angeles, Cal.	2,816,061	Providence, R.I. 179,213
Philadelphia, Pa.	1,948,609	Fort Wayne, Ind. 177,671
Detroit, Mich.	1,511,482	Worcester, Mass. 176,572
Houston, Tex.	1,232,802	Salt Lake City, Ut. ... 175,885
Baltimore, Md.	905,759	Gary, Ind. 175,415
Dallas, Tex.	844,401	Knoxville, Tenn. 174,587
Cleveland, O.	750,903	Arlington, Va. 174,284
Indianapolis, Ind.	744,624	Madison, Wis. 173,258
Milwaukee, Wis.	717,099	Virginia Beach, Va. ... 172,106
San Francisco, Cal.	715,674	Spokane, Wash. 170,516
San Diego, Cal.	696,769	Kansas City, Kans. ... 168,213
San Antonio, Tex.	654,153	Anaheim, Cal. 166,701
Boston, Mass.	641,071	Fresno, Cal. 165,972
Memphis, Tenn.	623,530	Baton Rouge, La. 165,963
St. Louis, Mo.	622,236	Springfield, Mass. 163,905
New Orleans, La.	593,471	Hartford, Conn. 158,017
Phoenix, Ariz.	581,562	Santa Ana, Cal. 156,601
Columbus, O.	539,677	Bridgeport, Conn. 156,542
Seattle, Wash.	530,831	Tacoma, Wash. 154,581
Jacksonville, Fla.	520,117	Columbus, Ga. 154,168
Pittsburgh, Pa.	520,117	Jackson, Miss. 153,968
Denver, Colo.	514,678	Lincoln, Nebr. 149,518
Kansas City, Mo.	507,087	Lubbock, Tex. 149,101
Atlanta, Ga.	496,973	Rockford, Ill. 147,370
Buffalo, N.Y.	462,768	Paterson, N.J. 144,824
Cincinnati, O.	452,524	Greensboro, N.C. 144,076
Nashville, Tenn.	447,877	Riverside, Cal. 140,089
San Jose, Cal.	445,779	Youngstown, O. 139,788
Minneapolis, Minn.	434,400	Fort Lauderdale, Fla. . 139,590
Fort Worth, Tex.	393,476	Evansville, Ind. 138,764
Toledo, O.	383,818	Newport News, Va. ... 138,177
Portland, Oreg.	382,619	Huntsville, Ala. 137,802
Newark, N.J.	382,417	New Haven, Conn. ... 137,707
Oklahoma City, Okla.	366,481	Metairie, La. 135,816
Oakland, Cal.	361,561	Colorado Sprgs, Colo. . 135,060
Louisville, Ky.	361,472	Torrance, Cal. 134,584
Long Beach, Cal.	358,633	Montgomery, Ala. 133,386
Omaha, Nebr.	347,328	Winston-Salem, N.C. .. 132,913
Miami, Fla.	334,859	Glendale, Cal. 132,752
Tulsa, Okla.	331,638	Little Rock, Ark. 132,483
Honolulu, Hawaii	324,871	Lansing, Mich. 131,546
El Paso, Tex.	322,261	Erie, Pa. 129,231
St. Paul, Minn.	309,980	Amarillo, Tex. 127,010
Norfolk, Va.	307,951	Peoria, Ill. 126,963
Birmingham, Ala.	300,910	Las Vegas, Nev. 125,787
Rochester, N.Y.	296,233	South Bend, Ind. 125,580
Tampa, Fla.	277,767	Topeka, Kans. 125,011
Wichita, Kans.	276,554	Garden Grove, Cal. ... 122,524
Akron, O.	275,425	Macon, Ga. 122,423
Tucson, Ariz.	262,933	Raleigh, N.C. 121,577
Jersey City, N.J.	260,545	Hampton, Va. 120,779
Sacramento, Cal.	254,413	Springfield, Mo. 120,096
Austin, Tex.	251,808	Chattanooga, Tenn. .. 119,082
Richmond, Va.	249,621	Savannah, Ga. 118,349
Albuquerque, N.Mex.	243,751	Berkeley, Cal. 116,716
Dayton, O.	243,601	Huntington Bch., Cal. 115,960
Charlotte, N.C.	241,178	Beaumont, Tex. 115,919
St. Petersburg, Fla.	216,232	Albany, N.Y. 114,873
Corpus Christi, Tex.	204,525	Columbia, S.C. 113,542
Yonkers, N.Y.	204,370	Pasadena, Cal. 113,327
Des Moines, Ia.	200,587	Elizabeth, N.J. 112,654
Grand Rapids, Mich.	197,649	Independence, Mo. ... 111,662
Syracuse, N.Y.	197,208	Portsmouth, Va. 110,963
Flint, Mich.	193,317	Alexandria, Va. 110,938
Mobile, Ala.	190,026	Cedar Rapids, Ia. 110,642

NATIONS OF THE WORLD

Nation	Population	Capital
Afghanistan	18,294,000	Kabul
Albania	2,188,000	Tirana
Algeria	17,910,000	Algiers
Andorra	29,000	Andorra la Vella
Angola	6,761,000	Luanda
Argentina	26,056,000	Buenos Aires
Australia	14,215,000	Canberra
Austria	7,506,000	Vienna
Bahamas	220,000	Nassau
Bahrain	265,000	Manama
Bangladesh	80,558,000	Dacca
Barbados	254,000	Bridgetown
Belgium	9,837,000	Brussels
Benin	3,286,000	Porto Novo
Bhutan	1,035,000	Thimphu
Bolivia	5,950,000	La Paz; Sucre
Botswana	710,000	Gaborone
Brazil	112,239,000	Brasilia
Bulgaria	8,804,000	Sofia
Burma	31,512,000	Rangoon
Burundi	3,966,000	Bujumbura
Cameroun	7,663,000	Yaoundé
Canada	23,316,000	Ottawa
Cape Verde	303,000	Praia
Central African Empire	2,370,000	Bangui
Chad	4,197,000	N'Djamena
Chile	10,656,000	Santiago
China	965,937,000	Peking
Colombia	25,048,000	Bogotá
Comoro Islands	370,000	Moroni
Congo	1,440,000	Brazzaville
Costa Rica	2,071,000	San José
Cuba	9,474,000	Havana
Cyprus	640,000	Nicosia
Czechoslovakia	15,090,000	Prague
Denmark	5,099,000	Copenhagen
Djibouti	81,000	Djibouti
Dominica	80,000	Roseau
Dominican Republic	4,978,000	Santo Domingo
Ecuador	7,556,000	Quito
Egypt	38,741,000	Cairo
El Salvador	4,123,000	San Salvador
Equatorial Guinea	286,000	Malabo
Ethiopia	28,981,000	Addis Ababa
Fiji	590,000	Suva
Finland	4,746,000	Helsinki
France	53,196,000	Paris
Gabon	500,000	Libreville
Gambia	553,000	Banjul
Germany, East	16,765,000	East Berlin
Germany, West	61,396,000	Bonn
Ghana	10,309,000	Accra
Greece	9,284,000	Athens
Grenada	105,000	St. George's
Guatemala	6,436,000	Guatemala City
Guinea	4,646,000	Conakry
Guinea-Bissau	544,000	Madina do Boe
Guyana	783,000	Georgetown
Haiti	4,749,000	Port-au-Prince
Honduras	2,831,000	Tegucigalpa
Hungary	10,678,000	Budapest
Iceland	222,000	Reykjavik
India	625,818,000	New Delhi
Indonesia	130,597,000	Jakarta
Iran	34,274,000	Tehran
Iraq	12,171,000	Bagdad
Ireland	3,192,000	Dublin
Israel	3,643,000	Jerusalem
Italy	56,601,000	Rome

NATIONS OF THE WORLD

Nation	Population	Capital
Ivory Coast	7,161,000	Abidjan
Jamaica	2,831,000	Kingston
Japan	113,863,000	Tokyo
Jordan	2,779,000	Amman
Kampuchea	7,973,000	Phnom Penh
Kenya	14,337,000	Nairobi
Korea, North	16,651,000	Pyongyang
Korea, South	36,436,000	Seoul
Kuwait	1,129,000	Kuwait
Laos	3,427,000	Vientiane
Lebanon	3,056,000	Beirut
Lesotho	1,214,000	Maseru
Liberia	1,796,000	Monrovia
Libya	2,444,000	Tripoli
Liechtenstein	24,000	Vaduz
Luxembourg	362,000	Luxembourg
Madagascar	7,900,000	Antananarivo
Malawi	5,572,000	Lilongwe
Malaysia	12,600,000	Kuala Lumpur
Maldives	141,000	Malé
Mali	6,035,000	Bamako
Malta	326,000	Valletta
Mauritania	1,481,000	Nouakchott
Mauritius	909,000	Port Louis
Mexico	64,594,000	Mexico City
Monaco	25,000	Monaco-Ville
Mongolia	1,531,000	Ulan Bator
Morocco	18,245,000	Rabat
Mozambique	9,444,000	Maputo
Nauru	7,000	—
Nepal	13,136,000	Katmandu
Netherlands	13,912,000	Amsterdam
New Zealand	3,152,000	Wellington
Nicaragua	2,312,000	Managua
Niger	4,859,000	Niamey
Nigeria	78,660,000	Lagos
Norway	4,051,000	Oslo
Oman	817,000	Muscat
Pakistan	72,368,000	Islamabad
Panama	1,771,000	Panama City
Papua New Guinea	2,756,000	Port Moresby
Paraguay	2,805,000	Asunción
Peru	16,358,000	Lima
Philippines	45,028,000	Manila
Poland	34,945,000	Warsaw
Portugal	9,733,000	Lisbon
Qatar	180,000	Doha
Rhodesia	6,740,000	Salisbury
Romania	21,658,000	Bucharest
Rwanda	4,368,000	Kigali
San Marino	21,000	San Marino
Sao Tome and Principe	82,000	Sao Tome
Saudi Arabia	7,629,000	Riyadh
Senegal	5,115,000	Dakar
Seychelles	62,000	Victoria
Sierra Leone	3,470,000	Freetown
Singapore	2,322,000	Singapore
Solomon Islands	207,000	Honiara
Somalia	3,354,000	Mogadishu
South Africa	26,129,000	Pretoria; Cape Town
Spain	36,672,000	Madrid
Sri Lanka	13,971,000	Colombo
Sudan	18,656,000	Khartoum
Surinam	448,000	Paramaribo
Swaziland	499,000	Mbabane
Sweden	8,271,000	Stockholm
Switzerland	6,421,000	Bern
Syria	7,845,000	Damascus
Taiwan	16,601,000	Taipei

311

NATIONS OF THE WORLD

Nation	Population	Capital
Tanzania	16,073,000	Dar es Salaam
Thailand	44,039,000	Bangkok
Togo	2,348,000	Lomé
Tonga	109,000	Nukualofa
Trinidad and Tobago	1,098,000	Port of Spain
Tunisia	6,065,000	Tunis
Turkey	42,134,000	Ankara
Uganda	12,353,000	Kampala
United Arab Emirates	656,000	Abu Dhabi
United Kingdom	55,992,000	London
United States	216,817,000	Washington
Upper Volta	6,319,000	Ouagadougou
Uruguay	3,047,000	Montevideo
U.S.S.R.	258,932,000	Moscow
Vatican City	1,000	—
Venezuela	12,737,000	Caracas
Vietnam	47,872,000	Hanoi
Western Samoa	153,000	Apia
Yemen	5,635,000	Sana
Yemen, Democratic	1,797,000	Aden
Yugoslavia	21,912,000	Belgrade
Zaire	26,376,000	Kinshasa
Zambia	5,138,000	Lusaka

NATIONAL PARKS OF THE UNITED STATES

Name	Location	Acreage
Acadia	Southern Maine	41,634
Arches	Southeastern Utah	73,234
Big Bend	Western Texas	708,221
Bryce Canyon	Southwestern Utah	36,010
Canyonlands	Southeastern Utah	257,640
Capitol Reef	South central Utah	241,671
Carlsbad Caverns	Southeastern New Mexico	46,753
Crater Lake	Southwestern Oregon	160,290
Everglades	Southern Florida	1,400,533
Glacier	Northwestern Montana	1,013,129
Grand Canyon	North central Arizona	673,575
Grand Teton	Northwestern Wyoming	310,358
Great Smoky Mountains	North Carolina and Tennessee	515,225
Guadalupe Mountains	Western Texas	77,518
Haleakala	Island of Maui	26,402
Hawaii Volcanoes	Islands of Hawaii and Maui	220,344
Hot Springs	Central Arkansas	3,535
Isle Royale	Northern Michigan	539,341
Kings Canyon	East central California	460,330
Lassen Volcanic	Northern California	106,933
Mammoth Cave	Southwestern Kentucky	51,354
Mesa Verde	Southwestern Colorado	52,073
Mount McKinley	South central Alaska	1,939,493
Mount Rainier	West central Washington	241,992
North Cascades	Northern Washington	505,000
Olympic	Northwestern Washington	896,599
Petrified Forest	Eastern Arizona	94,189
Platt	Southern Oklahoma	912
Redwood	Northwestern California	58,000
Rocky Mountain	North central Colorado	262,324
Sequoia	East central California	386,863
Shenandoah	Northern Virginia	193,538
Virgin Islands	Virgin Islands	15,150
Voyageurs	Northern Minnesota	219,431
Wind Cave	Southwestern South Dakota	28,059
Yellowstone	Northwestern Wyoming, Southwestern Montana, and Northeastern Idaho	2,221,772
Yosemite	East central California	761,320
Zion	Southwestern Utah	147,034

FACTS ABOUT THE EARTH

THE OCEANS
Area (sq. mi.)

Pacific	63,750,000
Atlantic	31,830,000
Indian	28,357,000
Arctic	5,440,000

PRINCIPAL SEAS
Area (sq. mi.)

Mediterranean	1,145,000
South China	895,000
Bering	876,000
Caribbean	750,000
Okhotsk	590,000
Yellow	480,000
East China	480,000
Japan	389,000
Andaman	300,000
North	222,000
Red	169,000
Caspian	169,000
Black	164,000
Baltic	163,000
Dead	370

PRINCIPAL LAKES
Area (sq. mi.)

Superior, *U.S.*	31,810
Victoria, *Africa*	26,200
Aral, *U.S.S.R.*	24,400
Huron, *U.S.*	23,010
Michigan, *U.S.*	22,400
Nyasa, *Africa*	14,000
Baikal, *U.S.S.R.*	13,300
Tanganyika, *Africa*	12,700
Great Bear, *Canada*	11,800
Great Slave, *Canada*	11,172
Erie, *U.S.*	9,940
Winnipeg, *Canada*	8,555
Ontario, *U.S.*	7,540
Balkhash, *U.S.S.R.*	7,200
Ladoga, *U.S.S.R.*	7,000
Chad, *Africa*	6,500

LONGEST RIVERS
Length (miles)

Nile, *Africa*	4,000
Amazon, *S. America*	3,900
Mississippi-Missouri, *U.S.*	3,870
Ob, *U.S.S.R.*	3,200
Yangtze, *China*	3,100
Congo, *Africa*	3,000
Amur, *Asia*	2,900
Yenisei, *U.S.S.R.*	2,800
Lena, *U.S.S.R.*	2,800
Hwang Ho, *China*	2,700
Mekong, *Asia*	2,600
Niger, *Africa*	2,600
Mackenzie, *Canada*	2,500
Missouri, *U.S.*	2,465
Paraná, *S. America*	2,450
Mississippi, *U.S.*	2,330
Murray, *Australia*	2,310
Yukon, *Canada & Alaska*	2,300
Volga, *U.S.S.R.*	2,300
Irtish, *U.S.S.R.*	2,250
St. Lawrence, *Canada*	2,100
Madeira, *S. America*	2,000
Indus, *India*	2,000

PRINCIPAL MOUNTAINS
Height (feet)

Everest, *Tibet, Nepal*	29,002
Godwin Austen (K2) *Jammu & Kashmir*	28,250
Kanchenjunga, *Nepal, Sikkim*	28,146
Makalu, *Nepal*	27,790
Dhaulagiri, *Nepal*	26,795
Nanga Parbat, *Jammu & Kashmir*	26,660
Annapurna, *Nepal*	26,500
Gosainthan, *Tibet*	26,291
Nanda Devi, *India*	25,645
Kamet, *India*	25,447
Namcha Barwa, *Tibet*	25,445
Gurla Mandhata, *Tibet*	25,355
Tirach Mir, *Pakistan*	25,263
Kula Kangri, *Tibet, Bhutan*	24,740
Muztagh Ata, *China*	24,388
Minya Kanka, *China*	24,000
Chomo Lhari, *Bhutan, Tibet*	23,930
Api, *Nepal*	23,899
Tengri Khan, *U.S.S.R.*	23,622
Aconcagua, *Argentina*	23,080
Ojos del Salado, *Argentina, Chile*	22,572
Mercedario, *Argentina*	22,211
Huascarán, *Peru*	22,180
Llullaillaco, *Argentina, Chile*	22,057
Kailas, *Tibet*	22,000
Tupungato, *Argentina, Chile*	21,810
Incahuasi, *Argentina, Chile*	21,719
Sajama, *Bolivia*	21,491
Illampu, *Bolivia*	21,489
Nanadas de Cachi, *Argentina*	21,325
Illimani, *Bolivia*	21,280
Antofalla, *Argentina*	21,129
Chimborazo, *Ecuador*	20,702
McKinley, *Alaska*	20,300
Logan, *Canada*	19,850
Kilimanjaro, *Tanzania*	19,321
Elbrus, *U.S.S.R.*	18,468
Popocatepetl, *Mexico*	17,888
Kenya, *Kenya*	17,040
Ararat, *Turkey*	16,915
Mont Blanc, *France*	15,781
Matterhorn, *Italy, Switzerland*	14,780
Whitney, *California*	14,501
Rainier, *Washington*	14,408
Pikes Peak, *Colorado*	14,110
Mauna Loa, *Hawaii*	13,675
Jungfrau, *Switzerland*	13,667
Fujiyama, *Japan*	12,395
Etna, *Sicily*	10,741
Olympus, *Greece*	9,793

313

PRESIDENTS OF THE UNITED STATES

	Name	Born	State	Pres.	Party	Died
1	George Washington	1732	Va.	1789	Fed.	1799
2	John Adams	1735	Mass.	1797	Fed.	1826
3	Thomas Jefferson	1743	Va.	1801	Rep.	1826
4	James Madison	1751	Va.	1809	Rep.	1836
5	James Monroe	1758	Va.	1817	Rep.	1831
6	John Quincy Adams	1767	Mass.	1825	Rep.	1848
7	Andrew Jackson	1767	N.C.	1829	Dem.	1845
8	Martin Van Buren	1782	N.Y.	1837	Dem.	1862
9	William H. Harrison	1773	Va.	1841	Whig	1841
10	John Tyler	1790	Va.	1841	Dem.	1862
11	James K. Polk	1795	N.C.	1845	Dem.	1849
12	Zachary Taylor	1784	Va.	1849	Whig	1850
13	Millard Fillmore	1800	N.Y.	1850	Whig	1874
14	Franklin Pierce	1804	N.H.	1853	Dem.	1869
15	James Buchanan	1791	Pa.	1857	Dem.	1868
16	Abraham Lincoln	1809	Ky.	1861	Rep.	1865
17	Andrew Johnson	1808	N.C.	1865	Rep.	1875
18	Ulysses S. Grant	1822	O.	1869	Rep.	1885
19	Rutherford B. Hayes	1822	O.	1877	Rep.	1893
20	James A. Garfield	1831	O.	1881	Rep.	1881
21	Chester A. Arthur	1830	Vt.	1881	Rep.	1886
22	Grover Cleveland	1837	N.J.	1885	Dem.	1908
23	Benjamin Harrison	1833	O.	1889	Rep.	1901
24	Grover Cleveland	2ND TERM		1893	Dem.	
25	William McKinley	1843	O.	1897	Rep.	1901
26	Theodore Roosevelt	1858	N.Y.	1901	Rep.	1919
27	William H. Taft	1857	O.	1909	Rep.	1930
28	Woodrow Wilson	1856	Va.	1913	Dem.	1924
29	Warren G. Harding	1865	O.	1921	Rep.	1923
30	Calvin Coolidge	1872	Vt.	1923	Rep.	1933
31	Herbert C. Hoover	1874	Ia.	1929	Rep.	1964
32	Franklin D. Roosevelt	1882	N.Y.	1933	Dem.	1945
33	Harry S. Truman	1884	Mo.	1945	Dem.	1972
34	Dwight D. Eisenhower	1890	Tex.	1953	Rep.	1969
35	John F. Kennedy	1917	Mass.	1961	Dem.	1963
36	Lyndon B. Johnson	1908	Tex.	1963	Dem.	1973
37	Richard M. Nixon	1913	Calif.	1969	Rep.	....
38	Gerald R. Ford	1913	Neb.	1974	Rep.	....
39	James E. Carter	1924	Ga.	1977	Dem.	....
40	Ronald Reagan	1911	Ill.	1981	Rep.	....

WEDDING ANNIVERSARIES

1st —Paper	7th—Wool or	14th—Ivory
2nd—Cotton	copper	15th—Crystal
3rd —Leather	8th—Bronze	20th—China
4th —Fruit and	9th—Pottery	25th—Silver
flowers;	10th—Tin or	30th—Pearl
silk	aluminum	35th—Coral
5th —Wood	11th—Steel	40th—Ruby
6th —Sugar and	12th—Linen	50th—Gold
candy; iron	13th—Lace	75th—Diamond

BIRTHSTONES

January	Garnet	July	Ruby
February	Amethyst	August	Sardonyx or
March	Bloodstone or		Peridot
	Aquamarine	September	Sapphire
April	Diamond	October	Opal or
May	Emerald		Tourmaline
June	Pearl, Moon-	November	Topaz
	stone, or	December	Turquoise or
	Alexandrite		Zircon

HALL OF FAME OF GREAT AMERICANS
(at New York University)

Alice Freeman Palmer	1855-1902	Educator
Francis Parkman	1823-1893	Historian
George Peabody	1795-1869	Merchant & Banker
William Penn	1644-1718	Colonizer
Edgar Allan Poe	1809-1849	Writer
Walter Reed	1851-1902	Bacteriologist
Franklin D. Roosevelt	1882-1945	32nd president
Theodore Roosevelt	1858-1919	26th president
Augustus Saint-Gaudens	1848-1907	Sculptor
William Tecumseh Sherman	1820-1891	General
John Philip Sousa	1854-1932	Composer
Joseph Story	1779-1845	Jurist
Harriet Beecher Stowe	1811-1896	Novelist
Gilbert Charles Stuart	1755-1828	Painter
Sylvanus Thayer	1785-1872	Educator
Henry D. Thoreau	1817-1862	Writer
Lillian D. Wald	1867-1940	Social worker
Booker T. Washington	1856-1915	Educator
George Washington	1732-1799	1st president
Daniel Webster	1782-1852	Statesman
George Westinghouse	1846-1914	Inventor
James A. McNeill Whistler	1834-1903	Painter
Walt Whitman	1819-1892	Poet
Eli Whitney	1765-1825	Inventor
John Greenleaf Whittier	1807-1892	Poet
Emma Willard	1787-1870	Educator
Frances Elizabeth Willard	1839-1898	Temperance leader
Roger Williams	1603-1683	Colonizer
Woodrow Wilson	1856-1924	28th president
Orville Wright	1871-1948	Inventor
Wilbur Wright	1867-1912	Inventor

HALL OF FAME OF GREAT AMERICANS
(at New York University)

John Adams	1735-1826	2nd president
John Quincy Adams	1767-1848	6th president
Jane Addams	1860-1935	Social worker
Louis Agassiz	1807-1873	Naturalist
Susan B. Anthony	1820-1906	Suffragist
John James Audubon	1785-1851	Ornithologist
George Bancroft	1800-1891	Historian
Henry Ward Beecher	1813-1887	Clergyman
Alexander Graham Bell	1847-1922	Inventor
Daniel Boone	1734-1820	Frontiersman
Edwin Booth	1833-1893	Actor
Louis Dembitz Brandeis	1856-1941	Jurist
Phillips Brooks	1835-1893	Clergyman
William Cullen Bryant	1794-1878	Poet
George Washington Carver	1864-1943	Botanist
William Ellery Channing	1780-1842	Clergyman
Rufus Choate	1799-1859	Jurist
Henry Clay	1777-1852	Statesman
Samuel L. Clemens	1835-1910	Novelist
Grover Cleveland	1837-1908	22nd and 24th president
James Fenimore Cooper	1789-1851	Novelist
Peter Cooper	1791-1883	Industrialist
Charlotte S. Cushman	1820-1887	Actress
James Buchanan Eads	1820-1887	Engineer
Thomas A. Edison	1847-1931	Inventor
Jonathan Edwards	1703-1758	Theologian
Ralph Waldo Emerson	1803-1882	Writer
David Glasgow Farragut	1801-1870	Admiral
Stephen Collins Foster	1826-1864	Composer
Benjamin Franklin	1706-1790	Statesman
Robert Fulton	1765-1815	Inventor
Josiah Willard Gibbs	1839-1903	Mathematician
William Crawford Gorgas	1854-1920	Sanitation expert
Ulysses Simpson Grant	1822-1885	18th president
Asa Gray	1810-1888	Botanist
Alexander Hamilton	1757-1804	Statesman
Nathaniel Hawthorne	1804-1864	Novelist
Joseph Henry	1797-1878	Physicist
Patrick Henry	1736-1799	Statesman
Oliver Wendell Holmes	1809-1894	Writer
Oliver Wendell Holmes	1841-1935	Jurist
Mark Hopkins	1802-1887	Educator
Elias Howe	1819-1867	Inventor
Washington Irving	1783-1859	Writer
Andrew Jackson	1767-1845	7th president
Thomas Jonathan Jackson	1824-1863	General
Thomas Jefferson	1743-1826	3rd president
John Paul Jones	1747-1792	Naval officer
James Kent	1763-1847	Jurist
Sidney Lanier	1842-1881	Poet
Robert Edward Lee	1807-1870	General
Abraham Lincoln	1809-1865	16th president
Henry W. Longfellow	1807-1882	Poet
James Russell Lowell	1819-1891	Poet
Mary Lyon	1797-1849	Educator
Edward A. MacDowell	1861-1908	Composer
James Madison	1751-1836	4th president
Horace Mann	1796-1859	Educator
John Marshall	1755-1835	Jurist
Matthew Fontaine Maury	1806-1873	Ocean cartographer
Albert Abraham Michelson	1852-1931	Physicist
Maria Mitchell	1818-1889	Astronomer
James Monroe	1758-1831	5th president
Samuel F. B. Morse	1791-1872	Inventor
William T. G. Morton	1819-1868	Dental surgeon
John Lothrop Motley	1814-1877	Historian
Simon Newcomb	1835-1909	Astronomer
Thomas Paine	1737-1809	Writer